China and Latin America

Economic and Trade Cooperation in the Next 10 Years

China and Latin America

Economic and Trade Cooperation in the Next 10 Years

Edited by

SU Zhenxing

Chinese Academy of Social Sciences, China

Translated by

ZHAO Hongling

Beijing Institute of Technology, China

中国社会科学出版社
CHINA SOCIAL SCIENCES PRESS

World Scientific

NEW JERSEY • LONDON • SINGAPORE • BEIJING • SHANGHAI • HONG KONG • TAIPEI • CHENNAI • TOKYO

Published by

World Scientific Publishing Co. Pte. Ltd.
5 Toh Tuck Link, Singapore 596224
USA office: 27 Warren Street, Suite 401-402, Hackensack, NJ 07601
UK office: 57 Shelton Street, Covent Garden, London WC2H 9HE

Library of Congress Cataloging-in-Publication Data
Names: Su, Zhenxing, editor.
Title: China and Latin America : economic and trade cooperation in the next 10 years / by Zhenxing Su (China Academy of Social Sciences, China).
Other titles: 880-01 Zhongguo yu Lading Mei Zhou. English
Description: [Hackensack,] New Jersey : World Scientific, 2017. | Includes bibliographical references.
Identifiers: LCCN 2016054701 | ISBN 9789813202283 (hc : alk. paper)
Subjects: LCSH: Latin America--Foreign economic relations--China. | China--Foreign economic relations--Latin America. | Latin America--Economic conditions--21st century.
Classification: LCC HF1480.5.Z4 C69 2017 | DDC 337.5108--dc23
LC record available at https://lccn.loc.gov/2016054701

British Library Cataloguing-in-Publication Data
A catalogue record for this book is available from the British Library.

《中国与拉丁美洲：未来10年的经贸合作》
Originally published in Chinese by China Social Sciences Press.

Sponsored by B & R Book Program (本书获得丝路书香工程资助)

Desk Editors: Chandrima Maitra/Dong Lixi

Typeset by Stallion Press
Email: enquiries@stallionpress.com

Printed in Singapore

Preface

Since the beginning of the 21st century, the economic and trade cooperation between China and Latin America and the Caribbean area has experienced a "Golden Period" of accelerated development. According to China's official statistical data, the value of the Sino-Latin American bilateral trade has increased 16.5 times, from \$14.9 billion in 2001 to \$261.2 billion, with an average annual growth rate of 29.7%. Within 12 years, China has become the third largest trade partner of Latin America, following the United States and the European Union (27 nations). In terms of direct investment, up to the end of 2011, China's stock of foreign direct investment (FDI) in Latin America had reached \$55.17 billion, occupying 13% of the overall Chinese FDI stock. China has become one of the most important foreign investors in Latin America. The leapfrog economic and trade cooperation is driving China and the Latin-American countries to move forward toward establishing "a comprehensive partnership". Latin America today is an important supplier of energy sources for China, a critical growing market for the Chinese commodity export, and an increasingly important place for China's investments abroad. Therefore, Latin America is playing an increasingly important role in the Chinese global diplomatic affairs.

Our study in this book is a basic research about the development of the Sino-Latin American economic and trade relations, aiming at exploring its prospect in the coming 10 years. The basic guiding ideology of our research is based on both the judgment in the report of the *Eighteenth National Congress of the Communist Party of China* that "The development of our country is still in an important period of strategic opportunities" and the requirement that "We have to accurately understand the changes of the meanings and conditions of the important period of strategic opportunities". The development in the past 10 years makes it clear that the Sino-Latin American economic and trade cooperation has entered a new period of historical opportunity. What are the factors that have contributed to this period of historical opportunity and how will the factors change in the following 10 years? The past 10-year development has manifested a continuous improvement of mutual benefit for China and the Latin-American countries, but some new interest conflicts also have occurred and they need to be dealt with in time. China and the Latin-American countries have a lot in common in their development processes, e.g., at present both are in the process of transformation and structural adjustment, but due to the differences in structure and development, they have particular focuses on self appeals in the cooperation process, which can only be satisfied through ways such as widening or deepening the bilateral cooperative activities. The international financial crisis in 2008 marked the beginning of important changes in the international economic system. On the one hand, the emerging market economies are increasingly becoming the driving force for the global economic growth; on the other hand, there are still more and more uncertainties in the world economy, and the trade protectionism is coming back. How will the new international economic situation influence the Sino-Latin American economic and trade cooperation? In short, we believe that the prospect of this cooperation in the coming 10 years involves many issues that need to be solved by carrying out comprehensive and fundamental researches.

This book contains 11 chapters and can be roughly divided into two parts. Chapters 1–8 provide a study about the Latin-American economic conditions. We believe that understanding the economic conditions of the target countries is both the basis on which bilateral economic and trade cooperations can be carried out and the precondition for determining historical opportunities. Chapter 1 provides a description of the current economic situation and its main developing trend of the whole areas of Latin America, covering four aspects: (1) A review of the effects and problems of the large-scale economic reforms of the Latin-American countries from the 1970s. (2) The Latin-American economic operation in the 10 years after getting rid of their long-term economic downturn in 2003. (3) The economic and social policy adjustments undertaken by the left-wing governments in power and the effect of them. (4) The fundamental developing path of the Latin-American countries — to continue to transform their economic growth modes and readjust their industrial structures.

Chapters 2–7 offer a review of the economic conditions of six countries — Argentina, Brazil, Chile, Mexico, Peru, and Venezuela. Although there are only 33 countries in Latin America, most of them are either small in size or island countries, and therefore, different in economic scales. In 2010, the economic aggregate of the six countries mentioned above occupied 83% of the total economy of Latin America. As a result, the Sino-Latin American economic and trade cooperation will concentrate on the major Latin-American countries for a long time. In fact, the economic and trade relations between the United States and Latin America, and between EU and Latin America, will basically have the same pattern. The content of the six chapters involves similar topics (resource endowment, industrial structure, economic system, development pattern, basic economic policy, economic environment, economic and trade relations with China, etc.), but varies in details. For instance, since the 1980s, Chile's economic policy began to stay away from neoliberalism, showing a strong decision-making autonomy, which led to only a little adjustment range in economic policy in the past 10 years. Venezuela, under the Chavez government, conducted a series of more radical economic and social changes. Argentina, in the 1990s, actively implemented the neoliberalism, which led to a severe economic crisis in 2001; thus, the new left-wing government in power had started a systematic economic policy adjustment. Mexico is another type. The right-wing National Action Party had been in power for 12 years, basically having a continuation of economic policy from the 1980s, but there is a major adjustment in its social policy. The resource advantages of these six countries have their own characteristics. The industrial structures, especially the levels of the differences in the manufacturing industry, are significant, and the regional distributions of foreign trade and economic cooperation are different (e.g., Mexico is highly dependent on the US market). This requires that we fully understand the respective advantages and characteristics of the main partner countries, making specific use of the potentials of the partners in cooperation. Chapter 8 is the study of the economic openness of the Latin-American countries. It is our new attempt in the research method, seeking to adopt new methods to expand and deepen our awareness and understanding of the cooperation environment in Latin America.

Chapters 9–11 focus on the analysis of the opportunities and challenges facing the Sino-Latin American economic and trade cooperation. Our analysis of this issue is done with a dual perspective — from both our visual angle and that of the other party. On the basis of a comprehensive review of the achievement of the Sino-Latin American economic and trade cooperation, Chapter 9 focuses on the revelations of the basic experience and policy instruments in the period of accelerated development, as well as emerging issues. Chapter 10 is a collection and analysis of the reactions of the Latin-American public and the international opinions to China's economic rise and the acceleration of the Sino-Latin American economic and trade cooperation and the changes of the reactions, confirming that the above opinions have changed from the "China Competition" theory to the "China Opportunity" theory. According to our so-called "dual perspective", we believe that in the next decade the Sino-Latin American economic and trade cooperation will still be in the period of an important historical opportunity, but with new changes in the constituents and challenges of the period of opportunity. Chapter 11 introduces the overall vision of the next phase of industrial restructuring of the Latin-American countries. A dialectical analysis is done of the so-called conflicts of interest between China and Latin America. It is believed that these are only interest demands for further cooperation, rather than the antagonistic interests, and by deepening cooperation, the conflicts could become converging interests. It is emphasized that both parties should adhere to the road of win–win cooperation. Corresponding policy suggestions are provided in this chapter.

Below is a brief introduction of some of the main points in this book.

1. The Economic Reforms in Latin America

In the 1970s, Latin-American countries experienced a so-called "structural crisis of development". Its essence is that the continuation of a half-century of the import substitution of industrialization mode had lost vigor. Because of the failure to transform the economic growth mode, the Latin-American countries ran into a debt crisis in the early 1980s, and had to carry out large-scale structural reforms. The reforms came to an end in the early 21st century, arriving at two changes, namely the transformation from the state-run economy to a market economy, and from the inward-oriented development mode to the outward, and thus achieved the initial transformation of the economic growth mode. The reforms were misled by the neoliberalism with high costs — between 1980 and 2002, Latin America experienced "the lost decade" and between 1998 and 2002 "another lost 5 years".

2. Policy Adjustments in the Past 10 Years

In the 1990s, the new liberalism was rampant, financial crises occurred frequently, and social conflicts and political turbulences were intensified, which had provided a historical opportunity for the rise of the left-wing political forces in Latin America. At the turn of the century, a large number of left-wing parties had come into power, and the political parties had formed a pattern of competition between the left and the right. Through the general election to realize the legal change of the regime, the political situation of the world has entered a period of relative stability and the achievement of economic and social development has become the main basis of the legitimacy of the regime. The left-wing governments have generally adjusted their policies systematically, emphasizing the inclusive development, playing the national economic function, and implementing the steady pragmatic macroeconomic policy and the active social policy, and therefore, the Latin-American region gradually formed the mainstream view of development which is different from the new liberalism and led the regional cooperation along its path toward the goal of independent development. At the same time, since 2003 Latin America had got rid of its economic downturn that had lasted over 20 years and entered a new period of growth. It had successfully withstood the impact of the international financial crisis of 2008–2009, accumulated substantial foreign exchange reserves, and greatly reduced its debt burden. The regional poverty had been reduced up to 15% from 43.8% in 1999 to 28.8% in 2012. All these have contributed to the many favorable conditions for the next phase of the economic and social development.

3. The Development Path for the Next 10 Years

The basic development path of the Latin-American countries for the next 10 years is to vigorously adjust the industrial structure and to continue to change the way of economic growth. In order to achieve inclusive development and social equality, the central government should plan the industrial structure adjustment to mobilize the investment enthusiasm of the public and private sectors, promote the technological innovation, and increase the export of technology- and knowledge-intensive high value-added products so as to improve the competitiveness abroad and increase the domestic employment and the resident income by stimulating domestic demand through the adjustment and upgrading of the industrial sectors. In terms of policy decision, the government should have a combination of the industrial policy, the macroeconomic policy and the active social policy.

4. Major Driving Forces Accelerating the Sino-Latin American Economic and Trade Cooperation in the Past 10 Years

From the implementation of reform and opening up to the beginning of the 21st century, China had obtained a substantial increase in its comprehensive national strength. After China became the "world factory", while its foreign economic cooperation continued to focus on attracting foreign capital and technology, there appeared a huge demand for energy and raw materials, so that Latin America's crude oil, minerals and bulk agricultural products had become the focus of cooperation, which is the most important new growth point in the Latin-American economic and trade cooperation. Hence, the so-called "China Effect" in the Latin-American countries — the "dual effect" of which the export of energy and raw materials surged, and the trade prices continued to significantly improve. At the same time, in the past 10 years, China had achieved the transition from a major invested country to a major foreign investment country — its direct investment in Latin America had increased rapidly. China, with its largest foreign currency reserves, is playing an increasingly important role with its financial advantage, e.g., during the international financial crisis, China and the Latin-American countries had carried out a series of financial cooperation, including the "Loan for Oil", both to meet their urgent financial needs and to expand the scale and scope of the bilateral trade cooperation. China has signed bilateral free trade agreements with Chile, Peru, and Costa Rica, which has effectively promoted the bilateral cooperation. These initiatives seem to have been creating "new growth points" for the bilateral cooperation, which is a successful experience for the Sino-Latin American economic and trade cooperation in the past 10 years.

5. The Expanding Market of Latin America

Thanks to the comprehensive role played by a variety of factors, the economy of Latin America experienced a strong growth between 2003 and 2008, and a rapid recovery from the impact of the international financial crisis in 2009. But it is undeniable that one of the key factors lies in the boom of the export of energy and raw materials and the sharp improvement in trade prices. To a certain extent it can be said that the "China Effect" has played a role in nurturing the Latin-American market. The growth of domestic production drives the demand of the renewal of equipment, the employment growth and the increased income of residents have improved the consumption demand, and the "double surpluses" of the public finance and the current account have strengthened the national import capacity. From an overall perspective, the recent 10 years has witnessed a continuous growth in the import of goods in the Latin-American regions. This is a factor that cannot be ignored in the study of the Sino-Latin American bilateral trade.

6. Current Issues in the Sino-Latin American Economic and Trade Cooperation

After more than 10 years of fast development, there are still some original contradictions in addition to some new problems in the Sino-Latin American economic and trade cooperation. According to our observation, currently the main problems are as follows. First, it is the commodity structure of the bilateral trade. At present, the basic pattern of trade between China and Latin America is that China mainly exports manufactured industrial goods while Latin America mainly exports raw materials and primary products. It is believed in Latin America that the pattern of trade is unfavorable for Latin America. In recent years, driven by China's strong demand for energy and raw materials, the export commodity structure of the Latin-American countries has been in the trend of the "re-primarization of the products", and thus they strongly demand increasing the export of high value-added products to China. Second, some Latin-American countries with higher levels of industrial development believe that China's industrial output is not only damaging their related industrial sectors, but also squeezing their export markets, and thus they constantly practice the trade protectionism against China. Third, the public opinion in Latin America is dissatisfied with China's investment which is mainly concentrated on energy and mineral areas, taking it for granted that China's goal is to focus on the acquisition of the Latin-American resources. Fourth, China's investment risk in Latin America is increasing. In the past, the policy of nationalizing oil and gas resources undertaken by a few Latin-American countries had brought some damage to the Chinese enterprises, and some Chinese enterprises had encountered the labor problem, and so on.

In the future, with the expansion of the scale of Chinese enterprises in the investment of Latin America and the expansion of business areas, similar problems will appear, and other risks, such as the non-normal change of governments, the policy changing, and the violation of agreed contracts, are likely to occur.

7. The Next 10 Years — Another Important Period of Historical Opportunity for the Sino-Latin American Economic and Trade Cooperation

The basic factors constituting this period of historical opportunity are as follows. First, in the post-financial crisis period, the economy of western developed countries will maintain a low growth, while the emerging economies will become the important engine of the world economy; the status of the South–South cooperation will rise and the Latin-American countries will further strengthen the cooperation with China and the Asia-Pacific region. Second, the Sino-Latin American cooperation in the field of energy and resources will continue to be strengthened. China's demand for these products will continue to be strong. Latin-American countries estimate that the current price of raw materials can be maintained for another 10 years or so, and they will make full use of this "resource dividend" period. Third, the two sides are optimistic about the economic outlook and the market is in a state of continuous expansion, but the commodity structure of bilateral trade needs to be adjusted gradually so as to create a new trade "growth point". Fourth, Latin America has a huge demand for funds, but the current investment rate is only about 20% of their GDP. The rigidity of social investment is too strong to be compressed, for otherwise it would become a challenge for the government. In the next 15 years, the minimum requirement for the infrastructure investment should account for 5% of the GDP, but currently it only occupies 0.8–0.9%. The establishment and development of strategic emerging industries are mainly based on FDI, etc. This situation provides favorable conditions for more Chinese enterprises to invest in Latin America and for China's huge foreign exchange reserves to exert their advantages. Fifth, in the next 10 years, the

Latin-American countries will enter the period of industrial structure adjustment. The overall industrial development level in China is higher than that in Latin America; therefore, the industrial cooperation can drive the export of technology and equipment and the transfer of some industrial overcapacity. The Latin-American countries also value China's status as a platform for Asian exports, believing that through cooperation between enterprises, more Latin-American enterprises will enter the chain of the Asian industries, which will be conducive to the adjustment of the industrial structure of Latin America.

8. Main Policy Recommendations

First, adhere to the basic principle of establishing a comprehensive cooperative partnership in the Latin-American region, focusing on the economic and trade cooperation. Second, establish a regional cooperation platform with Latin America, implementing the "two-wheel drive" bilateral cooperation mechanism between the regional cooperation platform and the countries. Third, try to implement the several cooperation initiatives proposed by Prime Minister Wen Jiabao during his visit to Latin America in June 2012 to inject new impetus to the bilateral economic and trade cooperation. Fourth, focus on the increase in the production and investment in the related industries in Latin America so as to lay a more solid foundation for the long-term development of bilateral economic and trade cooperation. Fifth, continue to promote the construction of bilateral free trade areas. Sixth, strengthen the economic and trade cooperation between China and the two sub-regions of Central America and the Caribbean area. To sum up, we have made great efforts in this research, striving to make some innovation in this achievement in order to offer some reference for decision making. However, due to the limitations of the writers, there is still room for improvement in this book regarding errors and shortcomings. Criticism from readers will be highly valued.

SU Zhenxing
April 2013

About the Editor

SU Zhenxing studied Russian in the Beijing Foreign Language College for one year from 1959 to 1960. From 1960 to 1964, he studied Spanish at the department of western languages and literature in Peking University. He is a Researcher and PhD student advisor at the Institute of Latin American Studies of the Chinese Academy of Social Sciences. His academic specialties are Latin American Studies. In 1964, he started working for the Institute of Latin American Studies of the International Department of the Central Committee of the Communist Party of China. From 1974 to 1977, he was the cultural attaché of the Chinese Embassy in Argentina. He has served as the Director of the Institute of Latin American Studies of the Chinese Academy of Social Sciences, and as a member of the 9th National Committee of the Chinese People's Political Consultative Conference.

About the Translator

Zhao Hongling is Associate Professor of English in the School of Foreign Languages, Beijing Institute of Technology (BIT); Master Supervisor of English Language and Literature; one of the tutors in the MTI (Master of Translating and Interpreting) Center of BIT. He got his Bachelor of Arts degree from Nanjing Normal University in 1986 and his master certificate from Shanghai Institute of technology in 1988. From 1988 to 2016, he has been working in the School of Foreign Languages, BIT, teaching English to English-major graduates and undergraduates and Non-English-major graduates and undergraduates, and doing researches. He has written a number of articles concerning English teaching and taken part in the compiling of several English textbooks for graduates and undergraduates.

List of Contributors

SU Zhenxing

Academician and Professor in the Institute of Latin American Studies, Chinese Academy of Social Sciences.

Lin Hua

Associate Professor in the Institute of Social and Cultural Studies of Latin America, Chinese Academy of Social Sciences.

Dr. Yang Zhimin

Professor and Deputy Director in the Institute of Economic Research of Latin American Studies, Chinese Academy of Social Sciences.

Dr. Zhang Yong

Associate Professor in the Institute of Economic Research of Latin American Studies, Chinese Academy of Social Sciences.

Dr. Huang Zhilong

Associate Professor, Research Department of the Chinese International Economic Exchange Center.

Dr. Sun Hongbo

Associate Professor in the International Relations Research of Latin American Studies, Chinese Academy of Social Sciences.

Dr. Zhao Lihong

Associate Professor in the Economic Research Office of the Institute of Latin American Studies, Chinese Academy of Social Sciences.

Dr. Chai Yu

Professor and Assistant Director in the Institute of Latin American Studies, Chinese Academy of Social Sciences; Director of the Economic Research Office.

Li Shenggang

PhD student of the Graduate School, Chinese Academy of Social Sciences.

Contents

Chapter 1

Reform and Development of the Latin-American Economy

SU Zhenxing

During the more-than-10-year period since the beginning of the 21st century, the economic situation in Latin America and the Caribbean region (hereinafter referred to as "Latin America" or "Latin-American region") has changed greatly. The main changes are: (1) The economic reform led by the new liberalism has come to an end, and the economic reform has entered a new period of reflection and policy adjustment; (2) The economic recession and downturn over 20 years has finally ended, and the economy entered a new growth period; (3) The pragmatic principle has gradually become the basic guiding ideology of Latin-American countries to develop their economic policies. The author believes that the three changes above will help us have an overall understanding of the basic features of the change of the economic situation in Latin America over the past 10 years, and make a basic judgment about the evolving economic tendency of the following 10 years. The basic structure of this chapter consists of four sections — the first three sections deal with the above three major changes respectively, and the last section focuses on how the Latin-American countries should continue to change the way of their economic growth.

Section 1 The Economic Reform Entering the Policy Adjustment Period

The economic reforms in Latin America led by the new liberalism started in the middle of 1970s, lasted for about 25 years, and ended at the turn of the century; hence the economic reforms entered a new period of policy adjustment. How had this change happened? What influence will this change have on the evolution of the Latin-American economic situation? In order to answer these two key questions, a series of related issues need to be analyzed.

I. Main Achievements and Failures in the Early Stage of the Reforms

There are different opinions as to the main achievements accomplished in the Latin-American economic reforms led by the neoliberalism. The author believes that the reforms beginning from the 1970s were the result of historic development. Regardless of the many mistakes in the process of neoliberal reform, there is no doubt that there have been some basic achievements.

1. The Reforms Have Transformed the Latin-American Development Mode from the Inward into the Outward Mode

The development mode of import substitution industrialization pursued by Latin-American countries in the 1970s has lost vitality — a structural crisis had occurred in the development, which was sharpened by the eruption of the debt crisis in the early 1980s. Therefore, there was no way out without reforms. The transformation from the inward development mode to the outward development mode was realized through removing tariff and non-tariff barriers and slashing the national economic functions. In order to better participate in international competition, Latin-American countries had selected two "production specialization modes": "On the one hand, in the last 20 years, the Southern Cone countries, particularly Argentina, Chile, Brazil, and Uruguay have played a more important role in the processing industry of primary products in the production of a wide range of industrial-use natural resources (such as iron and steel, petroleum industry products, non-ferrous metals, fish meal, vegetable oil, pulp, and paper). On the other hand, in Mexico and Mid-American States, the production specialization patterns have shifted decisively into the 'customers' industries (such as computer, audio–visual equipment, TV sets and clothing industries)".[1] The case of the Caribbean countries is more complicated. They can roughly be divided into three categories: the first one is in customer industries, such as the Dominican Republic; the second is resource processing industries, such as Belize, Trinidad and Tobago, Barbados, Suriname, and the third category is mainly engaged in tourism and offshore financial industry.

2. The Reform Has Enabled Latin-American Countries to Have Achieved the Transition from the State-led Economy into the Market Economy

The neoliberal economic reform in Latin America focused on the realization of the market, privatization, and financial liberalization. Although it is recognized that the general direction to the transition to a market economy is correct, in fact, the so-called "market" reform had gone too far — not only was the macro-economic function of the state excessively weakened, but also the opportunity to adjust the industrial structure was missed. "After 30 years of trade and financial liberalization, we have not been able to achieve the success of a structural reform. On the contrary, something has gone wrong with our past structural reforms: too much emphasis has been put on the market so that the structural differences of the country have been exacerbated".[2]

3. The Malignant Inflation of the Late Half of the 1980s and the Early Half of the 1990s Has Been Eliminated

As is shown in Table 1.1, from 1987 to 1994, the average inflation across the region had remained at a three or four-digit number, and

[1] Jorge Katz, "Cambios Estructurales y Productividad en la Industria Latinoamericana", 1970–1996, *Revista de las CEPAL*, No. 7, agosto de 2000, p. 66.
[2] Alicia Barcena, The Economic Development of Latin America and the Caribbean in 2012, *Latin American Studies*, No. 6, 2012.

Table 1.1 Consumer Price Index in the Latin-American Region (Selected High-inflation Countries) (Changes: December the Year Before–December the Next Year)

Country & Region	1987	1988	1989	1990	1991	1992	1993	1994	1995
Latin America & Caribbean	209.2	776.8	1, 212.5	1,991.3	199.7	418.9	887.6	337.3	25.0
Argentina	174.8	387.7	4,923.3	1,343.9	84.0	17.6	7.7	3.9	1.8
Brazil	394.6	993.3	1,863.6	1, 584.6	475.8	1,149.1	2,489.1	929.3	22.0
Ecuador	32.5	85.7	4.3	49.5	49.0	60.2	31.0	25.4	2.2
Mexico	159.2	51.7	19.7	29.9	18.9	11.9	8.0	7.1	48.5
Nicaragua	1,347.2	33,547.6	1,689.1	13,490.2	775.4	3.5	19.5	12.5	10.8
Peru	114.5	1,722.6	2,775.3	7,649.6	139.2	56.7	39.5	15.4	10.4
Uruguay	57.3	69.0	89.2	129.0	81.3	59.0	52.9	44.1	36.8
Venezuela	40.3	35.5	81.0	36.5	31.0	31.9	45.9	70.8	52.9

Source: CEPAL, *Balance Preliminar de las Economia de America Latina y el Caribe*, 1995, p. 51.

it tended to ease in 1995 as a whole. In this process, the Brazilian implementation of the "Real Plan" was successful. The practice of the "exchange rate anchor" or "Currency Board System" in other countries had caused a lot of negative consequences, and a few countries had adopted the practice of "dollarization".

4. The Enterprises Had Been Improved Efficiently Having Been Restructured

Latin-American businesses experienced a major reshuffle and a big restructuring in the reform process. First, the rapid market opening made local companies unable to resist the fierce competition of foreign goods. For example, in Chile, in the early period of the reform a tide of bankrupt enterprises occurred: in 1976, the number was 132, in 1979, it was 332, and in the first 10 months of 1980, there were 350 bankrupt enterprises. The second is the phenomenon of "de-industrialization". Between 1980 and 2009, the Latin-American manufacturing output in gross domestic product (GDP) changed from 27.8% to 15.3%, going down 12.5 points (see Figure 1.1). In this backdrop, many manufacturing industries declined significantly so that a number of related businesses could not continue to survive. The third is the privatization of state enterprises. Between 1990 and 1999, the total revenue of privatization of Latin-American state-owned enterprises was $177 billion, accounting for 56% of revenue over the same period of privatization in developing countries.[3] After the restructuring, in order to face the fierce market competition, the enterprises generally increased their investments, updated their production equipments, and improved their management and operation so that their production efficiencies were generally improved.

The author believes that the main mistakes of the neoliberal economic reform in Latin America are in the following three aspects: Firstly, too much emphasis was put on the market and liberalization;

[3] Gregorio Vidal, *Privatizationes en America Latina: Flujos Internationales de Capital, Regiolizacion y Desarticulacion Productiva, Consecuencias Financieras de la Globalizacion*, Universidad Nacional Autonoma de Mexico, Instituto de Investigaciones Economicas, Mexico, 2005, pp. 73–99.

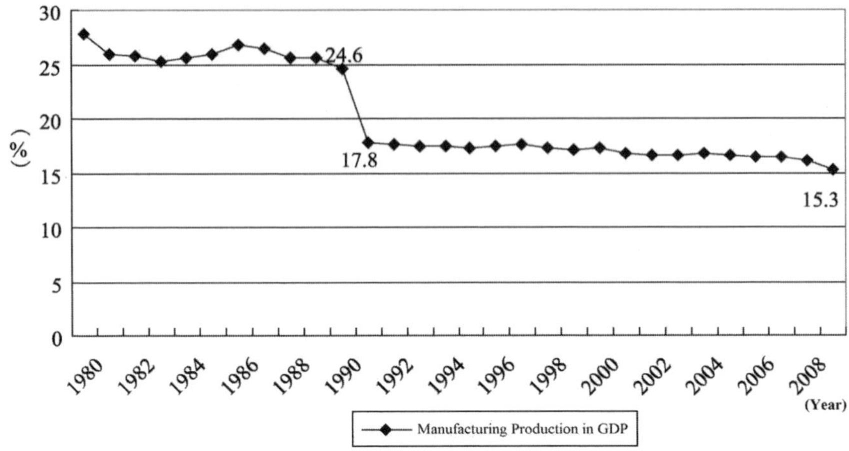

Figure 1.1 Manufacturing Production of Latin-American Countries[a] in GDP (1980–2009)

Note: [a]Means Caribbean countries are excluded. The economy of 1980–1990 was calculated on the basis of the constant dollar price of 1980; the data of 1991–2009 came from the Statistical Yearbook of Latin America 2010 (on the calculation of constant dollar price in 2000).

Source: CEPAL, *America Latina y el Caribe: Series Historicas de Estadisticas Economicas 1950–2008*, 2009; CEPAL, *Anuario Estadistico de America Latina y el Caribe*, 2010.

secondly, the relationship between the economic reform and economic growth was not well dealt with, and thirdly, social justice and social stability were ignored.

The mistake of neoliberalism in dealing with the relationship between the state and the market is the result of the domination of its theoretical idea of *laissez-faire* rather than simply a matter of a methodological issue. In the process of economic reform in Latin America, the *laissez-faire* ideology of neoliberalism can be understood in two ways. First, the state intervention in the economy rose to a height of ideology to be criticized — the state intervention is totalitarian, and the market is omnipotent. Second, the economic reforms in Latin America, although known as "structural reforms", in fact put almost all of the energy on the market-oriented reforms. The industrial structures of Latin-American countries not only failed to make any substantial adjustments, but experienced a process of "de-industrialization" up to 20 years. In its choice of the so-called "production specialization mode", the neoliberalism publicly aired "The best industrial policy is no industrial policy", advocating that Latin-American countries should choose their "production specialization mode" on the basis of their static comparative advantage of natural resources and labor resources.

The economic reform in Latin America in the 1970s was still in the pilot period of individual countries (Chile), and started the gradual expansion in the region after the outbreak of the debt crisis in the 1980s. In the context of the debt crisis, the difficulty of dealing with the relationship between the economic reform and economic growth had been very difficult; however, the governments had always stressed to accelerate the reform while ignoring how to protect growth. Many actions of the reform directly hurt the economic growth, for example, the rapid market opening led to a large number of enterprise bankruptcy, the use of "exchange rate anchor" or "Currency Board System" to counter inflation, resulting in a substantial appreciation of the currency, directly damaging the exports, and so on. After experiencing the "lost 10 years" in the 1980s, the economy of the Latin-American region began to have just a little improvement when a series of financial crises occurred. Between 1998 and 2002, another "lost 5 years" continued. As a result, the Latin-American region has experienced over 20 years of economic recession and depression from the 1980s. "In fact, in some Latin-American countries, this low-growth phase is as long as 25 years... 25 years of low growth caused up to 30% of the potential GDP losses".[4]

The problem of social injustice and rich–poor differentiation has long existed in Latin-American countries, and it turned more serious with the distress and economic downturn of the debt crisis of the 1980s. In 1990, the poverty rate hit the historical record of 48.3%. Neoliberals believe that as long as the economy grows,

[4]Development Research Center of the Organization Economic Cooperation and Development, *The Outlook of Latin American Economy of 2011*, Chinese version, translated by Zhao Lihong & Zhao Chongyang, Contemporary World Press, 2011, p. 28.

social problems will naturally dissolve. However, not only has the low economic growth been a long period in the countries, but many reforms are still increasing the rich–poor divide in the society. Thus, throughout the 1990s to the early 21st century, high unemployment continued, poverty rate was staying more than 40%, the absolute number of poor population increased, and growing social conflicts and the Indian Movement flourished. Between 1997 and 2001, seven Latin-American presidents had been ousted. In particular, the outbreak of the economic crisis of 2001 in Argentina triggered a sharp political crisis and a massive social protest.

II. The Rise of the Left-wing Party and Its Influence

The chaotic situation in the 1990s in Latin America, as described above, had created the necessary conditions for the growth of the left-wing party. The left-wing political parties of Latin America raised the banner of anti-neoliberalism, put forward the slogan of "Another world is possible", and won its foundation of the growing mass through the "St. Paul Forum" and the "World Social Forum" to expand its political influence. The "Fifth Republic Movement" led by Chavez in 1998 won the Venezuelan general election, starting the left-wing political power in Latin America at the turn of the century. In just a few years, a large number of left-wing parties in many of the Middle- and South-American countries became the ruling parties so that a new political landscape appeared in Latin America. The author believes that if the rise of the left-wing parties had been ignored, it would be difficult to fully observe and understand the current situation in Latin America, especially the new changes in the economic and social affairs.

Although the left-wing governments in Latin America are divided into radical and moderate in terms of their political overtones, not a single leftist government negated the main achievements of the early reforms, such as adhering to the opening policy and the implementation of market economy. A few countries focused the nationalization policy on the fields of oil and gas resources. Land reforms in Brazil, Venezuela and other countries were mainly carried out through the collection of the "idle" lands and the allocation of them to peasants so that the spontaneous "Land Grabbing Movement" of the landless peasants was eased. The leftist governments have advocated social equality and inclusive development, repositioned the state functions under the conditions of market economy, and restored the state macro-adjustment functions and the need to develop national industrial development planning and to implement positive industrial policies. They have emphasized the important responsibility of the state to improve the income distribution and provision of social services in the country so as to achieve the inclusive development. In fact, both in the ruling left-wing countries and in other Latin-American countries, these ideas have gradually become the dominant ideology. This indicates that the neoliberal influence in Latin America has basically subsided in the last 10 years. The author believes that in the Latin-American region the change in the mainstream concept of development is a fundamental change.

Latin-American leftist governments generally pursued an active social policy, increased government transfer payments and social spending, and implemented various forms of anti-poverty and social relief programs. With the increase of economic growth rate, the employment situation has improved accordingly. Thus, in the last 10 years, the incidence of poverty in Latin America has been declining and the absolute number of poor people has decreased significantly. The poverty rate was lowered 15.1 points from 43.9% in 2002 to 28.8% in 2012. Over the same period the absolute number of poor people was changed from 225 million to 167 million, with 58 million people free of poverty (see Figure 1.2). This change has had a profound political influence: it strengthened not only the social foundation of the ruling left-wing government, but also the social stability of Latin-American countries, gradually forming a domestic environment conducive to economic and social development. A brief review tells us that, from the end of the 1970s to 1990, Latin America experienced a process of political democratization through the action of "power back to the people" of military governments, universally restoring the institutions of representative democracy, changing the entire region into "a continent of democracy". It would have been an

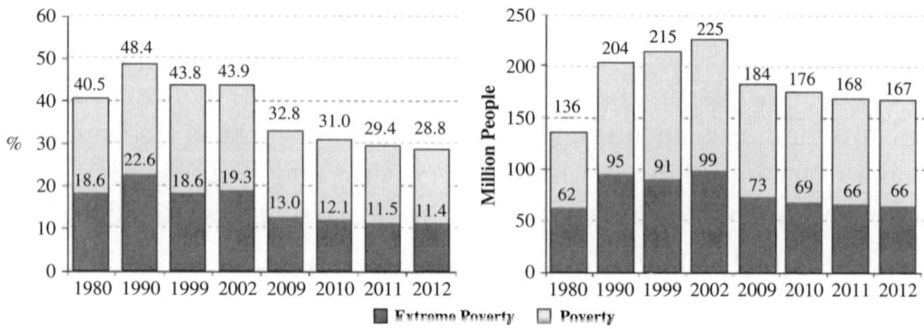

Figure 1.2 Extreme Poverty and Poverty in Latin America (1980–2012)
Source: CEPAL, *Panorama Social de America Latina 2012*, 2013, p. 14.

important political reform and a major reorganization of the political map of Latin America, but it had not brought about the desired effect of political stability in Latin America in the 1990s. The fundamental reason lies in that the desired political effect was "offset" by the serious social differentiation in the 1990s. After the left-wing governments came to power, they took advantage of the so-called "democratic deficit" which was an issue of fundamental importance, making efforts to solve social conflicts caused by the serious social differentiation, gradually restored social stability and achieved positive results in improving the environment for development.

Today in Latin America, the achievement of economic growth and social development has become an important basis for the legitimacy of the government. It is a growing consensus to maintain a high growth rate and achieve sustainable development; the main political parties, whether left or right, in power or off power, are increasingly having more and more in common regarding the economic and social policies, and the adjustments of the directions of the internal and external policies caused by the changes of governments are significantly reduced. A positive change resulting from the updating of concepts is an unprecedented pragmatic and robust attitude in the formulation of national economic policies.

On the basis of the above changes, it can also be seen that in the past 10 years the traditional spirit of solidarity and mutual assistance and seeking common development among Latin-American countries has been further promoted, and important new progress has been made in regional cooperation. The appearance of some institutions — the "Bolivarian Alliance for the Peoples of Our America" (ALBA), the "Southern Bank", the "Union of South American Nations" (Unasur), the "Community of Latin-American and Caribbean States" (CELAC) and others — is undoubtedly a number of landmark events. The establishment of these institutions is the result of some of the active advocacies and promotions of the left-wing governments. Some scholars have pointed out that "such a consensus in Latin America and the Caribbean area has been formed: a new form of regionalism and integration should be built. In this new form, political coordination is a priority in trade matters, and the sovereignty issue is to be placed in a special important position".[5] This shows that regional cooperation in Latin America has shifted from the past stress on the economic and trade cooperation to the emphasis on political coordination and the joint safeguarding of national sovereignty. The CELAC has made it clear that the core of the regional integration institutions and the regional cooperation platform without foreign participation will be built in Latin America. Brazilian former president Lula said, "We want to use our own responses to meeting the needs of welfare and wealth of the peoples of Latin America". Chilean former President Bachelet stressed, "Some people thought that globalization could be done by the unilateral way of governance, without any rules and only by the force of the market. However, the economic crisis, the climate change crisis, the energy crisis, the food crisis and other crises, have forced the international community to abandon the unstrained *laissez-faire* paradigm".[6]

In summary, we believe that in the last 10 years, although the Latin-American left-wing governments have made some mistakes in governing their countries, the political rise of the left-wing governments has made an important historical contribution.

This contribution mainly lies in the fact that the chaos of the development philosophy and basic policies of neoliberalism has been

[5]Francisco Rojas Aravena, "La Celac y la Integración Latinoamericana, Principales Claves y Desafíos", *Nueva Sociedad*, No. 240, Julio-agosto de 2012, Buenos Aires, Argentina, p. 17.
[6]*Ibid.*, p. 20.

substantially corrected in Latin America, so that Latin-American countries are back on a rational and pragmatic path of development. In the face of the crisis of the Western free market capitalism, what the Latin-American left-wing leaders had emphasized was to exercise national sovereignty, to choose their own path of development, and to meet the aspirations of welfare and wealth of the people with their own answers.

This is a huge and profound change compared with the blind pursuing of the neoliberalism, following the standard of the "Washington Consensus".

In recent years, the academic research on the Latin-American left seems to "have focused" too much on the abstract concepts of the so-called "21st century socialism" and "social socialism", ignoring the main practices of the Latin-American leftist parties. Therefore, some conclusions about the contributions of the Latin-American left-wing parties to the ideology and movement of the socialism in the world would inevitably be far-fetched and vague.

Section 2 Review of Latin-American Economy in the 10 Years

From 2003 onwards, 20 years of low economic growth came to an end and a new growth period came in the Latin-American region. Between 2003 and 2010, the average annual economic growth rate of Latin America reached 4.2%, and in South America the growth rate was even up to 5%, way higher than that between 1981 and 2002. In the last section, the main achievements of the early economic reforms in Latin America and the impact of the rise of the left parties were briefly discussed, and the overall changes of the development environment in Latin America were described. In this section, we will focus on the analysis of the main reasons for the acceleration of the economic development of Latin America, as well as the economic operation between 2003 and 2012.

I. Economic Expansion (2003–2008)

From 2003 to 2008, Latin America experienced a strong economic expansion — with 4.8% of an average annual GDP growth and the average annual per capita GDP growth of 3.4%, including a per capita GDP growth rate never seen in the previous 30 years.[7] Why did this turning point of economic growth in Latin America happen in 2003? The author believes that the emergence of this change is a particular time convergence of many favorable factors. In addition to internal factors, several important external factors need to be emphasized.

1. The World Economy was in a Period of Strong Growth

It was generally believed that the economic expansion of Latin America from 2003 to 2008 was to have benefited firstly from the favorable international economic situation. Statistics in Figure 1.3 indicate that during the period from 2003 to 2008, developed economies and emerging economies were in a relatively strong growth, and the growth in emerging economies was especially dramatic. According to the statistics of some scholars, in the 1990s, among the 125 emerging economies in the world, those with an average annual per capita GDP growth

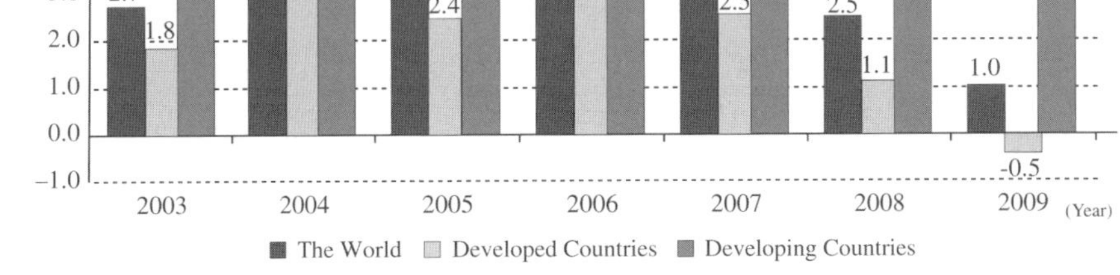

Figure 1.3 World GDP Growth Rate

Source: CEPAL, *Balance Preliminar de la Economias de America Latina y el Caribe 2008*, 2008, p. 14.

[7]The average annual GDP per capita of Latin America exceeded 3% during 1967–1973.

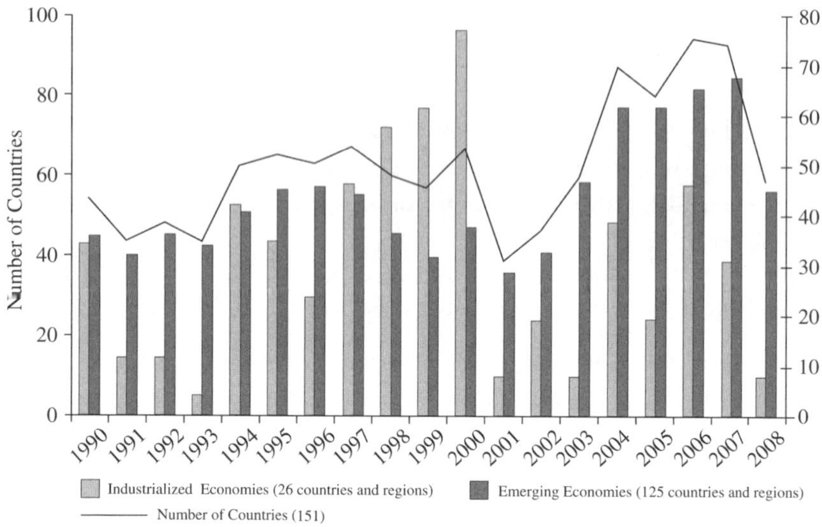

Figure 1.4 The Countries with the Number of GDP Per Capita Over 3% (1990–2008)
Source: Osvaldo Kacef, Rafael Lopez-Monti, "America Latina, del Auge a la Crisis: Desafios de Politica Macroeconomica", *Revista de la CEPAL*, No. 100, 2010, p. 43.

rate of over 3% occupied 38% of the total number, and from 2003 to 2008 this proportion rose to 57%. Over the same period, among the global 26 developed economies, the countries with an average annual per capita GDP growth rate over 3% fell from 33% down to 25% in the total number (see Figure 1.4). Under the above background, the international trade grew rapidly, the Foreign Direct Investment (FDI) inflows increased, the international market was awash in liquidity, and the international financing costs declined. All these had become the positive driving forces for the economic growth in Latin America.

2. The Huge Demand of China and Other Emerging Asian Economies for Energy and Raw Materials Have Boosted the Extraordinary Growth of the Commodity Exports from Latin America

Figure 1.5 shows that, from 2003 to 2008, there was a strong growth trend in Latin America's commodity exports — the annual

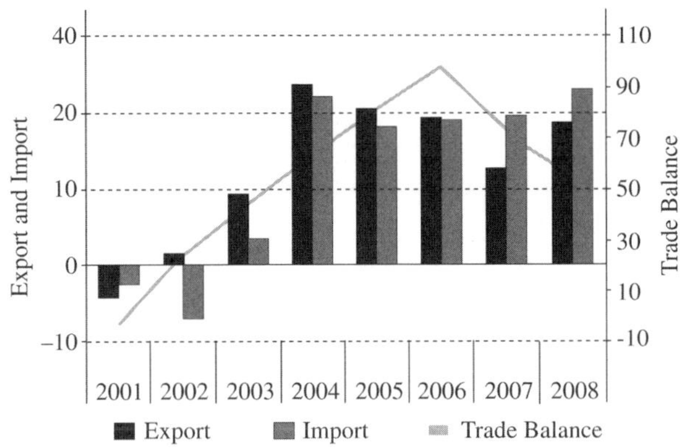

Figure 1.5 Annual Change of Merchandise Trade in Latin America (2001–2008) (Export & Import Annual Change Rate, Trade Balance in Billion Dollars)

Source: CEPAL, *Balance Preliminar de las Economias de America Latina y el Caribe 2008*, 2008, p. 68.

commodity trade surplus rose sharply: in 2006 it reached nearly $100 billion in size. In 2007 and 2008, although the import growth was significantly greater than that of the export, the trade settlement had always maintained a surplus. In 2008, the surplus was up to $48.3 billion.

3. The Trade Price Rate of Exports Over Imports Has Improved Substantially

The prices of primary products and crude oil in the international market continued to go higher, so that the purchasing power of the export countries of these products increased greatly. The relevant data from Figure 1.6 shows that, compared with the 1990s, the average value of the improvement of the trade price rate of exports over imports of the 19 countries in Latin America increased by 25.2%. Among those, Bolivia, Colombia, Ecuador, and Venezuela had benefited the most (the trade ratio reached 94.7%) because they were countries relying on the exports of crude oil and mineral products, while the trade price rate of the six countries in Central America, Haiti, and Dominica, which relied on the imports of energy, food and other products, got worse (down to 12.1%).

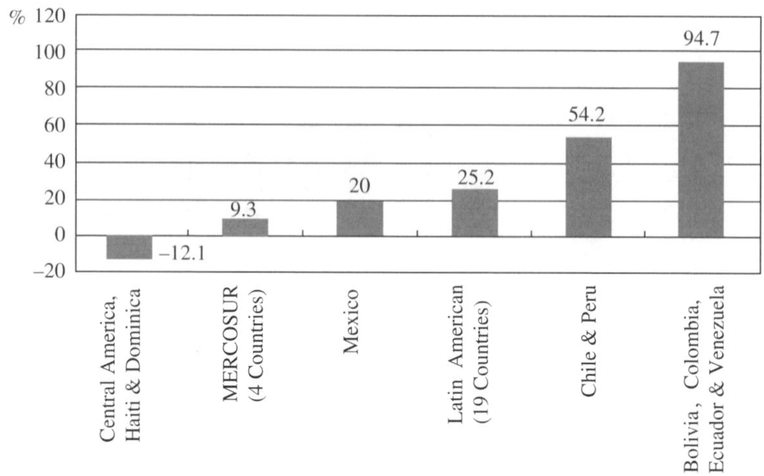

Figure 1.6 Improvement of Average Trade Parity (2003–2008 compared with 1990s)

Source: Osvaldo Kacef, Rafael Lopez-Monti, "America Latina, del Auge a la Crisis: Desafios de Politica Macroeconomica", *Revista de la CEPAL*, No. 100, Abril 2010, p. 44.

4. The Remittances of Overseas Workers Has Increased Substantially

There are a large number of Latin-American labor forces working in European and American developed countries; therefore, the remittances of overseas workers (*remesas de trabajadoris emigrados*) have become substantial foreign exchange earnings. From 2003 to 2008, the total annual remittances exceeded $50 billion, accounting for 1.7% of the regional GDP. This income is particularly important for Central American countries and Mexico because they have the largest number of overseas workers. Figure 1.7 shows that overseas workers' remittances received in Honduras each year amounted to 17.1% of its GDP, while the average value of the Central American countries was 9.2% of their GDP. The annual remittances of overseas workers in Mexico are equivalent to 2.4% of its GDP, roughly the same amount of its annual direct foreign investment.

About the role of the above factors in Latin America's economic growth, the Latin-American Economic Commission made the

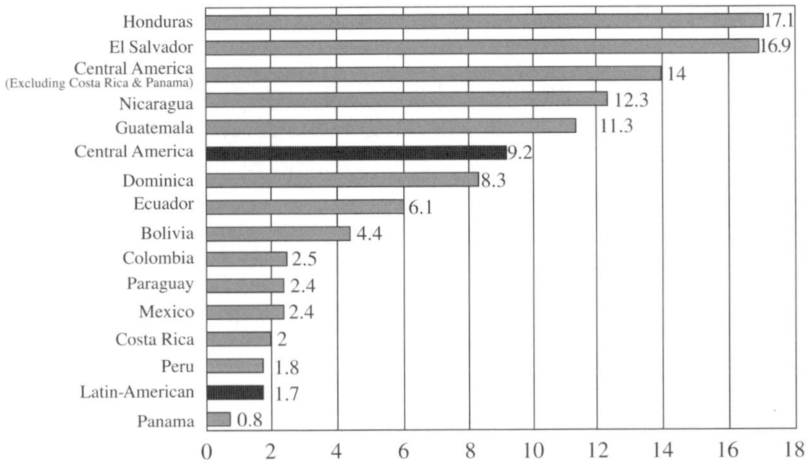

Figure 1.7 Overseas Workers' Average Annual Remittances Received (GDP %) (2003–2008)

Source: Osvaldo Kacef, Rafael Lopez-Monti, "America Latina, del Auge a la Crisis: Desafios de Politica Macroeconomica", *Revista de la CEPAL*, No. 100, Abril 2010, p. 44.

following explanation: "From 2003, especially since 2004, favorable external conditions began to exert positive impact on trade price rates, and thus led to the rise of export purchasing power and the expansion of export products because of the increase in the profit of such products. As a result, exports became the engine of the economic recovery. ... At the same time, from the perspective of the high unemployment rate, the low level of real wages, the inefficiency of operating equipments, and the previous economic instability, it was not surprising that the domestic demand did not respond timely".[8] The response of domestic demand was lagging behind because of the continuous impact of the Asian financial crisis (1998–2002), the Russian financial crisis, the Brazil monetary crisis (1999), and the Argentine economic crisis (2001). The Latin-American economy was in low growth, known as another "lost 5 years" in Latin America.

[8]CEPAL, *Balance Preliminar de las Economias de America Latina y el Caribe, 2004*, Santiago de Chile, pp. 12–13.

In the face of strong external demand and sluggish response of investment and domestic demand, the Latin-American countries have adopted two major policies. On the one hand, the Central Banks tried to lower interest rates, striving to support economic recovery by using flexible monetary policies. On the other hand, the public sectors tried to maintain the relative stability of prices by continuing to maintain a high level of savings. In addition, due to the relatively stable nominal rate of exchange, strong growth in exports and trade prices had led to a substantial improvement in export purchasing power and investment growth. The obvious increase of the investment of the production sectors of tradable commodities resulted in the growth of employment and real wages. If the cut of bank interest rate had a stimulating effect on the consumption of durable goods, the continuous rise in employment and real wages had driven the increase in the ordinary consumption.[9]

Looking back today, we find that Latin-American countries highly valued but also were very cautious with the arrival of the economic expansion cycle from 2003 to 2008. The reason why they highly valued it is that it was a good opportunity. The reason why they were cautious is that governments were aware that they had just gone through the "lost 5 years", the economic base was still quite fragile, and the conditions of a high-growth phase had not come. From this point of view, it is relatively easy to understand certain features of Latin-American economies from 2003 to 2008. First, the current accounts (except in 2008) and the public finances had maintained "double surplus". The current account could maintain a favorable balance because Latin-American countries took a moderate control over its import, which means they had broken their previous practice to have a substantial relaxation of import when a strong export growth occurred. The fact that the public finances could maintain a surplus indicated a significant change in the fiscal policy in Latin America — a widespread use of more stringent policy to increase revenue. Second, there was no rush to adopt expansionary

[9] *Ibid.*, p. 13.

policies and to pursue high economic growth. For example, the average annual growth rate of disposable income in Latin-American countries reached 5.7% from 2003 to 2008, exceeding the GDP growth rate (4.8%). The national savings rate was equivalent to 22% of the GDP annual growth and the average regional investment rate remained at the level before 2003 — slightly lower than the 20% of the GDP growth. Third, the policy of strict control or reducing the debt burden had been implemented, and even the debts of many countries had been paid ahead of schedule. Fourth, many active measures had been taken to intervene in the currency markets against the pressure of the continuous appreciation of the currency so that the international reserves of each country had different levels of increase. By the end of 2008, the total foreign exchange reserves in Latin America had more than $500 billion in size. Later it turned out that these factors had created very favorable conditions for Latin-American countries to respond to the impact of the international financial and economic crisis from 2008 to 2009.[10]

II. Dealing with the International Financial Crisis (2008–2009)

The international financial crisis triggered by the US subprime mortgage crisis began to impact the real economy of Latin America since the beginning of the third quarter of 2008, which means that the economic expansion in Latin America from 2003 to 2008 had come to an end. The impact of the international financial crisis on Latin America is mainly reflected in the following four aspects. First, the value and volume of exports of goods in Latin America dropped sharply. In 2009, exports fell by 9.6% and export value fell by 23.4%, compared with the previous year, in Latin America (see Figure 1.8), where oil and mining exporters (South American countries and Mexico) were the most seriously affected. Terms of trade in Latin America

[10]Osvaldo Kacef, Rafael Lopez-Monti, "America Latina, del Auge a la Crisis: Desafios de Politica Macroeconomica", *Revista de la CEPAL*, No. 100, abril de 2010, pp. 47–49.

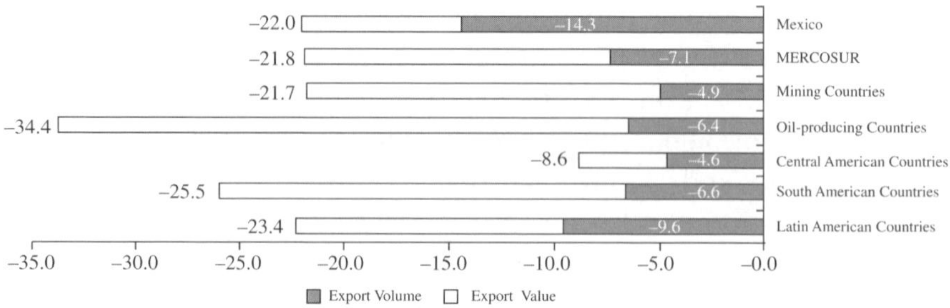

Figure 1.8 Changes in Exports of Goods Measured by Export Value and Export Volume in 2009 (%)

Source: Osvaldo Kacef, Rafael Lopez-Monti, "America Latina, del Auge a la Crisis: Desafios de Politica Macroeconomica", *Revista de la CEPAL*, No. 100, 2010, p. 55.

became worsened by 10% and exports declined 14% in purchasing power.[11]

Second, the remittances of the overseas workers had been reduced. This is related to the fact that the overseas labor force of Latin America is relatively concentrated in the United States and Spain that had got worst hit by the crisis. It is estimated that the remittances of overseas workers in the Central American countries, Colombia, Ecuador, Mexico and other countries in 2009 fell by about 10%. In addition, the crisis had also caused a greater negative impact on the tourism industry in the Caribbean countries.

Third, FDI in 2009 decreased by 35–40%, while domestic private bank loans shrank, especially in Chile, Peru, and Brazil (see Figure 1.9).

Fourth, due to the combined effect of the above factors, the business community and consumers are pessimistic about the economic outlook. In the first half of 2009, in the five categories of private consumption, the public consumption, export and import of goods and services, and fixed capital formation, only the public consumption was a positive (3.2), but the rest were negative (see Figure 1.10). It

[11]Development Center of the Organization of Economic Cooperation and Development, *The Outlook of Latin American Economy of 2011*, Chinese version, translated by Zhao Lihong & Zhao Chongyang, Contemporary World Press, 2011, p. 26.

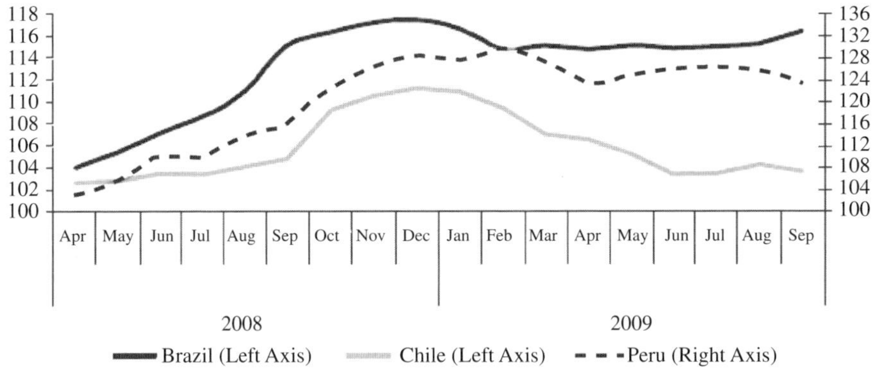

Figure 1.9 Private Bank Loans of Brazil, Chile, and Peru (Index of First Quarter 2008 = 100)

Source: Osvaldo Kacef, Rafael Lopez-Monti, "America Latina, del Auge a la Crisis: Desafios de Politica Macroeconomica", *Revista de la CEPAL*, No. 100, 2010, p. 56.

turned out that the economy in Latin America had a negative growth of 1.9% in 2009.

The time of the impact of this international financial crisis on Latin America is relatively short, lasting generally from the third quarter of 2008 to the second quarter of 2009. In the second half of 2009, most Latin-American countries had shown signs of economic recovery. Latin America had been able to successfully deal with this shock wave mainly due to the following factors: First, Latin-American countries had generally a more stable financial system not to be led to financial chaos by the impact of the international financial crisis. Second, the "counter-cycle" stimulus policy had been generally implemented. Unlike the 1990s, with the intervention of the international multilateral financial institutions, those countries were not allowed to carry out such policies even if they were able to. Third, the financial situation improved significantly in Latin America thanks to the economic prosperity from 2003 to 2008. Considerable foreign exchange reserves had been accumulated and become the necessary material basis for the implementation of "counter-cycle" policy. Fourth, some scholars believe that IMF loans to Latin-American governments also had had a positive effect on dealing with the crisis. It should be noted that the impact of the

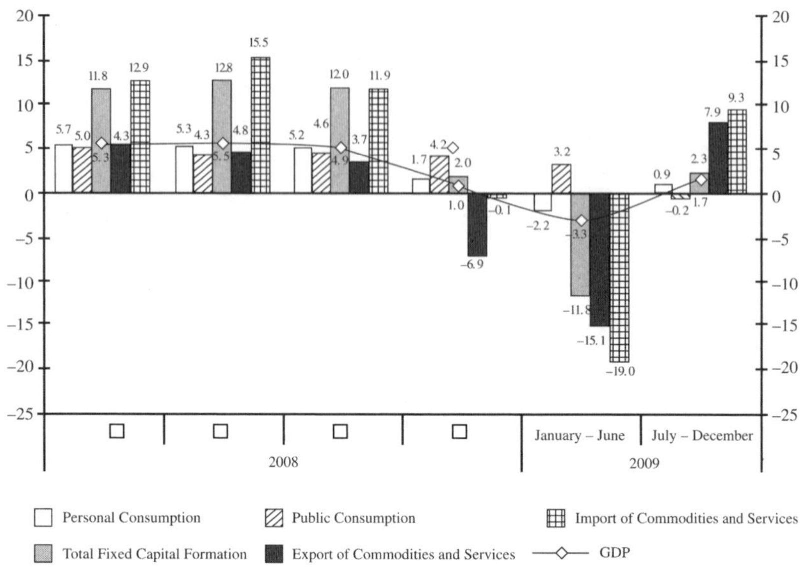

Figure 1.10 The Composition of the Total Demand and Supply of the Latin-American Region (Year-on-Year Change, %)

Source: Osvaldo Kacef, Rafael Lopez-Monti, "America Latina, del Auge a la Crisis: Desafios de Politica Macroeconomica", *Revista de la CEPAL*, No. 100, 2010, p. 57.

crisis on the economic recession of Latin-American countries have significant differences (see Figure 1.11). The explanation for the differences may mainly contain the following two aspects. First, Latin-American countries have different focuses of national foreign trade and economic cooperation on different countries, for example, exports of Mexico and Central American countries were highly dependent on the US market. Therefore, the seriously affected US economy by the crisis would inevitably lead to a drag in economic growth in the Mexican and Central American countries. China is the main import country of commodities from South American countries, and China's demand for commodities from South American countries from 2008 to 2009 still remained strong. Second, some Latin-American countries found it difficult to implement counter-cycle policies either because of the lack of interest in their basic economic policies for foreign investors, or because of their poor financial situations. Venezuela is probably a typical example in this regard.

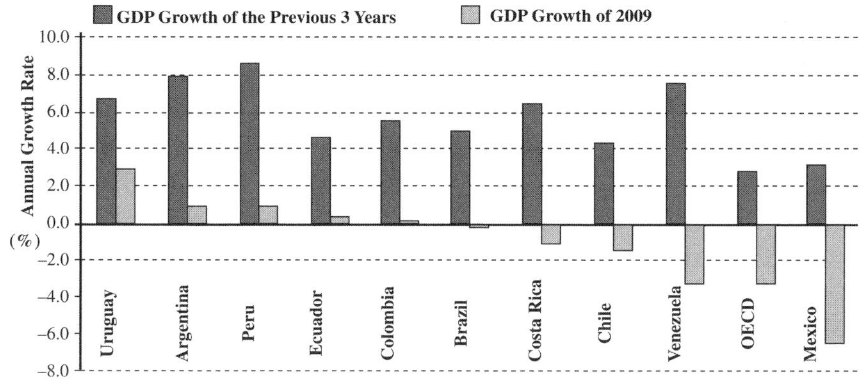

Figure 1.11 The Recession Impact of the Crisis on Latin-American and OECD Countries

Source: Development Center of the Organization of Economic Cooperation and Development: *The Outlook of Latin American Economy of 2011*, Chinese version, translated by Zhao Lihong & Zhao Chongyang, Contemporary World Press, 2011, p. 28.

As for the specific policies adopted by each country, it is impossible to give a comprehensive introduction because it is a question involving a very wide range of issues, and there are great differences between countries. From the regional perspective, we can sum up the policy measures that Latin-American countries had taken to deal with the international financial crisis from the following five aspects in Table 1.2. Generally speaking, the policies adopted by great powers involved a wide range of issues, even covering all of the five aspects, but the policies adopted by small countries were usually simple.

III. Economic Situations from 2010 to 2012

In 2010, 2011, and 2012, the economic growth of the Latin-American region was 5.9%, 4.3%, and 3.1%, respectively, and the per capita GDP growth was 4.8%, 3.1%, and 2%, respectively.[12] From the perspective of the whole region, the cause of the slowing-down economy can be understood from the following three aspects: First, the

[12]CEPAL, *Balance Preliminar de las Economias de America Latina y el Caribe 2012*, Santiago de Chile, diciembre de 2012, p. 72, Cuadro A2, p. 73, Cuadro A3.

Table 1.2 Overview of the Counter-cyclical Policy Adopted in Latin America

Counter-cyclical Policy	Main Content
1. Monetary and financial policies	To reduce the deposit reserve ratio, to relax the re-discount transactions, to increase the lending capacity of the Central Bank with the injection of the Exchequer, to lower interest rates, etc.
2. Fiscal policy	To implement tax relief or deferred tax for departments or enterprises affected seriously by the crisis, to reduce the purchase tax on vehicles and other commodities, to lower the personal income tax, to increase investment in infrastructure, to cut the public spending, etc.
3. Exchange rate and foreign trade policy	To increase the liquidity of foreign currency, e.g., Brazil reached a $30 billion currency swap agreement with the Federal Reserve, $10 billion agreement of "capital for oil" with China, increased import tariff or imposed the permit system for the introduction of some goods, and provided financial support for the export of goods, etc.
4. Department policy	To expand the scale of housing construction, to establish special funds to support SMEs, agriculture and animal husbandry, as well as some key industrial sectors, etc.
5. Labor and social policy	To expand unemployment insurance coverage, to adjust the minimum wage, to implement social assistance programs, etc.

Source: Quinta Cumbre de las Americas, *La Reaccion de los Gobiernos de las Americas Frente a la Crisis Internacional: Una Presentacion de las Medidas de Politica Anunciadas hasta 31 de marzo de 2009*, Puerto Espana, 17–19 de abril, 2009.

measures taken by Latin-American countries to deal with the international financial crisis triggered by the US subprime mortgage between 2008 and 2009 were successful because the economy of the entire region recovered rapidly and a high growth of 6% was obtained in 2010. But it is clearly difficult to maintain this growth rate. Second, the economic recovery in the United States and Europe was slow and weak, and especially the European countries intensified debt crisis at the end of 2009 started a new round of economic impact on the Latin-American economy. Third, it is also difficult for the current economic growth mode in Latin America to adapt to the changes in the international environment in the post-crisis era.

There are four reasons for the Latin-American high economic growth in 2010 as follows. First, this was the recovery of the economy after the recession of the previous year, including the restored use of the original idle production capacity and the change of the number of the countries with negative economic growth from 17 to 6, and so on. Second, the majority of the anti-cycle stimulus policies implemented by the governments of Latin America were still playing a role. Third, in 2010, except some of the Caribbean countries, the vast majority of Latin-American countries had a significant increase in exports of goods, especially in the growth of export of oil and mineral products. Fourth, domestic demand growth remained stable. The Economic Commission for Latin America (ECLAC) said, "The improvement of the labour market index, the growth of credit, and the general improvement of the economic outlook have stimulated the growth of private consumption. Coupled with the substantial increase in investment in machinery and equipment, together they have constituted one of the main boosters of demand growth".[13] From the perspective of the whole region, from 2010 to 2012, the domestic demand was the key factor in promoting the economic growth, while the shrinking of external demand was the main cause of the economic slowdown. In contrast, FDI had not been reduced, and the investment rate in most Latin-American countries showed a steady growth trend.

We emphasize that in 2010 the economic growth of Latin America is recovery in nature, which means that the economic slowdown in 2011 should be expected, including the limit of the use of idle production capacity, as well as the exit of stimulus policies. The effect could not last to 2011. Some problems occurred in the rapid recovery of the economy in Latin America in 2010, of which two had a greater impact. One is the increase in the pressure of currency appreciation.

[13]CEPAL, *Balance Preliminar de las Economias de America Latina y el Caribe 2010*, Santiago de Chile, diciembre de 2010, p. 7.

Because of the US Fed's quantitative easing policy and other reasons, the global liquidity was high, and in the asset market a large number of short-term capitals flowed to emerging countries, especially Latin-American countries, so that these countries were facing the pressure of increasing currency appreciation. For example, in the first nine months of 2010, the currency appreciation emerged in Brazil, Colombia, Costa Rica, Chile, Uruguay, and other countries, among which the highest currency appreciation happened in Brazil, reaching 13.6% and the lowest appreciation of Costa Rica also reached 8%. According to the analysis of some Latin-American relevant institutions, for some Latin-American countries, it was not sufficient to solve the problem simply through such measures as limiting the short-term capital inflows and increasing the foreign exchange reserves. It was also necessary to take counter-cyclical strategy in the fiscal and financial field as an auxiliary means to ease the pressure on the exchange market so as to reduce the pressure on internal demand and to prevent excessive credit. The other is a general rebound of inflation. In 2010, Latin America's consumer price index rose from 4.7% the previous year to 6.5% — not a great increase, but a common trend in regional countries. In terms of the causes, one is because the fuel and food prices in the international market continued to rise so that the imported inflation emerged in countries (such as the Central American and Caribbean countries) that imported such goods. The other is because the economic recovery prompted the growth of investment and consumption, driving the increase of prices, and therefore, the more economic recovery, the greater the pressure of inflation.

A problem worth discussing is the viewpoint in the economic community of Latin America that by the end of 2010 a "partial overheating" phenomenon had occurred in the Latin-American economy. This judgment may be due to the lack of understanding of the recovery of the high growth of the Latin-American economy in 2010, and the potential impact of the slow western economic recovery, especially that of the debt crisis in Europe. Brazil is one of the typical examples. With Brazil's economic growth in 2010 reaching a record high of 7.5%, coupled with the rebound in inflation, the Brazilian government had decided that its economy was overheating, and so it took cooling measures. For example, at the beginning of 2011, the government had compressed 50 billion reais (about 1.2% of its GDP) in its annual public budget, and from January to July, Brazil's Central Bank adjusted the benchmark interest rate several times, from 10.75% to 12.5%. To limit short-term speculative capital inflows, for the first eight months of 2011, the Central Bank raised the financial transaction tax up to 6%.[14] Under the influence of this policy, a rapid decline occurred in the economic growth in Brazil — during the first three quarters of 2011, an increase of only 3.2%, of which the manufacturing sector grew by only 1%, and the annual economic growth rate was only 2.7% in 2011. Being the largest economy in Latin America, Brazil's growth rate fell by 64% compared with the previous year, becoming an important factor in the economic slowdown in Latin America in 2011.

By 2012 the influence of a big power on the region's economic growth became more obvious. In order to reverse the economic downturn, in the second half of 2011, Brazil took the "maintaining-growth" policy. For example, from August 2011 to October 2012, the Central Bank of Brazil adjusted its benchmark interest rate 10 times, gradually from 12.5% to 7.25%; various measures were taken to protect and expand the market for industrial products, such as the implementation of a preferential credit plan of a total of 20 billion reais to encourage enterprises to update their equipments, tax cuts on the sales of cars and white home appliances, and a temporary increase in import tariffs of the goods of iron and steel, petrochemicals, pharmaceuticals, and other products. In August 2012, the federal government launched the infrastructure construction plan for a total investment of 133 billion reais (about $65 billion) over a period of 25 years, planning to build 7,500 kilometers of roads and 10,000 kilometers of railway, one of the key objectives of which was to attract private capitals to participate in the infrastructure construction. In 2012, despite

[14]Zhou Zhiwei, *Brazil*: "The 'Domino' Worry of the Cabinet Corruption Case", Wu Baiyi (ed.): *Report on the Development of Latin America and the Caribbean* (2011–2012), Social Sciences Literature Publishing House, 2012, pp. 137–139.

its efforts to promote domestic demand, the effect in Brazil was relatively limited since the annual economic growth rate ended up to only 1.2%, coupled with the decline in exports. During Brazil's economic downturn, the economic performance of the other two major countries — Argentina and Mexico — was also poor. Following the growth of 5.6% in 2010, Mexico kept a 3.8% or so in the past two years. In 2012, the high growth rate of Argentina fell from 9% several years before to only 2.2% mainly due to the decline in exports of industrial goods to Brazil and other major markets as well as the impact of the drought on its agriculture.

For the Latin-American region, the international trade environment in 2012 was generally unfavorable. In its three major trading partners, the EU economy was in recession, the United States' economy continued to grow slowly, and China's economy had slowed down significantly. Therefore, it was more prominent that the decline in exports had become the main cause of the economic slowdown. In 2011, the export value of Latin America grew by 22.3%, but in 2012, it was an increase of only 1.6%, of which exports to the EU fell by 4.9%, exports to China's fell by 0.9%, but exports to the United States increased 4.8%.[15] Based on the above major changes in the export markets, the foreign trade situation was relatively good in the countries relying on the markets of the United States (Mexico, Central American countries, as well as a number of oil exporting countries), while the foreign trade situation had deteriorated in the South American countries that exported natural resources to EU and China. From the perspective of commodity prices, oil and edible oil prices continued to remain strong; thus the Latin-American countries had a substantial reduction in trade prices; in other words, the growth of export value in 2012 mainly resulted from the increase in the volume of exports. For Brazil and Argentina, the value of exports in 2012 was also a going-down — Brazil fell by 4.5% compared with the previous year and Argentina by 2.4%. However, according to the forecast of ECLAC, the economy of Latin America wound hit bottom

[15]CEPAL, *Balance Preliminar de las Economias de America Latina y el Caribe 2010*, Santiago de Chile, diciembre de 2012, p. 7.

and rebound in 2013, expected to achieve a growth of 3.8% against that of 4.1% forecasted by the International Monetary Fund.

Statistics in Table 1.3 indicate that Latin America's economic situation had been significantly improved over the 10 years from 2003 to 2012. Although the economic growth rate had not yet been restored to the level of 1970s, it had gone out of the continuous downturn and violent fluctuations of the 1980s and 1990s into the track of basic normal growth. The current account and capital projects had some changes after a period of double surplus (2005–2007), but there had been no payment pressures — the majority of the primary fiscal years remained a state of surplus, the proportion of the central government debt to GDP fell from 57% in 2003 to 29.8% in 2012, and the foreign exchange reserves increased from $17.4175 billion in 2003 to $723.125 billion in 2012. These changes were conducive to the next stage of development.

Section 3 Pragmatic Tendency of the Economic Policy

Early in 2008, Javier Santiso, director of the Development Center of the Organization for Economic Cooperation and Development, pointed out, "Latin America's strong growth over the past five years to a large extent originated from the global macroeconomic prosperity of the new millennium, e.g., the rising commodity prices, favorable terms of trade, low price of capital, plenty of foreign investment, and so on. However, this growth has come from the sound and effective policy framework".[16] Santiso emphasized the "sound and effective policy" of Latin-American countries, which is very worthy of our attention.

At the beginning of the 21st century, with a number of left-wing governments in power, the development ideologies and economic policies of Latin-American countries had changed significantly. Such changes were mainly manifested in the choice of the economic policy not blindly following some "foreign dogma", such as the cult of

[16] Javier Santiso, The "Preface" of *The Economic Outlook of Latin America in 2009*, Translated by Yue Yunxia *et al.*, The World Knowledge Press, 2009, p. 2.

Table 1.3 Major Economic Performance in Latin America (2003–2012)

	2003	2004	2005	2006	2007	2008	2009	2010	2011	2012
Economic growth rate (%)	1.8	5.8	4.6	5.6	5.6	4.0	−1.9	5.9	4.3	3.1
Balance of current account ($100 million)	91.28	227.51	361.98	499.07	129.70	−330.82	−230.00	−554.82	−735.65	−886.06
Capital account balance ($100 million)	6.97	−71.81	248.56	134.53	1,126.17	715.75	692.17	1,417.50	1,793.99	1,413.93
Primary fiscal surplus /GDP	−0.2	0.6	1.5	2.4	2.3	1.4	−0.9	−0.1	0.2	−0.3
Central government debt/GDP	57.0	51.2	43.2	36.1	30.7	29.7	31.0	30.4	30.5	29.8
Foreign exchange reserves ($100 million)	1,741.75	1,964.35	2,246.88	2,732.19	4,138.37	4,531.72	5,141.85	6,104.94	7,231.25	7,231.25

Note: The data of 2012 are preliminary.
Source: CEPAL, *Balance Preliminar de las Economias de America Latina y el Caribe 2012*, p. 71.

the "Washington Consensus" in the 1990s, taking the initiative to correct the imbalance of the relationship between the state and the market, re-emphasizing the importance of the functions of the macro-control and the public service of the country, and making decisions from the actual situation in the country. Therefore, some foreign academic circles boiled the guiding ideology of policy adjustments in Latin America down to "pragmatism". Obviously, this change in decision making was not only an important factor in maintaining a good growth trend of the Latin-American economy in the past 10 years, but also a great significance in promoting the region's economy to continue to grow healthily and stably. The change of this kind of guiding ideology resulted mainly from the great setbacks experienced in the 1980s and 1990s. However, some foreign scholars believe that the rise of pragmatism in Latin America was related to the impact of the Chinese mode. Javier Santiso believed that although the China mode was difficult to be replicated in other places, "it is not possible to deny China's experience... In Latin America, the Chinese experience has led to a group of people represented by the Chilies who are also trying to create something new: the economic development based on the principle of pragmatic economic policies, rather than on the basis of laboratory tests or other modes of other countries that are directly derived from the economics textbooks".[17] Specific cases of economic policy adjustment in Latin America have been discussed above, such as the counter-cyclical policy adopted in the process of the international financial crisis. Below, some other cases will be added.

I. Fiscal Policy: Emphasis on Revenue Increase by Reducing Expenditure and Sustainable Growth

The financial revenue of Latin-American countries had been in good condition from 2003 to 2008. Such a good situation made it easy to get a fever after experiencing many years of financial difficulties.

---

[17] Javier Santiso, "La Emergencia de China y Su Impacto en America Latina", *Politica Exterior*, V. 19, No. 107, p. 108.

However, Latin-American countries did not immediately take the fiscal policy of expansion; instead, they continued to implement policies to increase revenue and reduce expenditure, seeking to consolidate the fiscal balance and the pursuit of sustainable growth. In terms of income, in addition to the expansion of taxes because of the economic recovery and the improvement of the situation of taxation, the national governments had generally improved their relevant tax rates. Take VAT — the main tax, for example. The average VAT in the region increased from 11.7% in 1994 to 14.6% in 2004. A sharp rise in commodity prices was a new source of income; for example, in Argentina, the export taxes on agricultural and animal products were enough to "pay most of the expenditure of the government". The increased income of those countries producing and exporting oil and mineral products was more impressive as these countries generally increased the corresponding tax rates, as shown in Table 1.4.

In terms of savings, the spending growth appeared below economic growth in all the countries, which could be described as "unprecedented" in Latin America. This phenomenon had benefited from the reform of the financial system of Latin America, such as the implementation of the "Fiscal Responsibility Law" in Brazil, the

Table 1.4 Some Latin-American and Caribbean Countries: Oil-related Tax Rates (%)

Country	Resource Tax	Income Tax	Profit Remittance Tax	Investment Incentives
Bolivia	18	25	12.5	Yes
Chile	28.0–45	15	35	Yes
Colombia	5.0–25	35	7	No
Ecuador	12.5–18.5	25	25	—
Guatemala	5.0–20	30	No	Yes
Guyana	No	35	10	Yes
Mexico	No	35	7.7	Yes
Trinidad and Tobago	12.5	50	—	Yes
Venezuela	30	50	No	Yes

Source: CEPAL, sobre la base de J.M. Davis R. Ossowski y A. Fedelino, *Fiscal Policy Formulation and Implementation in Oil-Producing Countries*, Washington, D.C., Fondo Monetario Internacional, 2008.

"Fiscal Prudence and Transparency Law" in Peru, and the "Fiscal Structure Balance Law" in Chile. Some countries had also made certain temporary decisions based on the changes. For example, the government of Argentina decided to set aside part of the 2004 income allocation for the payment of the annual expenditure of the following year due to its expectation of a decrease in its fiscal revenue in 2005; the Brazilian government decided to raise the interim primary surplus fiscal indicators in 2004, and so on.

Another important savings measure of Latin America is to establish a "stabilization and savings fund" (*fondos de estabilizacion de ahorro*). The purpose of establishing such a fund is to reduce the impact of the changes of export earnings on the public accounts due to the fluctuations in commodity prices. To be blunter, it is to avoid the phenomenon of "spending money like water when there is enough money and borrowing money to spend when there is no money". As a result, the countries exporting bulks of primary products generally have established such funds, such as Chile's "Copper Compensation Fund", Colombia's "National Coffee Fund" and "Oil Savings and Stabilization Fund", Ecuador's "Stability, Social and Production Investment and Public Debt-Reduction Fund", Mexico's "Oil Stabilization Fund", and Venezuela's "Macroeconomic Stabilization Fund". These funds typically have the following three elements: (1) to determine a reference price according to a conservative estimate of the medium-term outlook of certain commodities; (2) to develop appropriate investment guidelines for determining the investment of the increased revenue obtained during the export boom so as to be able to use the income when the export prices go down; (3) to develop operating rules to determine the proportion between price fluctuations and the spending of the fund.[18]

With the above measures, the fiscal accounts of the central governments of the Latin-American countries have made significant progress in reducing the deficit and increasing the primary surplus. According to the estimate of some scholars, in Latin America, from

[18]CEPAL, *Balance Preliminar de las Economias de America Latina y el Caribe 2004*, p. 41.

2002 to 2008, the total annual income increase was equivalent to 3.4% of its GDP, the increase of expenditure equaled 1.6% of its GDP, and the primary fiscal surplus growth was at an average annual rate of 1.8%. In the 19 countries with complete statistical data, only 7 achieved the financial surplus in 2002, 14 in 2008; only 3 countries — Guatemala, Haiti, and Honduras — continued to be in the state of fiscal deficit.[19]

In the discussion of the adjustment of fiscal policy in Latin America, attention also needs to be paid to the changes of the debt policy of these countries. In recent years, the proportion of the public debt and GDP in Latin America had continued to decline, from 58.4% in 2002 to 28% in 2008. The development of Latin America had long been disturbed by debt problems. Both the economic recession in the 1980s and the weakening of the ability to invest in the 1990s were directly related to the debt burden. Argentina triggered a crisis because of its debt default in 2001, indicating that the debt crisis was always there. Therefore, with the improvement of the economic situation at the beginning of the 21st century, the Latin-American countries had sought to reduce the debt burden to reverse the long-term passive situation. The achievements in reducing the burden of foreign debt both benefited from some objective factors, such as the general appreciation of the currency relative to the dollar, and from the adjustment of policies taken by Latin-American countries. First, as mentioned above, adhering to the implementation of the fiscal policy to increase revenue and reduce expenditure so as to maintain the primary fiscal surplus. Second, debt restructuring — issuing local currency bonds to replace foreign currency bonds. In Brazil, for example, the local currency bonds had replaced most of the Brady Bonds and the debt maturity was extended to an average of 3.7 years; the local currency bonds issued by Colombia and the real bonds and the peso bonds issued by Brazil and Mexico through the Inter American Development Bank had extended the deadline

[19]Osvaldo Kacef, Rafael Lopez-Monti, "America Latina, del Auge a la Crisis: Desafios de Politica Macroeconomica", *Revista de las CEPAL*, No. 100, abril de 2010, p. 50.

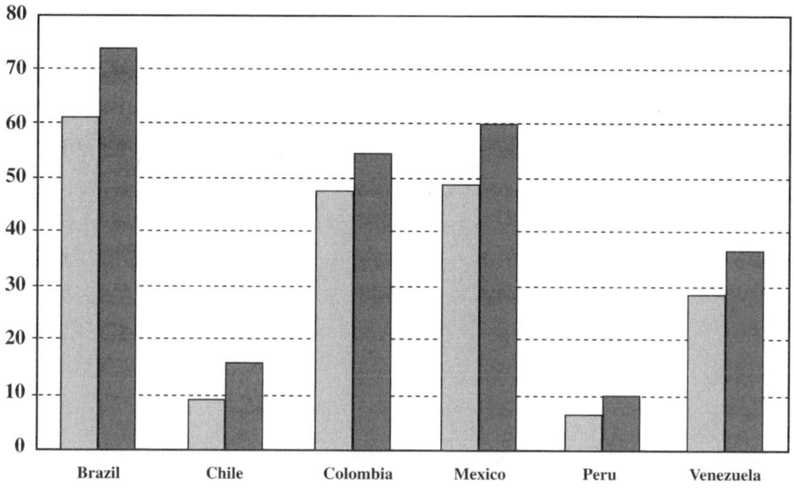

Figure 1.12 Ratio of Local Currency Denominated Bonds to the Total Amount of Government Bonds (%)

Source: CEPAL, *Balance Preliminar de las Economias de America Latina y el Caribe 2005*, 2005, p. 57.

with fixed interest rates. Figure 1.12 shows that the proportion of the local currency bonds in the total amount of government bonds in six major countries in Latin America increased significantly, among which Brazilian local currency bonds accounted for 70%. Third, many countries had paid their debts in advance taking advantage of the favorable financial situations. For example, Brazil had paid off all their debts to the International Monetary Fund ($15.46 billion) by the end of 2005.

II. Monetary and Exchange Rate Policy: Focus on Curbing Inflation and Currency Appreciation

The Latin-American countries were facing higher inflation expectations and currency appreciation pressures, both in the expansion phase (2003–2008) and in the post-crisis phase since 2009. The rise of the prices of international foods and fuels is the main reason for the rising pressure of inflation. Central America and most of the Caribbean countries faced even greater pressure of inflation because they needed to import large amounts of foods and fuels. The pressure of currency appreciation came from large inflows of capital, significant improvement of external trade price, and the increase in remittances. South American countries faced greater pressure of currency appreciation than Mexico and Central American countries.

In terms of monetary policy, the Latin-American countries can be divided into three categories. The first category refers to those implementing the inflation targeting system or about to implement the system, such as Brazil, Chile, Colombia, Mexico, Paraguay, Peru, Costa Rica, Guatemala, and Honduras. The Central Banks of these countries had to make great efforts to ensure the basic realization of their inflation targets, in which Mexico and Central American countries had taken price subsidy policies for foods and fuels. The countries of the second category increased their international reserves and limited their domestic credits as a priority target of monetary policy, such as Argentina, Bolivia, Nicaragua, and Dominica, in which Nicaragua and Dominica were trying to implement the relevant agreements with the International Monetary Fund. The countries of the third category were Ecuador, Salvatore, and Panama, whose economies were based on dollars, basically having no monetary policies of their own, and their levels of interest rates changing with the international interest rate. It should be noted that in the economic expansion from 2003 to 2008 the Latin-American countries basically had achieved success in the control of inflation, owing to the effective measures taken by the Central Banks and the effect of the currency appreciation on price increases in Latin-American countries. Because inflation was under control, interest rates in most Latin-American countries had declined.

According to the report of the ECLAC, the trend of currency appreciation in Latin-American countries lasted almost throughout the whole process of the economic expansion from 2003 to 2008. The pressure of currency appreciation had eased when the international financial crisis broke out in August 2008. For the sake of simplicity, we can take the year of 2005 as an example. During the first 10 months of 2005, the "extraregional" (excluding the trades between the local regional countries) effective exchange rate appreciation in Latin America increased by 3.8%, of which South American countries experienced an average appreciation of 5.5%, and Central America,

Mexico, and the Caribbean countries an average of 2.3%.[20] It is noteworthy that, in 2010, as the economic recovery in Latin America had been consolidated, a large influx of external funds made it possible for the currency appreciation trend to come back again. Compared with the same period the previous year, in the first 10 months of 2010, 11 countries in Latin America had nominal appreciations of the currency, among which the following countries had larger appreciations of their currencies: Brazilian real — 13.2%, Colombian peso — 13.6%, Uruguayan peso — 3.1%, Chilean peso — 9.4%, and Costa Rican colon — 8.0%.

Since the beginning of the 21st century, an important policy change of the Latin-American countries is a general strengthening of the capital control. The specific practices of different countries are not the same. First, it is the intervention of the foreign exchange market. This is almost universally adopted in the world, and therefore, the international reserves of Latin-American countries generally increased. The international reserves of some countries (such as Bolivia, Paraguay, and Peru) were close to or more than 25% of their GDP. Second, it is the reduction or limiting of the inflow of foreign short-term speculative capitals. The common measures include imposing a financial transaction tax or implementing the non-interest-bearing reserve policy. In Brazil, for example, the income financial transactions tax for foreign investment in fixed-profit products was increased first from 2% in 2009 to 4%, and then to 6% in October 2010, the futures transaction tax from 0.38% to 6%, and the stock transaction tax was fixed at 2%. Third, it is taking measures to promote domestic capital outflows. For example, in September 2010, Peru announced to allow their pension fund management companies to invest 30% of the funds overseas; in November 2010, Chile also announced that the limit of their pension overseas investment would gradually be increased to 80%.[21]

---

[20] CEPAL, *Balance Preliminar de las Economias de America Latina y el Caribe 2005*, p. 64.

[21] Development Center of Economic Cooperation and Development Organization, *The Economic Outlook of Latin America in 2012*, translated by Wang Wenxian, Zhao Lihong *et al.*, Contemporary World Press, 2012, p. 28.

III. Industrial Policy: Focus on Improving International Competitiveness

In the period of import in substitution of industrialization, the Latin-American countries had a clear industrial policy (*Industriales politicas*). According to the national industrial policy, the state made the long-term industrial development plan, determined new industry sectors to be established, and built the coordination mechanism between the industrial departments. For example, in the 1970s, Brazil proposed the "Second National Development Plan", and Mexico implemented the "National Industry Promotion Planning" from 1979 to 1982. They are the typical examples of the implementation of industrial policies. After the debt crisis broke out in the 1980s, the industrial policy had gradually lost its position in Latin-American countries, and later with the advance of the economic reform, the industrial policy had actually been canceled. The main reasons are: (1) In the days of the implementation of industrial policy, the creation of new industrial sectors was accomplished mainly by the state or state-owned enterprises to invest. After the economic reform, the state lost the main position of the investment, and the state-owned enterprises were either privatized or bankrupted. (2) The new economic mode established after the reform emphasized the realization of the balance of the public finance, focusing on the abolishment of the financial and credit subsidies. (3) The industrial policy had been criticized as one of the "culprits" of distorting resource allocations due to the decision-making errors or waste of investment in the planning of industrial development and implementation of investment projects. Therefore, the prevailing argument then was: "The best industrial policy is no industrial policy".

Since the mid-1990s, with the new economic mode gradually established, the Latin-American countries began to implement the so-called "Competitiveness Policy" (*competitividad de politicas*). Its purpose was to improve the competitiveness of domestic products in the international market. This policy covered a wide range, including the so-called "sectoral policies", such as the special support policies for automotive, electronics, footwear, and other industries, and the support policy for SMEs and micro-enterprises, involving financial, credit, tax, and other support, and the support in organization and coordination of the value chain or the production region. The importance of this policy was obvious, but it had its limitations. The ECLAC pointed out, "The competitiveness policy of Latin America, including those sectoral policies, is concerned with improving the effectiveness of the existing departments, rather than creating new departments; it seeks the expansion of participation in the international market on the basis of the static comparative advantage of natural resources and non-skilled labors".[22]

Specifically, there are two major issues involved here. First, the competitiveness policy is concerned about the immediate and static benefits. The biggest difference between competitiveness policy and industrial policy is that the former supported all the existing industrial sectors without priorities, and thus it was called "neutral policy". Therefore, it did not focus on creating a strategic emerging industry sector. Such a policy would inevitably lead to the solidification of the current industrial structures so that those non-promising industrial sectors could not be eliminated and those promising emerging industry sectors could not be established. In this background, the establishment of some of the emerging industry sectors in Latin America mainly relied on FDI. Second, the gap between the development of science and technology in Latin-American countries and the advanced level of technology of the world is becoming increasingly large. Before the 1980s, the development of science and technology in Latin America was not very satisfactory, but the public departments had done a lot of work in the building of scientific research institutions and scientific research mechanism and provided 80% of the national research and development investment. Some large state-owned enterprises (such as energy and

[22]CEPAL, *Cambio Estructural para la Igualdad: Una Vision Integrada del Desarrollo*, San Salvador, 27–31 de agosto, 2012, p. 246.

telecommunications companies) had played an important role in the research and development. After the economic reform, the development of science and technology in the country had not been clearly defined, and the development of science and technology had mostly lost its goal and power. The public policy and the public investment in the field of science and technology had been marginalized, and many research institutions had turned to the market to meet the needs of the market. It had become the main trend to buy foreign technology or to rely on direct foreign investment to get technology transfer. In today's rapid development of world science and technology, the situation in Latin America is facing a huge risk.

Since entering the 21st century, the gradual coming back of industrial policy has become an important manifestation of adjusting the development policies of the Latin-American countries. For example, after the economic crisis in 2001, Argentina set up the "National Forum of Production Chain Industrial Competitiveness" (*Foros Nacionales de Competitividad Industrial de las Cadenas Productivas*), choosing nine industrial sectors as the key ones. In 2011, Argentina had again launched the "2020 Industrial Strategic Plan" (*Plan Estrategico Industrial 2020*), increasing the key industrial sectors to 11. In 2002, Mexico promulgated the "Economic Policy of Competitiveness" (*Politica Economica Para la Competitividad*), identifying 12 priority industries; subsequently promulgated the "10 Suggestions to Improve the Competitiveness from 2008 to 2012", including promoting high-value-added industrial upgrading, accelerating the transformation of traditional industries, and using advanced technology. In 2005, Peru made the "National Competitiveness Plan" (*Plan Nacional de Competitividad*), identifying six key industries. In 2007, Chile promulgated the "National Innovation Strategy to Improve Competitiveness" (*Estrategia Nacional de Innovacion para la Competitividad*), the preferred industries including aquatic products, fruit, pig, poultry, functional food, mining, tourism, logistics and transportation, financial services, construction, etc. In addition, a number of countries had taken measures to encourage individual projects, e.g., the Peru government encouraged some of the large mining investment projects, the government of

Costa Rica encouraged the project of the introduction of Intel, the Uruguayan government gave tax incentives to projects in line with their national interests, etc. The above examples show that the return of industrial policy in Latin America has become a trend, but the progress is uneven between countries in progress. It is generally considered that at present Brazil is taking the lead in the recovery of industrial policy in the Latin-American region.

In November 2003, the Brazilian Lula government promulgated the *Directions of Industrial, Technological and Foreign Trade Policies* (*Directrices de Politca Industrial, Tecnologica y de Comercio Extirior*, PIT-CE), selecting semiconductors, software, pharmaceuticals and capital goods as four strategic industries, and established the "Brazilian Industrial Development Agency" as the coordination mechanism for the implementation of the policies. In May 2008, the government of Brazil launched a new industrial policy — "Production Development Policy" (*Politica de Desarrollo Produvtivo*, PDP), covering four aspects: (1) measures of financial and credit support; (2) the plan of six strategic technologies by the Ministry of Science and Technology responsible for coordination; (3) the plan of seven leading industries (including aviation, petroleum, natural gas and petrochemicals, bioethanol, mining, paper and pulp, and beef) coordinated by the national economic and social development bank; (4) the plan of 12 competitive industries (including the automotive industry, capital goods, textiles and clothing, wood and furniture, cosmetics, civil construction, service industry, shipbuilding, leather and footwear, agricultural products processing, bio-diesel, and plastics) coordinated by the ministries of development, industry, and foreign trade. However, no sooner had this policy come out then the international financial crisis had broken out. Therefore, the Brazilian government had to focus on the prevention of its economic downturn through fiscal and credit measures, ignoring the adjustment of economic structures.

After a strong recovery of the economy in 2010, the Rousseff Administration launched the Brasil Maior Plan (2011–2014) in August 2011 to put further stress on key industrial sectors, especially the development of resources and technology-intensive industries.

The program was launched in Brazil in the context of a huge appreciation of the currency, Real. In addition to emphasizing the promotion of innovation, investment and foreign trade, it included a series of measures to protect the domestic market and protect domestic manufacturing production, with clear trade protectionism. The above situation shows that great importance has been attached to Brazil's industrial policy, and the two governments in the policy have continuity. It also must be noted that after Brazil's "production development policy" and "Brasil Maior Plan" had been promulgated, with the interruption of the international financial crisis and currency appreciation, the government's main focus was on "growth", rather than "adjustment of structure"; therefore, the actual effect of the implementation of industrial policy was relatively limited.

According to the report of the ECLAC, with the return of industrial policies, Latin-American countries have generally put more emphasis on technology and innovation policies. It can be seen from the following three aspects: (1) Many countries have adopted the concept of "national innovation system", and realized that knowledge innovation is a complicated system, which needs to be promoted from the two aspects of supply and demand. Supply refers to the various supports such as providing the public resources to knowledge innovation (Brazil's research and development investment accounted for 1.2% of its GDP, being the highest in Latin America); demand refers to providing the corresponding policy stimulus for the demand of knowledge innovation of the production department. (2) All the countries have made progress in the study of how to design and how to implement the policy of technology and innovation. (3) Institutional construction has been emphasized, e.g., Argentina, Brazil, Costa Rica, Cuba, and Venezuela have determined the Ministerial-level agency in charge of determining the innovation project, and Chile, Mexico, and Nicaragua have established the "National Innovation Council" (*Consejo Nacional de Innovacion*) as a subsidiary to the Presidential Palace, the Ministry of Industry or the Ministry of Education.[23]

[23]CEPAL, *Cambio Estructural para la Igualdad: Una Vision Integrada del Desarrollo*, San Salvador, 27–31 de agosto, 2012, p. 248.

IV. Social Policy: Emphasis on Inclusive Growth

Latin America is known as "one of the areas in the world with the most unfair income distribution" and has always been criticized by the public opinions of the world. The social inequality in Latin America has its specific historical background and institutional factors, but from the perspective of government decision making, it is true that there has been a long-term bias of emphasizing the economic policy and ignoring the social policy. One of the social consequences of the "lost 10 years" in the 1980s is the record of a 48.3% of poverty rate in the whole area in 1990. In the structural reform of the 1990s, the new liberalism vigorously promoted that the so-called "social equity is the natural result of economic growth". The structural reform process in the 1990s was accompanied with intense social conflicts. Therefore, it is not hard to find that it failed to bring the positive result of social stability although the political democratization process of Latin-American countries had made significant progress. Since entering the 21st century, especially since 2003, the poverty rate in Latin America had continued to decline — in 2011 down 30.4%, 18 points less than in 1990. Although the index is still relatively high, it can be regarded as a historic progress for the Latin-American region. This result is mainly due to the sustained economic growth over the past 10 years and the corresponding improvement of employment and income; at the same time, it is closely related to the development ideology and policy adjustment of Latin-American countries. Since the early 21st century, in the implementation of the United Nation's "Millennium Development Goals", Latin-American countries strongly promoted the social cohesion concept, emphasizing inclusive growth so that the past bias in favor of economic growth but ignoring social development had been balanced to a certain degree, and more power had been put in making and implementing social policies. Take social spending for example. "Under more stringent fiscal disciplines than in the past, the national governments have increased their public spending; in particular, they have increased spending on social functions with a great effort".[24] Statistics show

[24]CEPAL, *Panorama Social de America Latina, 2009*, Santiago de Chile, noviembre de 2009, p. 24.

that from 1990 to 1991 Latin America's social spending accounted for 12.2% of its GDP, and from 2006 to 2007, the proportion of GDP rose to 17.4%, an increase of 5.2%. According to the dollar price in 2000, from 2006 to 2007, the social spending per capita of Latin America reached $820 (the highest per capita $1,000, the lowest per capita less than $200). Another example is the popular "Conditional Transfer Payment Plan" in Latin America. At present, there are 17 countries involved in the implementation of the plan, covering 22 million families and 101 million people, accounting for about 17% of the total population of Latin America, and the capital investment accounting for about 0.25% of the regional GDP. Brazil and Mexico are the best in implementing the program, the capital investments accounting for 0.41% and 0.43% of their GDP respectively, covering 83% and 71% of the country's poor population respectively. This program has been and recommended by the United Nations because of its positive social effects.

As have already mentioned in the last section, in the economic expansion period of 2003, because the economic foundation was still fragile, Latin-American countries did not pursue a higher growth rate by taking expansionary economic policy, but introduced the policy for Latin-American countries to cope with the international financial crisis. In this section, we further discussed the adjustment of the Latin-American countries in terms of fiscal policy, industrial policy, and social policy. We believe that the above examples have reflected the overall more stable and pragmatic trend of the economic and social policy of Latin-American countries in the past 10 years.

The author believes that in the economic policy adjustment of Latin-American countries in the past 10 years, in addition to a number of left-wing governments coming to power and becoming the main factor of economic policy adjustment, there are two important backgrounds not to be neglected: first, the big discussion on the development concept in the Latin-American academic circles from the latter half of the 1990s to the beginning of the 21st century, and the second, the impact of the Chilean mode.

In the second half of the 1990s, with the continuous shock of the financial crisis and the recession of the Latin-American economy, the academic world of Latin America had carried out a big discussion on the development concept. In the discussion, the criticism of neoliberalism gradually concentrated on the *laissez-faire* theory, emphasizing to rationally deal with the relationship between the state and the market. Around this central issue, scholars had put forward their views on a series of important issues. (1) Emphasizing the need to achieve "a new balance between the market and the public interest", considering it the goal of improving and supplementing the market to provide public goods rather than the anti-market act. (2) Emphasizing that the "public policy" should cover all the activities of the organization to achieve common interests, rather than just state operations, both to correct the government's mistakes and to correct the mistakes of the market. (3) The result of one-sided emphasis on market orientation and freedom is that the national state is weakened, leading to the unilateral liberalization of developing countries, as well as the weakening of government regulation. Developing countries should continue to maintain national sovereignty, especially in determining their economic and social development strategies by themselves. (4) Macroeconomic policies cannot be simplified into a single anti-inflation policy, and the positive role of anti-cyclical policies cannot be denied. (5) The production development is the key to economic development. The main problems involved in the production development strategy are as follows: first, the production sector and enterprises should play a leading role; the second is the "complementation or industry chain", i.e., the industry's forward and backward contact, and the third refers to "innovation", including institutional innovation, technological innovation, product innovation, etc. (6) Emphasizing social progress and the improvement of people's livelihood. Social progress is the common product of the following three elements: the long-term social policies to increase social justice and social inclusion; the economic growth rate to create a moderate scale of employment opportunities; and the reduction of the structural differences between different sectors so as to continuously reduce the differences between different departments and different types of enterprises.[25] The above are the basic points of view that we have summarized from some of the key literatures of the time. It can be seen that the mainstream concepts of the scholars are the emphasis on independent choice of development path, independent decision making, playing the role of the state in macro-control and providing public products, emphasizing the adjustment of industrial structure, institutional innovation, continuous development of social productive forces, emphasizing inclusive development, paying attention to social progress and improving people's livelihood. Looking back now, the big discussion at that time had precisely become the public opinion preparation and theoretical guidance for the national economic policy adjustment of Latin America in the recent 10 years.

In 2005, the author published an article on the adjustment of the economic policy of the Chilean government, stressing that the reason why the economy of Chile in the 1990s was the "only one of strong growth" different from the rest in the Latin-American area (from 1991 to 2000, Chile's economy grew at an average annual rate of 6.6%, doubling the average growth rate of Latin America in the same period) is not that Chile had implemented the new liberalism very effectively; on the contrary, it is the result of "deviation" from the framework of the new liberalism policy.[26] In the mid-1970s, the Chilean military government and the "Chicago Disciples had taken the lead in the "experiment" of the new liberal reforms in Latin America, but its initial reform was not successful — especially in 1975 and 1982, two serious economic recessions occurred, with 12.9% and 14.3% of negative growth, respectively. This kind of adverse situation caused the reflection of the Chilean military government and its economic team. They began to adjust their policies in the first half

[25]Jose Antonio Ocampo, "Mas alia del Consenso de Washington: Una Vision desde la CEPAL", *Revista de la CEPAL*, No. 66, diciembre de 1998; "Retomar la Agenda del Desarrollo", *Revista de la CEPAL*, No. 74, agosto de 2001.

[26]SU Zhenxing, "Chile's Economic Policy and Development Model", *Latin American Studies*, No. 5, 2005.

of the 1980s, such as re-raising the tariff, implementing the export-tax rebate system, and recovering the crawling exchange rate system. As the Chilean economist French Davis said, "In order to cope with the 1982 recession, Chile was forced to adjust its policy to deal with severe external restrictions and promote the domestic recovery. Thus, it emerged in the evolution from the established orthodox or neoliberal mode in the 1970s and early 1980s to a more pragmatic mode, including local regressions from some of the early reforms". He called the change "a deviation from the neoliberal orthodox" (*una desviacion de la ortodoxia neoliberal*).[27]

Spanish economist Javier Santiso gave a more in-depth review about the change of the Chilean military government and its economic team in his book *Pragmatic Economic Policies in Latin America*. He said, "In the first few years of the neoliberal revolution, the coup in 1973 and the script of the 'Chicago Disciples'" are not the beginning of the break, but they are a fragment of the patterned Waltz... Chile did not favor the implementation of the doctrine of a possible economic policy until after the 1982–1983 crisis, choosing the carefully tailored macroeconomic reform based on realism and pragmatism". "Therefore, the second wave of the 'Chicago Disciples' did not hesitate to give up the creed of the neoliberalism and money in order to adapt to the specific circumstances of the Chilean economy".[28]

After the Chilean military government's "power to the people" in 1990, during the process of continuing to advance structural reforms, the consecutive four left-wing literati governments further promoted the spirit "on the basis of realism and pragmatism". The author has pointed out that "in terms of the adjustment of the reform guidance ideology and the economic policy of the Chilean government, we should note that the reforms of Chile are consistent in their basic objectives in the pursuit of the establishment of market economy, the

[27] R. Ffrench-Davis, "El Impacto de las Exportaciones sobre el Crecimiento en Chile", *Revista de la CEPAL*, No. 76, abril de 2002, pp. 144–145.
[28] Javier Santiso, "*The Pragmatic Nature of Latin American Economic Policies*", translated by Gao Jing *et al.*, The World Knowledge Press, 2009, pp. 76–77.

implementation of free trade, a comparative advantage, and enabling private enterprises to play a leading role. Since the 1990s, the adjustment of the guiding ideology of the reform of the literati governments was mainly concentrated on the function of the state, focusing the state intervention or regulation on the relationship between reform and development".[29] Just because it had got rid of the doctrine of neoliberalism, the literati governments of Chile have carried out big adjustments and innovations of a series of policies, such as trade policy, exchange rate policy, fiscal policy, policy of coping with short-term speculative capital, policy of supporting SMEs, and social policy. As Gonzales said, "In spite of the fact that the country's weight is less than in the past, but the actual situation shows that the Chilean economy is not the economy without state intervention. The state retains its existence in all the areas where a modern state should appear, restricting the doctrine of neoliberalism".[30]

It can be seen that the Chilean economic thought and tendency of the pragmatic economic policy started in the late stage of the military government and were formed in the period of the literati governments since the 1990s. Although the military government represented by General Augusto Pinochet was controversial at home and abroad, the civilian government of Chile did not "draw a clear line" between themselves and the military government in the economic policy. "The return of democracy has solidified the great changes of Chile... Chile's new leadership has not abandoned the economic system that has been established; they continue to combine privatization and regulation, the trade openness and the state ownership of mining, the financial liberalization and capital controls... With the mode now known as 'equal growth', the pragmatic outline of Chile has become increasingly clear".[31]

---

[29]SU Zhenxing, "Chile's Economic Reform and Development Model", *Latin American Studies*, 2005, No. 5, p. 15.

[30]Raul Gonzalez, "Tres Decadas de un New Orden Economico: Chile, 1973–2003", *Revista Europe de E studios Latinamericanos y del Caribe*, CEDLA, Amsterdam, Paises Bajos, No. 77, octubre de 2004, p. 69.

[31]Javier Santiso, "*The Pragmatic Nature of Latin American Economic Policies*", translated by Gao Jing *et al.*, The World Knowledge Press, 2009, pp. 77–78.

If, in the 1980s, the economic policy adjustment of the Chilean military government is a remarkable example of the transition from conservatism to pragmatism, the economic policy adjustment of the Brazilian Lula government is considered to be a typical example of transition from radicalism to pragmatism. As the leader of the Brazil Labor Party, Lula participated in the four presidential campaigns in 1989, 1994, 1998, and 2002. The first three campaigns were not successful because the radical economic policy was one of the main reasons for the failure of his campaigns. "So, in the 2002 presidential campaign Lula repeatedly reassured the investors that he had given up his strong left-wing views on some sensitive issues (such as debt). The facts are contrary to the most pessimistic Wall Street prophecy — the economic policies of the elected President Barack Lula paid amazing attention to effectiveness. He changed his tune after taking office as president, supporting the progressive economic policies, combining the fiscal austerity and strict monetary policy with positive social policy".[32] It has been proved that during his reign of eight years (2003–2010), based on the large-scale structural reforms of his predecessor Fernando Henrique Cardoso, Lula continued to implement pragmatic policies and positive social policies, which played an important historical role in pushing Brazil to rise as the regional power.

We might as well have a review of the past 10 years. The regional economy of Latin America had been able to have a prosperous period of six years (2003–2008), to successfully withstand the impact of international financial and economic crisis, and to maintain a strong growth trend in the past three years due to the combination of the following three factors: the new economic growth mode and economic mechanism brought about by the former structural reforms, the relatively favorable international environment and the pragmatic economic policies. In today's Latin America, the wind of the pragmatic economic style blew from Chile to Brazil and from Brazil to more countries, which is a welcome and logical phenomenon.

[32] *Ibid.*, pp. 92–93.

First, as a summary of the development experience, the economic pragmatism first resulted from Latin America, easy to be identified by other Latin-American countries, to be learned, and to achieve practical results. Second, the Latin-Americans themselves brought about the economic pragmatism in the recent several decades when they had been interfered and misled by the doctrine of neoliberalism. It is helpful for people, especially the academic circles, to restore self-confidence and the past ideological line to deal with problems and make decisions from their own realities. Third, the practice has proved that the economic pragmatism is the most suitable for the complex and changeable external environment of the world.

Section 4 Continuing to Change the Way of Economic Growth

The economy in Latin America has experienced the growth of the last 10 years. What is the basic trend of the next 10 years? We believe that from the above analysis, the current economic foundation in Latin America is good. The economic trend of the next 10 years or so will depend mainly on whether substantial progress can be made in continuing to change the way of economic growth. There are two reasons why efforts should be made to continue the transformation of economic growth pattern. First, in terms of the problems appearing in the recent 10 years of development, Latin-American countries still shoulder heavy responsibilities in the transformation of economic growth pattern. Second, after the international financial crisis in 2008 and 2009, the international environment has undergone major changes. When studying the whole Latin-American area, we should always focus on the problem of imbalanced regional developments. In the past 10 years, the problem was still very obvious. The data in Table 1.5 show that from 2003 to 2010 the economic growth rates of three secondary Latin-American areas differed greatly, of which South America was the highest (5%), Central America the second (4.3%), and the Caribbean the lowest (2.9%). What are the reasons behind these differences? As mentioned above, the main driving

Table 1.5 GDP Growth Rates in the Sub-regions of Latin America (1971–2010) (%)

	1971–1980	1981–1990	1991–1997	1998–2002	2003–2010
South America	5.6	1.0	4.1	0.3	5.0
Argentina	2.6	−1.0	6.1	−3.1	7.5
Brazil	8.8	1.7	3.0	1.7	4.0
Chile	2.8	3.1	8.2	2.5	4.0
Colombia	5.5	3.4	4.0	0.7	4.4
Central America	4.3	1.0	4.5	3.5	4.3
Mexico	6.6	1.9	2.9	3.2	2.2
The Caribbean		1.6	1.9	3.0	2.9
Latin America & the Caribbean	5.9	1.5	3.6	1.3	4.2

Note: Calculated with the same price of 2005. GDP refers to the sum of the sub-regions.
Source: CEPAL, sobre la base de CEPAISTAT [base de datos en linea]. http://websie.eclac.el/sisgen/ConsultaIntegradad.asp/, 2012.

factors in the Latin-American economic expansion of this round are the strong demands of the international market for the raw materials of energy, minerals, bulk agricultural products and primary products. South American countries, a small number of Caribbean countries, and Mexico belong to this type of countries exporting these products, benefiting from a substantial increase in export volume and substantial improvement in trade prices. Central American countries are net importers of energy and food, not only unable to enjoy the export boom of this kind of goods, but also, because of its higher prices and increased imports, having to face the pressure of imported inflation and to increase the food subsidies for residents. However, the luck of Central American countries lies in: (1) The customer industry forms the main support for export; (2) Remittances from overseas workers provide a big source of foreign currency. Most of the economies of the Caribbean countries rely mainly on tourism and other services, having basically nothing to do with the prosperity of exporting raw materials and primary products. The economic growth of these countries has had no improvement, and their current debt ratios are generally very high. For example, in 2011, the entire

Caribbean public debt was equivalent to the proportion of 77.7% of its GDP, of which Jamaica reached more than 126%.

The situations in the recent 10 years also show that the economic performance of the Latin-American countries also is closely related to the economic situations of their main counterparts in their economic cooperations. One outstanding example is Mexico. The customer industry is the main support for exports in Mexico like in Central American countries. Its remittances of overseas workers occupy the first place in Latin America. It is one of the exporting countries of raw materials and primary products, but the annual economic growth rate of Mexico was only 2.2% from 2003 to 2010, the lowest in the Latin-American countries. The fundamental reason is that its economy was highly dependent on the United States market and the economic crisis occurred in United States and the slow recovery there have had the most serious negative impact on the economy of Mexico. Central American countries were naturally affected by the United States, but to a smaller extent. As exporting countries of raw materials and primary products, South American countries are more dependent on the demands of China, Asia, and the EU countries. The initial situation had been good, but in recent years, the negative impact on the exports of South America due to the economic downturn in Europe had appeared. The recession of tourism in the Caribbean region is apparently related to the bad economic situation in North America and Europe. There is also an interesting phenomenon: the overseas workers of Mexico and Central America are more concentrated in the United States, while the overseas workers of South American countries are more concentrated in Spain. In recent years, the Spanish economy was worse than that of the United States, and therefore, the adverse impact on overseas remittances in South American countries became more serious (see Table 1.6).

Another phenomenon in the last 10 years is that the export commodities of Latin-American countries constituted the so-called "re-primary products" trend. According to the added values, the export commodities of Latin-American countries are divided into five categories: high-tech finished goods, medium-tech manufactured

Table 1.6 Countries in Latin America and the Caribbean: Remittances of Overseas Workers ($ Million)

Country	2003	2004	2005	2006	2007	2008	2009	2010	2011	2012[a]
Brazil	2,018	2,458	2,479	2,890	1,809	2,913	2,224	2,189	2,134	1,497
Colombia	3,060	3,170	3,314	3,890	4,493	4,842	4,145	4,023	4,168	1,993b
Costa Rica	306	302	400	490	596	584	489	505	487	2,46b
Ecuador	—	—	—	—	3,335	3,083	2,736	2,591	2,672	1,221b
Salvador	2,105	2,548	3,017	3,471	3,695	3,742	3,387	3,431	3,649	2,893
Guatemala	2,107	2,551	2,993	3,610	4,128	4,315	3,912	4,127	4,378	3,590
Honduras	842	1,138	1,776	2,329	2,581	2,808	2,476	2,524	2,750	1,398b
Jamaica		1,466	1,621	1,770	1,964	2,021	1,792	1,906	2,025	1,520
Mexico	15,139	18,332	21,688	25,567	26,059	25,145	21,306	21,304	22,803	17,267
Nicaragua	439	519	616	698	740	818	768	823	912	741
Venezuela	2,061	2,230	2,430	2,378	3,046	3,222	3,042	2,998	3,200	1,528[b]

Note: [a]Means data before September; [b]means data before June.
Source: CEPAL, according to official data.

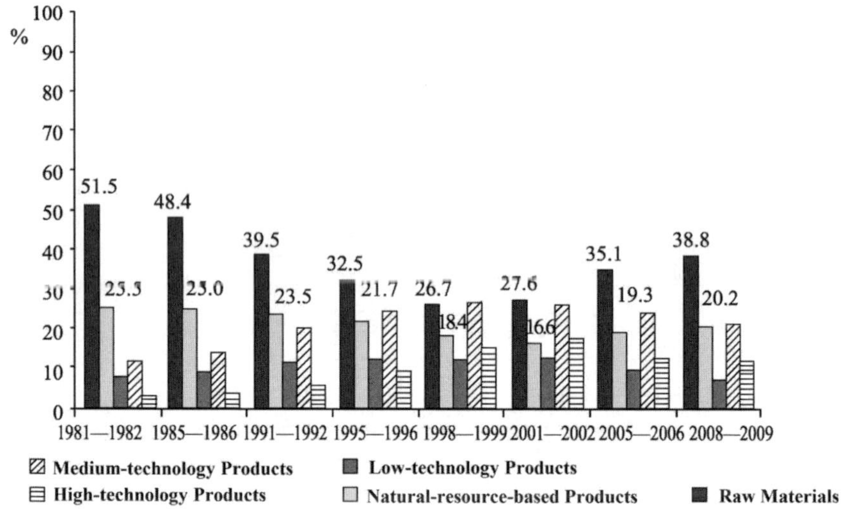

Figure 1.13 Changes of the Structure of Exports of Latin America to the World (by Proportion of Value) from 1981 to 2009

Source: Osvaldo Rozales, Mikio Kuwayama, *China y América Latina yel Caribe: Hacia Una Relación Económica y Comercial Estratégica*, CEPAL, p. 96.

goods, low-tech products, finished products on the basis of natural resources, and raw materials. The last two categories belong to primary products. Figure 1.13 shows that since the 1980s the proportion of primary products in Latin-American exports continued to decline, with the lowest proportion of 44.2% between 2001 and 2002. From 2003 onwards, the proportion of primary products rose again, to 59% between 2008 and 2009. There are two main reasons for this phenomenon. First of all, the strong demand of the international market and increase of price led to the growth of profit for the production sector of primary products, continuously attracting domestic and foreign investment into this sector, reducing correspondingly the investment into other industrial sectors, especially the manufacturing sector. Secondly, due to the large increase of export income and the great amount of short-term capital inflows resulting from the continuous implementation of the "Quantitative Easing" monetary policy by the western countries represented by the United States, the continuous appreciation of domestic currencies caused the export of manufacturing products to be in a disadvantageous position.

The above phenomena may explain from different angles that Latin-American countries have not done enough in the transformation of their economic growth modes. From the analyses of the academic circles from different perspectives, we believe that in the near future the efforts of the Latin-American countries to continue to transform the modes of economic growth will mainly focus on the following aspects.

I. Adjustment of the Industrial Structure

In the development mode of import substitution industrialization, due to the gradual replacement method — the non-durable consumer goods first, then consumer goods, and then the capital goods, a "small and comprehensive" industrial structure was formed in the industrial sector, which involves almost everything, but with no international competitiveness. Therefore, after Latin-American countries entered into the export-oriented development mode, they accordingly proposed the problem of implementing the "specialized production", which stressed the need to focus on the development of national industries with comparative advantages in order to compete in the international market. However, in the 1990s, Latin-American countries were disturbed by neoliberalism in their choice of the "specialized production" model, emphasizing on static comparative advantage of natural resources and labor resources. As we have already mentioned above, to date, there are two kinds of "specialized production" models in the Latin-American region: First, it is the model of developing customer industries; second, it is the mode of resource development and processing. The former mainly refers to Mexico, Central America and a few Caribbean countries (Dominican Republic, etc.), and the latter mainly refers to South American countries and a few Caribbean countries (such as Trinidad and Tobago, and Belize).

Although corresponding achievements have been made in the two specialized modes, it should be clearly noted that the two kinds of industries have significant limitations: it is very difficult for them to support the continued rapid growth of the entire national economy and to promote the national technological progress. From another perspective, the problem seems to be more prominent. Latin-American countries had long built an open economy, but they have not resolved the issue of how to effectively participate in the competition of the international market, and have so far mainly depended on some low-end products to conquer the world. As shown earlier in Figure 1.13, by 2008–2009, 60% of the exports were primary products, and the high-tech manufactured goods accounted for only over 10%. The ECLAC recently made it clear that, "Historical experience shows that both the low value-added processing and assembly industry and primary product specialization, in the long run, have the problem of the lack of the vitality of productivity, employment and economic growth. This type of specialized production must be weighed against the short-term gains and long-term costs, which is essential for determining the agenda of restructuring macroeconomic policies and industrial policies. As the development axis, the restructuring was, and still is, the main challenge facing Latin America, and its importance in the near future will continue to grow".[33]

When we discussed the economic policy adjustments in the third section of this chapter, it had been mentioned that in recent years many Latin-American countries have put forward their own industrial policies and long-term industrial development planning, having determined their emerging strategic industries. From this trend, in the next 10 years, industrial restructuring may become the top priority of the economic work in Latin America. The reason why ECLAC stressed the importance of the industrial restructuring as the "development axis" lies in that it emphasized the need to center around the industrial restructuring, focusing on the objective of developing and implementing the national development plan and establishing strategic emerging industrial sectors. In doing so, many other aspects of work can be activated, for example, to strengthen

[33]CEPAL, *Cambio Estructuml para Igualdad: Una Vision Integrada del Desarrllo*, San Salvador, 27–31 de agosto, 2012, p. 27.

the national innovation system and the research team building, to increase research and development investment, to actively promote scientific and technological progress, to improve labor productivity, to increase investment in education, to strengthen the development and accumulation of human resources, to increase the exports of high value-added products and the introduction of FDI and advanced technology in foreign trade and economic cooperation, and to strengthen the support and transformation of the majority of SMEs, and so on.

Latin-American countries have seized the key issues by adjusting the industrial structure as the focus of their work; therefore, it is worthy of attention to understand the actual progress. It is expected that certainly there are differences in the ways and efforts how Latin-American countries adjusted their industrial structures. For example, some countries have clearly stated the guiding ideology to "revive industrialization", while some other countries did not emphasize this point, e.g., the Chilean key industrial sectors covered only agriculture, forestry, fishery, and animal husbandry. In addition, entering into the stage of centering on adjusting the industrial structures does not mean immediately abandoning the existing customer industries and resource industries because these industries will still be the key industries for the participation in the international markets and the foreign exchange for some period of time.

II. Continuing to Boost Domestic Demand

We have done a study and found that during the 60 years since the 1950s, from the perspective of the three major demands the GDP ratio — consumption, investment and net exports, in Latin America, the final consumption (mainly private consumption) has accounted for about 80%, becoming the main driving force of economic growth in Latin America.[34] During the recent 10 years, although the prosperity of primary product export had contributed to reversing the

[34]SU Zhenxing, Zhang Yong, "The Transformation of Latin American Economic Growth Mode and the Twists and Turns of the Modernization Process", The *Latin American Studies*, No. 5, 2011.

economic stagnation of Latin America from 1998 to 2002, it is due to reliance on domestic demand that the economy could have sustained high growth. The rising domestic demand at this stage had benefited from two factors. First, the improvement of economic situation led to employment growth and the increase of wages and labor compensation, and at the same time, the inflation had been effectively controlled. Second, the active social policies taken by Latin-American governments had brought about a sharp decline in the proportion of poor population and a modest improvement in income distribution. Compared with 2002, in 2012, the absolute number of poor people in Latin America was reduced nearly 60 million. Statistical data from Table 1.7 show that in the first decade of the 21st century, there was a general decline in the proportion of poverty and extreme poverty

Table 1.7 Changes in Proportion of Poverty and Extreme Poverty between 2002 and 2010 in 18 Countries of Latin America (%)

Country	Around 2002	Poverty Rate	Extreme Poverty	Around 2010	Poverty Rate	Extreme Poverty
Argentina	2004	34.9	14.9	2010	8.6	2.8
Bolivia	2002	62.4	37.1	2009	42.4	22.4
Brazil	2001	37.5	13.2	2009	24.9	7.0
Chile	2000	20.2	5.6	2009	11.5	3.6
Colombia	2002	49.7	17.8	2010	37.3	12.3
Costa Rica	2002	20.3	8.2	2010	18.5	6.8
Ecuador	2002	49.0	19.4	2010	37.1	14.2
El Salvador	2001	48.9	22.1	2010	46.6	16.7
Guatemala	2002	60.2	30.9	2006	54.8	29.1
Honduras	2002	77.3	54.4	2010	67.4	42.8
Mexico	2002	39.4	12.6	2010	36.3	13.3
Nicaragua	2001	69.4	42.5	2009	58.3	29.5
Panama	2002	36.9	18.6	2010	25.8	12.6
Paraguay	2001	61.0	33.2	2010	54.8	30.7
Peru	2001	54.7	24.4	2010	31.3	9.8
Dominica	2002	47.1	20.7	2010	41.4	20.9
Uruguay	2002	15.4	2.5	2010	8.6	1.4
Venezuela	2002	48.6	22.2	2010	27.8	10.7

Source: Table from family questionnaire of relevant countries by the Latin-American and the Caribbean Economic Commission. From CEPAL, *Panorama Social de América Latina 2012*, Santiago de Chile, p. 14.

in Latin America, and the decline was huge. Bolivia is one of the counties with the highest poverty rates in Latin America. Compared with 2002, the poverty rate of 2009 dropped by 20%, and the extreme poverty rate dropped by 15%. Argentina originally belonged to the countries with the lowest poverty rate in Latin America, and the direct consequence of the economic crisis occurred in 2001 resulting in the respective 34.9% and 14.9% of the poverty rate and extreme poverty rate in 2004. By 2010 they returned to the pre-crisis level, indicating that the speed of recovery was very fast. In Latin America, the consumption of the small number of high-income population is not seriously affected by the change of the economic situation, but the consuming ability of the majority of the mid- and low-income population is closely related to the change. In the next 10 years, Latin-American countries will certainly continue to make efforts to seek steady and rapid economic growth, but it is difficult to predict whether the implementation of an active social policy will be changed due to a change of government in some countries. In fact, for the next stage, it is not easy to consolidate the achievements in poverty reduction over the past 10 years, but to continue to reduce poverty, we have to not only further deepen the existing social policy, but also change the systems such as the system of income distribution and labor system. Therefore, it is absolutely undesirable for the social policy to go backwards again.

III. Raising the Level of Investment

It is generally agreed that the slow economic growth of Latin-American countries is directly related to the long-term low investment rates. For example, in Latin America the average investment rate in 2008 was equivalent to 23.6% of their GDP — the highest level since 1980, but the investment rate was not only still below the level of the region in the 1970s, but also far from that of the developing countries in Asia — the investment rate of the latter reached 35% in the 1990s, and currently more than 40%. The historical evolution of the fixed capital formation rate in Latin America during the 60 years (1950–2010) (see Figure 1.14) shows that in the 1950s and 1960s, the

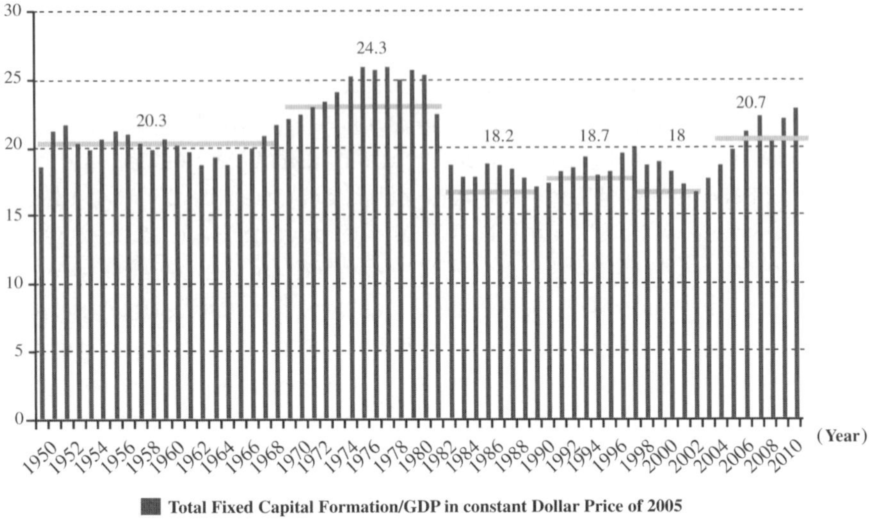

Figure 1.14 Ratio of the Total Amount of Fixed Capital Formation (1950–2010) in Latin America (Proportion of GDP in Constant Dollar Price of 2005, %)

Source: CEPAL, *Cambio Estructural para la Igualdad: Una Visión Integrada del Desarrollo*, 2012, p. 125.

average Latin-American fixed capital formation was equivalent to 20.2% of the GDP, 24.3% from 1970 to 1982, hovering at around 18% from 1982 to 2003, and restoring to 20.7% from 2004 to 2011, still below the 1970s. In the above background, in the last 30 years, the track of the changes in the public investment and private investment (regional average) of the whole regions showed some differences. From 1980 to 1981, the public investments were equivalent to 6.7% of the GDP, and thereafter they went on a declining trend — dropping to 3.9% from 1999 to 2003 and rising again to 4.8% from 2004 to 2010. The private investments from 1980 to 1981 were equivalent to 14.3% of the GDP, but dropped to 11.1% from 1982 to 1990. Although there were some ups and downs from 1991 to 2003, but they remained at 14–15.6%, and from 2004 to 2010 they further rebounded to 15.9%.[35]

[35]CEPAL, *Cambio Estructural para la Igualdad: Una Vision Integrada del Desarrollo*, San Salvador, 27 a 31 de agosto de 2012, p. 129.

Figure 1.14 shows that the turning point of the changing of the Latin-American fixed capital formation from decreasing into rising occurred in 1982 and lasted till 2003. There are three main reasons for it: (1) the debt crisis of the 1980s; (2) the regional hyperinflation in the late 1980s and early 1990s; (3) the continuity of internal and external financial crises from the mid-1990s to the early 21st century, such as the financial crisis of Mexico (1974), Brazil (1999), Argentina (2001), the Asian financial crisis, the Russian financial crisis, and the Turkish financial crisis. The rise of the investment rates between 2004 and 2010 resulted from not only the prosperity of the export of primary products and the significant improvement of the trade price ratio, but also a series of policy adjustments of the Latin-American countries, such as the effective control of inflation, the policies of prudent finance, monetary and exchange rate, the improvement of the public finances, the reduction of the debt burden, and the accumulated substantial foreign exchange reserves.

The reasons for the substantial shrinking of the public investment since 1982 can be classified into three aspects: (1) Under the pressure of a heavy debt burden, the public finances had been in trouble for a long time and the investment had to be reduced greatly. For example, the infrastructure investment in Latin America has long been compressed to a low level of 0.8–0.9% of the GDP, which is the fundamental cause why the current infrastructure is seriously lagging behind. (2) In the process of the dominant neoliberal economic reforms, too much emphasis had been put on weakening the role of the public sectors. (3) Under the constraints of international multilateral financial institutions, Latin-American countries could not take the counter-cyclical fiscal policies even if the conditions allowed. It is clear that since 2004 Latin-American countries not only needed to improve the level of the public investment, but also had a corresponding investment potential. The trend of the changes in private investment indicates that, except for the economic shrinking due to the debt crisis in the 1980s, the economic situations on the whole were in a tendency of gradual growth — if the economic outlook was more optimistic, this trend would become more evident.

The situation in the last 10 years shows that Latin-American countries are learning lessons of the past, seeking to restore the normal economic functioning of the state, to improve the public investment capacity through a mixture of a wide range of policies, and to continue to take positive policies in terms of attracting FDI. According to the judgment of the Latin-American academia, Latin America is still in the stage of emphasizing the amount of foreign investments.

IV. Adjusting the Regional Distributions of Foreign Economic and Trade Cooperation

At present, the power of global economy is in a historical process of rebalancing, which means that the center of economy is gradually turning from the "North" to the "South". This process was further accelerated by the international financial crisis between 2008 and 2009. According to the estimate of 2013 UNDP Human Development Report, by 2020, the gross domestic product of Brazil, China, and India together will exceed that of the United States, Canada, Britain, France, Germany, and Italy as a whole; by 2025, the annual spending of the domestic markets in the countries of the South will reach $30 trillion: from 1990 to 2010, the proportion of the global middle class in the South changed from 26% to 58%, and by 2030, more than 80% of the middle class in the world will come from the South.[36] Alicia Barcena, Executive Secretary of the UN Economic Commission for Latin America, also said, "'The South–South' trade prospects or 'South–South' economic interaction will exceed the 'North–North' trade in 2017. Between 2013 and 2017, the contribution of the emerging economies to the world economic growth is expected to reach 2/3".[37] In terms of the "accuracy" of these predictions, there may be different opinions, but there is probably no doubt about the rebalancing process of the strength of the global economy.

In this backdrop, it is imperative for Latin America to adjust the regional layout of its foreign trade and economic cooperation. In fact,

[36] "Reference News", March 16, 2013, p. 6.

[37] Alicia Barcena, The Economic Development of Latin America and the Caribbean in 2012, *Latin American Studies*, No. 6, 2012, p. 6.

as early as the 1960s and 1970s, Latin-American countries had put forward the policy of diversification of its external relations, striving to change the historical pattern of its foreign trade and economic cooperation which had put too much emphasis on North America and Europe. In the last two decades of the 20th century, the economic development of Latin-American countries was not smooth — limited progress had been made in the adjustment of their foreign trade and economic relations due to the debt problem. In foreign trade, for example, in the 1990s, Latin America's dependence on the US market had increased substantially (see Figure 1.15); in the last 10 years, the pace of adjustment had been significantly accelerated, especially in their trades with China and the Asia-Pacific region. However, in terms of the source of foreign investment, investments from the United States and Europe have been so far in absolute dominance in Latin America.

It is expected that in the next 10 years Latin-American countries will intensify their efforts to adjust the regional layout of their foreign trade and economic cooperation. There are two characteristics in the

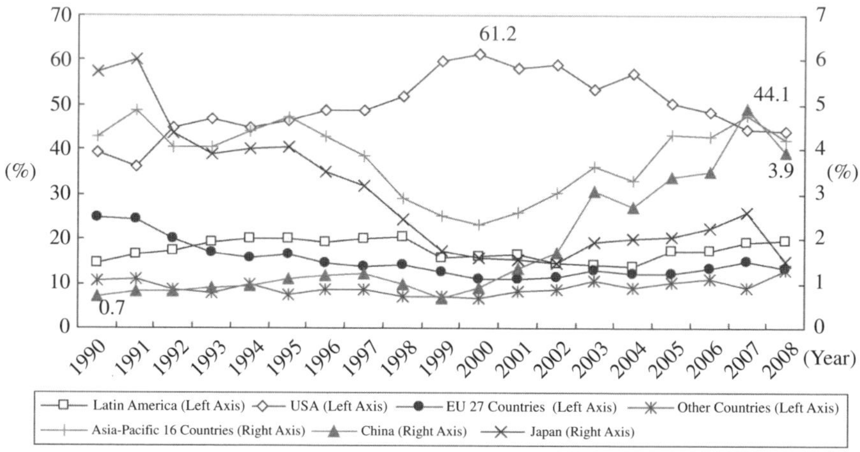

Figure 1.15 Export Diversification Trends in Latin America, by Destination of Export

Note: Including the Caribbean countries.
Source: Calculated and drawn according to CEPAL, *Panorama de la Inserción Internacional de América Latina y el Caribe, 2008–2009.*

process of this adjustment: First, in foreign trade, the proportion of their trade with the Asia-Pacific, Africa and the region itself will significantly increase, while the proportion of the trade with North America and Europe will relatively decline. In terms of foreign investment, the investment from the Asia-Pacific region is expected to increase, but it will not alter their predominant dependence on the US and Europe. Second, in terms of the trend of the changes in foreign economic and trade relations of the several sub regions, the South American regional trade and economic cooperation with the Asia-Pacific is expected to have a substantial increase, and Mexico, Central America and the Caribbean are likely to increase moderately their trade and economic cooperation with the Asia-Pacific region, but in the short term it is unlikely for both to change the traditional pattern of reliance on the US market.

Chapter 2

Economic Trend of Argentina and the Sino-Argentine Economic and Trade Relations

Lin Hua

With vast land and abundant resources, Argentina has a strong economic complementarity with China, being China's most important trade partner in Latin America. Although the crisis of 2001 had caused an unprecedented negative impact on the development of the country, the crisis contributed to its profound reflection on its economic development model. In 2002, Argentina made it clear to bid farewell to the neoliberal model and to explore new ways of economic growth. After coming to power in 2003, the Kirchner government further demonstrated its stance to adjust the economic policy. Over the next 10 years, Argentina had been exploring a kind of growth mode different from the past. In this process, the economic and trade cooperation between China and Argentina also entered a new stage of development. Both the trade and investment were showing unprecedented vigor. It should be acknowledged that the rapid development of the trade and economic relations between China and Argentina is inseparable from both the background of the economic, trade, and industrial policy adjustments over the past 10 years and the good environment of stable economic growth and improved trade balance. The future trend of the Sino-Argentine relations will continue to be affected by the Argentine economic growth and industrial restructuring. Therefore, in order to have a comprehensive analysis and understanding of the current situation and prospect of the Sino-Argentine economic and trade relations, we have to make a systematic interpretation of a variety of changes in Argentina's recent economic policy and trade patterns. Meanwhile, since Argentina is a big country with natural resources, it is the key factor in the future development of the Sino-Argentine relationship whether its rich resources and the complementary advantages of both countries can be made use of. Therefore, it is also necessary to give a summary of the latest changes of the current resource situation and industrial structure of Argentina.

Section 1 Economic Overview and Transformation of the Economic Growth Mode

In 2001, an unprecedented full-blown crisis broke out in Argentina. For a time, this country, once seen as a "model and example" of the neoliberal reform by Western countries and international financial institutions, had become synonymous with "failure and chaos" — the country's reputation plummeted. The severe crisis would inevitably lead to profound reflection. The neoliberal economic reform began from the late 1980s and brought a short-term boom in Argentina before 1994, but its drawbacks soon emerged in the latter half of the 1990s, eventually leading to a deadly disaster for Argentina. Argentina started the adjustment and correction of its economic policy during the ruling period of Duhalde (2002–2003). One of the most important reforms is the abolition of the implementation of the 11-year-old Currency Board System, abandoning the fixed exchange rate, and adopting a floating exchange rate. After becoming the president, Kirchner gradually established a general idea of reform, taking completely different macro-control measures from those in the Menem era, trying to explore a path of sustainable development. The macroeconomic developments of Argentina in the past 10 years can be divided into two stages. The first stage is from 2003 to 2007, during which the annual growth rate of the Argentine economy reached 8–9%. The five consecutive years of stable high growth was rare in the history of Argentina. The second stage refers to the years after 2008, during which the Argentine economy fluctuated due to the impact of the international financial crisis, but because of the changes in macroeconomic conditions in Argentina and the introduction of a series of government measures to maintain growth, the extent of impact on the Argentine economy was much smaller than in the past. This section will first give a brief review and evaluation of the neoliberal economic reform implemented in Argentina in the 1990s, and then focus on the adjustments of the Argentine economic policies, the main features of the new mode of growth, and the impact on the economic situation in the past 10 years; finally, in connection with the adverse environment under the international financial crisis, an analysis will be made of the main problems currently facing the economic development.

I. The Neoliberal Reform and Economic Crisis

In the 1980s, Argentina suffered from the debt crisis, and its economy fell into a full-blown recession. In this background, after Menem was in power in 1989, the original economic policies were immediately changed and massive neoliberal economic reforms began to be embarked on. Early in the period of military rule in the 1970s, Argentina tried the neoliberal reforms, but for various reasons, the reforms did not achieve the expected results. In contrast, the economic reforms carried out in Argentina in the 1990s were more comprehensive and thorough. From the perspective of the breadth of the reforms, not only all the areas such as finance, trade, fiscal, monetary and other economic fields, but also the labor and social security system had been covered; from the perspective of the depth, the reforms had overturned the original model of economic development, implementing a comprehensive opening policy in finance and trade, and a large-scale privatization as the main feature, which were the content not involved in the early attempts at reform.

As a starting point, the wave of privatization began in 1990 by the sale of state-owned telecommunications and airlines. By 1999, the vast majority of the state-owned enterprises of production and service had been sold to private capital, including a vital lifeline department for the economic development. Except the transfer of shares, a number of oil companies, railways, ports, highways, water supply and broadcast television industry were transferred to private managements through the way of transferring the franchise by the government. The 10-year privatization process made the important companies in all Argentine sectors almost entirely controlled by foreign capital. It was obvious that the economy was characteristic of foreignization and multinational corporationization. In the case of the full control and monopoly of foreign economy, the government could not play a role in regulating the economy.

The reform of the monetary system undoubtedly played a key role in the change of the macroeconomic situation throughout the 1990s. In 1980s, Argentina suffered hyperinflation — the index of consumer price in 1989 went up to 4924%.[1] In 1991, in order to curb inflation, the Argentine government issued the famous "Convertibility Plan", i.e., the Currency Board System. The main contents included: (1) The exchange rate was fixed at 10,000 Austral[2] = \$1. (2) The monetary base was fully supported by the foreign exchange reserves of the Central Bank. (3) The Central Bank was not allowed to grant loans to the government and the banking system. (4) The dollars needed for the transactions of frequent items and capital projects were free to exchange. (5) Debts, contracts, and bank deposits could be settled in US dollars. Under the Currency Board System, the Central Bank could not make up the deficit through the issuance of currency, so inflation had been effectively curbed (see Table 2.1). In 1992, the government adopted the "Organic Law of the Central Bank", on the one hand establishing the independence of the Central Bank, and on the other hand weakening the ability of the Central Bank to regulate the economy through adjusting interest rates or the monetary policy. Due to the long-term fixed exchange rate, the peso had been overvalued, which led to the decline in exports due to

---

[1]CEPAL, *Estudio Economico de America Latina y el Caribe 1998–1999*, p. 140.
[2]In January 1992, the australe was replacing by the peso, 1 peso = 10,000 australes, peso and dollar exchange rate as 1:1, the sale of foreign exchange still unrestricted.

the poor price competitiveness and a substantial increase in imports, resulting in the continuing expansion of the trade deficit. The Currency Board System needed to guarantee adequate foreign exchange reserves, but the lack of export revenue made the government unable to use the fiscal revenues to enrich foreign exchange reserves. Therefore, the external debts had become an important source of foreign exchange reserves.

Generally speaking, the economic reforms of the 1990s had played a role in stabilizing the macroeconomy, curbing inflation, improving the financial situation, and attracting foreign investments. From 1990 to 1998, except in 1995 when Argentina suffered an economic backdraft due to the Mexican financial crisis, there was a more rapid growth in the other years (see Table 2.1). The hyperinflation rate

Table 2.1 Argentina's Main Economic Indicators (1990–1998)

	1990	1991	1992	1993	1994	1995	1996	1997	1998
GDP Growth Rate (On the fixed price of 1986, %)	−1.8	10.6	9.6	5.7	8.0	−4.0	4.8	8.6	4.2
GDP Growth Rate Per Capita (%)	−3.2	9.1	8.1	4.3	6.6	−5.3	3.4	7.2	2.9
Consumption Price Indicator (%)	1,344	84.0	17.6	7.4	3.9	1.6	0.1	0.3	0.7
Fixed Investment Ratio in GDP (%)	11.9	14.1	17.1	18.7	20.8	18.0	18.8	22.0	22.5
Foreign Debt Ratio in GDP (%)	—	32.3	27.4	28.0	30.4	35.2	36.9	38.4	42.1
Fiscal Deficit Ratio in GDP (%)	−3.8	−1.6	−0.1	1.4	−0.2	−0.6	−1.8	−1.4	−1.2
Export of Commodity and Service ($100 million)	148	143.9	154.2	164.6	194.5	250.2	284.7	309.4	308.2
Import of Commodity and Service ($100 million)	68.5	115.7	192.8	220.4	272.8	259.9	300.8	372.4	383.3
Capital Account Balance of Payments ($100 million)	−51.7	−15.9	86.3	110.4	111.7	29.2	99.8	153.4	188.2
City Public Unemployment (%)	7.4	6.5	7.0	9.6	11.5	17.5	17.2	14.9	12.9

Source: CEPAL, *Estudio Económico de América Latina y el Caribe 1998–1999*, pp. 142–143.

lasting several years had been effectively controlled, maintaining a single digit level since 1993. As a result of a series of measures to increase revenue, coupled with privatization receipts and external borrowing, the fiscal balance had been improved. Except in 1990, the deficit ratio to gross domestic product (GDP) was less than 2%, and in 1993 a surplus was even achieved. With the opening of financial markets and a high interest rate policy, a large number of foreign capitals were attracted to have flown into Argentina. From 1992 to 1998, except for 1995 when the net inflow of foreign capital decreased because of the Mexican crisis, the surplus of Argentine capital account remained at a high level. In foreign trade, after the implementation of trade liberalization, the volume of import and export increased year by year, but due to the reasons such as the overvalued currency as a result of the fixed exchange rate, the import growth rate was significantly higher than the export growth, so that the trade balance showed a deficit in most years. All in all, the macroeconomy of Argentina during Menem's reign remained basically stable.

However, due to excessive privatization, marketization, and liberalization, the reform had not only brought a series of negative effects, but also foreshadowed the full-blown economic, political and social crisis for Argentina in 2001.

In the fourth quarter of 1998, negative growth appeared in the Argentine economy, which began a four-year recession and in the late 2001 the economic and financial crisis broke out. Notable characteristics of the economic situation in these four years were: stagnation of production, contraction of consumption, insufficient investment, growth of external debt, fiscal tightening, financial collapse, and weakness of import and export. In 2002, the Argentine economy fell back to 10.9%,[3] to the bottom. The output of almost all the sectors of the economy was declining, with the industry and construction sector suffering the greatest loss in the recession. The problem of underinvestment existed throughout the period of the crisis. The fixed capital formation of 2002 accounted for only 10.8% of the GDP, about half of

[3]Data of this part came from CEPAL, *Estudio Economico de America Latina y el Caribe 2002–2003*, p. 144.

that before the crisis. Due to excessive borrowing, the external debt to GDP ratio exceeded 50%. With the intensification of the recession, the country risk index of Argentina continued to grow, making it difficult to raise more funds in the international capital markets to pay debts. The government had announced to stop paying debts, plunging into the most serious bad debt crisis. The turmoil in the financial market led to massive capital fleeing Argentina. The capital account (excluding Foreign Direct Investment, FDI) had remained a net outflow for four years. The net outflow of 2002 reached a record of nearly $27 billion. The imports contracted severely due to the decline in domestic demand and the impact of currency devaluation, and the import volume in 2002 was only 28.7% of that in 1998.

In terms of the crisis at the beginning of the 21st century, Chinese scholars have conducted a detailed analysis and study of the root causes of it. They reached a basic consensus — the neoliberal economic reform was the culprit of the crisis. Firstly, the process to economic reforms, the implementation of almost unconditional opening, unreserved privatization and unrestricted market not only increased the dependence of Argentine economy on the international market, but also seriously undermined the ability of the national macro-control of the economy. Secondly, the overvaluation of currency as a result of the rigid exchange rate policy not only put the domestic products in an unfavorable condition in the competition of international trade, but also made the government lost the ability to regulate the economy with the use of monetary means. Thirdly, the long-term implementation of the debt-development and deficit-fiscal policy led the government into a vicious cycle of "borrowing the new debt to pay the old", and ultimately made it lose its solvency. Finally, the economic reform departed from the principle of social justice at the expense of the interests of ordinary people, resulting in a surge of unemployment, poverty, and the deterioration of income distribution.

II. Adjustment of Economic Policy

Since 2003, the Argentine economy re-entered the growth phase after experiencing a continuous decline of four years. It is in 2003 that the

Kirchner government came to power. Therefore, many people think that the economic recovery of Argentina should be attributed to the adjustment of the economic policy by the Kirchner government. In fact, during the several months before the Kirchner presidency, the Argentine economy was showing signs of recovery. After he came to power, Kirchner not only kept Roberto Lavagna, former economic minister of the Duhalde government, and followed the main economic policy of the former government. In the ruling of Duhalde in 2002, Argentina witnessed a year of the most serious economic and financial crisis — many of the measures taken by the government had not been effective in the short term. The decision to devalue the peso had even intensified the turmoil of the financial market. However, it is because the Duhalde government had taken a series of economic reforms that it was possible for Argentina to overcome the crisis and achieve recovery. It is reasonable to say that the Duhalde government was the transitional period of the Argentine economy from the dominance of neoliberalism to the new development period, laying the foundation for the more comprehensive and in-depth policy adjustments of the later Kirchner government. The next three sessions of the government had inherited the floating exchange rate system, export taxes and the "Economic Emergency Law" that the Duhalde government had implemented. They had become important means of government regulation of the economy.

Here the main features of the policy adjustment since 2002 will be discussed from the four aspects of finance, monetary, exchange rate, and social policy, as well as the differences from the neoliberal era. The adjustments of trade policy and industrial policy will be analyzed in the two following sections.

1. The Prudent Expansionary Fiscal Policy

In the first half of the 1990s, the Argentine government obtained a lot of revenue through privatization of state-owned enterprises. Due to the reform of the tax system, combined with the stabilizing macroeconomic situation, the significant growth in revenue improved the financial situation, and in 1993 a surplus of total revenues even

Table 2.2 Financial Revenue and Expenditure of Argentina (1991–1998) (GDP Ratio, %)

Year	1991	1992	1993	1994	1995	1996	1997	1998
Recurrent income	15.0	17.4	21.5	19.3	18.9	17.2	18.6	18.8
Recurrent expenditure	16.2	16.8	18.7	18.4	18.8	18.2	19.1	19.1
Savings	−1.2	0.6	2.8	0.9	0.1	−0.9	−0.4	−0.3
Capital expenditure	0.4	0.7	1.3	1.2	0.7	1.0	1.1	1.1
Total revenue and expenditure	−1.6	−0.1	1.5	−0.3	−0.6	−1.9	−1.5	−1.4

Source: CEPAL, *Estudio Economico de America Latina y el Caribe 1999–2000*, p. 145.

appeared. However, with the gradual ending of the privatization process, the revenue could only rely on tax, and the fiscal pressure on the government was growing. In 1994, in order to increase taxes, the government had taken a series of tax reforms such as increasing the value-added tax rate from 18% to 21% and raising the import taxes. However, these measures did not make a fundamental improvement in the financial situation; instead, they caused the tax systems of Argentina to have changed from simple to complex. Under the Currency Board System at that time, the government could not cover the deficit by printing money, and the only way out was large-scale borrowing. From 1992 to 1999, the ratio of external debt to GDP increased from 27.4% to 51.5%, and the proportion of interest payment to that of the exports also increased from 10.2% to 21.6% (see Table 2.2).[4]

In 1999, the Argentine economy went into recession with a sharp drop in revenue and the fiscal deficit of 3.1% of the GDP.[5] Under the pressure of the deficit reduction required by the IMF, the government had to take a comprehensive austerity. However, in the case of a recession, the austerity policy could not play the role of stimulating the economy and promoting economic recovery. The country

[4]CEPAL, *Estudio Economico de America Latina y el Caribe 2000–2001*, p. 106.
[5]CEPAL, "Argentina", *Estudio Economico de America Latina y el Caribe 2006–2007*.

thus was trapped in a vicious cycle of "recession-austerity". The serious domestic situation caused the Argentine reputation to plummet in the international capital market so that it could not make up the deficit through borrowing and therefore, its financial situation deteriorated further. In 2001, the deficit ratio to GDP reached 4%.[6] After coming to power, President Duhalde continued to implement the contractionary fiscal policy to increase revenue. Thanks to the change in the exchange rate system, the tax reform had achieved some success, and in 2002 the tax revenue increased significantly, easing the financial pressure.

After coming to power in 2003, the Kirchner government drew a lesson from the failure of the austerity policy in the period of the crisis, deciding not to succumb to pressure from the international financial institutions, to give up its usual practice adopted in the past to achieve a surplus by tightening, establishing a prudent expansionary fiscal policy to promote the production and stimulate the recovery and growth of the economy. The so-called prudent expansion means to expand revenue and expenditure at the same time, but to control the speed of spending growth and to maintain a fiscal balance and achieve a surplus as a primary objective. To reverse the situation of the financial difficulties, the Government had taken a number of measures, including increasing the categories of taxes, stimulating consumption through increasing wages, promoting the recovery of production and markets, expanding the value-added tax and income tax, cracking down on tax evasion, etc. Between the four years from 2003 to 2006, the tax revenue as the government's main source of income increased by 50.6%, 36%, 21.3%, and 25.8%, respectively.[7] Although expenditures maintained a high growth rate, the growth rate was less than that of the revenue, so the government was able to maintain a balanced revenue and expenditure. From 2003 to 2008, double surpluses of primary finance and total fiscal revenue

[6]CEPAL, "Argentina", *Estudio Economico de America Latina y el Caribe 2006–2007.*

[7]CEPAL, *Estudio Economico de America Latina y el Caribe 2003–2004, 2004–2005, 2005–2006, 2006–2007.*

and expenditure had been achieved. Such a good financial situation was rare in the history of Argentina (see Table 2.3).

In the analysis of the causes why the financial situation had improved significantly from 2003 to 2008, three factors should be taken into account, which had played a role in increasing revenues.

First, the Kirchner government completed the debt restructuring in 2005, greatly reducing the debt pressure. In 2002, the public debt of Argentina had accounted for 145.9% of its GDP.[8] After taking office, the Kirchner government had been striving to succeed in restructuring the debts. However, due to the considerable differences between the Argentine government and the international creditors, debt negotiations had been difficult. In March 2005, significant progress had finally been made for the debt restructuring plan. About 76% of the old debt had been converted into new debt, totaling \$62 billion, and 44% of the new debt was issued in pesos. In the process of debt negotiations, the policy adopted by the government of Argentina was relatively appropriate — both adhering to the principles and making compromises and concessions, and eventually led to the fundamental success of the protracted debt restructuring plan. The substantial reduction in debt and interest and debt rescheduling had reduced the financial burden of the government and increased the freedom of the government to arrange the public spending. In January 2006, the government paid off all the debt owed to IMF using its international reserves so as to enhance its autonomy in deciding its fiscal policy with no more interference and restrictions.

Secondly, the export tax had become an important source of government tax revenues. In the early 1990s, the government had canceled the export tax, but recovered this tax as a provisional duty for a period of one year during the economic crisis in 2002 in order to increase revenue. However, the later sessions of the government had not only failed to abolish the export tax, but also repeatedly raised

---

[8]CEPAL, "Argentina", *Estudio Economico de America Latina y el Caribe 2005–2006.*

Table 2.3 Financial Revenue and Expenditure of Argentina (2001–2011) (Ratio in GDP, %)

Year	2001	2002	2003	2004	2005	2006	2007	2008	2009	2010	2011
Total revenue	14.3	14.2	16.1	16.3	16.7	17.2	18.2	19.4	21.0	22.5	21.8
Recurrent revenue	14.2	14.1	16.1	16.2	16.5	17.0	18.1	19.3	20.8	22.4	21.6
Tax receipt	12.9	12.1	14.5	15.4	15.8	16.0	17.2	18.1	18.2	19.6	19.9
Capital income	0.1	0.0	0.1	0.1	0.2	0.2	0.1	0.1	0.2	0.1	0.1
Total expenditure	18.3	14.8	15.9	14.4	16.3	16.2	17.5	18.7	21.8	22.6	24.1
Recurrent expenditure	17.4	14.1	15.1	12.9	14.3	13.6	15.3	16.4	19.1	19.6	21.1
Interest expenditure	4.0	2.1	1.9	1.3	1.9	1.7	2.1	2.1	2.3	1.6	2.2
Capital expenditure	0.9	0.7	0.8	1.5	2.0	2.6	2.2	2.2	2.7	3.1	3.0
Primary fiscal balance	0.0	1.5	2.1	3.2	2.3	2.7	2.7	2.8	1.4	1.5	−0.1
Fiscal balance	−4.0	−0.6	0.2	2.0	0.4	1.0	0.6	0.7	−0.8	−0.1	−2.3

Source: Data of 2001–2008 came from CEPAL, *Estudio Económico de América Latina y el Caribe 2009–2010*, pp. 98–99; Data of 2009–2011 came from CEPAL, "Argentina", *Informe Macroeconómico*, julio 2012.

Table 2.4 Export Tax Revenue and Its Proportion in Total Revenue

Year	2006	2007	2008	2009	2010
Export tax revenue (million pesos)	14,712	20,450	36,055	32,042	45,547
Proportion in total revenue (%)	9.5	10.0	13.1	10.3	10.9

Source: Official website of INDEC, http://www.indec.mecon.ar.

the export tax.[9] In March 2008, the Government announced that it would change the tax of the export of soybeans, sunflower seeds, wheat, corn and other agricultural products from the fixed rate to the floating rate,[10] which led to a nationwide agricultural strike for several months. There were two considerations for the government to stay firm in the export tax issue: first, because of the rising international prices of agricultural products, a substantial increase in tax revenue from the exports was undoubtedly a huge contribution to the government finance; second, the export taxes could restrict the export of certain necessities of life, and thus played a role in stabilizing the domestic market price (see Table 2.4).

Finally, the nationalization of the pension system in 2008 injected a lot of money into the government finance. Since the entire private pension companies of the country had been nationalized, the annual financial social security funds collected were very impressive. The income of the government pension contribution was 52.57 billion pesos in 2008. In 2009, it was 77.23 billion pesos, and in 2010, it was 102.46 billion pesos, an increase of 46.9% and 32.7%, respectively.[11] The proportion of the social security income to the total tax revenue also increased from 19.1% to 24.6%, the second largest source of revenue behind the VAT.[12]

[9]In 2004, the export taxes of oil and its by-products were raised from 20% to 24%; in 2006, the export taxes of meat and dairy products were raised from 5% to 15% and 10%, respectively; in January 2008, the export tax of soybeans was raised from 27.5% to 35%; the export taxes of wheat and corn were raised from 20% to 28% and 25%, respectively.

[10]The bill was not passed in the Senate.

[11]Official website of Argentina National Bureau of Statistics and Survey (INDEC), http://www.indec.mecon.ar.

[12]The data were calculated from the official website of Argentina National Bureau of Statistics and Survey (INDEC).

Beginning from 2009, the financial pressures facing Argentina had increased, but a relatively loose fiscal policy was still maintained. The government considered that in the context of the global economic crisis, it was essential for them to rely on expanding domestic demand and implement appropriate fiscal stimuli to maintain steady economic growth. The main reasons for the rapid expenditure growth were: first, the government had strengthened social assistance for low-income groups; second, after the nationalization of the pension system, the expansion of the coverage and the increase of the standard of social security pension led to the increase of pension payments. Third, it was related to the high-subsidy policy implemented by the government in recent years. After the cancellation of fixed exchange rates in 2002, the devaluation of peso plummeted. To control inflation, the government froze the prices of domestic public services and fuels. In order to avoid business losses, the government subsequently adopted subsidies. With the improvement of the economic situation, the government had neither thawed the prices, nor removed the subsidies, but rather expanded the subsidy amount and scope of subsidies. The government spent $4.7 billion on the subsidies in 2005, and $16.7 billion in 2007, i.e., in just two years the expenditure increased by 3.4 times.[13] To reduce the financial burden, the government had reduced subsidies for gas and electricity in 2009, but the trade unions and consumers were extremely dissatisfied with the subsequent rising of prices. The Government had to make compromises. Between 2009 and 2011, a cumulative increase of 228% of the government subsidies were provided to the energy and transport sectors, while growth in current expenditure over the same period was 139%.[14] In November 2011, with the increasing financial pressure, the government announced the cancellation of all the subsidies of the water, electricity and gas for the financial, insurance, mobile phone, aviation and port transport, mining, oil and gambling industries, and the cancellation of all the subsidies for the large profit companies

[13]Fundacion para el Cambio, Los Subsidios ee Argentina, Buenos Aires, marzo de 2009, p. 10.
[14]EIU, *Country Report: Argentina*, London, United Kingdom, August 2011.

and the subsidized public services provided to high-income groups. Although the reduction of subsidies accounted for only a small part of all subsidies, it had already had a positive financial impact. In the first nine months of 2012, the growth rate of subsidy spending dropped to 18%.[15]

2. The Reform of the Central Bank and the Monetary Policy

The Central Bank is the maker and implementer of monetary policies, and therefore, changes of the monetary policy in Argentina in recent years are closely related to the reform of the Central Bank. From the 1990s to date, Argentina had experienced a total of five major reforms of the Central Bank.

The implementation of the *Convertibility Law* (i.e., "Convertibility Plan") in 1991 should be regarded as a major adjustment of the functions of the Central Bank. Under the plan, issuing currency should be guaranteed with the international reserves. That is, the money supply was no longer determined by the Central Bank, but by the amount of international reserves. This provision deprived the Central Bank of the function of the "issuing bank", so that the Central Bank could no longer regulate the money supply in accordance with the economic performance. The "Convertibility Plan" also prohibited the Central Bank to provide loans and loan guarantees to the government and financial institutions, but allowed a certain number of dollars in government bonds to be held in the Central Bank reserves. This provision limited the Central Bank to provide financing to the government and as a "lender of last resort" function, so that no financial support from the Central Bank would be given to maintain a government fiscal balance and relieve the losses of commercial banks. In 1992, with the implementation of the "Convertibility Plan", the government promulgated the *Organic Law of the Central Bank*, clearly stating that the basic function of the Central Bank was to maintain a stable currency value in addition to the responsibility of financial supervision and independent making of monetary policies.

[15]CEPAL, *Balance Preliminar de las Eeconomias de America Latina y el Caribe 2012*, diciembre de 2012.

Table 2.5 Argentina's Foreign Exchange Reserves and M2 Growth Rate (1992–2001)

Year	1992	1993	1994	1995	1996	1997	1998	1999	2000	2001
Increase in reserves (%)	32.74	42.50	6.82	−1.02	38.82	32.73	34.38	12.01	−4.39	−120.83
Growth rate of M2 (%)	51.5	34.0	13.4	1.7	10.6	14.6	1.0	−2.0	−6.2	−19.2

Source: Data of 1992–1999 came from CEPAL, *Estudio Economico de America Latina y el Caribe 2000–2001*, p. 106; Data of 2000–2001 came from CEPAL, *Estudio Economico de America Latina y el Caribe 2001–2002*, p. 104.

Through the above two laws, the independence of the Central Bank had increased, but the function of it was greatly reduced.

In the 11 years of the implementation of the "Convertibility Plan", since the Central Bank was unable to decide on the amount of currency issuance, the monetary policy had been completely passive, difficult to play the function of regulating the economy. In order to stimulate the economy, the government needed to adopt the expansionary monetary policy, but this depended on the increase of the foreign exchange reserves. There were mainly two ways to expand the reserves: first, it was the trade surplus; second, it was capital inflows. In the late 1990s, due to the overvalued currency of peso, the exports became non-competitive and the foreign trade suffered continuous annual deficit, so that the foreign exchange reserves could not be substantially increased. To attract foreign capital, it was necessary to raise interest rates. As a result, the credit and investment would be suppressed, resulting in production declines. In this case, the fiscal policy had become the only means to stimulate the economy. Since the problem of the fiscal deficit generated could not be solved by the Central Bank issuing the currency to provide support to the government, the last way out could only be borrowing. The huge debt burden would eventually drag Argentina into the abyss of the crisis (see Table 2.5).

No sooner had the "Convertibility Plan" been abolished than the Argentine government immediately had issued the new "Central Bank Organic Law", reforming comprehensively the functions of the

Central Bank and the monetary system, abolishing the restrictions of the Currency Board System on the Central Bank. Under the new law, the Central Bank restored its function as a currency issuer and regained the control of the discretion of the money supply. When necessary, the Central Bank could provide financial support to the government and financial institutions. In addition, the new law also stipulated that the Central Bank could use the foreign exchange reserves to repay debt.

With the change in the functions of the Central Bank, the monetary policy had been transformed from the exchange-rate targeting system into the money-supply targeting system. The intermediate target initially referred to the quarterly growth rate of the monetary base, but from 2006 it was changed into the quarterly growth of M2. The ultimate goal of monetary policy was to control inflation and maintain the stability of the currency peso. The Central Bank announced the quarterly monetary aggregate target and provided a floating ceiling. All in all, after 2002, the Argentine Central Bank had adopted a positive expansionary monetary policy with a very large scale of money supply for the pursuit of a high economic growth and the stabilization of the exchange rate through the intervention of the foreign exchange market. As for the excessive supply of currency due to the intervention in the foreign exchange market, the Central Bank hedged against the excess liquidity through the issuance of LEBAC documents (Letras del Banco Central, the Central Bank documents) and NOBAC bills (Notas del Banco Central, Central Bank bills) in the open market.

Before 2006, in order to stimulate production and demand, the Central Bank maintained a low interest rate. However, with the problem of the increasing inflation, the interest rate rose and in 2008 the lending rate reached the level of 19.5%.[16] After 2009, the interest rate came down.

After the crisis of 2001, in order to encourage investment and expand production, the government had taken various measures to

---

[16]EIU, *Country Report*, Argentina, London, United Kingdom, December 2012.

Table 2.6 Argentine Monetary and Credit Indicators (%)

Year	2003	2004	2005	2006	2007	2008	2009	2010	2011
The ratio of private sector loans in GDP	10.8	10.5	11.7	13.0	14.5	13.7	13.5	14.6	16.6
M2 ratio in GDP	25.1	25.9	26.6	27.0	26.1	22.4	23.2	25.0	28.9
Ration of liquidity in GDP	26.5	28.4	28.8	29.4	28.8	25.4	26.9	29.3	—

Source: Data of 2003–2009 came from CEPAL, "Argentina", *Estudio Economico de America Latina y el Caribe 2010–2011*, Data of 2010–2011 came from CEPAL, "Argentina", *Informe Macroeconomico*, julio 2012.

promote the credit, easing the lending restrictions on SMEs and consumers. The size of credit issued to the private sectors gradually expanded, and in 2011 the ratio was 16.6% of the GDP,[17] but still did not reach the highest level of 25% in the 1990s.

In March 2012, Argentina once again amended the "Central Bank Organic Law", listing the promotion of social justice with economic growth as one of the targets of the Central Bank. After the reform, the basis of monetary circulation was no longer inflation, but economic growth. In other words, the Central Bank could expand the money supply so as to achieve the targets of economic growth. The reform also abolished the provision of a monetary base supported by the foreign exchange reserves, so that the Central Bank could use more reserves to repay the foreign debt. In addition, the maximum limit of the short-term loans provided by the Central Bank to finance, i.e., the so-called "temporary advance amount", was changed from 12% to 20% in the amount of the monetary base.[18] The responsibilities of the Central Bank governor also had been expanded. He had the sole responsibility for the operation of the money and foreign exchange markets (formerly the responsibility of the Central Bank council), and he should play a greater role in the financial regulation (formerly the responsibility of the relatively independent monetary and foreign exchange institutions). The government considered that in view of the severe crisis environment, the monetary authorities should be directly responsible for the financial regulation

[17]CEPAL, "Argentina", *Informe Macroeconomico*, julio 2012.
[18]EIU, *Country Report*, Argentina, London, United Kingdom, April 2012.

and supervision. The Central Bank council was supposed to supervise the issuance of domestic and foreign debt, which used to be the job of the financial and foreign exchange institutions. Overall, the Central Bank would have more power and space to implement monetary policies and to provide funds to finance after the reform. It would play a greater role in promoting the economic growth and economic intervention (see Table 2.6).

3. The Competitive Floating Exchange Rate

After the collapse of the Currency Board System, the Argentine government enacted measures of peso devaluation and the peso system, leading to upheavals in the financial market — a rapid depreciation of the peso against the dollar peaked at the level of 4:1. The government took a series of interventions to stabilize the currency market, including selling a large sum of dollars to the foreign exchange market, and shortening the settlement deadlines. By the end of 2002, the exchange rate gradually had become stabilized, but the international reserves of the Central Bank fell to $10.48 billion.[19] After taking office, Kirchner made it clear to take "a competitive, stable and floating exchange rate system under the management of the Central Bank." Although the Central Bank did not pre-set the future level of the exchange rate, the real goal was to control the exchange rates within the range of 2.8–3.1 pesos per dollar. The Central Bank kept a stable exchange rate by frequently trading dollars in the foreign exchange market. It should be acknowledged that the active intervention had achieved remarkable results, not only reducing the fluctuation of exchange rates, but also dispelling the doubts of the market exchange rate. After the stabilization of the foreign exchange market, the Central Bank began the implementation of controls on the capital account from June 2005 in order to ease the upward pressure on the peso and to reduce dependence on the intervention of the Central Bank. The new measures required that, except for the newly issued public debt, the foreign trade financing and FDI, all capital inflows had to pay

[19]CEPAL, *Anexo de Balance Preliminar de las Economias der America Latina y el Caribe 2011*, p. 114.

30% as the non-interest reserve for no less than 365 days, aiming to curb short-term capital inflows. However, since the relevant provisions of this measure were not strict, it was easy for foreign capitals to find channels to avoid paying the reserve; therefore, the effect was not obvious. The government acknowledged a symbolic significance of the measure — mainly to show that the government had a strong attitude towards maintaining a competitive exchange rate regime.

Changes in the exchange rate regime had a positive impact on the Argentine economic recovery and steady growth. The most direct impact was reflected in foreign trade. The currency devaluation increased the price competitiveness of export products, and so greatly promoted the export; on the contrary, the devaluation was not conducive to imports, which reinforced the import substitution, so that the industrial sectors that were previously unable to compete with imported commodities recovered their production. As for the growth in exports, on the one hand, fiscal revenues had been expanded because of the export taxes; on the other hand, the foreign exchange reserves had also been greatly enriched, so that the countries had obtained the capacity to withstand external shocks and to repay foreign debt. In 2010, Argentina's foreign exchange reserves increased to $52.15 billion,[20] in which exports played a key role. The currency devaluation also made the labor cost down, leading to the expansion of employment. Therefore, to maintain a competitive exchange rate had become an important means for the successive governments to rebuild the economy after 2003.

From 2003 to 2007, the nominal peso-dollar exchange rate had remained stable. In 2006 and 2007, a slight devaluation occurred. Starting from 2008, the peso nominal exchange rate against other major currencies had maintained a trend of depreciating slightly, but the real exchange rate showed a trend of appreciation. According to the report of the Argentine "Thought Fund", from 2008 to 2010, the Argentine multilateral real exchange rate appreciated by 20%.[21]

[20] *Ibid.*, p. 114.

[21] Fundacion Pensar, *Un Modelo Agotado, la Economia Argentina bajo Cristina Fernandez de Kirchner, 2008–2011, abril de 2011*, p. 15.

Table 2.7 Exchange Rate Changes of Argentina

Year	2003	2004	2005	2006	2007	2008	2009	2010	2011	2012
Annual growth rate of nominal exchange (%)	−4.9	−0.2	−0.6	5.2	1.3	1.5	17.9	4.9	5.6	—
Real growth rate of nominal exchange (%)	−7.8	5.0	0.2	1.8	1.9	−4.1	2.4	−0.8	0.5	−4.0

Note: Represents appreciation.

Source: Data of the nominal exchange rate came from CEPAL, "Argentina", *Informe Macroeconomico*, julio 2012; Data of the actual exchange rate came from CEPAL, *Balance Preliminar de las Eeconomias de America Latina y el Caribe 2005–2013*.

The report concluded that the nominal exchange rate depreciation and the real exchange rate appreciation resulted from inflation. If the inflation problem could not be solved, this trend would continue. However, according to ECLAC statistics, Argentina's real exchange rate appreciation was not so large (see Table 2.7). In 2012, the Argentine economic slowdown increased the market demand for the dollars and the concerns about the currency, resulting in a weak peso. By September 2012, the nominal exchange rate of peso against the dollar had dropped 11%, a depreciation larger than the previous year. However, due to inflation, the real exchange rate appreciation trend remained. The strict foreign exchange controls and the dollar shortage led to rampant black markets — in the black markets peso against the US dollar had been close to 7:1 at the end of the year, 44% higher than the official rate.

4. The Adjustment of Social Policy and Improvement of Social Situation

In the neoliberal period, the government hoped to solve social problems with the help of the self-generated power of the economic growth, deeming that once the growth was achieved, its effect would inevitably spread to all social classes. This is the so-called "drip effect." This led to the fact that Argentina never put social development as a long-term task for the government, nor develop a complete strategy for social development and planning. The economic crisis of 2001 caused a heavy blow on Argentine social development. In the recession of four years (1999–2002), per capita GDP in Argentina fell from $7,874 to $6,456 (at prices in 2000),[22] a drop of 18%. Urban unemployment rate grew from 14.3% to 19.7%. Only in 2002, the real average wage and urban minimum wage decreased by 13.9% and 19.5%, respectively. Under the influence of unemployment, wage reduction and other factors, the degree of impoverishment of Argentine society increased rapidly — the proportion of poor people nationwide climbed from 23.7% to 45.4%. Even 40% of the employment in the public sectors was living below the poverty line. Such a huge change is rare in the history of Latin America. The worsening social situation also affected the concentration of wealth. With the Gini coefficient rising from 0.542 to 0.590, Argentina had become one of the Latin-American countries with the most inequitable distribution of income (see Table 2.8).

After taking office, Kirchner had repeatedly stressed the importance of social justice, proposing to regard fighting poverty as the most important work of the government. Faced with the severe domestic social situation, the government had taken a number of measures, including the promotion of employment, implementation of social assistance for the special populations,[23] labor reform, raising the minimum wage, etc., so that the social situation had improved.

---

[22]If there is no special note, the data here all came from CEPAL, *Anexo Estadistico de Panorama Social de America Latina 2006.*

[23]In April 2002, the Duhalde government introduced a "Male and Female Head-of-Household Unemployment Plan". It was not implemented as a general social policy at first, but as an emergency measure to deal with the social crisis, for a period of one year. But the Kirchner Administration continued the plan. Its purpose was to provide financial assistance to families that had lost their sources of income, but had children that needed to be brought up. According to the plan, the beneficiaries could receive 150 pesos per month, which was equivalent to half of Argentina's per capita income in 2002. A total of 2 million people had benefited from the year since the scheme was implemented. By October 2005, 1.47 million people were still receiving funding from the program. In 2005, with the improvement of the economy, the government of Argentina announced that the "Male and Female Head-of-Household Unemployment Plan" was changed into a long-term social policy — the "Social Integration into Family Plan". The prerequisite of acceptance of funding was to ensure that their children would go to school and complete a certain period of study, the amount of funding to be

The Fernandez government further improved the social awareness of vulnerable groups. In addition to retaining the original social policies, in 2008 the government conducted a reform of the social security system. Since 2009, in order to alleviate the impact of domestic economic slowdown and inflation on ordinary people, on the basis of the existing social programs, the government had gradually taken on new measures of relief and compensation. The new measures included the basic living subsidy program[24] for unemployed families with children, the year-end grant program for the retirees, and raising the threshold of personal income tax four times.[25] To sum up, at present, a social policy system of the combination of a long-term protection and emergency relief had been formed in Argentina. It had become a long-term mechanism for the governments after 2003 to strengthen social protection by providing grants for special populations and regularly raising the levels of the minimum wages and pensions.[26] The social spending of the government increased year by year, and the proportion of it against GDP increased from 20.9% in 2001 and 2002 to 27.8% in 2009 and 2010.[27] This level was second only to Cuba in Latin-American countries (see Table 2.9).

After 10 years of social policy adjustment, the social situation in Argentina had been significantly improved. Proportion of the population in poverty and extreme poverty in 2012 had dropped to

---

determined by the number of children, and each family could receive a maximum of 275 pesos.

[24]The plan began to be implemented since December 2009. Direct beneficiaries were juveniles whose parents were unemployed or had income less than the minimum wage and who were not officially registered as unemployed and domestic service personnel. At the beginning of the implementation of the plan, eligible children could receive a monthly allowance of 180 pesos; the disabled children could get 720 pesos. After three times of adjustments in 2010, 2011, and 2012, the above two grants were raised to 340 pesos and 1,200 pesos. The number of beneficiaries of this plan reached 3.8 million.

[25]After the fourth times of upward adjustment in 2013, the income tax threshold of all workers was 15,000 pesos.

[26]The minimum pension levels were adjusted two times in March and September each year since 2008. From 2003 to 2013, the minimum pension increased from 150 pesos to 2,477 pesos.

[27]CEPAL, *Panorama Social de America Latina 2010*, p. 165.

Table 2.8 Minimum Wage Level of Argentina

Year	2003	2004	2005	2006	2007	2008	2009	2010	2011	2012	2013
Minimum monthly wage (peso)	200	350	450	630	800	980	1,240	1,500	1,840	2,300	2,875
Minimum increase of wages (%)	—	75	28.6	40	27	22.5	26.5	21	22.7	25	25

Source: Official websites of the Ministry of Labor, Employment and Social Security of Argentina.

Table 2.9 Real Wage Increase of Argentina (%)

Year	2002	2003	2004	2005	2006	2007	2008	2009	2010	2011
Real average wage increase	−19.4	12.2	9.2	7.5	8.9	9.1	8.8	11.7	12.9	20.3
Real minimum wage increase	−19.6	3.3	54.5	31.8	12.9	13.7	15.3	15.3	10.0	13.4

Source: CEPAL, "Cuadro 1", *Anexo Estadistico de Panorama Social de America Latina 2012.*

4.3% and 1.7% respectively,[28] the lowest in Latin-American countries. The income distribution tended to improve with the Gini coefficient dropped to 0.492.[29]

III. Features of the New Growth Pattern

In the 1990s, Argentina achieved its economic growth, relying on the influx of foreign capital due to its large-scale privatization and financial liberalization and the expansion of consumption stimulated by imports. However, this growth had great vulnerability and uncertainty because it was excessively dependent on external market forces. Under the impact of foreign investment and imported products, the domestic industry experienced a serious recession, declining in production capacity and exports caused by overvalued currency. There was a serious shortage of endogenous economic growth momentum. At the same time, due to the over privatization and marketization of the economy, the state lost the means and tools to regulate the

[28]CEPAL, *Panorama Social de America Latina 2013*, p. 86.
[29]CEPAL, *Anexo Estadistico de Panorama Social de America Latina, 2012.*

economy and stimulate the growth, and thus could not implement effective macro-control measures. The intervention in the economy went down to a minimum.

Argentina's denial of neoliberalism began from the period of Duhalde, but at that time the primary task was to stabilize the situation, to overcome the crisis and to restore national order; thus a lot of policies and measures were born with the emergency nature. After Kirchner became the president, the general idea of policy adjustments came to be set down, and so Argentina really took to explore a new growth path. In 2007, after Fernandez, Mrs. Kirchner became the president. She not only inherited the basic policies, but also, in some ways, strengthened them, so that the continuity of policy had been maintained.

The new mode of economic growth mainly has three different aspects from the neoliberal governing ideas. First, the role of government domination and intervention was emphasized in the economy. Second, expanding domestic demand, consumption and production was treated as the driving force of economic growth to enhance the endogenous growth. Third, emphasis was put on the importance of trade surplus and lowering the level of economic opening — strengthening the consciousness of protectionism. Below, we will do some analysis on the two issues of the transformation of the economic growth mode and state intervention. Trade related issues will be discussed in Section 3.

1. Production Growth Model and Economic Growth

From the Duhalde government, Argentina had got a clear reform route — to replace "financial accumulation" with a "production accumulation", to set up a "production-oriented economic growth model", and to reduce external dependence. After taking office, Kirchner adopted the economic policy of the development of domestic production and the expansion of domestic demand that had further implemented the work to transform the economic growth mode.

This adjustment had been able to be implemented smoothly because, first of all, it had benefited from the currency devaluation that started in 2002. In the effect of peso devaluation, the imports fell by 50% in 2002, mainly capital goods and consumer goods, which had reinforced the import substitution to a large extent, and also stimulated the growth of export-oriented industrial sectors. Due to the reduction of imports and the decrease of commodity supply, those industrial enterprises targeting the domestic market began to re-invest and expand production to meet the needs. By 2004, the production capacity of steel industries almost reached its limit. For those products still unable to compete with imported goods, the government implemented a protectionist measure, mainly for light industrial products. Since 2003, the manufacturing output had maintained a double-digit growth for two consecutive years, becoming one of the main driving forces for the economic growth. In 2009, the Argentine economy decelerated with the impact of the international environment. In 2010 and 2011, the growth rate of manufacturing exceeded that of the economic growth, becoming a major factor driving the economic recovery again.

In the "production model of economic growth", the contribution of the construction industry was also very prominent. In the inaugural speech, Kirchner proposed to follow the US experience in the 1930s — through the development of the public works to revive the economy, suggesting that the state play a leading role in the public investment. Facts have proved that this decision had played an important role in driving the entire economic recovery. In 2003, the budget of the Argentine government in the public works was 1.76 billion pesos, but in 2006 it was 7.9 billion pesos.[30] The growth rate was very alarming. Large-scale infrastructure construction enabled the entire construction industry to restore vigor and vitality. The annual growth rate in 2003 and 2004 reached 34.4% and 29.4%, respectively.[31] In addition to the leading role in the economic recovery, the expansion of the public works also attracted thousands of large and small businesses, creating a lot of jobs. By the end of 2005,

[30]Official website of Argentina Public Works Secretariat, www.obraspublicas.gov.ar.

[31]CEPAL, "Argentina", *Informe Macroeconomico*, julio 2012.

Table 2.10 Economic Indicators of Argentina, 2003–2011 (%)

Year	2003	2004	2005	2006	2007	2008	2009	2010	2011
GDP growth rate	8.8	9.0	9.2	8.5	8.7	6.8	0.9	9.2	8.9
Growth rate of consumption	7.0	8.3	8.5	7.4	8.8	6.6	1.5	9.1	10.7
Rate of fixed capital formation against GDP	14.1	18.7	20.9	23.0	24.2	25.1	21.2	24.5	26.2

Source: CEPAL, "Argentina", *Informe Macroeconomico*, julio 2012.

the number of employees in the construction industry had reached 320,000, an increase of 20 million more than in the third quarter of 2002, becoming one of the sectors with the largest opportunities for the creation of formal employment. After taking office, Fernandez continued to increase government investment in the public works — to stimulate the economy. At the end of 2008, the government announced a public works program, totaling up to $32 billion.

In the expansion of production, with the recovery and rising of incomes, the demand and consumption were also growing rapidly. The Government had repeatedly raised the minimum wage and the pension level, and provided incentives for consumers in terms of taxation and credit. These measures had largely enhanced the confidence of the consumers, improved the purchasing power and stimulated the consumption. The average annual growth rate of private consumption from 2003 to 2005 reached over 8%, and in 2007, further to 9%.[32] Expansion of the production scale and strong domestic demand had greatly promoted the investment. The domestic fixed capital investment maintained a rapid growth rate, with an increased annual proportion of the GDP — in 2008 it reached 25.1%,[33] which was much higher than the level of around 20% of the 1990s (see Table 2.10).

Some scholars contributed the sustained economic growth of Argentina since 2003 to the favorable external environment, e.g., low interest rates, rising prices of international raw materials, rising demands from emerging economies such as China, the economic prosperity of world and the like. It is true that the economic growth

[32]CEPAL, *Estudio Economico de America Latina y el Caribe 2008–2009*, p. 114.
[33]CEPAL, "Argentina", *Informe Macroeconomico*, julio 2012.

of Argentina had been driven by the above favorable conditions, but if there had not been the contribution of domestic production sectors such as the industry and construction and the internal demand, high growth might be limited to only those export-related sectors. If you compare the economic growths of other export-oriented Latin-American countries exporting the same primary products in the same period, it is not difficult to find that not all countries had made good use of the external force to promote the economy of their countries. Thus, since 2002 the "production-oriented economic growth model" initiated by the Argentine government had indeed played a positive role in sustaining the economic growth.

2. Strengthening State Intervention

Another important feature of the Argentine economic policy adjustment is that the state intervention in the economy and management had significantly been enhanced, changing the past economic situation of over-relying on market regulation. It can be said that after 2002 the government began to play a leading role in a full range of economic life.

First, in terms of macroeconomic policy, restoring the functions of the Central Bank and strengthening them are an important manifestation of this interventionism. Since the two reforms of the Central Bank from 2002 had greatly enhanced the functions of the Central Bank, the monetary, fiscal and exchange rate policies had therefore become an important means of the government to regulate the economy (see the second part of this section).

Secondly, in terms of legislation, several important regulations had provided a legal guarantee for the government intervention in the economy. The temporary regulations implemented during the economic crisis were repeatedly extended, so that not only the executive power of the government had been consolidated, but also they had become an important tool for government intervention in the economy. For example, in December 2001 during the period of President De la Rua, the government amended the *Financial Management Law*, giving the government the right to make changes in the structure of the budget without congressional authorization, the so-called "super powers." This right was subject to Parliament for regular renewal. In 2006, the parliament passed a resolution declaring that the government would permanently have this right. In 2009, the Senate adopted the bill of the amendment of Article 37 of the *Financial Management Law*, ruling that the proportion of 5% was the limit that the government could modify the budget without congressional authorization. In addition, although Argentina had long been out of the economic crisis in 2001, the Kirchner government and the Fernandez government repeatedly extended the temporary law enacted during the Duhalde Ruling — the *Economic Emergency Law*. The law authorized the government to adopt a series of measures to intervene the economy without the approval of the Parliament. In other words, even if the ruling party did not have the majority in parliament, the government could still take advantage of this law — by presidential decrees, government orders and other administrative decrees, and reform measures, to promote the transformation of economic growth mode. Many measures enacted since 2002 had been carried out under the framework of this law.

Thirdly, in terms of price control, the Government had taken various interventions. In recent years, Argentina had been facing greater inflationary pressures. Because of this, in addition to the regulation and control of monetary and other macro-policies, the government also tried to curb the rising prices or adjust unreasonable prices through measures such as negotiating with the relevant industries and signing price agreements, developing reference prices, imposing export taxes on certain products in order to limit the priority of export to ensure domestic supply, wage bargaining, and freezing the public utility charges. The industries which were involved were mainly meat and food, fuel, water, electricity, transportation, telecommunications and other public services. Take natural gas, for example. Before the devaluation of the peso, the price of natural gas was calculated on the basis of dollars; in 2002, the *Economic Emergency Law* stipulated that natural gas prices be decided by 1:1 exchange rate of peso against dollar. This resulted in the dollar price of natural gas becoming only about one-third of the original, which caused strong dissatisfaction of the gas production enterprises and the tensions of energy supply. To ensure the benefits of the natural gas producers, in May 2004, the Kirchner government announced the timetable to raise the price of natural gas. Large users of natural gas, such as industrial enterprises and power plants would negotiate prices directly with the producers. However, the residential natural gas prices rose slightly in the government intervention. As for the loss of corporate profits, the government had taken to provide financial subsidies to compensate them.

Finally, the government had improved the status of the national capital in the economy by re-nationalization of privatized enterprises or the establishment of new state-owned enterprises. As mentioned earlier, an important feature of the economic reforms in the 1990s was a large scale of privatization of state enterprises. After coming to power, the Kirchner government emphasized the role of the state intervention in the economy, but did not include re-nationalization as the main content in the economic growth adjustment, only strengthening the supervision and management of privatized enterprises, issuing measures such as price freeze, limit of profit remittances, and compulsory investment. The government only nationalized a minority of the enterprises which had been in trouble — mismanagement, serious loss or poor quality — during the economic crisis.

During the governance of Fernandez, with the gradual deepening of reforms, the government became increasingly aware of the importance of the nationally owned part of the priority sectors, which would contribute to the implementation of macro-control and strengthen the control of important resources. From 2008 onwards, the government had gradually nationalized the national pension system, the Argentina Airlines, the country's largest oil companies — Oil Deposits Administration (namely, Argentina's state oil company, YPF company hereinafter), and the railway system, and in 2009 the *Audiovisual Media Services Law* was passed ready to nationalize 2/3 of the national broadcasting frequencies and television channels.

Generally speaking, the nationalization process since 2003 has the following characteristics. First, in terms of the industry distribution, the nationalization mainly was concentrated in the public service, involving the sectors including postal services, water supply, railways, aviation, social security, radio and television, etc. In the areas of production only few enterprises had been nationalized so far, e.g., the military aircraft factory and YPF. Second, the nationalization had experienced the process from "rescuing loss-making enterprises" to "meeting the needs of development". The enterprises nationalized during Kirchner's reign were mostly companies with operational problems. For example, the Argentine Post Office and Argentine water companies were no longer able to fulfill the concession contract due to serious losses; San Martin Railway not only was losing money, but also often had accidents, offering poor quality of service. The purpose of the government to have nationalized these difficult companies lacking private investment was for the sake of rescuing them. After nationalization, the government had declared that once these companies had turned profitable, they would be privatized again. However, the 2008 nationalization of the pension system and the 2012 nationalization of the YPF Company clearly reflected the intentions of the government to hold the key sectors in order to meet the needs of development. Third, the way of nationalization was no longer the same as before — entirely by the state. The state adopted the approach to control or hold part of the shares of the joint ventures. For example, after the nationalization of YPF, the "Federal Organization of Oil-producing Provinces" formed by the Government and the oil-producing provinces held a 51% of the total shares, YPF Company's original second-largest shareholder, Argentine Petersen Group held 25% of the shares, and the original holding company of Spain's Repsol held 6.4% of the shares. Founded in 2004, the Argentina Energy Company (Enarsa) was made up of three kinds of shareholders: the federal government holding 53% of the shares, the provincial government 12%, and 35% of the shares in the hands of small shareholders in the equity markets. After the Argentina Airport 2000[34] had been nationalized, the government only had a 15% of the stake.

[34]An enterprise operating the airport business, owning 33 airports nationwide.

Both from the perspective of size and magnitude, the proposed re-nationalization of the past 10 years cannot be compared to the privatization process in the 1990s; therefore, it is hard to draw a conclusion about the impact on the domestic economy. For now, the biggest benefit for the government is the nationalization of the pension system, and one of the examples of successful nationalization is the Argentina Post Office becoming out of the red after being nationalized. However, the continued implementation of nationalization could weaken the confidence of the investors in the short term and cause some negative impact on the inflow of foreign capitals.

IV. Dealing with the Financial Crisis and the Current Problems

From 2008 onwards, there had been some changes in the Argentine economy. First, the external conditions of the economic growth had been changed by the international financial crisis and began to have impact on the domestic economy. Secondly, the ending of the term of the Kirchner government marked the completion of its task to lead the Argentine economy to recovery. The several years of economic reform practice had basically established the features of the new mode of growth, and the development of the domestic economy gradually went onto the right track. However, some problems began to come out and present new challenges for the sustainability of growth. Below, we will offer an analysis of the main problems affecting the Argentine economy and the government's countermeasures in the last 10 years from both the external and internal perspectives.

1. Dealing with the Global Financial Crisis

From the beginning of the second half of 2008, the impact of the global financial crisis on the Argentine economy was gradually emerging, but owing to the smooth running of the economy in the first half of that year, the annual economic growth still reached a high level of 6.8%. In 2009, the impact of the financial crisis turned exacerbated, causing Argentina's failure to continue to maintain high growth for six consecutive years — the annual GDP growth was only 0.9%.[35] In 2010 and 2011, the Argentine economy achieved a strong recovery — the annual growth rate reached 9.2% and 8.9%, respectively. In 2012, affected by the global economic downturn and a weak Brazilian economy, the economic growth of Argentina was slowing down, with an annual GDP growth of only 2.2%,[36] not only far lower than in 2011, but also lower than the average growth rate of 3.1% of Latin America and the Caribbean states. In 2013, the Argentine economic situation was still grim. The issues, such as the high rate of inflation, the excessive depreciation of the exchange rate, the reduction of foreign exchange reserves, and the widened current account deficits, became the major factors constraining economic growth. It can be concluded that since 2008 unstable characteristics occurred in the macroeconomic growth of Argentina, which were mainly influenced by external factors.

However, in general, the impact of the global financial crisis on Argentina in recent years was still limited compared with the past. There are five reasons. First, after the 10-year adjustment of economic policies, the Argentine government had gained more means of macroeconomic control and policy tools, therefore; its ability to respond to crises had improved. Second, since 2003 the government had achieved an unprecedented double surplus of fiscal and trade balance so that the government could have sufficient funds to intervene the economy. Third, since the problem of part of the debt owed during the 2001 crisis had remained unresolved, the international capital market had not opened its doors to Argentina. Therefore, the conduction effect of the financial crisis was limited. Fourth, learning from the lesson of the last crisis, Argentina strengthened its supervision of financial institutions and the control of capital flows. Fifth, in recent years, Argentina paid attention to controlling the size of

[35] CEPAL, *Anuario Estadistico de America Latina y el Caribe* 2012.

[36] Except special notes, the data of this part were derived from CEPAL, *Balance Preliminar de las Economias de America Latina y el Caribe 2012*, diciembre de 2012.

the external debt and thus its solvency was strengthened gradually, reducing the debt levels.

Since 2008, the Argentine government had adopted a series of anti-crisis measures, mainly in the following aspects. First, it was to adhere to expansionary fiscal policies, increasing financial investment to stimulate economic growth. For example, a large-scale public works project had been implemented in 2008 and 2009. Second, the Central Bank stepped up its intervention in the foreign exchange market to stabilize the exchange rate and avoid excessive fluctuation range, and also made sure that in the case of stabilized exchange rates it would timely buy dollars in order to enrich its foreign exchange reserves. Third, to encourage domestic production and consumption, the government had issued a number of credit incentives. For example, in December 2008, the government unveiled a plan to encourage the consumption of automobiles. In January 2009, the government introduced a policy to encourage residents to purchase home appliances and other consumer durables. In July 2009, the government announced the projects to provide preferential loans to people who were going to build new houses, expand their shelters or buy new houses. In 2012, to respond to the decline in domestic investment, the government enacted new measures to force the banks to provide preferential loans, requiring all the banks whose deposits were more than 1% of the total deposits of the financial sectors to come up with more than 5% of the company's private deposits for the loans to companies, half of which had to be lent to SMEs. The loan period was supposed to be at least three years, and the interest rate must not exceed 15%. Fourth, the government insisted on using the foreign exchange reserves to repay foreign debt in order to boost investor confidence and enhance the credibility of the debt so as to get prepared to return to the international credit market as soon as possible. Fifth, to support domestic enterprises, strengthen import substitution, and save foreign exchange, the government implemented strict import controls, showing a strong trend of trade protectionism. Sixth, the exchange controls were strengthened. Since the investors lacked confidence in the future economic trend of Argentina, in the second half of 2011 the situation of capital outflows had become serious. To prevent capital fleeing and buying dollars, the government adopted a series of foreign exchange control measures so that the trend of capital out-flowing had been curbed. In 2012, the economic slowdown of Argentina intensified the demand of investors and the public for the dollars. To prevent the loss of foreign exchange reserves, the government continued to strengthen exchange controls. Businesses and residents were banned to do transactions of purchasing foreign exchange savings for the purpose of hedging, and the foreign exchange that residents needed to buy for traveling abroad had also been severely restricted. Dividends paid to foreign investors, debt of principal and interest, and the payment of import trade payment should be declared in advance and audited.

2. Main Problems at Present

(1) The Inflation

Since 2003, with the devaluation of the peso, the increased money supply and rapid economic growth, Argentina had been facing inflationary pressures. During Kirchner's reign, the government tried to control inflation in the single digit by means of price controls, but in 2005 the consumer price index still climbed to 12.3%.[37] Although the inflation rate had dropped slightly since then, it was still very high. Beginning from 2007, with the changes in the calculation method by the National Bureau of Statistics and Survey and the replacement of the director, serious discrepancies began to appear between the official statistics, the provincial statistics and the statistics of private institutions. This led to the doubt of the public whether the government had intervened in the statistical work, and therefore, distrust was generated on the official inflation rate. Over the next few years, it was always heard the voices of doubt, both domestic and foreign, on the inflation statistics of Argentina. The IMF had also repeatedly requested Argentina to modify the existing index system, but the Argentine government did not give a positive response.

[37]CEPAL, "Argentina", *Informe Macroeconomico*, julio 2012.

According to the statistics of some private institutions, it is estimated that in recent years Argentina's inflation rate had reached a level of 20–25% — twice of the official statistics.

There are five main causes for the high inflation: (1) too large scale fiscal spending and the money supply; (2) increased liquidity on the currency market resulting from the foreign exchange control and the low interest rate policy to stimulate the economy; (3) the high demand with insufficient supply; (4) the exacerbated supply and demand due to measures to restrict imports of cheap goods abroad to enter the Argentine market; (5) too fast wage rises. The Argentine government controlled prices mainly by means of signing price agreements with the suppliers, freezing part of the utility prices, providing financial subsidies and restricting exports. The measures of raising the interest rates and appreciating exchange rates to deal with the problem of inflation had not been adopted because they were contradictory to the objectives of the Argentine government to stimulate the economy and maintain a trade surplus.

In terms of the current effect, the means of price-control was limited in curbing inflation, and led to a vicious cycle of price controls and inflation to some extent. Regulatory measures affected corporate profit margins, suppressed the production enthusiasm and the willingness to invest, and caused companies to reduce the scale of investment, being reluctant to expand production. The final result was stagnant or declining production, short supply and intensified demand. The subsidy policy also was between the devil and the deep sea. If high subsidies were maintained, the government was bound to face increased financial pressure; if the subsidies were removed, prices would inevitably go up. Whether it was price controls or subsidies, both began to be implemented from the ending of the crisis in 2001. They were very effective for the control of inflation in the early period of the currency depreciation and during the economic recovery, but with the stable exchange rate and steady development of economic activities, the government should reduce its intervention in the prices and let the market mechanism play a greater role. The recent inflation has affected not only the real exchange rate, savings rate and credit, but also social stability.[38] At the same time, the rapid rise in the cost of labor wages is not conducive to enhancing the competitiveness of Argentine products. If this problem were not well solved, under the condition of the economic downturn, the stagflation situation of "low growth and high inflation" might occur in Argentina.

(2) The Debt Problem

During the period of Kirchner's presidency, Argentina had restructured most of the arrears of debt occurred in the economic crisis of 2001. Still nearly a quarter of the debt had not been resolved, totaling approximately $20 billion. Since then, the Argentine government had not given up its efforts of debt restructuring. In April 2010, the government announced the restructuring plan for the $30 billion of debt and interest that had not been dealt with in the debt restructuring in 2005. The new plan was welcomed by most of the creditors; 66% of the bondholders agreed to participate in the bond exchange, so that Argentina had successfully resolved some of the remaining debt. With the improvement of the solvency of Argentina, the Standard & Poor's (S&P) raised the rating of Argentine domestic and foreign currency debt to level "B" in September 2010. However, because there was still a small part of the debt difficult to reach an agreement on the debt rescheduling, Argentina had not been able to return to the international capital market; therefore, its financing capacity had been greatly restricted.

In addition, although the debt restructuring had eased the pressure of debt on Argentina, its external debt still remained large — $141.1 billion in 2012, an increase of $27.3 billion[39] more than that of the debt restructuring in 2005, and it was also huge to the size of the corresponding economy. In 2012, the foreign debt accounted for 29.6% of its GDP, not only higher than the other two big countries in Latin America — Brazil (13.9%) and Mexico (19.3%), but also

[38]Since 2011, large-scale protests and strikes broke out in Argentina, demanding the government to raise wages.
[39]CEPAL, *Anuario Estadistico de America Latina y el Caribe 2013*.

Table 2.11 External Debt Scale of Argentina

Year	2003	2004	2005	2006	2007	2008	2009	2010	2011	2012
Total external debt ($100 million)	1,646	1,712	1,138	1,089	1,246	1,249	1,164	1,293	1,407	1,411
Debt-to-GDP ratio (%)	127. 0	111.8	62.1	50.8	47.5	38.0	37.7	34.9	31.4	29.6

Source: CEPAL, *Anuario Estadistico de America Latina y el Caribe 2011*, 2013.

higher than the national average in Latin America (20.9%).[40] This indicated that the external debt burden was still heavy in Argentina, which was the inevitable result of the long-term debt-development model (see Table 2.11).

Over the last two years, due to the changes in domestic and international economic situation, the solvency of Argentina has been questioned. On the one hand, the government had been restructuring the domestic and external debts, so that the risk of debt had declined; on the other hand, it had insisted on using the foreign exchange reserves to repay the debt interest in order to dispel the market concerns. The several sessions of governments since 2003 had been trying to change the debt-development path, adhering to the principle of "growth first, debt second", refusing to pay off foreign debt at the expense of economic development. This position was consistent with the Argentine national interests and long-term development needs, but in any case, it was necessary to continue to control the volume of foreign debt, avoiding the debt peak period coinciding with the economic slowdown so as to maintain solvency.

(3) The Government Intervention

As mentioned earlier, one of the differences between the existing policies of Argentina and the neoliberalism lies in that the government had stepped up intervention in the economic activity. There is no doubt that the government intervention is absolutely necessary for the achievement of economic recovery and economic growth. However, many measures taken in the government intervention in economy had encountered much resistance because the economic interests

[40] *Ibid.*

of some groups had been involved. The measures of freezing price and the peso price taken during the Kirchner reign had been strongly opposed by private enterprises, especially multinational companies, but Kirchner had made outstanding achievements in the economic field, which had enabled him to get higher prestige and support rate in the population. After Fernandez took office, the Argentine economy had come out of recovery and began to move to a new height. This situation required that the Fernandez government have greater ability to govern the country, i.e., this government was facing a more severe test than the previous administration. In this case, the governing style of the Fernandez government tended to be tough, and hence more efforts were taken to further enhance the government intervention in the economy. In May 2008, after the government announced that the export tax rate of agricultural products was changed from a fixed rate to a floating rate, the farming community set off a nationwide strike after unsuccessful negotiations, leading to a several-month-long agricultural crisis, resulting in a series of chain reactions: huge losses in the agricultural production, the dropping of the government support rate, changes of several members of the Cabinet, and the ruling coalition's defeat in the mid-term elections the next year. Although the agricultural crisis came to an end after the Senate had rejected the government's bill, it led to the nationwide questioning of the strong intervention of the Argentine government in the economy. In 2012, a series of protests were triggered by the measures of foreign exchange controls and import restrictions taken by the government because the vital interests of the enterprises and the general public had been involved. The method of the forcible acquisition of YPF also had aroused strong repercussions at home and abroad, criticized by foreign investors.

Over the past 10 years, the interventionist policy pursued by the Argentine Government has corrected the bias of over marketization in the neoliberal era, but if this approach of "strong government intervention with little market regulation" were adopted for a long time, it would be possible to go to the other extreme. At present, many contradictions and problems encountered by the Argentine economy, such as inflation and energy shortages, to some extent, have too much to do with the excessive intervention of the government and the failure of market regulation mechanisms. In addition, the government frequently uses the administrative directives and promulgates measures with the *Economic Emergency Law*, which is conducive to improving the government authority. However, it is not conducive to the consolidation of democratic institutions because in the long run it will lead to the executive power overriding the legislation. Therefore, it is necessary for the government to adjust the government intervention efforts in government-led economy, giving play to the role of market self-regulation in order to ensure sustainable economic growth.

Section 2 Changes of Industrial Structure and Adjustment of Industrial Policy

From the 1980s to the 1990s, the adjustment of industrial development strategy by the government and the impact of the economic opening-up on the industrial sectors had greatly affected the industrialization process, resulting in a clear phenomenon of "de-industrialization" in Argentina. While the industry had declined in the national economy, the rapid expansion of the tertiary industry was gradually becoming a pillar industry in the economic development. "De-industrialization" and the expansion of tertiary industry did not mean the optimization and upgrading of industrial structures, but a step backward. For this change was mainly due to many causes such as slow agricultural development, decreased capacity of industrial production, simplification of manufacturing structures and unbalanced development of the departments of services. After 2003, the manufacturing sector grew at a faster pace, playing an important role in economic recovery. After taking office, Kirchner pursued the "production growth model" aiming at the development of the domestic production and the expansion of domestic demand, playing a role in optimizing the industrial structure to a certain extent. The role of agriculture in the economy had increased and the "de-industrialization" trend had been checked. In this section, from the perspective of the correlation between the resources and the structures of the industry and foreign trade, we will first of all make a brief introduction about Argentina's advantage of resources, then focus on the analysis of the changes of the industrial structure of Argentina since 2003, especially the results of re-industrialization, and finally give an overview of the changes of the industrial policies.

I. Resource Advantage

Argentina has a vast territory, rich in minerals, oil and gas, forestry, animal husbandry, fisheries, water, and other resources. Since its population have higher level of education, its human resource has the feature of a high quality.

Argentina is rich in oil, gas, uranium, beryl, gypsum, sulfur, and other minerals, in addition to abundant limestone, granite and other stone resources, but it is limited in coal, iron, and aluminum, which cannot meet its domestic demand. In recent years, the geological exploration work has made great progress, so that a number of new deposits have been discovered — reserves of copper, lead, zinc, gold, silver, and molybdenum have increased. Mineral resources are mainly distributed in the Northwest, the central mountainous areas and the Southern Patagonia. The reserves of beryl from which rare metal beryllium is extracted are second to Brazil, ranking No. 2 in the world. Argentina is rich in uranium ore resources, being one of the few countries in Latin America that have uranium resources. According to the report *Uranium: Resources, Production and Demand (2009)*, published by the Organization for Economic Co-operation and Development (OECD) in 2010, Argentina's uranium reserves are 19,000 tons, accounting for 0.4% of the total world reserves.[41] As an important nuclear energy, uranium resources provide the conditions to develop nuclear power for Argentina.

Oil and gas resources are concentrated in the Northern province of Salta, the Midwest province of Neuquén and Mendoza, the Southern province of Chubut and Santa Cruz, as well as the Southern tip of Tierra del Fuego. In 2012, Argentina had proven oil reserves of 374 million cubic meters and natural gas reserves of 315.5 billion

[41] http://en.wikipedia.org/wiki/List_of_countries_by_uranium_reserves.

cubic meters.[42] In recent years, the Argentine oil and gas reserves are declining. By the end of 2011, its oil and natural gas reserves and production ratio were 11.4 times and 8.8 times, respectively.[43] According to the current production rate, the conventional oil and gas reserves in Argentina could last only about 10 years of exploitation. After 2010, Argentina's shale oil and gas exploration had made significant progress — astonishing reserves of shale oil and gas resources have been discovered in Neuquen Province and Mendoza Province. According to the *World Shale Gas Resources: An Initial Assessment of 14 Regions Outside the United States*, a research report issued in April 2011 by the US Energy Information Administration, the technically recoverable reserves of Argentina's shale gas reached 774 trillion cubic feet (equivalent to 219 trillion cubic meters),[44] second only to China and the United States among the 32 assessed countries, ranking No. 3. This further confirms the huge oil and gas resource potential in Argentina. However, in terms of the difficulty and high cost of the production of shale oil and gas, full development is still to be expected.

Due to favorable natural conditions and fertile land, Argentina has abundant land and agricultural resources. After Brazil, its agricultural land and arable land in Latin America rank the second, showing a gradual trend of expansion in the last 20 years (see Table 2.12). The main agricultural area has mild climate and abundant rainfall, and therefore relies mainly on rainfall for irrigation. The mechanical irrigation area is only about 5% of all arable land. Argentina's forestry resources are less prominent in the Latin-American countries. The total forest area is declining and the forest coverage rate dropped from 12.5% in 1990 to less than 11% in 2009. But in addition to the forest, Argentina also has 61.47 million hectares of forest, accounting for 22% of its total land area.[45] With

[42]Official website of Argentina National Bureau of Statistics and Survey, http://www.indec.mecon.ar.

[43]BP, *BP World Energy Statistics Yearbook*, June 2012, pp. 6, 20.

[44]Website of U.S. Department of Energy Information, http://www.eia.gov/analysis/studies/worldshalegas/.

[45]FAO, *Evaluacion de los Recursos Forestales Mundiales 2010*, Roma, Italia, 2010, p. 234.

Table 2.12 Agricultural Resources of Argentina (10,000 Hectares)

Year	1990	1995	2000	2005	2009
Agricultural Land Area	12,739	12,794	12,877	13,440	14,050
Arable Land Area	2,640	2,700	2,790	2,950	3,100
Mechanical Irrigation Area	148	155	157	160	165
Grassland and Pasture Area	9,997	9,992	9,987	10,390	10,850
Forest Coverage	3,479	3,333	3,186	3,060	2,963

Source: FAO Database, http://faostat.fao.org/site/377/DesktopDefault.aspx? PagelD = 377#ancor.

numerous rivers and lakes, its national water area covers 4.71 million hectares, accounting for 1.6% of its total land area.[46] This provides favorable conditions for the development of its inland aquaculture industry, and also makes hydroelectric power generation an important way of power generation for Argentina. It has a coastline of more than 4,000 kilometers long and a vast fishing area with numerous species of fish — one of the major fishing grounds of the Atlantic coast of South America.

Argentina is sparsely populated, with a total population of 40.37 million people (2010),[47] ranking No. 4 in Latin America. The annual population growth rate from 2010 to 2015 was 8.5%, lower than the Latin-American average. In 2010, the economically active population reached 19 million people. With a high degree of urbanization, 93.1% of the population is concentrated in urban areas. Nearly a third of the residents live in the country's capital Buenos Aires and its surrounding satellite towns. Due to the lower birth rate and the rise of average life expectancy, Argentina has formally entered the aging society — in 2010, the population of 65-year-olds accounted for 10.5% of the total population. The life expectancy has reached 76 years. Argentina is one of the countries with the highest level of human development in Latin America. In the UN Human Development Index in 2010, Argentina was the 46th, ranking No. 2 in Latin America, behind

[46] *Ibid.*

[47] Data in this part came from CEPAL, *Anuario Estadistico de America Latina y el Caribe 2012.*

Chile. Argentina's advantage lies in the fact that its education, science, culture, and health (ESCH) are relatively developed, with a population of high quality and less discrimination against women. For a long time, due to the relative average distribution of wealth, the overall standard of living is higher, and therefore, Argentina is recognized as a "middle-class nation" in Latin America.

With adequate educational resources, Argentina has a good development of higher education. It is one of the few countries in Latin America where the last year of pre-school education is also included in the scope of compulsory education. The primary education has become universal, and the level of universal secondary education is also higher than the national average in Latin America. The national higher educational institutions are divided into multiple levels, with a total of 80 comprehensive universities. The University of Buenos Aires is the largest in size in the country, with over 300,000 students. In 2006, the number of students registered in the universities of Argentina reached 2,080,000, of which 74.1% were undergraduate and graduate students, and 25.7% were college students.[48] In 2011, of the country's economically active population of over 15 years old, 40.1% had 10–12 years of education, and 33.1% had more than 13 years of education.[49]

II. Characteristics and Changes of the Industrial Structure

After the 1990s, with the adjustment of the industrial development strategy of the government and the impact caused by the economic opening up on the industrial sectors, new changes occurred in the industrial structure of Argentina. In the composition of the three major industries, the position of the first and the second industry decreased significantly in the national economy — a serious decline happened in the commodity-producing sector; however, driven by

[48] Juan Carlos Moreno-Brid, Pablo Ruiz-Nupoles, *La Educacion Superior y el Desarrollo Economico en America Latina*, CEPAL, Mexico, D.F., enero de 2009, p. 29.

[49] CEPAL, *Anuario Estadistico de America Latina y el Caribe 2012*.

the real estate industry and the transportation industry, the tertiary industry was experiencing a rapid expansion, becoming the most dynamic economic sector. In the second industry, the manufacturing sector was the most seriously affected by the adjustment of economic and industrial policies, of which the growth rate was significantly lower than the economic growth rate. After the reform of the 1990s, Argentina's industrial structure was going further toward "de-industrialization" and "tertiary industrialization" that appeared since the end of the stage of import substitution industrialization. In other words, the economic reform had made the irrationality of the industrial structure more prominent rather than improved the industrial structure (see Table 2.13).

All in all, the Argentine industrial structure had the following characteristics before 2003: First, the overall layout of the industrial structure was irrational. The declining proportion of the first and second industry in GDP was not the optimization of industrial structure, but the result of the unbalanced industrial development. Agricultural development was slow due to the lack of investment, the development of the manufacturing sector was blocked with the impact of the imported goods, and the service sector achieved a rapid development in the wave of privatization due to a lot of foreign investment. Second, the structure within the industry was irrational. Its agriculture was dominated by farming, and its soybean crops accounted for more than half of the total output. With the high dependence on a single crop, the development of the internal diversity of agriculture was insufficient. The direction of the adjustment of industrial structure shifted from the comprehensive import substitution to the priority of the development of industries with comparative advantages. The proportion of technology-intensive industries, such as cars, mechanical equipment and electronics, and labor-intensive industries, such as textile, leather, and footwear, had declined, while the proportion of resource-intensive industries, such as the farm-product-processing industry and mineral-processing-oriented industry, had increased. In the structure with resource-processing industry as a pillar industry of manufacturing, on the one hand, it was difficult to have a more substantial upgrade for the added value; on the other hand,

Table 2.13 Growth Rate of Various Economic Sectors in Argentina (1993–2002) (%)

Year	1993	1994	1995	1996	1997	1998	1999	2000	2001	2002
Agriculture	2.4	7.5	5.6	−1.2	0.5	8.7	2.5	−1.7	1.1	−2.3
Mining	9.9	13.8	16.4	4.5	0.7	−3.8	−3.3	6.7	4.7	−3.7
Manufacturing	4.6	4.5	−7.2	6.5	9.2	1.8	−7.9	−3.8	−11.6	−11.0
Construction industry	10.9	5.8	−12.2	8.4	16.6	8.7	−7.9	−9.3	−12.1	−33.4
Water, electricity and natural gas	11.1	10.8	7.4	4.1	8.2	7.6	3.6	6.6	1.1	−3.0
Transportation, storage and communications	5.3	10.3	1.7	6.9	11.2	8.9	−1.3	1.7	−4.6	−7.9
Commerce and catering	3.4	6.7	−7.5	7.9	10.9	3.4	−6.9	−2.4	−7.8	−16.8
Finance, insurance, real estate, and business service	9.9	9.5	−0.9	6.1	7.3	7.0	−0.5	1.2	−4.1	−9.6
Community, social and personal services	—	1.5	0.6	2.3	3.9	1.5	1.9	1.7	−0.2	−3.3

Source: CEPAL, *Estudio Economico de America Latina y el Caribe 2001–2002, 2003–2004*.

Table 2.14 Sector Composition in GDP of Argentina (%)

Year	Farming, Forestry, Animal, Husbandry and Fishery	Mining	Manuf-acturing	Water, Electri-city and Natural Gas	Const--ruction Business	Comm-odity Produ-ction Depart ment	Business and Repair	Hotel and Catering Services	Traffic Transport and Storage Industry	Fin-ance	Real Estate	Public Adminis-tration and National Defense	Educa-tion, Social Services and Medical treat-ment	Other Serv-ices	Ser-vice Sector	Others
1993	5.2	1.5	18.2	1.9	5.7	32.5	14.3	2.3	6.8	3.9	14.4	6.2	7.7	5.4	61.1	6.4
1994	5.1	1.5	17.8	1.9	5.6	31.8	14.2	2.4	7.1	3.5	15.5	6.0	7.6	5.2	61.6	6.6
1995	5.3	1.9	17.2	2.0	5.2	31.7	13.5	2.4	7.4	3.8	16.1	6.0	7.9	5.1	62.3	6.0
1996	5.6	2.2	17.5	1.9	5.0	32.2	13.9	2.5	7.5	3.6	15.6	5.7	7.5	5.0	61.4	6.4
1997	5.2	1.9	18.2	1.9	5.1	32.4	14.2	2.6	7.8	3.5	15.2	5.4	7.3	4.9	60.8	6.8
1998	5.2	1.4	17.8	1.9	5.5	32.0	14.0	2.8	8.2	3.7	15.1	5.6	7.4	4.8	61.5	6.5
1999	4.5	1.6	17.0	2.2	5.4	30.7	13.3	2.8	8.3	4.1	15.7	6.2	8.2	5.0	63.5	5.8
2000	4.7	2.5	16.5	2.3	4.7	30.7	12.7	2.7	8.5	4.1	15.7	6.3	8.5	5.1	63.5	5.8
2001	4.6	2.5	16.1	2.4	4.3	29.8	12.2	2.7	8.5	5.1	15.9	6.4	9.0	5.3	65.1	4.5
2002	10.3	6.0	20.3	1.7	2.5	40.8	10.8	2.1	7.4	5.3	12.8	5.4	7.3	3.8	54.8	4.4
2003	10.3	5.5	22.5	1.6	3.1	43.0	11.0	2.2	8.0	3.6	11.2	5.0	6.5	3.6	51.0	6.0
2004	9.7	5.3	22.3	1.6	3.9	42.6	10.8	2.2	8.4	3.8	10.3	4.8	6.1	3.6	50.0	7.4
2005	8.7	5.4	21.4	1.6	4.5	41.7	10.9	2.4	8.4	4.0	10.1	5.0	6.5	3.8	50.9	8.4
2006	7.8	5.5	20.6	1.5	5.3	40.7	10.6	2.5	8.2	4.3	10.1	5.1	7.2	3.8	51.7	7.6
2007	8.6	4.4	19.5	1.4	5.7	39.6	10.6	2.5	7.9	4.5	10.1	5.4	7.6	3.8	52.2	8.2
2008	9.0	3.5	19.5	1.2	5.5	38.6	10.9	2.4	7.8	4.7	10.1	5.6	7.8	3.7	53.1	8.3
2009	6.9	3.4	19.6	1.2	5.3	36.3	11.2	2.4	7.6	5.2	10.6	6.4	8.5	4.2	56.0	7.7
2010	9.2	3.3	18.8	1.1	5.1	37.5	11.2	2.3	7.4	5.3	9.7	6.3	8.0	3.8	54.2	8.3
2011	9.7	3.1	18.9	1.0	5.3	37.9	11.6	2.2	7.3	5.2	9.1	6.5	8.2	3.5	53.5	8.6

Note: "Others" means in the form of "value-added tax + import tax − indirect statistics of financial intermediation.
Source: www.cei./ov.ar/userfiles/pib_a.xls.

the overall international competitiveness of the industrial products was not strong. In the tertiary industry, finance, telecommunications, and transportation sectors developed rapidly, with a high degree of concentration of enterprises. Sectors that could create a lot of employment, such as the commercial sector and the public services, developed slowly, and even shrank. Third, the international competitiveness and labor productivity of large private enterprises and foreign-funded enterprises increased significantly, establishing a dominant and leading role in the three major industries. In the top 500 enterprises, the foreign-funded enterprises increased from 219 in 1993 to 340 in 2002, in which the foreign-controlled enterprises changed from 161 to 293.[50] SMEs were struggling in the competition, characterized by limited production and low degree of specialization, technically below the level of the international requirements, and therefore, they could hardly survive in the competition (see Table 2.14).

The irrational industrial structure directly affected the trade structure. In exports, the primary products and processed products accounted for two-thirds, and the industrial products one-third. This led to Argentina's exports vulnerable to the fluctuations of international market price of raw materials and agricultural products. Once the price dropped, in turn the development of related industries would be affected. Similarly, due to the industrial structural imbalances, the capital goods and intermediate goods were still dependent on imports. In addition, the impact of changes in the industrial structure on employment was obvious. In the process of "de-industrialization", the ability to create formal employment in the industrial sector declined significantly, forcing a large number of unemployed workers to flow into services. The service sector was not developed on a strong industrial and agricultural foundation, unable to absorb surplus labor, which led to an increase in unemployment and irregular employment.

After 2003, the Argentine economy entered a new stage of development — the international and domestic environment had changed. In the process of the adjustment of economic policy and improved

[50] http://www.indec.mecon.ar.

economic situation, the industrial structure had also undergone some changes. Its agriculture had improved significantly in the national economy, the proportion of the manufacturing sector had been restored, the signs of "re-industrialization" emerged, and the share of services declined. Below, we will analyze the main changes in the internal production structure from the two aspects of agriculture and manufacturing.

1. Agriculture

After the crisis in 2001, the development pace of agriculture in Argentina was significantly faster, thanks to the rise of agricultural profitability after the currency devaluation. Moreover, the demand of emerging countries, such as China and India, for agricultural products continued to expand, making the international agricultural market become increasingly active, pushing up international prices of agricultural products. In addition, to support agriculture, the government heavily subsidized the agricultural production. These factors greatly stimulated the production enthusiasm of the farmers.

In the sectors of agriculture, farming was still dominant. Crop acreage and yields increased significantly. In the agricultural year of 2010–2011, the crop acreage reached 34.5 million hectares, and the total output exceeded 100 million tons,[51] hitting a record. The importance of soybeans in farming unabated. In recent years, the soybean price was soaring because of the rising demand from the international market for soybeans. This provided favorable conditions for the development of Argentine soybean farming. Today, Argentina has become the third-largest soybean producer in the world behind the United States and Brazil. In the 1990s, the crop yield was higher than oil crops, so the soybean crops occupied at most 30% of the total output, but in recent years, this proportion increased to 50–60%. The output of the production of the single crop of soybeans was more than that of the total production of food crops. Therefore, the harvest of soybeans played a decisive role in agriculture. In food crops also

[51]INTA, *Evolucion del systema Productivo Agropecuario*, junio del 2011, p. 3.

Table 2.15 Agricultural Output of Argentina

Agriculture Year	2005–2006	2006–2007	2007–2008	2008–2009	2009–2010
Food crops (10,000 tons)	3,164.7	4,172.8	4,459.5	2,665.6	3,787.9
Wheat	1,259.3	1,454.8	1,634.8	837.3	875.1
Corn	1,444.6	2,175.5	2,201.7	1,312.1	2,267.7
Oil crops (10,000 tons)	4,471.6	5,167.3	5,155.7	3,418.9	5,560.4
Soybean	4,053.7	4,748.3	4,623.8	3,099.3	5,267.7
Number of cattle slaughter (10,000)	1,341.5	1,495.6	1,466.0	1,605.3	1,188.3
Number of sheep slaughter (10,000)	447.4	445.1	414.0	405.0	406.0
Number of pig slaughter (10,000)	305.8	320.0	312.2	334.0	323.4
Number of poultry slaughter (10,000)	450,000	487,000	539,000	573,000	616,000
Milk production (100 million liters)	101.6	95.3	100.1	100.6	103.8
Fishing capacity (10,000 tons)	106.8	91.6	93.4	77.6	75.3

Source: Official website of Argentine National Bureau of Statistics and Survey, http://www.indec.mecon.ar.

existed the problem of insufficient diversity. The yields of wheat and corn accounted for almost 80–90%. Sorghum yields changed little compared with the 1990s, while the production of other crops was low and unstable. Since farming was heavily dependent on a few crops such as soybeans, wheat and corn, the changes of weather conditions had a very big impact on agriculture. In the agricultural year of 2008–2009, a drought rarely seen in the Argentine history caused a significant decline in crop acreage, resulting in a production decrease by one-third (see Table 2.15).

Compared with farming, the development of animal husbandry was relatively slow. Cattle and sheep herds had suffered different degrees of decline. In the 1990s, the number of cattle maintained was more than 50 million, but after reaching 53.16 million in 1994, a downward trend began and in 2005, the number was only 46.81 million. The number of sheep herds had reached 18.44 million in

1993, but in 2005 it was reduced to 12.47 million.[52] In terms of the production of beef, the output was rising steadily before 2009, but then the slaughter rate dropped due to the negative impact on the production enthusiasm of the cattle industry with the government's restrictions on exports. In the animal husbandry, only the poultry industry developed rapidly. Prior to 2001, Argentina imported poultry to meet domestic market demand, but by 2009, self-sufficiency in poultry had been achieved, and the exports reached 222,000 tons.[53]

The marginalized status of forestry and fishery in agriculture has not changed. In recent years, the amount of forest exploitation stabilized at around 10 million tons. The rich fishery resources and freshwater resources have not been well utilized. Seafood catches declined year by year, far lower than in Brazil and Mexico, and even less than in Chile and Peru.

All in all, in recent years, agriculture has achieved rapid development. This is mainly attributed to the expansion of farming, especially the production of soybeans. Soybeans are becoming more and more important to agriculture because they are the most competitive products. The position of agriculture in the national economy rebounded significantly — accounting for almost 10% of GDP in 2011. However, the uneven development inside agriculture had intensified, resulting in more prominent reliance on agricultural planting and soybean farming. This structural defect caused agricultural production vulnerable to changes of climatic conditions and fluctuations of market prices, and therefore the uncertainty increased. After 2003, the agricultural growth turned unstable (see Table 2.16), which had much to do with the structural characteristics of a single crop.

2. Manufacturing

After 2003, the development of the manufacturing sector could be divided into two stages. The first stage was between 2003 and 2004 when the growth rate reached a double-digit level, belonging to the

---

[52]http://www.indec.mecon.ar.

[53]INTA, *Evolucion del systema Productivo Agropecuario*, junio del 2011, p. 7.

Table 2.16 Growth Rates of All the Economic Sectors of Argentina (2003–2011) (%)

Year	2003	2004	2005	2006	2007	2008	2009	2010	2011
Agriculture	6.9	−1.5	11.1	2.6	9.8	−2.5	−15.7	28.0	−2.2
Mining	3.7	−0.4	−0.2	3.0	−0.5	1.1	−1.1	−1.5	−3.5
Manufacturing	16.0	12.0	7.5	8.9	7.6	4.5	−0.5	9.8	11.0
Water, electricity, and gas	6.9	6.5	5.0	5.0	5.7	3.4	0.9	6.2	4.6
Construction industry	34.4	29.4	20.4	17.9	9.9	3.7	−3.8	5.2	9.1
Commerce and restaurants	11.7	12.4	9.5	7.9	10.7	7.9	−0.1	12.1	13.6
Transportation, storage, and communications	8.2	13.4	14.8	13.5	13.7	12.1	6.5	10.6	9.3
Finance, insurance, real estate, and business services	−1.1	2.2	7.1	8.2	8.1	9.3	3.1	5.5	9.8
Community, social, and personal services	2.8	4.4	5.6	5.4	5.0	4.9	4.3	4.1	4.2

Source: CEPAL, "Argentina", *Informe Macroeconomico*, julio 2012.

resumption of growth after the crisis. The second stage was after 2005. Except in 2009, which was affected by the international financial crisis, the rest of the years maintained steady growth. In the recovery phase, with the recovery of domestic demand, a large number of idle production capacities were re-used. Devaluation of the peso led to the decline of the cost of the enterprises, resulting in profit rise — enterprises had accumulated more liquidity to lay the foundation for later expanded reproduction. Starting from 2005, the production capacity of many companies reached its limit, resulting in the need for new investment. Initially the limited scale of investment was mainly used to increase the employees, buy new machinery, and expand the plants, but with the full recovery of the economy and the strong growth of market demand, the scale of business investment increased, turning to new projects. The manufacturing sector entered the stage of stable development.

Next, we will analyze the changes in the manufacturing structures from the four aspects of the contribution of the manufacturing sectors to manufacturing growth, the composition of the manufacturing sectors, the manufacturing employment and the manufacturing export. Subject to data limitations, here the period between 2003 and 2008 will be studied mainly.

Table 2.17 Contribution of Various Sectors to the Added Value of Manufacturing (%)

Year	1993–1998	2002–2007
Food, beverage and tobacco	31.6	19.0
Cars	9.7	9.9
Technology-intensive industries	0.5	21.4
Natural resource intensive industries	17.6	10.7
Labor intensive industries	19.4	24.8
Basic metal processing and chemical engineering	21.2	14.2

Note: The technology-intensive industries refer to metal products, mechanical equipment, electrical appliances, audio–visual equipment, telecommunications equipment, medical equipment, precision instruments, and transport equipment; natural resource-intensive industries refer to wood processing, paper, oil refining, rubber, and non-metallic mineral processing; labor-intensive industries refer to textiles, clothing, leather, shoes, publishing and printing, and plastics.
Source: German Herrera, Andres Tavosnanska, "La Industria Argentina a Comienzos del Siglo XXI", *Revista CEPAL*, No. 104, agosto de 2011, p. 107.

(1) The Contribution of Various Sectors to the Manufacturing Growth

Two significant changes can be seen from Table 2.17. One is the increase of the contribution of technology-intensive industries and labor-intensive industries to the manufacturing sector, almost accounting for nearly half of all manufacturing value-added growth. The other is the decline of the contribution of the food sector and natural resource-intensive industries. This suggests that the manufacturing growth momentum has changed. In the 1990s the fastest growing sectors were the production departments of basic industrial products, such as steel, fuel, and food. Most of these industries were capital and resource intensive, and large and medium-sized, with a high degree of business concentration. The labor-intensive industries are the sectors most affected by the open policy of the 1990s, with a large number and distribution. The recovery of them on the one hand indicates the increase of the contribution of SMEs to the manufacturing sector, and on the other hand helps to increase industrial employment.

Table 2.18 Composition of the Sectors of the Added Value of Manufacturing Industries in Argentina (1993–2007) (%)

Year	Food, Beverage and Tobacco	Auto Mobiles	Technology-intensive Industries	Natural Resource Intensive Industries	Labor Intensive Industries	Basic Metal Processing and Chemical Engineering
1993	22.7	6.5	16.3	15.4	25.1	13.9
1998	24.0	7.0	14.0	15.7	24.3	15.0
1999	26.8	5.3	12.4	16.2	23.7	15.6
2000	26.6	5.7	12.3	15.8	23.2	16.4
2001	28.0	4.5	11.6	16.5	21.8	17.6
2002	30.5	4.7	9.9	17.3	19.1	18.6
2003	28.0	4.3	11.5	16.9	21.2	18.0
2004	26.4	5.0	13.0	16.9	21.4	17.4
2005	26.4	5.6	13.6	15.9	21.6	16.9
2006	25.9	6.3	14.2	15.2	2.0	17.4
2007	25.7	6.8	14.7	14.5	21.5	16.8

Source: German Herrera y Andres Tavosnanska, "La Industria Argentina a Comienzos del Si/lo XXI", *Revista CEPAL*, No. 104, agosto de 2011, p. 107.

(2) The Changes in the Composition of the Manufacturing Sectors

In the 1990s, the trend of "primary products" of the Argentine manufacturing sectors was obvious. The fastest growing sectors during this period were associated with primary product processing industries, including food processing, natural resource-intensive industries, basic metal processing and chemical industry. In 1993, these industries accounted for 52% of the added value of manufacturing, and in 2002, this proportion increased to 66%. During the same period, the proportion of automobile manufacturing, technology-intensive industries and labor-intensive industries in the manufacturing structure dropped from 48% to 33% (see Table 2.18). After 10 years of adjustment, in 2007, the share of primary products in the manufacturing industry dropped to 57%. It is worth noticing that during the five years the technology-intensive industries, including machinery equipment manufacturing, achieved the fastest recovery, with an increase of almost 5%, while this type of industries was the most seriously impacted in the economic reforms of the 1990s.

Table 2.19 Growth Rate of Manufacturing Sectors and Growth Rate of Employment in the Manufacturing Sectors of Argentina (%)

Year	1975–1982	1983–1988	1989–1990	1991–2001	2002	2003–2008
Annual average growth rate of manufacturing industry	−2.1	1.2	−9.6	0.9	−9.7	11.2
Annual average growth rate of employment in manufacturing	−6.8	−0.9	−12.9	−4.2	−9.1	5.8

Source: German Herrera y Andres Tavosnanska, "La Industria Argentina a Comienzos del Siglo XXI", *Revista CEPAL*, No. 104, agosto de 2011, p. 109.

(3) The Employment in Manufacturing

During the over 20 years after 1975, the employment in manufacturing had been in a declining state. Even in the years when the manufacturing production was increasing, the employment also declined. This feature was the most evident in the 1990s (see Table 2.19). Since 2003, the employment in manufacturing began a resumption of growth after experiencing successive years of decline, driven in large part by the expansion of labor-intensive industries and technology-intensive industries.

Table 2.20 shows the distribution of the newly increased employment in manufacturing in different sectors. From 2002 to 2007, a total increase of more than 410,000 manufacturing jobs accomplished the growth rate of 54.2%. Employment in all sectors had increased, but the growth rate ranged from 15.6% to 20.5%. There were two industries contributing the most to new jobs. First, it was the labor-intensive industry, including textiles, clothing, furniture manufacturing, and other such industries, which were mainly for the domestic-market orientation, with relatively a high level of protection. Second, it was the technology-intensive industry, including metal, all kinds of equipment manufacturing and automobile manufacturing, whose employment growth exceeded the average. This suggests that the changing trend of the distribution of new jobs in the manufacturing sector and that of the composition of the value added

Table 2.20 New Jobs in the Manufacturing Sectors of Argentina (2002–2007)

Manufacturing Sector	New Employment (person)	Employment Growth (%)	Proportion in Total Employment (%)	1996–2001 Proportion in Total Employment of Manufacturing (%)
Food and beverage	73,996	30.5	18.2	29.7
Tobacco	1,091	23.2	0.4	0.5
Textile	26,345	62.9	6.8	5.8
Clothing	25,782	99.7	6.3	3.9
Leather and footwear	11,574	39.1	3.0	3.9
Wood processing	13,697	68.7	3.6	2.6
Paper and paper products	9,230	38.5	2.4	2.9
Publishing and printing	12,589	33.8	2.6	4.6
Oil refining	1,472	15.6	0.4	0.9
Chemical products	28,144	40.9	6.7	8.3
Rubber and plastics	24,030	62.7	5.9	4.8
Non-metallic mineral processing	17,675	73.8	4.2	3.6
Common metal	13,400	48.4	3.3	3.7
Metal products	45,030	100.2	11.0	6.4
Mechanical equipment	30,177	85.2	7.6	4.9
Office equipment	1,644	200.5	0.4	0.1
Electric appliance	9,375	85.0	2.1	1.7
Audio–visual and communications equipment	4,059	93.8	0.7	0.9
Medical equipment and precision instruments	2,922	60.5	0.7	0.6
Automobile	36,977	95.7	8.2	6.1
Transportation equipment	5,325	100.9	1.3	0.8
Furniture and others	17,314	84.3	3.9	3.3
Total	411,848	54.2	100.0	100.0

Source: German Herrera y Andres Tavosnanska, "La Industria Argentina a Comienzos del Siglo XXI", *Revista CEPAL*, No. 104, agosto de 2011, p. 111.

manufacturing sectors was consistent. The fastest growing sector was also the sector that provided the most new jobs.

After 2008, with the rise in labor costs, the effect of the labor-intensive industries to create new employment was restrained. Together with the macroeconomic instability, the ability to create jobs in the manufacturing sector decreased sharply. From 2008 to 2011, only 53,000 new jobs were created in industry,[54] way fewer than in the services.

(4) The Manufacturing Trade

From 2003 to 2008, the manufacturing export grew by 130%. In the exports, the share of food, leather, footwear, refining and chemical industries declined, while the proportion of cars, machinery and equipment increased. However, if you compare the data with 10 years ago, you will find that the overall structure of commodities exported changed little (see Table 2.21), still dominated by natural resource processing products. The growth rate of imports far exceeded exports mainly because the imports dropped more obviously than the exports during the crisis in 2001. In the imports, the fastest growing were consumer durables, including automobiles, televisions, cell phones, air conditioners, as well as basic raw materials, such as steel, aluminum,

Table 2.21 Proportion of Some of the Manufactured Goods in the Exports of Manufactured Goods of Argentina (%)

Year	1998	2003	2007
Food and beverage	43.9	45.4	43.4
Oil	3.9	11.2	10.2
Chemical products	9.9	11.4	10.1
Common metals	5.9	7.4	7.4
Mechanical equipment	3.1	2.4	2.9
Automobile	17.4	7.7	13.6

Source: German Herrera y Andres Tavosnanska, "La Industria Argentina a Comienzos del Si/lo XXI", *Revista CEPAL*, No. 104, agosto de 2011, p. 113.

[54]http://www.indec.mecon.ar.

petroleum, and its by-products. In other words, the intermediate goods and capital goods remained the main imported goods.

The trade of processed agricultural and animal husbandry products remained in the surplus state, but the situation of manufactured industrial goods was just the opposite, and deficits had continued to expand. This also caused the deficit to have appeared in the entire trade of manufactured goods after 2005. Still three commodities caused the trade deficit: The first one was the capital goods such as electrical and mechanical equipment, the second was the intermediate products such as industrial parts, and the third was the final consumer goods such as textiles and metal products. The trade deficit of manufactured goods had a direct relationship with the imbalance of industrial structures, which was the legacy of the economic reforms in the 1990s. Because since 2003 Argentina maintained a surplus trade balance, the manufacturing trade imbalance was covered up (see Table 2.22).

As can be seen from the above analysis, the changes in Argentine manufacturing sector from 2003 to 2008 were mainly reflected in two aspects. First, the labor-intensive industries and technology-intensive industries rose up, resource-intensive industries were no longer the main driver of growth and the trend of "primary products" in manufacturing got a certain degree of containment. Second, the shift of the industrial growth model had a positive impact on employment, and the manufacturing sector once again became an important channel for the creation of employment. However, the imbalance of the internal structure of the manufacturing sector still existed. From the perspective of import and export trade of manufactured goods, the processing products of agriculture and animal husbandry played an important role in exports because they had a comparative advantage, while capital goods and intermediate products occupied an important position in imports. The process of the significant import substitution did not appear and some products relied on imports more severely than before (see Table 2.23).

Table 2.22 Proportion of Imports of Some of the Manufactured Goods in the Total Consumption and in the Total Imports of Manufactured Goods of Argentina (%)

	Proportion of Imports in the Total Consumption			Proportion of Import in the Total Imports of Manufactured Goods		
	1998	2003	2007	1998	2003	2007
Textile	13.5	17.2	21.1	2.6	3.0	2.1
Paper	22.1	15.3	19.1	3.4	3.4	2.2
Refined oil	3.0	2.3	14.4	1.1	1.4	4.4
Chemical products	25.6	29.3	36.9	16.8	30.4	20.1
Common metals	19.8	13.3	20.4	4.1	4.6	5.5
Metal products	19.3	14.4	19.2	3.4	2.5	2.5
Mechanical equipment	45.8	38.8	46.8	14.9	13.6	13.9
Office equipment	93.8	92.9	97.4	4.2	3.9	3.3
Electric appliances	49.5	48.5	54.6	6.2	4.0	4.8
Audio–visual equipment and communication equipment	58.3	80.2	90.3	6.8	3.8	7.8
Medical equipment, optical instruments and precision instruments	64.8	71.8	77.6	2.6	2.7	2.4
Automobile	40.7	38.2	49.8	17.8	12.5	17.4
Transportation equipment	46.0	81.0	90.3	2.3	1.4	3.3

Source: German Herrera y Andres Tavosnanska, "La Industria Argentina a Comienzos del Si/lo XXI", *Revista CEPA, No. 104*, agosto de 2011, p. 118.

3. Change of Industrial Policy

During the last 10 years of the policy adjustment, Argentina had put great emphasis on the importance of the production sector, establishing a new mode of economic growth driven by the production growth. To be objective, this development strategy had played a role in optimizing the industrial structure, so that the position of the production sector in the national economy had been raised (see Table 2.14).

Table 2.23 Trade Balance of Manufactured Goods of Argentina ($100 Million)

Year	1993	1998	2002	2003	2004	2005	2006	2007	2008
Export of agricultural and animal husbandry products	49.30	87.61	81.38	99.38	119.26	131.41	152.44	191.87	238.03
Import of agricultural and animal husbandry products	84.0	13.89	3.95	5.39	6.48	7.15	8.12	10.65	12.96
Trade balance of agricultural and animal husbandry products	40.89	73.72	77.43	93.99	112.79	124.26	144.32	181.22	225.07
Export of manufactured goods	36.78	86.24	76.01	76.75	96.16	119.85	148.26	173.21	219.70
Import of manufactured goods	150.24	282.40	76.83	121.03	199.79	253.92	303.95	389.90	486.54
Trade balance of manufactured goods	−113.46	−196.16	−0.82	−44.29	−103.63	−134.07	−155.69	−216.69	−266.84

Source: German Herrera y Andres Tavosnanska, "La Industria Argentina a Comienzos del Siglo XXI", *Revista CEPAL, No. 104*, agosto de 2011, p. 119.

However, in this process, the Argentine government had not proposed a complete industrial plan in order to adjust the irrational industrial structures.

In 2011, the Argentine government had promulgated two important industrial development plans — the 2020 *Industrial Strategic Plan* and the "*2010–2020 Agricultural Strategic Plan*", putting forward the industrial and agricultural development objectives of Argentina for the next 10 years, showing the determination of Argentina to become one of the industrial and agricultural powers of the world. Below, we will make a brief analysis of the direction of industrial policy in the two plans and the recent adjustment of energy policy by the Argentine government.

(1) The 2010–2020 Agricultural Strategic Plan

Over the years, agriculture has been the traditional advantageous industry sector in Argentina. In recent years, driven by the soybean industry, agriculture has made great progress. However, the lack of product diversity, the short industrial chain, and the low value-added problem are fundamentally not conducive to the long-term sustainable development of agriculture. The *2010–2020 Agricultural Strategic Plan* was made for this reason. The plan proposed that the development goal of Argentine agriculture over the next 10 years is to transform the agricultural development mode from "the production of low value-added primary products and the primary product-oriented export" into "increasing the added value of products through industrialization of primary products". In the process of the mode-transformation, it is necessary to create more jobs in agriculture to achieve social inclusion, taking into account environmental sustainability and geographical balance. This means that Argentina will be changed from a "big cereal producing country" to " the world's largest producer of high-quality agricultural products."

To achieve the above goal, the government of Argentina presented the industrial chain of eleven key supported agricultural products, including beef, poultry, eggs, pork, dairy products, wheat, corn (dry and wet), beans, soybeans, and agricultural machinery. The development strategy was to extend the industrial chain and improve

Table 2.24 Added Values of Some of the Export of Agricultural Products and the Added Value of Employment of Argentina (2010–2020)

	Increase in Exports ($100 Million)	Added Direct Jobs
Poultry meat		29,000
Eggs	84	21,000
Pork	1.5	22,800
Beef	19.1	40,000
Dairy products	23.2	38,600
Wheat and its processed products	24.0	70,800
Wet corn		2,375
Dry corn	19	930
Beans	8.7	21,900
Soybean and its processed products	31.0	44,500
Agricultural machinery	6.8	27,500
Total	124.6	319,405

Source: INTA, *Evolucion del Sistema Productivo Agropecuario Argentino*, junio de 2011, p. 24.

the industrial linkage, forming a complete industrial chain of going from the production, processing, storage and transportation to the final sales of products. Crop production not only needs transverse combination, forming its own industrial chain, but also should finance animal husbandry, forming the vertical industry chain, changing vegetable protein into animal protein, to adapt to the reality of rising meat demand in the international market. The above chain of eleven industries would have the potential to create 319,000 direct jobs and increase exports of $12.46 billion (see Table 2.24).

The plan also has the targets for production and exports. By 2020, Argentina plans to increase crop acreage by 27%, from the current 34 million hectares to 42 million hectares, aiming at the increase of 60% of crop production, from the current total output of about 100 million tons to 160 million tons, in which the production of corn, wheat and soybean will increase to 50 million tons, 23 million tons and 71 million tons; the beef production will increase by 46%, with export reaching $7 billion; the poultry production will increase by 88%, to 3 million tons, and the pork production will increase 2-fold, reaching 800,000 tons. The agricultural product exports will double to $100 billion.

In terms of the goals in the *2010–2020 Agricultural Strategic Plan*, in the next 10 years, the Argentine agricultural development will follow two principles: The first one is to develop comparative advantages and the second is to upgrade the industrial structure. In other words, Argentina needs to continue to make use of its upstream edge of the development foundation of high-quality agricultural products and try to promote the industrialization process of the traditional strengths of the "primary agricultural products", putting their advantages of agricultural production into the food industry. Through the realization of the diversification of the final products, agriculture will stay away from dependence on a few agricultural products. It should be acknowledged that the direction of the adjustment of agricultural structure in the plan is in line with the development needs of Argentina. In September 2009, the Argentine government provided the institutional guarantee for the implementation of the *2010–2020 Agricultural Strategic Plan* by upgrading the Secretariat of Agriculture, Animal Husbandry, Fisheries and Alimentation to the ministerial level. However, at present there are still some factors that might restrict the implementation of the planning, such as seeds, pesticides and land, which are controlled by foreign companies, and large-scale agro-processing commonwealths are mostly foreign-funded enterprises. Therefore, it will be necessary to take more specific and detailed policy measures.

(2) The Adjustment of Energy Shortages and Energy Policy

In the early 1990s, Argentina achieved energy self-sufficiency, having few surplus available for export. In recent years, the rapid economic growth and low domestic energy prices led to the increase of the demand of production and living for energy. However, limited by the investment, the natural gas and oil production fell down instead of increasing, resulting in several energy crises due to shortage of market supplies. After 2003, gas production had maintained a steady growth, but after 2007, gas production experienced successive years of decline, resulting in serious supply shortages.

Although the government expanded its imports of natural gas and stopped exporting, still domestic demand could not be met. In 2011, Argentina imported 3.6 billion cubic meters of pipeline natural gas from Bolivia, and imported 4.4 billion cubic meters of liquefied natural gas from other countries,[55] becoming a net importer of energy again. Since 1998, the oil production had been in decline, but sales in the domestic market had been in the state of growing. By 2011, the oil production and sales had become basically flat. Due to lack of fuel, the electricity supply also had a serious gap. Every year during the winter peak hours of electricity and gas supply, the government had to cut the supply to industrial enterprises, greatly affecting the industrial production.

Apart from the problem of insufficient energy production, the unreasonable structure of energy consumption of Argentina also made it difficult to alleviate the contradiction of energy supply and demand. Non-renewable energy sources such as oil, gas and coal accounted for 85% of the total fuel consumption, while renewable energy sources such as hydropower account for only 11–12%. In contrast, the energy consumption structures of Brazil and Colombia had the features of diverse nature — hydropower and other renewable energy sources accounted for one-third of their total energy consumption (see Table 2.25).

Facing the increasingly serious problem of energy supply and demand, the Argentine government realized the necessity to adjust the policy of energy industry. In terms of the recent policy direction, the government tried to change the relation between energy supply and demand, mainly from three aspects.

First of all, it was to strengthen the control of oil, gas, and power resources. In the 1990s, Argentina's oil and gas companies experienced a large-scale privatization — the largest oil company YPF had also been sold to Spain's oil company Repsol. After 2002, the Argentine government strengthened its intervention in the oil and gas industry through measures such as the implementation of

[55]BP, *BP World Energy Statistics Yearbook*, June 2012, p. 28.

Table 2.25 Production and Consumption of Oil and Natural Gas of Argentina (2001–2011)

Year	2001	2002	2003	2004	2005	2006	2007	2008	2009	2010	2011
Oil production (1,000 barrels per day)	830	818	806	754	725	716	699	682	676	652	607
Oil consumption (1,000 barrels per day)	425	394	405	425	449	471	523	534	518	550	609
Oil refinery capacity (1,000 barrels per day)	619	619	620	623	627	623	634	634	636	640	649
Natural gas production (100 million cubic meters)	371	361	410	449	456	461	448	441	414	401	388
Natural gas consumption (100 million cubic meters)	311	303	346	379	404	418	439	444	432	433	465

Source: BP, *BP World Energy Statistics Yearbook*, June 2012, pp. 8–23.

Table 2.26 Installed Electric Power Capacity and Power Consumption of Argentina

Year	2006	2007	2008	2009	2010	2011
Hydro (MW)	9,920	9,945	9,991	10,024	10,024	10,025
Wind (MW)	28	28	28	28	28	60
Nuclear (MW)	1,018	1,018	1,018	1,018	1,018	1,018
Thermoelectric (MW)	7,684	7,762	9,170	10,002	8,972	9,257
Hybrid generation (MW)	7,027	7,027	7,147	7,257	8,968	9,508
Total installed capacity (MW)	25,678	25,781	27,354	28,330	29,009	29,868
Electricity consumption (MW/h)	86,556,866	90,507,603	93,013,607	91,901,372	96,554,996	102,107,455

Source: Official website of Argentina National Bureau of Statistics and Survey, http://www.indec.mecon.ar.

controls on oil and gas prices, forcing the companies to invest, creating new state-owned oil companies, and providing subsidies. In 2012, the nationalization of YPF meant major adjustments of the Argentine energy industry policy. First, through the strategy of implementation of oil nationalization, the Argentine government had gained the control of energy, becoming not only the energy policy maker, but also the direct producer of energy, which would help alleviate the energy shortage in Argentina and achieve energy self-sufficiency. Second, because the top priority of future oil production was to meet domestic market demand, the profits of foreign oil companies would have to be used more for reinvestment and expansion of production — their production and operational autonomy would be limited. However, although the Government had regained control of the country's largest oil company, a lot of financial and technical support would be required for the future full development of oil and gas resources, so the participation of foreign capital was still essential (see Table 2.26).

In addition to the oil sector, the government also strengthened its intervention in the power sector. After the economic crisis of 2001, the government froze the electricity price, providing financial subsidies to power enterprises. However, due to lack of investment, the power supply could not satisfy the demand. In recent years, with the rising costs, many transmission companies fell into deficit. In August 2012, the government announced the establishment of a special committee to analyze the cost, productivity and investment plans of electricity enterprises, and on the basis of the analysis determine the prices, income levels of employees and profit rate of the enterprises. This means that the government would play a greater role in corporate decision making.

Secondly, it was to promote the construction of nuclear power. In the 1950s, Argentina started to develop nuclear technology, but for various reasons the first nuclear power plant was not established until 1974. At present, there are two nuclear power plants in Argentina, with a total installed capacity of 1018 MW. In 2011, Argentina announced that it would invest $1.3 billion for the renovation of the second nuclear power plant, expecting an extended deadline to run for another 30 years, with an increase of installed capacity by 35 MW. Meanwhile,

Table 2.27 Production and Export of Biomass Fuels of Argentina

	2008	2009	2010	2011	2012	2013
Biodiesel production (10,000 tons)	71.2	117.9	181.5	242.7	245.5	199.7
Biodiesel exports (10,000 tons)	68.8	114.8	135.8	168.2	155.7	114.1
Ethanol production (ton)	—	18,439	96,034	134,137	199,454	374,167

Source: Official website of Argentina National Bureau of Statistics and Survey, http://www.indec.mecon.ar.

the government also decided to build two new reactors and expand uranium production to increase its nuclear generating capacity.

Thirdly, it was to promote the positive development of bio-energy. Argentine biofuels are mainly biodiesel, ethanol, biogas, and bio-gasoline. Biodiesel initially mainly supplied the international market. Sales in the domestic market has increased since 2010, now accounting for a third of the total output, while ethanol production is mainly for the domestic market. Both fuels are extracted from plants, belonging to new types of renewable energy. Soybeans and corn are Argentine traditional prestigious products that can be used to extract biofuels, which provide the necessary conditions for the promotion of biofuels. The Argentine government has developed bio-energy as an important strategy to encourage the construction of bio-fuel plants, and decreed that from 2010 onwards all the gasoline and diesels are to be blended with 5% of the renewable fuels. In the active guidance of the government, in recent years the pace of the development of bio-energy in Argentina is very fast (see Table 2.27). The proportion of bioenergy in Argentine energy consumption structure is still very low, but if the government can remain a stable policy, the future of the development of bio-energy will be very promising.

(3) The 2020 Industrial Strategic Plan

In February 2011, the Fernandez government announced the 2020 *Industrial Strategic Plan*, putting forward the Argentine economic growth target and industrial development goals in the next 10 years.

According to the plan, in the next 10 years, the average annual GDP growth rate is to be maintained 5%, the GDP value will increase to $580.709 billion by 2020, the per capita GDP will be raised from the current $8,700 to $12,900, the investment rate will increase to 28%, 1.5 million jobs will be added, and the unemployment rate will gradually decline to 5%. In foreign trade, the import and export volume will reach $139 billion and $167 billion respectively, with trade surplus of $28 billion. The gross industrial production will have an average growth rate of 7%, reaching $140 billion in 2020. In the next 10 years, the Argentine government will focus on supporting eleven industries — food (including poultry, dairy products, and pork), leather and footwear, textiles and clothing, wood processing, automobile and parts, agricultural machinery, capital goods, building materials, petrochemicals, pharmaceuticals, software and information services. They will account for 80% of the total value of manufacturing and 60% of the employment in manufacturing production.

The above eleven key industries cover the labor-intensive industries (footwear, textiles and clothing), the resource-intensive industries (food, building materials, petrochemicals, timber processing) and the technology-intensive industries (automobiles and parts, agricultural machinery, capital goods, software and information services, drugs), reflecting the strategic intent of the Argentine government to revitalize the industry, reconstruct the complete industrial system, and promote the balanced development of intra-industry. The future direction of industrial restructuring has the following characteristics. First, it is to continue to support industries with comparative advantages, making it a major source of trade surplus, such as the food industry. Second, it is to strengthen the import substitution, increase local production of industrial products in order to strengthen the protection of the weak recovering sectors in recent years that had experienced the most serious damage in the 1990s, such as footwear, textiles and clothing, capital goods, agricultural machinery, and petrochemicals. Third, it is to promote the development of high-tech industries, improve product quality, and increase technology and knowledge content of the products, such as the various technology-intensive industries.

Table 2.28 Growth Targets of the Argentine Key Manufacturing Sectors in 2020

	Output or Output Value	New Jobs	Export	Import	Trade (Surplus)
Poultry meat	3 million tons	50,000	$2.475 billion	$57 million	$2.418 billion
Dairy products	18.2 billion liters	11,660	$3.248 billion	$127 million	$3.121 billion
Pork	822,000 tons	18,400	$0.451 billion	$21 million	$430 million
Shoes	200 million pairs of shoes (80 million of them of high grade)	12,000	50 million pairs	36 million pairs	14 million pairs
Textiles and garments	$9.29 billion	25,000	$2.395 billion	$2.321 billion	$74 million
Cars and accessories	1.9 million (domestic accessories accounted for 60%)	230,000	$41.5 billion	$32.26 billion	$8.24 billion
Agricultural machinery	$2.5 billion	20,000	$0.87 billion	$415 million	$455 million
Capital goods	$18.2 billion	44,000	$6.37 billion	$6 billion	$370 million
Building materials	20.1 million tons of cement, 0.79 million tons of aluminum, 9.3 million tons of raw steel	44,000	—	—	—
Petrochemical industry	14 million tons	75,100	$7.5 billion	$7.3 billion	$200 million
Software and information services	$7.33 billion	74,000	$2.96 billion	—	—
Drugs	1.35 billion pills	30,000	$3.985 billion	$2.447 billion	$1.538 billion
Wood processing	$27.273 billion	63,000	$2.821 billion	$2.279 billion	$542 million

Source: "Plan Estrategico Industrial 2020, Un Buen Punto de Partida", *Informe Industrial*, edicion 231.

From the perspective of the Argentine manufacturing industry trend since 2003, there is a certain degree of difficulty to achieve the above goals. Firstly, most of the eleven key industries rely heavily on imports, in a serious state of foreign trade deficit; therefore, it is relatively difficult to reverse this situation in 10 years. Secondly, in terms of job creation, a total of 410,000 new jobs had been created in the manufacturing industry from 2003 to 2007, but the ability to create jobs in the next few years declined. Thus, the target to create 1.5 million jobs in the next 10 years will face serious challenges. Finally, the development of high-tech industries need to invest more in R&D funding and to train more talents, but Argentina has done far from enough in this regard. In 2011 the ratio of the expenditure of research activities to GDP is only 0.73%,[56] more than 70% of the funding for research activities and R&D funding came from the government, and the funding from enterprises accounted for only less than 25%. The main means of business improvement technique was to purchase new machinery and equipment, but the investment in independent research and development in order to improve the technological innovation capability was very limited (see Table 2.28).

Section 3 Foreign Trade and Economic Relations

In the 1990s, trade liberalization was an important part of the economic reform. Under the influence of the open-policy guidance and a fixed exchange rate system, the Argentine imports grew faster than exports; the trade balance in most years was imbalanced. After 2003, Argentina's foreign trade re-entered the high growth period — the foreign trade had become one of the main engines of economic growth; its status in the national economy had improved significantly.

In terms of foreign investment, Argentina has undergone great changes. In the period of import substitution industrialization, with

[56]Country statistics of Iberian American and Pan American Science and Technology Network (RICYT), http://db.ricyt.org/query/AR/1990, 2011/calculados.

the rise of large-scale nationalization movement, the position of foreign capital was greatly weakened. In the 1990s, the economic liberalization and privatization led to the influx of foreign capital and Argentina once again became the focus of foreign investment. The capital of Spain and the US dominated in foreign capital. In recent years, a wide range of trends in the source and flow of direct foreign investment appeared.

In this section we will analyze the main features of Argentina's foreign trade in recent years, changes in trade policy and the case of the use of foreign capital so as to have the knowledge and understanding of the development of foreign trade and economic relations of Argentina.

I. Foreign Trade Development

1. The Change of the Total Amount of Foreign Trade and the Situation of Trade Balance

In the 1990s, Argentina's foreign trade growth rate was relatively fast. Between 1990 and 1999, the exports rose from $12.35 billion to $23.31 billion, an increase of 88.7%; the imports went up from $4.08 billion to $25.51 billion, an increase of 525.2%.[57] The import growth rate was significantly higher than the export — there were trade 6 years of trade deficit out of 10 years. From 2003 to 2011, the import and export volume increased by 4.37 times and 1.81 times, respectively. The total foreign trade topped $100 billion in 2007, and in 2011 close to $160 billion. Due to severe contraction of imports during the 2001 economic crisis, dropping to the level of the early 1990s, while exports barely affected by the crisis, with export prices rising more than imported products, although the increase of exports was less than the imports, the trade balance also remained a surplus. With the expansion of the total import and export, the position of foreign trade in the national economy increased significantly. The proportion of imports in GDP rose from 13% in 1997 to 20% in 2011, and in the same period the proportion of exports in GDP rose

[57]INDEC, *Comercio Exterior Aegentino 2011*, Buenos Aires, 2012.

Table 2.29 Total Imports and Exports and Trade Balance of Argentina

Year	Exports ($100 Million)	Export Increase (%)	Imports ($100 Million)	Import Increase (%)	Trade Balance ($100 Million)
1990	123.5	—	40.8	—	82.8
1995	209.6	—	201.2	—	8.4
2000	263.4	—	252.8	—	10.6
2002	256.5	—	89.9	—	166.6
2003	299.4	16.7	138.5	54.1	160.9
2004	245.8	17.9	224.5	62.1	21.3
2005	403.9	64.3	286.9	27.8	117.0
2006	465.4	15.2	341.5	19.0	123.9
2007	559.8	20.3	447.1	30.9	112.7
2008	700.2	25.1	574.6	28.5	125.6
2009	556.7	−20.5	387.9	−32.5	168.9
2010	681.9	22.5	567.9	46.4	113.9
2011	840.5	23.3	743.2	30.9	97.3

Source: INDEC, *Comercio Exterior Argentino 2012*, Buenos Aires, 2013. The increased results were calculated by the author.

from 11% to 22%.[58] Due to the growth of foreign trade in recent years faster than the growth of the world trade, Argentina's share of the total world trade has increased. The proportion of exports in the total world exports rose from 0.39% in 2003 to 0.46% in 2011, and in the same period, the proportion of imports in the total world imports increased from 0.18% to 0.40% (see Table 2.29).

There are three main causes for the increase in exports since 2003: first, the price competitiveness of export products had increased due to the change of the exchange rate regime; second, the international demand rose, and third, the prices of the major international export products of Argentina kept rising. From 2005 to 2011, in the export products of Latin-American countries, the price of agricultural products rose 85.2%, the food price rose 84%, the oil price rose 138.4%, and the soybean price rose 96.8%.[59] The Argentine exports had benefited greatly. The main reason for the import growth is mainly due

[58]World Bank official website, http://datos.bancomundial.org/indicator.
[59]CEPAL, *Anuario Estadistico de America Latina y el Caribe 2012*.

to the strong demand for raw materials resulting from the economic recovery and expansion of production in the domestic market and the need to import large quantities of capital goods to update the production equipment.

2. The Change of the Geographic Distribution of Foreign Trade

In the 1990s, the geographic distribution of Argentine exports was very concentrated, with the main export destinations in the South Common Market (Mercosur) countries, the EU and the US. In 1997, Mercosur occupied 36% of the total exports of Argentina,[60] the EU 15%, and the United States 8%. The share of these three regions and countries in Argentine exports totaled 59%. After 2003, the Argentine export market was more diversified, with a more balanced geographical distribution. In 2011, the proportion of the exports of Argentina to the Mercosur countries dropped to 25%, to the United States dropped to 5%, but to the EU increased to 17%. In the original non-traditional export markets, the status of China and Southeast Asian countries increased significantly.

In the sphere of import, Argentina's main trading partners remained to be Mercosur, the EU and the United States. In 1997, of total imports, the Argentine imports from the above three regions and countries accounted for 25%, 27%, and 20%, respectively. Geographical distribution of imports was more concentrated than exports. After 2003, the sources of imports also showed a variety of features, but the status of Mercosur in Argentine imports had improved. In 2011, the share of the United States and the EU in imports decreased by 10% and 16% in Argentina; Mercosur increased to 31%. Argentina had a substantial increase of imports from China, making China the third-largest source of imports next to Mercosur and the EU.

It is worth noticing that, in addition to the South American countries, the EU countries of free trade agreements, North America,

[60]The data of this part were obtained by the author according to the data of country statistics of the official website of the Argentina National Bureau of Statistics and Investigation.

Southeast Asian countries, Japan, and the Middle East countries, other regions of the world with Argentina's foreign trade has also had a rapid development. These areas include Africa, Oceania, the Caribbean, and South Asian countries. As a whole, they are on the rise in the proportion of total imports and exports in Argentina — in 2011, 16% and 18%, respectively.

There was an occurrence of reversal in the Argentine trade balance with the European Union and Brazil. In the latter half of the 1990s, Argentina maintained a trade surplus with and Brazil, but a deficit with the EU. After 2003, the trade between Argentina and Brazil went into a deficit and the trade with EU into a surplus. In the trade with the United States, Argentina was still in a deficit position, but with other developing countries in trade, Argentina was still in a surplus position.

3. The Change of Import and Export Commodity Structure

Since 2003, the changes of the Argentine export structure had occurred mainly in the following aspects. First, the export of primary products showed an upward trend, which was mainly due to the expanded demand for primary products in the international market in recent years, resulting in the commodity prices continuing to rise. Second, the proportion of manufactured exports in the total exports improved significantly, mainly due to export growth of food, metal products, motor vehicles and other products. Third, the share of energy exports declined significantly, which was related to the Argentine energy shortage in recent years. Although the share of manufactured exports increased, there was little structural change in export commodities (see Section 2), still with the low-tech resource processing products. From 2002 to 2010, in the exports of manufactured goods, on average, only 13.6% of the products were the mid-high-tech products, and high-tech products accounted for only 3.3%.[61]

---

[61] Andres Wainer y Martin Schorr, "Insercion de la Industria Argentina en el Mercado Mundial. Reflexiones sobre la Postconvertibilidad", *Apuntes para el cambio*, Ano2, No. 2., Buenos Aires, marzo/abril de 2012, p. 2.

Compared with the 1990s, changes in the structure of Argentine imports mainly are reflected in three aspects. Firstly, the share of fuels increased significantly, which was caused by the stagnation of the Argentine energy production capacity and strong demand. Secondly, the proportion of the imports of consumer goods decreased significantly, which had a direct relationship with the restrictive import measures that the government had introduced in recent years. Finally, the proportion of capital goods first increased and then decreased, which was a trend consistent with the changes in the fixed investment in equipment needed for the domestic production activities. The changes in the proportion of intermediate products and components in imports remained steady, still accounting for about 50%.

Through the brief analysis of the structure of Argentina's import and export commodities, we can see little change in the degree of specialization in the international division of labor of Argentina, which is still in the low-end position of the global value chain. Its foreign trade has obvious characteristics of inter-industry trade. Its export is still characteristic of low value-added processing of primary products and resource-based products. There is no trend of diversification and structural change. Its imports are still based on capital goods and intermediate goods. Except for consumer goods, the import substitution effect is not obvious. The technological content of export products is significantly lower than that of imported products; the level of competitiveness of the manufactured goods is still not high. Although the import and export structure is subjected to the combined effect of many factors, such as the industrial structure, international competitiveness of products, changes of domestic demand and fluctuation of international market, the adjustment of the domestic industrial layout and improvement of the innovation ability are the key factors in the optimization and upgrading of the trade structures. Argentina has done far from enough in these areas; therefore, although the "quantitative change" occurred in foreign trade, the "qualitative change" might still require a lengthy process (see Table 2.30).

Table 2.30 Export Commodity Structure of Argentina ($100 Million, %)

	Primary Products		Agricultural Products		Industrial Products		Fuel and Energy	
	Value of Export	Proportion	Value of Export	Proportion	Value of Export	Proportion	Value of Export	Proportion
1993	32.7	24.9	49.3	37.6	36.8	28	12.4	9.4
1997	57.1	21.6	91.0	34.4	83.4	31.5	32.9	12.4
2003	64.6	21.9	99.9	33.8	77.0	26	54.1	18.3
2007	124.9	22.3	192.1	34.3	173.3	31	69.5	12.4
2011	196.3	24	275.5	33.6	284.1	34.7	63.7	7.8

Source: Official website of Argentina National Bureau of Statistics and Survey, http: //www.indec.mecon.ar.

4. The Change of Trade Policy

In the 1990s, trade liberalization was an important part of the economic reform, and the main goal of trade policy was to collaborate with the strategy of the full opening of the economy and to meet the needs of the export-oriented economic development. Through measures such as lowering tariffs and reducing non-tariff barriers, the government promoted the opening of domestic market to the outside world. During this period, Argentina, Brazil, Uruguay, and Paraguay together formed the Mercosur in order to expand the intra-regional trade and deepen the process of regional integration.

After 2003, with the rapid development of foreign trade, the trade policy objectives had also changed. First of all, the foreign trade had to serve the macroeconomy. The government tried three ways to achieve this goal. One was to maintain a trade surplus, using accumulation of export revenues and substantial foreign exchange reserves in order to enhance the national capacity to withstand external shocks and the ability to repay debt. Another was to impose export taxes in order to expand the revenue for the implementation of the economic stimulus plan. The third was to change the relation between supply and demand by limiting the export of necessities in order to achieve the purpose of curbing inflation. Secondly, the foreign trade policy should help the implementation of the strategy

Table 2.31 Import Commodity Structure of Argentina ($100 Million, %)

	Capital Goods		Intermediate Products		Fuels		Spare Parts		Consumer Goods		Automobiles		Other	
	Value of Import	Proportion	Value of Import	Proportion	Value of Import	Proportion	Value of Import	Proportion	Value of Import	Proportion	Value of Import	Proportion	Value of Import	Proportion
1993	41.1	26	50.6	32	3.9	2.5	28.1	17.8	35.3	22.4	8.5	5.4	0.4	0.3
1997	77.2	25.3	101.0	33.2	9.7	3.2	55.4	18.2	45.4	14.9	15.6	5.1	0.3	0.1
2003	25.3	18.3	62.7	45.3	5.5	4	22.6	16.3	17.2	12.4	5.1	3.7	0.1	0.0
2007	107.0	23.9	155.2	34.7	28.5	6.4	78.3	17.5	49.9	11.2	27.1	6.1	1.2	0.3
2011	147.5	20	216.5	29.3	94.0	12.7	138.2	18.7	85.1	11.5	55.9	7.6	2.1	0.3

Source: Official website of Argentina National Bureau of Statistics and Survey, http://www.indec.mecon.ar.

of "re-industrialization" and import substitution. The trade liberalization in the 1990s led to the import of an influx of a large number of cheap products that had caused a huge impact on the domestic market, resulting in bankruptcies of a large number of uncompetitive industrial enterprises. Therefore, in order to promote the "re-industrialization" process and improve the localization rate of industrial products, the adjusted trade policy was supposed to have restrictions on some imported goods to protect the weak domestic industry and employment (see Table 2.31).

Under the guidance of the above objectives, the Argentine trade policies began to have increasingly strong protectionist tendencies, and the degree of trade openness declined. In terms of the specific measures, the government had implemented various tariff and non-tariff barriers to limit imports. In expanding exports, the government tried to maintain the price competitiveness of export products mainly through the exchange rate policy of a slight depreciation, but had been less successful in improving the structure of export products and increasing added values. Some measures, such as the export taxes and quotas on the exports of agricultural products, to a certain extent, also hindered exports.

After the international financial crisis broke out in 2008, to ensure trade surplus Argentina further strengthened the import restrictions. Specific measures include: to carry out anti-dumping investigations and impose anti-dumping duties, to implement the non-automatic import licensing system requiring companies to do imports and exports equivalently, to give reference customs prices for imported goods, to set up the State Secretariat of Foreign Trade under the Ministry of Economic Affairs to strengthen import management, etc. In recent years, Argentina practiced more stringent management on the imports. In February 2011, the government increased the management of non-automatic import license for the products from 412 kinds of species to 600. In early 2012, the government announced that all imported goods must be declared in advance and obtain the approval of the Secretariat of State for Foreign Trade before they were imported. The matching system of import and export, import advance declaration system and non-automatic import licensing system became the most important means of Argentine import restrictions. Importers must pass the check of all the three systems in order to purchase foreign exchange for importing products.

The stringent import controls had produced a variety of adverse effects. First, trade frictions frequently happened between Argentina and Brazil, the EU, China, the United States and other major trading partners. According to statistics, Argentina is one of the countries to have adopted the most frequent trade protectionist measures. The United States and the European Union repeatedly complained to the World Trade Organization (WTO), requesting Argentina to cancel a series of protectionist measures, including the non-automatic import licensing and trade balance. Brazil also had to take retaliatory measures to restrict imports from Argentina. Second, the increase of domestic industrial production capacity was restricted. The raw materials and components of Argentine manufacturing and assembly industries were more dependent on imports. The import controls made supply of such products tense, leading to improper function of business capacity. Third, the export was impacted indirectly. Because some export products also relied on imported parts, restrictions on imports resulted in limitations of some exports. The automobile manufacturing was the most seriously affected. Fourth, the imbalance between supply and demand in the domestic market was not conducive to price stability. The import restrictions touched the interest of multi-stakeholders, but if the two main objectives of trade policy had not changed, the possibility for the government to relax regulation was not great. In early 2013, the Argentine government announced the abolition of the much-maligned non-automatic import licensing system, but before that, the import tariffs on hundreds of products had already risen to 35%. Thus, the future of Argentina would continue to pursue protectionist trade policies, but might make minor adjustments according to the functioning of the domestic economy and the trade balance.

II. Foreign Direct Investment (FDI)

The opening up and privatization policies of the 1990s greatly enhanced the attractiveness of Argentina to foreign investors. From

Table 2.32 Net Flows of Foreign Direct Investment of Argentina (2003–2011) ($100 Million)

Year	2003	2004	2005	2006	2007	2008	2009	2010	2011
FDI	16.5	41.2	52.7	55.4	64.7	97.3	40.2	70.6	72.4

Source: CEPAL, *La Inversion Extranjera Directa ee America Latina y el Caribe 2011*, p. 50.

1992 to 1995, the average annual FDI inflows reached $4 billion, between 1996 and 1998 they increased to $8 billion, and in 1999 $24 billion.[62] All in all, the FDI in the 1990s was achieved mainly through the purchase of Argentine state-owned and private enterprises. From the perspective of the flow of foreign investments, from 1992 to 2000, 41.3% of the FDI went into services, the petroleum sector absorbed 35.5%, and the foreign investment in manufacturing accounted for 21.7%.[63] Spain and the United States were the most important investors of Argentina and between 1992 and 2002 about 60% of foreign investment came from these two countries. The prosperity of the foreign investment of the 1990s made the importance of foreign companies in the Argentine economy greatly improved, becoming an important driving force of economic growth. In the 1,000 largest enterprises, the number of foreign companies increased from 199 in 1992 to 427 in 2000, and the proportion of sales also increased from 39% to 67%.[64] After 10 years of privatization, almost all the important companies in the industries of Argentina were controlled by foreign capitals, and thus the degree of economic dependence on foreign capitals was becoming increasingly high (see Table 2.32).

[62]Gabriel Bezchinsky, Marcelo Dinenzon, Luis Giussani, Omar Caino, Beatriz Lopez, Silvia Amiel, *Inversion Extranjera Directa en la Argentina. Crisis, Reestructuracion y Nuevas Tendencias Despues de la Convertibilidad*, CEPAL, junio de 2011, p. 10.
[63]*Ibid.*, p. 12.
[64]Gabriel Bezchinsky, Marcelo Dinenzon, Luis Giussani, Omar Caino, Beatriz Lopez, Silvia Amiel, *Inversion Extranjera Directa en la Argentina. Crisis, Reestructuracion y Nuevas Tendencias Despues de la Convertibilidad*, CEPAL, junio de 2011, p. 15.

The economic crisis in 2001 had a significant impact on the foreign investment. In 2003, the net flow of FDI in Argentina was only $1.65 billion.[65] Beginning in 2004, the FDI gradually restored. However, with the transformation of the economic growth mode and the adjustment of foreign policy, the sources and direction of flows of foreign capitals had changed a lot.

Firstly, the sources of FDI tended to be diversified. In addition to the traditional countries such as the United States, Spain, the Netherlands and Chile, the countries that had the smaller share of investment in Argentina in the 1990s, such as Switzerland, Luxembourg, China and Brazil, were regarding Argentina as an important stage to pursue their international strategies, of which Brazil and China were the most prominent. Brazil has become one of the important sources of FDI in Argentina. Its investment is mainly concentrated in the industries of steel, oil, food, building materials, automobiles, and so on. There are four reasons for Brazil to expand investment in Argentina. First, the Brazilian multinational companies have got a rapid development in recent years, with improved international competitiveness and financial strength, having sufficient funds to implement the strategy of internationalization and foreign expansion. Second, the Brazilian Development Bank actively has promoted and subsidized the foreign investment enterprises in order to strengthen the competitive position of Brazilian enterprises in the international market. Third, Mercosur has provided a favorable platform for Brazilian foreign investment. Fourth, after 2003, the Argentine economy was running smoothly, and with the prosperity of domestic market, the attractiveness of foreign investment increased. Although Brazil's investment in Argentina was growing fast, the motivation was still to seek markets and resources. In Section 4 of this chapter, a detailed analysis will be made of the Chinese investment in Argentina (see Table 2.33).

Secondly, the way of FDI was more balanced, and the profits reinvested in the share of foreign capital had improved significantly. As mentioned above, the absorption of foreign investment in

[65] CEPAL, *La Inversion Extranjera Directa en America Latina y el Caribe 2011*, p. 50.

Table 2.33 Main Sources of FDI in Argentina (2005–2010) ($ Million)

Year	2005	2006	2007	2008	2009	2010
Brazil	1,231	443	862	1601	407	1,678
Chile	609	520	490	869	273	1,290
USA	1,273	820	720	2,051	905	1,179
Spain	953	2,397	1,759	722	1,206	1,176
Switzerland	282	39	274	735	197	748
Germany	72	255	471	370	339	548
Holland	1,054	123	601	1,139	108	208

Source: CEPAL, *La Inversion Extranjera Directa ee America Latina y el Caribe 2011*, p. 54.

Argentina in the 1990s was mainly by foreign takeovers, mergers and acquisitions of domestic enterprises or equity participation. The proportion of greenfield investment, reinvested earnings and long-term loans between the parent company and the subsidiaries was relatively low in foreign direct investments. After 2003, the importance of equity investments through acquisition, mergers and acquisitions, equity participation, and the increase of shares had declined, while the reinvestment of earnings had increasingly become an important form of direct investment. Several reasons could explain the changes in the composition of foreign capitals. First, the privatization process had ended; the expansion of foreign capitals turned to acquisitions of local private capitals, so the scale had been constrained. Second, after 2003, several sessions of the government had strengthened the management of foreign investments, made restrictions on repatriation of profits to foreign parent companies and required part of the industry profits be used to expand production. Thirdly, with the resumption of economy and recovery of the domestic market, the production capacity of many companies gradually hit the limit, needing additional investment, while the profit growth after the economic recovery had become an important source of funding (see Table 2.34).

Finally, the distribution of industries of FDI had changed. In the 1990s, the services and oil and gas extraction were the most favored departments for foreign investment; after 2003, more foreign capitals flowed into the manufacturing. The most attractive for foreign

Table 2.34 Main Ways of FDI in Argentina (2005–2011) ($ Million)

Year	2005	2006	2007	2008	2009	2010	2011
Equity capital	3,813	1,939	2,297	3,838	2,133	2,298	3,984
Inter company loans	296	490	2,126	5,491	−1,010	2,484	1,045
Reinvested profits	1,156	3,108	2,050	396	2,894	2,273	2,214

Source: CEPAL, *La Inversion Extranjera Directa ee America Latina y el Caribe 2011*, p. 57.

Table 2.35 Flows of FDI Investment in Argentina (2005–2011) ($ Million)

Year	2005	2006	2007	2008	2009	2010	2011
Natural resources	2,043	2,756	2,586	1,550	1,103	3,143	1,541
Manufacturing	2,680	3,049	3,408	5,760	156	4,945	784
Services	1,803	1,590	1,889	3,549	2,216	2,303	1,283

Source: CEPAL, *La Inversion Extranjera Directa ee America Latina y el Caribe 2011*, p. 51.

investment were still the advantageous sectors such as automobile, chemicals, metal processing, food and beverage. The foreign capitals absorbed by the service sector not only were distributed in the traditional industries of finance, telecommunications, commerce and so on, but also began to invest in the relatively-weak-technology and human-capital-intensive industries, which used to be ignored by foreign capitals in the past, such as the software industry, business services, information technology, tourism and certain sectors of the cultural and creative industry (see Table 2.35).

These three changes show that the sources and flow directions of the foreign investments in Argentina in the last 10 years are more diversified, which is conducive to the rational use of foreign investments, the expansion of external financing, the diversification of risks, and the absorption of and learning from more advanced experiences of business management. However, in the absorption and utilization of foreign investments, there are still some problems in Argentina (see Table 2.35).

First, the scale of foreign investment is not large in relation to the total size of economy. Although the flow of foreign investment had expanded since 2004, it did not exceed the level of the mid-late 1990s. The share of FDI in GDP in 2011 was less than 2%, lower than in the 1990s. In Latin-American countries, the size of foreign investment of Argentina was not only much smaller than that of Brazil and Mexico, but also smaller than the moderate countries like Chile and Colombia.

Second, the main goal of FDI in Argentina was to seek resources and markets, which determined that Argentina could not be integrated into the global value chains or could only participate in the low-end segments of the value chains. Although Argentina's automobile industry got a rapid development driven by foreign capitals, the high-end segments of the value chains, such as the product research and development and the production of key parts, were basically in the hands of multinational companies. In the true sense, Argentina did not form an automobile manufacturing center, but more of an assembly center that utilized the mature technology and design of multinational corporations, with spare parts mostly dependent on imports; its independent research and innovation content was very low. In addition, Argentina's automobile production was mainly for domestic sales or exports to Brazil, so it played a limited role in the international division of automotive industry.

Third, restrictions on foreign investment and management had been strengthened; some macro-control measures had conflicted with the interests of multinational corporations. For example, the implementation of the "freezing" or "peso-oriented" approach for the prices of utilities had led to strong resentment among European companies; later, the price controls and increase of export taxes resulted in an impact on corporate profits, leading to the lack of motivation for business investment. The nationalization initiatives being implemented in recent years, the requirements for enterprises to expand investment and the restrictions on profits remitted abroad, have increased the concerns of investors with the safety of their investments and the security of their interests.

Fourth, the investment environment needed to be improved. According to *The Global Competitiveness Report 2012–2013* released by the World Economic Forum, compared with the previous year,

Argentina's global competitiveness ranking fell by 9, ranking No. 94 among 144 countries, its position being even behind Guatemala in Latin-American countries. In the 12 indicators to measure the level of competitiveness, only the three indicators of health and basic education, higher education and training, and market size scored higher, while the competitive disadvantages were obvious, including the imperfect systems, inadequate infrastructures, low efficiency of commodity market and labor market, underdeveloped financial market and weak innovation ability. In the report of *Doing Business in 2012* issued by the International Finance Corporation, the private-sector arm of the World Bank, the Argentina business environment ranked No. 113 among 183 countries, positioned in the middle or after the middle. According to the report, the weaknesses in the investment environment of Argentina lay in the aspects of "starting a business", "applying for a construction permit", "registering properties", "paying taxes", and "investor protection". All in all, many areas of the investment environment in Argentina need to be improved.

Section 4 Development of Economic and Trade Relations with China

Since the establishment of diplomatic relations between China and Argentina in 1972, the Sino-Argentine relations have been developing steadily. Since 2003, the bilateral economic and trade cooperation has shown a trend of leaping development. China has already become Argentina's second largest trading partner behind Brazil. However, with the rapid development of the Sino-Argentine trade, some contradictions and problems have inevitably appeared. In this section, we will analyze the development of the relations of the Sino-Argentine economic trade and the obstacles from the two aspects of trade and investment and provide corresponding strategic suggestions.

I. The Sino-Argentine Bilateral Trade Development and Unbalanced Trade Problems

In the 1990s, the trade between China and Argentina had already started a momentum of rapid growth. According to the statistics of Argentina, from 1990 to 1999, China's imports from Argentina increased from $240 million to $510 million, and exports to Argentina from a $32 million to $990 million,[66] both of the growth rates exceeding that of the total imports and exports over the same period in Argentina. Except in 1990 and 1991, China had maintained a surplus position in the rest of the years. In the four years of recession in Argentina (1999–2002), China's imports from Argentina was not affected — increasing from $510 million to $1.09 billion, while exports to Argentina experienced a serious setback, dropping to $3.3 billion. The main reason for this contrast is because the domestic economic contraction in Argentina led to a sharp decrease of demand for imports, while over the same period China's economy had maintained a rapid growth, with an increasing demand for Argentine products. After the Argentine economic crisis, the Sino-Argentine trade grew rapidly. According to the statistics of China, the bilateral trade volume increased from $3.15 billion in 2003 to $14.76 billion in 2011, an increase of almost five times. However, in the process of rapid development in trade, the problem of unequal trade had gradually become more and more obvious, drawing the attention of both countries, especially Argentina. Here we need to do a brief analysis, and propose some countermeasures.

1. The Problems of Statistical Differences of Trade and Trade Deficit

In 1990, although Argentina kept a deficit in trade with China, the problem of trade imbalance was not unduly concerned with due to the limited volume of the trade, coupled with the fact that there was a deficit in the total revenue of Argentina's foreign trade. After 2003, with the adjustment of Argentine trade policy to achieve the goal of trade surplus, and the growth of bilateral trade and China's rising share of Argentina's foreign trade, the difference between the trade statistics of both countries and the problem of trade imbalance gradually emerged. According to the Argentine statistics, Argentina

[66] http://www.indec.mecon.ar.

Table 2.36 Chinese Customs' Statistics of Import and Export Volume and Trade Balance between China and Argentina ($100 Million)

Year	2003	2004	2005	2006	2007	2008	2009	2010	2011
Export of China	4.5	8.5	13.3	20.0	35.7	50.5	34.8	61.2	85.0
Import of China	27.3	32.5	38.0	37.0	63.3	93.6	43.2	68.0	62.6
Trade balance	−22.8	−24.0	−24.7	−17.0	−27.6	−43.1	−8.4	−6.8	22.4

Source: *China's Foreign Trade Statistics Yearbook 2005–2012*, China Statistics Press.

Table 2.37 Argentine Statistics of Import and Export Volume and Trade Balance between China and Argentina ($100 Million)

Year	2003	2004	2005	2006	2007	2008	2009	2010	2011
Export of China	7.2	14.0	22.4	31.2	50.9	71.0	48.2	76.5	105.7
Import of China	24.8	26.3	31.9	34.8	51.7	63.6	36.7	58.0	62.4
Trade balance	−17.6	−12.3	−9.5	−3.6	−0.8	7.4	11.5	18.5	43.3

Source: Official website of Argentina National Bureau of Statistics and Survey, http://www.indec.mecon.ar.

had maintained a trade surplus for six consecutive years from 2002 to 2007, but the favorable balance declined year by year and after 2008 the surplus changed into a deficit — deficit in 2011 reached an unprecedented $4.3 billion (see Table 2.37). However, the statistics of the Chinese Customs have shown that from 2003 to 2010 Argentina had maintained a surplus position in the Sino-Argentine trade, and in most years the surplus value had reached more than $2 billion; it was not until 2011 that the surplus was changed into deficit, with only half of the amount in the Argentine statistics (see Table 2.36).

The statistical contrast of the two countries shows two very distinct differences. First of all, the Chinese statistics of Chinese imports are higher than the statistics of Argentine exports to China, while the Chinese statistics of Chinese exports are less than the Argentine statistics of imports from China. In other words, in the Argentine statistics, there is the problem of insufficient statistics of Chinese imports and over statistics of China's exports. Secondly, the difference of the statistics of Chinese exports by both sides is greater than the difference of statistics of Chinese imports. Except in 2008, the statistical differences of Chinese imports did not exceed 30% of the total exports of Argentina, and in 2011, there was even a very close case. However, the statistical differences of China's exports accounted for 40–50% of Argentina's total imports before 2008, only with a slight narrowing after 2009. The above two differences led to serious different understandings of the bilateral trade imbalances, resulting in Argentina's frequent launching of protectionist measures against China in recent years.

2. The Importance of China and Argentina in the Foreign Trade of Both Countries

According to the Argentine statistics, China's importance in the Argentine foreign trade continues to increase. In 2007, the Argentine exports to China for the first time exceeded the exports to the United States; China became Argentina's second largest export destination country.[67] In 2008, the Argentine imports from China also exceeded its imports from the United States, ranking second. The proportion of the bilateral trade volume in Argentina's total foreign trade rose from 7.4% in 2003 to 10.6% in 2011. Since 2003, China has been occupying 7–8% of the total exports of Argentina, in some years up to 9%. The proportion of the imports from China in the total imports of Argentina increased from 6.2% in 2004 to 14.3% in 2011. That is to say, the importance of China in Argentina's imports exceeded that in its exports, also showing a trend of increasing.

In contrast, the importance of Argentina in China's foreign trade is much smaller. According to the Chinese statistics, the proportion of Argentina is less than 1% in China's foreign trade, remaining at the level of 0.4%, in some years reaching 0.6%. In the trade between China and Latin-American countries, the status of Argentina has declined. In 2003, Argentina was China's fourth largest trading partner in Latin America, and its total volume of trade with China ranked relatively close to that of the third partner of Chile, with only a difference of $350 million. By 2011, Argentina fell to the fifth place in the Sino-Latin

[67]If the EU is seen as a whole, China is Argentina's third largest trading partner.

American trade, behind Venezuela, also very close to the trade volume of Panama and Peru with China. The Sino-Argentine trade value dropped to less than half of that of the Sino-Chilean trade.

The above analysis shows that China's trade dependence on Argentina is far less than Argentina's trade dependence on China. There are two main reasons for this asymmetry. One is the differences of trade scale between the two countries — in 2011, China's total foreign trade had already reached $3,642.06 billion,[68] but Argentina's foreign trade was only $157.89 billion. The other reason is the growth rate of the Sino-Argentine trade lagged behind that of China's trade with other major Latin-American countries, particularly Venezuela and Chile. Therefore, it is not surprising to see the share disparity of foreign trade in the respective foreign trade of China and Argentina. It is undeniable that Argentina occupies a pivotal position in China's imports of agricultural products, becoming one of the major suppliers of Chinese soybeans and soybean oil. According to statistics, from 2007 to 2009, 73.3% of China's imports of soybean oil came from Argentina.[69]

3. The Imbalance of Trade Structure

The composition of the Argentine products exported to China has three distinct characteristics. First, most of the products are the low-tech primary products and processed agricultural products, with the manufactured goods accounting for only 2.5% (2010).[70] Second, most of the products are renewable resources, with the non-renewable resources accounting for only 12.1% (2010),[71] most of which are oil, in

---

[68]Website of Chinese Ministry of Commerce, http://zhs.mofcom.gov.cn/article/aa/201201/20120107923402.shtml.

[69]Osvaldo Rosales, Mikio Kuwayama, *China y America Latina y el Caribe, acia una Relacion Economica y Comercial Estrategica*, CEPAL, marzo de 2012, p. 101.

[70]Eduardo Daniel Oviedo, "Modernizaciones, Intereses y Relaciones Estrategicas entre Argentina y China", Ponencia Presentada al Seminario Internacional: "Como Enriquecer la Asociacion Estrategica entre China y Argentina ante las Nuevas Situaciones Internacionales" Instituto de Relaciones Internaciona- les Contemporieneas (CICIR) Beijing, China, octubre de 2011.

[71]*Ibid.*

Table 2.38 Main Commodities of Argentina's Export to China in 2010

	Exports ($ Million)	Proportion in Total Exports	Main Commodities and the Proportions
Seeds and fruits	4,121	71.1%	Soybean (99.9%)
Oil	666	11.5%	Crude oil (100%)
Animal and vegetable fats and oils	353	6.1%	Soybean oil (66.2%)
Leatherwear	143	2.5%	Tanned leather (77.4%)
Meat	67	1.2%	Poultry meat (99.5%)
Total	5,350	92.4%	—

Source: Ministerio de Economia y Finanzas Publicas, *El Comercio Exterior Bilateral Argentina-China*, agosto de 2011.

addition to a small amount of refined copper, lithium and iron. Third, the product structure is single, with five main commodities accounting for more than 90% of the total exports to China, of which the total amount of the export of soybeans and soybean oil accounted for about three-quarters of the total exports (see Table 2.38). Compared with the other major trading partners of China, the product range of Argentina's exports to China's is very limited. According to statistics, from 2008 to 2009, as many as 3,858 kinds of the products of Argentina were exported to other Latin-American countries, 2,263 kinds of products were exported to the EU, 1,470 kinds of products were exported to Asian countries, but only 529 kinds of products were exported to China.[72] Such an export structure determined that the added value of Argentina's exports to China was relatively low, depending on a few commodities. From 1995 to 2005, the soybeans and soybean oil contributed 59.4% and 23.8%, respectively to Argentina's exports to China.[73] In other words, 80% of Argentina's exports to China grew from these two products.

[72]CEPAL, *La República Popular China y America Latina y el Caribe: Hacia una Nueva Fass ee el Vinculo Economico y Comercial*, junio de 2011, p. 20.
[73]Andres Lopez y Daniela Ramos, *A la Sombra del Gigante Chino! Hay Lugar parr la Argentina en el New Mundo?* Boletin Informativo Techint 326, mayo-agosto de 2008, p. 78.

Compared with exports, Argentina's imports from China have the features of diversification and equalization. In 2010, the two major categories of electronic and mechanical equipment products accounted for 55% of the total imports, but in each category of products, no one product accounted for more than 50%. Specifically, in the front row of Chinese imports to Argentina the first eight kinds of products in turn were computers (10%), telephones (8.5%), chemical products (3.5%), motorcycles (3.3%), toys (1.3%), plastic products (0.7%), medical equipments (0.3%) and steel casting tools (0.3%).[74] The above eight kinds of products accounted for only 27.9% of China's total exports to Argentina (see Table 2.39). According to statistics, 98% of China's exports to Argentina belong to industrial products, the proportion of primary products accounting for less than 2%.[75]

There is a trend of balanced development in the import structure divided from the use. In the 1990s, the products of Argentina's imports from China were mainly consumer goods, most of which were cheap goods. However, with the change of the Chinese export model and professional model, the proportion of consumer goods from China decreased in the imports of Argentina from China, while the proportion of capital goods and intermediate goods had increased, and the product quality had already started to be widely recognized. By 2007, 11.4% of the Argentine imported capital goods, spare parts and intermediate products came from China.[76]

The structure of import and export commodities indicates that the Sino-Argentine trade has two important features. First, it is the strong complementarity — the merchandise exports are their advantageous products with competitiveness, while the imported products

[74]Ministerio de Economia y Finanzas Publicas, *El Comercio Exterior Bilateral Arjgentina–China*, agosto de 2011.

[75]Eduardo Daniel Oviedo, *Modernizaciones, Intereses y Relaciones Estrategicas entrr Argentina y China*, ponencia presentada al Seminario Internacional: "Como Enriquecer la Asociacion Estrategica entre China y Argentina ante las Nuevas Situaciones Internacionales", Instituto de Relaciones Internacionales Contemporieneas (CICIR) Beijing, China, octubre de 2011.

[76]Andres Lopez, Daniela Ramos, *A la Sombra del Gigante Chino: Hay Lugar parr la Argentina en el New Mundo?* Boletin Informativo Technt 326, mayo-agosto de 2008, p. 82.

Table 2.39 Argentine Main Imports from China in 2010

	Imports ($ Million)	Proportion in Total Imports	Main Commodities and their Proportions
Electronic equipment	2,191	28.6%	Telephone and other transmission equipment (29.5%)
Mechanical equipment	2,015	26.3%	Automatic data processing equipment (38%)
Organic chemical products	600	7.8%	Other organic and inorganic products (44.2%)
Automobiles	415	5.4%	Motorcycles (61.5%)
Toys and games	220	2.9%	Children's toys (43.6%)
Plastics and plastic products	209	2.7%	Other plastic products (24.4%)
Optical and medical devices	131	1.7%	Lighting equipment and fittings (42.8%)
Casting equipment	120	1.6%	Medical instruments and tools (18.1%)

Source: Ministerio de Economia y Finanzas Publicas, *El Comercio Exterior Bilateral Argentina–China*, agosto de 2011.

Table 2.40 Structure of Argentine Imported Products from China (%)

Year	1995	2000	2004	2005	2006	2007
Capital goods	14.5	22.3	26.6	30.2	31.2	32.8
Spare parts of capital goods	5.5	10.6	15.7	17.3	16.9	14.9
Intermediate products	19.7	19.2	29.8	26.3	24.5	27.4
Consumer goods	60.3	47.4	26.0	24.9	27.1	24.2
Other	0.0	0.53	1.96	1.36	0.33	0.6
Total	100	100	100	100	100	100

Source: Andres Lopez, Daniela Ramos, *A la Sombra del Gigante Chino: Hay Lugar parr la Argentina en el New Mundo?* Boletin Informativo Techint 326, mayo-agosto de 2008, p. 82.

are relatively rare or insufficient in production. Second, the traded products have significant features of inter-industry trade. A vast majority of the Sino-Argentine import and export products are one-way flow, with almost no overlap between imports and exports (see Table 2.40).

II. Trade Frictions

In recent years, Argentina continued to adopt the trade protectionism measures against China, such as anti-dumping, quotas, technical limitations, and setting the minimum reference prices, and thus deeply influencing Chinese exports to Argentina. Argentina is the country that has carried out the most anti-dumping investigations among the Latin-American countries. Most of the investigations were against Chinese products. For example, from the fourth quarter of 2008 to the fourth quarter of 2009, Argentina had launched a total of 33 anti-dumping investigations, among which 20 Chinese products were involved.[77] The Chinese products that suffered the anti-dumping sanctions of Argentina were mainly those that were competing with the domestic production in Argentina and the government-protected products, such as textiles, footwear, toys, car and motorcycle parts, wood products, building materials, household appliances, chemicals, and hardware tools.

Argentina frequently has set limits on Chinese products, resulting in a very negative impact on the Sino-Argentine trade, even trade between China and Latin America. First, protectionism seriously has restricted the development of the Sino-Argentine trade, especially China's exports to Argentina. In recent years, the growth rate of the Sino-Argentine trade has been significantly lower than the trade between China and other major Latin-American countries. One of the reasons that cannot be ignored is the trade remedy measures successively taken in the context of crisis in Argentina to ensure the trade surplus. Secondly, Argentina also has a negative role model for other Latin-American countries by frequently launching attacks on the Chinese products. In 2009, Argentina joined forces with Brazil to launch a joint anti-dumping investigation and sanction for Chinese products. In 2011, Argentina suggested that Mercosur countries take unified action to work together to build trade barriers and collective boycott for the imports from China. Finally, the continued

---

[77] CEPAL, *La República Popular China y America Latina y el Caribe: Hacia una Nueva Fass ee el Vinculo Economico y Comercial*, julio de 2011, p. 216.

implementation of the anti-dumping sanctions made China lost some of the markets. Once the Chinese products had been identified as dumping, high anti-dumping duties would be imposed, of which some of the periods would last up to five years. For example, in 2009, Argentina declared to levy an anti-dumping duty of up to 873.81% for the circuit devices made in China; in 2010, it levied an anti-dumping duty of 202.79% for the China-made multi-functional food processing machines; in 2011, an anti-dumping duty of 136.92% was imposed on China-made electric fans. The sanctioned Chinese products had lost price competitiveness, and had to give up part of the market.

China has responded to a range of irrational trade remedy measures that Argentina had adopted against the Chinese products. In April 2010, through the implementation of new quality standards, China suspended the import of soybean oil from Argentina. In October of that year, through consultations and negotiations, the two countries resolved the trade disputes of soybean oil and restored the import and export business of the soybean oil.

One of the main causes leading to the Sino-Argentine trade frictions is that Argentina has considered the unequal the Sino-Argentine trade a threat to their own interests. In addition to the trade deficit, Argentina is more concerned about the structural problems of import and export commodities, i.e., China's exports are mainly industrial products, while Argentina's exports are mainly primary products. This contrast leads to the discrepancies between the added values of the export and import products in the Sino-Argentine trade. According to Argentine statistics, in 2006, the average price of Argentine exports to China was $336 per ton, while the average price of goods imported from China reached $3,469 per ton.[78]

It should be emphasized that the presence of the unequivalence in the Sino-Argentine foreign trade was not caused by China, but the result of the respective resources and industrial advantages of

[78]Andres Lopez, Daniela Ramos, *A la Sombra del Gigante Chino! Hay Lugar parr la Argentina en el New Mundo?*", Boletin Informativo Technt, mayo-agosto de 2008, p. 85.

China and Argentina, as well as the patterns of import and export. Argentina itself has very obvious advantages in resources, but lacks industrial competitiveness; the characteristics of the import and export model are the exports of primary products and processed agricultural products and the imports of manufactured goods and intermediate industrial products. China is a big consumer of resources, requiring a lot of resources and raw materials to meet the needs of its domestic production. Compared with the 1980s and 1990s, the manufacturing level of China has been already significantly improved, and its exports have changed from the cheap consumer goods to the manufactured goods with a certain degree of technology and fine processing. Thus, the Sino-Argentine trade is actually more representative of a very distinct complementary characteristic, and also reflects the characteristic of their respective foreign trade structure.

III. Thoughts on the Soybean Oil Event

In 2010, the war in soybean oil trade sparked the concern among all the parties. On the surface, it is a kind of response to Argentine trade protectionism for China to suspend the import of Argentine soybean oil, but the soybean oil crisis also reflects the conflict of interest in the strategic development of soybean processing industry of the two countries.

As mentioned earlier, the share of soybeans and soybean oil accounted for about three-quarters in Argentine exports to China, and three-quarters of China's soybean oil imports were from Argentina. From this perspective, the two countries have an interdependent relationship in the trade of soybeans and soybean oil. It is also for this reason that the importance of the trade of soybeans and soybean oil in the Sino-Argentine trade is self-evident.

Then, why is there some kind of conflict of interest in the soybean processing industry between China and Argentina? From a horizontal perspective, the Argentine soybean oil has provided a complementation for China's domestic production shortage, but from a longitudinal point of view, both China and Argentina need to improve their level of industrialization through oil crushing industry. In this

Table 2.41 Changes of the Yield, Import and Consumption of Soybean Products in China (1995–2008)

	Kind	1995–1996 Agricultural Year (10,000 Tons)	2007–2008 Agricultural Year (10,000 Tons)	Growth Rate (%)
	Soybean	1,350	1,430	5.93
Output	Soybean flour	605.1	3,017	398.6
	Soybean oil	115	680	491.3
	Crushing capacity	747	3,805	409.37
Import	Soybean	79.5	3,400	4, 176.73
	Soybean flour	117.9	30	−74.55
	Soybean oil	144.5	300	107.61
Consumption	Soybean	1,407.3	4,825	242.86
	Soybean flour	712.3	2,982	318.64
	Soybean oil	257.5	979	280.19

Source: Andres Lopez y Daniela Ramos, *A la Sombra del Gigante Chino: Hay Lugar parr la Argentina en el New Mundo?* Boletin Informativo Techint 326, mayo-agosto de 2008, p. 78.

sense, there is competition in this area between China and Argentina. The changes in China's soybean industry chain can illustrate this competition.

It can be seen from Table 2.41 that in the mid-1990s, the consumption pattern of the Chinese soybean products was to import a small amount of soybeans, with 55% of soybean oil and 17% of soybean flour imported. By 2008, China's soybean import had increased by 40 times, import of soybean flour accounted for only about a quarter of the original, and despite an increase in oil import more than doubled, the proportion of domestic soybean oil in the total consumption had already increased to nearly 70%. The main reason for this change is that after the end of the 1990s, in order to achieve self-sufficiency in fuel oil, the Chinese government began to actively support the soybean crushing industry and introduced a number of incentives. Promoted by this policy, along the southeast coast of China a boom to build oil processing enterprises emerged. China's oil processing capacity therefore had been greatly improved. In 2005, China became the world's second largest soybean flour and soybean oil producing country behind the United States. In the process to develop the oil crushing industry in China, the domestic soybean production could not meet the processing needs; so the surge in soybean imports came into existence.

These changes have had a significant impact on the Argentine export of soybeans and soybean oil to China. In the mid-late 1990s, the bean pulps were Argentina's main soybean export to China, and after 2000, the bean pulps were substituted with soybean flour and soybean oil. Compared with soybeans, Argentina was more willing to export soybean oil to China. The main reasons are: first, soybean oil belongs to processed products, its value is far higher than soybeans, and the increase rate of oil prices in recent years has risen more than that of soybeans; second, soybeans are Argentina's advantageous resources; the soybean oil processing is an important way to realize the re-industrialization by way of using this advantage. This intent is in conflict with China's strategy to import raw materials of soybeans to process soybean oil in the country to achieve oil self-sufficiency, which becomes a challenge for the Sino-Argentine trade of soybeans and soybean oil.

As "sensitive products" in the Sino-Argentine trade, the soybean oil crisis in 2010 is indeed worthy of concern. Although after China had suspended the import of soybean oil from Argentina, Argentina's loss was made up to a certain extent by seeking new markets, and China filled the vacancy left by the Argentine soybean oil import by turning to importing it from Brazil, but the degree of dependence on soy oil trade between the two countries was not lowered. After China re-opened the market to the Argentine soybean oil, the confidence of Argentine related industries was quickly boosted, and the active soybean trade also boosted the rise in the soybean price. The trend for China to need the import of soybean oil to meet its domestic demand will not change for the time being. The soybean oil crisis ultimately had been resolved through consultation and coordination. From this perspective, this storm is not entirely something bad. It has provided an opportunity for the two parties to have mutual communication and understanding of each other. Both of them are aware that there should be more exchanges and consultations on the issue that concerns the interests of both countries in order to find a point of balance in the bilateral trade relations for sharing the benefits.

IV. China's Direct Investment in Argentina

The 1990s is the heyday for Argentina to absorb foreign capitals, but few Chinese companies were involved, with very limited investment from China. After the crisis in Argentina, with the warming up of the Sino-Argentine trade relations and the Chinese government's strategy of "going out", China began to pay attention to Argentina. More and more Chinese enterprises went to Argentina to invest by building factories there. According to the statistics of the United Nations Economic Commission for Latin America (ECLAC), from 1990 to 2009, China's direct investment in Argentina had already reached $143 million, which was a rare phenomenon in the Latin-American countries. In addition, in 2010, due to the acquisitions of the Chinese oil companies in Argentina, the confirmed investment of China in Argentina reached $5.55 billion,[79] accounting for about one third of China's confirmed investment of that year in Latin America, secondary to Brazil. Argentina had thus become one of China's most important countries of investment in Latin America.

Different from the early investment that was confined to specific sectors, in recent years the area of China's investment is showing a variety of features. Currently, the Chinese companies have got involved in about 30 Argentine industries, such as oil, chemicals, telecommunications, agriculture, fisheries, mechanical equipment, shipping, infrastructure, mining, electronics, and finance, with different scales of investment. The ways of investment also varied, including establishing new enterprises, acquisitions of local businesses and setting up joint ventures or cooperative enterprises. With the Chinese enterprises have been increasingly strengthened, the practice of cross-border acquisitions is no longer an isolated phenomenon. In May 2010, the China National Offshore Oil Corporation (CNOOC) acquired a 50% stake in Bridas Corporation in Argentina with $3.1 billion. In September 2012,

[79]CEPAL, *La Inversion Extranjera Directa ee America Latina y el Caribe 2010*, p. 111.

Bridas Corporation acquired Esso — a subsidiary of the US Exxon Mobil Oil Company in Argentina. By the end of 2010, another Chinese major oil company — China Petroleum & Chemical Corporation (the Sinopec) spent $2.45 billion in the acquisition of the US subsidiary of Occidental Petroleum in Argentina, which became the fourth largest oil and gas producer in Argentina. In November 2012, the Industrial and Commercial Bank of China (ICBC) spent more than $600 million in the acquisition of the Argentina Standard Bank, acquiring 80% of the shares, becoming the first Chinese investment in the Argentine banks.

The main motivation of Chinese enterprises to invest in Argentina is to seek resources and markets. The Chinese enterprises seeking resources are represented by the oil companies such as the Sinopec and CNOOC, the mining companies such as China Metallurgical Group Corporation and the Shandong Gold Group, the grain and oil companies such as the Hopeful Group, and the fisheries aquaculture companies such as the Global Fishing Company under the China Agricultural Development Group, which value the rich Argentine oil mineral and agricultural resources. The Chinese enterprises seeking markets are represented by the high-tech enterprises such as ZTE, Huawei and Nuctech, the manufacturing companies such as TCL, Midea, Lenovo, and Shanghai SVA Group, and the transportation companies such as China Ocean Shipping Company and China Shipping Group, whose goal is to use quality products and services to develop and dominate the markets.

ZTE and Huawei are among the relatively early Chinese enterprises to have invested in Argentina. The biggest advantage of them is that they all belong to the emerging high-tech industries, which is what Argentina needed to develop, and the types of industry that the Argentine government encouraged and supported, and therefore they were affected little by policy changes. Another success lies in the goal not pursuing short-term benefits, but valuing the long-term interests. Shortly after Huawei entered Argentina in 2000, a serious economic crisis broke out, and in Argentina, the Chinese products were under the impression of "poor quality and low price". These made it difficult for Huawei to win the Argentine market. But Huawei took advantage of the opportunity of the divestment of some of the European and American companies during the economic crisis with increasing efforts to promote its products, gradually winning more and more regular customers, and ultimately established a foothold.

Early in 1999, Shanghai SVA Group established a color TV factory in Tierra del Fuego. TCL, Midea, and Lenovo began to invest in Argentina a few years after the 2001 economic crisis. Their advantages were having their own brands, excellent product qualities and reasonable prices. As to how to invest, they had a lot in common: establishing a cooperative relationship with the local well-known enterprises to achieve the localization of production and territorial management. TCL cooperated with Radio Victoria Fueguina Company in the appliance production and sales. Lenovo Group cooperated with the local businesses in Tierra del Fuego to set up factories to assemble laptops. Media acquired the business ownership of air conditioning in the three countries of Argentina, Brazil, and Chile from the local company of Carrier, setting up a joint venture, assembling air conditioners in Tierra del Fuego. Currently, Lenovo's market share in Argentina reached 17%, becoming Argentina's third-largest notebook vendor. TCL also found a place in the mainstream household appliance market, expanding its product range. After its realization of the localization of production, in early 2013, Media had already produced the Media-brand air conditioning products.

In addition to the above-mentioned high-tech companies and manufacturing companies, in Argentina, the development of more successful Chinese companies also include shipping- and- fishery-related businesses. Most of them were stationed in Argentina in the mid-1990s. The main advantage of them is that before investing in South America, they had already accumulated a certain amount of experience in international investment and cooperation abroad. Since their development had already been in Argentina for many years, they were familiar with the local laws and regulations, political, economic and cultural environment, and the labor system. After the difficult time of their beginning and the 2001 crisis in Argentina, the capacity of overseas survival and development of these enterprises was greatly enhanced.

The Sinopec, CNOOC, China Metallurgical, and Shandong Gold are Chinese companies that started to invest in Argentina only in recent years. They are characterized by strong capitals, and therefore their investments were achieved by acquisitions of local companies. At present, these companies are experiencing varying degrees of difficulties and obstacles. In 2010, the joint venture of CNOOC and Bridas planned to acquire BP's subsidiary Pan American Energy in Argentina in order to secure the determined position in oil and gas industry in Argentina, but ultimately failed to acquire it. After the acquisition of the subsidiary of the Western Oil Company in Argentina, the Sinopec had not got the $184 million in export subsidies promised by the Government of Argentina; so its production and business activities were affected to a certain extent. China Metallurgical Group Cooperation (MCC) and Shandong Gold encountered the problem of beneficiation. In 2006, MCC acquired a stake of 70% of the Sheila Grande iron ore in Argentina. Because the iron ore mine belonged to high phosphorus magnetite with high cost of mining, coupled with technical problems of water supply difficult to solve, large-scale production could not be achieved, resulting in a loss of mining. After the acquisition of a gold mine in Argentina, Shandong Gold found that the mine reserves were too low to have the mining feasibility, so the company had to continue to look for other gold mines. In addition, the business activities of the Sinopec, CNOOC, and MCC had been affected by the workers' strikes. Before entering the Argentine market, these enterprises had done the preparatory work of upfront information collection, research, and inspection, but they had underestimated the unexpected difficulties and problems.

V. Opportunities and Challenges of the Sino-Argentine Economic and Trade Relations

For China, Argentina is both an important trading partner in Latin America and an emerging market with the potential of development. Although the importance of Argentina in the external economic relations of China is less than that of Brazil, the linkage effect and the demonstration effect of the Sino-Argentine relations in

Latin-American countries cannot be ignored. From the perspective of long-term and strategic development of relations between China and Latin America, the strategic partnership between China and Argentina has to be further consolidated and deepened.

There is a good foundation for the development of the economic and trade relations between China and Argentina. First of all, since the establishment of diplomatic ties between China and Argentina, the bilateral relations have been developing steadily and there has been no serious conflict of interest or contradiction. Secondly, the two countries share identical or similar views on many major international issues, with common interests and aspirations in international affairs. Thirdly, the two governments have given high priority on the development of the Sino-Argentine relations — Argentine Presidents Nestor Kirchner and Fernandes visited China respectively in 2004 and 2010, and the Chinese President Hu Jintao also visited Argentina in 2004. Finally, in 2004, China and Argentina signed *The Memorandum of Understanding about the Trade and Investment Cooperation* to establish a strategic partnership, and meanwhile Argentina officially recognized China's status of market economy.

There are three important supports for the Sino-Argentine economic and trade exchanges. The first is complementarity, not only in bilateral trade, but also in the area of investment. China has accumulated huge foreign exchange reserves and the strength of companies is increasingly growing, needing to find new markets and open up investment channels; while Argentina lacks investment in many areas, needing to use the power of foreign capital in order to have better development. Therefore, the two countries also complement each other in the investment. The second is the existing and more and more obvious interdependence between the two countries. In the aspect of trade, China is Argentina's second largest trading partner, and Argentina is one of China's most important agricultural importers. In the area of investment, after years of development, many Chinese enterprises have already formed a firm foothold in the Argentine market, hoping to go into other Latin-American countries on the basis of Argentina. Argentina has become an important overseas market for these companies. After the 2008 economic crisis, the pace of foreign investment in the United States and Europe has slowed down, while China's investment has contrarily increased. This has not only expanded the sources of investment in Argentina, but also made up for the lack of investment from the European companies to a certain extent. The third is mutual benefit. The rapid development of the Sino-Argentine trade has played an important role in promoting the strong recovery of the Argentine economy. Both the foreign exchange reserves and the financial income benefited from an increase in the Argentine exports to China. For China, in the case of continuing growth of the domestic demand for food and energy, new sources of raw materials must be found to diversify the supply of important resources. Argentina is undoubtedly a suitable choice. In summary, it is no doubt that the relationship in the field of economy and trade between the two countries is of mutual attraction, mutual needs, interdependence, and mutual benefit. This has formed the foundation for the current and future development of the Sino-Argentine relations to be more cooperative than competitive, and more of consensus than of conflict, and provided a wider space and more opportunities for the future development of both countries.

Argentina is rich in resources, but many oil fields and mines have not been effectively developed and utilized. Its agricultural arable land area is vast, with enormous potential for development. After experiencing the "de-industrialization" in the 1990s, the manufacturing sector is in the stage of revival and re-development, which also contains unlimited business opportunities. These are attractive factors for China. However, at present, China has not done enough in-depth study of the Argentine market, lacking understanding of many products and the relevant policies, and therefore, marketing is still in the exploratory stage. China has a large population and a huge market, and in recent years as the income level and quality of life of the people have improved, the demand for high-grade consumer goods and requirement for product quality are getting higher and higher. However, Argentina's exploitation of the Chinese market is far from enough. One manifestation of that is that, due to the lack of competitiveness of industrial products, its exports to China can only be limited to a small number of low-degree processed agricultural products and fuels; the second is the limited size of investment in China. Many of the traditional advantageous industrial sectors, such as food and beverage, have not or hardly entered the Chinese market. Therefore, both China and Argentina need to further explore each other's markets, seeking the potential to achieve maximum benefits.

In the area of trade, the main obstacle facing the Sino-Argentine relation is the trade protectionism. Although Argentina had adopted the protectionist measures for their own interests, but in the long run, protectionism is not conducive to the development of bilateral trade, and has an impact on the country's own economic development. Thus, protectionism is only effective in the short term, rather than a permanent solution. About this issue, the two countries should enhance understanding and strengthen communication and coordination to avoid trade frictions and disputes. This is a mutual responsibility. From the Chinese perspective, imbalances that exist in the Sino-Argentine trade should be paid attention to, the crux of the problem should be found and effective countermeasures should be adopted. First of all, a follow-up study should be done of the changes in the Argentine industrial structures and the adjustment of the industrial policies, especially the strategic planning of industry and agriculture put forward in the past two years, so that the companies of import and export products can actively adapt to these changes. Those capable enterprises can enter each other's markets by way of direct investment and local production, changing the traditional model of relying solely on exports. Secondly, as to the continued implementation of anti-dumping investigations in Argentina, the Chinese enterprises should join forces actively to respond to protect their own interests so as to reduce losses. Third, Chinese companies can circumvent the anti-dumping investigation by entrepot trade in order to hold the hard-won markets.

In the area of investment, the biggest problem that the Chinese enterprises encountered is the insufficient and not detailed market research, underestimating the difficulties that might arise. The main reasons for these difficulties are as follows: first, Argentina is in the process of exploring new ways of economic growth, lacking policy stability. In addition, in recent years, the government intervention in the economy has been strengthened, constantly introducing restrictions on investment activities. Second, the investment environment in Argentina itself is not perfect, with low efficiency and poor credit of the business administrations. The infrastructure development should also be strengthened. Third, there are great differences between the two countries in terms of corporate culture, communication, business management, labor system, and so on. To overcome these difficulties, Chinese enterprises need to strengthen their work in three dimensions. First, a good job must be done of information gathering, research and early assessment. A detailed inspection of the project must be done to fully estimate the problems that may arise. Second, a sense of risk is necessary, the prevention must be well in advance, and risks must be avoided and controlled. Third, Chinese enterprises should seek the integration into the local community, strengthen social responsibility and improve the "soft power" of the companies by ways of the localization of management, hiring local workers, and participating in public and cultural activities,.

China should attach importance to the issues of the structure of trade and investment that has been the concern of Argentina. In recent years, some scholars in Argentina defined the relationship between Argentina and China, using the "periphery center" theory of the known economist Raul Prebisch, or "North–South relations", deeming that the rising Chinese demand for raw materials led to prosperity for the trade of agricultural products, but undermined the industrial competitiveness. They proposed that Argentina should no longer sell non-renewable energies in order to achieve modernization of its own. Although this view is unfair, and is not in line with the *status quo* of the development of the Sino-Argentine relations, but the issues raised are indeed worthy of attention. One is how to achieve the shared interests and the balance of interests; the second is how to avoid contradictions and conflicts between the two countries in the process of the industrialization of both countries. These two issues are to be considered by the Chinese authorities. The diversification of cooperation may be a solution. In other words, China and Argentina should continue to expand the scope of cooperation on the basis of the existing cooperation, deepen cooperation in the high-end areas of manufacturing, high-tech industries, development and utilization of new energies, finance, and commerce, so as to help the bilateral economic and trade relations to develop in depth.

Chapter 3

Brazilian Economy and the Sino-Brazilian Economic and Trade Relations

Yang Zhimin

Brazil is the largest country in Latin America, with an area of 8.547 million square kilometers and a population of 198 million (2012). Brazil is known to the world for its resources — in recent years rich marine reserves have been found enriching the variety of its resources. During the stage of the import substitution industrialization between the 1930s and the 1970s, Brazil had developed into a new industrial country with a relatively complete industrial system. In the last 20 years of the 20th century, Brazil experienced an economic downturn — from 1981 to 1990, its average annual economic growth rate was 1.6%, and from 1991 to 2000, its average annual economic growth rate was 2.6%. At the same time, Brazil had carried out a large-scale economic reform, and realized the transformation from inward to outward development and the transition from the system of state-led economy to the market economy. Since the beginning of the 21st century, driven by the boom of the export of primary products, the flourishing domestic demand, and active investments, Brazil has been in the process of significant accelerating economic growth, becoming not only one of the BRIC (Brazil, Russia, India, and China) countries, but also the sixth largest economy in the world.

Section 1 The Vast Territory and Abundant Resources of Brazil

The population of Brazil ranks the fifth in the world, but the population density is only 22 people per square kilometers, being one of the countries with the smallest population density in the world. From this point of view, Brazil is a country with vast land and few people.

At the same time, Brazil has a wealth of mineral, forest, land, water, and other natural resources. Therefore, Brazil without doubt has a vast territory and abundant resources.

I. Agricultural and Forestry Resources

Brazil has a vast territory and abundant land resources. According to statistics, Brazil covers a land area of 851.488 million hectares, of which the agricultural area is 275.03 million hectares, and the forest area is 517.3276 million hectares. In terms of land use, the permanent arable land area covers 7.1 million hectares, accounting for 0.84%; the arable land area is 0.07193 million hectares, accounting for 8.5%; the permanent grassland and pasture area covers 196 million hectares, accounting for 23.17%; the rest land area is 53.5844 million hectares, accounting for 6.33%, and the forest area is 517.3276 million hectares, accounting for 61.15%. In 2010, the total population of Brazil was 195 million. The agricultural population was 21.074 million, among which the female labor force was 2.71 million, and the male labor force was 8.339 million.[1]

Brazil is one of the world's leading producers and exporters of agricultural and livestock products. Its main agricultural products and their production, the three kinds of main livestock products and their production are listed in Tables 3.1–3.3.

Brazil is extremely rich in forest resources, with the world's largest tropical rain forest and an area of 544 million hectares, covering about 64% of its land area. In its natural forest area of

[1] FAO database, http://faostat3.fao.org/home/index.html#VISUALIZE_BY_AREA.

Table 3.1 Brazilian Main Agricultural Products in 2011 (In Order of Production, Tons)

No.	Agricultural Products	Value ($1,000)	Note	Production	Note
1	Sugar cane	23,885,831	*	734,006,000	
2	Soybean	18,160,269	*	74,815,400	
3	Corn	2,959,193	*	55,660,400	
4	Milk (whole, fresh)	9,914,191	*	32,091,000	
5	Cassava	1,328,863	*	25,441,700	
6	Orange	3,828,654	*	19,811,100	
7	Rice	3,695,030	*	13,477,000	
8	Local chicken	15,726,308	*	11,040,600	F
9	Local beef	24,962,227	*	9,240,560	Fc
10	Banana	2,064,206	*	7,329,470	
11	Wheat	837,047	*	5,690,040	
12	Tomato	1,632,235	*	4,416,650	
13	Potato	615,798	*	3,917,230	
14	Dried beans	1,972,006	*	3,435,370	
15	Local pork	4,962,690	*	3,228,310	Fc
16	Cottonseed	1,031,199	*	3,194,550	*
17	Coconut	325,488	*	2,943,650	
18	Fresh vegetable	533,254	*	2,829,820	Im
19	Green coffee	2,901,245	*	2,700,440	
20	Pineapple	660,771	*	2,318,120	

Note: *Non-official data, Fc: Estimate of FAO, F: Calculated value, Im: Replacement method data of FAO.
Source: FAO, http://faostat.fao.org/site/339/default.aspx.

about 412 million hectares, 124 million hectares are national forestry, including national forests, the Indian reserves, national parks and other protected areas, while most of the remaining 288 million hectares of forests are privately owned. The artificial forest area is about 6 million hectares, of which the eucalyptus plantation area accounts for 59%, the pine plantation area accounts for 37%, and the other tree species account for 4%. The timber stock volume of the artificial forest is about 775 million cubic meters, out of which 113 million cubic meters of timber can be produced. In addition, the non-timber forest products, such as Brazil nuts, rubber, and palm

Table 3.2 World Ranking of Major Agricultural Products of Brazil in 2011

Ranking	Agricultural Products
1	Orange juice, yerba mate, lint (cotton), vegetable wax, syrup, bagasse, oilseed meal, concentrated orange juice, green coffee, beef products, waffles, centrifugal raw cane sugar, centrifugal sugar, cashew, coffee extract, sisal and other fiber crops, sugar cane, oranges, feed pulp, non-edible alcohol and other dry meat, etc.
2	Cassava, Brazil nuts (shelled), boneless beef (cattle and calves), whole milk powder, pork sausage, refined sugar, pineapple, papaya, beef, Brazil nuts (hulled), beef, black wheat flour, triticale wheat bran, soybean, edible offal of bovine, canned chicken, turkey and oil, etc.
3	Whole milk, condensed pineapple juice, tobacco (untreated), cow fat, castor oil, dried beans, non-centrifugal sugar, etc.

Source: FAO, http://faostat.fao.org/site/339/default.aspx.

cores, are very important, becoming an important source of local employment and income.[2]

II. Oil and Related Resources

The statistical report of BP in 2012 shows that since 1999 the record of oil reserves of Brazil has continued to be refreshed, from 8.2 billion barrels in 1999 to 15.1 billion barrels in 2011 (see Figure 3.1).

At present, the Brazilian oil reserves account for about 0.9% of the total global reserves, ranking the 14th in the world's major oil producing countries, after the United States, Canada, Venezuela, Kazakhstan, Russia, Iran, Iraq, Kuwait, Saudi Arabia, Qatar, the United Arab Emirates, Libya, and Nigeria. Since 2007, giant oil and gas fields have been found in the Southeastern coast of Brazil, with expected oil reserves to be more than 50 billion barrels, and therefore Brazil is expected to enter the world's top 10 oil countries (see Figure 3.2).

In addition, Brazil is the world's most important producer of biofuels, especially bio-ethanol. In the recent 10 years, the development of bio-fuel industry in Brazil has developed rapidly. According to

[2] *Source*: http://www.fao.org/foresty/country/57478/en/bra/.

Table 3.3 Three Kinds of Main Livestock Products of Brazil (2001–2011) (10,000 Tons)

	2001	2002	2003	2004	2005	2006	2007	2008	2009	2010	2011
Whole fresh milk	2,115	2,232	2,294	2,420	2,538	2,619	2,614	2,844	2,909	3,072	3,209
Eggs (10,000)	3,078	3,095	3,142	3,232	3,350	3,521	3,558	3,689	3,844	3,896	4,073
Chicken meat	622	706	777	868	789	818	902	1,024	997	1,073	1,104

Source: FAO database, http://faostatfao.org/home/index.html#VISUALIZE_BY_AREA.

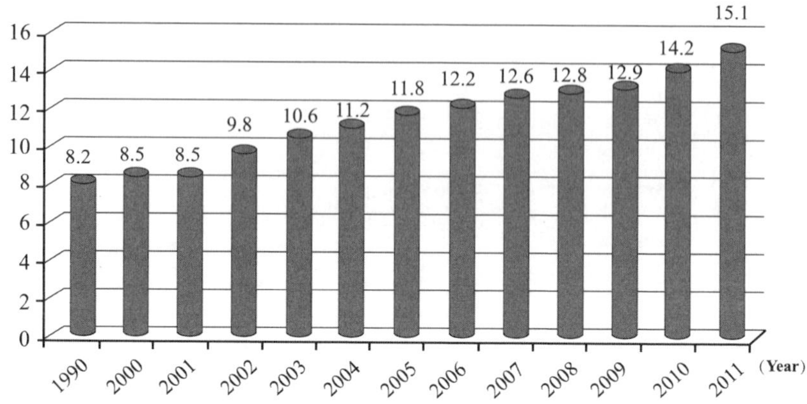

Figure 3.1 Proven Oil Reserves of Brazil (1 billion barrels)
Source: BP, http://www.bp.com/.

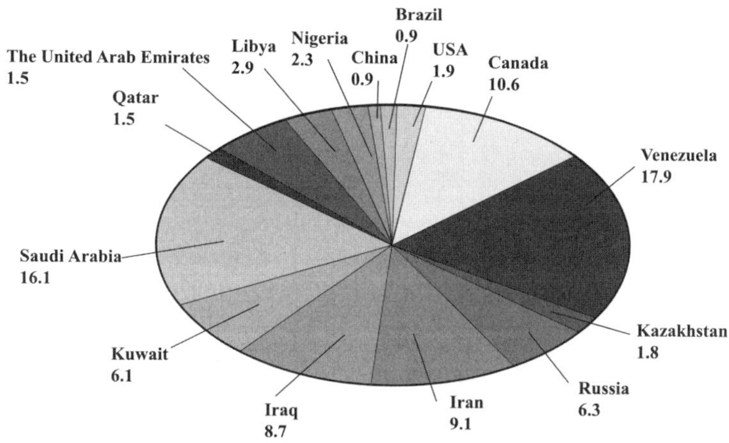

Figure 3.2 Proportion of Oil Reserves of Major Countries (%)
Source: BP, http://www.bp.com/.

statistics, in 2001, Brazil's bio-fuel production was 5.6 million tons; in 2007, it rose to 11.323 million tons, reaching a peak of 15.557 million tons in 2010. Since then, in 2011 the output had declined to 13.196 million tons, dropping 15.3% less than the previous year (see Figure 3.3).

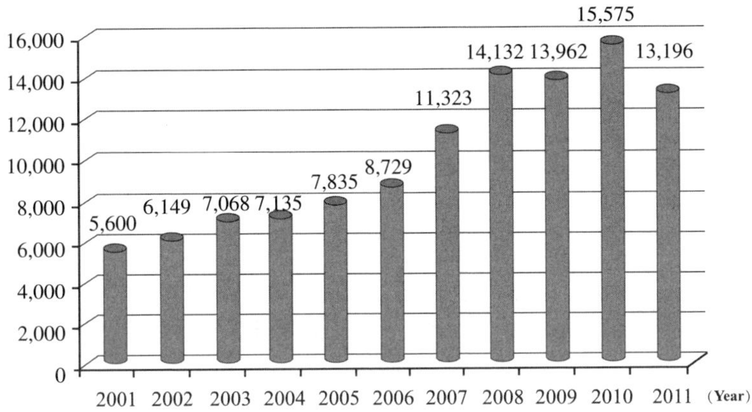

Figure 3.3 Brazil's Annual Bio-fuel Production (1,000 tons)
Source: BP, http://www.bp.com/.

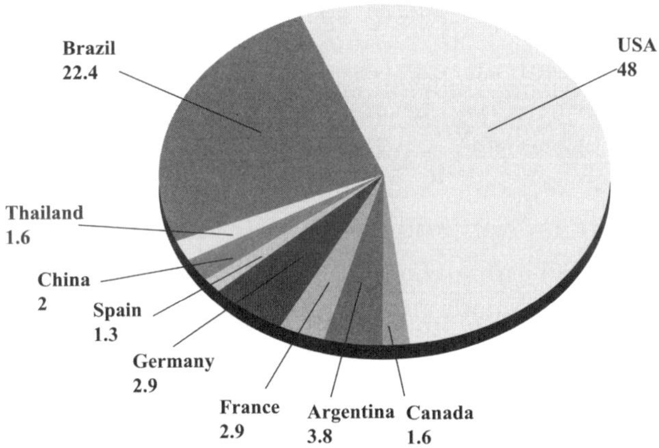

Figure 3.4 Proportion of Brazilian Bio-fuel Production (%)
Source: BP, http://www.bp.com/.

In 2011, as a major producer of bio-fuels, Brazil's share of global production reached 22.4%, after the share of 48% of the United States, resulting in the second place in the world. The rest of the major producers include Canada, Argentina, France, Germany, Spain, China, and Thailand, but the shares of these countries are not more than 5% (see Figure 3.4).

III. Mineral Resources

Brazil has the largest reserves of mineral resources in the world, and is one of the largest producers and exporters. Its proven iron ore reserves are 33.3 billion tons, accounting for 9.8% of the world's total reserves, ranking the fifth in the world, with an annual output of 355 million tons, ranking the second in the world. Its exports are also among the top few in the world. Its nickel reserves account for 98% of the world's total reserves, and other metal reserves such as manganese, bauxite, lead, and tin, account for more than 10% of the total reserves of the world. 4.559 million tons of niobium ore reserves have been ascertained for the world to use for 800 years according to the current speed of consumption. In addition, there are rich mines of chrome ore, gold ore, and asbestos. The proven reserves of coal mines account for 10.1 billion tons, but with very low grade.[3]

1. Bauxite

The total world bauxite reserves are 34 billion tons. With 3.8 billion tons of metallurgical bauxite reserves, Brazil ranks the fifth largest in the world. The world's top four countries of the reserves are Australia, Guyana, Vietnam, and Jamaica. At the same time, Brazil is the world's third largest producing country of bauxite ore — in 2010, its production reached 31.7 million tons, accounting for 15% of the global output. The main production enterprises of bauxite ore in Brazil are MRN (accounting for 52% of the national output), Vale (12%), CBA (11%), Mineracao Curimbaba (8.4%), and other enterprises (16.6%), located mainly in the state of Para (85%), Minas Gerais (14%), and other areas (1%).

2. Kaolin

Global reserves of kaolin are estimated to be 15 billion tons, mainly in four countries (95% of the world's reserves), in which the United States, Brazil, Ukraine, and India account for 53%, 28%, 7%, and 7%, respectively. The estimated reserves of Brazil are 9.4 billion

[3]Business Office of Chinese Embassy in Brazil, http://br.mofcom.gov.cn/article/ddgk/zwdili/200905/20090506245659.shtml.

tons. Brazil is the sixth largest producer of kaolin in the world. Its production in 2010 accounted for 7.8% of the total global output. The United States is the largest producer. The main production enterprises of kaolin in Brazil are Imerys Rio Capim Caulim SA (52%), Caulim da Amazonia SA (CAD AM/Vale, 24%), Para Pigmentos SA (PPSA/Imerys, 19%), and other enterprises (5%). In 2010, the amount of Brazilian kaolin exports reached $280 million, an increase of 11% more than in the previous year. The Brazilian kaolin is mainly exported to Belgium (21%), the United States (20%), Japan (14%), the Netherlands (13%), Finland (11%), and other regions (21%).

3. Copper Mines

Brazil's copper reserves have 17.3 million tons, mainly distributed in the states of Para, Goias, Bahia, Alagoas and Ceará, and the ratios of reserves are 83%, 7%, 5%, 3%, and 2%, respectively. Brazil is the 15th largest copper producer in the world, with a production capacity of 0.213 million tons in 2010. The main production enterprises are Vale (61%), Mineracao Maraca (Yamana, 29%), and Mineracao Caraiba (10%).

4. Tin Mines

Brazil tin (contained Tin) reserves, ranking the fourth in the world, accounting for 11% of the total reserves, is the world's sixth largest producer of tin ore. In 2010, its tin production was 12,000 tons, accounting for 4.6% of the global output (261,000 tons) of the year. The main tin ore production enterprises in Brazil are Mineracao Taboca (66%), Coopersanta (20%) and other enterprises (14%). They are mainly distributed in the states of Amazon and Rondonia, whose outputs account for 60% and 40%, respectively.

5. Iron Ores

Brazil's iron ore reserves rank the fourth in the world, with 29 billion tons (global reserves are 160 billion tons). The iron content of the Hematite iron ore in the state of Para is as high as 60% and that of the Itabirite iron ore in the state of Minas Gerais is 50%. Brazil is the second largest producer of iron ore in the world. According to statistics, in 2010, its output reached 372 million tons, accounting for 15% of the global output (240 million tons) of the year. The main Brazilian iron ore production enterprises and their production proportions are: VALE (81.7%), SAMARCO (6.6%), CSN (2.9%), MMX (1.03%), NAMISA (0.9%), and other enterprises (6.8%).

6. Gold Mines

Brazil's gold reserves are 1,590 tons, accounting for 3.3% of the total global reserves, mainly distributed in the states of Para (41.5%), Minas Gerais (37%), Goias (6.5%), Bahia (6.3%), and other regions (8.%). Brazil is the world's 12th largest gold producer — in 2010, its annual yield was about 58 tons. The main gold production enterprises are Kinross (29%), Anglo Gold Ashanti (22%), Yamana Gold (17%), Garimposor Gold Digging (12%), Jaguar Mining (7%), and other enterprises (13%). The major gold producing area is Minas Gerais (64%), Goias (11%), Bahia (11%), and Para (3%).

7. Niobium Ores

Brazil is the world's largest country of niobium reserves, with reserves of 8.42 tons. They are distributed mainly in the states of Minas Djilas (75.08%), and Amazon (21.34%).

8. Other Minerals

Brazil is the world's fifth largest country of nickel reserves and the 10th largest producer. Its reserves amount to 8.7 million tons, accounting for 12% of the global reserves. With 235 million tons of manganese reserve, mainly distributed in the state of Minas Gerais, Brazil is the world's second largest producer of manganese. Out of only 30% of the land area of Brazil, 309,000 tons of uranium reserve have been ascertained, ranking the seventh in the world. It is estimated that the total reserve of uranium is up to 800,000 tons. With the zinc reserve of 650,000 tons (global reserves are 200 million tons), Brazil is the 12th largest producer of zinc in the world.

Table 3.4 Global Status of Brazilian Mineral Resources

Production and Type of Brazilian Mineral Resources				
Global Export Status of Mineral Resources (Strategically Significant)	Available for Export	Self-sufficient Minerals	Minerals to be Imported	Minerals Depending on External Sources (Strategically Significant)
Niobium (No.1)	Nickel	Limestone		Coking coal
Iron ore (No.1)	Magnesium	Industrial jewels		Potassium
Manganese (No.2)	Kaolin	Titanium		
Tantalum (No.2)	Tin			
Graphite (No.3)	Vermiculite	Copper	Phosphate	Sulfur
Bauxite (No.2)	Chromium	Tungsten	Diatomite	Tombarthite
Ornamental stones	Gold	Mica	Zinc	

Source: Brazil Mining Association (IBRAM), *Mining Sector is Brazil 2011*, http://www.ibram.org.br/.

Brazil's mineral resources can be divided into four categories: the world's major export minerals, mineral resources available for export, self-sufficient mineral resources and imported external minerals. Among them, the first and last categories of minerals have an important strategic significance for Brazil itself because the first category affects the global market and the last relies heavily on imports. (see Table 3.4)

Brazil is an important seller in the global mining industry, but it also has a significant reliance on the import of the mineral resources that greatly affects its economy. For example, Brazil is the fourth largest fertilizer consumer in the world, consuming an equivalent to 2% of the world's fertilizer production, and 91% of the potassium which is crucial to fertilizer industry and 51% of phosphate need to be imported.[4]

[4]Brazil Minerals Association (IBRAM), *Mining Sector in Brazil 2011*, http://www.ibram.org.br/.

Section 2 The Industrial Structure of Brazil

Over the past 10 years, many factors have promoted the growth of the domestic investment and Foreign Direct Investment (FDI) in Brazil. First, the export of bulk agricultural and mining commodities has boomed; second, a lot of oil resources continue to have been discovered; third, the government has implemented active industrial policies, emphasizing the development of the production and export of high value-added products; fourth, the climax of infrastructure construction came about to meet the 2014 football World Cup and the 2016 Summer Olympic Games. The active investment situation has not only promoted the economic growth (average annual economic growth rate of 2007–2011 is 4.2%), but also brought about new changes in the development trend of industrial structures.

I. Brazilian National Economic Structure

According to the United Nations Committee on Trade and Development (UNCTAD) statistics, in the Brazilian national economic structure, in 2001, the output values of agriculture, industry, and service industry were respectively \$28.438 billion, \$128.718 billion, and \$319.464 billion; in 2010, the output values of the above three industries increased respectively to \$103.379 billion, \$479.465 billion, and \$1.2 trillion (see Table 3.5).

Although the output values of agriculture, industry and service industry had increased rapidly in the 10 years from 2001 to 2010, the proportions of each individual industry in the national economy had remained stable. According to calculation, in 2001, the proportions of the three industries were 6%, 27%, and 67%, respectively; in 2010, they were 6%, 27%, and 67%, respectively (see Figure 3.5).

In order to further investigate the various specific sectors in the Brazilian national economy, we will compare the different proportions of economic activities in the gross domestic product (GDP). Specifically, we will take 2011 as an example, using the data released by the UN Economic Commission for Latin America. We can see that in the composition of Brazil's GDP that year, the social and personal services accounted for 30.9%, financial intermediary 15.3%, manufacturing industry 14.6%, wholesale and retail trade

Table 3.5 Composition of Brazil's GDP (2001–2010) ($ Million, Current Price)

Year	2001	2002	2003	2004	2005	2006	2007	2008	2009	2010
Agriculture	28,438	28,849	35,295	39,381	43,199	51,287	65,364	83,038	83,616	103,379
Industry	128,718	117,933	133,065	171,539	221,527	269,202	326,790	392,627	348,173	479,465
Service	319,464	289,167	309,504	358,718	492,036	615,035	782,879	931,334	937,599	1,201,337

Note: According to a statistical method based on UNCTAD, agriculture includes farming, forestry, animal husbandry and fishery; industry includes mining and stone mining, manufacturing industry, electric power, gas, water supply, and construction; services include all the other economic activities.
Source: UNCTAD, http://unctadstat.unctad.org/TableViewer/tableView.aspx.

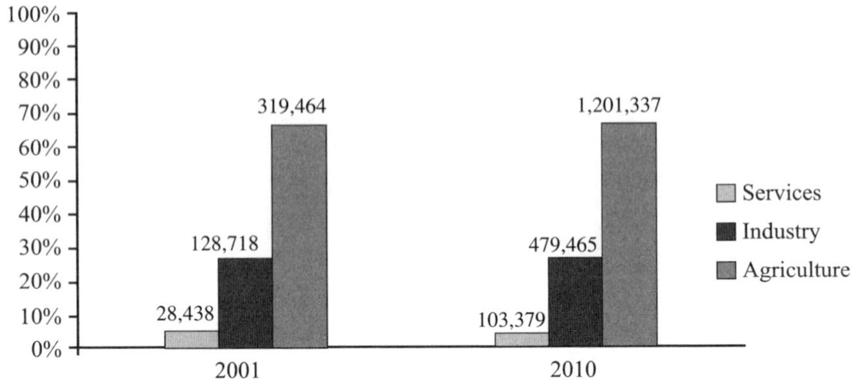

Figure 3.5 Proportions of the Production of Brazilian Services, Industry, and Agriculture

Source: UNCTAD, http://unctadstat.unctad.org/TableViewer/tableView.aspx.

12.6%, transportation, storage, and communications industry 8.2%, agriculture, forestry, animal husbandry and fisheries 5.5%, mineral and quarry industries 4.1%, and electricity, gas and water supply accounted for 3.1% (see Table 3.6).

II. Strategic Industries of Brazil[5]

At present, the Brazil government has clearly proposed to develop the strategic industries, including oil and gas, biotechnology, tourist hotels, mineral resources, electronic components, agriculture and cattle industry, and industry. The government of Brazil has formulated specific policies to encourage and support the recovery and development of the above industries, and to encourage foreign investors to enter the industries. The specific plans to promote the strategic industry sectors can be seen in Table 3.7.

1. The Oil and Gas Industry

The discovery of the sub-salt oil resources in Brazil in 2007 has brought about a great opportunity for the coastal zone of Brazil, which is about 800 kilometers long. It is reported that 72% of the

[5] *Source*: http://www.brasil.gov.br/.

Table 3.6 Production and Proportion of Various Economic Activities in Brazilian GDP in 2011 ($ Million, Current Price; %)

No.	Economic Activities	Production	Proportion
1	Public administration, national defense, social security, education, health and social work, and other community, social and personal service activities	651,583	30.9
2	Financial intermediaries, real estate, leasing and business activities	323,334	15.3
3	Manufacturing	308,125	14.6
4	Wholesale and retail trade, goods repair, hotels and restaurants	266,977	12.6
5	Transportation, storage and communications	172,514	8.2
6	Construction	121,989	5.8
7	Agriculture, forestry, animal husbandry and fishery	115,167	5.5
8	Mineral sources and stone mining	86,036	4.1
9	Electric power, gas and water supply	64,994	3.1

Source: ECLAC, http://interwp.cepal.org/cepalstat/WEB_ce-palstat/Perfil_nacional_economico.asp? Pais=BRA (idioma=i).

area of the sub-salt oil resources (about 107,200 square kilometers) will be tendered in the next several rounds. The Brazilian government expects that over 80 oil companies will invest in them; in the next 10 years, the oil field will absorb $330 billion of investment, and the vast majority of these enterprises will be foreign companies.

In fact, many foreign enterprises had participated in the first round of the project. Some of the globally well-known oil enterprises have set up R&D centers in Brazil, such as the German Semens and many American companies like Baker Hughe, GE, Halliburton, IBM, Schlumberger, and FMC Technologies. The Danish Maersk Oil and Spanish Repsol announced that the size of their businesses in Brazil had reached $3 billion. The well-known Swiss ABB Group with the world's leading energy technology announced plans for the construction of drilling rigs for the oil wells of Brazil; and some Russian and

Table 3.7 Brazil's Plan of Strategic Industries and Incentives

No.	Strategic Measure	Plan	Policy Maker	Measures
1	Oil and gas			
2	Biotechnology	Biotechnology Development Policy	Federal government of Brazil	To support the industrialization of biological technology and promote the development of economy and society
3	Tourist hotel	World Cup Tourism Plan (Pro-CupTourism)	Brazilian National Economic and Social Development Bank	Renovation, expansion, upgrading and construction of hotel facilities
4	Mineral resources	National Mining Planning of 2030 (PNM2030)	Federal government of Brazil	Strategic tools to guide the long-term policy of mining industry
5	Electronic parts	Semiconductor and Display Industry Development Support Plan	Federal government of Brazil	Financial support, helping financing arrangements
		One Student, One Computer Plan (ProUCA)		Tax reduction and other preferential measures
		National Broadband Special Program (REPNBL)		
		Special Support Policies for the Development of Digital TV Technology and Equipment		
6	Agriculture and cattle raising	Brazil Agricultural Enterprise Plan for 2010/2011–2020/2021	Ministry of Agriculture of the federal government of Brazil	Growth planning
		Harvest Plan		Credit support
		Agricultural Insurance		Reducing the loss of planting and breeding
7	Industry	Major Planning of Brazil, Strong Brazil Plan (Plan Brasil Maior)	Ministry of Development, Industry and Foreign Trade of the federal government of Brazil	Investment, innovation, trade support and a package of measures to protect the domestic industry and the market

Source: Data from the website of Brazilian government, http//www.brasil.gov.br/.

Chinese oil and gas companies also plan to set up representative offices in Brazil.[6]

2. The Biotechnology Industry

At present, Brazil has 237 biotechnology companies, 63% of which were established in the past 10 years. Brazil's development of biotechnology is designed to enhance human health and animal health, as well as for the application of reagents, agriculture, environmental protection and bio-energy. The application of biotechnology in the bio-energy area has been effective, which will be able to substitute for fossil energy and bring a reasonable price. Since 1980s, Brazil began to invest in related technology and personnel training, to support the industrialization of the technology through the introduction of the "Biotechnology Development Policy", and to promote economic and social development. At the same time, in the field of agriculture, the Brazilian Agricultural Research Corporation has spent 20 years on carrying out biological technology research, and made progress in medical treatment, the development of new vaccines, livestock asexual reproduction, application of the breeding of molecular markers, the development of the genetically modified crop farming and bio-pesticides.

It is reported that the Brazilian government had provided 10 billion reais for biotechnology enterprises. 70% of the enterprises relied on the operation of the fund, of which the vast majority are small and micro-enterprises. 77% of the Brazilian biological enterprises need to import reagents, and 64% of the enterprises need to import equipment. In 2011, the Brazilian Biotechnology Association (Brazi BrBiotec) was established to play a role in the organization and leadership of the industry.

3. The Tourism Hotel Industry

According to the statistics of Brazilian tourism agencies, in 2011 Brazil received 5.4 million foreign tourists, an increase of 5.3% than

[6] *Source*: http://www.brasil.gov.br/para/invest/strategic-sectors.

in 2010. As Brazil is to host the 2014 Football World Cup and the 2016 Summer Olympic Games, the number of visitors will be increasing steadily. It is expected that 8 million visitors will have arrived at the opening of the 2014 World Cup, and in the place where the 2016 Olympic Games is to be held, 600,000 visitors will be ushered in in the first month.

In order to meet the needs of tourists brought about by the two major events, the federal government of Brazil has taken measures to enhance the country's hotel system. Among them, the Brazilian National Economic and Social Development Bank (BNDES) — the largest development bank of Latin America — launched the "World Cup Tourism Plan" (ProCup tourism) to promote the transformation, expansion, upgrading and construction of the hotel facilities of the host cities of the World Cup and other cities. For example, the city of Aparecida 179 kilometer north of Sao Paulo — one of the host cities of the Games — has become one of the beneficiaries of the tourism plan. This religious tourism resort has obtained the financial support to build a 330-room hotel. In addition, the Gloria Hotel located in Rio De Janeiro City also has benefited from the program. Opened in 1922, the hotel is the second largest hotel in Brazil. With the funds obtained from BNDES, at the original site, the hotel has been rebuilt from the aspects of the international standards of safety and sustainability to meet the requirements of the upcoming accommodation of the two events. The government of Brazil required that from 2011 to 2014 the federal bank should provide funds to the private sectors reaching 14 billion reais. According to this, the Brazilian Ministry of Tourism expected that by 2014 the number of hotels in Brazil can reach 35,394. At the same time, Brazil encouraged foreign enterprises to invest in Brazil's tourism industry. According to the information of Brazilian Department of Tourism, the current foreign capitals can be invested through three ways: investment in fixed assets, securities, and direct investments. According to the laws of Brazil, the inflow and outflow of foreign capitals only need to be registered, and foreign direct investments shall be entitled to the national treatment.

4. The Mineral Resource Industry

The mineral resource industry is of strategic significance for Brazil to develop. In recent years, the huge demands for mineral resources from the international market and the continued high prices of mineral products have provided a new impetus for the development of this industrial sector.

According to statistics, the mining and mineral processing industry together accounted for 5% of Brazil's GDP. However, from the perspective of foreign trade, the trade of iron and steel, non-ferrous metals and non-metallic mineral products accounted for 21% of the exports and for 13% of the imports, accounting for 43% of the trade surplus. In order to promote the development of the mining sector, the Brazilian government introduced the *2030 National Mining Planning* (PNM2030), as strategic guidelines for the long-term development of mining to ensure that the industry would become the pillar industry of sustainable development in the next few decades. The planning also stressed the strengthening of the management of mineral resources to constantly improve the added values of the products and the more reasonable distribution of the interests of the mining sector.

Since Brazil has made remarkable achievements in its economic reform and its domestic macroeconomic situation is relatively stable, with great potential and unique advantages in mineral resources, it is expected that its mining sector will continue to be a key area to attract foreign investment. It is estimated that in the next five years the Brazilian iron ore industry will attract foreign investment of more than $32 billion.

5. The Electronic Component Industry

Brazil is one of the world's five largest personal computer markets, with annual mobile phone sales reaching 70 million units. Such a huge demand makes it one of the most attractive centers for semiconductor and display manufacturers. In order to reduce its dependence on imports and to further increase its domestic production, the Brazilian government had introduced a series of plans to encourage the production.

The electronic component industry has a broad and important influence on the development of the industries such as aviation, automobile and medical equipment, and therefore Brazil has adopted the *Support Plan for the Development of Semiconductor and Display Industries*. The plan provided support for those enterprises engaged in research and development and sales in Brazil, promising the commitment by the Brazil National Economic and Social Development Bank to provide financing for the design and implementation of relevant projects. The scheme was also applicable to the manufacturing companies that invested in the semiconductors and displays as electronic equipment. In April 2012, the program was extended to duty-free areas of domestic purchase and import of the necessities required for the investment of the semiconductor industry, covering important strategic investors of the semiconductor and display industry, such as the suppliers of computer motherboards, LCD and LED displays.

The Brazilian federal government also enacted the *One Student, One Computer Program* (ProUCA) by 2015. The plan canceled the taxes and social contributions, e.g., the industrial product tax (IPI) and the payment of social integration scheme (PIS), the wealth plan for the civil servants (PASEP), the social security financing (COFINS) and the economic field regulation (CIDE), and the raw materials and intermediate products that portable computer manufacturers obtained for sales. The plan means that the fiscal income of the Brazilian government will be reduced.

In addition, the Brazilian government has also developed other special plans, e.g., the *National Broadband Special Plan* (REPNBL) to speed up the development of communications network and promote the development of domestic industry and technology, the *Special Support Policy for the Development of Digital TV Technology and Equipment*, and so on. Similarly, the state has given tax reliefs for the above-mentioned industries to import capital goods and input products.

6. The Agriculture and Cattle Raising Industry

According to the *2010/2011–2020/2021 Brazilian Agricultural Enterprise Plan*, the production of livestock and crops (soybeans, maize, wheat, and beans) will be increased from 143 million tons in 2011 to 175 million tons in 2021, with 32 million tons more than the current Brazilian yields. Cotton is expected to increase 47.8%, soybean yield 25.9%, beef, pork, and poultry will be increased by 26.5% than in 2011. At the same time, through the *Harvest Plan*, the Brazil government provided credit loans for the purchase of agricultural equipment with interest rates lower than the market in order to encourage the expansion of the agricultural sector. Meanwhile, there were other measures, such as the protection for the planting industry and livestock breeding industry through providing the "Agricultural Insurance". In addition, the Brazilian Agricultural Research Corporation (Embrapa) also actively provided technical support for the production sector.

7. The Industry

The Brazilian industrial system is relatively complete, especially the relatively complete manufacturing sector, but the current international competitiveness of the industry is relatively weak. In other words, the adjustment of industrial structure has lagged behind. In the recent 10 years, the Brazilian government has introduced some policies or plans, trying to identify a number of key industries, especially the strategic emerging industries, to achieve the whole industrial upgrading, increasing the added values of the products of the industrial sectors, in order to improve the international competitiveness of the industry. In November 2003, the Lula government promulgated the *Policy Guidelines for Industry, Technology and Foreign Trade* (*Directrices de Politica Industrial, Tecnologica y de Comercio Exterior*, PITCE), identifying the semiconductor, software, pharmaceuticals and capital goods as the four major strategic industries, and the established the Brazilian Industrial Development Bureau as the coordination mechanism for the implementation of the industrial policy.

In May 2008, the Lula Administration also announced the *Production and Development Policy* (*Politica de Desarrollo Productivo*, PDP), specifically proposing 19 key industries. In addition to the ones mentioned above, among the 19 industries, the automobile manufacturing, capital goods, textiles and clothing, wood and furniture, cosmetics, shipbuilding, aviation, plastics, paper and pulp belong to the manufacturing industry. In August 2011, the Rousseff Administration launched the *Strong Brazil Plan* (Brasil Maior Plan, 2011–2014), once again stressing the development of key industrial sectors, in particular, resources and technology intensive industries.

The above-mentioned documents issued by the Brazilian federal government reflects its emphasis on the adjustment of industrial structure and its positive attitude toward the formulation of the industrial policy and industrial planning, but this does not mean that Brazil has made much progress in its adjustment of the industrial structure. The main reason is that the *Policy Guide of Industry, Technology and Foreign Trade* (hereinafter referred to as the *Guide*) is just a rough document. The *Production Development Policy* was put forward for the further implementation of the *Guide*, hence more specific, but no sooner had this file been introduced than came the impact of the 2008 international financial crisis, and the main focus of the Brazilian government was steered to take counter-cyclical policies to deal with the crisis and therefore the adjustment of industry did not receive enough attention. The *Strong Brazil Plan* itself is only a short-term plan. The main background of its introduction is that the currency Real was in the process of strong appreciation in Brazil, which was extremely unfavorable for the export of manufactured goods. Therefore, the plan focused more on how to improve the technology, knowledge content and added values of industrial products to improve the competitiveness of the export, and what measures should be taken to limit more external industrial products to enter the domestic market.

In summary, it can be said that in the next period, the adjustment of industrial structure will become the focus of economic work in Brazil because it is related to the international competitiveness of Brazil and the overall level of its economic development. This outlook provides an important opportunity for qualified foreign enterprises to invest in Brazil and to carry out enterprise cooperations and technological cooperations.

III. The Important Economic Sectors

Brazil has not only a vast territory and abundant resources, but also a complete national economic system. In the economic structure of Brazil, agriculture, mining and energy industry, including bio-fuels, are the three major sectors occupying important positions, which form the important pillar industries of the national economy. For this reason, we will introduce the above three major sectors.

1. The Agricultural Sector[7]

The agriculture and related industries are one of the most important economic activities in Brazil. Agriculture includes farming, animal husbandry and related economic activities. The development speed of the Brazilian agriculture is faster than the world average. According to statistics, the grain production of Brazil accounts for 7% of the world's total output, i.e., out of the 2,300 million tons of the world's grain yield, 160 million tons come from Brazil. Brazil is one of the world's largest exporter of agricultural products.[8]

(1) Production of Major Agricultural Products

According to the statistics of FAO of the United Nations, in 2011, the top 10 of the agricultural products of Brazilia, sorted according to the yield, are as follows: sugarcanes, soybeans, corn, milk, tapioca, oranges, rice, local chicken, local beef and banana. After these top 10, they are respectively: wheat, tomatoes, potatoes, dried beans, local pork, cottonseeds, coconuts, fresh vegetables, coffee, pineapples, watermelons, eggs, milo, papaya, and cashew. See Table 3.1 in the first section of this chapter.

[7]FAO database, http://faostat3.fao.org.
[8]*Source*: http://www.brasil.gov.br/.

(2) Major Exports of Agricultural Products

In 2010, according to the rank of export quantity, the top 10 of Brazilian agricultural products are as follows: soybeans, centrifugal sugar, soybean cakes, corn, refined sugar, chicken, green coffee, soybean oil, orange juice, and wheat. The quantity and amount of the main 24 kinds of agricultural products exported by Brazil are shown in Table 3.8.

Table 3.8 Number and Amount of 24 Major Agricultural Products Exported by Brazil in 2010

Product	Number (Ton)	Note	Amount ($1,000)	Note	Price (Dollar/Ton)
Soybean	25,860,785	*	11,042,996		427
Centrifugal sugar	20,938,703		9,306,851		444
Soybean cake	13,668,599		4,719,373		345
Corn	10,815,275		2,214,956		205
Refined sugar	7,060,788		3,454,554		489
Chicken meat	3,460,760		5,789,272		1,673
Green coffee	1,791,064		5,182,002		2,893
Soybean oil	1,559,776		1,347,663		864
Orange juice	1,510,776		1,089,227		721
Wheat	1,324,208		226,872		171
Boneless beef (cattle and calves)	947,659		3,853,303		4,066
Feed pulp	663,213		98,809		149
Ginned cotton	512,498		821,547		1,603
Untreated tobacco	493,003		2,706,674		5,490
Concentrated orange juice	466,861		685,512		1,468
Pork	394,607		1,101,649		2,792
Canned chicken	250,619		738,468		2,947
Dried meat	190,106		553,391		2,911
Other melons	177,828		121,970		686
Bean bran	168,674		54,151		321
Banana	139,540		45,269		324
Mango	124,380		119,645		962
Beef products	124,266		497,868		4,006
Kitchen waste	120,915		115,756		957

Source: FAO, http://faostat3.fao.org/home/index.html,VISUALIZE_TOP-20.
*: Non-official data.

Brazil is an important exporter of agricultural products in the world. In 2010, Brazil was the world's largest exporter of centrifugal sugar, chicken, and green coffee, and one of the largest exporters of soybeans. According to the sorting of the amount in the exports of a single global agricultural product, Brazil's exports of soybeans, centrifugal sugar, chicken, and green coffee reached $11.04 billion, $9.31 billion, $5.79 billion, and $5.18 billion, respectively, ranking the 4th, 8th, 17th, and 20th in the world's exports of single agricultural products.[9]

(3) Major Imports of Agricultural Products

In 2010, the imported agricultural products of Brazil were mainly wheat, malt, wheat flour, corn, barley, frozen potatoes, onions, natural rubber, pears, and beans. The quantity and amount of the first 25 products imported at present are shown in Table 3.9.

2. The Mining Sector[10]

From the beginning of 2000, the huge demand for mineral products in the international market has promoted the rapid growth of the output of Brazil's mineral products. From 2001 to 2011, the output of mineral products increased by 550%, and the output value increased from $7.7 billion to $50 billion (see Figure 3.6).

According to statistics, in 2010 totally there were 7,809 mining companies in Brazil, of which 942 were in the Midwest, 1,258 in the Northeast, 439 in the Northern region, 3,392 in the Southeast and 1,901 in the Southern region.

According to the data of the Brazilian "Compensation Fund for Development of Mineral Resources" (CFEM), in 2010, the states with the largest yields of ore products and their proportions respectively were: Minas Gerais (48%), Para (28%), Goias (5%), Sao Paulo (4%), Bahia (2.7%), Mato Grosso do Sul (1.8%), Sergipe (1.7%), and other states (8.8%). At the same time, the compensation fund for the

[9] *Source*: FAO, http://faostatfao.org/home/index.html#VISUALIZE_TOP-20.

[10] This part of information came from *Brazilian Mineral Economic Information and Analysis in 2011* of the Brazil Mining Association.

Table 3.9 Number and Amount of 25 Major Agricultural Products Imported by Brazil in 2010

Product	Number (Ton)	Amount ($1,000)	Price (Dollar/Ton)
Wheat	6,323,216	1,702,319	269
Malt	845,176	485,502	574
Flour	653,127	249,148	381
Corn	462,539	80,268	174
Barley	295,805	70,079	237
Frozen potato	242,560	211,058	870
Onion (including scallion)	238,490	121,595	510
Natural rubber (dry)	232,161	756,312	3,258
Pear	189,863	189,134	996
Beans (dry)	181,162	135,004	745
Palm kernel oil	176,793	190,330	1,077
Palm oil	155,813	134,130	861
Garlic	153,141	275,561	1,799
Soybeans	117,840	44,792	380
Olive confects	84,810	136,900	1,614
Kitchen waste	82,867	171,997	2,076
Apples	76,879	73,204	952
Wine	75,315	266,434	3,538
Other unnumbered food	68,873	281,327	4,085
Virgin olive oil	52,504	236,916	4,512
Non-alcoholic beverage	47,984	50,061	1,043
Cocoa beans	47,609	147,942	3,107
Tomato paste	46,034	47,628	1,035
Other fruits	42,939	60,475	1,408
Dried peas	41,105	18,596	452

Source: http://faostat3.fao.org/home/index.html#VISUALIZE_TOP_2.

exploitation of mineral resources also created records: 742 million reais in 2009, 1 billion reais in 2010, and 1.3 billion reais in 2011.

From 2006 to 2011, the trade surplus of mineral products increased rapidly, from $6.54 billion to $33 billion, and the proportion of the trade surplus in Brazil increased from 14% to 143% (see Table 3.10).

Currently, the iron ore still is Brazil's export product of the highest income: in 2010 the export value was $28.912 billion, accounting for 81.8% of the value of Brazil's total mineral exports of primary

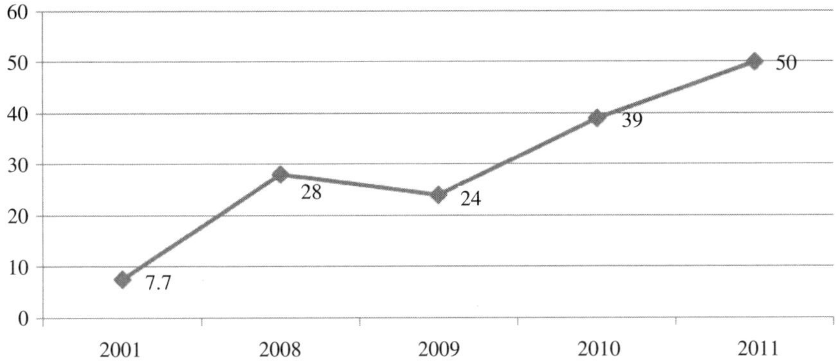

Figure 3.6 Amount of Brazilian Mineral Products (2001–2011) ($ billion)

Note: Data of 2011 are an estimate.
Source: Brazil Mining Association: Brazilian Mineral Economic Information and Analysis in 2011.

Table 3.10 Surpluses of Brazilian Import, Export, and Trade of Mineral Products (2006–2011)

Year	2006	2007	2008	2009	2010	2011
Export ($ million)	11,030	15,196	22,841	18,096	35,360	43,000
Import ($ million)	4,490	5,185	9,729	5,497	7,756	10,000
Surplus ($ million)	6,540	10,011	13,112	12,599	27,604	33,000
Trade surplus ($ billion)	46	40	24	25	20	23
Mineral surplus trade/Commodity trade surplus (%)	14	25	53	50	136	143

Source: Brazil Mining Association, *Brazilian Mineral Economic Information and Analysis in 2011.*

products; in 2011, the export were estimated at $35.7 billion. In addition to the iron ore, the Brazilian export of other major mineral products include: gold, niobium, copper, silica, kaolin, manganese ore, bauxite, tin, lead, and granite, while the imports of the mineral products are mainly coal, potassium chloride, copper, zinc, and sulfur. According to statistics, in 2010 and 2011, the trade surpluses of import and export of Brazil were $27.6 billion and $33.6 billion, respectively (see Table 3.11).

Table 3.11 Import and Export Amount of Mineral Products in Brazil in 2010 and 2011 ($ Million)

Export of Mineral Products	Amount		Import of Mineral Products	Amount	
	2010	2011		2010	2011
Export of primary products	35,360	43,595	Import of primary products	7,756	10,023
Iron ore	28,912	35,745			
Gold bars	1,786	1,988			
Niobium (iron niobium)	1,557	2,034			
			Coal	3,575	5,078
Copper	1,238	1,806			
			Potassium chloride	2,204	2,904
Silicon	460	637			
			Copper	952	1,232
Kaolin	275	258			
			Zinc	157	10
Manganese ore	357	276			
			Sulfur	246	176
Bauxite	270	322			
			Other	623	623
Tin	8	20			
Lead	12	12			
Granite	219	230			
Other	268	268			
Trade surplus	2,010	27,604	2,011	33,572	

Note: Data of 2011 are an estimate.
Source: Brazil Mining Association, *Brazilian Mineral Economic Information and Analysis in 2011.*

Since 2007, every year, the Brazil Mining Association released a report about the investment in the mineral sector in the next five years, i.e., to do statistics and predictions of the investment situation in the mineral industry at a time period of five years. According to the data of the association, from 2007 to 2011, 2008 to 2012, 2009 to 2013, 2010 to 2014, and 2011 to 2015, the investments in the

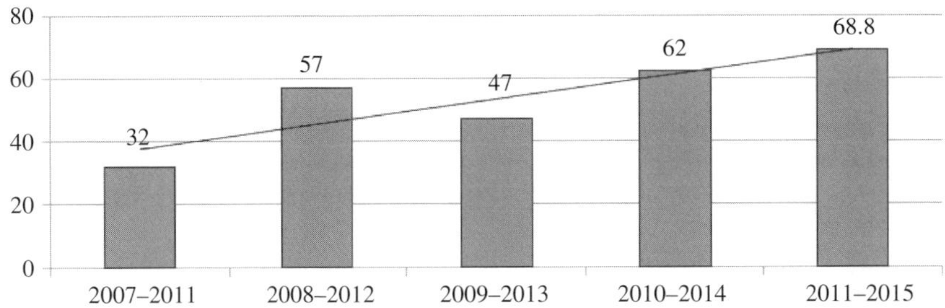

Figure 3.7 Investment in Brazilian Mining Sector ($ billion)

Source: Brazil Mining Association, *Brazilian Mineral Economic Information and Analysis in 2011.*

mineral sector respectively were $32 billion, $57 billion, $47 billion, $62 billion, and $68.8 billion. Except the release of the decline in 2009 of the investment in the five years (2009–2013), (affected by the international financial crisis at the end of 2008), in the investment data released for the next five years, there was always an upward trend (see Figure 3.7).

The Mineral Association of Brazil expected that the amount of investment in the mineral sector from 2011 to 2015 would be $68.8 billion, an increase of 10.5% more than the investment from 2010 to 2014. During that period, most of the investment would be absorbed by the iron ore industry; 63% of the total investment was expected to enter into the mining industry, i.e., the iron ore industry would absorb $44.969 billion. The specific investment flows can be seen from Figure 3.8.

Brazil has increased its investment rapidly in the field of mineral production and processing, while its investment in the exploration is very little. According to statistics, in 2009 and 2010, in the field of mineral exploration Brazil's investment accounted for only 3% of the world's total private investment in mineral exploration; its ratio was not only lower than other big powers, but also lower than the Latin-American Peru and Chile. It is reported that only 30% of the territory of Brazil has been surveyed comprehensively through detection and identification (see Table 3.12).

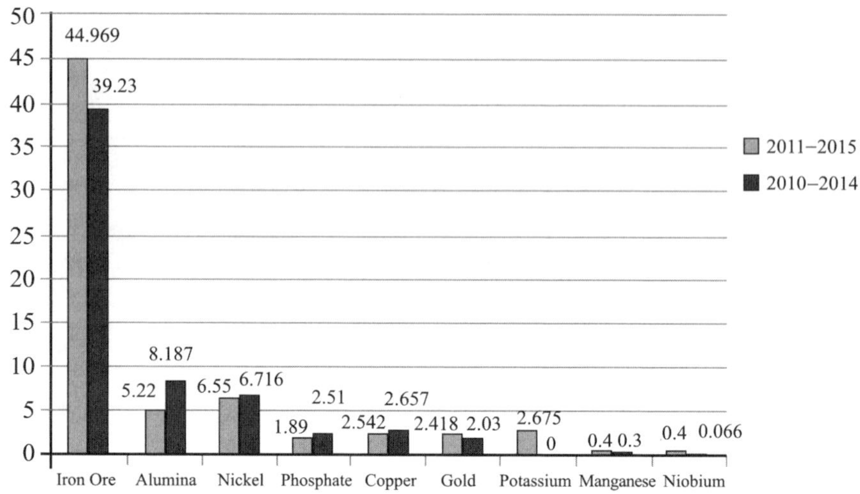

Figure 3.8 Sectors of Brazilian Mineral Investment in 2010–2014 and in 2011–2015 ($ billion)

Source: Brazil Mining Association, *Brazilian Mineral Economic Information and Analysis in 2011.*

Table 3.12 Comparison of Investments in Mineral Exploration in the Global Top 10 Mining Countries ($ Million)

No.	Country	Investment	Investment/ Total Global Mining Exploration (%)
1	Canada	2,033	19
2	Australia	1,284	12
3	USA	856	8
4	Mexico	642	6
5	Peru	535	5
5	Chile	535	5
6	Russia	428	4
6	China	428	4
7	Argentina	321	3
7	Brazil	321	3

Source: The author's summary of Brazil Mining Association, *Brazilian Mineral Economic Information and Analysis in 2011.*

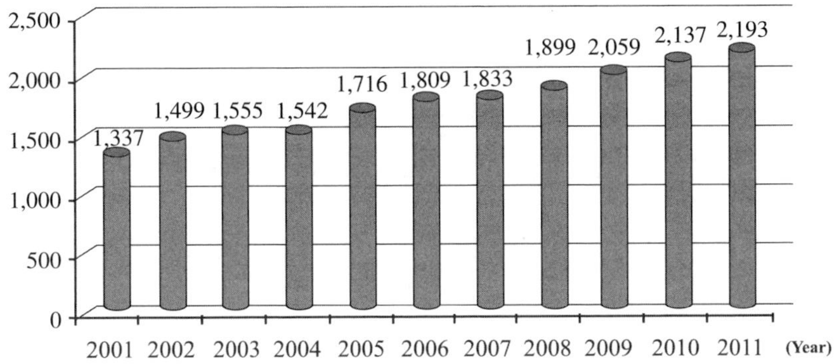

Figure 3.9 Oil Production of Brazil (1,000 barrels/day)

Source: BP, BP Statistical Review of World Energy June 2012, www.bp.com/statisticalreview.

3. The Energy Sector

(1) Oil

According to statistics, in 2011, the Brazilian oil production reached 2.193 million barrels per day, 114.6 million tons per year; compared with 2010, there was an increase of 2.5%. It accounted for 2.9% of the global total output that year, after the United States, Canada, Mexico, Venezuela, Russia, Iran, Iraq, Kuwait, Saudi Arabia, the United Arab Emirates, and China. Its production was equal to that of Nigeria, becoming the 11th largest producer in the world (see Figures 3.9 and 3.10).

In 2011, the oil consumption of Brazil reached 2.653 million barrels per day, 120.7 million tons per year, and a year-on-year increase of 2.3%; its consumption accounted for 3% of the total global oil consumption in the year. In addition, its oil refining capacity was 2.116 million barrels per day, accounting for 2.3% of the total global refining capacity, a growth of 1.1% than the previous year (see Table 3.13).

(2) Natural Gas

By the end of 2011, 500 billion cubic meters of natural gas reserves had been ascertained in Brazil, accounting for 0.2% of the total global reserves. From a global perspective, its natural gas resources are not

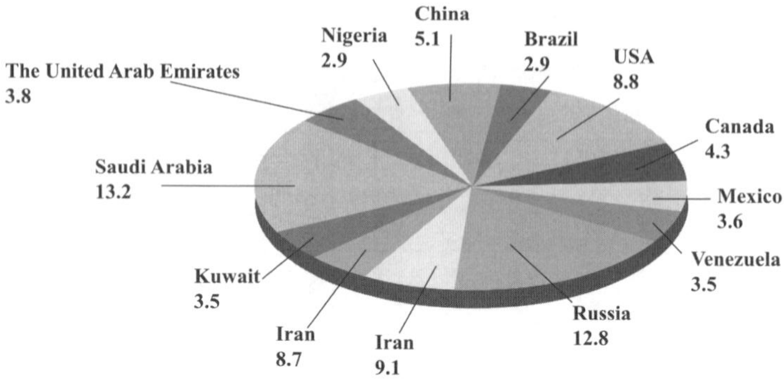

Figure 3.10 Proportions of Oil Production of the Global Major Oil Producers (%)

Source: BP, *BP Statistical Review of World Energy June 2012*, www.bp.com/statisticalreview.

rich; from the output point of view, in 2011 its production reached 16.7 billion cubic meters, an increase of 16.2% compared with the previous year, accounting for 0.5% of the world's total output. In 2011, Brazil's natural gas consumption was 26.7 billion cubic meters, a reduction of 0.3% than the previous year, accounting for 0.8% of the total global consumption. Bolivia is the only source of natural gas import of Brazil — in 2011, the import was 9.7 billion cubic meters. (see Table 3.14)

(3) Bio-fuel

Brazil is the world's leading producer of bio-fuels. In 2011 its bio-fuel production was 13.2 million, accounting for 22.4% of the global production that year, secondary to the United States (28.251 million tons), ranking second in the world. The world's other major bio-fuel producers and their shares of the world's total output are: Germany — 4.8%, Argentina — 3.8%, France — 2.9%, and China — 2%. (see Table 3.15)

Section 3 The Achievement and Enlightenment of Brazil's Economic Reform

A review of Brazil's nearly a 100 years of development tells us that prosperity and crisis always occurred in alternation; therefore,

Table 3.13 Oil Production, Consumption and Refining Capacity of Brazil (2001–2011)

	2001	2002	2003	2004	2005	2006	2007	2008	2009	2010	2011		
											Production	Increase Over the Previous Year (%)	Propor-tion in the World (%)
Production (1,000 barrels/day)	1,337	1,499	1,555	1,542	1,716	1,809	1,833	1,889	2,029	2,137	2,193	2.5	2.9
Consumption (1,000 barrels/day)	2,030	2,005	1,953	2,024	2,070	2,090	2,235	2,395	2,415	2,629	2,653	2.3	3.0
Production (million tons)	70.1	78.6	71.3	80.8	89.3	94.2	95.5	99.2	106.0	111.7	114.6	2.5	2.9
Consumption (million tons)	92.7	91.0	88.6	91.5	93.8	95.0	100.7	107.9	108.0	118.0	120.7	2.3	3.0
Refining capacity (1,000 barrels/day)	1,849	1,854	1,915	1,915	1,916	1,916	1,935	2,045	2,093	2,093	2,116	1.1	2.3

Source: BP, *BP Statistical Review of World Energy June 2012*, www.bp.com/statisticalreview.

Table 3.14 Natural Gas Reserves, Production, Consumption and Import of Brazil (2001–2011) (Billion Cubic Meters)

											2011		
Year	2001	2002	2003	2004	2005	2006	2007	2008	2009	2010	Production	Increase Over the Previous Year (%)	Proportion in the World (%)
Production	7.7	9.2	10	11	11	11.3	11.2	13.7	11.7	14.4	16.7	16.2	0.5
Consumption	11.9	14.1	15.8	18.8	19.7	20.8	21.1	24.6	19.8	26.8	26.7	–0.3	0.8
Trade											9.7		

Source: Summary of Bp statistical data, *BP Statistical Review of World Energy June 2012*, www.bp.com/statisticalreview.

Table 3.15 Production of Biofuels of Brazil (2001–2011) (1,000 Tons)

							2011		
Year	2001	2003	2005	2007	2009	2010	Production	Proportion Compared with the Previous Year (%)	Proportion in Global Output (%)
Production	5,600	068	7,835	11,323	13,962	15,575	13,196	−15.3	22.4
Other main producers							28,251		48
USA									
Germany							2,829		4.8
Argentina							2,233		3.8
France							1,720		2.9
China							1,149		2.0

Source: Summary of the data of BP statistics, *BP Statistical Review of World Energy June 2012*, www.bp.com/statisticalreview.

Brazil's development is vividly called the "pendulum type" of development — an economic crisis was ushered in after an economic boom; a choice of development path and adjustment of economic policy had to be made after a crisis. In the latter half of the 1980s, especially in the early 1990s, Brazil began its economic reform process with neoliberalism as the core content. In 2003, Lula's Labor Party came to power and Brazil's economic reform entered a new stage of development.

I. Historical Debts Resulting from the Economic Reform in the 1990s

In the 1990s, Brazil's economic reform was mainly around the privatization of state-owned enterprises, trade liberalization and financial liberalization. Its aim was to reduce government intervention and to play the role of the market. Through the reform, in most years Brazil's economy maintained growth, serious inflation was curbed, foreign trade was increased, enterprise efficiency got improved, the government financial burden had been reduced, and therefore the reform had achieved remarkable results. However, there are also some problems in the reform of this stage, for example, privatization had weakened the ability of the state to control the economy, social fairness and justice had been ignored, and so on.

Among them, the privatization policy had weakened the country's economic control to a certain extent. From the 1980s to 1990s, under the policy orientation of the new liberal reform, Brazil had carried out the privatization of state-owned enterprises many times. At that time, the privatization of the state-owned enterprises seemed to be a global trend. However, most countries and regions had implemented privatization in order to improve the efficiency and competitiveness of enterprises, while Brazil's main purpose was to ease the deteriorating financial pressure of the public sectors. The sale of state-owned enterprises could not only quickly increase the income of the government, get rid of the money-losing enterprises, and reduce the burden of government, but also increase the government tax in the future through the transformation of state-owned enterprises into profit-making private enterprises.

By the end of the 1990s, a large number of state-owned enterprises in Brazil, and even some of the state-owned enterprises with strategic status, had been privatized. Among them, the most famous were the privatization of the state steel company of Minas Gerais during the reign of Collor and the privatization of CVRD during the rule of Cardoso. The Brazil National Petroleum Corporation (Petrobras), the largest state-owned oil company in Brazil, was lucky not to have been privatized because of the constitutional limit. It is said that Brazil's privatization plan was the world's most massive privatization program. In the 1990s, a big source of the public finance was the income of the privatization of state-owned enterprises. According to statistics, from 1990 to 1999, the revenue of Brazil's privatization reached $71.7 billion, of which the privatization of the industrial sector accounted for three-quarters of the total income of privatization.[11]

However, although the privatization of state-owned enterprises in Brazil had improved the public financial situation, it also had weakened the ability of the state to control the economy. Therefore, in the general election of 2002, it triggered a heated debate in the country. According to some analyses, it was the privatization policies that had abandoned the Brazilian national research and development institutions, which were replaced by the import of technology from multi-national companies. According to statistics, Brazil's import of capital goods rose from $7.5 billion in 2001 to $14.8 billion in 1994, and over the same period its import of the semi-manufactured goods rose from $600 million to $27.3 billion. Despite the large amount of foreign capital inflow, Brazil's fixed capital investment rate was low. "Under the leadership of the multi-national corporations in the economic modernization of Brazil, neither the capital accumulation rate of Brazil has been increased, nor has the international competitiveness of Brazil been promoted".[12]

---

[11]Jiang Shixue, *Prediction of the Prospect of Latin American Development*, China Social Sciences Press, 2011.

[12]Mary Lodha, *Brazil: Development Path of Neo-liberalism and New Economic Dependence*, abridged translation by Zhou Tong, http://www.cnki.net.

In addition, in the development process, there has been the concept of "heavy growth, light distribution" in Brazil, resulting in the serious unfair distribution of social income and the wide gap between the rich and the poor. In the latter part of the reform in the 1990s, the Brazilian government noticed the problem, began the development of culture, education, and public health, formulated measures to reduce poverty, and carried out the reform of the social security system in order to ease the social contradictions and lighten the mood of discontent. However, the market-oriented reform and the decline of the government's financial control had not effectively resolved the above social problems. This had made the social fairness and justice seriously neglected, which has become one of the legacies of historical debts of the reform in 1990s.[13]

II. The Targeted Economic Reform Measures by the Labor Government

Winning the general election in 2003, so far the Brazilian Labor Party has been in power for 11 years, experiencing three terms of governments (the Lula Government: 2003–2006, and 2007–2010; MS Rousseff's Government: 2011–present). The Labor Party government had, on the one hand, inherited the basic policies of domestic reform and opening to the outside world implemented by the Cardoso government during the eight years of his administration, and on the other hand, taken positive measures to correct or remedy the problems left over by the pre-reforms.

(1) Active Social Policies

The three labor party governments have consistently focused on the issue of social equity, launching a number of redistribution adjustment programs such as the "Zero Hunger Program", the pension reform and the tax reform. Among them, in the implementation of the "Zero Hunger Program", the new government had greatly reduced the administrative cost and set up a special agency for the

[13]Lv Yinchun, *Economic Development and Social Justice*, World Knowledge Publishing House, 2003.

social development and the elimination of hunger to implement a variety of social assistance programs. At the same time, the government also took measures to alleviate poverty through the distribution of the uncultivated land, increasing the support of fund for crop planting, establishing aboriginal residential areas, restarting the Northeast Development and Administration Bureau, reducing the tax burden on the rural cooperatives, and encouraging private banks to provide small loans to farms and cooperatives. In addition, the policy of the "Family Assistance Plan" to expand the redistribution had been adopted. The "Conditional Cash Transfer Payment Plan" implemented first in Brazil, regarded as a successful experience of anti-poverty, had been promoted to other countries by the related agencies of the United Nations. The active social policies, together with the improved economic situation and increase of employment, had enabled Brazil to have achieved remarkable results in reducing social poverty in the first 10 years of the 21st century. In 2001, Brazil's poverty rate was 37.5%, and the extreme poverty rate was 13.2%; in 2011, they were reduced to 20.9% and 6.1%, respectively, with reductions of 16.6% and 7.1%, respectively.[14] Such a low poverty rate level has not been in existence in the history of nearly half a century of Brazil.

(2) The Prudent and Pragmatic Macroeconomic Policies

Since the beginning of the 21st century, due to the continued strong demand for energy, minerals and agricultural commodities in the international market, a substantial increase has occurred in exports of such products in Brazil, and trade prices have been continuing to improve, resulting in the fact that the trade income and tax income of the government have continued to increase. With a significant improvement in the fiscal revenue, the Brazilian government had implemented the *Fiscal Responsibility Act*, adhering to strict principles to increase revenue. In 2004, the Brazilian government increased the annual fiscal earning index, striving to leave some leeway in

[14]CEPAL, *Panorama Social de America Latina 2012*, Santiago de Chile, p. 14, Cuadro 1.

the high-income years in order to put the surplus into use in the years when the prices of export commodities fell. At the same time, Brazil made use of the opportunity of the improved fiscal situation to actively repay its debt and improve the debt structure. For example, by the end of 2005, Brazil had repaid in advance all the debt owed to the International Monetary Fund. Another example, by issuing local currency bonds Brazil had replaced most of the Brady bonds and extended the average maturity of the debt to 3.7 more years. At present, the local currency bonds have accounted for more than 70% of the total government debt in Brazil.

In the recent 10 years, the Brazilian government has successfully overcome the inflationary pressure through the implementation of the inflation targeting measures. In contrast, the pressure of the currency appreciation is more serious than the inflation problem. A variety of reasons had caused the continued pressure of currency appreciation, for example, the boom of the export of primary products had brought about a large trade surplus, every year a large number of FDI flowed in, the monetary policy of "quantitative easing" of the western countries had caused a large number of short-term speculative capitals to have poured into emerging markets like Brazil, and so on. The government of Brazil has failed to avoid the trend of currency appreciation and the damage caused by the trend of currency appreciation, although it had adopted various measures, such as the financial transaction tax, the active intervention in foreign exchange market and the increase of foreign exchange reserve.

(3) The Success in Dealing with the Impact of the International Financial Crisis

The serious impact on the Brazilian economy caused by the international financial crisis of 2008 lies mainly in the following aspects: the dramatic shrinking of export volume and export value, the rapid deterioration of the trade price, the decline in export purchasing power, the sharp contraction of FDI, the tightening or quitting lending of domestic private banks, the reduction of private investment and private consumption, and so on. In the face of this sudden change, the Labor Party government resolutely adopted a counter cyclical policy to deal with the situation. The specific policies included: to reduce the deposit reserve ratio, to lower the interest rates, to inject capitals to the Central Bank by the Treasury to increase its lending capacity, to offer tax relief for the severely affected sectors by the crisis, to reduce the purchase taxes of vehicles and some commodities, to reduce personal income tax, to cut the public spending, to increase foreign currency liquidity, to have reached the agreement of "$10 Billion Fund for Oil" with China, and to have signed the swap agreement of $30 billion, to implement the import license system for some commodities, to expand the scale of the construction of infrastructure and housing, to establish a special fund to support small and medium enterprises, agriculture and animal husbandry industry and some key industrial sectors, etc.[15] Due to the timely and effective measures taken by the government to deal with the crisis, the recovery of the Brazilian economy began to occur in the middle of 2009, and in 2010 a historical record of 7.5% of its economic growth was achieved. However, in view of the particularity of this international financial crisis, because of the slow economic recovery of the western countries, especially European countries with the adverse effects of a serious debt crisis, Brazil's economic growth rate slowed down significantly in the last two years.

(4) The Emphasis on the Adjustment of the Industrial Structure

One of the "shortcomings" of Brazil's early economic reform was its excessive emphasis on the marketization and privatization, but the adjustment of the industrial structure was ignored. Since the Labor Party came to power, it began to re-emphasize the positive role of the national industrial policy in order to speed up the adjustment of industrial structure and to improve the international competitiveness of the manufacturing sector. The industrial policy and industrial planning of the Labor Party government have been dealt with above. Although Brazil so far has made limited progress in adjusting

[15]CEPAL, Quinta Cumbre de las Americas, *La Reaccion de los Gobiernos de las Americas Frente a la Crisis Internacional: Una Presentacion de las Medidas de Politica Anundadas Hasta 31 de Marzo de 2009*, Puerto Espana, 17–19 de abril, 2009.

its industrial structure, it cannot be denied that Brazil had started earlier in its development of industrial policy and industrial restructuring plan than the other Latin-American countries.

Based on the continuity of its policies and economic and social achievements, the public support rate of the Brazilian Labor Party government has been steadily rising. It is reported that the growing middle class is an important new support force. According to a poll, 15 months after the inauguration of President Rousseff, her support rate was as high as 77%, an increase of 5% higher than in December 2011, much higher than the polled support rate of Lula (54%) and Cardoso (57%) when they were in office. What is particularly notable is that Rousseff had won not only in the poorer Northeast region with up to 82% of the support rate, but also with 75% support rate in the Southeastern region where the opposition support rate used to be higher.[16]

III. The Achievement of the Brazilian Economic Reform in the Past Ten Years

First of all, the middle class has been continuously growing, which, to a certain extent, is conducive to maintaining the social stability. Since 2003, Brazil has created 5,000 new consumers. In 2005, 15% of the Brazilians belonged to "Class A" (with family income more than 6,745 reais) and "Class B" (5,174–6,745 reais), 34% belonged to "Class C" (1,200–5,174 reais), and 51% belonged to "Class D" (751–1,200 reais) and "Class E" (less than 751 reais). After a few years, the proportions were changed into: the "Class A" and "Class B" population accounted for 18%; "Class C" (middle class) rose to 36%; "Class D" and "Class E" dropped to 46%. Then in 2007, the proportion of "Class C", that is, the middle class, increased to 46%; "Class D" and "Class E" dropped to 39%. The latest statistics show that the proportion of the middle class has reached 55.05%, while "Class D" and "Class E" further dropped to 33.2%.[17]

[16] EIU, *Country Report — Brazil*, May, 2012.
[17] *Source*: http://www.brasil.gov.br/para/invest/timeline-of-the-brazilian-economy.

Secondly, with the rating of a historical record of investment security, Brazil had boosted the confidence of foreign investment. In 2008, for the first time the S&P gave Brazil a "Reliable Investment Grade", from which Brazil had entered into the ranks of reliable countries with no risk of default for foreign capitals. For this reason, foreign capitals had continued to feel optimistic about the basic economic situation of Brazil. According to statistics, in 2011 the Latin-American region had attracted more than $153 billion of FDI, accounting for 10% of the total amount of global FDI that year, which was a historical record of FDI in the region. Among them, Brazil became the biggest winner, with the absorption of $66 billion of FDI, accounting for about 44% of the total FDI in Latin America. There are mainly two factors contributing to the good performance of Latin America, including Brazil, in attracting foreign investment: first, it is the recovery of global FDI flows; second, it is the good macroeconomic situation of Latin America. The foreign capitals that flowed into the developing countries, especially into Latin America, mainly were the increase of green investment. The current activity of corporate mergers and acquisitions in the Latin-American region is not active.

However, from 2011 to 2012, due to the slowing down of the growth of the Brazilian economy, recently the S&P credit rating for its outlook of the next two years was changed from "stable" down to "negative"; its sovereign credit rating of "BBB" remained unchanged. The S&P's announcement showed that three consecutive years of low growth might appear in Brazil. The GDP growth rates of 2011 and 2012 were 2.7% and 0.9%, respectively, but it was expected that in 2013 the economic growth rate would be 2.5%. Due to the decline in exports and the recession in the field of private investment, the government's stimulus measures gradually let investors lose confidence and the economic growth became weak.[18]

At the same time, according to the report issued by the international agencies of development research and the Brazilian Don Cabral Fund, in 2013, the global competitiveness ranking of Brazil fell by 5, becoming the 51st in the 60 countries listed for research. Since

[18] *Source*: http://br.mofcom.gov.cn/article/jmxw/201306/20130600157542.shtml.

2010, Brazil's ranking continued to decline, from 38th, 44th, and 46th down to the current ranking. It is reported that the poor performance of Brazil's economic growth is the direct consequence of its poor economic competitiveness. At the same time, the management problems resulted in poor infrastructure, high tax burden, and high cost of logistics and transportation.[19]

Thirdly, Brazil has achieved a historic shift from a debtor country of the IMF to a creditor country. In 2005, Brazil stopped borrowing money from IMF, and in 2006 achieved self-sufficiency of oil. In 2009, in the case of the global crisis, Brazil announced that it would inject $10 billion to IMF, becoming one of the 47 member states that are able to provide regular funding to IMF. These funds are mainly used to help developing countries.

Finally, in the background of the global economic crisis, Brazil had become the sixth largest economy in the world. In 2011, Brazil surpassed Britain to be the world's sixth largest economy, behind the United States, China, Japan, Germany, and France. In the same year, Brazil's foreign exchange reserves for the first time exceeded $350 billion, resulting in an improved balance of payment for Brazil's international trade, with exports reaching $256.04 billion. In addition, the data of the Brazil Department of Labor show that in 2010 the number of regular jobs in Brazil increased by 2.8 million, resulting in a regular employment of workers reaching 44 million people.[20]

However, Brazil's economic development still faces many challenges and some of the challenges are long-standing headaches for Brazil and the rest of Latin America. First of all, the problem of unfair income distribution and land ownership may become a long-term concern for Brazil's economic reform. Secondly, the task of reducing poverty and narrowing the regional development gap is arduous. At present, there are still 40 million people living in poverty in Brazil. At the same time, the issues of uneven regional development are still outstanding. According to statistics, from 2002 to 2010, the proportion of the Northern part of Brazil in the GDP

[19] *Source*: http://br.mofcom.gov.cn/article/jmxw/201305/20130500146831.shtml.
[20] Website of Brazilian Government: http://www.brasil.gov.br/.

increased from 4.7% to 5.3%, and the proportion of the Northeast region increased from 13% to 13.5%, but the proportion of Southeastern region decreased from 56.7% to 55.4%.[21] Thirdly, the problem of the relationship between the external demand and domestic demand for the economic growth needs to be solved. The external economic environment is still grim. Brazil's economic growth rate in 2012 was only 0.9%. The global demand for mineral products and the prices were falling, the economic growth of China — Brazil's main trading partner — has slowed down and the economic situation of the euro zone has been worsening, resulting in a certain degree of influence on Brazil's exports of mineral products such as iron ore. However, the proportion of domestic demand in Brazil's GDP reached 60%, while its net export accounted for at most 25%, an average of only 10%. Therefore, expanding domestic demand is the key to economic growth in Brazil. In addition, the bottlenecks, such as the inadequate transport and telecommunications infrastructure, the heavy and complex taxes, and the imperfect education and health care system, also limited the development of Brazil.[22]

IV. Important Enlightenments of Brazil's Economic Reform

First, the endogenous power of economic growth in Brazil is still insufficient. At present, the economic structure of Brazil shows that its dependence on the external market is still relatively large. Despite the fact that over the past 10 years Brazil has achieved the diversification of its export destinations, of its export products, and of its export surpluses, the degree of diversification of the above three levels is still insufficient; especially in the context of the financial crisis, its economic growth is more vulnerable to the impact of external shocks. By 2010, in Brazil's export destinations, China had become the largest export destination; exports to China accounted for 18%

[21] Regional Development and Regional Inequality, "An Overview of the Brazilian Economy", http://www.econ.fea.usp.br/nereus/eae0503_1_2006/hadch199.pdf.
[22] Adriana Ursell Abdenour, "The Brazilian Economy Has Walked Out the Shadow of the "Lost Decade"", *Chinese Social Sciences*, December 5, 2012.

of its total exports; in the export structure, the primary products ranked first, accounting for 36.9% of Brazil's total export; in the diversification of the export earnings, oil, minerals and agricultural products were still the main sources of earnings.[23] However, this foreign trade was highly dependent on a country and focused on the primary products and raw materials; once facing the deterioration of the external conditions, its risks would emerge suddenly. In 2012, Brazil's economy was poor — its GDP growth rate reaching only 0.9% — mainly because it was affected by the adverse effects of the reduction of the needs for primary products and raw materials of trading partners such as China and the European Union. Therefore, some scholars believe that at present Brazil should make sure whether it has been trapped in the mire of the "resource curse".[24]

Second, more efforts are needed to improve people's livelihood and to meet the needs of the people. As the Chinese saying goes, "Water can carry a boat, but it can also capsize it". If the people's livelihood is ignored, it may cause social unrest at least, and it may impact the stability of the state power finally. This is reflected in the election — voters can "vote with their feet". In 2002 the Brazilian Labor Party took office for the first time because of the drawbacks in the 1990s when the neoliberalism reform had ignored the social fairness and justice. In 2010 the Labor Party won the election again also because the people had recognized the governing effect of Brazil's "left" government in past eight years. In 2012, the polls gave a high support rate to the current government because the Labor Party's economic reform had been effective in correcting the mistakes of the reform in the 1990s and in reducing poverty and promoting the growth of the middle class. However, Brazil still has a long way to go in its improvement of the livelihood of the people, such as the "Zero Hunger Program", which has not yet achieved the goal to let every Brazilian citizen eat three meals a day.

[23] Roberto Dumas Damas, "The History and Prospect of the Brazilian Economy", *Economic Studies of Big Powers*, No. 2, 2010.

[24] Xiang Jun, "Why People in Brazil Protest", *United Morning Post of Singapore*, June 29, 2013, p. 21.

For more than 10 years, the Brazilian Labor Party government has made considerable achievements in the reduction of poverty, and the growing middle class is one of its specific reflections. The middle class had also been an important supporter of the Rousseff Administration. However, in June 2013, the outbreak of the mass protest in Brazil started with the rising of bus and subway fares as the fuse. Some analysts said that in this protest it was precisely the middle class in Brazil that had acted as the protagonist. Due to the gap between the needs of the people and the commitment of the government, the economic downturn and corruption, the growing middle class began to pursue the equality to share social reform and political power.[25]

Finally, Brazil's task of economic reform is still arduous. The unfair distribution of income, backward land ownership, and imbalance of regional development are not only the long-term chronic disease that hinders Brazil's economic development and the fundamental issue, but also the future direction of economic reform and long-term task. This reform may need to span several governments, decades, and even a 100 years. Among them, take the unbalanced regional development, for example. Since the 1960s, successive governments of Brazil have been endeavoring to narrow the development gap between regions, taking a series of policies and measures with remarkable results, having accumulated experiences in dealing with the development problem of the management of backward areas. The Constitution of Brazil of 1988 wrote: The elimination of inequality is one of the fundamental objectives of the federal government of Brazil. After taking office, Lula also reiterated the provisions of the Constitution: The elimination of regional development imbalances should become one of the central tasks of the national development strategy.

Section 4 The Brazilian Foreign Economic Cooperation and the Sino-Brazilian Economic and Trade Relations

Brazil is the largest economy in Latin America and its economic output accounts for about 50% of the whole region. Brazil has paid

[25] *Ibid.*

attention to the diversification of the layout of its foreign trade markets, having trade relations with more than 200 countries and regions in the world. Since entering the 21st Century, Brazil's economic growth rate has accelerated, and its foreign trade and investment have developed rapidly, especially in attracting FDI. In 2011, Brazil's economic growth was weak. In 2012, its growth rate was only 0.9% and its foreign trade had a negative growth. At present, Brazil's trade weighted tariff rate is 7.6%. Its non-tariff barriers and use of anti-dumping measures are worrying the world. Generally speaking, foreign investors enjoy their national treatment in Brazil, but in some industries, the investment activities are restricted, and the complex taxes and the management environment also pose a challenge to investors.

Statistics show that in 2013 Brazil's trade freedom was 69.7 points, at a "more free" level, but below the world average. Since 2003, Brazil's trade freedom showed a rising trend, but from 2009, Brazil's trade freedom level decreased compared with 2006–2009 and since 2007, it had been below the world average level (see Figure 3.11).

In 2013, Brazil's investment freedom was 50 points, on the demarcation line of "very not free" and "depressed" level. Affected by the

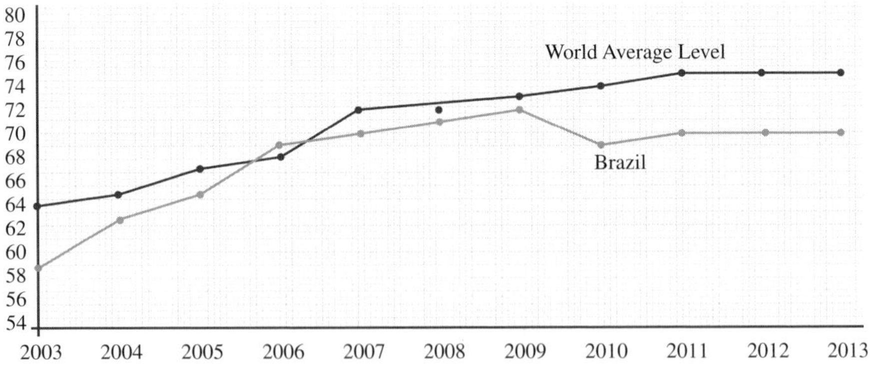

Figure 3.11 Trade Freedom of Brazil (2003–2013) (points)

Source: 2013 Index of Economic Freedom, http://www.heritage.org/index/country/brazil.

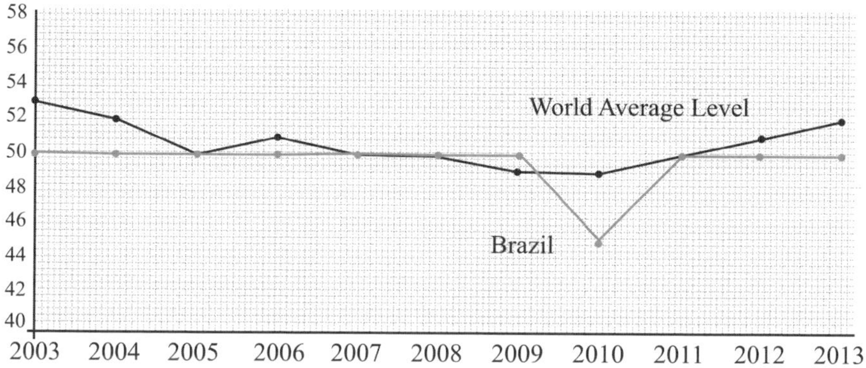

Figure 3.12 Investment Freedom of Brazil (2003–2013) (points)

Source: 2013 Index of Economic Freedom, http://www.heritage.org/index/ country/brazil.

global financial crisis, Brazil's degree of investment freedom declined sharply in 2009; in 2010, it began to rise, but declined from 2011 to 2013 (see Figure 3.12).

I. The Brazilian Foreign Economic and Trade Relations

In 2010, Brazil's foreign trade amounted to $383.7 billion; its exports and imports grew by 26.8% and 24.5%, respectively; in 2011, its trade volume reached $482.3 billion, a year-on year increase of 25.7%. However, the foreign trade of Brazil declined in 2012.[26] According to the statistics of Brazil Foreign Trade Secretariat, in 2012 the amount of import and export of goods in Brazil was $465.73 billion, a decrease of 3.4% compared with the same period the previous year (the same below). Among them, its export was $242.58 billion, a decrease of 5.3%; its import was $223.15 billion, a decrease of 1.4%, and its trade surplus was $19.43 billion, a decrease of 34.8%.

From the perspective of countries (areas), in 2012, the exports of Brazil to China, the United States, Argentina, and the Netherlands accounted for 17.0%, 11.0%, 7.4%, and 6.2%, respectively of the total Brazilian exports; the amounts of exports were $41.23 billion, $26.7

[26] *Source*: http://www2.apexbrasil.com.br/.

billion, \$18 billion, and \$15.04 billion, respectively, among which its exports to the United States and the Netherlands grew by 3.5% and 10.3%, respectively compared with the previous year, but its exports to China and Argentina decreased by 7.0% and 20.8%, respectively. In the same year, the proportions of Brazil's imports from China, the United States, Argentina, and Germany accounted for 15.4%, 14.5%, 7.4%, and 6.4%, respectively in its total imports, and the imports amounted to \$34.25 billion, \$32.36 billion, \$16.44 billion, and \$14.21 billion, respectively, among which imports from the United States, Argentina, and Germany decreased by 4.7%, 2.7%, and 6.6%, respectively compared with the previous year, but the imports from China grew by 4.5%. The sources of the top five trade surpluses of Brazil are Holland, China, Venezuela, Egypt, and Iran; the surpluses were \$11.93 billion, \$6.98 billion, \$4.06 billion, \$2.46 billion, and \$2.16 billion, respectively. Its deficits mainly came from Nigeria, Germany, and the United States, amounting to \$6.95 billion, \$6.93 billion, and 5.66 billion, respectively (see Tables 3.16 and 3.17).

In terms of goods, the three categories of products — mineral products, food, beverages and tobacco, and plant products — are

Table 3.16 Brazil's Exports to Its 10 Largest Trading Partners in 2012 (\$ Million)

Country and Region	Amount	Compared with the Previous Year (%)	Proportion (%)
Total Value	242,580	−5.3	100.0
China	41,228	−7.0	17.0
USA	26,701	3.5	11.0
Argentina	17,998	−20.8	7.4
The Netherlands	15,041	10.3	6.2
Japan	7,956	−16.0	3.3
Germany	7,277	−19.5	3.0
India	5,577	74.2	2.3
Venezuela	5,056	10.1	2.1
Chile	4,602	−15.1	1.9
Italy	4,581	−15.8	1.9

Source: Chinese Ministry of Commerce, *Country Trade Report*, http://countryreport.mofcom.gov.cn.

Table 3.17 Brazil's Imports from Its 10 Major Trading Partners in 2012 ($ Million)

Country and Region	Amount	Compared with the Previous Year (%)	Proportion (%)
Total Value	223,149	−1.4	100.0
China	34,248	4.5	15.4
USA	32,357	−4.7	14.5
Argentina	16,444	−2.7	7.4
Germany	14,209	−6.6	6.4
South Korea	9,098	−9.9	4.1
Nigeria	8,012	−4.5	3.6
Japan	7,735	−1.7	3.5
Italy	6,199	−0.4	2.8
Mexico	6,075	18.4	2.7
France	5,910	8.2	2.7

Source: Chinese Ministry of Commerce, *Country Trade Report*, http://countryreport.mofcom.gov.cn.

Brazil's main exports. In 2012, the exports of the three categories were $60.48 billion, $31.42 billion, and $31.36 billion, respectively, accounting for 24.9%, 13.0%, and 12.9% of Brazil's total exports. The global economic downturn made a portion of the Brazilian exports decline, with the modest export growth only in textiles and raw materials, precious metals and their products, plant products, live animals and animal products, and leather bags. The increases of these products were 12.4%, 9.4%, 4.4%, 1.0%, and 0.9%, respectively. Mechanical and electrical products, mineral products and chemical products are the first three categories of goods imported by Brazil; in 2012, the total imports of them were $138.01 billion, accounting for 61.9% of the total imports of Brazil. Among them, the amount of imports of fossil fuels was $40.19 billion, a drop of 4.2% compared with the previous year, accounting for 18% of the total imports (see Tables 3.18 and 3.19).

In attracting foreign investment, according to the statistics of UNCTAD, in recent years, Brazil is one of the world's five largest destinations of FDI. In 2011, the amount of FDI that Brazil had attracted was $66.7 billion, an increase of 37.8% compared with the previous year; an increase of 157%, compared with 2009. In 2012, the

Table 3.18 Brazil's Main Export Commodities in 2012 ($ Million)

Customs Classification	HS Code	Commodities	2012	Same Period of the Previous Year	Compared with the Previous Year (%)	Proportion (%)
Type	Chapter	Total Value	242,580	256,040	−5.3	100.0
5	25–27	Mineral products	60,483	71,785	−15.7	24.9
4	16–24	Food, beverage, tobacco	31,420	31,787	−1.2	13.0
2	06–14	Plant products	31,357	30,041	4.4	12.9
17	86–89	Transport equipment	19,437	19,575	−0.7	8.0
16	84–85	Mechanical and electrical products	18,806	19,225	−2.2	7.8
15	72–83	Base metals and products	17,240	18,941	−9.0	7.1
1	01–05	Live animals; animal products	15,365	15,215	1.0	6.3
6	28–38	Chemical products	11,570	12,258	−5.6	4.8
10	47–49	Cellulose pulp, paper	6,716	7,248	−7.3	2.8
7	39–40	Plastics, rubber	6,113	6,611	−7.5	2.5
11	50–63	Textiles and raw materials	3,386	3,013	12.4	1.4
14	71	Precious metals and products	3,239	2,962	9.4	1.3
3	15	Animal and vegetable fats and oils	2,539	2,590	−2.0	1.1
8	41–43	Leather products; bags	2,180	2,160	0.9	0.9
9	44–46	Wood and wood products	1,891	1,903	−0.6	0.8
		Other	10,840	10,725	1.1	—

Source: Chinese Ministry of Commerce, *Country Trade Report*, http://country-report.mofcom.gov.cn.

attracted foreign investment was also more than $50 billion. According to some analysis, due to the fact that Brazil is the host country of the 2014 football World Cup and the 2016 Olympic Games, its service industry and its construction of major infrastructures are the major areas to attract foreign investment.[27]

[27] *Source*: http://www2.apexbrasil.com.br/.

Table 3.19 Brazil's Major Import Commodities in 2012 ($ Million)

Customs Classification	HS Code	Commodities	2012	Same Period of the Previous Year	Compared with the Previous Year (%)	Proportion (%)
Type	Chapter	Total Value	223,149	226,243	−1.4	100.0
16	84–85	Mechanical and electrical products	60,163	60,098	0.1	27.0
5	25–27	Mineral products	42,219	44,559	−5.3	18.9
6	28–38	Chemical products	35,628	34,601	3.0	16.0
17	86–89	Transport equipment	25,208	26,374	−4.4	11.3
15	72–83	Base metals and products	13,788	14,247	−3.2	6.2
7	39–40	Plastics, rubber	12,507	13,207	−5.3	5.6
18	90–92	Optics, watches and clocks, medical equipment	6,913	6,762	2.2	3.1
11	50–63	Textiles and raw materials	6,613	6,567	0.7	3.0
2	06–14	Plant products	5,217	5,024	3.8	2.3
4	16–24	Food, beverage, tobacco	2,925	3,091	−5.4	1.3
1	01–05	Live animals; animal products	2,330	2,298	1.4	1.0
20	94–96	Furniture, toys, miscellaneous products	2,253	1,946	15.8	1.0
10	47–49	Cellulose pulp, paper	2,203	2,384	−7.6	1.0
13	68–70	Ceramics; glass	1,951	1,835	6.3	0.9
3	15	Animal and vegetable fats and oils	958	1,051	−8.9	0.4
		Other	2,273	2,198	3.4	

Source: Chinese Ministry of Commerce, *Country Trade Report*, http://countryreport.mofcom.gov.cn.

II. The Bilateral Economic and Trade Relations between China and Brazil

1. A General Review of the Bilateral Trade

At present, Brazil is China's largest trading partner in Latin America, and China is Brazil's largest trading partner in the world, largest export market and the second largest import market. According to the statistics of Chinese Customs, in 2010 the Sino-Brazilian bilateral trade amounted to $62.55 billion, an increase of 47.5% compared with the previous year, achieving a historical record. Among them, China's exports were $24.463 billion, and imports were $38.087 billion, an increase of 73.3% and 34.7%, respectively compared with the previous year.[28]

China's main exports to Brazil were machinery and equipment, computer and communications technology, instrument and apparatuses, textiles and yarns, weaving materials and weaving products, photoelectric technology, LED display plates, steel, transportation tools, automatic data processing equipment and their spare parts, and air conditioners. Brazil's main exports to China involve iron ore stones and concentrates, soybeans, crude oil, paper pulps, soybean oil, cow leather and horse leather, aerospace technology, aircraft, manganese ores and concentrates, and copper and copper products.

According to the statistics of Brazil, the mineral products are the main products of Brazilian export to China. In 2012, the export amounted to $20.21 billion, dropping 19.9% compared with the previous year, accounting 49% of Brazil's total exports to China. Plant products are the second major category of goods that Brazil exports to China, amounting to $12.07 billion, an increase of 9.8% compared with the previous year, accounting for 29.3% of Brazil's total exports to China. The steady growth of China's economy led to Brazil's significant growth of the export of related products. In 2012, Brazil's exports to China — chemical products, transport equipment and animal products — increased by 59.9%, 41.8%, and 31.2%, respectively compared with the previous year. Brazil's

[28]According to the statistics of Brazil Foreign Trade Secretariat, in 2012 the import and export volume of the bilateral goods between Brazil and China was $75.48 billion, a decrease of 2.1%, among them Brazil's exports to China was $41.23 billion, a decrease of 7.0%; Brazil's import from China was $34.25 billion, an increase of 4.5%; the surplus of Brazil reached $6.98 billion, a decrease of 39.5%. China is the largest trading partner of Brazil, the largest export destination and the largest source of imports.

imports from China were mainly mechanical and electrical products, textiles and raw materials and chemical products. In 2012, the total imports of these products were $24.05 billion, accounting for 70.3% of Brazil's total imports from China. China is continuing to maintain its edge in the export of labor-intensive products. Its light industry products of textiles and raw materials, furniture and toys, and leather and bags occupy important positions (No. 2, No. 7, and No. 10) in Brazil's imported large commodities (HS) from China. In terms of these products, India, Indonesia, Bangladesh, Italy, France, Argentina, Uruguay, and Vietnam are China's major competitors[29] (see Tables 3.20 and 3.21).

2. Mutual Investments

By the end of 2010, China's non-financial direct investment in Brazil came up to a total of $860 million, mainly involving mining, timber processing, motorcycle production and household appliances assembly. By the end of 2010, Brazil's real investment in China amounted to $388 million, mainly in the areas of regional aircraft manufacturing, compressor production, coal, real estate, manufacturing of automobile spare parts, hydro-electric power generation, and textile and garment manufacturing.

According to the statistics of Brazil's Central Bank, during the 10 years from 2001 to 2010, Brazil's stock of foreign investment grew from $50 billion to $189 billion, of which the stock of investment in China grew from $15 million to $148 million, accounting for 0.06% of the total foreign investment of Brazil over the same period. According to the statistics of the Chinese Ministry of Commerce, from 2001 to 2010, the stock of Brazil's investment in China rose from $39 million to $573 million, accounting for 0.04% of the total foreign investment in China in the same period. At present, a total of 57 investment enterprises in China come from Brazil. Among them, 29 service enterprises in China are mainly engaged in trade, trade consulting, law firms and other business; 16 industrial production enterprises in

[29]The Chinese Ministry of Commerce, *Country Trade Report*, http://countrynpon.mofcom.gov.cn/record/view110209.asp.

Table 3.20 Brazil's Main Commodities Exported to China in 2012 ($ Million)

Customs Classification	HS Code	Commodities	2012	Same Period of the Previous Year	Compared with the Previous Year (%)	Proportion (%)
Type	Chapter	Total Value	41,228	44,315	−7.0	100.0
5	25–27	Mineral products	20,205	25,212	−19.9	49.0
2	06–14	Plant products	12,066	10,988	9.8	29.3
4	16–24	Food, beverage, tobacco	1,701	1,773	−4.1	4.1
10	47–49	Cellulose pulp, paper	1,314	1,396	−5.9	3.2
3	15	Animal and vegetable fats and oils	1,005	823	22.1	2.4
15	72–83	Base metals and products	996	940	6.0	2.4
17	86–89	Transport equipment	928	654	41.8	2.3
11	50–63	Textiles and raw materials	741	590	25.5	1.8
1	01–05	Live animals, animal products	591	450	31.2	1.4
8	41–43	Leather products; bags	487	401	21.3	1.2
16	84–85	Mechanical and electrical products	462	380	21.8	1.1
7	39–40	Plastics, rubber	294	361	−18.4	0.7
6	28–38	Chemical products	275	172	59.9	0.7
9	44–46	Wood and wood products	49	61	−19.6	0.1
14	71	Precious metals and products	38	44	−14.6	0.1
		Other	77	70	10.2	

Source: Chinese Ministry of Commerce, *Country Trade Report*, http://country-report.mofcom.gov.cn.

China are mainly engaged in procurement operations; 12 enterprises in the fields of mineral resources, energy and agricultural products processing are mainly engaged in the sales business of their products in China.[30]

[30]Business Office of Chinese Embassy in Brazil, http://br.mofcom.gov.cn/article/zt<dy/201207.

Table 3.21 China's Main Exports to Brazil in 2012 ($ Million)

Customs Classification	HS Code	Commodities	2012	Same Period of the Previous Year	Compared with the Previous Year (%)	Proportion (%)
Type	Chapter	Total Value	34,248	32,788	4.5	100.0
16	84–85	Mechanical and electrical products	17,734	16,543	7.2	51.8
11	50–63	Textiles and raw materials	3,320	2,910	14.1	9.7
6	28–38	Chemical products	2,999	3,031	−1.1	8.8
15	72–83	Base metals and products	2,629	2,724	−3.5	7.7
7	39–40	Plastics, rubber	1,454	1,292	12.6	4.3
17	86–89	Transport equipment	1,259	1,535	−18.0	3.7
20	94–96	Furniture, toys, miscellaneous products	1,236	1,087	13.6	3.6
18	90–92	Optics, watches and clocks, medical equipment	939	945	−0.7	2.7
13	68–70	Ceramics; glass	727	694	4.8	2.1
8	41–43	Leather products; bags	431	447	−3.5	1.3
10	47–49	Cellulose pulp, paper	284	223	27.5	0.8
2	06–14	Plant products	284	235	20.9	0.8
1	01–05	Live animals, animal products	270	278	−2.8	0.8
5	25–27	Mineral products	230	439	−47.6	0.7
12	64–67	Shoes, boots, umbrellas and other light industrial products	228	217	5.0	0.7
		Other	225	189	18.8	

Source: Chinese Ministry of Commerce, *Country Trade Report*, http://country-report.mofcom.gov.cn.

3. Contract Services and Cooperations of Designing and Consulting

China's economic cooperation with Brazil began in 1984, mainly including contracted projects and labor service cooperation, successfully completing the projects of Land-photogrammetric Engineering and Port-dredging Remediation. By the end of 2010, China and Brazil had signed contracts for labor services and design consulting totaling $7.442 billion, of which $4.392 billion had been finished.[31]

III. Some Concerns in the Sino-Brazilian Economic and Trade Relations

1. The Interactive Economic Relationship between China and Brazil

In recent years, the rapid growth of China's economy has become an important factor in stimulating the economic growth in Latin America; Latin America's supply of raw materials and primary products is also conducive to easing the problem of resource constraints that China's development faces. China's impact on Latin America, especially Latin-American countries with exports of mineral and agricultural products such as Brazil, can be seen through two aspects: one is the demand, and the other is the price. China's huge demand for mineral products and agricultural products led to higher prices of such products in the international market so that the export countries had got more earnings. Among them, China's demand for iron

Table 3.22 Impact of China's Demand on Global Demand for Iron Ore and Soybeans in 2007 (%)

	Demand Growth (2002–2007)		
	China	Other Countries and Regions	Impact of China's Demand
Iron ore	224.9	19.5	38.4
Soybean	37.2	17.7	3.1
Bean oil	54.2	18.4	6.4

Source: Rhys Jenkins, *The "China Effect" on Commodity Prices and Latin American Export Earnings*, CEPAL, April, 2011.

[31]Chinese Ministry of Commerce, http://mds.mofcom.gov.cn/article/Nocategory/200812/20081205968627.shtml.

Table 3.23 Impact of China's Demand on the Global Market Price of Iron Ore and Soybeans in 2007 (%)

	Impact of China's Demand	Price Elasticity of Supply		Impact of China's Demand on Prices	
		Minimum	Maximum	Maximum	Minimum
Iron ore	38.4	0.25	0.4	153.6	960
Soybean	3.1	0.4	0.6	7.7	5.1
Bean oil	6.4	0.4	0.6	16.0	107

Source: Rhys Jenkins, *The "China Effect" on Commodity Prices and Latin American Export Earnings*, CEPAL, April, 2011.

ore accounted for about 40% of the total global demand; therefore, the "China Factor" had an important impact on iron ore prices. Similarly, China's demand also had an obvious impact on the international market of soybeans and other agricultural products. This is evident from the relevant data in 2007 (see Tables 3.22 and 3.23).

As a major exporter of iron ore and soybeans, Brazil benefited significantly from China's huge demand. The study of relevant scholars showed that because of China's huge demand for mineral products and agricultural products, the Latin-American export countries can be divided into four types in accordance with the benefit or the extent of the damage. In the three beneficiary groups, the first group benefited the highest reaching 20–50%; the second group 7–20%; the rest belonged to the third group. Brazil was in the second group (see Table 3.24).

2. The Problems about China as a Major "Buyer" of Brazilian Resource Products

The commodity structure of the bilateral trade between China and Brazil shows that in Brazil's export to China the top two commodities are iron ore and its concentrates and soybeans. However, in the iron ore trade, the Chinese side did not have a corresponding influence on the price of the product because it was one of the largest buyers of it; on the contrary, China was in a passive position. In terms of soybeans, China's import from Brazil once was equivalent to 80% of the total output of Brazilian soybeans in the Midwest (data

Table 3.24 Impact of "China Factor" on the Net Export Earnings of South American Countries (%)

Country	Maximum	Minimum
Argentina	11.9	6.9
Bolivia	40.0	23.8
Brazil	16.0	11.9
Chile	47.8	28.8
Colombia	9.1	3.3
Ecuador	17.4	7.9
Peru	48.2	29.3
Uruguay	−9.4	−3.9
Venezuela	21.4	10.1

Source: Rhys Jenkins, *The "China Effect" of Commodity Prices and Latin-American Export Earnings*, CEPAL, April, 2011.

2003), so that the Midwest has become a region with faster speed in its economic development in recent years. However, just because of the importance of soybean products to Brazilian growers, Brazil was more concerned about China's measures taken in the inspection and quarantine of the products, and therefore some frictions occurred.

In Latin America, on the one hand, the importance of China's huge market was paid attention to; on the other hand, some negative public opinions also emerged. For example, some people said that China regarded Latin America only as China's "warehouse of raw materials", that China participated in the construction of the Latin-American infrastructure only to create convenient conditions for their own obtaining of industrial materials and grains, and that if the current pattern of the trade development between China and Latin America had continued, Latin America might have remained to be China's exporter of raw materials for a long time, unable to get rid of poverty and backwardness, not to mention "to rise up" with China's help.[32] According to statistics, about 60% of the Brazilian exports to China were concentrated on iron ore, soybeans and their products,

[32]Latin America should know "China is not a 'British Empire', but a friendly cooperative partner", *International Herald Tribune*, November 19, 2004.

and China's exports to Brazil mainly were concentrated on electronic components, machinery, and communications equipment and were increasingly showing a trend of diversification, of which not one kind of products could account for 5% of China's total exports to Brazil. Therefore, an analysis showed that the trade between China and Brazil was asymmetric.

3. The Recognition of the Status of China's Full Market Economy and the Actual Implementation of It

The Lula government of Brazil had resisted the great pressure from the industrial sector, and in 2004 announced the recognition of China's status of full market economy, regarding it as a "strategic partnership" between China and Brazil. However, due to the impact of a variety of factors, China has not actually enjoyed the status of full market economy in Brazil. According to the provisions of Article 7 in Brazil's "On the Administrative Procedure Regulations of the Implementation of the Anti-dumping Measures", there were three ways to determine the normal price of the involved products of the non-market economy countries: the first one was to refer to the price of similar products in a third country of market economy, the second was to refer to the price of similar products exported to other countries by the third country of market economy, and the third was based on other reasonable prices.[33] Therefore, only when Brazil has recognized China's status of full market economy and implemented it actually in accordance with the provisions of the World Trade Organization (WTO) will Brazil be able to use the price of similar products of the third country (market economy country) as the reference standard for Chinese products when adopting anti-dumping investigations of them.

We know that China's status of full market economy is closely related to the occurrence of the bilateral trade frictions between China and Brazil. In the rapid growth of the bilateral trade, a

---

[33]Yu Yang's compiled translation: *Regulations on Administrative Procedures for the Implementation of Anti-dumping Measures in Brazil*, http://www.cacs.gov.cn/.

prominent issue in the bilateral trade is Brazil's anti-dumping measures against Chinese products. According to the statistics of the Chinese Ministry of Commerce, since the first anti-dumping investigation against Chinese products initiated by Brazil in December 1989, by the end of 2005, Brazil had launched 21 anti-dumping investigations against Chinese products, involving over 10 kinds of commodities such as mechanical and electrical products, metal chemicals, light industry, textile, and food. Its trade remedy measures mainly included: anti-dumping measures, safeguard measures and special safeguard measures.[34] According to the statistics of WTO, from 1980 to 2003, the anti-dumping cases initiated by Brazil against China reached 31, behind Argentina and Mexico, accounting for 9% of the anti-dumping cases of developing countries against China.[35] Despite the slight differences in the above two statistics, it is shown that Brazil is not only one of the Latin-American countries, but also one of the developing countries that have most frequently adopted the anti-dumping measures against Chinese products.

[34]Chinese Ministry of Commerce, Country Trade Report: Brazilian Economic and Trade Situation in 2005 and the Sino-Brazilian Trade Relations, No. 1 (Total No. 61), 2006, http://countryreport.mofcom.gov.cn/assay/view.asp?news_id=2747.

[35]Ran Zongrong, "The Anti-dumping Motivations of Developing Countries Against China and China's Countermeasures", *International Trade Issues*, No. 4, 2005.

Chapter 4

Economic Trend of Chile and the Policy Choice of the Sino-Chilean Economic and Trade Cooperation

Zhang Yong

Chile has been hailed by the World Bank and the West as a model for the Latin-American economy. According to the *2011 World Competitiveness Report* released by the International Institute of Management Development (IMD) in Lausanne, Switzerland, Chile ranked 25th in the world's 59 countries and regions, leaving three more countries behind compared with 2010, ranking first in Latin America. According to the *2010–2011 Global Competitiveness Report* released by the World Economic Forum (WEF), the global competitiveness of Chile ranked 30th in the 139 countries and regions, becoming No. 1 in Latin America. As the world's most authoritative two institutions of the evaluation of international competitiveness, the former focuses on national attention to providing enterprises with a competitive environment, and the latter tends to study the factors deciding a country's economic growth. Therefore, the two ratings of Chile proved that it had both of the competitive advantages. Specifically, its political stability had brought the continuity of economic policy; its macroeconomy had maintained low inflation and high growth; its opening trade and growth of investment had become the "double engines"; its public fiscal surplus had provided "escort" for the reform of the social field; its efficient business environment and positive industrial policy had given the micro-enterprises great vitality. The fact that in January 2010 Chile and the Organization for Economic Cooperation and Development (OECD) signed an agreement, officially becoming the 31st member of the organization also confirms this point. At the same time, due to the rise of commodity prices in 2003 and the policy adjustment and consolidation in recent years, the Latin-American countries, including Chile, could ride out the global economic crisis of 2008–2009; obviously, the position of emerging market countries in the world economy has risen significantly. Under this background, we look forward to the prospect for the economic and trade cooperation between China and Chile. In this chapter, we will analyze Chile's economic structure and potential from the perspective of resources and industries and make a prediction about the future economic trend by summarizing the economic policy adjustment to lay a good foundation for the expansion of the policy choice of the economic and trade cooperation between China and Chile.

Section 1 Overview of Resources

Generally speaking, a country's economic development model is closely related to its resource endowments and in the initial stage of economic development its economic growth is also driven by its resources. Studies have shown that in the process of modernization the Latin-American countries have experienced three stages: the primary-product-oriented export, the import substitution industrialization and the post-structural-reform outward development. In addition, in the pendulum model of the development, the resource-type products have always played an important role. From 1870 to 1930, the export of primary products was dominant; from 1930 to 1982, the export of primary products became the main source of foreign exchange for supporting the import substitution; during the period of outward development, with the favorable terms of trade the primary products had created the conditions for all the countries to accumulate funds for social development and to have weathered the financial crises. Chile has a wealth of copper resources; so its development path generally followed the above rules. However, the United Nations Economic Commission for Latin America had given a warning of the risk of this "production specialization" of primary products that the economy of Latin America had long been dependent on. In Chile, there are also arguments about the "resource curse" — people expressed concern of the slowdown of the economic growth of the countries with rich natural resources resulting from rent-seeking activities, the "Dutch Disease" and the lack of contact with the domestic economy. This section will focus on the resources of Chile in order to lay the foundation for analyzing the policies of Chile and the channels of expanding economic and trade cooperation between Chile and China. Of course, the concept of "resources" is broad, including minerals, energy and population. It is worth emphasizing that the population resources also have an important impact on a country's development model and social policies.

I. The Extremely Rich Copper Mines Have Become One of the Pillars of the Economic Development

In the world's mineral economy, Chile's position is unique: it has the reputation of the "copper kingdom" because it is known for its rich copper mines, being the biggest supplier of many minerals in the forms of coarse ore, ore and concentrates. By the end of 2009, Chile's reserves of copper, lithium, rhenium, and selenium ranked first in the world, its reserve of iodine ranked second in the world, and its reserve of molybdenum ranked third in the world. In addition, because a large number of gold and silver ores exist together with some of the major porphyries of copper reserves, Chile's reserves of gold and silver also occupy an important position in the world, equal to or even more than 5% of the world's total reserves. As shown in Table 4.1, by the end of 2009, Chile's copper reserve reached 153 million tons, accounting for 29% of the world's total reserve, ranking first in the world. Its reserves of lithium, selenium, and rhenium also ranked first in the world, with the proportions of respectively 76%, 52%, and 23% of the world's total reserves. Although its potassium reserve accounted for less than 2% of the total global reserve, with 130 million tons of reserve, Chile still ranked seventh in the world.

Table 4.1 Estimation of Main Mineral Reserves in Chile

		2008			2009		
Type	Unit	World Reserve	Global Ranking	Ratio	World Reserve	Global Ranking	Ratio
Boron	1,000 tons	35,000	NA	NA	35,000	NA	NA
Coal	million tons	155	NA	NA	155	NA	NA
Copper	1,000 tons	152,000		29%	153,000		29%
Gold	Ton	3,100	4	6.4%	3,400	4	7%
Iodine	1,000 tons	1,800	2	23%	1,800	2	23%
Iron ore	1,000 tons	520,000	NA	0.7%	535,000	NA	0.7%
Lithium	1,000 tons	7,500		76%	7,500		76%
Molybdenum	1,000 tons	1,950	3	20%	1,950	3	20%
Natural gas	million cubic meters	98,000	NA	NA	98,000	NA	NA
Saltpeter	1,000 tons	225,000	NA	NA	225,000	NA	NA
Oil	1,000 barrels (42 gallons)	150,000	NA	NA	150,000	NA	NA
Potassium	1,000 tons	130,000	7	1.6%	130,000	7	1.6%
Rhenium	Ton	1,300		52%	1,300		52%
Selenium	Ton	20,000		23%	20,000		23%
Silver	Ton	70,000	NA	NA	70,000	NA	NA
Sulfuric acid	1,000 tons	44,800	NA	NA	47,100	NA	NA

Note: "NA" means "Non-existence". Unless specially noted, the data of reserves are by the end of the year.

Source: US Department of the Interior, US Geological Survey, *2009 Minerals Yearbook: Chile*, April 2011, Table 4.3, p. 23.

From the perspective of production, many minerals in Chile occupy important positions in the world, the most important being copper, in addition to lithium, rhenium, molybdenum, iodine, and others. According to the statistics of the Central Bank of Chile, in 2011, the output of the main minerals in recent years is shown in Table 4.2. It can be seen that the production of copper and gold remained stable, but the output of other minerals experienced big fluctuations. Although mining was affected during the international financial crisis of 2008–2009, in view of the strong demand of the emerging markets for resource-based products, the production of copper and other minerals rose bucking the trend. In 2009, the production of copper reached 5.39 million tons, with a year–on-year increase of 1.2%.

Table 4.2 Output of the Main Mining Products of Chile (2005–2009)

	2005	2006	2007	2008	2009
Copper (10,000 tons)	532.1	536.1	555.7	532.8	539
Molybdenum (10,000 tons)	4.79	4.31	4.48	3.36	3.48
Gold (Ton)	40.5	42.1	41.5	39.2	40.8
Silver (Ton)	1,399.5	1,607.2	1,936.5	1,405.0	1,301.0
Iron sand (10,000 tons)	786.21	862.9	881.8	931.6	824.2
Saltpeter (10,000 tons)	128.28	111.18	116.04	115.76	104.87
Iodine (10,000 tons)	1.53	1.65	1.55	1.55	1.74
Coal (10,000 tons)	73.24	67.37	28.8	53.38	63.61

Source: Banco Central de Chile, *Statistical Synthesis of Chile 2005–2009*, 2011.

From the perspective of geographical distribution (see Figure 4.1), the Chilean mining regions are mainly concentrated in the central and northern areas, namely the Tarapaca District (The First District), Antofagasta District (The Second District) and the Atacama District (The Third District). The copper companies based on the mines are inductive to playing the industrial cluster effect, and the mining area has made an important contribution to the economy of the whole region. The Tarapaca District has three major mines: Collahuasi, Cerro Colorado, and Quebrada Blanca, located in the border area between Chile and Bolivia. The infrastructures of developed ports and highways closely connect the Tarapaca District with Northern Chile, Southern Peru, and Bolivia. At the same time, the district also has two tax-exempt areas and enjoys the exemption of certain taxes. In the Antofagasta District, mining accounts for 70% of the entire economic activities in the region. From a global perspective, here are reserved great amounts of the world's mineral resources: 28% of copper, almost all of nitrate, 43% of lithium, 20% of molybdenum, 15% of gold, 15% of iodine and 3% of silver. Chuquicamata and Escondida are the major copper mines in the main area. The mining investment of the region aims to reach $6.6 billion from 2007 to 2010.

In addition, in the Atacama District, the main mines are Candelaria Mine (Freeport MacMoran Company), El Salvador (Codelco Company), and the Paipote Smeleter (Enami Company). Mining

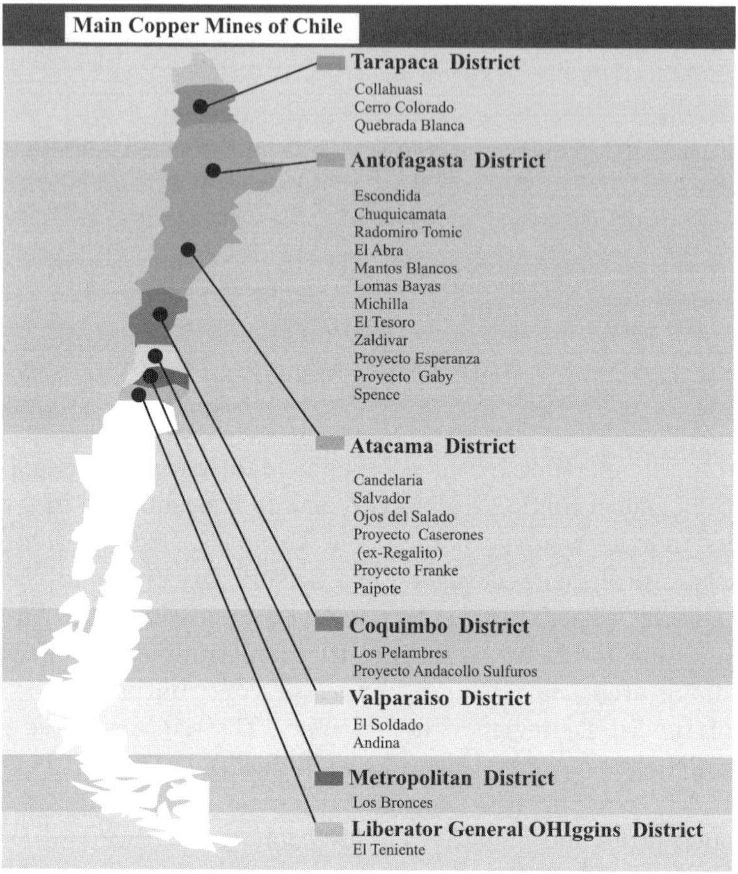

Figure 4.1 Main Copper Mines of Chile

accounts for 45.4% of the region's gross domestic product (GDP), and 83% of the export volume.[1]

Chile's copper mining industry is made up of the production enterprises with the integration of mining, mineral processing, and metallurgy. Most of the copper production units can complete the whole production process from ore dressing to smelting copper products, and recover the products of molybdenum, rhenium, gold, silver, tellurium, and selenium. Chile's copper production comes mostly

[1] *Mining Cluster in Chile*, CORFO/Chilean Economic Development Agency, p. 13.

from large mines, including Chuquicamata, Teniente, El Salvador, Escondido, and Andina. From the perspective of the industrial structure of copper mines, Chile has formed the pattern of the state-owned enterprises as the dominant, supplemented by foreign enterprises. As the world's largest copper company, Chile's state-owned copper company (Codelco) is made up of five branch companies — the North Company (Note Division), El Teniente Company (EL Teniente Division), Ventanas Company (Ventanas Division), Andina Company (Andina Division), and Salvador Company (Salvador Division), with a production capacity totaling 2.02 million tons in 2009. And the biggest foreign enterprise is the Escondida Mining Company (Minera Escondida Ltd.) jointly invested by BHP, Rio Tinto, the Japanese Consortium and the International Finance Corporation, with a production capacity reaching 1.3 million tons in 2009 (see Table 4.3).

II. Lack of Energy Has Become an Important Factor Restricting the Economic Growth

Although rich in copper resources, Chile lacks energy reserves. Chile's dependence on external energy is becoming more and more prominent due to the supply gap resulting from its growing demand for energy. According to BP 2011 World Energy Statistics, the Chilean oil consumption in 2010 reached 14.7 million tons, down 6% compared with the previous year; by oil-equivalent calculation, its consumption of hydropower, natural gas and coal reached 4.9 million tons, 4.2 million tons, and 3.7 million tons, respectively. From the perspective of historical trends, the consumption of oil grew the fastest, natural gas was influenced by external factors, and other renewable energy sources, except for the hydropower consumption, grew the slowest (see Figure 4.2).

It is noteworthy that since 1995 Chile decided to import natural gas from Argentina, and its consumption of natural gas grew rapidly; but since 2004, due to the domestic energy crisis, Argentina began to restrict its gas exports so that the Chilean energy sector was in big trouble. To make matters worse, the Argentine government subsequently increased the export tax on fossil fuels, which had made

Table 4.3 The Structure of the Chilean Copper Mining Industry in 2009

Main Operating Company	Shareholder Structure	Main Factory Location	Annual Production (10,000 Tons)
Minera Escondida Ltd	BHP (BHP Billiton plc), 57.5%; Rio Tinto (Rio Tinto plc), 30%; Japanese Consortium (Japan Escondida Corp.), 10%; International Finance Corp. (International Finance Corp.), 2.5%.	Escondida (surface mine). There are two mineral processing plants: one is the cathode copper oxidation plant (SX-EW2), and the other is the cathode copper sulfide plant, Second District	130
Minera Spence S.A.	Rio Tinto, 100%	Spence (mine & cathode copper oxidation plant), Second District	20
Companla Minera Cerro Colorado	Rio Tinto, 100%	Cerro Colorado (mine & cathode copper oxidation plant), First District	10
Compania Minera Dona Ines de Collahuasi SCM	Anglo American Resources Group (Anglo American plc), 44%; British Xstrata (Xstrata plc), 44%; Companies led by Mitsui Co. Ltd., 12%.	Collahuasi (surface mine), (mineral processing plant & cathode copper oxidation plant), First District	59
Corporacion Nacional del Cobre (CODELCO)	The Chilean government, 100%	CODELCO North Company (Norte Division), including Chuquicamata, Mina Mina Sur, Radomiro Tomic and Chuquicamata cathode copper oxidation plant, smelting and refining plants (oxides and sulfides) Radomiro Tomic cathode copper oxidation plant, Second District	90
Corporacion Nacional del Cobre (CODELCO)	The Chilean government, 100%	El TenienteCompany (El Teniente Division) and mines, Caletones smelter (anode) and refinery, Sixth District	43

(*Continued*)

Table 4.3 (Continued)

Main Operating Company	Shareholder Structure	Main Factory Location	Annual Production (10,000 Tons)
Corporacion Nacional del Cobre (CODELCO)	The Chilean government, 100%	Ventanas Company (Ventanas Division), Ventanas (smelter & refinery) (cathode), Fifth District	40
Corporacion Nacional del Cobre (CODELCO)	The Chilean government, 100%	Andina Company (Andina Division), including Rio Blanco and Sur Sur mine (refinery), Fifth District	21
Corporacion Nacional del Cobre (CODELCO)	The Chilean government, 100%	Salvador Company (Salvador Division), including Campamento Antiguo and Damiana Norte (surface mine), Inca (underground mine), Potrerillos (cathode copper oxidation plant & refinery), Third District	8
Minera Gaby S.A.	The State Copper Company (CODELCO), 100%	Gabriela Mistral (mine & cathode copper oxidation plant), Second District	15
Compania Minera Los Pelambres S.A.	Antofagasta Company (Antofagasta plc), 60%; Japanese Consortium, 40%.	Los Pelambres (surface mine & processing plant, Fourth District	34
Minera El Tesoro S.A.	Antofagasta Company (Antofagasta plc), 100%	El Tesoro (surface mine & cathode copper oxidation plant), Second District	10
Minera Michilla S.A.	Antofagasta Company (Antofagasta plc), 74.2%; other Chilean private investors, 25.8%	Michilla (mine & cathode copper oxidation plant/sulfide plant), Second District	4.5
Empresa Nacional de Mineria (ENAMI)	The Chilean government, 100%	Hernan Videla Lira (Smelting plant), Paipote, Third District	34
Empresa Nacional de Mineria (ENAMI)	The Chilean government, 100%	Processing plants: Manuel Antonio Matta, Paipote; Osvaldo Martinez, El Salado; Vallenar, Second District; Jose Antonio Moreno, Taltal, Second District	18

(Continued)

Table 4.3 (*Continued*)

Main Operating Company	Shareholder Structure	Main Factory Location	Annual Production (10,000 Tons)
Anglo American Sur S.A.	Anglo American Resources Group (Anglo American plc), 100%	Los Bronces (mine) (concentrate) and Tortolas (cathode copper oxidation plant), Santiago Metropolitan Region	25
Anglo American Sur S. A.	Anglo American Resources Group (Anglo American pic), 100%	Chagres (smelting plant), Fifth District	17.5
Anglo American Sur S.A.	Anglo American Resources Group (Anglo American plc), 100%	El Soldado (mine) (concentrate), Fifth District	5
Empresa Minera de Mantos Blancos S.A.	Anglo American Resources Group (Anglo American plc), 99.9%; other private capital, 0.1%	Mantos Blancos (surface mine & cathode copper oxidation plant), Second District	10
Empresa Minera de Mantos Blancos S.A.	Anglo American Resources Group (Anglo American plc), 99.9%; other private capital, 0.1%	Mantoverde (surface mine & cathode copper oxidation plant), Third District	6.5
Xstrata Copper Chile S.A.		Altonorte (smelting plant), La Negra, Second District	28
Compania Minera Xstrata Lomas Bayas	British Xstrata (Xstrata plc), 100%	Lomas Bayas (mine & cathode copper oxidation plant), Second District	7.5
Sociedad Contractual Minera El Abra	US Freeport-McMoRan Copper & Gold Inc. (Freeport-McMoRan Copper & Gold Inc.), 51%; the State Copper Company, 49%	El Abra (mine & cathode copper oxidation plant), near Calama, Second District	22.5
Cia. Contractual Minera Candelaria	US Freeport-McMoRan Copper & Gold Inc., 80%; SMMA Candelaria Inc., 20%	Candelaria (surface min, underground mine & processing mine), near Copiapo, Third District	15

(*Continued*)

Table 4.3 (*Continued*)

Main Operating Company	Shareholder Structure	Main Factory Location	Annual Production (10,000 Tons)
Cia. Contractual Minera Ojos del Salado	US Freeport-McMoRan Copper & Gold Inc., 80%, SMMA Candelaria Inc., 20%	Ojos del Salado (mine & processing mine), near Copiapo, Third District	3.5
Compania Minera Zaldivar	Barrick Gold Corp. (Barrick Gold Corp.), 100%	Zaldivar (surface mine & cathode copper oxidation plant), Second District	15
Compania Minera Quebrada Blanca	Canadian Teck Cominco Ltd. (Teck Cominco Ltd.), 76.5%; Inversiones Mineras S.A., 13.5%; Chilean State Mining Company (Empresa Nacional de Mineria, ENAMI), 10%	Quebrada Blanca (surface mine & cathode copper oxidation plant), First District	10
Compania Minera Carmen de Andacollo	Canadian Teck Cominco Ltd., 90%; Chilean State Mining Company, 10%	Carmen de Andacollo (mine & cathode copper oxidation plant), Fourth District	2.2
Alliance Copper Ltd.	Chilean National Copper Technology Co. Ltd. (Codelco Technologies Ltd.), 100%	Second District	2

Source: US Department of the Interior, US Geological Survey, *2009 Minerals Yearbook*: *Chile*, April 2011, Table 4.2.

many power plants in Chile switch to more expensive diesel fuels. In early 2008, electricity price in Chile increased 40% more than in 2006, and businesses of all sectors were subject to varying degrees of impact. These were sufficient to show that Chile had gone into the problem of the "energy bottleneck" in promoting economic growth.

From the perspective of the total amount of energy consumption of Chile, in 2010 it reached 28.4 million tons of oil equivalents, ranking sixth in the Latin-American region, behind Brazil, Mexico, Venezuela, Colombia, and Argentina. From the perspective of composition, in 2010, the proportion of oil consumption reached 51.8%, the consumption of hydropower 17.3%, the consumption of natural

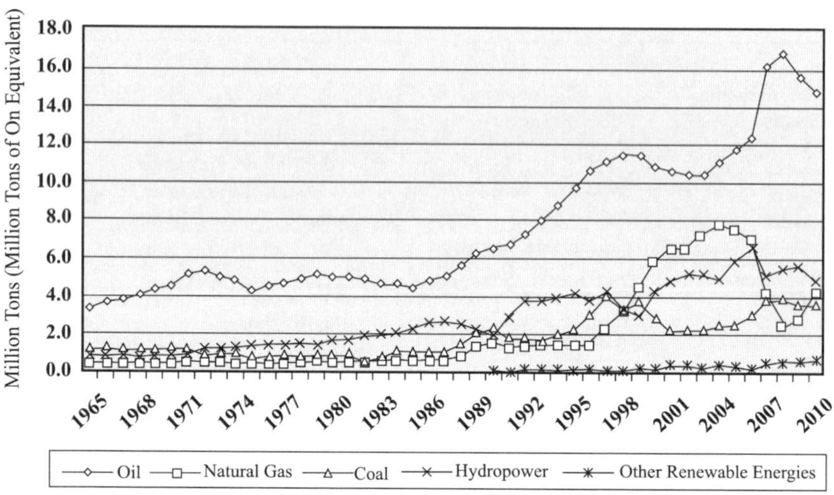

Figure 4.2 Chile's Main Energy Consumption Trends (1965–2010)

Source: BP Statistics of World Energy in 2011, http://www.bp.com/sectionbodyco-py.do?categoryld=7500&contentId=7068481.

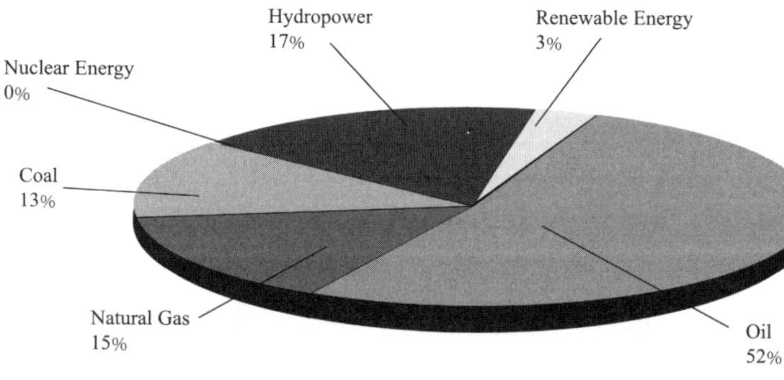

Figure 4.3 The Composition of Energy Consumption of Chile in 2010

Source: BP Statistics of World Energy in 2011, http://www.bp.com/sectionbodyco-py.do?categoryld=7500&contentId=70684810.

gas 14.9%, the consumption of coal accounted for 13.2%, the consumption of renewable energy accounted for 2.8%, and there was no consumption of nuclear energy (see Figure 4.3). It can be seen that the consumption of oil is still occupying the "half" of the total consumption, and the consumption of hydropower has been the focus of Chile's attention because it has the advantages of zero pollution and low cost.

In recent years, in order to solve the problem of energy supply, Chile is working hard to build a new solar energy development center in the world. According to media reports, a total investment of nearly $1.3 billion of solar power station projects have been on a number of different levels of progress. Although the cost is high, the uncertainties of the power supply in Chile and the focus on environmental sustainability have provided support for the development of solar power. At present, totally there are seven solar projects being invested in Chile, of which two projects of the Spanish company Solarpark in the second district have passed the environmental assessment; other projects are still under the assessment. The hydropower stations are expected to have been built before 2020.

Although investment in solar power station is three times of the power stations with traditional technology, with the passage of time, undoubtedly the cost will decrease. The Chilean electricity cost is the highest in Latin America area, so it is possible that solar power will not have been able to gain a competitive advantage until 2015. Moreover, although the power plant construction investment is huge, once put into operation, the marginal cost is zero because there is no need to use any fuel. The construction of Chilean solar power plants is built mainly with the participation of the mining companies to provide electricity for mining. Many traditional power plants are also willing to increase the proportion of renewable energy power generation in order to reduce the overall operating cost and to reduce carbon emission, which is also of great significance.

III. The Aging of the Population Presents Challenges to Chile's Economic and Social Policies

The population factor is very important because not only it is the input element to promote the economic growth — the source of labor, but also its structure has an important impact on social development and policies. For the Latin-American region, the peak of population birth passed in the late 1960s, but as the newborn population gradually go into the working age, the relative proportion of the working age population (15–64 years old) began to increase year by year since 1970 (53.5%). By 2010, its share of the total population proportion will have reached 65.4% so that the employment pressure will begin to be highlighted; but precisely because of this, the curve of dependency ratio and that of the proportion of working age population showed an opposite trend, i.e., the time when the proportion of the working age population reaches the maximum is the period when the social burden becomes the lightest (48%). In other words, from 1970 to 2025 Latin America is in the fermentation period of "demographic dividend", with a significant working age population ratio, which means a light social burden. This population structure in general is beneficial to the economic development. On the other hand, the aging of the population will challenge the social policies. It is generally believed in the world that when 7% of the population becomes the elderly aged over 65 in a country, it means that the country has entered into an aging society. According to the prediction of the Population Statistics Center of the Latin American Economic Commission, Latin America will break through this standard in 2015 (7.8%), and then aging will tend to accelerate.[2]

As is shown in Figure 4.4, Chile basically followed the above trend. The difference lies in that it entered the aging society early and so its "demographic dividend period" ended early. In 2000 the population aged over 65 accounted for 7.2% of the total Chilean population, 15 years earlier than the rest of the Latin-American area to have entered the aging society, and the dependency ratio is expected to have rebounded the bottom in 2015, 10 years earlier than the time of ending population dividend of the whole area. This will propose two major challenges for Chile: first, the decline of the proportion of working-age population will lead to the transformation of the development mode from depending on the amount of labor input to relying on the total-factor productivity model of economic development; second, the aging of the population will lead to increased spending

[2]See CELADE-Division de Poblacion-CEPAL database, http://www.eclac.org/celade/proyecciones/basedatos_BD.htm.

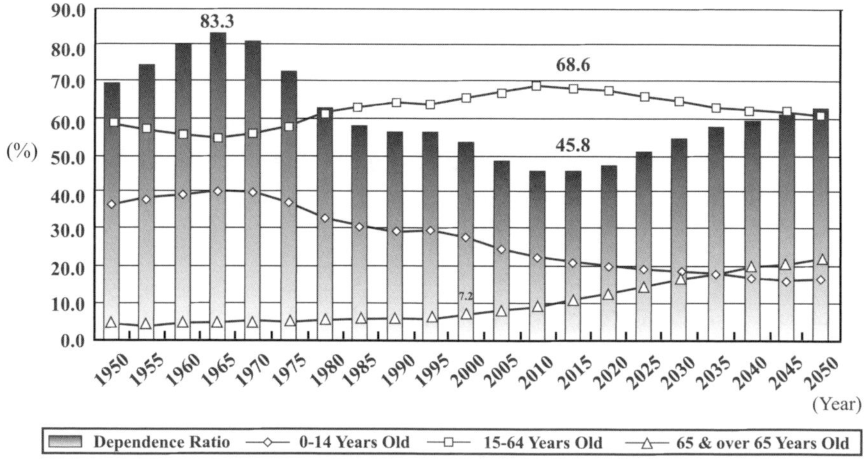

Figure 4.4 The Proportion of the Working-Age Population and the Change of the Trend of Dependence Ratio of Chile

Note: Dependency ratio, GDR, also known as the total burden coefficient, refers to the ratio of the total non-working age population over the working age population, used to reflect the basic relationship between population and economic development from the perspective of population. Calculating formula: GDR $= [\mathrm{P}(0{\sim}14) + \mathrm{P}(65+)] + \mathrm{P}(15 \sim 64) \times 100\%$.

Source: http://www.eclac.cl/celade/proyecciones/basedatos_BD.htm.

on the social security, leading to higher requirements for the social security system and the profit pattern of the social security fund.

To sum up, from the perspective of resources, with rich copper resources, Chile has made the mining industry become one of the pillar industries of its national economy. To avoid the occurrence of the phenomenon of the "resource curse" in the background of the soaring prices of primary products, it may be necessary to consider how to improve the added value of mineral products, extend the industrial chain and expand the connection with its domestic economy. For energy, due to its lack of traditional fossil fuels, Chile's heavy dependence on external energy will be the salient feature of its midterm energy supply. In the future, in addition to the breakthrough in nuclear energy development, the first and the most likely is that the government will favor the renewable energies such as the hydro power, solar energy, and bio-energy, which will provide opportunities for the investment of domestic and foreign private capitals. Chile stepped into the aging society at the beginning of the 21st century, earlier than most Latin-American countries, which required that its mode of economic development should adapt to its population structure. Therefore, an important topic facing Chile is to adjust its development strategy timely and to transform its mode of economic growth.

Section 2 Economic Growth Trend and Industrial Structure

Generally speaking, there are four basic frameworks for the analysis of a country's economic growth mode. First, from the perspective of the demand structure, it is how to balance the relationship between consumption, investment and net export. Second, from the perspective of industrial structure, it is how to promote the structural adjustment of agriculture, industry and service industry. Third, from the perspective of the elements of input, it is how to gradually upgrade the dependence on resources, capitals, labor and productivity to promote economic growth. Fourth, from the perspective of income distribution, it is how to increase the proportion of residents in the distribution of national income to increase consumption and promote growth. This section will mainly give an analysis of Chile's economic growth trends and characteristics from the two aspects of the demand structure and industrial structure, and then offer a discussion about the corresponding industrial policies.

I. The Source of Economic Growth

From the perspective of historical process, the Latin-American countries experienced a "pendulum" mode of development: "outward-inward-outward". Specifically, from 1870 to 1930, characterized by the prosperity of the export of primary products and the early industrial development, each country had implemented the development mode of the export of primary products. From 1930 to 1950, under the impact of the capitalist Great Depression of the

1930s, some Latin-American countries entered into the stage of the exploration of import substitution industrialization; from 1950 to 1980, the Latin-American countries had been involved in the tide of import substitution industrialization and hence came the climax period of post-war industrialization, and social transformation also entered the accelerating phase universally. After 1980, Latin America went into a structural adjustment phase because of the outbreak of the crisis of structural development. During this period, the Latin-American countries started a large-scale structural reform, completing the transformation of the development mode from the inward development to the outward, and the transformation of the state-dominated economy to the market economy. From 2003 onwards, Latin America went into a new cycle of economic expansion. Chile is one of the earliest countries to have explored the import substitution industrialization in Latin America. Its growth is similar to the whole region, but it also has different characteristics.

First of all, from the perspective of the growth of nearly 60 years, the characteristics of economic fluctuations are very obvious. Chile's growth had continued to be above the average level of the Latin-American countries during the periods of 1977–1981, 1986–1998, and 2000–2005, and most of the rest of the time its economic growth was lower than the average level. Chile belongs to the first Latin-American countries to have started the import substitution of industrialization. Because of the relatively small domestic market, it is the first country to have shown signs of decline in its economy. In the late 1950s, Chile's model of import substitution development lost its vitality, and the mistakes of the economic policy of the People's Unity government in the early 1970s led to a sharp deterioration of the economy and a military coup in September 1973. After the military government came to power, the economic reform was carried out and the economic development began to enter a new stage. With the impact of the debt crisis at the beginning of the 1980s, the Chilean economy had a severe recession (−13.6%) in 1982, but in the situation of a general continuous decline of Latin America economy in the 1980s, Chile was the earliest to have recovered its stable economic growth (see Figure 4.5).

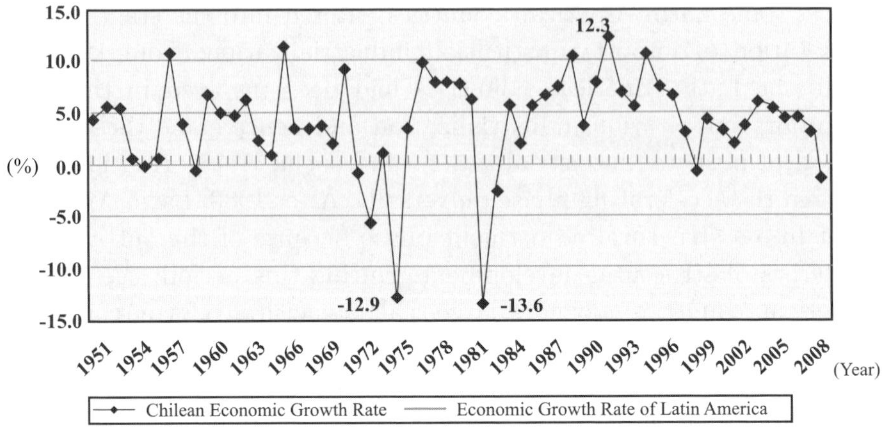

Figure 4.5 Economic Growth Rate Trends of Chile and Latin-American Countries (Excluding the Caribbean) (1951–2009)

Note: Calculated on the basis of the price of US dollars in 2000.

Source: Data of 1950–2008 came from http://www.cepal.org/deype/cuademo37/esp/in-dex.htm; data of 2009 came from *Statistical Yearbook for Latin America and the Caribbean 2010*.

Secondly, from the perspective of the proportions of the three needs (see Table 4.4), the proportion of the final consumption accounted for as high as 80% of GDP, of which the private consumption accounted for more than 70% before 1980, followed by a decline. In spite of this, the final consumption (accurately speaking *private consumption*) still was the main driving force for Chile's economic growth, which was consistent with the overall trend of the Latin-American countries. Therefore, how to improve the income distribution system so as to promote consumption was the challenge that the Chilean government faced. In terms of investment, take 1990 as a cutoff point. Its ratio of fixed capital formation was below the average level of the Latin-American countries in the early period, but higher than the average level in later period, especially from 2000 to 2008, its investment rate reaching 24%, which was inseparable with Chile's experience of actively attracting foreign investment. As for the ratio of net export, there were relatively large fluctuations in the demand structure of the three needs, which means external demand was one of the important factors that had caused the economic fluctuations.

Table 4.4 The Proportions of the Three Needs of Consumption, Investment and Net Export of Chile and Latin-American Countries in GDP (%) (1950–2008)

	1950–1960		1961–1970		1971–1980		1981–1990		1991–2000		2000–2008	
	Latin America	Chile	Latin America	Chile	Latin America	Chile	Latin America	Chile	Latin America	Chile	Latin America	Chile
Ultimate consumption												
Government ultimate consumption	10.6	11.5	10.6	11.9	3.5	15.5	3.8	12.5	15.3	12.9	14.4	12.2
Private ultimate consumption	71.6	73.1	70.9	72	73.8	74.8	72.8	69.9	65.4	64.1	66.2	67.1
Total capital formation												
Changes in inventories	1.2	−2.8	1.9	−0.5	2	0.3	0.3	0.1	2.3	0.8	2.2	0.9
Fixed capital formation	17.5	14.3	17	14.8	23.1	16.6	18.3	17.2	18.2	20.4	18.8	23.1
Net export of goods and services												
Export	9.4	15.7	8.7	15.6	9.7	16.5	14.3	26.8	15.5	27.6	21.7	34.5
(Minus)Import	9.8	9.4	8.6	12.9	12.5	22.9	9.9	23.2	16.4	26.4	23	37.6
Difference items	−0.5	−2.6	−0.4	−1.0	0.4	−0.8	0.4	−3.3	−0.2	0.6	−0.2	−0.2
GDP Calculated by expenditure	100	100	100	100	100	100	100	100	100	100	100	100

Note: GDP data of 1950–1970 were calculated on the basis of the price of the US dollar in 1970; GDP data of 1971–1990 were calculated on the basis of the price of the US dollar in 1980; GDP data of 1991–2008 were calculated on the basis of the price of the US dollar in 2000.

Source: Historical data from the economic statistics of 1950–2008 of the United Nations Economic Commission for Latin America, http://www.cepal.org/deype/cuaderno37/esp/index.htm.

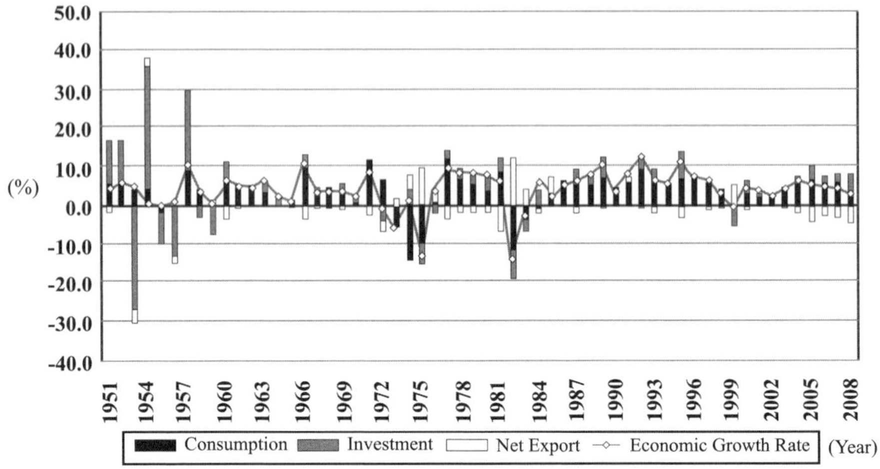

Figure 4.6 Chile's Economic Growth and Contribution of the Factors by Expenditure Approach (1951–2008)

Note: GDP data of 1950–1970 were calculated on the basis of the price of the US dollar in 1970; GDP data of 1971–1990 were calculated on the basis of the price of the US dollar in 1980; GDP data of 1991–2008 were calculated on the basis of the price of the US dollar in 2000.

Source: The author calculated and drew according to the historical data of the economic statistics of 1950–2008 of the United Nations Economic Commission for Latin America, http://www.cepal.org/deype/cuademo37/esp/index.htm.

Finally, from the perspective of the Troika of stimulating economic growth — consumption, investment and net export, first, whether it was in the period of import substitution industrialization or in the export-oriented development period, the consumption (especially, private consumption) had always been the main force. Second, the investment was very important; the decline in investment tended to cause significant fluctuations of the economy. Third, the effect of promoting economic growth with the net export was reflected more obviously in years of recession (1975 and 1982 in Figure 4.6), but the culmination of the trade surplus of primary products to ease the crisis tended to deepen the dependence of the export of primary products.

II. The Characteristics of Industrial Structure

1. The General Trend

The industrial structure of Chile is characterized by stages (see Figure 4.7). First of all, in the 50 and the 60 of the 20th century the ratio of the first industry was showing a downward trend, from 9.7% in 1950 dropping to 6.9% in 1970; the second industry remained at the level of 42%, despite some fluctuations, and over the same period the tertiary industry also fluctuated with the second

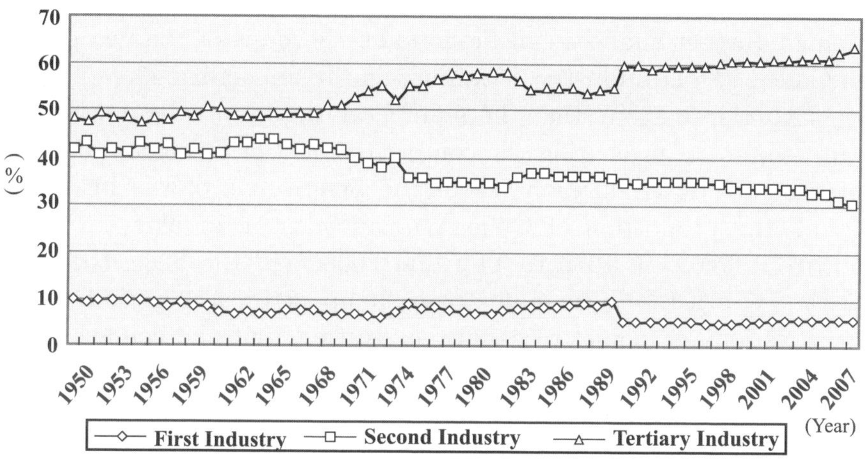

Figure 4.7 The Three Trends of the Changes of Chilean Industrial Structure (1950–2008)

Note: The first industry includes agriculture, forestry, animal husbandry, and fishery; the second industry includes production and supply industries of mining, manufacturing, electricity, gas and water, and the construction industry; the tertiary industry includes wholesale, retail, catering, transport, storage, communications industry, financial and insurance services, community, and social and personal services. The output values of 1950–1970 were calculated on the basis of the price of the US dollar in 1970; the output values of 1971–1990 were calculated on the basis of the price of the US dollar in 1980; the output values of 1991–2008 were calculated on the basis of the price of the US dollar in 2000.

Source: The author calculated according to the historical data of the economic statistics of 1950–2008 of the United Nations Economic Commission for Latin America, http://www.cepal.org/deypZcuaderno37/esjD/index.htm.

industry. Secondly, in the 1970s and 1980s, in view of the structural imbalance in Chile earlier than other Latin-American countries, the "de-industrialization" process started beginning with the decline of the ratio of the manufacturing industry. The proportion of the first industry rebounded, rising to 9.7% in 1990, returning to the level of 1950. Finally, since the 1990s, the proportion of the first industry basically maintained at 5–6%, while the proportion of the second industry continued to decline, and correspondingly the proportion of the third industry rose in the same period. This trend of industry change did not represent the arrival of the "post-industrial era". On the contrary, Chile was still in an "unfinished" state of industrialization. A further analysis can be done on the basis of the two pillars of Chile's second industry — mining and manufacturing.

Experience shows that the manufacturing industry is an important symbol of measuring the competitiveness of a country and the degree of industrialization. From the perspective of the historical trend, the proportion of Chilean manufacturing industry in GDP fell from 25.6% in 1950 to 14.9% in 2008, and the biggest decline of the growth rate of manufacturing happened in the period of the most serious economic recession, suggesting that the conditions of the growth of the manufacturing industry and a country's economic growth were highly relevant. In addition, for the mining, in most years before 1990, it accounted for more than 10%; since the 1990s, its share gradually dropped to 5–7% (see Figure 4.8). This shows that the mining industry is still occupying an important position in Chile, but its influence has been less than before.

2. The Analysis of the Specific Sectors

Since 2003, the composition of the sectors of Chile's gross domestic product (GDP) had experienced the following changes (see Table 4.5). First, there were four sectors accounting for more than 10%: manufacturing, financial and business services, personal services, and commercial, hotel and catering industry (since 2005). Moreover, since 2007 the proportion of the "financial and business services" had caught up with the manufacturing sector, which shows that in Chile the high-end and efficient service industry has developed

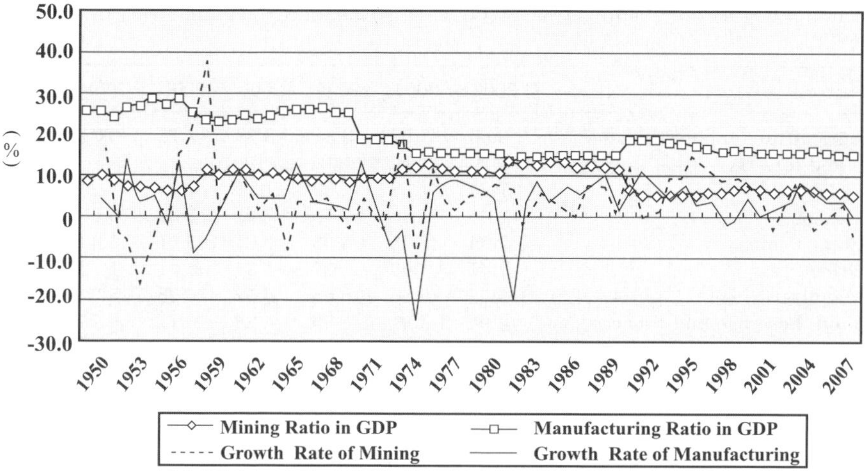

Figure 4.8 The Proportions of GDP and Annual Growth Rate of the Chilean Mining Industry and Manufacturing Industry (1950–2008)

Note: The output values of 1950–1970 were calculated on the basis of the price of US dollar in 1970; the output values of 1971–1990 were calculated on the basis of the price of US dollar in 1980; the output values of 1991–2008 were calculated on the basis of the price of the dollar in 2000.

Source: The author's calculation came from the historical data of the economic statistics of 1950–2008 of the United Nations Economic Commission for Latin America, http://www.cepal.org/deype/cuademo37/esp/index.htm.

rapidly. Second, the copper production accounted for more than 80% of the mining industry, so the decline of its share directly led to the decline of the proportion of the mining sector year by year. Third, the manufacturing sector was impacted by the international financial crisis of 2008–2009, falling from 16.28% to 15.04%. Although "food, beverage and tobacco products" and "chemical, oil, rubber and plastics" were the two major sectors in the manufacturing industry, their proportion had shown a downward trend before the international financial crisis. Fourth, the proportion of the "commercial, hotel and catering industry", "transportation", "communications", and "financial and business services" in the tertiary industry basically showed a rising trend, especially the communications industry characteristic of technology progress getting good momentum of development, with its ratio increasing year by year.

Table 4.5 Sector Composition of GDP (%, Calculated on the Price of Peso in 2003)

Sector	2003	2004	2005	2006	2007	2008	2009
Agriculture, animal husbandry, and forestry	3.60	3.68	3.81	3.88	3.73	3.71	3.95
Fishery	1.23	1.38	1.32	1.21	1.18	1.23	1.09
Mining	8.45	8.45	7.70	7.41	7.32	6.66	6.67
Copper mines	7.04	7.03	6.33	6.07	6.01	5.44	5.52
Other	1.41	1.43	1.37	1.34	1.31	1.22	1.15
Manufacturing	16.42	16.56	16.63	16.52	16.28	15.92	15.04
Food, beverage and tobacco products	4.94	4.91	4.93	4.88	4.77	4.75	4.67
Textiles, clothing and leather	0.77	0.80	0.81	0.82	0.74	0.65	0.54
Wood and furniture	1.10	1.17	1.14	1.11	1.00	0.93	0.73
Paper and printing	1.71	1.81	1.72	1.73	1.96	1.98	2.01
Chemicals, oil, rubber and plastics	4.62	4.58	4.61	4.65	4.39	4.25	4.07
Non-metallic minerals and basic metal products	1.34	1.40	1.41	1.38	1.39	1.30	1.10
Metal products, machinery and equipment and others	1.95	1.90	2.01	1.94	2.02	2.05	1.92
Electricity, gas and water	2.86	2.77	2.70	2.78	1.89	1.79	2.10
Construction	6.90	6.72	7.01	6.97	6.97	7.40	7.12
Commerce, hotels and catering	9.68	9.79	10.07	10.29	10.44	10.55	10.43
Transportation	6.92	6.81	6.89	7.08	7.26	7.30	7.17
Communications	2.29	2.35	2.39	2.41	2.60	2.84	3.09
Finance and commercial services	14.96	15.21	15.62	15.62	16.34	16.26	16.27
Real estate	5.82	5.63	5.51	5.44	5.39	5.38	5.65
Personal services (education, medical services, etc.)	11.56	11.27	11.03	10.94	10.94	10.99	11.34
Public management	4.33	4.17	4.10	4.05	4.01	3.98	4.19
Others	5.00	5.20	5.23	5.41	5.64	5.98	5.88
Total	100	100	100	100	100	100	100

Note: Add-ups may not equal to the total values due to rounding.

Source: Statistical Synthesis of Chile 2005–2009, Banco Central de Chile, p. 17.

In terms of the internal situation of the manufacturing industry, there are some important features (see Table 4.6). According to the data from the Chilean National Bureau of Statistics, since 2003, in the 39 sectors of the manufacturing industry, the production index of five sectors had increased gradually, mainly involving the manufacturing of raw materials; four sectors had decreased gradually, involving mainly the labor-intensive textile and garment industry. From

Table 4.6 Changing Trends of the Index of Production and Sales of the Manufacturing Industry from 2003 to 2011 (2002 = 100)

Classification of Manufacturing Industry	Production Index					Sales Index				
	2003	2005	2007	2009	2011	2003	2005	2007	2009	2011
151 Production, processing and preservation of meat, fish, fruit, vegetables, oil and fat	103.6	116.3	130.3	114.2	119.0	106.0	117.7	125.3	113.8	109.5
152 Production of milk products	106.0	112.2	117.4	115.3	120.3	110.1	113.8	115.4	113.4	115.3
153 Manufacturing of grain mill products, starch products and fine fodder for livestock	105.8	125.4	148.8	112.3	136.8	107.5	126.6	151.8	112.1	137.5
154 Other food manufacturing	97.2	105.0	108.9	110.0	115.3	103.8	111.7	115.5	115.0	119.2
155 Beverage manufacturing	104.3	117.2	139.7	149.9	151.5	106.1	117.5	136.6	145.0	146.3
160 Manufacture of tobacco products	99.6	120.1	135.0	125.2	144.9	105.5	123.2	138.7	129.0	156.4
171 Spinning, weaving and finishing of textiles	99.7	83.0	69.1	51.0	32.9	100.0	83.4	71.2	53.3	32.1
172 Other textile manufacturing	218.4	449.5	456.8	302.2	310.1	199.9	399.2	397.9	266.5	279.1
173 Manufacture of knitted and crochet fabrics and their products	101.1	83.1	83.3	55.4	53.2	94.2	91.8	84.3	60.6	51.5
181 Clothing manufacturing, except fur clothing	100.1	89.5	68.7	45.5	37.1	104.5	101.4	81.8	59.6	48.4
191 Tanning and dressing of leather; manufacturing of luggage, handbags and harnesses	95.4	77.7	73.3	61.8	50.8	85.6	77.0	78.1	61.2	48.3
192 Manufacturing of shoes	97.7	100.1	76.9	50.3	45.5	97.8	100.8	82.9	48.0	49.3
201 Sawing and planning	107.8	120.8	113.5	79.7	79.0	107.2	122.1	113.2	82.9	77.0
202 Manufacture of wood products and cork products; manufacture of straw goods and woven material goods	112.2	123.4	127.4	98.0	118.7	115.1	136.7	142.0	107.6	125.2

(Continued)

Table 4.6 (*Continued*)

Classification of Manufacturing Industry	Production Index					Sales Index				
	2003	2005	2007	2009	2011	2003	2005	2007	2009	2011
210 Manufacturing of paper and paper products	107.4	121.6	153.4	167.5	172.3	106.6	119.1	149.7	168.3	164.3
221 Press	109.1	128.7	129.1	117.0	93.8	107.1	129.1	127.6	115.7	90.8
222 Printing and related services	112.1	108.4	109.9	96.3	95.4	95.9	97.5	101.9	88.6	87.5
232 Manufacture of refined petroleum products	104.6	114.6	99.2	99.5	95.0	107.8	102.9	105.8	104.4	101.1
241 Manufacture of basic chemicals	114.6	136.5	135.6	133.4	146.8	106.8	121.8	112.6	111.4	126.7
242 Manufacture of other chemicals	97.5	123.0	131.1	135.6	150.4	100.0	127.3	134.0	138.7	154.6
251 Manufacture of rubber products	123.3	155.9	142.4	80.3	112.8	112.3	145.7	132.3	75.1	106.1
252 Manufacture of plastic products	102.8	117.5	131.4	128.1	122.2	105.8	129.6	143.6	141.4	133.3
261 Glass and glass products	107.5	150.2	174.5	155.5	156.8	102.8	137.2	163.4	146.8	127.9
269 Manufacture of non-metallic mineral products	105.0	118.6	125.7	99.1	111.1	107.6	121.1	129.0	104.4	112.7
271 The manufacture of basic steel	101.4	114.8	130.7	104.0	130.3	98.3	121.5	133.3	103.8	126.0
272 Basic precious metals and non-ferrous metal manufacturing	118.7	164.8	168.8	135.6	118.0	116.8	158.0	182.8	133.9	108.0
281 Manufacture of structural metal water tanks and metal containers	92.7	104.6	108.2	159.0	153.7	94.0	104.3	110.4	157.5	153.8
289 Manufacture of other metal products; service activities for metal processing	106.5	106.5	114.2	88.6	115.4	105.3	115.4	159.4	103.3	117.6
291 General machinery manufacturing	110.8	153.6	125.7	124.7	121.2	103.7	140.9	121.0	115.9	110.6
292 Manufacture of special machinery	94.6	109.5	125.3	138.0	167.1	96.7	120.6	146.0	170.5	203.2
293 Non-other classified manufacturing of household appliances	102.4	118.1	137.3	103.1	131.2	99.8	109.0	128.1	100.7	127.8

311 Manufacture of motors, generators and transformers	99.9	175.1	210.2	202.2	289.3	90.6	179.5	203.7	232.7	290.1
312 Manufacturing of power distribution and control equipment	93.4	216.6	86.2	86.2	88.5	96.6	220.5	87.7	89.6	89.4
315 Manufacture of electric lights and lighting equipment	112.9	62.9	36.7	35.6	62.7	111.2	70.7	40.6	36.2	64.4
331 Manufacture of instruments and equipment for the measurement, inspection, test, and navigation	179.8	236.0	384.4	350.2	444.3	177.0	235.8	380.5	350.0	443.9
341 Automobile manufacturing	68.1	58.1	62.7	0.0	0.0	66.3	54.1	58.6	0.0	0.0
343 Manufacture of automobile and engine parts and accessories	91.9	109.4	88.0	78.3	75.9	101.0	117.7	101.4	89.7	93.6
361 Furniture manufacturing	100.2	112.8	126.1	86.7	110.2	99.7	109.5	123.1	86.2	108.9
369 Non-other classified manufacturing	96.7	82.1	61.4	57.9	57.5	91.3	100.7	80.3	71.9	62.3

Note: Manufacturing was classified according to *The International Standard Industrial Classification Version 3.0.* Data of 2011 lasted till July.

Source: Summary of the data from Chile National Bureau of Statistics (www.ine.cl). *Produccion Fisica de la Industria Manufacturera, por Grupo*: 2002; *Venta Fisica de la Industria Manufacturera, por Grupo*: 2002.

the perspective of sales index, in the 39 sectors the four increasing sectors and the three decreasing sectors roughly corresponded with the trend of the production index. Especially the three sectors with the index of falling sales were concentrated in the textile and garment industry, which shows that the industry was facing a severe pressure of competition.

3. The Corresponding Adjustment of Industrial Policies

Unlike the monetary and fiscal policies, the industrial policy is always controversial from definition to practice. The neoliberalism pursuing the supremacy of the market believes that the market can automatically select the departments and enterprises to ensure the efficiency of resource allocation. Therefore, it does not need any industrial policies. But the comprehensive school of the theory of Schumpeter, the evolutionary theory and structuralism believe that due to the differences between the sectors, it is necessary to implement the public intervention in the development of the industry in order to explore technology opportunities to achieve the goal of the accumulation of knowledge and ability.[3] In general, no matter when and where to start, industrialization is always accompanied with and driven by a combination of policies to promote and support the growth of the immature industry or sector, as well as to accelerate the creation of strategic sectors and capacity.

The industrial policies of the Latin-American countries are closely linked with the economic development model, and the stage characteristics are very obvious. During the period of the import substitution industrialization, the industrial policies were a combination of trade protection and promoting investment, to create "new departments" as a priority, to change the patterns of the specialization of previously popular primary products, and to achieve the diversification by increasing the proportion of technology intensive activities in the production structure. After the "lost decade" resulting from the debt crisis, the industrial policies began to be gradually

[3] See Wilson Peres, Annalisa Primi, *Theory and Practice of Industrial Policy: Evidence from the Latin American Experience*, CEPAL, February 2009.

declining due to the conflict with the economic reform advocating the market, but some countries in the east and Southeast of Asia had obtained competitiveness of domestic production and the technical ability by virtue of the active department policies that continued till the mid-1990s. Under the influence of the "Washington Consensus" in the 1990s, the industrial policy of Latin America was embodied in the "policy of competitiveness" in order to improve the economic competitiveness of a country through the planning and design. Specifically, there were three groups. The first group included mainly Brazil, Mexico and some English-speaking Caribbean countries, which had paid special attention to the position of industrial sectors in the national competitiveness and to its link with technology development and the effective participation in international trade, but compared with the previous industrial development planning, the industrial policy lacked substantive content. The second group involved the Andean and Central American countries. Different from the former group that had focused on manufacturing, they mainly concentrated on improving the overall competitiveness of the economy, whose national competitiveness strategy was usually in the form of industrial agglomerations. The third group referred to countries such as Argentina, Chile and Uruguay that did not carry out official industrial policies or selective strategies of national competitiveness. They focused on the most basic "levels" or "neutral" intervention policies, i.e., non-discrimination against production departments and sectors targeted by the enterprise needs. However, the policies of these countries were very pragmatic — whenever there was a demand, they would practice priority policies for the department or sector. Chile was a typical example whose policy of neutrality did not interfere with the long-term government support for forestry, mining and some of the key export activities.

The period of Chile's import substitution industrialization was approximately from 1938 to 1973, during which the industrial policies were paid attention to; not only the government tried to protect domestic industries through high tariffs, but also the country's institutions became the most important business owners. In this case, large numbers of industries emerged, such as iron and steel, oil exploitation and processing, sugar, vertical integration of power generation and distribution, and telecommunications. At the same time, the financial repression policies such as the tilted credit or subsidies, and the negative interest rates came out. After the military coup in 1973 (1973–1990), Chile had basically abandoned the vertical industrial policy. However, three industrial policy tools deviated from the neutral policy stance, one of which was the policy of forestry, i.e., the No. 701 "Law to Promote the Forestry" in 1974 providing incentives widely for the development of commercial afforestation, which had laid the foundation for the important position of forest products in Chile export today. The second was the various activities promoted by the semi-official Chile Foundation (*Foundacion Chile*), promoting production and development, covering the fields of agriculture, forestry, marine resources and quality. In the late 1970s the Foundation was responsible for the promotion of the salmon farming technology of Norway and the establishment of Chile's first company exporting salmon. This decision made a significant contribution to the subsequent export boom of salmon and other fisheries. The third was the rapid development of fruit industry, originating from an agreement (Program Chile-California) between the University of Chile and the University of California (UC) on the exchange of students and scholars. Under the protocol, many Chilean agronomists went to study fruit planting at the University of California, and some professors from UC came to Chile to create and strengthen the existing fruit planting projects. These had greatly promoted Chile's export of fruits.

In recent years, Chile has implemented industrial policies through agencies such as the Production and Promotion Association (CORFO) and the Export Promotion Agency (ProChile). The main policy tools are shown in Table 4.7. Despite Chile's commitment of the "level" policy to all sectors, allowing the "vertical" policy to exist for special sectors had proved the practicality of its economic policy. For example, the R&D and training subsidies had laid the foundation for improving human capitals, the financing business policies for all small and medium-sized enterprises had promoted the development of small- and medium-sized enterprises (SMEs) in Chile, and

Table 4.7 Chile Policy Intervention Matrix

	Level Characteristics	Vertical Characteristics
Public Investment	R&D subsidies: in the charge of the "Entrepreneurship Education Fund" (Chile Innova)	Food safety: in the charge of the Agriculture and Animal Husbandry Service under the Ministry of Agriculture (SAG)
Market Intervention	Training: in the charge of the National Training and Employment Services (SENCE) and the Supplier Development Plan (PDP) and Technical Support Fund (FAT)	Forestry: No. 701 Forest Promotion Law
	All small and medium enterprises: in the charge of the Technical Cooperation Services (SERCOTEC)	Agricultural protection: levy higher tariffs for four groups of products that have price ranges (wheat, sugar, vegetable oil, and oilseeds)
	Credit for small and medium enterprises: in the charge of the Small Business Guarantee Fund (FOGAPE)	Public Entrepreneurship: in the charge of the Chilean Foundation (such as salmon and oyster industry)
	Credit for small and medium enterprises: through the implementation of the "Loan Evaluation Program"	Education related to special departments: Chile–California Project (fruit industry)
	Economies of scale: the implementation through the "Project Development" (PROFO) program	
	Export promotion: the implementation of the "Tax Rebate System" (Reintegro simplificado), by the end of 1996	
	General export promotion: in the charge of the Export Promotion Agency (ProChile)	
	Different types of market failure: to be overcome with the projects of the Production Promotion Commission (CORFO) under the government's Ministry of Economic Affairs	

Source: The author's summary of relevant literatures.

the system of traditional export tax rebates and the simplified tax rebates had promoted Chile's export boom. In addition, forestry, the salmon industry and fruit industry supported by the corresponding policies for a long time had maintained a strong international competitiveness, but the tariff protection for key agricultural products would gradually step out of the stage of history because of the conflict with the free trade agreement signed by Chile.

It can be expected that the future industrial policy of Chile will pay more attention to the improvement and development of "level" tools; at the same time, it will still have a certain degree of "selectiveness". Otherwise, the realization of the economic growth would not be enough to overcome the state of underdevelopment and to eradicate poverty. In addition, the "chosen" industries should not only have a good prospect for the world market, but also meet the competition advantages of Chile, for example, copper mining, aquaculture, fruit production, pork, poultry, offshore services, tourism, food processing, financial services, transportation and logistics, the construction industry, etc. Moreover, in the development of industrial policies three points need to be paid attention to: first, the ability to narrow the gap between policy design and the effective implementation of institutions should be improved. Second, the gap between the implementation of the plan or policy incentives and the ultimate goal to be achieved should be assessed in order to allocate the limited resources to the industries with potential. Third, in view of the "selective" department policies, the behaviors of rent-seeking and bureaucratic occupation should be avoided.

Section 3 Adjustment of the Economic Policies from the Beginning of the 21st Century

According to the statistics of the Central Bank of Chile, in 2010 Chile's GDP reached $203.925 billion, per capita GDP reaching $11,929. In accordance with the division of low, medium and high income countries by the World Bank, in 2011 Chile was likely to be the first to be among the rank of high income countries in

South America.[4] The development model in constant adjustments and pragmatic economic policies were hidden behind these enviable economic achievements. After 1980s, Chile opened its market, strengthened its macro-control, and adjusted its industrial structure, resulting in a great growth of its economy. Especially since 2003, the government had implemented a prudent fiscal policy and monetary policy, and due to the continuous rising of the prices of its pillar export products, such as copper, salmon and pulp, it had achieved a steady economic growth. Since 2008, affected by the spread of the international financial crisis, the real economy of Chile had been impacted, resulting in a slowdown in economic growth. Since the second half of 2009, its economy began to recover. However, in 2010 the sudden "2-27" earthquake caused up to $30 billion of economic loss of Chile, accounting for about 17% of its GDP. The Pinera government tried to strengthen the macroeconomic regulation and control, focusing on the restoration of the four areas of transportation, housing, employment and fisheries to start post-disaster reconstruction work. With the favorable conditions of the warming external market and higher copper prices, the Chilean economy had bottomed out, showing a rapid upward trend.

I. The Basic Institutional Framework of the General Economic Policy

Since 1990, the Chilean center–left coalition government had formed a consensus, i.e., to maintain the free market economic system. Under this stable framework of the system, through its well-implemented progressive reforms, Chile had avoided economic fluctuations. The macro-institutional framework mainly included: the independent Central Bank had implemented the monetary policy, responsible and predictable fiscal policies and the comprehensive regulation and supervision of the financial system, to promote economic

[4] According to the per capita income criteria of the world bank, low-income countries — below $995, lower middle income countries — $996–3,945, upper middle income countries — $3,946–12,195, high income countries — more than $12,196.

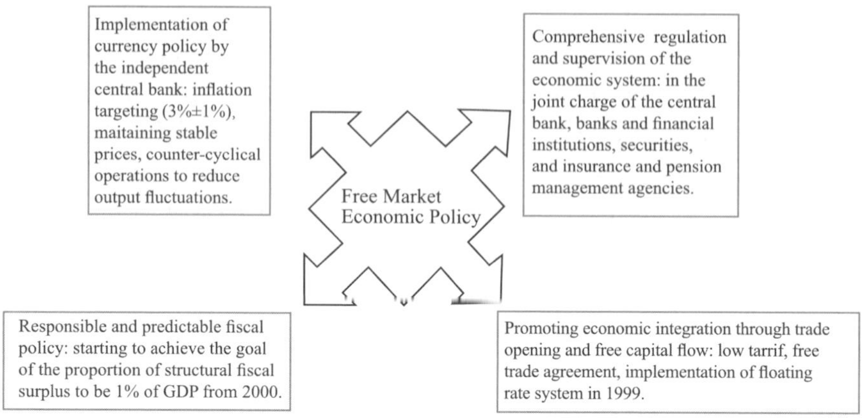

Figure 4.9 The Institutional Framework of Chile's Economic Policy

integration through openness of trade and the free flow of capitals (see Figure 4.9).

Inflation targeting was the monetary policy system that the Central Bank had directly targeted the inflation and announced the goal of inflation. In this system, the traditional system of monetary policy had changed greatly — no intermediate target was set up between the policy tools and the ultimate goal, and the decision making of monetary policy relied mainly on the forecast of inflation on a regular basis. Chile's Central Bank determined in advance the country's mid-and-long-term inflation target in the next coming period in the third quarter of each year according to forecasts. The target was set to 3%, up and down 1%, most of the time. Under the supervision of the public, the Central Bank made use of the corresponding monetary policy tools to make the actual value of inflation match with the forecasted targets.

Since coming to power, the civilian government of Chile had done beneficial exploration of the fiscal and tax policy suiting to its national conditions in the background of financial globalization. The country gradually formed a relatively stable and responsible fiscal policy through a variety of means, such as limiting the public expenditure, establishing the stabilization fund and maintaining the structural surplus of the public finance. The function of the policy in recent years is mainly reflected in the following three aspects: first, to maintain macroeconomic stability and promote economic growth; second, to provide a stable and balanced financing for the social security system to ensure that it had a healthy development with favorable conditions; third, to promote the perfection of the social security system with its effect on the framework of the system of social policies. This fiscal norm with the structural surplus no less than 1% of GDP had made the public expenditure decisions based on a more sustainable financial availability. In other words, the temporary high fiscal surplus brought about by the economic cycle was not the foundation of spending decisions; also a temporary drop of earning would not necessarily lead to spending cuts.

Financial liberalization was the main content of economic reform in Latin America in the 1990s, including deregulation and privatization. Chile had taken effective measures in this regard, not only to have ensured a balance between a free market system and a reasonable banking regulation, but also to have promoted the capital market to develop in depth.

As early as 1970s, Chile began its reform in the field of trade. The main content of it was from the export policy, encouraging domestic export to increase its income of foreign exchange, then changing the traditional policy of import restrictions, and ultimately promoting the liberalization of the trade. Reducing tariffs and eliminating non-tariff barriers became the core of the trade liberalization measures. At the same time, through a wide range of bilateral tax and free trade agreement network, Chile had firmly established its status as an attractive investment destination.

With the rise of the Latin-American leftism in the political arena at the turn of the century, the neoliberalism began to lose popularity, and many countries started to re-adjust their macroeconomic policies after the reform. The re-adjustments can be broadly divided into three categories. First, the "radical" governments, such as Venezuela, Ecuador, and Bolivia, tried to re-strengthen the country's economic control through the nationalization of oil and gas resources. Second, the "mild" governments, such as Brazil and Argentina, stressed that the adjustment should be done through public policies to promote economic growth and to correct the serious imbalance in the field of society. Third, even those non-left-wing ruling countries had a great magnitude of adjustment of their economic policies, especially in the ability to use counter cyclical macroeconomic policies to "iron" economic fluctuations. The typical representative is the president Piniella of the government of Chile. He tried to practice his election platform — "Hope, Change and Future" — through the principle of "seeking change in stability".

II. The Policy Adjustment to Deal with the International Financial Crisis (2008–2009)

The global financial crisis, which was marked by the collapse of Lehman Brothers in the United States and upgraded from the sub-prime mortgage crisis since the 2008, had greatly hit the global economy. The end-of-year report of the Economic Commission for Latin America (CEPAL) pointed out that, in 2009, Latin America experienced an economic recession of 1.8%, per capita GDP declining by about 2.9%, thus cutting off the 2003–2008 growth cycle (with an average annual growth rate of about 5%, per capita GDP growth of more than 3%). The Latin-American economy suffered the most serious impact of the crisis in the fourth quarter of 2008 and the first quarter of 2009. From the beginning of the second quarter of 2009, it began to rebound in the bottom and fully recovered in the second half of that year. As can be seen from Table 4.8, in 2009, Chile's economic recession was 1%, and the per capita GDP fell 2%, ending the period of growth (2000–2008). The crisis had affected the real economy mainly through the channels of the atrophy of external demand, deteriorating terms of trade, and the reduction of foreign direct investment; at the same time, with the rising of the cost of external borrowing and the reduction of the availability of international financing, the crisis began to spread to the financial market, resulting in the shortage of domestic liquidity.

In order to deal with the foreign-sourced international financial crisis, Chile decisively had taken an anti-cyclical policy to actively

Table 4.8 Chile's Main Economic Indicators (2000–2012)

Main Economic Indicators	2000	2003	2008	2009	2010	2011	2012
Economic growth rate (%)	4.5	3.9	3.7	−1.0	6.1	6.0	5.5
Per capita GDP growth rate (%)	3.2	2.8	2.7	−2.0	5.1	5.0	4.6
CPI (%)	3.8	2.8	8.7	1.5	2.4	3.3	2.9
Export of commodities and services ($ million)	23,293.2	26,753.7	75,248.5	63,955.5	81,727.7	93,817.8	92,862
Import of commodities and services ($ million)	21,893.1	23,677.6	70,382.1	50,605.9	68,209.1	85,441.8	88,083
Commodity trade condition index (the year of 2005 = 100)	71.6	73.5	117.9	119.3	146.0	146.9	130.5
Current account balance ($ million)	−897.5	−829.6	−5,800.1	3,518.1	3,268.6	−3,220.2	−6,064
Current account balance/GDP (%)	−1.1	−1.1	−3.2	2.0	1.5	−1.3	—
Unemployment (%)	9.7	9.5	7.8	9.7	8.2	7.1	6.4
Poverty (%)	20.2	18.7	—	11.5	—	11.0	—
Total external debt ($ million)	37,177.0	430,67.0	64,318.0	74,041.0	73,578.0	77,090.0	101,875
Total external debt/GDP (%)	46.8	55.3	35.8	42.9	34.0	31.0	—
International reserve ($ million)	15,238.4	14,932.7	23,675.9	25,446.7	27,974.3	42,292.0	38,943

Note: The year of 2012 is an estimate.

Source: This is the author's summary of the data from *Statistical Yearbook for Latin America and the Caribbean 2012* and *Preliminary Overview of the Economies of Latin America and the Caribbean 2012*. ECLAC, *Statistical Yearbook for Latin America and the Caribbean 2012*, *Preliminary Overview of the Economies of Latin America and the Caribbean 2012*.

deal with it from the five aspects of currency and finance, fiscal policy, exchange rate and trade, industry and labor, and social policy. Specific measures are shown in Table 4.9. First, the Central Bank injected liquidity to the financial system to ensure the normal operation of the local credit market. The liquidity could be guaranteed and the interest rates could be as low as possible, but the greater liquidity could not guarantee the increase of credit supply and the increase of the supply of credit and could not guarantee the increase of demand for goods. Therefore, how to rebuild the lost confidence was very important. Second, the fiscal policy was a powerful tool, and which specific type of policy should be implemented was also very important. Measures to increase spending had more potential than measures based on the reduction of taxes because the former could directly stimulate demands while the latter would increase the disposable income of the private sectors, but in the face of uncertainty about the future, the increased income was likely to be saved rather than spent. In view of the implementation of the counter cyclical fiscal policy, the proportion of primary fiscal finance of Chile in GDP changed from surplus (5%) in 2008 to deficit (−3.9%) in 2009, while the debt proportion of the central government in GDP rose from 5.2% to 6.1%.[5] Finally, the department policy was still a continuation of the pragmatic style of Chile's industrial policy, focusing on supporting the "needs" of the sectors, especially to help SMEs to weather the storm.

To sum up, from the beginning of the 21st century, Chile has implemented pragmatic policy adjustments on the basis of following the basic free market economic system, with an outstanding performance in its ability to develop anti-cyclical monetary and fiscal policy. Although the dual impact of the economic recession in 2009 and the earthquake in 2010 made the Chilean Piniella government to have reduced the proportion of structural fiscal surplus, most of the "unexpected earnings" from the income of copper mines continued to be saved in the two sovereign wealth funds (Pension Reserve Fund &

[5]ECLAC, *Preliminary Overview of the Economies of Latin America and the Caribbean 2010*, 2010.

Table 4.9 Measures Taken Up To 31 December 2009

Combination of Policies	Measures
	Adjusting the statutory deposit reserve: temporarily relaxing the requirements for the statutory deposit reserve;
	Injecting local currency into the liquidity: 1. Repurchase operations for the 28-day and 60–90-day bonds; 2. Requiring local banks to bid for financial resources in the form of US dollars; 3. Adjusting the tax rate to increase liquidity and improving the public-bond demand to make bonds more attractive as an alternative source of financing. Encouraging the emerging medium enterprises to use the tool by means of a subsidy to the restructuring of the bonds, the intermediary and the issuing expense; 4. Expanding the financing mechanism of the Production Promotion Council (CORFO) for the financing of banks and non-banks; implementing the CORFO as a new mechanism to ensure the re-arrangement of the loans; 5. As a supplement to the monetary policy measures, in July 2009, the Central Bank announced the establishment of a "short-term liquidity facility" (Tem Liquidity Facility, FLAP) for the banks, i.e., with the current monetary policy interest rates to provide liquidity support for 90 and 180 days. The Central Bank also adjusted the issuing plan for Central Bank notes (PDBC) with a period of less than one year. Finally, the Central Bank decided in the remaining time of 2009 to suspend the issuance of bonds with a period of more than one year (including one year);
	Adjusting the policy rate of currency: throughout 2009 the Central Bank gradually cut the interest rates in its monetary policy, from 8.25% in January to the minimum value of 0.5% in July. At the same time, the Central Bank announced that it would maintain the interest rate unchanged for a long period of time.
	Cutting taxes or increasing benefits and subsidies: 1. Temporarily increasing the housing subsidies and new subsidies for the middle-income families; 2. In January 2009 announcing the fiscal stimulus plan of a total of $4 billion, equivalent to 2% of GDP, aiming to stimulate the economic growth and employment through the implementation of short-term measures and structural reforms. The plan included an increase of the public spending, a tax cut and an injection of capital. At the same time it also provided direct and targeted incentives to produce a direct effect on the economy.

(Continued)

Table 4.9 (*Continued*)

Combination of Policies	Measures
	The Economic and Social Stabilization Fund (FEES) would be the first to provide funding for the project, and other income came from the issuance of bonds (no more than $3 billion) authorized in the 2009 budget and the financial control goal that had been cut;
	3. The measures to be taken were as follows: (1) Stimulating investment and consumption: abolishing stamp duty for all credit transactions in 2009; in the first half of 2010 levying half of the tax rates; (2) Corporate financing: on the basis of the past profits, temporarily reducing the tax payment of the monthly provisional enterprise income. In 2009, the amount of the taxes of the SMEs was to be reduced by 15%; large enterprises by 7%; (3) Personal support: in the 2010 financial year, tax rebates was to be implemented for the income tax of natural persons;
	4. In March 2009, as part of the fiscal stimulus plan, $70 would be provided for each member of the most vulnerable families;
	5. In August 2009, low-income families eligible to enjoy the birth subsidy or family allowance would again receive a subsidy of $70 per family member. An estimate of 4 million people would receive the grant;
	6. In August and September of 2009, part of the income tax refund was paid almost nine months earlier than the normal date. The amount returned was based on the average of the past three years, with the maximum limit of $420. An estimate of one million people had benefited from this policy.
	Increasing or advancing the payment of the public expenditures:
	1. Implementing the counter-cyclical fiscal policy in accordance with the 2009 budget law. The actual increase of the total expenditure (2.5% of GDP) was 5.7%. Social spending increased 7.8% (69% of total spending). Infrastructure spending increased 8%;
	2. Public investment was about $7 billion. In the first half of 2009 it focused on the implementation of the public projects. The largest invested departments were the Ministry of Public Works ($2.5 billion), the Ministry of Housing and Urban Development ($1.46 billion), the Ministry of Health ($300 million), and the Department of Regional and Administrative Development ($1.07 billion);
	3. In the public works, an increase of 14.6% was invested in the projects of improving connectivity, infrastructure and transportation. Investment in regional development funds would increase 7.3%, mainly owing to the National Regional Development Fund;

(*Continued*)

Table 4.9 (*Continued*)

Combination of Policies	Measures
	4. The real growth of residential investment was 10%. The goal was to build 140,000 new homes. More main and secondary roads would be built. Grant of $50,000 would be provided to protect family property; 5. As part of the fiscal stimulus plan, another $700 million was provided to be used for a large public investment project, including construction of urban and rural roads, housing and irrigation facilities. **Other measures**: Providing an economic stimulus package of $1.15 billion for the purchase of houses and support of small business financing.
Exchange rate and foreign trade policy	**Liquidity injection of foreign currency**: Requiring bidding for foreign exchange swaps (1–6 months) of $5 billion. **Financing and support for export**: 1. Strengthening the banks to provide loans to exporters; 2. Speeding up the VAT refund for exporters.
Department policy	**Housing policy**: 1. The real growth of the residential investment in 2009 was 10%; 2. Temporarily increasing the housing subsidies; increasing additional subsidies of housing for middle-income families; 3. Expanding the coverage of the insurance of housing foreclosure; 4. For housing loans with state subsidies, the maximum limit increased from 80% of the value of the house to 90%; 5. For residential purchase, the government would accelerate the use of transferable mortgage secured loans and authorize the social security agencies to issue loans. **Policy for SMEs**: 1. Expansion of $500 million to the Investment Guarantee Fund (FOGAIN); 2. Increasing loans to SMEs through the capitalization ($500 million) of national banks; 3. Making the seed capital for micro-enterprises doubled through injecting a total of $8.3 million of additional funds to the Technical Cooperation Services Department (SERCOTEC); 4. Injecting $2.5 million to the Unity and Social Investment Fund (FOSIS) so that the project fund capacity increased three times, which could subsidize the operating cost of those credit institutions providing financing to micro-enterprises;

(*Continued*)

Table 4.9 (*Continued*)

Combination of Policies	Measures
	5. The longest period of re-negotiation for the tax debt of micro-enterprises was extended to three years, and any restrictions or detention of the default account of micro-enterprises using this rule were immediately suspended; 6. Due to the upgrading of the function of the Small Enterprise Guarantee Fund (FOGAPE), the businesses of mutual guarantee cooperatives and the companies would be supported, and the availability of capital operation coverage would be improved. As a transitional measure, when the larger scale enterprises needed to be supported in order to maintain their operations, they could apply for a small-business guarantee fund to keep the employment status of the workers; 7. Supporting the securitization of loans of smaller companies to reduce the credit cost of the sector. **Agricultural policy**: 1. Increasing income with the No. 701 Act of promoting forestry development; 2. Providing an as high as $120 million credit through the Production Promotion Association (CORFO) to guarantee the support of the salmon industry development. **Industrial policy**: 1. National Copper Corporation of Chile raised $1 billion in capital raising to promote its investment plans; 2. Supporting the small-scale mining industry through the price support fund of a $18 million. **Other measures** 1. One-time payment of $41 million to the Municipal Common Fund; 2. Increasing the lending capacity of the insurance companies, putting more resources into the credit channel; also taking some measures to make the companies to be able to participate in the syndicated loans.
Labor force and social policy	**Labor policy**: 1. Allocating additional budget to the labor-intensive employment or investment plan. If the unemployment rate increased or the economic growth rate was beyond the expected level, the government would begin to use this part of the fund; 2. (Additional) employment subsidies had been put on the agenda;

(*Continued*)

Table 4.9 (*Continued*)

Combination of Policies	Measures
	3. Providing subsidies to low wage workers between the ages of 18 and 24; 4. Planning to expand the Unemployment solidarity Fund to all the unemployed workers, rather than just to permanent-contracted workers; 5. The Government recommended encouraging enterprises to retain and train their employees through tax incentives and subsidies. If the employers maintained the level of the employee fund that they had invested in April, the measure would increase the tax deduction on the expenditures incurred by the enterprises for the employee training. Or the worker and the employer reached a consensus of a temporary departure (the longest period for five months), in which the worker did not have to work, but need to receive training, and he or she would get only half of the revenue equivalent to the average income of his or her recent six months, no more than $320. This part of the income would be paid by the enterprise, and at the same time the unemployment insurance should provide subsidies. **Social policy**: From March 2009 onwards, the non-workers from the country's 1.7 million low-income families would receive direct subsidies; each non-worker could receive a one-time subsidy of $70. There were more than 3.5 million people in the country to have benefited from this policy.

Source: *The Reactions of the Governments of the Americas to the International Crisis*: *An Overview of Policy Measures Up To 31 December 2009*, ECLAC, January 2010.

Economic and Social Stabilization Fund). At the same time, the government had implemented a tax-increase policy (such as the mining tax), and in the case of low cost at that time increased the local and external debts. These measures would help to make up the short-term unexpected social spending when new policies were adopted to support low-income groups. As for the monetary policy, the Central Bank would continue to adhere to the inflation target system in the long run, but with certain flexibility. In the medium term, the monetary policy rate would be stable at 5–5.5%, which could meet the requirements of inflation targeting and promote the stable growth of the economy in the medium and long term. The Central Bank was given a priority to maintain price stability, which shows that the government would not hesitate to accelerate monetary policy tightening in the face of sudden inflation or overheating. As long as inflation remained low and the economy was limitedly overheating, the Central Bank would choose to fight against the appreciation of the peso in the current level of policy interest rates.

Section 4 Pattern and Trend of the Foreign Trade and Economic Cooperation

As mentioned earlier, with a transparent and low-risk business environment, excellent infrastructure, high-quality human capital and government support, Chile has become Latin America's most competitive, stable and open economy. Its foreign trade pattern has the obvious characteristic of "Hub and Spoke".

I. The Establishment of a Wide Range of International Agreement Network by Signing Free Trade Agreements

Chile has signed free trade agreements with many countries (or regions) in order to enter the markets of these countries (or regions). These countries (or regions) include: the United States, Canada, Mexico, the European Union, Central America, South Korea, the European Free Trade Union, Singapore, New Zealand, Brunei, Japan, China, and India. As shown in Table 4.10, by October 2010, Chile has signed 25 free trade agreements with 57 countries in the world.

China–Chile free trade agreement negotiations were jointly announced by President Hu Jintao and President Lagos on November 18, 2004. Since then, both countries have had five rounds of consultations about the issues such as the market access, rules of origins, technical trade barriers, sanitary and phytosanitary measures, trade remedy, dispute resolution, and cooperation, and on November 18, 2005, agreed on all the content of the trade agreement. According to the agreement, both countries began the process of reducing tariffs on trade of goods on July 1, 2006. Among them, 97% of the total number of product items of the two countries would be lowered to

Table 4.10 Chile's International Agreements in Operation and under Negotiation (up to October 2010)

	Bilateral Tax Agreements		Free Trade Agreement
In operation	Argentina, Brazil, Canada, South Korea, Croatia, Denmark, Ecuador, Spain, France, Ireland, Malaysia, Mexico, Norway, New Zealand, Paraguay, Peru, Poland, Portugal, the United Kingdom, and Sweden	In operation	Australia, Canada, China, Colombia, Costa Rica, El Salvador, the European Free Trade Union (EFTA), Honduras, Japan, Mexico, Panama, Peru, South Korea, and the United States
Signed agreement	Belgium, Colombia, Russia, Thailand, and Switzerland	Economic organization agreement	EU, Singapore, Brunei, and New Zealand
Negotiation finished	South Africa	Economic supplementary agreement	Mercosur (Argentina, Brazil, Paraguay, and Uruguay), Bolivia, Colombia, Ecuador, and Venezuela
Under negotiation	Australia, Austria, China, Cuba, the United States, Finland, Holland, Hungary, India, Italy, Kuwait, Czech, Uruguay, and Venezuela	In partial agreement	Cuba and India
		Under negotiation	Guatemala, Malaysia, Nicaragua, Thailand, Turkey, and Vietnam

Source: *Mining Cluster in Chile*, InvestChile CORFO/Chilean Economic Development Agency, October 4, 2010.

zero tariff step by step within 10 years. The two countries would further cooperate in the fields of economy, SMEs, culture, education, science and technology, environmental protection, labor and social security, intellectual property, investment promotion, mineral resources, industry, and so on.

II. The Foreign Trade Showing a Rapid Growth Trend

Chile's foreign trade was in the slow growth phase in the 1990s. Since 2003 it started to go into the period of rapid growth, mainly due to the boom cycle of the rising of the world commodity prices and strong external demand. This trend continued to last till 2008 but stopped by the outbreak of the international financial crisis. However, with the global economic recovery, its foreign trade soon returned to the fast growth track. As is shown in Figure 4.10, from 1991 to 2002, the total foreign trade of Chile increased from \$16.4 billion to \$32.9 billion, a doubled growth, and from 2003 to 2008, its trade increased from \$37.4 billion to \$125.9 billion, an increase of about 2.4 times. With the impact of the international financial crisis in 2009 its foreign trade fell by 29.5%, but after two years of recovery, its total trade volume achieved a historical record of \$147.7 billion in 2012.

From the perspective of the structure of import and export, the major exports of Chile to the world are "food and live animals", "non-edible raw materials (excluding fuels)" and "manufactured goods according to the classification of raw materials"; the major imports of Chile from the world are "fossil fuels, lubricating oil and related

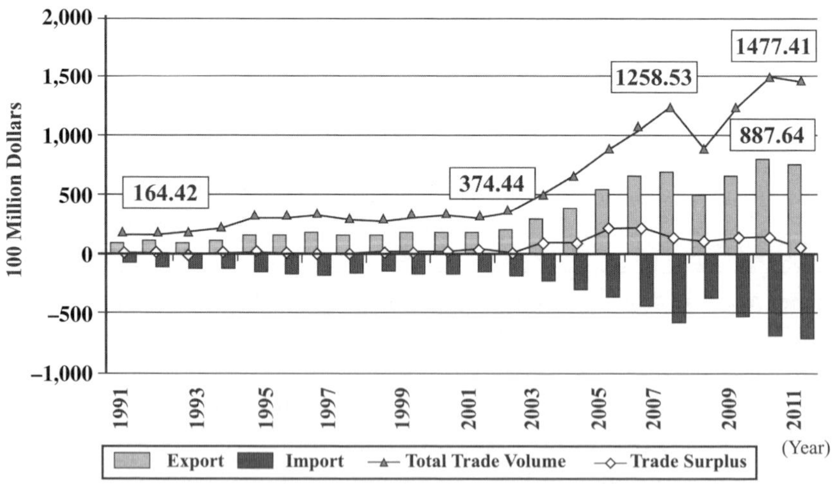

Figure 4.10 Trends of Chile's Foreign Trade Development (1991–2011)

Source: CEIC Database Chilean Sub-database (Date of Update: April 7, 2013).

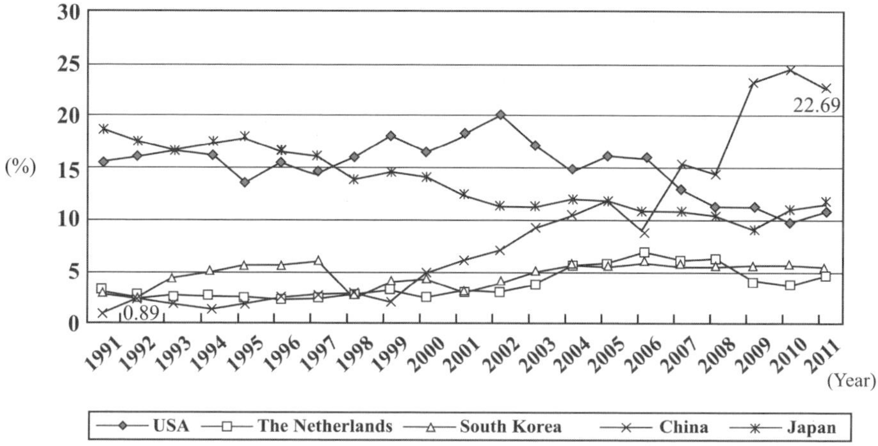

Figure 4.11 Trends of the Change of the Proportion of Chile's Main Export Markets

Source: CEIC Database Chilean Sub-database (Date of Update: January 17, 2012).

materials", "manufactured goods according to the classification of raw materials" and "machinery and transport equipment". According to the calculation of the CEIC database, in 2010, the first three kinds of export products accounted for 88.9% of the proportion of its total export, and the first three kinds of imported products accounted for 66.6% of the proportion of its total import.

From the perspective of export destination, the market share of the United States and Japan in Chile's export declined significantly, while China's share rose significantly, especially since 2006. As is shown in Figure 4.11, from 1991 to 2011, the share of the United States in Chile's export dropped from 15.4% to 10.9%, Japan's share fell from 18.7% to 11.4%, but China's share had soared from 0.9% to 22.7%.

From the perspective of the country origin of imports, from 1991 to 2011, the proportion of the United States in Chilean import experienced the changes of the "rise-fall-rise", and in 2011 the US share returned to the level of 1991 — 21%; while Argentina was experiencing the changes of increase first and then decrease, in 2011 accounting for roughly the same as in 1991 — about 7%. However, over the same

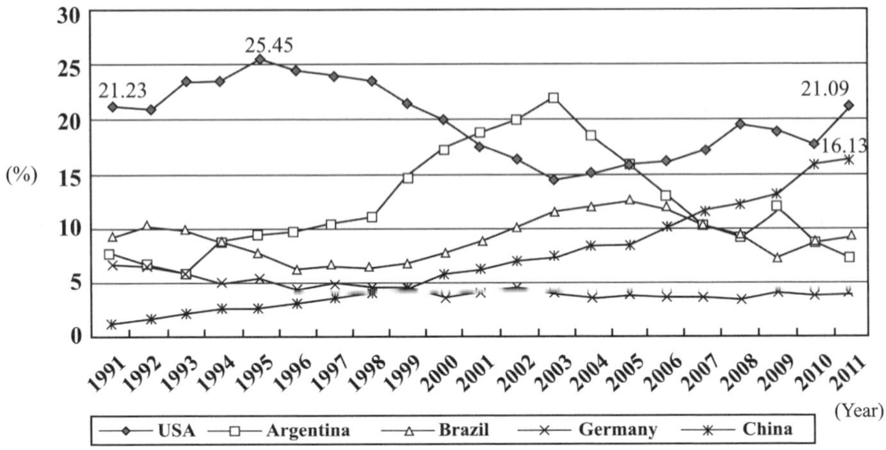

Figure 4.12 Trends of the Change of the Proportion of Chile's Main Sources of Imports

Source: CEIC Database Chilean Sub-database (Date of Update: January 17, 2012).

period, the proportion of China in Chile's import had been in an upward trend, rising from 1.28% to 16.13% (see Figure 4.12).

III. The Important Role of FDI in the Economic Development

The fact that Chile has become a very attractive country for foreign investment has been internationally recognized. According to the *2010 World Investment Report* released by the United Nations Committee on Trade and Development (UNCTAD), in 2009 Chile's Foreign Direct Investment (FDI) stock reached $121.64 billion, ranking second in Latin America after Brazil. In 2010 $1.82 billion of FDI flowed into Chile, 43.3% higher than in 2009. According to the monitoring report of the global investment trends issued by the UNCTAD, that ratio was much higher than the average growth rate of 21.1% of foreign investment that Latin America had absorbed. This made Chile the third country with the highest growth rate of the absorption of foreign investment in the region, and also the third largest foreign investment receiving country. Moreover, according to the *2010 Report of FDI in Latin America and the Caribbean Region* released by ECLAC of the United Nations, in Chile, FDI accounted for about 8% of its GDP, the highest in the region.[6] According to the statistics of the Central Bank of Chile, Chile's FDI in 2011 reached $17.299 billion, an increase of 12.5% ($15.373 in 2010); its FDI in 2012 reached $28.152 billion, an increase of 62.7%.[7] The proportion of FDI in GDP rose from an annual average rate of 6.8% (1998–2008) to an average annual rate of 7.3% (2009–2011) (see Figure 4.13).

There are two mechanisms for investing in Chile. The first one is the *No. 600 Act of Foreign Investment Regulation* in effect since 1974; the other one is Chapter 14 in the *International Exchange Regulation* of the Central Bank of Chile, which rules that if foreign investors are willing to use this mechanism, they have to be registered under this regulation. Under the mechanism of the No. 600 Act, investors have to sign a contract with the state to transfer capital or other

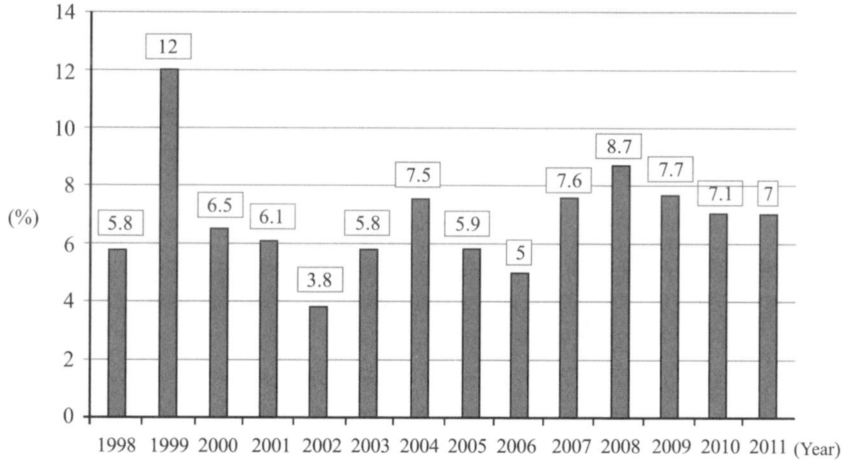

Figure 4.13 Proportions of FDI in Chile's GDP (1998–2011)

Note: Here the FDI includes the investments under Chapters 14 and 19 of *The Complete Works of the Central Bank International Foreign Exchange Regulations* and the *Foreign Investment Laws and Regulations* (DL600).

Source: Chile's Central Bank (www.bcentral.cl).

[6] http://www.foreigninvestment.cl/index.php+option=com_content&view=article&id=136&Itemid=99.

[7] *Ibid.*

forms of investment, meanwhile obtaining some special protection and rights. From 1974 to 2011, the amount of investment using this mechanism amounted to $82.021 billion, accounting for 56.5% of the total amount of FDI through the above two mechanisms.[8]

From the perspective of sectors, from 1974 to 2011, 34.1% of FDI obtained through the implementation of the No. 600 Act flowed into the mining sector. Next, the service sector accounted for 22.4%, electricity, natural gas and water sector accounted for 18.4%, manufacturing accounted for 10.9%, transport and communications accounted for 11.1%, the construction sector accounted for 1.7%, and agriculture and fisheries accounted for 1.4% (see Figure 4.14). In the subsectors of the service sector, the financial intermediaries (including banks and investment companies) received the most FDI, accounting for 41.5%, followed by the retail industry (26.6%), and the third was the insurance industry (15.6%).[9]

From the perspective of the source of investment, from 1974 to 2011, 24.6% of the FDI through the implementation of the No. 600 Act came from the United States. Other sources included: Spain

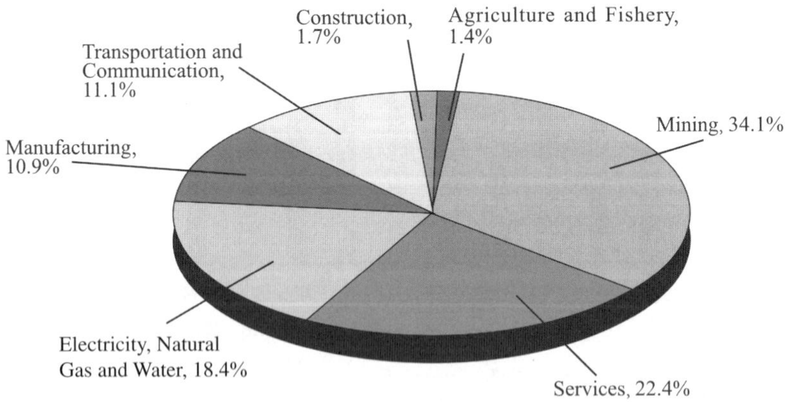

Figure 4.14 FDI Achieved through the No. 600 Act (1974–2011) (Divided by Sectors, a Total of $82.021 Billion)

Source: Chilean Foreign Investment Commission, www.foreigninvestment.cl.

[8] *Ibid.*

[9] *Ibid.*

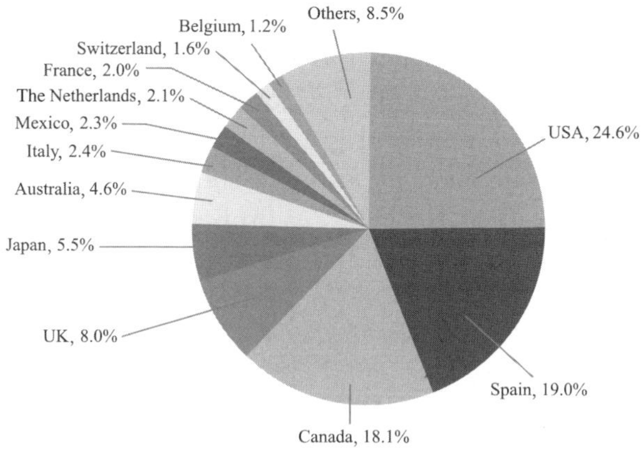

Figure 4.15 FDI Achieved through the No. 600 Act (1974–2011) (Divided by Sources, a Total of $82.021 Billion)

Source: Chilean Foreign Investment Commission, www.foreigninvestment.cl.

accounted for 19%, Canada 18.1%, the UK 8%, Japan 5.5%, and Australia 4.6% (see Figure 4.15).

In summary, through years of reform Chile has established a relatively sound, stable and more open market economic system, with more typical characteristics of openness in its foreign strategy: to have constructed the "Hub and Spoke" network by signing free trade agreements to strengthen the close relationship with the world economy; through its comparative advantages and division and cooperation to have promoted the trade to develop by leaps and bounds so as to improve its international competitiveness; to have vigorously attracted foreign investment to make it an important force in promoting economic growth, and to have absorbed the advanced management experience and expertise to expand the spillover effect of FDI. At the same time, Chile's outward development strategy also has presented a new trend. First, located in the Pacific Rim, Chile has become an important bridge for Asia to communicate with Latin America. While maintaining close ties with the traditional European and American developed countries, it began to strengthen its ties with Asia and the emerging market countries. Secondly, due to the rise of the status of emerging market countries in the world economy, the trade proportion of Chile has increased with the emerging market countries, and for its industrial upgrading needs Chile had to strengthen the intra industry trade with its trading partners. Finally, although Chile's ability to attract foreign investment is strong in terms of the total amount and growth speed, still it has the characteristics of the over concentration of the fields of investment and the source countries. With the rising proportion of emerging market countries in Chile's foreign trade, investments from these countries will gradually increase to make up for the situation of weak foreign investment capacity of Europe and the United States due to the downturn of their economies. The new trend above is a huge opportunity for China; especially the signing of the China–Chile Free Trade Agreement has provided a good opportunity for Chinese enterprises to enter the markets of Chile and Latin America.

Section 5 Present Situation and Policy Choice of the Economic and Trade Cooperation between China and Chile

In the 10 years of China's accession to the World Trade Organization (WTO), the total amount of trade between China and Latin America has achieved a leapfrog growth. In 2000, it topped \$10 billion; in 2007 it exceeded \$100 billion, with seven years, and in 2011 it went over \$200 billion (\$241.5 billion), within four years. With the sharp increase in the Sino-Latin American trade, China's investment in Latin America has also increased rapidly. According to the data from ECLAC, in 2010 China's investment in Latin America soared, reaching \$15.3 billion — 2.1 times of the total investment of the first 10 years (\$7.3 billion). Therefore, if 2007 were identified as the "first year" of the Sino-Latin American trade, 2010 would be the "first year" of China's investment in Latin America. With the rapid growth of trade and investment, the demand of China and Latin America for further development of financial cooperation was "ripe", and the international financial crisis had objectively prompted both sides to accelerate the financial cooperation. In the background of the economic and trade cooperation between China and Latin America, the economic and trade relations between China and Chile will also follow the development path of the "leapfrog trade growth — steady increase of investment — vigorous financial cooperation".

I. Trade Still Being the Main Body of Economic and Trade Cooperation, but the Trade Structure Needing to Be Optimized

In the 1980s and 1990s, the Sino-Chilean trade development was relatively slow — the bilateral trade volume did not reach 1 billion US dollars until 1998, but since the beginning of the 21st century the Sino-Chilean trade began to show a rapid growth (see Figure 4.16). In 2012 the bilateral trade volume reached \$33.219 billion, an increase of 14.7 times of the year 2001, of which China's export to Chile reached \$12.608 billion and the import from Chile reached \$20.611 billion, increasing respectively 14.5 times and 14.8 times compared with 2001. In the 33 years from 1980 to 2012, China maintained a surplus status for six years (in 1990, 1994–1998); in the remaining 27 years, China had been in the status of deficit, and since 2001 the

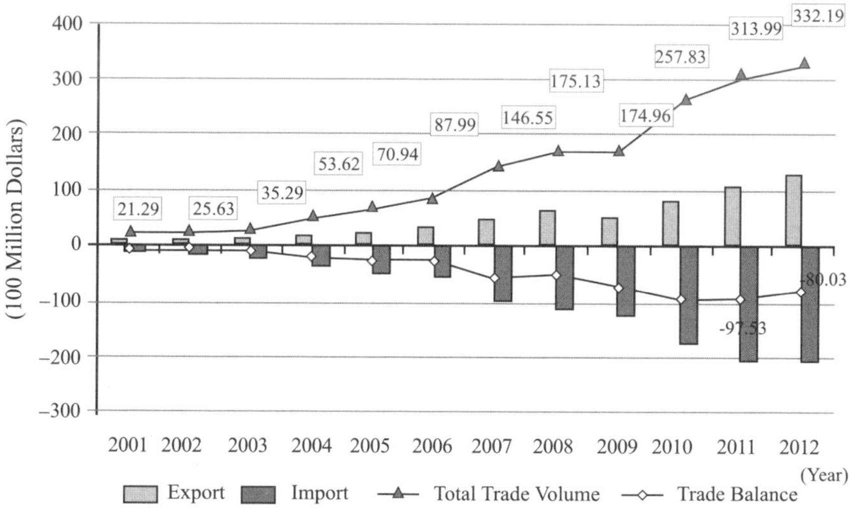

Figure 4.16 Trends of the Trade Development between China and Chile (2001–2012)

Source: CEIC Database Chinese Economic Database (Date of Update: March 21, 2013).

deficit was showing a gradual expanding trend, increasing from \$487 million to \$9.753 billion in 2011, an increase of 19 times. In 2012, China's deficit to Chile had been reduced. The vast majority of the deficit came from the import of primary products from Chile, which confirms the existing inter-trade pattern of "finished products for primary products". In particular, the strong demands for resource products of emerging markets such as China and India had played a positive role in helping the Latin-American countries (especially South American countries) to have recovered from the international financial crisis.

From the perspective of trade structure, China and Chile have strong economic complementarity. China exports mainly textile products and mechanical and electrical equipment to Chile, while importing from Chile mainly mineral products and base metals and their products. As is shown in Table 4.11, in all the trade commodities in accordance with HS codes, in 2011 the first three kinds of commodities that China exported to Chile accounted for a total of 63.92% of its total export, including textile materials and textile products (26.85%), the mechanical and electrical products, audio–visual equipment and parts and accessories (26.3%), and base metals and their products (10.77%). The first two kinds of commodities that China imported from Chile accounted for 88.32% of its total import, including base metals and their products (61.33%) and mineral products (26.99%). It can be seen that there is a very high degree of concentration of the goods that China exported to Chile and imported from Chile. In the future in order to reduce to the trade deficit and promote trade balance, China should maintain the stability in import, and at the same time, strive to diversify its export structure, upgrading export commodities from the simple manufactured goods to high value-added goods, for example, the industries with export potential, such as chemical products and vehicles, aircraft, ships and transportation design equipment, should be given policy support. For Chile, when its production and its technical ability were in non-symmetrical distribution between economic units, the market mechanism may promote the self-reinforcing of specialization on the basis of static rather than dynamic comparative advantages. Chile

Table 4.11 Structure Details of the Sino-Chilean Trade in 2011

Imports from Chile			Exports to Chile	
Proportion (%)	$ Million	All Goods in Accordance with the HS Encoding Classification	$ Million	Proportion (%)
0.69	142.08	Live animal; animal products	7.50	0.07
2.54	523.59	Plant products	19.88	0.18
0.04	7.53	Animal, vegetable oils, fats; waxes; refined edible oils and fats	9.46	0.09
1.57	322.66	Food; beverage, wine and vinegar; tobacco and tobacco products	121.77	1.13
26.99	5,553.83	Minerals	16.92	0.16
1.10	227.00	Chemical industry and its products	467.55	4.32
0.03	7.07	Plastic and its products; rubber and its products	547.67	5.06
0.05	11.03	Leather; fur and fur products; bags; catgut products	176.16	1.63
0.63	129.89	Wood and wood products; charcoal; cork; knitting goods	49.68	0.46
4.86	999.16	Cellulose pulp; waste paper; paper, paperboard and its products	78.84	0.73
0.07	13.71	Textile materials and textile products	2,906.44	26.85
0.00	0.00	Shoes, hats and umbrella; feathers; artificial flowers; human hair products	652.14	6.03
0.00	0.00	Mineral products; ceramics; glass and glass products	227.68	2.10
0.00	0.60	Jewelry, precious metals and their products; imitation jewelry; coins	1.34	0.01
61.33	12,619.35	Base metal and its products	1,165.18	10.77
0.09	18.45	Mechanical and electrical equipment, audio and video equipment and their spare parts and accessories	2,846.73	26.30
0.00	0.01	Vehicles, aircraft, ships and transport equipment	738.64	6.82
0.00	0.05	Optical, medical and other instruments; clocks; instruments	115.15	1.06
0.00	0.00	Weapons, ammunition and their parts and accessories	0.71	0.01
0.00	0.03	Miscellaneous products	673.27	6.22
0.00	0.00	Works of art, collectibles and antiques	0.34	0.00
0.00	0.00	Special deals and non-classified goods	0.05	0.00
100	20,576.04	Total	10,823.08	100

Source: The author's summary of the data from Chinese Economic Database in the CEIC database.

should be aware of the risks hidden behind its specialized production of copper mining and its export model.

II. Increasing Direct Investment in Chile and Having a Reasonable Industrial Layout While Raising the Total Amount

According to the latest statistics of the ECLAC, in 2010, China's investment in the Latin-American countries reached \$15.251 billion, after the United States (17%) and the Netherlands (13%), becoming Latin America's third biggest investment-source country (9%). However, as China's investment in Latin America increased, the concerns of some Latin-American scholars also began to increase, mainly in three aspects. First, from the perspective of industry distribution, 90% of the investment was concentrated in mining areas of natural resources such as oil, natural gas, and mining, which would hinder the industrial development and technological upgrading of Latin America, for the specialized production of natural resources would deepen the degree of "de-industrialization". Second, China's large transactions in the field of natural resources in Latin America were mostly dominated by state-owned enterprises, so the Latin-American scholars worried that the assets acquired in different transactions would eventually be concentrated in the hands of the Chinese government. They believed that the United States had set obstacles to the investment of the Chinese state-owned enterprises, but there were few Latin-American countries to have set limits for the investment for national security considerations. Third, the economic activities that the China companies were engaged in were not sensitive to local social responsibility and environmental issues of Latin America, so labor disputes and environmental disputes occurred occasionally. The above issues deserve the attention of Chinese enterprises in Chile.

As is shown in Table 4.12, more than 90% of China's direct investment in Latin America flowed to the Cayman Islands and the British Virgin Islands, and a relatively small investment flowed to other countries. The reasons behind this imbalance are worth studying, perhaps due to the nature of the "tax havens" of the two places.

Table 4.12 China's Investment in Major Latin-American Countries ($ Million)

Year	Latin America	Argentine	British Virgin Islands	Brazil	The Cayman Islands	Chile	Ecuador	Mexico	Peru	Venezuela
2003	1,038.15	1.00	209.68	6.67	806.61	0.20	0.27	0.03	0.12	6.22
2004	1,762.72	1.12	385.52	6.43	1,286.13	0.55	0.30	27.10	0.22	4.66
2005	6,466.16	0.35	1,226.08	15.09	5,162.75	1.80	9.07	3.55	0.55	7.40
2006	8,468.74	6.22	538.11	10.09	7,832.72	6.58	2.46	−3.69	5.40	18.36
2007	4,902.41	136.69	1,876.14	51.13	2,601.59	3.83	3.58	17.16	6.71	69.53
2008	3,677.25	10.82	2,104.33	22.38	1,524.01	0.93	−9.42	5.63	24.55	9.78
2009	7,327.90	−22.82	1,612.05	116.27	5,366.30	7.78	17.90	0.82	58.49	115.72
2010	10,538.27	27.23	6,119.76	487.46	3,496.13	33.71	22.06	26.73	139.03	94.39
2011	11,935.82	185.15	6,208.33	126.40	4,936.46	13.99	−35.06	41.54	214.25	81.77

Source: CEIC Database Chinese Economic Database (Date of Update: September 13, 2012).

In 2011 China's investment in Chile was $13.99 million. By of the end of 2011, China's direct investment stock in Chile was $97.94 million.[10]

With little direct investment in Chile, when entering Chile, the Chinese companies can learn from the experiences and lessons in their investments in other countries, getting ready a reasonable industrial layout in advance. First, China itself contains a huge demand, a steady enterprise financial status, the national policy support, and lower commodity prices, which means that it is currently a good opportunity for the Chinese enterprises to invest in resources and to purchase in Chile, but the enterprises should also be aware of the risks of "going out": one is the investment involving strategic resources may be confronted with possible boycott mood of the relevant interest groups, and even attract criticism from the third party; second, after the completion of the transaction, management and operation may incur greater risks due to factors such as the country's laws and regulations, the labor system and customs and culture. For example, strikes of copper mine workers in Chile occur now and then. Therefore, it is suggested that the radical full acquisition of equity should be avoided in the merger and acquisition (M&A) of overseas resources; the form of M&A of a portion of the equity can be considered more, or the M&A can be done in combination with other countries. If the enterprise's interests were tied together with the interests of the existing shareholders of the acquired enterprise, the risk thereby would be reduced. Secondly, China should increase the market-oriented FDI based on the information industry and the efficiency-oriented FDI based on manufacturing to form the pattern of "three pillars" with the resource-oriented FDI so as to disperse the negative pressure of the international public opinion. Finally, the economic cooperation is the important content of the economic and trade cooperation; therefore, with a wealth of experience in contracted projects, labor cooperation and design consultation, China can accomplish a great deal in Chile.

---

[10]CEIC Database Chinese Economic Database.

III. Promoting the Development of Financial Cooperation in a Timely Manner in the Process of the Internationalization of the RMB

Financial cooperation is an internal requirement for the growth of trade and investment, and the international financial crisis has led to the acceleration of financial cooperation between China and Latin America. For example, on January 12, 2009, China officially became the 48 member of the Inter-American Development Bank, China signed the bilateral currency swap agreement with Argentina, China signed the agreement of "Loans for Oil" with Brazil, Venezuela and Ecuador, and China and Venezuela increased the capital to the joint investment fund. In the above context, China and Chile have great potential in financial cooperation. Chile has a relatively sound financial system and capital market, and it is one of the few countries in Latin America capable of obtaining international financing. At present, the Central Bank of Chile is studying to put the RMB into the portfolio of its foreign exchange reserves, which may be a direction. In addition, it is also a subject worthy of study the use of RMB for clearing trade and the direct investment in Chile. The premise of all these cooperations is that China should continue to improve the mechanism for the RMB exchange rate formation and establish an effective RMB trading market outside China.

Chapter 5

Economic Policy Adjustment of Mexico and the Prospect of the Sino-Mexican Economic and Trade Cooperation

Huang Zhilong

In the 20th century, Mexico experienced a process of industrialization for half a century, creating a remarkable economic miracle, but became the first Latin-American country to have the outbreak of the debt crisis in 1982. Since then, Mexico had been in the process of economic reform and adjustment for 30 years. Through joining the North American Free Trade Area, Mexico became the exclusive emerging market country in the G20 to enjoy the US market; after the first generation of economic reform in the 1990s, Mexico began to be known as the model of neoliberal reform in the developing countries, and became the first member of the club of developed countries — the Organization of Economic Cooperation and Development (OECD); by signing free trade agreements with the world's major economies such as the United States, the European Union, Japan and the Latin-American countries, Mexico became one of the world's most opening countries, becoming the main practitioner of "Open Regionalism". However, the intense market reform and opening to the outside world, together with the lack of supporting measures such as financial regulations, led to the first financial crisis of the era of globalization in Mexico in 1995.

Mexico's recent 30 years of economic reform and opening up is a combination of success and failure, experience and lessons of emerging market countries involved in globalization. At present, Mexico's macroeconomic policy, financial system, trade rules and fiscal policy have achieved the international standards in nature; however, Mexico is facing common problems of the "Middle Income Trap", such as low investment rate, the stagnation of manufacturing industry, serious unemployment and poverty and deterioration of social security. Since the 21st century, Mexico's average annual economic growth rate has been less than 2%. The biggest challenge facing the government of Mexico is how to speed up economic growth and how to solve the social problems of poverty and unemployment and social security in its development.

Section 1 Resource Endowments and Industrial Advantages of Mexico

I. The Advantage of Resource Endowments

1. The Big Land Area and Superior Climate Condition

Mexico is the third largest country in Latin America with a land area of 1.96 million square kilometers. About 5/6 of the land are plateaus and mountains, with an average of about 1,800 meters above sea level. The country is divided into 31 states and one federal district (Mexico City); the 31 states are divided into five regions: the northern region consists of 7 states, the Gulf of Mexico is made up of 5 states, the North Pacific region is composed of 5 states, the South Pacific region covers 4 states and the central area includes 10 states. Each state consists of cities (towns); there are 2,394 cities. With complex and diverse climates, most parts of Mexico are divided into two seasons of drought and rain throughout the year, 4.8% of the land area are hot and humid regions, 23% are dry and hot regions, 23.1% are temperate regions, 28.3% are arid areas, and 20.8% are extremely arid regions. The Mexican territory is mainly covered with high altitude terrains, with no cold in winter, no heat in summer, and evergreen trees in the four seasons, enjoying the laudatory title of the "Pearl of the Plateau".

2. The Abundant Human Resources

In 2010, with a total population of 113 million, Mexico was the second country with the largest population in Latin America after Brazil, accounting for 18.8% of the total population of the region. Historically, Mexico's population growth rate had been higher than the Latin-American average, but its population growth rate of 1985–2010 was 1.56%, lower than the average level of 1.62% of Latin America (see Figure 5.1). Of its population of 113 million, the rural population was 25.18 million, accounting for 22.2%. The proportion of the population over 60 years old was 9.44%, and the proportion of the population over 65 years old was 6.58%, which was close to 10% and 7% of the population aging society. In 2010, the national economically active population was 4,879 million, with the rate of labor force participation (the proportion of the population above 15 years old in the economically active population) of 61.7% below the average of 66% in Latin America, only slightly higher than that of Cuba and Venezuela in the major countries in Latin America, reflecting a still high proportion of informal employment of Mexico (see Figure 5.2).

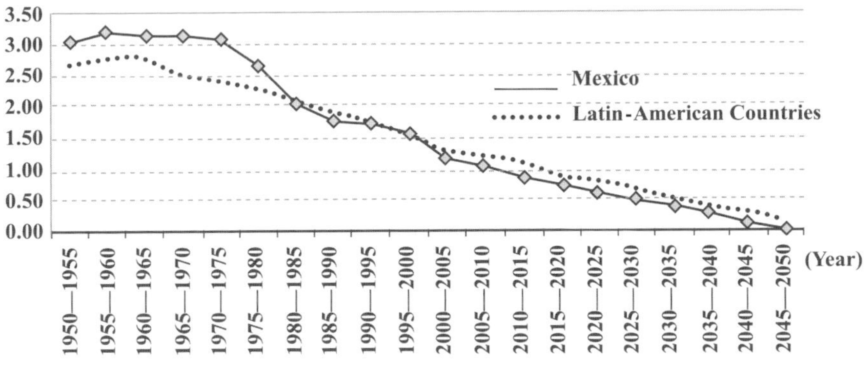

Figure 5.1 Population Growth of Mexico and Latin America (%)

Source: ECLAC, www.cepal.org.

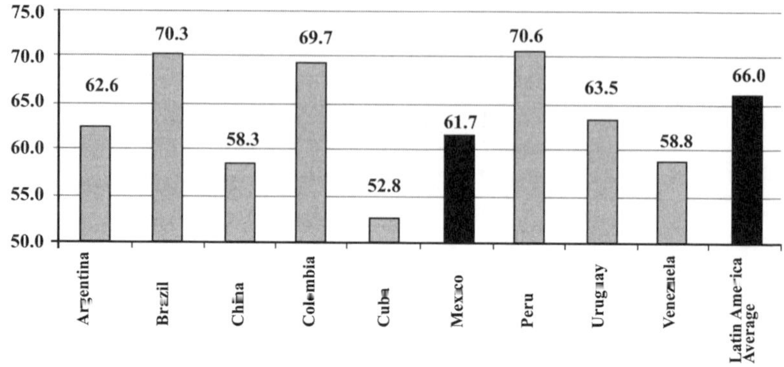

Figure 5.2 Proportion of Mexico's Economic Active Population (Work Participation Ratio) (%)

Source: ECLAC, www.cepal.org.

3. The Downward Trend of Oil and Gas Resources

Mexico is a big country of the reserve, production and export of oil in the world. In 2010, with proven oil reserve of about 11.4 billion barrels, it had the 5th largest crude oil reserve in the western hemisphere after Canada, Venezuela, the United States and Brazil, ranking the 18th in the world. Mexico is also one of the world's major non-OPEC countries, producing and exporting oil. Due to the declining of the oil field production in its traditional regions and the insufficient input on crude oil exploration and technology of the government, Mexico's crude oil production continued to decline (see Figure 5.3). The highest daily production of crude oil fell from 3.82 million barrels in 2004 to 2.96 million barrels in 2010, a decline of about 22.6%. The decline in production capacity and the strong domestic consumption of crude oil led to a clear downward trend of the export volume of crude oil in Mexico. Since the 1980s, Mexico's capacity of crude oil production was basically half for export and half for domestic consumption. However, after its production reached its highest historical level in 2004, its crude oil export fell from the highest level of 2.115 million barrels per day in 2003 to 1.539 million barrels per day in 2010. In the meantime, its domestic consumption of crude oil had been steadily increasing and it almost doubled from 1980 to 1994. In recent years, with the implementation of the diversification policy

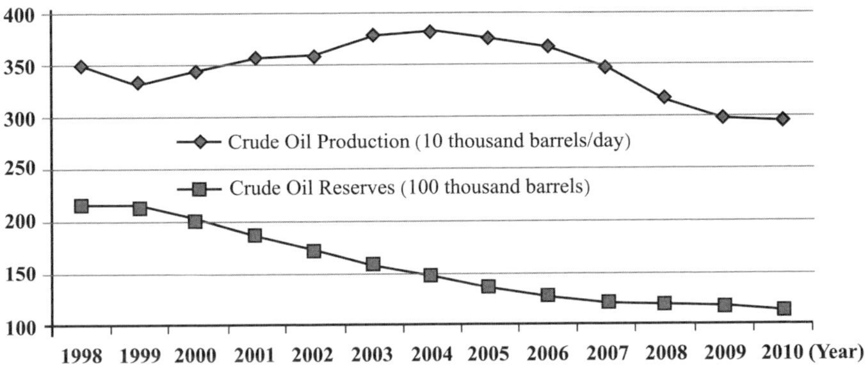

Figure 5.3 Mexican Crude Oil Reserves and Production Variation Trends

Source: BP, *Statistical Review of World Energy*, June 2011.

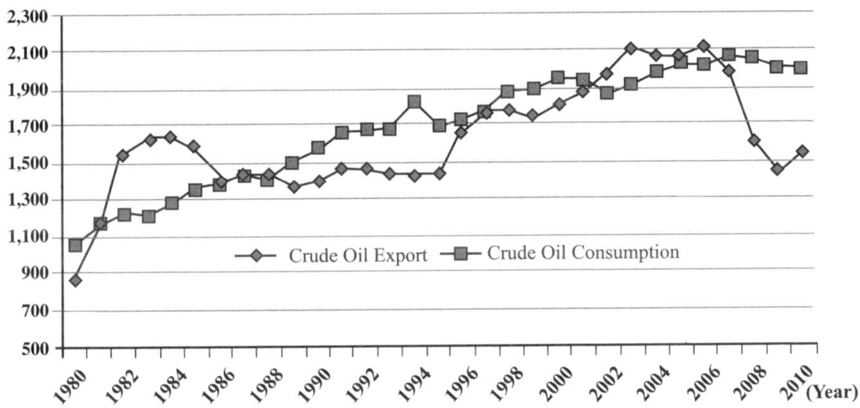

Figure 5.4 Mexican Crude Oil Domestic Demand and Export (1,000 barrels/day)

Source: BP, *Statistical Review of World Energy*, June 2011.

of energy-saving emission reduction and energy supply, the domestic crude oil consumption had been stable at around 2 million barrels per day. In terms of natural gas reserves and production capacity, in 2010, the proven recoverable reserves of Mexican natural gas were 452.65 billion cubic meters, accounting for 0.3% of the world's total reserves, ranking the 35th in the world; its natural gas production capacity was 55.3 billion cubic meters and its domestic demand was

68.9 billion cubic meters. Its import and export of natural gas as a whole showed a net import (see Figure 5.4).

4. The Great Potential for the Development of Mineral Resources

Mexico is one of the world's major countries of mineral resources. At present, more than 50 species of minerals have been found, mainly silver, lead, zinc, copper, gold, molybdenum, mercury, iron, cadmium, graphite, barite, fluorite, gypsum, etc. Its silver reserve ranks the 2nd in the world; its mineral reserves of gold, lead, zinc, copper, mercury, barite and fluorite also rank the forefront in the world.

Mexico is known as the "Country of Silver" — in 2008, with reserves of 37,000 tons, accounting for 13.7% of the world's total reserves, ranking the second in the world (after Peru), it was the world's second largest producer of silver. In 2008, its silver mine production was about 3,236 tons, an increase of 3.2% over the previous year, setting a historic record.

In 2008, Mexico's copper reserves were 38 million tons, accounting for 6.9% of the world's total, ranking the third in the world; its copper production was 269,000 tons, with a decrease of 19.9% compared with 2007. The main reason was because the workers of Cananea Copper Mine continued to hold strikes in 2008, and the production was interrupted throughout the year, resulting in a serious influence on the growth of copper production.

In 2008, Mexico's iron ore reserves were 700 million tons, with about 400 million tons of metal, distributed mainly in the Pacific coast and the northern plateau area. Mexico is the third largest iron ore producer in Latin America and the Caribbean, behind Brazil and Venezuela. In 2008 its production was about 11.69 million tons, an increase of 7.1% over the previous year.

Mexico's mineral mining and processing of gold, manganese, zinc, and barite are among the first ranks in the world. Mining is playing a more and more important role in Mexico in its national economy — in 2008, its total output value of mining industry was $12.4 billion (excluding fuel mineral resources), an increase of 29.3% over the previous year, in which the total metal mineral value was about

Table 5.1 Reserves and Production of Major Mineral Products of Mexico in 2008

Mineral	Unit	Reserve	Reserve Base	Production
Silver	ton	37,000	40,000	323.6
Gold	ton	1,400	3,400	5.1
Lead	(metallicity) 10,000 tons	150	200	14.1
Zinc	(metallicity) 10,000 tons	700	2,500	45.36
Copper	(metallicity) 10,000 tons	3, 800	4,000	26.87
Molybdenum	(metallicity) 10,000 tons	13.5	23	0.78
Manganese	(metallicity) 10,000 tons	400	800	17.0
Iron ore	(ore quantity) 100 million tons	7	15	0.117
Trona	100 million tons	2	4.5	—
Barite	10,000 tons	700	850	—
Graphite	10,000 tons	310	310	—
Fluorite	10,000 tons	3, 200	4, 000	—

Source: *Mineral Commodity Summaries*, 2009; *Minerals Yearbook*, 2008.

$11.3 billion, accounting for 91.1% of the national non-fuel mineral. Among the mining production value (excluding oil and gas), copper provided the highest contribution rate, accounting for 21% of mining production; the second was gold, accounting for 17%, followed by silver (15%), zinc (9%), iron (7%), coal (6%), sulfur (4%), lead (2%), etc. Thus, Mexico has a great potential of mining development (see Table 5.1).

II. The Industrial Structure

Since its accession to the North American Free Trade Agreement (NAFTA) in 1994, the liberalization of trade and investment has made Mexico fully integrated into the tide of economic globalization. The full depth of its economic opening to the outside world had enabled Mexico's manufacturing enterprises to process or assemble the final products by importing with lower cost, high quality and low price of intermediate products, spare parts and capital goods, making use of rich and relatively low human resources. NAFTA and the geographical advantages of Mexico had provided a unique convenient condition for Mexico's industrial products to enter the US market. At the same time, the opening up of its service industry and a large number of foreign capitals participating in the process of privatization of state-owned enterprises had promoted the development of the service industry of Mexico. However, the foreign capitals had invested very little in the production departments lagging behind in Mexico such as agriculture. In addition, due to the influx of agricultural products from the United States and Canada, the agriculture in Mexico had been affected unprecedentedly, resulting in the fact that the agricultural sector had become the weakest part in the chain of Mexico's participation in international competition. In 1996, in the composition of Mexico's gross domestic product (GDP), the proportions of agriculture, industry, and service industry, respectively were 6.26%, 28.36%, and 65.36%; in 2010 they were 3.92%, 34.35%, and 61.74%; the proportions of the number of labor force engaged in the three industries respectively were 13.7%, 23.4%, and 62.9% (see Figure 5.5).

Specifically, agriculture (covering agriculture, animal husbandry, forestry, and fishery) plays an important role in the economic life of Mexico. The span of its agricultural production modes is large — there is not only the mode of traditional small peasant and family agriculture, but also the mode of large-scale modern high-tech agricultural production. Its national arable land area is 35.6 million

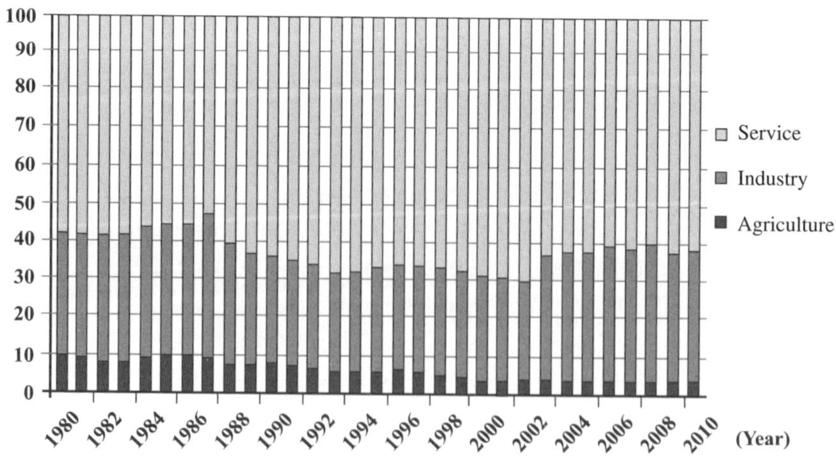

Figure 5.5 Proportions of Mexico's Three Sectors in GDP in 1980–2010 (%)
Source: ECLAC, www.cepal.org.

hectares, of which 23 million hectares have been cultivated. The main crops are corn, wheat, sorghum, barley, soybeans, rice and potatoes; important economic crops include coffee, cotton, sugar cane, fruit, and vegetables. Its national pastures cover an area of 79 million hectares, mainly feeding cattle, pigs, sheep, horses, and chickens. Mexico has a long coastline of 11,500 kilometers, with 25,000 square kilometers of freshwater lakes; its fishery resource is rich, with competitive advantages of abalone, tuna, sharks, sardines, lobster, shrimp, and octopus in the international market. Since its entry into NAFTA took effect in 1994, Mexico began to adjust its agriculture; the diversity and export of its agricultural products had increased; however, the growth of the agricultural sector lagged behind the other sectors of the economy, becoming the most affected sector in its opening to the outside world. At present, a large number of the Mexican domestically required products such as beef, pork, and cotton are imported from the United States; the traditional Mexican advantages in the agricultural sector such as corn, coffee, and sugar have been severely impacted by the products from the United States and Canada.

Industry is the most important sector in the national economy of Mexico. Through decades of import substitution industrialization, Mexico has established a relatively complete and diversified industrial system, with not only a light industry of food, textile, leather, clothing, paper, etc., but also a heavy industry of iron and steel, chemicals, automobiles, machinery manufacturing, and so on. Its energy industry is relatively developed, and its oil industry and mining industry also have a long history. The manufacturing industry covers Mexico's main industrial sectors, creating more than 80% of its total export income and of about 1/4 of its GDP. Its manufacturing includes more than 20 sectors such as steel, automobile, chemicals, electronic, metal processing, machinery manufacturing, food, textiles, paper, clothing, rubber, and pharmaceuticals. The proportion of the output value of manufacturing in the GDP increased from 18.1% in 1995 to 20.3% in 2000. Since China joined the World Trade Organization (WTO) in 2001, Mexico has been under enormous pressure from Chinese products; its manufacturing output fell to 17.8% in 2010, less than its share before its entry into the NAFTA.

It is noteworthy that since the NAFTA came into force, the automotive industry has become the largest manufacturing sector in Mexico. The liberalization of trade and investment has greatly improved the productivity and competitiveness of Mexico's auto industry. Nowadays Mexico has become the fifth largest auto producer after Japan, the United States, the European Union, and Canada, with especial advantages in producing small and medium-sized cars, light trucks, car engines, and spare parts. Mexico's major automobile manufacturing and assembly plants are: Chrysler, GM, Volkswagen, Ford, and Nissan. These five enterprises have 30 assembly plants in Mexico, mostly concentrated in the central and northern regions, with an annual output of cars reaching almost 2 million units. The production process includes metal smelting, molding and the automotive assembly. According to the data from the Association of Mexican Industry of Automobiles (AMIA), in 2006 the automobile production was 1.98 million, with the export of cars of more than

Table 5.2 Changes in the Value Added Industries of Mexico from 1990 to 2010 (%)

	1990	1995	2000	2002	2004	2006	2008	2010
Agriculture, forestry, animal husbandry, and fishing	4.0	3.9	3.3	3.4	3.5	3.3	3.3	3.3
Mining industry	8.6	8.3	7.5	7.6	7.5	7.0	6.5	6.4
Manufacturing	18.4	18.1	20.3	19.2	18.6	18.6	17.9	17.8
Water, electricity and gas	1.3	1.4	1.4	1.4	1.4	1.5	1.4	1.6
Construction	7.4	6.6	6.9	6.6	6.8	7.0	7.1	6.6
Business tourism	17.8	16.6	18.1	17.7	18.0	18.2	18.3	17.9
Transportation and storage	6.6	7.2	8.2	8.6	9.2	9.5	9.8	10.1
Financial service	17.5	19.6	18.1	19.4	20.0	20.6	21.5	21.6
Social service	18.4	18.5	16.1	16.0	15.1	14.4	14.1	14.5
Total	100.0	100.0	100.0	100.0	100.0	100.0	100.0	100.0

Source: A summary of the data from ECLAC, www.cepal.org.

1.557 million, of which more than 80% were exported to the US market (see Table 5.2).

The service industry in Mexico not only has the highest proportion of output value, but also is the industry that has created the most employment opportunities, providing nearly 60% of the country's jobs. Mexico's service sector mainly includes commerce, finance, telecommunications, real estate, tourism, insurance, advertising, media, etc. Hotels, restaurants and commerce have maintained around 18% in Mexico's GDP; financial service industry developed rapidly after Mexico's entering the NAFTA — from 2000 to 2010, the proportion of its output value in GDP increased from 18.1% to 21.6%, ranking first in all the sectors of the national economy.

Section 2 Economic Reform and Policy Adjustment of Mexico

I. An Overview of the Reform from 1980s to 1990s

After the outbreak of the debt crisis in 1982, Mexico first carried out an emergent policy adjustment and a local reform within a period of time. The government had formulated the *Recent 10-Point Adjustment Plan* and the *1983–1988 National Development Plan*, implementing the policies of the liberalization of trade and investment and privatization of state-owned enterprises. At the same time, through the compression of government spending, the control of import and increase of non-oil export, the government alleviated the pressure of domestic finance and the imbalance of international payments. At the same time, through negotiations with multilateral financial institutions, through the channel of "Beck Plan", Mexico got a loan of $12.5 billion, and temporarily eased the debt crisis. From 1987 to 1990, the Mexico government began to change the original austerity policies, emphasizing the "debt repayment by development", and developed a *Revitalization and Growth Plan*, striving to achieve moderate economic growth. In 1989, International Monetary Fund (IMF) and other institutions confirmed that Mexico had achieved success in its economic and structural reforms, allowing it to enter into the negotiations about debt rescheduling of the Brady Plan.

After arduous negotiations, 450 creditor banks agreed to reduce debt and cut interest rates about Mexico's long-term debt of \$48.5 billion; \$7 billion of its debt principal was cut and \$675 million of its interest was removed, leading to a preliminary relief for Mexico's debt pressure. From 1987 to 1989, Mexico's economy had achieved growth for three consecutive years, and its fiscal deficit fell to a proportion of 6.6% of its GDP, with an inflation rate of 19.7%, the lowest level after the debt crisis. After the Salinas Administration took office in 1988, with the gradual stabilization of the debt and the economic situation, Mexico began to start a comprehensive new liberal reform. Its main content included the following aspects.

First, NAFTA was signed to further promote the liberalization of trade. With the promotion of the reform, Mexico's tariff taxes were significantly reduced; the average tariff rate fell from 22.6% in 1986 to 13.1% in 1989. At the same time, in 1990, the Salinas Administration changed the position of the former government, regarding joining the NAFTA as a strategic step for Mexico's economic development in the future. In addition to joining the NAFTA (1994), Mexico had signed free trade agreements with Chile (1991), Costa Rica (1994), Colombia and Venezuela (1994). In 1993, Mexico joined the APEC, becoming a member of the OECD.

Second, with the full liberalization of foreign capitals, the liberalization of capital projects was implemented. In order to join the NAFTA and the OECD, in 1989 and 1993, Mexico had made two amendments to the foreign investment law. According to the new foreign investment law, foreign investments in Mexico enjoyed the national treatment; except some key sectors such as oil, electricity, and nuclear power that were related to its national economic lifeline, all the other sectors were open to foreign investments, with foreign equity participation ratio able to reach 100%. The inflow of foreign capitals had increased greatly from \$24.087 billion in 1988 to \$50.401 billion in 1994. At the same time, Mexico also fully opened its capital projects, abolishing restrictions on foreign investments in its domestic security market, and making up for the increasing current account deficits of international balance of payment through attracting a large number of foreign short-term capitals. During the six years of the reign of Salinas, the inflow of security capital of Mexico reached $71.609 billion, accounting for 70.3% of the total amount of the attracted foreign investment.

Third, a large scale of state-owned enterprises had been privatized. The privatization policy of the government of Salinas was expanded gradually from general businesses to the banks, steel, airlines, and other backbone enterprises, covering all the sectors except petroleum, electric power, and nuclear industry. Cardenas Iron and Steel Company, Telmex, Cananea Copper Company and 18 state-owned banks had all been sold. The number of state-owned enterprises was reduced from 412 in 1988 to 209 in 1994. The government's privatization revenue reached $20 billion, accounting for 7.6% of its GDP. Among them, the privatization of state-owned banks was divided into two stages: in 1990, Mexico allowed only private capitals to go into the banking sector. The goal of privatization of banks was to maximize revenues, without taking into account the banking business qualifications and experience of the private capitals; therefore, the initial acquisition of 18 state-owned banks was completed by the newly established 20 private financial groups in 1992. After the financial crisis in 1995, the government had to allow these banks to be transferred to foreign financial institutions at a low price. At present, 80% of Mexico's banking assets and earnings are controlled by foreign capitals.

Fourth, a strict fiscal policy and inflation targeting monetary policy were implemented. In order to suppress the long-term inflationary pressure, the government had formulated the *Mexico Bank Law*, strengthening the independence of the Central Bank's monetary policy, cutting off the financial relations between the Central Bank and the government. During the financial crisis of 1995, after the exchange rate system had been changed from the Pegged Exchange Rate System into a fully Floating Exchange Rate System, Mexico began the implementation of inflation targeting monetary policy framework, regarding the price stability as the only policy objective of the Central Bank. In 2000, the Central Bank began to publish its quarterly report on inflation; according to the changes of the domestic and foreign economic environment, the annual inflation target was publicly announced at the beginning of each year. With the use of the instruments such as zero average reserve policy and the dollar auction mechanism, the Central Bank had imposed its impact on the money supply to the financial market, thereby affecting the level of interest rates, and affected the level of exchange rate through its intervention in the foreign exchange market. This shows that Mexico's monetary policy is a fully market-oriented regulatory tool to achieve the international standard.

II. The Economic Policy Adjustment since 2000

In 2000, the National Action Party came to power replacing the Institutional Revolutionary Party. The Fox and Calderon Administrations basically maintained the neoliberal policies of the previous government, but with greater emphasis on the importance of social justice, paying attention to the social problems such as poverty, employment, social security, and the social safety net. The adjustment of economic policy mainly involved the following aspects.

1. Further Privatization

Although the Fox Administration had repeatedly said it would not implement the privatization of the oil and electric power industry, it encouraged private capitals at home and abroad to invest in oil and power industries. Fox had decided to let four domestic private entrepreneurs to participate in the Mexico Petroleum Company Management Committee, and allow private capitals to hold shares of two airlines, Mexico City International Airport, Mexico Foreign Trade Bank, Hidalgo Insurance Company, 20 harbor bureaus, the Northwest Railway, the Valley Railway Bureau and the Southern Railway Bureau. In August 2002, Fox put forward the reform program of the power sector, but failed to get passed in the Parliament because of some amendments to the Constitution and the boycott of the Opposition Party. In the reign of Felipe Calderon, the most important reform was the reform of the energy, i.e., allowing Mexico's National Oil Company to bring in foreign and domestic private capitals and giving the company more autonomy to expand its ability of reproduction and exploration. In June 2008, Felipe Calderon put forward the reform bill, but was strongly opposed by the opposition Democratic Revolution Party led by Offut Ladoire. Finally the Congress passed the compromised energy reform package proposed by the Institutional Revolutionary Party — promising to increase the autonomy of Mexico National Petroleum Company, allowing the introduction of a part of the domestic private capitals and allowing the purchasing of foreign exploration equipment and technology, but not the implementation of full privatization.

2. The Comprehensive Financial Reform

In March 2001, in Congress, Fox proposed a comprehensive tax reform program to increase taxes and to make the tax system more equitable and effective. The reform plan tried to unify the value-added tax, cancel the exemption policy of food and medicine, and cancel the single tax system of agriculture and animal husbandry and transportation industry. However, the tax reform had also been opposed by the Opposition Party; only in 2006 the budget and fiscal responsibility law were passed to strengthen the fiscal discipline of the governments at all levels. In September 2007, the reform of the public finance proposed by Calderon was passed by the Congress. The content of the reform included: to levy the unified tax of the establishment of new enterprises — any enterprise could choose to pay the enterprise unified tax or net profit tax (rate of 28%); to levy fuel tax with the tax rate of 5.5%; the tax revenue was directly controlled by the state government; to strengthen tax administration, severely punishing tax evasion behaviors; to reform the public expenditure system to strengthen the sense of responsibility, improving the efficiency and transparency of the expenditure of governments at three levels; to implement the financial reform of the Mexican Petroleum Company, reducing the tax burden of the company — its tax rate was set at 79% in 2007 and to be reduced to 74% in 2008 and 71.5% in 2012 to promote its use of profit for reinvestment and technological innovation. The increased revenues would be used focusing on infrastructure, human capital investment and job creation.

3. Increasing the Support for Small- and Medium-Sized Enterprises

The two governments of Fox and Calderon had recognized that small- and medium-sized enterprises (SMEs) were the main channels to solve the problem of unemployment and the support of such enterprises should be strengthened. Fox newly established the SME Bureau in the Ministry of Economic Affairs and introduced the planning to promote SMEs and support micro-enterprises, allocating the funds of $500 million and $200 million, respectively to enable them to get a support of loans and technical assistance. In his *2007–2012 National Development Plan*, Calderon clearly pointed out that strengthening micro-enterprises and SMEs was an important part of the government's strategy to increase productivity and employment opportunities. The plan pointed out that Mexico's micro-enterprises and SMEs accounted for 99% of the total number of enterprises, accounting for 50% of the GDP, and creating 70% of the employment opportunities. At the same time, Calderon also developed a series of specific measures to promote the development of micro-enterprises and SMEs.

III. The Measures to Cope with the International Financial Crisis in 2008

In order to deal with the great impact of the international financial crisis, Mexico had taken a series of measures such as taxation, currency, and industry. On October 8, 2008, the government introduced the "Stimulus Plan for Growth and Employment". In January 2009, the government implemented the "Home Economy and National Employment Contract Plan", freezing the price of natural gas, reducing the price of liquefied petroleum gas by 10%, strictly controlling the rising of diesel price, reforming the pricing mechanism of electricity and lowered the price of electricity, and increasing subsidies to public utilities. In March, the government introduced a policy to reduce and abolish the taxes of enterprises and various administrative fees. In order to ease the financial pressure, the government pulled out $1.5 billion from the oil stabilization fund and cut down the administrative expense by cutting the wages of civil servants and the streamlining of agencies. At the same time, in order to alleviate the burden of import tariffs of enterprises, in January 2009, the government launched the policy of tariff cut in the industrial field; by 2013, the import tariff of industrial products in Mexico dropped from 10.4% in 2008 down to 4.3%.

In response to the financial crisis, the Central Bank decreased the benchmark interest rate from 8.25% at the end of 2008 to 4.5% and implemented policies such as the interest rate swap agreement of $6 billion proposed at the end of 2008 and changed the long-term fixed income holdings into short-term floating rate notes to inject liquidity into the market. In addition, the government also injected capitals to the two state-owned banks — the Mexico Development Bank (NAFIN) and the Mexico Foreign Trade Bank — to support them to provide loans to 1.3 million enterprises.

In order to maintain the stability of the peso, during the depreciation period of the peso in February 2009, the Central Bank intervened in the foreign exchange market through the dollar auction mechanism putting in $100 million in the foreign exchange every day, and promised if the peso fell over 2% within one day, up to 300 million dollars would be sold every day in the foreign exchange market. In addition, the government also actively sought loans from international financial institutions or other external assistances to deal with the problem of insufficient foreign exchange reserves. The Central Bank signed a currency swap agreement of $30 billion with the Federal Reserve Board. In April, the IMF adopted a resolution to provide $47 billion of "flexible loans" to Mexico. In November, the World Bank approved a loan of about $2 billion to Mexico.

In 2009, the government had constructed and renovated 800,000 sets of housing, creating 2.5 million temporary jobs for the construction industry, provided $550 million in funding for poor families to purchase a house or to improve their living conditions, and allocated $53 million for the implementation of the "Old for New Program of Home Appliances". The Mexico Development Bank (NAFIN) and the Mexico Foreign Trade Bank successively had provided a preferential loan of $1.65 billion for the automobile industry. The Ministry of Economic Affairs launched the "Car Scrappage Plan", providing certain subsidies for the replacement of more than 10-year-old cars with new cars. Under the framework of "Home Economy and National Employment Contract Pan", in 2009 the SME support policies included: in government procurement, the proportion of SMEs accounted for 20%; to ease the financing difficulties of SMEs, through the policy banks the government provided loans of $534 million to SMEs and subsidies of $779 million to commercial banks, achieving loans of $17.69 billion to the SMEs from 2009 to 2012.

IV. The Effect of the Economic Reform and the Direction of the Future Reform

After 30 years of reform and adjustment since the debt crisis, Mexico's policies of fiscal, monetary, trade and investment gradually began to be in line with the international standards. Through the implementation of inflation the targeting monetary policy and the strengthening of the independence of the Central Bank, the long-term problem of inflation had basically been solved. From 1981 to 1990, the average annual inflation rate reached 69.1%; from 1991 to 2000 it decreased to 18.7%; from 2001 to 2011 it was only 4.6%; in recent years, the inflation rate had been basically within the government's targeted range of 4.5%. However, Mexico's economic growth indicators had showed signs of deterioration. From 1991 to 2000, Mexico's average annual rate of GDP growth was 3.6%; from 2001 to 2011 it was only 1.9%. There had been substantial economic recessions during the two periods. In 1995 the financial crisis resulted in a sharp economic downturn of 6.1% and in 2009 the global financial crisis once again caused a decline of 6.6%. The rate of economic growth in the last 10 years has been even below the average of the "lost 10 years" of the 1980s. Thus, Mexico is still facing the biggest challenge of how to speed up the economic growth to reduce poverty and increase human capital and education expenditure, and how to alleviate the prominent social problems of social security and crimes.

Table 5.3 Changes of the Main Economic Indicators of Mexico from 1980 to 2011 (%)

	Growth Rate of GDP	Investment Rate	Deposit Rate	Inflation Rate	Import Growth Rate	Export Growth Rate	Unemployment Rate	Fiscal Deficit Rate	Government Debt Rate	Current Account Deficit Rate	Increment of Foreign Exchange Reserve ($100 Million)
1981–1990 Annual average	1.9	22.4	21.6	69.1	6.2	11.5	3.9	−3.0	N.A.	−0.7	5.7
1991–2000 Annual average	3.6	26.5	23.3	18.7	14.3	14.0	3.6	−3.1	45.6	−3.2	25.4
2001–2011 Annual average	1.9	24.6	23.6	4.6	5.4	5.8	4.0	−2.5	42.0	−0.9	103.3
2001	−0.9	22.8	20.3	6.4	−3.8	−3.6	2.8	−3.2	42.0	−2.5	92.3
2002	0.1	23.5	21.5	5.0	0.8	1.4	3.0	−3.5	45.7	−2.0	58.5
2003	1.4	22.9	21.9	4.6	−1.1	1.7	3.4	−2.3	45.6	−1.0	83.4
2004	4.0	24.8	24.2	4.7	10.7	11.5	3.9	−1.3	41.4	−0.7	51.7
2005	3.2	24.3	23.7	4.0	8.4	6.8	3.6	−1.4	39.8	−0.7	99.0
2006	5.1	26.1	25.7	3.6	12.7	10.9	3.6	−1.0	38.4	−0.5	22.1
2007	3.2	26.5	25.6	4.0	7.1	5.7	3.7	−1.2	37.8	−0.9	108.6
2008	1.2	26.9	25.5	5.1	3.0	0.5	4.0	−1.1	43.1	−1.4	80.8
2009	−6.3	23.7	23.1	5.3	−18.8	−13.7	5.5	−4.7	44.6	−0.6	45.3
2010	5.5	23.8	23.5	4.2	23.5	25.6	5.4	−4.3	42.9	−0.3	206.2
2011	3.94	25.1	24.2	3.4	16.4	17.2	5.2	−3.4	40.3	0.96	288.7

Source: IMF, *World Economic Outlook Database*, April, 2012. www.imf.org.

The OECD report said that the following aspects would be the priority areas of the future reforms of Mexico (see Table 5.3).

First, the efficiency of the public sectors should be enhanced. Above all, the performance evaluation system of the public sectors should be strengthened, the perfect process of the target evaluation mechanism of government decision making should be introduced, the public service and the public management should be optimized, and the quality of the public service should be improved. At the same time, the efficiency of utilities such as water supply, electricity, and gas industries should be improved, the subsidies to these areas should be reduced, and the incentive mechanism of private capital investment in these areas should be improved.

Second, it was the reforms of trade and investment. In the area of trade, non-tariff barriers and various technical barriers, including complex customs procedures and a wide range of technical standards should be reduced. In the field of investment, the restrictions on foreign investment in telecommunications, domestic land transport, maritime transport and aviation should be reduced, the technology spillover effect of foreign investment in these industries should be increased, and the improvement of the investment environment in the field of infrastructure should be promoted.

Third, the overall competitiveness of the economy should be improved with the promotion of enterprise innovation. Competitiveness and innovation are the source of economic growth. Mexico should establish a competitive mechanism and regulatory framework in the public institutions of post service, natural gas, and electricity to strengthen the construction of innovative mechanisms. In the areas of aviation, railway and telecommunications, the barriers to entry into them should be reduced to allow new competitors to participate in. At the same time, the procedures to deal with the consumer complaints should be simplified to improve the efficiency of the regulatory authorities. Therefore, the federal government should strengthen the power and responsibility of the Federal Competition Commission, giving it more resources and the coordination responsibility of the supervision of the departments.

Fourth, the reform of labor and social security system should be sped up. The labor reform and improving the efficiency of social policy are the driving force of economic growth in the future. At present, the registered unemployment rate is low, but there is still a large scale of informal employment and low productivity employment. Therefore, the creation of new jobs also depends on the accumulation of human capital. The labor reform should be focused on strengthening the labor training and enhancing the competitiveness to improve the flexibility of the labor market, strengthening the role of protection of the unemployment insurance and improving the operating mechanism of the formal labor market to improve the efficiency of labor market and liquidity. Specifically, the convenience of the transfer of the accounts of individual social insurance in the formal sectors should be improved, the management cost of the old-age insurance fund should be reduced, the legal protection for employees in the formal sectors should be improved, and the temporary labor contracts and part-time jobs in the formal sectors should be increased. These measures will improve the attractiveness of the employment of the formal sectors and promote the formalization of the employment in the informal sectors.

Section 3 Diversified Foreign Trade and Economic Cooperation Strategy

I. The Accession to NAFTA Marking a New Stage for Mexico's Opening

Formally established in January 1994, the NAFTA so far is still the world's largest free trade zone, the first truly "North–South" organization of the regional economic integration composed by the developed and developing countries. Mexico's accession to the NAFTA marked a new stage of development in its opening to the outside world. The purpose of the NAFTA is to cancel trade barriers, create conditions for fair competition, increase investment opportunities, provide appropriate protection of intellectual property rights, establish valid procedures for the implementation of agreements and for settlement of disputes, and promote trilateral, regional, and multilateral cooperation. Among them, the core content is cutting tariffs and the abolition of non-tariff barriers. Actually, in 1998 the tariffs between the United States, and Canada had been abolished, but Mexico was allowed to gradually reduce the trade barriers, taking into account the differences between their levels of development. There was a transitional period of 15 years for the abolishment of tariffs between Mexico and the United States.

In addition to the traditional trade, the NAFTA also covered the field of service trade, including the cross-border transport, ports, communications, financial services, and government procurement. The opening up of these areas is an important symbol of Mexico's entering a new stage of opening to the outside world. Mexico has always seen oil as the industry related to its state sovereignty. Its constitution expressly forbade foreign countries to meddle in its oil industry, but the provisions of its final agreement with the United States and Canada ruled that under the premise of ensuring Mexico's ownership and right of monopoly of oil, the capitals of the United States and Canada were allowed to enter into the secondary petrochemical product sectors and the electricity sector, and the restrictions were to be reduced in stages within 10 years until the complete abolition of restrictions. At the same time, the opening of the financial service industry was the most intense debate in the NAFTA negotiations. The financial service sector was one of the areas that the United States most wanted to enter into. The final agreement allowed the banks, financial companies and insurance companies of the United States and Canada to enter Mexico freely. At present, the financial sector in Mexico has been fully controlled by the international financial institutions of Spain, the United States, and so on. Therefore, the successful establishment of the NAFTA had provided a timetable for the opening of the market of Mexico in system and in procedure, and greatly promoted the breadth and depth of the opening of Mexico.

During the 10 years after the establishment of the NAFTA, the openness of Mexico was promoted in the round. To measure with the percentage of the trade volume in GDP, in 1994 Mexico's open rate was 35%, lower than the 54% of Chile and the 54% of Venezuela. In

1995, Mexico's openness rose sharply to 53%, and in 2000, Mexico's openness continued to rise to 58.3%, becoming the country with the highest degree of opening in the major Latin-American countries. After 2000, despite the decrease of the opening degree of Mexico, most of the years it remained more than 55%, after the opening level of Chile in the major Latin-American countries, way higher than the opening degrees of Brazil and Argentina (see Table 5.4).

II. The Diversified Strategy of Foreign Trade and Economic Cooperation

To reduce the excessive dependence on the US market and to achieve the target of a diversified foreign trade and economic cooperation

Table 5.4 Comparison of Opening Degrees of Mexico and other Latin-American Countries (%)

	Latin-American Average	Mexico	Brazil	Argentina	Chile	Colombia	Peru	Venezuela
1990	30.2	34.9	14.1	16.9	62.3	27.7	29.5	61.0
1991	29.7	32.5	15.5	15.6	58.4	26.6	26.7	58.8
1992	30.8	32.3	18.0	16.8	56.6	27.0	28.0	56.4
1993	31.3	31.4	18.3	16.2	54.2	29.4	28.8	55.3
1994	30.3	35.1	17.4	18.1	54.1	29.2	28.9	54.3
1995	32.2	53.0	16.0	19.8	56.0	28.9	30.7	50.0
1996	32.9	56.7	14.9	21.5	56.1	29.3	31.2	59.2
1997	34.1	55.3	15.8	23.3	56.1	28.9	32.7	51.2
1998	34.9	57.9	15.9	23.4	55.7	29.2	31.9	43.6
1999	39.1	57.6	20.2	21.4	56.8	29.0	32.0	42.1
2000	41.6	58.3	21.7	22.6	61.2	32.7	34.0	47.9
2001	41.4	52.3	25.7	21.9	64.9	33.9	33.3	42.1
2002	44.6	50.6	26.7	41.8	65.5	33.0	33.4	48.6
2003	45.6	52.2	27.1	40.6	68.9	36.5	35.3	50.6
2004	47.9	55.1	29.0	44.1	72.3	35.9	39.3	55.4
2005	47.3	55.8	26.6	44.3	74.1	35.6	44.3	60.1
2006	47.5	57.4	25.8	44.0	76.5	38.2	48.4	58.7
2007	46.5	57.6	25.2	45.0	80.5	36.3	51.4	56.2
2008	47.2	58.5	27.1	45.1	85.8	38.2	53.4	51.8
2009	39.6	57.0	22.1	37.4	70.2	34.1	43.3	38.5
2010	40.8	62.0	22.8	40.1	73.8	33.6	47.3	46.1

Source: ECLAC, www.cepal.org.

had always been the focus of Mexico's opening up strategy since the 21st Century. At present, Mexico has been more and more deeply integrated into the process of globalization — becoming members of organizations such as the WTO, the OECD, the Asia Pacific Economic Cooperation (APEC), and the Latin American Integration Association (ALADI). Through signing bilateral or multilateral free trade agreements, Mexico had reduced its over reliance on the United States in its foreign trade and investment. At present, Mexico, Chile, South Korea, and Singapore have become the countries that have signed the most free trade agreements in the world. Since the NAFTA came into force, Mexico had signed free trade agreements not only with Venezuela, Colombia, Chile and almost all Central American and the Caribbean countries, but also with the world's major economies such as Japan and the European Union. At the same time, despite the failure of Free Trade Area of the Americas (FTAA) due to various divergences, Mexico is still an active supporter of FTAA (see Table 5.5).

At present, Mexico is actively participating in the negotiation of the Trans-Pacific Partnership Agreement (TPP) launched by Chile, Singapore, New Zealand, and Brunei, led by the United States and joined by Japan. Mexico hoped to join the TPP as a driving force so that Mexico could regain the priority position in the global trade development after 18 years since signing NAFTA with the United States and Canada. Only by joining higher standards and higher levels of negotiations of trade rules could Mexico avoid being marginalized in the global economy. In addition, TPP negotiations would also be conducive to further consolidating the dominant position of Mexican products in the US market.

III. The Fast Foreign Trade Development and Obvious Trend of Market Diversification

From 2001 to 2011, despite the competition from China, Vietnam and other East-Asian countries, Mexico had achieved a steady growth in its foreign trade and import and export. During this period, the total amount of import and export of Mexico increased from $326.8 billion

Table 5.5 Free Trade Agreements Signed by Mexico

	Free Trade Agreement	With Country (or Organization)	Time of Implementation
1	NAFTA	USA & Canada	January 1, 1994
2	"3-Country" FTA	Venezuela & Colombia	January 1, 1995
3	Mexico–Costa Rica FTA	Costa Rica	January 1, 1995
4	Mexico–Bolivia FTA	Bolivia	January 1, 1995
5	Mexico–Nicaragua FTA	Nicaragua	July 1, 1998
6	Mexico–Chile FTA	Chile	October 1, 1999
7	Mexico–Uruguay Economic Cooperation Agreement	Uruguay	July 15, 2004
8	Mexico–EU FTA	EU	July 1, 2000
9	Mexico–Israel FTA	Israel	July 1, 2000
10	Mexico–Europe Free Trade Association FTA	Norway, Iceland, Switzerland & Luxembourg	July 1, 2001
11	Mexico–El Salvador, Guatemala & Honduras FTA	El Salvador, Guatemala & Honduras	March 15, 2001 with El Salvador; June 1, 2001 with Honduras
12	Mexico–Japan FTA	Japan	April 1, 2005
13	Mexico–Peru FTA	Peru	February 1, 2012

Source: Summaries of the public materials.

to $700 billion. Except the contraction of trade caused by the 2009 international financial crisis, Mexico had achieved growth in trade in the rest of the years, most of which the growth rate remained more than 10%. According to the statistics of Mexico, in 2011 Mexico's import and export of commodities reached $700.43 billion, an increase of 16.8% over the previous year. Among them, the export was $349.57 billion, an increase of 17.2% and the import was $350.86 billion, an increase of 16.4%. Its trade deficit was $1.29 billion, a decrease of 60.4%.

In terms of countries, in 2011 the United States was still Mexico's largest trading partner. Its exports to the United States were $274.71 billion, an increase of 15.2%, accounting for 78.6% of Mexico's total export; its imports from the United States were $174.36 billion, an increase of 20.2%, accounting for 49.7% of the total import of Mexico. Although the trade pattern of Mexico's dependence on the US had not changed, Mexico was also gradually strengthening its trade links with other countries and regions. Its proportion of trade with the EU and Asia increased steadily. In terms of import, in 2011, the proportion of Mexico's imports from the European Union and China increased 10.8% and 14.9% in its total import. Mexico's trade deficits came mainly from China, Japan, and South Korea, with $46.28 billion, $14.24 billion, and $12.14 billion, respectively. Its trade surplus came mainly from the United States, with $100.36 billion.

From the perspective of the trade structure, the first three types of goods that Mexico exports are mechanical and electrical products, transport equipment and mining products, in 2011 with exports of respectively $118.96 billion $65.06 billion, and $59.67 billion, increasing 5.0%, 22.8%, and 37.3%, accounting for 34%, 18.6%, and 17.1% in the total export of Mexico. In 2011 Mexico achieved growth in its export of the main commodities, most of which increased two digits. The top three commodities in Mexico's imports are mechanical and electrical products, mineral products and transport equipment, in 2011 with imports of respectively $129.69 billion, $36.66 billion, and $30.1 billion, increasing 10.2%, 45.1%, and 18.5%, accounting for 37.0%, 10.5%, and 8.6% in the total import of Mexico. In 2011, Mexico achieved growth in its import of main commodities, most of which increased two digits, except for a small amount of goods (see Figure 5.6).

From the perspective of the status of manufactured goods in export from 1991 to 2010, Mexico is the biggest export country of manufacturing industry in the Latin-American region. Especially since its joining the NAFTA, the export of Mexican manufacturing developed rapidly, the northern customer industry was unprecedentedly prosperous, and the proportion of the manufactured goods in the total export increased from 74.6% in 1993 to 85.1% in 1999. Over the same period the proportion of the entire Latin-American region rose from 46.4% to 58.6%, and its growth came from the main driving force of Mexico's export of manufactured goods. The

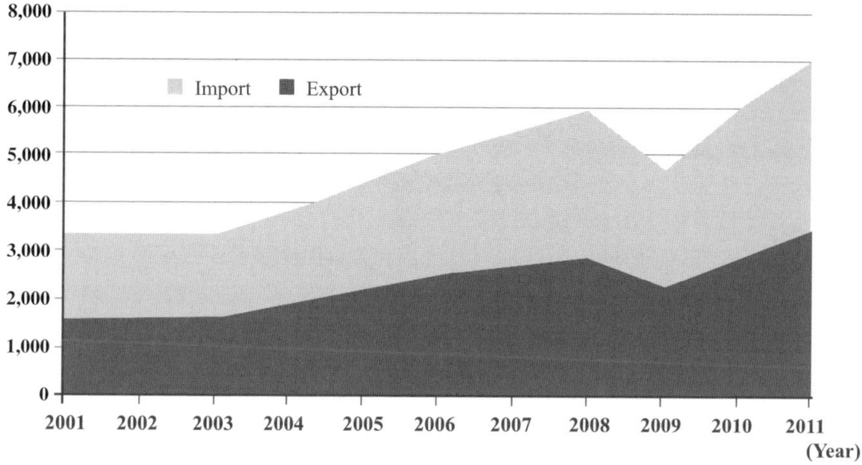

Figure 5.6 Mexico's Import and Export Situation (2001–2011) ($100 million)
Source: CEIC database, sub-database of Mexico.

trend of the change in the proportion of manufactured goods in Latin America was almost identical with that of Mexico, which shows that the export of manufactured goods of Mexico has a great impact on the whole export of the Latin-American manufacturing industry.

In terms of the diversification of export markets, Mexico has made some progress. The proportion of Mexico's export to the United States fell in its total export from 85% in 2005 to 78.6% in 2011; the markets of China, Germany, Brazil, Colombia, and Canada in Mexico's export share remained a steady growth; especially the Chinese market jumped from the 10th largest export market in 2005 to the 3rd largest export market in 2011, and its market share also increased from 0.5% to 1.7%. The progress of Mexico's import market diversification was more significant: from 2005 to 2011, the proportion of Mexico's imports from the United States dropped from 53.5% to 49.7%; on the contrary, since China's imports rose sharply, the proportion rose from 8% to 14.9% (see Figure 5.7). At present, its import from China had greatly increased, with the increase of the proportion from 8% to 14.9%. At present, China has become the second largest trading partner of Mexico behind the United States (see Table 5.6).

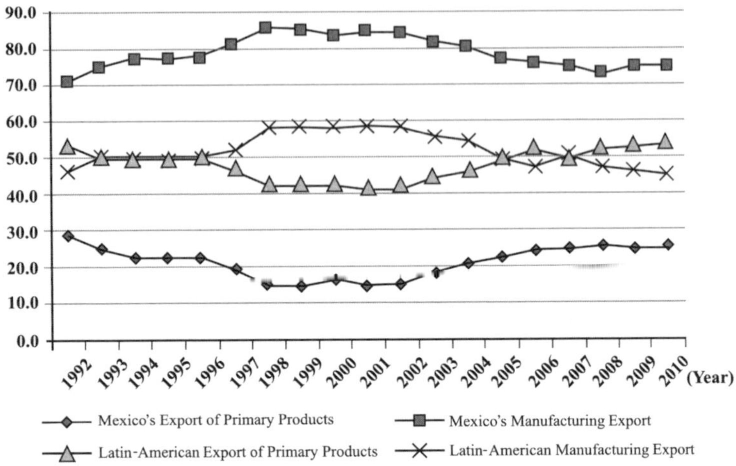

Figure 5.7 The Export Structure of Mexico and Latin America (%)
Source: ECLAC, www.cepal.org.

Table 5.6 Mexico's Main Trading Partners and Their Shares in 2011 (%)

Export Destination & Share		Source of Import & Share	
USA	78.6	USA	49.7
Canada	3.1	China	14.9
China	1.7	Japan	4.7
Colombia	1.6	South Korea	3.9
Brazil	1.4	Germany	3.7
Spain	1.4	Canada	2.8
Germany	1.2	Other	20.3
Other	11		
Total	100	Total	100

Source: CEIC database, sub-database of Mexico.

From 2001 to 2011, Mexico's foreign trade continued to show a deficit state, with an annual deficit of about $8 billion. In 2011, the main sources of trade deficit came from manufacturing powers such as China, Japan, South Korea, and Germany, with trade deficits of about $46.3 billion, $14.2 billion, $12.1 billion, and $8.5

Table 5.7 Mexico's Main Sources of Foreign Trade Surplus and Deficit in 2011 ($100 Million)

Main Sources of Deficit		Main Sources of Surplus	
China	−462.8	US	1,003.6
Japan	−142.4	Colombia	48.1
South Korea	−121.4	Venezuela	12.9
Germany	−85.2	Guatemala	12.4
Malaysia	−54.9	Canada	10.2
Chinese Taiwan	−53.0	—	—
Italy	−34.3	—	—
Thailand	−27.7	—	—
France	−26.4	—	—
Costa Rica	−16.5	—	—

Source: CEIC database, Sub-database of Mexico.

billion, respectively. At the same time, the United States was still the most important source of surplus for Mexico: in 2011, the trade surplus of Mexico against the United States was about $100.4 billion; against Colombia, Mexico's surplus was $4.81 billion (see Table 5.7).

IV. The Significant Improvement of the Investment Environment

Through joining NAFTA and signing free trade agreements with the European Union and other major economies, Mexico has become one of the world's most open economies and its investment environment has improved significantly. The competitiveness of Mexico's investment environment is mainly reflected in the aspects of exchange rate, labor cost, transportation cost, raw material prices, taxes, etc. According to the statistics of the US ALIX PARTNERS, in 2011 the cost of manufacturing in Mexico was lower than in Vietnam, India, Russia, and China, while in 2005 the lowest cost of manufacturing was in China (see Table 5.8). According to the statistics of the Economist Intelligence Unit (EIU), the investment environment in Mexico was graded "ordinary" from 1997 to 2001 and was "fine"

Table 5.8 Business Environment Score and Ranking of Major Latin-American Countries

	1997–2001		2002–2006				General Assessment	
Country	Score	Ranking	Score	Ranking	Score Change	Ranking Change	1997–2001	2002–2006
Chile	7.14	21	7.95	21	0.81	0	Fine	Fine
Mexico	6.32	32	7.21	28	0.89	4	Ordinary	Fine
Peru	5.55	37	6.28	39	0.73	−2	Ordinary	Ordinary
Brazil	5.36	40	6.27	40	0.91	0	Poor	Ordinary
Argentina	6.51	28	6.17	42	−0.34	−14	Fine	Ordinary
Colombia	5.34	41	5.96	46	0.62	−5	Poor	Ordinary
Ecuador	4.15	56	5.38	52	1.23	4	Very bad	Poor
Venezuela	5.30	44	5.30	56	−0.00	−12	Poor	Poor

Source: Country Report of *Economist Intelligence Unit* (EIU).

from 2002 to 2006; its global ranking rose from 32 up to 28, which was few in the major countries of Latin America.

According to the *Global Business Environment Report in 2011* published by the World Bank, in the world's 200 countries, Mexico's business environment ranked the 35th in the world, ranking the 1st in Latin America (see Table 5.9). Despite Mexico's backward ranking in the OECD member states, in the Latin-American region and even in all emerging market countries it occupied a leading position. From the perspective of the major sub-indexes, in Mexico's procedures for setting up a business, the time belonged to the shortest, and the cost was relatively low; its law index and investor protection index were higher than the average level of the Latin-American countries; its total tax burden of up to 50% was still below the Latin America average of 53.5%. From the perspective of the overall changes of the main indexes in the business environment from 2006 to 2010, the magnitude of the improvement within five years in Mexico was up to 15%, ranking the 4th in the Latin-American region, slightly lower than the degrees of improvement in Colombia, Peru, and Guatemala. Therefore, although since the National Action Party came to power Mexico's economic growth was lower than in the 1990s, the improvement of its investment environment would be conducive to Mexico's maintaining its attractiveness to foreign investment in the future (see Figure 5.8).

Table 5.9 Leading Position of Mexico's Business Environment in Latin America in 2010

	Comprehensive Ranking	Procedures to Set up a Business (1–20)	Time to Set up a Business (Day)	Cost to Set up a Business (Proportion in GDP per capita) (%)	Law Soundness Index (0–10)	Investor Protection Index (0–10)	Total Tax Rate (Proportion in Profit, %)
Mexico	35	6	9	12.3	5	6.0	50.5
Peru	36	6	27	13.6	7	6.7	40.2
Colombia	39	9	14	14.7	5	8.3	78.7
Chile	43	8	22	6.8	4	6.3	25.0
Panama	72	6	9	10.3	6	4.7	50.1
El Salvador	86	8	17	45.0	5	4.3	35.0
Guatemala	101	12	37	49.1	8	4.0	40.9
Paraguay	106	7	35	55.1	3	5.7	35.0
Argentina	115	14	26	14.2	4	4.7	108.2
Nicaragua	117	6	39	117.9	3	5.0	63.2
Uruguay	124	11	65	42.1	5	5.0	42.0
Costa Rica	125	12	60	10.5	5	3.0	55.0
Brazil	127	15	120	7.3	3	5.3	69.0
Ecuador	130	13	56	32.6	3	4.0	35.3
Honduras	131	13	14	47.2	6	3.0	48.3
Bolivia	149	15	50	100.8	1	4.0	80.0
Venezuela	172	17	141	30.2	2	2.3	52.6
Regional Average	100	10.5	43.6	32.6	4.4	4.8	53.5

Source: *Doing Business 2011 in Latin America: Making a Difference for Entrepreneurs*, 2011, the World Bank.

V. The Stable Growth of Attracted Foreign Investment

As an important supplement to the domestic capital, foreign capital had played an important role in the economic development of Mexico. After the debt crisis of 1982, to promote the recovery and development of the economy, the government of Mexico managed to relax the control of foreign investment and actively introduced the Foreign Direct Investment (FDI). After NAFTA came into force, the FDI in Mexico increased rapidly. From 1990 to 1993, the average annual net inflow of FDI was $4.02 billion; from 1994 to 2000 it

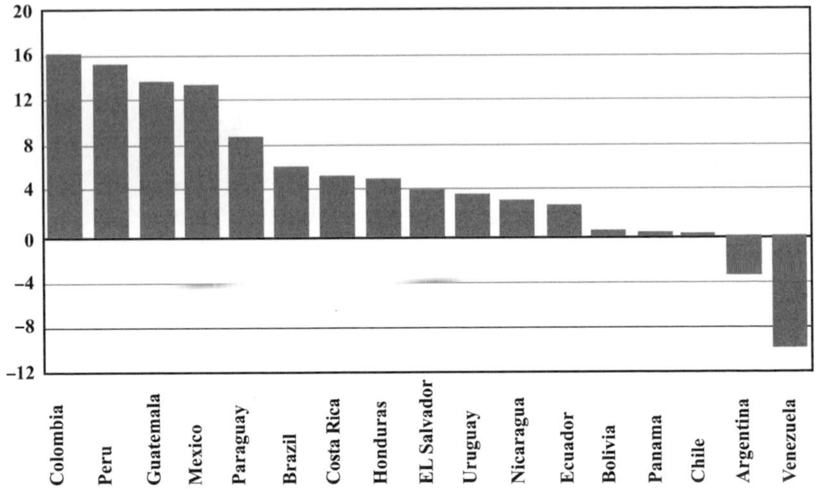

Figure 5.8 Business Environment of Latin-American Countries in 2006–2010 (%)
Source: *Doing Business 2011 in Latin America: Making a Difference for Entrepreneurs*, 2011, the World Bank.

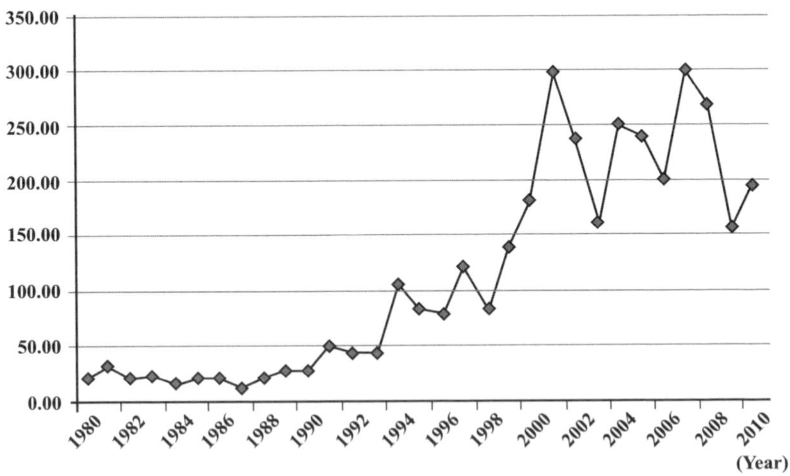

Figure 5.9 Net Inflow of FDI into Mexico from 1980 to 2010 ($100 million)
Source: CEIC database, sub-database of Mexico.

increased to $12.4 billion; from 2001 to 2010 it reached $22.8 billion. In the past 10 years, Mexico has remained one of the countries with the largest FDI in the emerging market countries, only behind the BRIC countries such as Brazil, Russia, India, and China. Even in the most serious period of the 1994 Mexican financial crisis and the 2009 international financial crisis, the large-scale withdrawal of FDI did not occur in Mexico.

From the perspective of FDI sources, since the NAFTA came into force, the United States has been the largest source of FDI in Mexico. From 1995 to 2001, the direct investment of the United States had been more than 60% in Mexico. However, since the beginning of the 21st Century, the FDI sources of Mexico had become increasingly diversified. Spain, Holland, the United Kingdom, and other countries increased investment sharply in Mexico through large-scale mergers and acquisitions in the financial sector and the reinvestment of the profit of the financial sector. Especially since the international financial crisis in 2008, the US investment in Mexico declined sharply, less than 50% of that before the financial crisis; in 2010 it was down to $5.3 billion. On the contrary, the investment from the Netherlands to Mexico increased substantially: in 2010, it reached $8.8 billion, more than that of Spain and the United States, and hence the Netherlands became the largest investment country of Mexico (see Figure 5.9).

From the perspective of the structure of the foreign investment of Mexico, the new investment had been the main body of foreign investment. From 1995 to 1999, the average annual foreign investment was $11.6 billion, of which the new investment was $6.9 billion and the profit reinvestment was $2.4 billion (see Table 5.10). During this period, the multi-national corporations were optimistic about the prospect of the economic development of Mexico after its joining the NAFTA, but more investments were involved in the large-scale privatization of Mexico, especially the privatization of state-owned banks. From 2000 to 2010, while the new investment was still the main foreign investment in Mexico, the profit reinvestments and new investments of parent companies increased significantly. Especially

Table 5.10 Mexico's Main Sources of FDI ($100 Million)

	USA	UK	Spain	Canada	Netherlands	Other	Total
1994	49.67	5.93	1.46	7.41	7.58	34.43	106.47
1995	55.15	2.24	0.50	1.71	7.45	16.71	83.75
1996	52.81	0.82	0.78	5.42	4.93	13.71	78.48
1997	74.20	18.37	3.29	2.41	3.70	19.50	121.46
1998	54.67	1.81	3.45	2.15	10.71	10.95	83.74
1999	74.98	−1.88	10.42	6.91	10.86	37.41	138.70
2000	130.00	2.86	21.17	6.70	26.97	−6.57	181.13
2001	214.40	1.38	28.94	10.27	26.54	17.07	298.59
2002	131.36	12.61	50.08	2.38	17.34	25.36	239.13
2003	88.77	10.82	28.49	3.04	7.65	23.69	162.47
2004	91.36	3.08	78.86	6.50	33.78	34.61	248.19
2005	116.82	13.48	16.79	4.79	40.11	50.81	242.80
2006	129.10	9.50	14.37	6.17	28.01	13.99	201.14
2007	124.38	6.00	53.81	4.76	57.53	54.22	300.69
2008	109.95	12.55	48.81	30.43	21.38	45.92	269.03
2009	69.73	3.45	26.70	16.00	20.66	18.20	154.75
2010	53.02	5.46	14.05	11.42	88.62	21.48	194.05

Source: CEIC database, sub-database of Mexico.

before the outbreak of the financial crisis in 2008, the global economy was prosperous unprecedentedly: from 2006 to 2008 the profit reinvestment was nearly $8 billion; at the same time, the annual new investments of parent companies were close to $7 billion (see Table 5.11).

Section 4 Sino-Mexican Economic and Trade Relations Developing in Twists and Turns

I. The Bilateral Trade between China and Mexico

From 2001 to 2011, the bilateral trade between China and Mexico developed rapidly. According to the statistics of the Chinese Customs, in 2001, the bilateral trade volume between China and Mexico was only $2.25 billion. Ten years later, in 2011, the trade volume between China and Mexico had reached as high as $33.36 billion, in which China's export to Mexico was $23.98 billion, China's import from Mexico was $9.38 billion, and China's surplus was $14.6 billion.

Table 5.11 Types of FDI in Mexico ($100 Million)

	Total of FDI	New Investment	Reinvestment of Profit	Investment of Parent Company
Annual Average Value of 1995–1999	116.36	68.89	23.05	24.41
2000	181.10	84.22	38.99	57.88
2001	298.59	228.70	38.70	31.18
2002	239.13	155.19	24.84	59.10
2003	162.46	70.08	21.05	71.34
2004	248.18	148.59	25.25	74.34
2005	242.80	129.29	40.32	73.20
2006	199.51	60.45	77.50	61.56
2007	300.70	162.38	80.80	57.52
2008	269.48	112.90	77.96	78.62
2009	155.75	69.72	43.79	42.24
2010	196.27	129.95	26.57	39.75

Source: CEIC database, sub-database of Mexico.

Compared with 2001, the trade volume between China and Mexico increased by 12 times and the trade surplus had increased by 13 times.

However, despite the big difference between China and Mexico in statistic data, the trend of the rapid development of bilateral trade is basically the same. According to the statistics from the Ministry of Economic Affairs of Mexico, in 2011, the trade volume between China and Mexico amounted to $58.22 billion, increasing 16.9%. Among them, Mexico's export to China was $5.97 billion, increasing 42.1%; its import from China was $52.25 billion, increasing 14.6%. The trade deficit of Mexico was $46.28, increasing 11.8%. China was Mexico's third largest export destination and the second largest source of import.

In 2011, the mineral products, base metals and base metal products, and transportation equipment were the first three categories of goods that Mexico exported to China; the export volumes of them were $2.9 billion, $900 million, and $890 billion, respectively, increasing 64.8%, 23%, and 39.1%, together accounting for 78.7% of Mexico's total export to China. Due to its low export base of

Table 5.12 Trends of the Sino-Mexican Trade ($100 Million)

	Sino-Mexican Trade Volume	China's Export to Mexico	China's Import from Mexico	China's Trade Surplus
1995	3.89	1.95	1.94	0.01
1996	5.18	2.21	2.97	−0.76
1997	5.98	4.14	1.84	2.30
1998	8.36	6.89	1.47	5.42
1999	9.51	7.92	1.59	6.33
2000	18.23	13.35	4.88	8.47
2001	25.51	17.90	7.61	10.29
2002	39.79	28.64	11.15	17.49
2003	49.44	32.67	16.77	15.90
2004	71.13	49.73	21.40	28.33
2005	77.64	55.38	22.26	33.12
2006	114.31	88.24	26.07	62.17
2007	149.70	117.08	32.62	84.46
2008	175.59	138.51	37.08	101.43
2009	161.81	122.99	38.82	84.17
2010	246.90	178.73	68.17	110.56
2011	333.59	239.78	93.81	145.97

Source: CEIC database.

the previous year, Mexico's export of cellulose pulp, paper, animal products, and wood and wood products to China increased greatly (see Table 5.12).

The mechanical and electrical products are the major commodities that Mexico imported from China. In 2011 the import volume was $35.65 billion, increasing 10%, accounting for 68.2% of Mexico's total import from China. The main rivals of China's products were the United States, South Korea, Japan, and Germany. In addition, China has a strong competitive strength in Mexico's import market of furniture and toys, accounting for 41% of the market share of the import of similar products in Mexico. China is the second largest source of import of base metals and their products, optical medical equipment, plastics and rubber behind the United States.

Table 5.13 Mexico's Import of Major Commodities from China in 2011 ($100 Million)

HS Coding	Commodity	2011	2010	Year-on-Year Ratio (%)	Ratio (%)
Chapter	Total Value	522.48	456.08	14.6	100.0
84–85	Mechanical and electrical products	356.49	324.13	10.0	68.2
72–83	Base metals and their products	31.83	17.68	80.0	6.1
90–92	Optics, watches and clocks, medical equipment	24.34	21.6	12.7	4.7
94–96	Furniture, toys, miscellaneous products	22.27	21.04	5.8	4.3
39–40	Plastics, rubber	18.21	15.5	17.5	3.5
28–38	Chemical products	15.09	12.12	24.5	2.9
86–89	Transportation equipment	10.92	8.5	28.5	2.1
50–63	Textiles and raw materials	10.75	8.69	23.8	2.1
68–70	Ceramics; glass	4.56	3.58	27.4	0.9
41–43	Leather products; bags	3.67	3.02	21.6	0.7
64–67	Shoes, shoes, umbrellas and other light industrial products	2.54	2.03	25.3	0.5
47–49	Cellulose pulp; paper	2.3	1.66	39.1	0.4
01–05	Live animals; animal products	1.67	1.67	35.5	0.3
25–27	Mineral products	1.63	1.68	–0.6	0.3
06–14	Plant products	1.38	1.69	15.9	0.3
	Other	14.85	1.7	18.9	2.8

Source: CEIC database.

II. The Bilateral Investment between China and Mexico

The bilateral investment between China and Mexico is still in its initial stage. In 1997, Mexico's investment in China was only $17 million; in 2004 it was increased to $21.2 million. During the financial crisis in 2009, Mexico's investment in China dropped to $0.91 million; in 2010 it rose to $15.25 million (see Table 5.13). In recent years, China's investment in Mexico increased sharply: in 2003 it was only $0.3 million, but in 2010 it reached $26.73 million. From

Table 5.14 Mexico's Export of Major Commodities to China in 2011 ($100 Million)

HS Coding	Commodity	2011	2010	Year-on-Year Ratio (%)	Ratio (%)
Chapter	Total Value	59.65	41.98	42.1	100.0
25–27	Mineral products	28.97	17.58	64.8	48.6
72–83	Base metals and their products	8.98	7.29	23.2	15.1
86–89	Transportation equipment	8.92	6.41	39.1	15.0
84–85	Mechanical and electrical products	5.15	4.99	3.2	8.6
28–38	Chemical products	2.87	2.3	25.1	4.8
39–40	Plastics, rubber	1.8	1.36	32.5	3.0
50–63	Textiles and raw materials	0.88	0.67	32.3	1.5
47–49	Cellulose pulp; paper	0.46	0.22	105.7	0.8
01–05	Live animals, animal products	0.45	0.2	130.6	0.8
90–92	Optics, watches and clocks, medical equipment	0.37	0.32	17.4	0.6
41–43	Leather products; bags	0.29	0.26	11.7	0.5
16–24	Food, beverage, tobacco	0.29	0.18	55.2	0.5
44–46	Wood and wood products	0.07	0.02	215.0	0.1
06–14	Plant products	0.06	0.05	17.3	0.1
94–96	Furniture, toys, miscellaneous products	0.04	0.02	109.1	0.1
	Other	0.05	0.12	−61.4	0.1

Source: CEIC database.

2003 to 2010, China's investment stock in Mexico had increased from $97.18 million to $153 million. In the field of engineering contract, important progress had been made in the cooperation between China and Mexico. According to the statistics of the Chinese Ministry of Commerce, by the end of 2011, the Chinese contracted companies in Mexico had completed the total turnover of $370 million, and a total of 159 people of various kinds of labor had been sent to Mexico (see Table 5.14).

According to the statistics of the Chinese Ministry of Commerce, China's investment in Mexico's industry is mainly in the distribution of trade and manufacturing sectors, such as commerce and trade,

Table 5.15 The Sino-Mexican Bilateral Investment Volume ($ Million)

	Mexico's Increased Amount of Direct Investment in China	China's Increased Amount of Direct Investment in Mexico	China's Cumulative Investment in Mexico
1997	0.17	—	—
1998	1.98	—	—
1999	0.33	—	—
2000	0.93	—	—
2001	1.82	—	—
2002	7.31	—	—
2003	5.55	0.03	97.18
2004	21.29	27.10	125.29
2005	7.10	3.55	141.86
2006	12.34	−3.69	128.61
2007	5.66	17.16	151.44
2008	3.85	5.63	173.08
2009	0.91	0.82	173.90
2010	15.25	26.73	152.87

Source: CEIC database.

clothing, machinery and equipment, and plastic products. The investment of these four types accounted for about 80% of China's investment in Mexico. In the regional distribution of investment, China's investment is mainly distributed in the Federal District of Mexico City, the Yucatan state, and Chihuahua state. From the perspective of the future direction of investment, in the *Guidance Catalogue of Countries and Industries of Foreign Investment* published by the Chinese Ministry of Commerce and other agencies, the guidance catalog of Mexico's investment industries include: crop planting, textile and garment manufacturing, electronic equipment manufacturing and petroleum technical service industry, etc. (see Table 5.15).

III. The Problems in the Bilateral Economic and Trade Cooperation

In recent years, the bilateral trade between China and Mexico has been growing rapidly; at the same time, there are still some prominent issues to be resolved between the two sides. They are mainly reflected in the following aspects:

1. The Too Large Gap between the Statistics of the Bilateral Trade

In the past 10 years, the bilateral trade between China and Mexico had increased greatly, and the trade disputes had also increased. Among them, one of the biggest problems was the great difference in the statistical standards and statistical data of the Sino-Mexican trade scale and trade balance, leading to different understandings of the bilateral trade. Take the year of 2010 for example. The Chinese statistical data of the Sino-Mexican trade volume was $24.69 billion, of which China's trade surplus was $11.056 billion; in contrast, the statistical data of the Mexican Ministry of Economic Affairs was that the volume of the Sino-Mexican trade was $49.79 billion and China's trade surplus was $41.4 billion. China has become the source of Mexico's largest trade deficit, playing the decisive role for Mexico's trade balance.

The fundamental reason for the huge difference in the statistics of the Sino-Mexican trade is due to the big difference between the two statistical standards. China's statistics dealt with only the goods shipped to Mexico from mainland China; entrepot trades of China from Hong Kong, Panama and other important areas were not included in China's export to Mexico. But Mexico directly followed the rules of origin: as long as the origin of products was China, regardless of the export side, whether it was Chinese Hong Kong, Panama or any other non-production places, all the goods were counted as China's export to Mexico. According to China's statistics, in 2010, China's export to Hong Kong and Panama was $218.3 billion and $11.9 billion, respectively. Mexico's statistics of Hong Kong's export to Mexico showed only $0.343 billion, while Chinese Hong Kong's statistics of its export to Mexico gave as high as $14.3 billion. At the same time, the Mexican statistics of Panama's export to Mexico showed only $0.03228 billion, while Panama's volume of export to Mexico in its statistics was up to $4.934 billion. Chinese Hong Kong and Panama's largest trading partner is China; after general calculations, only the entrepot trades of Chinese Hong Kong and Panama had statistically produced differences close to $20 billion for

Table 5.16 Huge Differences in the Bilateral Trade Statistics between China and Mexico ($100 Million)

	Mexico's Statistics		China's Statistics	
	The Sino-Mexican Trade Volume	China's Trade Surplus	The Sino-Mexican Trade Volume	China's Trade Surplus
1995	5.58	4.84	3.90	0.01
1996	7.98	7.21	5.18	−0.76
1997	12.93	12.02	5.98	2.29
1998	19.25	17.13	8.37	5.42
1999	20.47	17.95	9.51	6.32
2000	30.83	26.76	18.24	8.47
2001	43.09	37.46	25.51	10.29
2002	69.28	56.21	39.79	17.49
2003	103.75	84.26	49.44	15.90
2004	153.60	133.88	71.13	28.33
2005	188.32	165.61	77.64	33.12
2006	261.26	227.50	114.31	62.17
2007	316.39	278.48	149.69	84.46
2008	367.35	326.46	175.59	101.43
2009	347.37	303.21	161.81	84.17
2010	497.91	414.25	246.90	110.56
2011	—	—	333.59	145.96

Source: CEIC and China's Ministry of Commerce.

the Sino-Mexican trade, becoming the root cause of the huge gap between the bilateral trade statistics.

2. Mexico's Very Serious Trade Protectionism against China

With the rapid growth of China's economy, while the trade frictions between China and developed countries are increasing, its trade frictions with developing countries have also become a problem of concern. Among them, China's trade frictions with the major Latin-American countries, including Mexico, are particularly striking. As one of the most active countries in the implementation of trade protection, from 1995 to the end of June 2011, Mexico had launched 102 anti-dumping investigations, in which 30 anti-dumping investigations were against China, more than the 27 cases against the

United States. At present, Mexico is among the top 10 countries in the implementation of anti-dumping measures against China, and China has become the biggest victim of Mexico's trade protection. In comparison, China has launched external anti-dumping investigations against the main targets of the United States, South Korea, Japan, China, Taiwan, and other economic bodies, with only one against Mexico. This shows that the investigations of the two countries against each other are completely not equal. According to the rulings of the anti-dumping investigations, 85 out of the registered cases by Mexico had got verdicts, among which 18 cases had been carried out against Chinese products. According to Chinese statistics, in the products that China exported to Mexico, so far, still more than 1,300 tariff item numbers (such as textiles, clothing, shoes, bicycles, toys, mechanical and electrical products and accessories, and part of the organic chemicals, and electronic equipment and components) are under the position of being imposed anti-dumping duties by Mexico (see Table 5.16).

3. The Competitive Relations between China and Mexico in the Exports to the US

Another important dispute between China and Mexico is the intense competition of the two countries in the global market, especially in the US market, which is reflected in the manufacturing sector in particular. Since 1980, although the two countries had maintained a rapid growth in exports to the United States, but the time nodes marking the most obvious changes were in 1994 when Mexico joined NAFTA and in 2001 when China joined the WTO. In 1993, Mexico's export to the United States was $40.7 billion, and China's export to the United States was $33.5 billion; by 2001, the former rose to $132.8 billion, and the latter increased to $109.4 billion, both with basically a consistent growth rate. The proportion of the exports of Mexico and China to the United States rose to 11.25% and 9.27% in the total US import. During this period, the market share of Mexico was significantly higher than that of China. After China's entry into WTO in 2001, China's export to the United States began to grow significantly, and Mexico's export to the United States also continued

Table 5.17 Market Share Changes of China's and Mexico's Exports in the US Import Market ($100 Million, %)

	China's Export to USA	Mexico's Export to USA	China's Proportion	Mexico's Proportion
1980	11.6	128.4	0.45	4.99
1985	42.2	193.9	1.17	5.36
1990	163.0	308.0	3.15	5.96
1993	335.1	407.4	5.56	6.76
1994	413.6	503.6	6.00	7.30
1995	485.2	627.6	6.29	8.14
2001	1,093.9	1,327.8	9.27	11.25
2002	1,334.9	1,361.4	11.10	11.32
2003	1,632.6	1,397.0	12.51	10.70
2004	2,105.3	1,578.2	13.80	10.35
2005	2,598.4	1,724.9	15.00	9.96
2006	3,057.9	2,005.2	15.93	10.45
2007	3,401.2	2,128.9	16.86	10.55
2008	3,563.2	2,180.9	16.45	10.07
2009	3,095.6	1,783.4	19.30	11.12
2010	3,829.8	2,319.2	19.46	11.78

Source: CEIC database.

to maintain growth, but its growth rate was significantly lower than China's export to the United States. In 2010, the exports of China and Mexico to the United States rose to $383 billion and $231.9 billion, respectively, accounting for 19.46% and 11.78% of the total US import. During these 10 years, the proportion of Chinese export in the United States increased significantly, while the proportion of Mexican export had stalled, maintaining at the range of 10–11% (see Table 5.17).

The fierce competition of Chinese and Mexican commodities in the US market came from the relatively high homogeneity of the exports of finished products from the two countries, resulting in a prominent competition between them. From 2002 to 2011, the Mexican export of finished products to the United States rose from $9.44 billion to $19.03 million, with rising proportions in US imports of manufactured goods from 7.44% to 8.25%. In striking contrast, China's

Table 5.18 Changes of the Exports of China's and Mexico's Manufactured Goods in the Market Share of US Import ($100 Million, %)

	US Import	China's Export	Mexico's Export	China's Proportion	Mexico's Proportion
1996	916.5	45.6	56.9	4.98	6.21
1997	1,009.7	57.9	66.4	5.73	6.58
1998	1,120.7	69.7	74.7	6.22	6.66
1999	1,170.0	83.1	79.9	7.11	6.83
2000	1,339.7	102.9	91.3	7.68	6.81
2001	1,230.6	108.0	87.3	8.78	7.09
2002	1,269.4	133.7	94.4	10.54	7.44
2003	1,329.3	162.2	94.8	12.20	7.13
2004	1,702.6	218.9	121.1	12.86	7.11
2005	1,907.8	281.3	137.5	14.75	7.21
2006	2,230.8	362.6	150.0	16.26	6.72
2007	2,271.9	402.6	159.6	17.72	7.03
2008	2,316.8	437.9	159.1	18.90	6.87
2009	1,518.8	320.1	115.0	21.08	7.57
2010	1,944.8	376.8	148.1	19.38	7.62
2011	2,306.6	423.8	190.3	18.38	8.25

Source: CEIC database.

export of finished products to the United States rose from $13.37 billion to $42.38 billion, with rising proportions in the US import of manufactured goods from 10.54% to 18.38% (see Table 5.18).

4. The Recognition of China's Status of Full Market Economy

As for the problem of China's accession to WTO, Mexico was the last Latin-American country to have reached an agreement with China, and had retained restrictive measures to impose countervailing duties on Chinese goods within six years. In the treatment of the status of China's market economy, Mexico had taken a relatively strong opposing stance. Shortly after taking office, Mexican ambassador Guajardo said that Mexico would not recognize China's status of market economy within 15 years after China's accession to the WTO. According to the agreement with the United States upon China's accession to the WTO, China would automatically gain market economy status within 15 years after its accession to the WTO. This shows that Mexico is also acting in accordance with the terms of the standard of limit.

In accordance with the provisions of the price discrimination (dumping) in the basic principles of anti-dumping in Mexico: price discrimination means the act that exporters sell products to Mexico with prices lower than the normal value of the country of origin. In terms of the export products of non-market economy countries, the Mexico Trade Administration would choose a market economy as a surrogate country, regarding selection of domestic market sales price of the surrogate country, export prices to the third country and structured prices as the normal value, to compare with the export prices to Mexico to determine whether there was price discrimination and the corresponding magnitude of it. However, it is precisely because of Mexico's regarding China as a non-market economy country to have implemented anti-dumping investigations against China comparing the prices of the third country with China's, resulting in unfavorable situations for China.

Chapter 6

Economic Characteristics of Peru and the Sino-Peruvian Economic and Trade Cooperation

Sun Hongbo

Peru is rich in mineral resources, being one of the major countries with mineral reserves, mineral production and mineral export in the world (see Table 6.1). Since the 21st century, Peru has entered a new period of growth and prosperity, belonging to important emerging economies in the world. With a good macroeconomic operation, Peru's growth is driven by its domestic demand, the investment has a large contribution to its growth, and the mining and construction industry are the two fastest growing major industries. Its macroeconomy has remained stable for many years and the inflation has been kept at a low level. Its domestic savings rate has increased, resulting in the ability to enhance its independent growth. The contribution of Foreign Direct Investment (FDI) to the economic growth is increasing. The primary fiscal surplus of the public sectors has maintained a stable growth and the situation of financial revenue and expenditure continues to improve. With ample foreign exchange reserves, Peru uses its financial surplus to actively repay its external debt, resulting in a good sovereign credit and good financing channels in the international financial market. Peru has actively implemented the free trade strategy and achieved an initial success in its diversification of foreign trade.

Section 1 Overview of the Peruvian Economy

Peru has a land area of 1.2852 million square kilometers, with a population of 29.3998 million people (by the end of 2011).[1] Peru is located in western South America, bordering Ecuador and Colombia in the north, neighboring Brazil and Bolivia in the east, bordering Chile in the south, and connecting the Pacific Ocean in the West. Peru is rich in natural resources. With the development potential of its mineral resources, it is an important country producing gold, silver, zinc, tin, and lead in Latin America. In recent years, the investment in the fields of Peru's mining and oil and gas resources is very active, with an increasing production and export volume. In addition, Peru is rich in tourism resources because it is the birthplace of the ancient Inca civilization.

I. The Economic Geography of Peru

Peru is one of the world's 12 largest mining countries, with a forest coverage rate as high as 60%, after Brazil in South America. It has rich fishery resources, with fishmeal production ranking the forefront of the world. With diversified climates, Peru is one of the countries in the world with diversities of biological populations, genetic resources and culture. Its edible plants rank first in the world. Its rivers belong to the Pacific water system and the Atlantic water system, and there is an inland water system centering on Lake Titicaca — a plateau lake. In the plateau region there are more than 12,000 lakes and more than 1,000 rivers and streams.

1. The Regional Division of Economic Geography

Economically Peru has three major geographical spaces, namely, coastal areas, high altitude areas and tropical rain forests; each region is divided into a number of small areas. From west to east, the whole area is divided into three types of climate — tropical desert, plateau, and tropical rain forest.

---

[1]http://www.worldbank.org/en/country/peru.

(1) The Western Coastal Areas

The Peruvian climate is extremely dry, most of its area is desert, and its population is concentrated in the valley. The rainwater on the west slope of the Andes Mountains has formed more than 50 rivers, flowing through small valleys traversing in the panhandle, giving birth to more than 50 oases — the areas with the most developed agriculture, the most concentrated industry and the densest population.

The western coastal region is an important agricultural area, with an area of arable land accounting for one-third of the total arable land, mainly for growing crops like sugar cane, cotton, coffee, rice, etc.; the western seas are rich in fishery resources, making it one of the world's most famous fishing grounds.

(2) The Central Mountain Area

The central mountain area is in the middle of the Andes Mountains, with complex terrain structures and undulating hills and mountains. There is a large population in the central region, mainly concentrated in the valleys and the mining and industrial centers. The Quechuans — the most populous American Indians — are living in the mountainous provinces of Puno, Cuzco, Ayacucho, and Huancavelica.

There are a lot of fertile lands and pastures in the central mountain. Most of the crops in the mountain valleys are wheat, corn, barley, potatoes, and beans. Cattle, sheep, and pigs are the main animals fed in the cold zone of the high mountains. Especially the alpacas with soft and long wool are of high economic value there.

(3) The Eastern Tropical Rain Forest Areas

With a tropical rain forest climate, the eastern tropical rain forest areas are humid and rainy. With abundant river water, abundant water resources are provided in the east for the development of industry and agriculture, but because of the hot and humid climate and the dense forests, they have not yet been fully utilized.

The Amazon plain located in the eastern part is vast in area, but sparsely populated. The primeval forests there provide rich valuable timbers, and the agriculture there relies on the cultivation of coffee, cocoa and beans.

2. The Agricultural Resources

Due to the special terrain and climate diversity, the arable land in Peru accounts for about 2.84% of the total area of the country (2011).[2] The national agricultural planting area is relatively limited, about 5.4758 million hectares.[3] The main agricultural products are corn, rice, wheat, potato, and so on. The main economic crops are sugar cane, cotton, coffee, etc. Peru has maintained a dual agricultural pattern of traditional agriculture and modern export agriculture, and different geographical regions and natural environments have provided good conditions for the development of a variety of agricultural crops and animal husbandry. The accumulation of rich guano exists on the islands near the coast of the Pacific Ocean. In history, the guano export had brought considerable revenue to Peru; today, the guano is still providing a large volume of high-quality fertilizer for crop planting.

Animal husbandry accounts for a small proportion in agriculture, but because of the good natural conditions and abundant resources, its position in Peru's national economy cannot be ignored. The main breedings are cattle, horses, sheep, poultry, alpacas, and vicunas. 80% of the animal husbandry are concentrated in the mountains, and 20% in the coastal areas and the virgin forest area.

The Peruvian government encourages the export of agricultural products, mainly coffee and asparagus. In recent years, the international market demand for primary products and the continuously rising prices have had a stimulating effect on the agricultural production of Peru. Since 2006, the government has introduced a number of support policies for agricultural development, for example, tax breaks, improving agricultural infrastructure, expanding credit, providing technical support and attracting foreign investment

[2]https://www.cia.gov/library/publications/the-world-factbook/geos/pe.html.

[3]La Oficina de Estudios Economicos y Estadisticos del Ministerio de Agricultura del Peru, *Dinamica Agropecuaria 2002–2011*, p. 15, http://www.minag.gob.pe/portal/herramientas/estadisti-cas/din% C3% A1 mica-agropecuaria.

Table 6.1 Output of Peru's Main Agricultural and Animal Husbandry Products (10,000 Tons)

	2005	2006	2007	2008	2009	2010	2011
Sugar cane	680.4	725.1	822.9	939.6	993.7	966.1	988.5
Potato	329.0	324.8	338.8	359.7	376.5	381.4	407.4
Unhusked rice	246.8	236.2	225.6	277.6	299.1	283.1	262.5
Banana	169.7	177.8	183.5	179.3	186.6	200.7	196.8
Fresh milk	132.9	148.3	145.6	156.6	165.2	167.8	174.6
Yellow corn	124.0	126.9	136.8	148.1	156.0	N.A.	N.A.
Cassava	100.5	114.0	115.8	117.2	116.6	124.0	111.7
Chicken	65.7	71.2	77.1	87.9	96.6	102.1	108.6

Source: FAO database, http://faostat.fao.org/site/339/default.aspx.

in the agricultural development.[4] In October 2006, the government launched the "Mountain Export Plan" to open up land as the export base of special agricultural products.

Peru has a coastline of 2,400 kilometers, with about 600,000 square kilometers of waters. With very rich marine fishery resources, it has one of the world's four major fishing grounds, which is mainly due to the favorable conditions of the marine climate. As the most important fish species, the anchovy is the main raw material for the production of fishmeal. The development of the Peruvian marine fishing and processing industry started in the 1950s, and it had become one of the world's largest producers of fishery products in the 1960s. The fishery products include fishmeal, fish, canned fish, fish oil, etc. Chinport (Chimbote) has also developed into an important port because of the rise of the fishery.

3. Transportation

Highways play an important role in Peru's transportation — road freight traffic accounts for 80% of the total transport of the country.

[4]La Oficina de Estudios Economicos y Estadisticos del Ministerio de Agricultura del Peru, *Dinamica Agropecuaria 2002–2011*, p. 81, http://www.minag.gob.pe/portal/herramientas/estadisti-cas/din%C3% A1 mica-agropecuaria.

Water transport is very developed, and its foreign trade mainly relies on maritime transport. By 2012, Peru has 58 airports, 1,907 kilometers of railways, over 140,000 kilometers of highways, and more than 8,800 kilometers of waterways.[5] The main highways are arterial roads, i.e., the Pan-American highways running through the north and the south and the Central Roads crossing the east and the west; the railways are mainly distributed in the central, southern and southeastern areas, used for the transportation of mountain agricultural and mineral products and passenger travels.

Peru has a long coastal line along the Pacific Ocean, with many excellent ports. Especially the inland rivers in the Amazon region have provided convenient transportation by water. There are 19 sea ports, 4 river ports, and 1 lake port.[6] In the 1980s and 1990s, Peru invested way from enough in infrastructure construction, which led to the lack of infrastructure and became one of the "bottlenecks" restricting the development. In recent years, although the government has increased investment in infrastructure, with consecutive years of rapid growth of economy and the expansion of foreign trade, the existing infrastructure, including port capacity, still cannot meet the demand.

II. The Peruvian Population

In 2012, the total population of Peru was 29.948 million, increasing by 15.17% compared with the year of 2000.[7] According to the forecast of ECLAC, by 2020 the population of Peru will reach over 32.7 million people. Peru's proportion in the population of Latin America dropped from 4.99% in 2000 to 4.97% in 2012.

The growth peak of the Peruvian population happened between 1960 and 1965, with an average annual growth rate of 2.87%, after which the population growth rate began to decrease. From 2005 to 2010, the average annual growth rate of population dropped to 1.08%;

---

[5] *Ibid.*

[6] http://www.fmprc.gov.cn/mfa_chn//jhdq_603914//_603916/nmz_608635/1206608709/.

[7] http://websie.eclac.cl/anuario_estadistico/anuario_2012/es/contents-es.asp.

from 2010 to 2015, the average annual growth rate rose only to 1.14%. It is forecasted that the average annual growth rate of population will continue to decline to 1.08% from 2015 to 2020.[8]

From the perspective of the structure of population age, due to the decline in the birth rate, the problem of aging population will gradually appear. In 2010, the 0-to-14-year-old population accounted for 29.9% of the total population, the 15-to-34 year-old accounted for 35.4%, the 35-to-49-year-old accounted for 17.5%, the 50-to-64-year-old accounted for 10.5%, and the over-65- year-old accounted for 6% of the total population.[9]

The total labor force in Peru was about 15.9 million, and the urban public unemployment rate was 6.1% (January 2013). The current outstanding problem in the labor market is the proportion of too high non-formal employment, accounting for about 60%. This means that most of the employment of the labor force cannot enjoy the social security and the other benefits that regular workers are enjoying. The poverty rate in Peru had reached 42.4% in 2007. As a result of the sustained economic growth in recent years and the continuous implementation of the poverty reduction plan by the government, the proportion of poor people showed a decreasing trend, down to 25.8% in 2012. In the long run, to increase the normal employment is still the main way to reduce poverty.

III. The Mineral Resources of Peru

Since entering into the 21st century, the international market demand for mineral products has remained strong and the prices have continued to go high, providing an important opportunity for the economic development of Peru. Therefore, the mining industry has become the focus of the development of the government of Peru and the industry to have attracted the most FDI. Peru's bismuth and alum reserves rank the first in the world, copper reserves rank the third in the world, and lead and zinc reserves rank the first and second, respectively in Latin America. It has been proven that it has rich reserves of copper,

---

[8] http://websie.eclac.cl/anuario_estadistico/anuario_2012/es/contents-es.asp.
[9] *Ibid.*

Table 6.2 Peru's Main Proved Mineral Reserves in 2011

Coal	1,100 million tons
Copper	90 million tons
Gold	2,762 tons
Iron ore	10.853 million tons
Lead	9.106 million tons
Molybdenum	450,000 tons
Natural gas	823 billion cubic meters
Crude oil	3,100 million barrels
Phosphate rock	820,000 tons
Silver	120,000 tons
Sulfur	150 million tons
Tin	160,000 tons
Coal	1.1 billion tons
Uranium	100,000 tons
Zinc	251.37 billion tons

Source: Alfredo C. Gurmendi, *The Mineral Industry of Peru, 2011 Minerals Yearbook*, US Geological Survey, April 2013, p. 14.

gold, iron, lead, molybdenum, and silver, ranking among the first in the world. In 2011, Peru had been proved to have 90 million tons of copper reserves, 10.853 million tons of iron ore reserves, 9.106 million tons of lead reserves, 450,000 tons of molybdenum reserves, 120,000 tons of silver reserves, 820,000 tons of phosphate rock reserves, 150 million tons of sulfur reserves, and 160,000 tons of tin reserves (see Table 6.2).

According to the data of the US Geological Survey, in 2011, Peru was an important global mining output power, with its copper production ranking the second place in the world, after Chile; its gold production ranked the sixth globally; its production of lead and molybdenum ranked the fourth globally; its silver output ranked the second only behind Mexico, and its production of tin and zinc ranked the second in the world.[10] In 2011, Peru was the largest producer of gold, lead, tin, and zinc in Latin America, and the second largest

[10] Alfredo C. Gurmendi, *The Mineral Industry of Peru, 2011 Minerals Yearbook*, US Geological Survey, April 2013, p. 1.

Table 6.3 Production of Major Mineral Products in Peru

Year	2009	2010	2011
Copper (10,000 tons)	127.47	124.71	123.52
Iron (10,000 tons)	448.95	604.26	701.10
Zinc (10,000 tons)	150.91	147.05	125
Gold (ton)	182.4	163	164.01
Silver (ton)	3,854.02	3,637.41	34,144.01
Oil (10,000 barrels)	5,302.7	5,436.4	5,775.5

Sources: Summary of the statistics of the National Bureau of Peru and the Peruvian Department of Energy and Mineral Resources.

producer of cadmium, copper, mercury, molybdenum, phosphorus ore, silver, and selenium in Latin America.[11]

It is expected that between 2012 and 2016 Peru's mining will continue to be a hot industry to attract foreign investment. In 2011, the mining industry (see Table 6.3) in Peru had attracted foreign investment of about $5.4 billion, and between 2012 and 2013 it is expected to rise to $6 billion.[12] By the end of 2012, in the Peruvian mining the investments of China, the United States, Canada, Switzerland, Australia, Mexico, and Brazil, respectively had been $10.7 billion, $8.9 billion, $6.8 billion, $6.7 billion, $4.7 billion, $3.5 billion, and $2.1 billion. From the perspective of the distribution structure of mining investment, copper, gold, iron, zinc, respectively had attracted foreign investments of $35.4 billion, $6.9 billion, $6.8 billion, and $2.1 billion.[13]

IV. The Change of Peruvian Industrial Structure

Peru is a traditional agricultural and mining country; its industry is based on processing and assembly. From 2001 to 2010, the main industry in Peru had maintained a rapid development. According to the data of ECLAC, on the basis of the price of the year, the value

[11] *Ibid.*
[12] *Ibid.*
[13] *Ibid.*

of the economic activity of each industry rose from \$49.425 billion to \$144.086 billion, increasing 191.53% (see Table 6.4).

The nine industries listed in Table 6.4 basically reflect the status of the composition of the three major industries in Peru. Serial number 1 — agriculture, forestry, and fishery — belongs to the first industry, with an output value of about 7% in the total output value; serial numbers 2–5 belong to the second industry, with an output value of about 36% in the total output value, and serial numbers 6–9 belong to the tertiary industry, with an output value of about 57% in the total output value. From 2001 to 2011, the economic growth characterized by the export boom of mineral products had obviously caused the corresponding changes in its industrial structure.

First, the mining and construction are the two fastest growing industries. From 2001 to 2010 the output value of the mining industry increased from \$2.655 billion to \$16.658 billion, the output value of construction industry increased from \$2.818 billion to \$11.571 billion, and both of the two major industries respectively increased by 527.42% and 310.61% (see Table 6.4). Agriculture, forestry and fishery, manufacturing, and retail and catering also had achieved growth; from 2001 to 2010, their growth rates respectively were 139.54%, 163.24%, and 176.69%, but the scales of increase were obviously much smaller.

Second, the mining, construction and business have maintained a high annual growth rate. According to the data of the Peruvian Central Bank, from the perspective of the annual growth rates of the industries, mining, construction, and business have maintained a high growth rate (see Table 6.5). Agriculture and animal husbandry have maintained a steady growth, mainly driven by the growth of animal husbandry; from 2004 to 2010, the annual growth rate exceeded 5%. The growth of the primary product processing industry is flat, but the primary product manufacturing industry has had a strong growth. The construction sector is the fastest growing in the industry — from 2005 to 2010 the annual growth of it was more than 8%. Affected by the international financial crisis, from 2009 to 2010, Peru's fishery, metal and non-metallic mining industry had two consecutive years of negative growth.

Table 6.4 Output Value of Each Industry at Current Price ($100 Million)

Year	2001	2002	2003	2004	2005	2006	2007	2008	2009	2010
1. Agriculture, forestry, and fishery	40.77	40.95	42.82	46.24	52.12	58.66	68.81	85.22	88.16	97.66
2. Mining	26.55	31.17	37.17	53.51	70.21	107.66	122.80	134.28	127.36	166.58
3. Manufacturing	79.09	82.34	87.26	103.64	118.57	135.11	156.76	187.80	169.01	208.20
4. Electricity, gas, and tap water industry	12.36	12.63	13.37	14.34	16.32	17.28	19.26	22.36	24.62	27.33
5. Construction	28.18	30.53	33.24	37.75	43.13	52.30	65.20	82.45	89.93	115.71
6. Retail and catering	96.06	99.90	105.40	116.89	129.06	147.72	171.99	212.40	222.30	265.79
7. Traffic and communications	42.75	43.81	48.15	53.40	60.91	69.55	91.50	110.14	115.59	135.98
8. Finance and insurance	75.85	81.15	86.38	93.20	104.50	115.47	133.77	161.66	171.21	198.31
9. Community and personal service industries	92.63	97.24	106.22	115.49	128.34	140.02	154.63	182.19	196.02	225.30
Gross economic activity	494.25	519.73	559.99	634.46	723.15	843.76	984.68	1178.49	1204.20	1440.86

Note: There are statistical differences in the sums of the total value of the economic activities, GDP value, and the value of each economic activity, mainly caused by the statistical differences in the conversion of current prices and exchange rates.

Source: ECLAC Statistics Database.

Table 6.5 Annual Growth Rate of the Major Industries in Peru (%)

Year	2001	2002	2003	2004	2005	2006	2007	2008	2009	2010
Agriculture and animal husbandry	0.6	6.1	3.0	−1.4	5.4	8.4	3.2	7.2	2.3	4.3
Agriculture	−2.1	6.5	1.4	−1.8	4.2	8.4	2.0	7.4	0.9	4.1
Animal husbandry	0.8	3.8	3.0	3.0	6.9	8.2	5.3	6.0	4.4	4.4
Fishery	−11.1	6.1	−10.3	30.7	3.2	2.4	6.9	6.3	−7.9	−16.4
Mining	9.9	12.0	5.5	5.3	8.4	1.4	2.7	7.6	0.6	0.1
Metals and non-metals	10.9	13.0	6.3	5.1	7.3	1.1	1.7	7.3	−1.4	−4.8
Oil	−2.0	0.7	−4.3	7.1	23.4	5.7	6.5	10.3	16.1	29.5
Manufacturing	0.7	5.7	3.6	7.4	7.5	7.5	11.1	9.1	−7.2	13.6
Primary product processing industry	−1.7	4.8	3.2	8.0	3.9	4.1	−2.7	7.6	0.0	−2.3
Non primary product manufacturing	1.4	5.9	3.7	7.2	8.5	8.5	14.0	8.9	−8.5	16.9
Electricity and water supply	1.6	5.5	3.7	4.5	5.6	6.9	8.4	7.8	1.2	7.7
Construction industry	−6.5	7.7	4.5	4.7	8.4	14.8	16.6	16.5	6.1	17.4
Business	0.9	3.3	2.4	6.2	6.2	11.7	9.7	13.0	−0.4	9.7
Other services	−0.5	4.0	4.7	4.4	6.4	7.0	9.6	8.6	4.2	7.4
GDP	0.2	5.0	4.0	5.0	6.8	7.7	8.9	9.8	0.9	8.8

Source: Peru Central Reserve Bank Database, http://www.bcrp.gob.pe/estadisticas/cuadros-anuales-historicos.html.

Third, the mining industry output value accounted for a substantial increase in the proportion of economic activity, while other industries had declined in varying degrees. From the perspective of the proportion of each industry in the economic activities, from 2001 to 2010, the proportion of the mining industry increased from 5.37% to 11.56%, and the proportion of the construction industry increased from 5.7% to 8.03%; agriculture, manufacturing industry, finance, insurance, retail and other service industries had varying degrees of decline, a decrease of about two percentage points.

Section 2 Macroeconomic Policy of Peru

Like most Latin-American countries, Peru experienced a recession and downturn phase in the 1980s and 1990s: from 1981 to 1990, its economic growth rate was −1.2%, and from 1991 to 2000, its economic growth rate was 4.2%. At the beginning of the 21st century, Peru entered a new round of growth cycle, becoming one of the countries with the highest economic growth rate in Latin America. In the 1990s, in Peru the Fujimori Administration launched an economic reform guided by neoliberalism, centering on liberalization and marketization, namely the so-called "Fujimori Shock" (FujiShock). After entering the 21st century, the Toledo Administration (2001–2006) and Garcia Administration (2006–2011) had done pragmatic adjustments according to the changes of the domestic and foreign environment, implementing prudent fiscal policies and a flexible monetary policy, increasing investment in the infrastructure construction, focusing on the development of mining and agriculture, expanding opening to the outside world, actively signing free trade agreements with foreign countries, and attracting foreign investment to become deeply integrated with the world economy.

In response to the international financial crisis, Peru had taken effective fiscal and monetary policies to reduce the adverse impact of external shocks, and from 2009 to 2010 it had achieved a rapid economic recovery. After President Humala came to power (July 2011 to date), the framework of macroeconomic regulation and control has been maintained, and the steady growth model of economic, financial and trade openness has been adopted. Peru's investment environment continues to improve, and its business environment is considered to be superior to any other countries in Latin America, second only to Chile.[14]

I. The Economic Growth

The international public opinion believes that prudent macroeconomic policies, structural reforms, the improvement of terms of trade and a large number of FDI inflows have enabled Peru to have become one of the economies in Latin America with the fastest and

---

[14]World Bank, *Doing Business 2013: Peru*, 10th edition, 2013, pp. 5–9.

stablest growth in the past 10 years.[15] In 2010, according to the actual exchange rate of that year, the amount of Peru's gross domestic product (GDP) was $157.324 billion, with per capita GDP of $5333.9, increasing respectively 8.8% and 7.5% compared with 2009 (see Table 6.6). In the last 10 years, Peru's economic growth has the following characteristics.

First, high growth, low inflation. During the 10 years from 2001 to 2010, on the basis of the GDP in 2001, the total volume of the economic GDP of Peru increased 1.92 times; per capita GDP increased 1.6 times. Such a growth rate is rare in the history of the development of Peru. Peru has implemented the inflation targeting system, with the inflation of the capital of Lima as the reference system and a dynamic regulation and control system frame.[16] From 2002 to 2004, the consumer price index increased rapidly leading to the increasing inflationary pressure, mainly due to rising food prices. From 2003 to 2004, the consumer price index reached 3.66%, of which the food price index reached 5.56%, but the core consumer price indexes, excluding food and energy prices, had maintained a low level of only 0.73% (see Table 6.7).

In 2005, the inflation pressure had slowed down, and consumer prices, food prices and core consumer prices had dropped significantly compared with 2004. From 2006 to 2008, with the acceleration of economic growth, the inflation went into a new round of rising cycle. Affected by the factors of rising prices of international crude oil and commodities, in 2008, the consumer price index and food price index were up to 5.79% and 9.16%, the highest level in the past 10 years. The government reacted quickly, taking measures to tighten monetary release by the Central Bank; between 2009 and 2010, the pressure of inflation was greatly eased while maintaining a rapid economic growth.

[15]IMF, *Peru: 2012 Article IV Consultation*, Country Report No. 13/45, February 2013, p. 5.
[16]Deigo Winkelried, Jose Enrique Gutierrez, *Dinamica Inflacionaria Regional y el Esquema de Metas de Inflacion de el Peru, Revista Estudios Economicos, Banco Central de Reserva del Peru*, No. 24, Diciembre 2012, pp. 79–98.

Table 6.6 Economic Growth Situation of Peru

Year	2001	2002	2003	2004	2005	2006	2007	2008	2009	2010
GDP ($100 million)	539.56	567.75	613.56	697.01	793.89	923.19	1075.24	1,291.07	1,303.55	1,573.24
Economic growth rate (%)	0.2	5.0	4.0	5.0	6.8	7.7	8.9	9.8	0.9	8.8
Per capita GDP ($)	2,045.2	2,122.0	2,262.2	2,536.3	2,852.3	3,276.5	3,771.6	4,477.3	4,469.9	5,333.9
Growth rate of per capita GDP (%)	−1.2	3.6	2.6	3.6	5.5	6.4	7.6	8.5	−0.3	7.5

Source: Summary of ECLAC database, calculated by prices of the current year.

Table 6.7 Price Index of Peru (2001–2010, %)

Year	2001	2002	2003	2004	2005	2006	2007	2008	2009	2010
Consumer price index	1.98	0.19	2.26	3.66	1.62	2.00	1.78	5.79	2.94	1.53
Food price index	0.49	−0.25	0.77	5.56	0.94	2.43	2.50	9.16	4.23	2.54
Core consumer price index	3.34	1.86	1.27	0.73	0.92	1.28	1.74	2.70	3.62	1.47

Source: Summary of the data from ECLAC database.

For some time in the future, Peru is still likely to maintain a steady growth trend. The Humala Administration has maintained a policy of stability and continuity; its fiscal policy is rather robust in expanding investment in the field of infrastructure.[17] Specifically, in order to make Peru deeply integrated into the world economy, the government tried to control the growth of the public debt, expand investment in electricity, transportation, energy and other fields, and continue to sign free trade agreements with other countries. However, it cannot be ignored that the economic fluctuations in the world may give external impact on the Peruvian economy, especially the debt crises in Europe and the United States, as well as the international market price fluctuations of the primary products.

Second, the drive of domestic demand and the great contribution of investment. From the perspective of expenditure approaches, growth contribution sources of Peru's economy include the factors of government consumption, private consumption, investment and net export, in which the investment refers to gross capital formation, including gross fixed capital formation and investments in the construction industry, machinery and equipment.[18]

Peru's economy belongs to the growth driven by domestic demand, of which domestic consumption and investment have

[17]IMF, Peru: *2012 Article IV Consultation, Country* Report No. 13/45, February 2013, pp. 10–16.
[18]World Bank, *Public Expenditure Review for Peru: Spending for Results*, Report No. 62586, June 2012, pp. 19–20.

contributed a lot to the economic growth. Although the contribution of foreign trade to economic growth has increased, the proportion of the net export in GDP is not high.

Number 1, from the perspective of the variation of each part of growth in the composition GDP, from 2001 to 2010, the capital formation was the fastest growth, which had increased 310.18%, while the growth of government expenditure and private consumption was relatively flat, increasing 159.37% and 144.65%, respectively. In 2010, the expenditure of government consumption, private consumption and capital formation were $14.963 billion, $95.447 billion, and $41.531 billion, respectively (see Table 6.8).

In the formation of capital, the formation of fixed capitals included the fixed capital investment in the construction industry, machinery and equipment. In 2010, the fixed capital investment in the construction industry, and machinery and equipment were $26.206 billion and $15.202 billion, respectively, accounting for 63.29% and 36.71% in the total fixed capital investment of that year.

Number 2, from the perspective of the proportion of the composition of GDP, the largest increase happened in domestic investment, while the decline occurred in private consumption. In 2010, the private consumption, the public consumption, domestic investment and net export accounted for 61.9%, 10.1%, 25.3%, and 2.7% in GDP (see Table 6.9). From 2001 to 2010, the share of private consumption in GDP showed a decreasing trend, dropping 10.4%, but the share of domestic investment in GDP rose 6.5%, in which the proportion of private investment in GDP rose from 15.5% to 19.2% and the proportion of the public investment in GDP rose from 3.1% to 5.9%. The foreign trade had become one of the main pillars of the economic growth in Peru as its economic openness had increased and the free trade agreements with many countries had taken effect. From 2003 to 2007, the proportion of net export in GDP kept rising, with as high as 8.7% in 2006.

Third, the largest increase of domestic investment and relatively stable consumption growth. Analyzing the growth of the elements of GDP composition from the perspective of demand, the annual

Table 6.8 Composition of GDP Calculated by the Price of the Current Year According to the Expenditure Method ($100 Million)

Year	2001	2002	2003	2004	2005	2006	2007	2008	2009	2010
Government consumption expenditure	57.69	57.42	63.00	69.44	79.79	87.10	96.38	113.91	131.00	149.63
Private consumption expenditure	390.14	409.63	435.14	477.09	525.06	570.08	659.16	811.58	829.79	954.47
Changes of inventories	1.07	4.57	3.70	0.45	−3.51	6.69	14.14	14.94	−20.00	1.23
Total capital formation	101.25	104.48	113.10	125.12	142.03	185.03	246.75	351.71	292.85	415.31
Total fixed capital formation	100.18	99.91	109.39	124.66	145.54	178.35	232.61	336.78	312.85	414.09
Fixed capital formation of construction industry	60.79	66.41	72.20	82.25	94.35	114.44	146.02	199.75	203.56	262.06
Fixed capital formation of machinery and equipment	39.39	33.51	37.20	42.42	51.18	63.90	86.59	137.02	109.30	152.02
Balance of trade of goods and services	−9.54	−3.78	2.32	25.36	47.02	80.09	72.95	13.86	49.91	53.83

Source: Calculated according to ECLAC.

Table 6.9 Change of the Domestic and External Demand of Peruvian Economy in GDP (%)

Year	2001	2002	2003	2004	2005	2006	2007	2008	2009	2010
Private consumption	72.3	72.1	70.9	68.4	66.1	61.8	61.5	64.0	65.4	61.9
Public consumption	10.7	10.1	10.3	10.0	10.1	9.5	9.0	9.0	10.3	10.1
Domestic investment	18.8	18.4	18.4	17.9	17.9	20.0	22.8	26.9	20.7	25.3
Fixed investment	18.6	17.6	17.8	17.9	18.4	19.5	21.5	25.9	22.9	25.1
Private investment	15.5	14.8	15.0	15.1	15.5	16.4	18.2	21.5	17.7	19.2
Public investment	3.1	2.8	2.8	2.8	2.9	3.1	3.4	4.3	5.2	5.9
Net export	−1.8	−0.67	0.4	3.6	5.9	8.7	6.7	0.2	3.6	2.7

Source: Peru Central Bank Database, http://www.bcrp.gob.pe/estadisticas/cuadros-anuales-historicos.html.

increase of domestic investment is the largest, while the growth of private and public consumption is relatively stable.[19]

From 2001 to 2010, the total demand had maintained a stable growth. From 2002 to 2006, the growth rate of the total demand exceeded 4.5%; except for 2009, from 2007 to 2010, the growth rate of the annual total demand exceeded two digits (see Table 6.10). Since 2001, the domestic investment has become an important driving force for Peru's economic growth; especially the investment in transportation infrastructure such as the construction of ports, airports and highways had attracted a large number of private investment, which had a greater contribution to the economic growth.[20] From 2002 to 2005, the domestic investment growth increased from 2.9% to 9.2%; except for the decline in investment in 2009, from 2006 to 2010, the domestic investment had maintained a two-digit growth rate; in 2010 the annual growth rate reached 36.3% (see Table 6.10). In terms of the external demand, from 2001 to 2005, the export growth had been lager than the import growth; except for 2009, from 2006 to 2010, the import growth became larger than the export growth.

[19]World Bank, *Public Expenditure Review for Peru: Spending for Results*, Report No. 62586, June 2012, p. 19.

[20]CEPAL, *Perfiles de Infraestrutura y Transporte en American Latina: Caso Peru*, Unidad de Ser-vicios de Infraestrucutura de CEPAL, 2012, pp. 36–40.

Table 6.10 Changes of Aggregate Demand of Peru and the Decomposition (%)

Year	2001	2002	2003	2004	2005	2006	2007	2008	2009	2010
Aggregate demand	0.6	4.6	4.1	5.6	7.4	8.6	10.9	11.6	−2.8	11.2
Domestic demand	−0.4	4.1	3.7	3.8	5.8	10.3	11.8	12.3	−2.8	13.1
Private consumption	1.5	4.9	3.4	3.6	4.6	6.4	8.3	8.7	2.4	6.0
Public consumption	−0.8	0.0	4.0	4.6	8.5	7.6	4.5	2.1	16.5	10.0
Domestic investment	−7.1	2.9	4.7	4.3	9.2	26.5	25.8	25.8	−20.6	36.3
Fixed investment	−8.2	−0.5	5.9	7.8	12.3	20.2	22.6	27.1	−9.2	23.2
Private investment	−4.7	0.2	6.3	8.1	12.0	20.1	23.3	25.9	−15.1	22.1
Public investment	−22.4	−4.1	3.9	6.1	13.8	20.7	18.9	33.6	21.2	27.3
Export	6.8	7.5	6.2	15.2	15.2	0.8	6.9	8.2	−3.2	1.3
Import	2.9	2.3	4.2	9.6	10.9	13.1	21.4	20.1	−18.6	24.0

Source: Peru Central Reserve Bank Database, http://www.bcrp.gob.pe/estadisticas/cuadros-anuales-historicos.html.

The above situation shows that the boom of exporting minerals and energy resources had improved the fiscal state of the country, and the sustained rapid economic growth had driven the rise of domestic demand.

Fourth, the domestic savings rate increased and the ability of independent growth was enhanced. Compared with the past, in recent years, the savings rates of Peru's public and private sectors have been increasing, in which the savings rate of the public sectors has increased significantly, providing the maximum contribution to the national savings rate. External savings have also been improving, mainly in the inflow of foreign capital.

Over the past 10 years, the macroeconomic basis of Peru's economic growth has become increasingly stable. From the perspective of the proportion of domestic savings in GDP, it has been in an upward trend, indicating that the mechanism and quality of economic growth have been continuously improved. From 2001 to 2010, the proportion of domestic savings in GDP rose from 16.5% to 22.8%, increasing 6.3%; the financial condition of the public sectors had improved greatly: the proportion of the savings rate of the public sectors in GDP rose from 0.5% in 2001 to 6% in 2010, but the proportion of the savings rate of the private sectors in GDP has a little change (see Table 6.11).

Table 6.11 Change of the Proportion of Savings in GDP in Peru (%)

Year	2001	2002	2003	2004	2005	2006	2007	2008	2009	2010
Domestic savings	16.5	16.5	16.9	18.0	19.3	23.2	24.3	22.7	20.1	22.8
Public sectors	0.5	0.7	1.2	1.7	2.6	5.5	6.3	6.8	4.6	6.0
Private sectors	16.0	15.8	15.7	16.3	16.8	17.7	18.0	15.9	15.5	16.8
External savings	2.2	1.9	1.5	−0.1	−1.5	−3.2	−1.4	4.2	0.6	2.5

Source: Peru Central Reserve Bank Database, http://www.bcrp.gob.pe/estadisticas/cuadros-anuales-historicos.html.

Table 6.12 Net FDI ($100 Million)

Year	2001	2002	2003	2004	2005	2006	2007	2008	2009	2010
Net FDI	10.70	21.56	12.75	15.99	25.79	34.67	54.25	61.00	51.80	71.13
Proportion in GDP (%)	1.98	3.80	2.08	2.29	3.25	3.76	5.05	4.72	3.97	4.52

Source: Calculated on the basis of the data from ECLAC.

Fifth, the contribution of foreign capital to the economic growth is increasing. Due to the long-term high prices of global mining commodities, combined with the improvement of the investment environment as well as the active encouragement of the government for the development of mining, the FDI that Peru has attracted has continued to increase, increasing from $1.07 billion in 2001 to $7.113 billion in 2010, a percentage of up to 564.77% (see Table 6.12). From 2001 to 2010, the proportion of the net FDI in GDP increased from 1.98% to 4.52%.

From 2001 to 2006, the net FDI had increased from over $1 billion to more than $3 billion. From 2007 to 2010, the annual net FDI exceeded $5 billion. For some time in the future, Peru will maintain a high growth rate of foreign investment, and the sources of investment and the invested fields will be more diversified.

II. The Financial Situation and the Fiscal Policy

With the rapid economic growth and the strengthening of financial disciplines, the financial situation of the Peruvian government has greatly improved. In order to eliminate the periodic impact brought about by the export of primary products and the change in the terms of trade, the government had adopted the system of the structural fiscal balance index as the parameter tool for the adjustment of fiscal policies so that the impact of fiscal expenditure had been avoided and the fiscal sustainability had been ensured.[21]

Except the years affected by the international financial crisis, the fiscal deficit had been effectively controlled, and the fiscal surplus had been realized, which had laid the foundation for the fiscal policy to counter the international financial crisis. From the end of 2008 to August 2009, the main policy measures that Peru had taken in response to the financial crisis included: the economic stimulus plan of $4 billion between 2009 and 2010, the expansion of investment of $1.65 billion in infrastructure, providing credit and tax support to the export industries and enterprises affected by the financial crisis, expanding social protection and social assistance expenditures, and so on.[22]

First, the primary fiscal surplus of the public sectors has maintained a stable growth. From 2001 to 2005, the fiscal deficit had been declining, and the fiscal surplus had been achieved from 2006 to 2008. From 2003 to 2008, the primary fiscal surplus of the central government continued to increase, from 588 million new SOL to 12.977 billion new SOL, and the primary fiscal surplus of other departments had also maintained a stable growth (see Table 6.13). In terms of the primary fiscal surplus of the public sectors as a whole, the size of the surplus had maintained a synchronous growth, reaching 14.778 billion new SOL in 2008. However, the increase in the interest payments for the public debt had partially offset the contribution of primary fiscal surplus to the total fiscal surplus.

Second, the tax revenue is the main body of fiscal revenues. Regular incomes of the central government include two parts: tax revenue and non-tax revenue. From 2001 to 2010, the regular incomes had

[21] Alejandro Granda, Cesar Liendo, Carlos Rojas, *El Indicador de Balance Estructural*, Ministerio de Economia/Finanzas del Peru, Junio de 2012, pp. 28–29.

[22] ECLAC, *The Reactions co the Governments oo the Americas to the International Crisis*: An Overview of Policy Measures up to 31 August 2009, September 2009, p. 40.

maintained a rapid growth. In 2010, the regular revenue was 74.712 million new SOL, and the income tax and non-tax revenue respectively were 64.429 billion new SOL and 10.283 billion new SOL. From the perspective of the proportion of tax revenue and non-tax revenue, the proportion of the two incomes in recurrent incomes had changed little from 2001 to 2010. The scale of capital income of the central government was small, with the highest income of only 747 million new SOL in 2010.

Third, the capital expenditure is greater than the recurrent expenditure. The central government's fiscal expenditure includes two parts: the recurrent expenditure and capital expenditure. From 2001 to 2010, the scale of fiscal expenditure expanded from 28.58 billion new SOL to 70.49 billion new SOL, an increase of nearly three times. From 2008 to 2010, the increase in fiscal expenditure had been great, mainly due to the expansionary fiscal policy taken in response to the international financial crisis. In terms of the changes in the content of fiscal expenditure, from 2001 to 2006, the recurrent expenditure grew rapidly, but the capital expenditure had a slow growth; from 2007 to 2010, the capital spending had maintained a substantial growth, but the growth of the recurrent expenditure was slow due to the increasing public investment by the government.[23]

Fourth, the fiscal surplus has been used for the active repayment of foreign debt. In terms of the change in financing needs, from 2001 to 2008, the financing needs of the central government had continued to decline. In 2001, among the financing needs of 5.049 billion new SOL, the international debt financing was 1.755 billion new SOL, the domestic debt financing was 2.16 billion new SOL, and the privatization revenue was 1.14 billion new SOL (see Table 6.13). From 2006 to 2008, the central government had achieved a surplus; therefore, there was no need for financing, and the fiscal surplus had repaid part of the debt. In 2008, the new international debt repayment was 3.472 billion SOL, and the domestic debt repayment was 5.578 billion new SOL. As a result of the implementation of countercyclical

[23]World Bank, *Public Expenditure Review for Peru: Spending for Results*, Report No. 62586, June 2012, pp. 39–49.

Table 6.13 Peru's Financial Situation (100 Million New SOL)

Year	2001	2002	2003	2004	2005	2006	2007	2008	2009	2010
Regular income of the central government	267.03	286.66	316.58	353.25	410.19	530.36	607.13	680.03	608.31	747.12
Tax revenue	231.84	241.68	274.95	310.88	355.62	458.06	523.44	582.87	525.66	644.29
Non-tax revenue	35.18	44.98	41.63	42.38	54.58	72.29	83.68	97.16	82.65	102.83
Capital income of the central government	2.91	3.71	3.61	1.89	3.86	3.61	3.85	3.94	4.44	7.47
Fiscal expenditure of the central government	285.80	292.41	314.32	341.72	384.46	433.28	503.38	554.20	621.14	704.90
Regular expenditure	243.49	252.85	273.69	298.77	335.50	373.49	431.08	465.38	475.77	514.41
Capital expenditure	42.31	39.56	40.63	42.95	48.96	59.79	72.30	88.82	145.37	190.48
The primary fiscal surplus of the central government	−15.86	−2.04	5.88	13.42	29.60	100.69	107.60	129.77	−8.39	49.69
The primary fiscal surplus of other sectors	8.03	0.97	4.35	9.69	12.32	26.24	49.70	18.02	8.52	−12.39
The primary fiscal surplus of the public sectors	−7.83	−1.07	10.22	23.12	41.92	126.92	157.30	147.78	0.13	37.3
Debt interest	42.66	42.82	46.06	48.67	50.62	56.60	60.08	58.84	50.11	50.85
Fiscal surplus	−50.49	−43.89	−35.83	−25.55	−8.70	70.32	97.22	88.94	−49.98	−13.54
Financing requirement	50.49	43.89	35.83	25.55	8.70	−70.32	−97.22	−88.94	49.98	13.54
International debt financing	17.55	41.44	29.28	35.98	−38.13	−17.90	−63.98	−34.72	40.69	−20.77
Domestic debt financing	21.60	−12.59	4.75	−14.32	44.98	−55.46	−37.73	−55.78	8.27	30.13
Income from privatization	11.34	15.03	1.81	3.89	1.85	3.04	4.49	1.56	1.02	4.19

Source: Peru Central Reserve Bank Database, http://www.bcrp.gob.pe/estadisticas/cuadros-anuales-historicos.html.

fiscal policy, the central finance in 2009 produced the financing need of 4.998 billion SOL, completed mainly through the issuance of the international debt, indicating good international reputation of Peru with fine financing channels.

Fifth, the proportion of the fiscal deficit in GDP has showed a downward trend. In the past 10 years, from the perspective of the proportion of the main financial revenue and expenditure indicators in GDP, Peru's financial situation had been in the process of continuous improvement — the government's financial base had been increasingly consolidated. From 2001 to 2005, the proportion of the fiscal deficit in GDP fell from 2.7% down to 0.3%; in 2006 a fiscal surplus was achieved, occupying 2.3% of GDP; between 2009 and 2010, the fiscal deficit re-emerged, but the proportion of the amount of deficit in GDP showed a downward trend (see Table 6.14).

Sixth, the proportion of tax revenue in GDP is still not stable. From 2001 to 2007, the proportion of the central government's recurrent revenue in GDP rose from 14.4% to 18.3%, and later there came a downward trend, mainly due to the slowdown in economic growth and the government's implementation of a tax-cut policy. From 2001 to 2007, the proportion of tax revenue in GDP increased from 12.1% to 15.7%; between 2007 and 2010, it went down to 12.1%. The proportion of the non-tax revenue and the capital income in GDP basically did not change (see Table 6.15). From 2006 to 2010, the proportion of the government's fiscal expenditure in GDP had a substantial increase, about 1.9%, mainly due to largely increased proportion of capital expenditures in GDP.

Seventh, the sales tax is the main body of the tax revenue. From the perspective of the source of financial revenue, the tax revenues mainly include the income tax, import tax, sales tax, consumption tax and other taxes, in which the sales tax and income tax accounted for more than 70% of the proportion of the total tax revenue.[24] In 2010, among the tax revenue of 64.429 billion new SOL, the income tax was 25.802 billion new SOL, and the sales tax was 35.536 billion

---

[24]World Bank, *Public Expenditure Review for Peru: Spending for Results*, Report No. 62586, June 2012, pp. 27–32.

Table 6.14 Expenditure of the Peruvian Central Government (100 Million New SOL)

Year	2001	2002	2003	2004	2005	2006	2007	2008	2009	2010
Regular expenditure	243.49	252.85	273.69	298.77	335.50	373.49	431.08	465.38	475.77	514.41
Salary expenditure	82.28	89.22	96.68	105.05	115.91	125.52	130.19	138.70	151.60	158.23
Commodities and services	74.24	68.73	73.37	82.14	89.38	100.30	101.12	108.49	133.41	155.37
Transfer payment	86.97	94.90	103.64	111.57	130.21	147.68	199.77	218.18	190.77	200.81
Capital expenditure	42.31	39.56	40.63	42.95	48.96	59.79	72.30	88.32	145.37	190.48
Interest expenditure	40.60	39.53	41.91	43.81	47.94	54.18	55.25	51.28	48.67	47.66
Interest of domestic debt	4.66	4.85	4.69	4.60	6.57	11.21	12.79	18.14	18.01	18.75
Interest of foreign debt	35.94	34.69	37.22	39.21	41.38	42.97	42.47	33.14	30.66	28.91
Total	326.40	331.94	356.22	385.53	432.40	487.46	558.63	605.48	669.82	752.56

Source: Peru Central Reserve Bank Database, http://www.bcrp.gob.pe/estadisticas/cuadros-anuales-historicos.html.

Table 6.15 Proportion of the Main Fiscal Indicators in GDP (%)

Year	2001	2002	2003	2004	2005	2006	2007	2008	2009	2010
Regular income of the central government	14.4	14.8	14.8	15.7	17.5	18.1	18.3	15.9	17.2	14.4
Tax revenue	12.1	12.9	13.1	13.6	15.2	15.6	15.7	13.7	14.8	12.1
Non-tax revenue	2.3	2.0	1.8	2.1	2.4	2.5	2.6	2.2	2.4	2.3
Capital income of the central government	0.2	0.2	0.2	0.1	0.1	0.1	0.1	0.1	0.1	0.2
Fiscal expenditure of the central government	15.1	14.6	14.7	14.4	14.7	14.3	15.0	14.9	16.2	16.2
Regular expenditure	12.9	12.7	12.8	12.6	12.8	12.4	12.8	12.5	12.4	11.8
Capital expenditure	2.2	2.0	1.9	1.8	1.9	2.0	2.2	2.4	3.8	4.4
Primary fiscal surplus of the central government	−0.1	0.3	0.6	1.1	3.3	3.2	3.5	−0.2	1.1	−0.1
Primary fiscal surplus of other sectors	0.4	0.0	0.2	0.4	0.5	0.9	1.5	0.5	0.2	−0.3
Primary fiscal surplus of the public sectors	0.4	0.0	0.2	0.4	0.5	0.9	1.5	0.5	0.2	−0.3
Interest of debt	2.3	2.1	2.2	2.0	1.9	1.9	1.8	1.6	1.3	1.2
Fiscal surplus	2.7	2.2	1.7	1.1	0.3	2.3	2.9	2.4	−1.3	−0.3
Financing requirement	2.7	2.2	1.7	1.1	0.3	−2.3	−2.9	−2.4	1.3	0.3
Foreign debt	0.9	2.1	1.4	1.5	−1.5	−0.6	−1.9	−0.9	1.1	−0.5
Domestic debt	1.1	−0.6	0.2	−0.6	1.7	−1.8	−1.1	−1.5	0.2	0.7
Income from Privatization	0.6	0.8	0.1	0.2	0.1	0.1	0.1	0.0	0.0	0.1

Note: This table does not include the financial sector, the sign of "-" represents "debt repayment".

Source: Peru Central Reserve Bank Database, http://www.bcrp.gob.pe/estadisticas/cuadros-anuales-historicos.html.

new SOL, accounting for 40.05% and 55.16% of the tax revenues respectively (see Table 6.16). From 2001 to 2010, the proportion of the revenue of sales tax and income tax showed an increasing trend.

From the perspective of the change of the proportion of the types of tax revenues in GDP, the proportion of the sales tax and income tax had a substantial increase, but the proportion of the import tax and consumption tax showed a downward trend. From 2001 to 2010, the proportion of the sales tax in GDP increased from 6.2% to 8.2%, and the proportion of the income tax increased from 3% to 5.9% (see Table 6.17). In contrast, over the same period the proportion of the consumption tax in GDP decreased from 1.9% to 1.1%, while the proportion of the imports in GDP decreased from 1.5% to 0.4%.

III. The Financial Situation and Policy Adjustment

Peru's financial system is becoming more and more perfect. Except for the short-term fluctuations of a few years, the financial market has been relatively stable, which has created a favorable external condition for the economic growth. The Central Bank had effectively alleviated the inflationary pressure and improved the ability of counter-cyclical macro-control to deal with the external shocks by using the policy instruments, such as the interest rate, the exchange rate, the credit and the international bond issuance.[25] The independence of the Central Bank has been strengthened, the monetary policy has become an important tool for the macroeconomic regulation and control, and the monetary policy and fiscal policy have coordinated and cooperated with each other. From the end of 2008 to August 2009, in response to the financial crisis, the government had taken the monetary policies such as reducing the deposit reserve ratio, injecting liquidity in the form of local currency, and continuously cutting the benchmark interest rates.[26]

[25]IMF, *Peru: 2012 Article IV Consultation*, Country Report No. 13/45, February 2013, p. 5.

[26]ECLAC, *The Reactions of the Governments of the Americas to the International Crisis*: an Overview of Policy Measures up to 31 August 2009, September 2009, p. 40.

Table 6.16 The Fiscal Revenues of the Peruvian Central Government (100 Million New SOL)

Year	2001	2002	2003	2004	2005	2006	2007	2008	2009	2010
Tax revenue	231.84	241.68	274.95	310.88	355.62	458.06	523.44	582.87	525.66	644.29
Income tax	56.30	60.11	79.71	90.26	111.88	184.14	228.47	241.46	203.46	258.02
Import tax	27.86	24.83	25.50	27.44	31.43	28.47	21.98	19.11	14.93	18.03
Sales tax	118.15	126.13	141.10	162.06	183.02	215.17	252.58	315.83	295.19	355.36
Consumption tax	35.61	41.84	45.25	44.68	40.66	40.42	42.91	34.61	41.46	46.70
Other taxes	26.02	17.38	14.14	21.62	29.80	33.69	38.48	43.71	44.00	45.66
Non-tax income	35.18	44.98	41.63	42.38	54.58	72.29	83.68	97.16	82.65	102.83
Total	267.03	286.66	316.58	353.25	410.19	530.36	607.13	680.03	608.31	747.12

Source: Peru Central Reserve Bank Database, http://www.bcrp.gob.pe/estadisticas/cuadros-anuales-historicos.html.

Table 6.17 Proportions of the Fiscal Revenues of the Peruvian Central Government in GDP (%)

Year	2001	2002	2003	2004	2005	2006	2007	2008	2009	2010
Tax revenue	12.3	12.1	12.9	13.1	13.6	15.2	15.6	15.7	13.7	14.8
Income tax	3.0	3.0	3.7	3.8	4.3	6.1	6.8	6.5	5.3	5.9
Import tax	1.5	1.2	1.2	1.2	1.2	0.9	0.7	0.5	0.4	0.4
Sales tax	6.2	6.3	6.6	6.8	7.0	7.1	7.5	8.5	7.7	8.2
Consumption tax	1.9	2.1	2.1	1.9	1.6	1.3	1.3	0.9	1.1	1.1
Other taxes	1.4	0.9	0.7	0.9	1.1	1.1	1.1	1.2	1.2	1.1
Non-tax income	1.9	2.3	2.0	1.8	2.1	2.4	2.5	2.6	2.2	2.4
Total	14.1	14.4	14.8	14.8	15.7	17.5	18.1	18.3	15.9	17.2

Source: Peru Central Reserve Bank Database, http://www.bcrp.gob.pe/estadisticas/cuadros-anuales-historicos.html.

Table 6.18 Money Supply and Change of Domestic Loans (%)

	2003	2004	2005	2006	2007	2008	2009	2010	2011
Base money	7.2	19.6	27.8	17.1	25.2	38.2	2.1	24.2	31.3
Supply of M1	10.9	22.9	29.0	17.1	30.6	31.3	8.8	28.0	19.9
Supply of M2	10.3	17.1	28.9	7.7	37.7	48.5	−2.2	27.8	18.8
Domestic loans	8.8	12.1	6.1	23.2	38.0	9.4	9.9	23.9	12.3

Source: ECLAC, *Preliminary Overview of the Economies of Latin America and the Caribbean 2012*, pp. 67–95.

First, the change of the money supply. According to the changes of the macroeconomic trends, from 2003 to 2011, the timely adjustment of the money supply and a credit transfer mechanism through the banking system had played an important role in the adjustment of the money supply to the real economy.[27] From 2003 to 2005, the supply of basic currency of M1 (narrow money) and M2 (broad money) increased significantly. To prevent the economy from overheating, the Central Bank had tightened the money supply in 2006, increasing the supply of base money, M1 and M2 by only 17.1%, 17.1%, and 7.7% (see Table 6.18).

[27]Cesar Carrera Yalan, "El Canal del Credito Bancario en el Peru: Evidencia y Mecanismo de Transmision", *Revista Estudios Economicos*, Banco Central de Reserva del Peru, No. 22, Diciembre 2011, pp. 63–82.

From 2007 to the first half of 2008, despite the economic overheating, due to the sudden breakout of the international financial crisis in the second half of 2008, the Central Bank had to implement the counter-cyclical monetary policy, with more than 30% of the growth of the three kinds of monetary supply. In 2009, the money supply got reversed: the supply of the base currency and M1 increased by only 2.1% and 8.8%, respectively, while the supply of M2 had dropped by 2.2% (see Table 6.18). From 2010 to 2011, a larger increase in the supply of the amount of money had promoted the economic recovery.

In addition, the domestic lending has become one of the important tools of the monetary policy. From 2003 to 2007, the amount of loans maintained a rapid growth, injecting a large amount of funds for the economic growth. Between 2008 and 2009, there was a tightening of loans, but in 2010, the amount of loans appeared to have restored growth.

Second, the change of the interest rate. The interest rate policy is a key monetary policy tool of the Central Bank of Peru; especially the stability of the banking system and a good level of profitability have left a large space for the Central Bank to adjust the policy.[28] From the perspective of the adjustment of the benchmark interest rate of the monetary policy, from 2003 to 2008, with the emergence of the economic overheating due to the rapid economic growth, the benchmark interest rate was on the rise cycle. In 2008, the benchmark interest rate was 5.9%, with 2.7% higher than in 2003. In order to cope with the international financial crisis and reduce corporate financing burden, between 2009 and 2010, the benchmark interest rate had been lowered from 3.3% to 2.1%, but in order to prevent the overheating, in 2011, the Central Bank again raised the benchmark interest rate (see Table 6.19).

From the perspective of the market average loan interest rate, the adjustment of the interest rate is related with the change of the economic cycle, showing a downward trend. From 2003 to 2005, the loan interest rate was relatively stable, with a slight rise. From 2006 to

[28]IMF, *Peru: 2011 Article IV Consultation*, Country Report No. 12/26, February 2012, p. 22.

Table 6.19 Interest Rate Indicators (%)

	2003	2004	2005	2006	2007	2008	2009	2010	2011
The benchmark interest rate of monetary policy	3.2	2.7	3.0	4.3	4.7	5.9	3.3	2.1	4.0
The average loan interest rate	21.0	24.7	25.5	23.9	22.9	23.7	21.0	19.0	18.7

Source: ECLAC, *Preliminary Overview of the Economies of Latin America and the Caribbean 2012*, pp. 67–95.

2011, the loan interest rate fell sharply, from 23.9% in 2006 down to 18.7% in 2011. As an important monetary policy tool, the interest rate policy had continuously improved its transmission mechanism and effectively played a role in the regulation of the financial market.[29]

Third, the change of the exchange rate. From 2001 to 2010, the exchange rate of the Peruvian new currency new SOL against the US dollar was in the rising period. From 2001 to 2004, the new SOL had maintained a steady rise, and between 2005 and 2008, it entered the period of accelerated appreciation. In terms of the annual appreciation rate, in 2008 the appreciation rate was up to 6.49%, mainly due to the large inflow of US dollars in the first half of 2008. The Central Bank started to implement the intervention policy, acquiring $8.5 billion from the financial market as its foreign exchange reserve.[30] From September to December in 2008, despite the small devaluation of the new SOL, in the whole year of 2008, the new SOL still showed a trend of appreciation because of the lag effect of the spreading of the international financial crisis, Peru's solid macroeconomic fundamentals and the Central Bank's timely injection of dollar liquidity

[29]Paul Castillo, Fernando Perez Forero, "Los Mecanismos de Transimsion de la Politica Monetaria en Peru", *Revista Estudios Economicos*, Banco Central de Reserva del Peru, No. 21, Junio 2011, pp. 41–63.

[30]IMF, Peru: *Staff Report for the 2008 Article IV Consultation*, Country Report No. 09/40, February 2009, p. 6.

Table 6.20 Change of the Exchange Rate of Peru's New SOL

Year	2001	2002	2003	2004	2005	2006	2007	2008	2009	2010
Exchange rate of dollar against new SOL	3.51	3.52	3.48	3.41	3.30	3.28	3.13	2.93	3.01	2.83
Appreciation of the exchange rate of new SOL against dollar (%)	−0.52	−0.27	1.09	1.88	3.43	0.67	4.45	6.49	−2.95	6.19

Source: Peru Central Reserve Bank Database, http://www.bcrp.gob.pe/estadisticas/cuadros-anuales-historicos.html.

into the financial market. However, in 2009, the new SOL depreciated by 2.95%, but in 2010 it got a rapid appreciation of 6.19% (see Table 6.20).

It is noteworthy that the phenomenon of "de-dollarization" also appeared in Peru. In the past 10 years, the dollar deposit and the dollar denominated commercial loans have declined, mainly due to the macroeconomic stabilization, the macro prudential policy of exchange rate management and the development of local currency capital market.[31] Compared with the change of the exchange rate of Brazil, Colombia, and Uruguay, the fluctuation of the exchange rate of the Peruvian new SOL is relatively stable.[32]

Fourth, the change of the external debt. From 2002 to 2006, the scale of the Peruvian foreign debt had been relatively stable, mainly due to the rapid economic development, the improvement of the fiscal situation and the surplus of balance of payments for several years, resulting in a continuous decline of the proportion of foreign debt in GDP and the income of foreign exchange. Peru had further reduced the risk of the debt maturity structure and financing cost and got more relaxed financing channels in the international capital market by making use of its trade surplus and its advantage of international

[31]Mercedes Garcia Escribano, *Factores que Impulsan la Desdolarizacion en el Peru*, Banco Central de Reserva del Peril, No. 21, Junio 2011, pp. 23–40.
[32]IMF, *Peru, 2011 Article IV* Consultation, Country Report No. 12/26, February 2012, pp. 19–20.

reserves, with an early repayment of the outstanding bonds and bond exchange.[33]

In 2010, the total external debt amounted to $40.236 billion, an increase of $13.041 billion compared with 2001, rising 47.95% (see Table 6.21). From 2001 to 2004, the total amount of its external debt rose slightly; between 2005 and 2006, the scale of its external debt had declined, but from 2007 to 2010, the total amount of its external debt had risen sharply, mainly due to its counter-cyclical fiscal policy. Although the scale of Peru's total external debt had been expanding from 2007 to 2010, the external debt burden evaluated in the proportion of GDP had continued to decline for many years. In 2001, the proportion of its external debt in GDP was as high as 50.4%; in 2010 it dropped to 25.6%, with the debt burden greatly reduced (see Table 6.21).

IV. The Foreign Trade and Policy Adjustment

Peru has actively carried out its foreign economic and trade cooperation, expanded its import and export trade, and attracted much FDI. For a long time, the traditional products such as mineral products and agricultural products has had a high proportion in the export commodity structure of Peru and its export market also has been concentrated. In order to get rid of its dependence on the export of primary products, Peru has been trying to achieve the diversification of its industrial structure, striving to increase the high value-added export products, especially reducing the proportion of the export of traditional and non-traditional products and adjusting the geographical layout structure of the importers.[34]

First, Peru has expanded the scope of the global network of the free trade zones, emphasizing the potential of the value of the development of the economic and trade relations with Asian countries.

[33] IMF, Peru, *Staff Report for the 2010 Article IV Consultation*, Report No. 09/40, February 2010, pp. 38–40.

[34] Javier Illescas, Felipe Jaramillo, *Export Growth and Diversification: The Case of Peru*, World Bank, Policy Research Working Paper 5868, November 2011, pp. 19–20.

Table 6.21 Change of the Peruvian Foreign Debt ($100 Million)

Year	2001	2002	2003	2004	2005	2006	2007	2008	2009	2010
Issuance of international bonds	N.A.	N.A.	12.5	13.05	26.75	7.33	18.27	—	21.50	46.93
Total foreign debt	271.95	278.72	295.87	312.44	286.57	288.98	328.94	348.38	357.31	402.36
Proportion of total foreign debt in GDP (%)	50.4	49.1	48.2	44.8	36.1	1.3	30.6	27.0	27.4	25.6

Source: Calculated according to ECLAC.

Since entering the 21st century, Peru has actively promoted the bilateral FTA negotiations. According to incomplete statistics, in addition to the economic complementarity agreements (Acuerdo de Complementacion Economica) signed with the Andean Community (Bolivia, Ecuador, Colombia, effective in 1969), Cuba (effective in 2001) and the South American Common Market — Mercosur (effective in 2005), Peru had also signed free trade agreements (TLC) with the following countries: The United States (effective 2009), Chile (effective in 2009), Canada (effective in 2009), Singapore (effective in 2009), China (effective 2010), South Korea (effective in 2011), Mexico (effective in 2012), Japan (effective in 2012), Panama (effective in 2012), Switzerland, Liechtenstein, Iceland, and Norway (effective in 2011), EU (effective in 2013), and Costa Rica (effective in 2013). Peru has completed negotiations or been under the negotiation process of bilateral free trade agreements with Guatemala, Venezuela, El Salvador, Honduras, and the Union Pacific (Mexico, Chile, and Colombia).

Peru has a very positive attitude toward the development of the economic and trade relations with the Asia-Pacific countries. In addition to the above free trade agreements with Singapore, China, South Korea, Japan, and other countries, in July 2011, Peru started the negotiation of the promotion and protection of bilateral investment with India. In April 2012, the free trade negotiation between Peru and Thailand in terms of market access, rules of origin, and services had made progress. At the same time, Peru had also joined the negotiation of the US-led Trans-Pacific Strategic Economic Partnership (TPP).

Second, the trade in goods has maintained a rapid growth, but the trade surplus is greatly influenced by the economic cycle. From 2001 to 2011, its total trade in goods increased from \$14.126 billion to \$83.675 billion, an increase of nearly seven times. Among them, the export of goods rose from \$6.85 billion to \$45.666 billion, and the import of goods increased from \$7.276 billion to to 38.009 billion (see Table 6.22). In 2011, the volume of import and export increased by 28.7% compared with that in 2010, of which the export was \$45.666 billion, an increase of 30.8% over the previous year; the import was

Table 6.22 Peru's Commodity Trade ($100 Million)

Year	2001	2002	2003	2004	2005	2006	2007	2008	2009	2010	2011
Export	68.50	75.65	87.10	123.70	170.01	234.31	275.88	311.94	256.93	349.09	456.66
Growth rate (%)	−0.3	10.4	15.1	42.0	37.4	37.8	17.7	13.1	−17.7	31.6	30.8
Import	72.76	75.01	84.17	101.11	125.02	153.27	204.64	299.42	217.06	301.27	380.09
Growth rate (%)	−2.3	3.1	12.2	20.1	23.6	22.6	33.5	46.3	−27.6	37.8	26.2
Trade surplus	−4.26	0.64	2.93	22.59	44.99	81.04	71.24	12.52	39.87	47.82	76.57
Growth rate (%)	N.A.	115.02	357.81	670.99	99.16	80.13	−12.09	−82.43	218.45	19.94	60.12
Total trade volume	141.26	150.65	171.27	224.82	295.02	387.59	480.52	611.36	473.99	650.36	836.75
Growth rate (%)	−1.3	6.6	13.7	31.3	31.2	31.4	24.0	27.2	−22.5	34.4	28.7

Source: Chinese Ministry of Commerce, *Overview of Peruvian Commodity Trade and the Sino-Peruvian Bilateral Trade in 2011*, http://countryreport.mofcom.gov.cn/record/view110209.asp? news_id = 282500.

$38.009 billion, an increase of 26.2% over the previous year, and the surplus was $7.657 billion, an increase of 60.12% over the previous year. From 2001 to 2007, the surplus of goods trade rose sharply, mainly due to the expansion period of the demand for global mining products and agricultural products and the great improvement of trade conditions.

Due to the outbreak of the international financial crisis and its lagged impact, between 2008 and 2009, a substantial decline occurred in the trade surplus; from 2010 to 2011, the trade surplus had been restored, but had not reached the best level in the previous few years.

Third, the diversification strategy of foreign trade has achieved initial success, but its trade partners are still very concentrated. In 2011, the volumes of Peru's export to China, Switzerland, the United States, and Canada were $6.96 billion, $5.92 billion, $5.81 billion, and $4.18 billion, respectively, occupying 15.2%, 13.0%, 12.7%, and 9.2% in Peru's total export, increasing $28.3%, 54.7%, 2.4%, and 26.5%; the volumes of imports from the United States, China, Brazil, and Ecuador were 7.39 billion, $6.37 billion, $2.44 billion, and $1.88 billion, accounting for 19.5%, 16.8%, 6.4%, and 4.9% in Peru's total import, increasing $26.8%, 24.5%, 11.6%, and 31.7%.[35]

In 2011, the five largest sources of trade surplus of Peru were Switzerland, Canada, Spain, Japan, and Germany, with respectively $5.77 billion, $3.5 billion, $1.1 billion, $0.87 billion, and $0.78 billion; its trade deficits came mainly from Argentina, the United States, and Brazil, with respectively $1.65 billion, $1.59 billion, and $1.16 billion.[36]

Fourth, the primary products are still the major commodity export, and the proportion of the industrial products in the export has declined. Peru's commodity export structure is characterized by its high dependence on primary products; the export of industrial manufactured goods grows slowly, and the proportion of it in the export of goods has dropped significantly.

---

[35]Chinese Ministry of Commerce, *Overview of Peruvian Trade of Goods and the Sino-Peruvian Bilateral Trade in 2011*, http://countryreport.mof-com.gov.cn/record/view110209.asp? news_id = 28250.
[36]*Ibid.*

In 2010, the export of primary products was $30.779 billion, increased by nearly six times compared with that in 2001, with the proportion in the total export of goods rising from 81.4% in 2001 to 89.1% in 2010 (see Table 6.23). In 2010, its export of manufactured goods was $3.756 billion, increasing about three times than that in 2001, with the proportion in the export of goods falling from 18.6% in 2001 down to 10.9% in 2010.

Fifth, the mineral products and the situation that oil and fishery products are the dominant products of its foreign export have not changed. Peru's structure of export commodities has not changed, mainly relying on the export of traditional products such as mining products and fishery products. Peru's main export commodities are mineral products, precious metals and their products, and base metals and their products, with the exports in 2011 respectively $18.48 million, $10.29 million, and $4.52 billion, accounting for 40.5%, 22.5%, and 9.9% in Peru's total export.[37]

From 2001 to 2010, the proportion of mineral products in its export of goods rose from 45.6% to 61.1%; the proportion of the oil export in its exports of goods rose from 5.6% to 8.7% (see Table 6.24). The proportion of these two categories of traditional products in its exports of goods rose by 16% and 3%. Fisheries are the traditional industries of Peru's exports, but the proportion in the exports of goods fell from 13.2% in 2001 to 5.3% in 2010. The proportion of the export of agricultural products has declined slightly.

From the perspective of the classification of the traditional products and non-traditional products, the proportion of traditional products in the exports of goods has had a substantial increase; in contrast, the proportion of non-traditional products has showed a downward trend. From 2001 to 2010, the proportion of traditional products in the total export rose from 67.4% to 77.8%, increasing more than 10%, but the proportion of non-traditional products fell from 31.1% to 21.5%, down nearly 10%.

[37]Chinese Ministry of Commerce, *Overview of Peruvian Trade of Goods and the Sino-Peruvian Bilateral Trade in 2011*, http://countryreport.mof-com.gov.cn/record/view110209.asp? news_id = 28250.

Table 6.23 Structure of Peru's Commodity Export ($100 Million)

Year	2001	2002	2003	2004	2005	2006	2007	2008	2009	2010
Export of primary products	55.54	62.17	72.65	100.44	152.10	199.97	234.85	263.59	227.47	307.79
Proportion of the export of primary products in commodity export (%)	81.4	83.0	83.0	83.1	85.3	88.0	87.6	86.6	87.8	89.1
Export of industrial products	12.71	12.73	14.84	20.39	26.14	27.39	33.39	40.66	31.58	37.56
Proportion of industrial products in commodity export (%)	18.6	17.0	17.0	16.9	14.7	12.0	12.4	13.4	12.2	10.9
The terms of trade of commodity	80.1	82.4	85.6	93.2	100	127.3	132.0	114.4	108.1	127.7

Note: The terms of trade is based on the period of 2005, with the base of 100 for comparison.

Source: Statistic database of ECLAC.

Table 6.24 Proportions of Peru's Export of Products in the Total Export (%)

Year	2001	2002	2003	2004	2005	2006	2007	2008	2009	2010
	Classification of Industries									
Fishery	13.2	11.6	9.0	8.6	7.5	5.6	5.2	5.8	6.2	5.3
Agriculture	3.0	2.8	2.5	2.5	1.9	2.4	1.6	2.2	2.4	2.7
Mining	45.6	49.4	51.6	55.6	56.4	61.8	62.1	58.4	60.8	61.1
Oil	5.6	5.8	6.8	5.0	8.8	7.6	8.2	8.6	7.1	8.7
Others	32.6	30.4	30.1	28.3	25.4	22.6	22.9	25.0	23.5	22.2
	Classification of Traditional and Non-traditional Products									
Traditional products	67.4	69.6	69.9	71.7	74.6	77.4	77.1	75.0	76.5	77.8
Non-traditional products	31.1	29.2	28.8	27.2	24.6	22.2	22.5	24.4	22.9	21.5
Others	1.5	1.2	1.3	1.1	0.8	0.4	0.4	0.6	0.6	0.7

Source: Peru Central Reserve Bank database, http://www.bcrp.gob.pe/estadisticas/cuadros-anuales-historicos.html.

V. The International Balance of Payments

Since the beginning of the 21st century, the situation of Peru's international balance of payments has improved significantly, with continuous increase of its foreign exchange reserves. There are three main reasons for the improvement of its international balance of payments: first, its exports have increased and its trade in goods has achieved earnings for years; second, the terms of trade of primary products such as mining products have been improved, playing the role in enhancing the trade income. Third, due to the large inflows of FDI, its financial account has remained in surplus. The improvement of the balance of payments not only has improved the solvency of Peru, but also enhanced the government's macro-control ability, which is conducive to resisting the impact of the external risks.[38]

First, Peru's foreign exchange reserves have continued to increase, enhancing its ability to respond to its foreign debt repayment and the external adverse shocks. In 2010, the surplus of its international balance of payments was $10.956 billion, and the international reserves

[38]Paul Castillo Bardález, Daniel Barco Rondán, "Crisis Financieras y Manejo de Reservas en el Peru", *Reista E studios Economicos*, Banco Central de Reserva del Peru, No. 17, Junio 2009, pp. 86–112.

reached $43.187 billion, respectively 25 times and 4 times of those in 2001 (see Table 6.25). From 2001 to 2003, the current account had been in deficit, but the proportion of the balance of deficit in GDP fell from 2.2% to 1.5%; from 2004 to 2007, the current account achieved surplus, with the proportion of surplus in GDP up to 3.1% in 2006; in 2008, the deficit of the current account reached as high as $5.318 billion, 4.1% of GDP, the highest in recent years.

Second, the trade of goods has remained a surplus, but the services and revenue projects have been in the state of a long-term trade deficit. From 2001 to 2010, the current account deficit had been caused mainly by the deficits in the service trade and revenue projects, with the sizes of the deficits of the two major items continuing to expand. In 2010, the deficit of the service trade was $2.037 billion and the revenue projects were $10.053 billion, respectively about 2 times and 10 times of the corresponding deficits in 2001 (see Table 6.25). The main reason of the income deficit was due to the increase of the remittance of FDI profits.

Third, a large number of FDI inflows have made the financial account maintained a surplus for many years. Over the past 10 years, a major change in Peru's international balance of payments is due to a large inflow of FDI, its financial account has maintained a surplus for many years, and the size of the surplus has showed an expanding trend. In 2001, the balance of its financial account was $1.534 billion, and by 2010 it reached $12.347 billion.

The surplus of the financial account for many years has contributed greatly to the improvement of the Peruvian international balance of payments and the scale of the international reserve has been expanded. Although the capital account has been in a deficit state for 10 consecutive years, the size is not large, showing a downward trend.

Section 3 Sino-Peruvian Economic and Trade Cooperation and Its Prospect

Since the beginning of the 21st century, high-level exchanges between China and Peru have been frequent, the development of economic and

Table 6.25 Peru's International Balance of Payments ($100 Million)

Year	2001	2002	2003	2004	2005	2006	2007	2008	2009	2010
Current account	−12.03	−11.10	−9.49	0.19	11.48	28.73	14.60	−53.18	2.11	−23.15
Proportion of current account in GDP (%)	−2.2	−2.0	−1.5	–	1.4	3.1	1.4	−4.1	0.2	−1.5
Surplus of commodity trade	−1.79	3.21	8.86	30.04	52.86	89.86	85.04	25.69	59.51	67.50
Surplus of service trade	−9.63	−9.94	−9.00	−7.32	−8.34	−7.37	−11.92	−20.56	−11.44	−20.37
Benefit items	−11.01	−14.57	−21.44	−36.86	−50.76	−75.62	−83.59	−87.74	−74.84	−100.53
Transfer payments	10.40	10.19	12.09	14.33	17.72	21.85	25.08	29.43	28.87	30.26
Capital account	−1.55	−1.12	−1.12	−0.86	−1.23	−1.26	−0.67	−0.64	−0.42	−0.96
Financial account	15.34	19.83	8.20	22.86	0.24	8.44	90.69	89.61	23.62	123.47
Errors and omissions	2.55	2.49	8.01	2.36	3.62	−3.69	−1.39	−1.23	−6.24	10.19
Surplus of international balance of payments	4.32	0.10	0.06	24.56	14.11	32.22	103.24	34.56	19.07	109.56
International reserve	91.94	93.84	97.98	122.27	147.59	172.07	269.82	320.6	320.64	431.87

Source: Statistical database of ECLAC.

trade relations between the two countries have been rapid, the scale of cooperation has been expanding, and the fields of cooperation have been enlarged. In December 2004, the Peruvian government announced its recognition of China's status of market economy. In November 2008, during President Hu Jintao's visit to Peru, the two countries announced the establishment of a strategic partnership. In 2009, the two countries signed the free trade agreement, taking effect officially in March 2010. In April 2013, Peru's President Humala visited China, and the relationship between China and Peru had been promoted to a comprehensive strategic partnership.

Since 2008, the Sino-Peruvian economic and trade relations have achieved three breakthroughs: First, the heads of state of the two countries have realized exchange of visits and high-level visits have been frequent to have promoted the rapid development of bilateral economic and trade relations; second, the bilateral relations have been set at strategic partnership, and further enhanced to the comprehensive strategic partnership, significantly enhancing the status of each other in each other's global diplomacy and economic and trade cooperation; thirdly, the bilateral free trade agreements have enhanced the level and quality of the economic and trade cooperation between the two countries, the scale of trade have continued to expand, and the range of products have increased, promoting the rapid growth of Chinese direct investment in Peru.

I. The Sino-Peruvian Bilateral Trade

Over the past 10 years, the Sino-Peruvian bilateral trade has showed a trend of rapid growth. Especially after the formal implementation of the bilateral free trade agreement in March 2010, the trade between the two countries had been significantly expanded, the trade structure had been improved, and the types of products in trade have also been increasingly rich. China's position in Peru's diversification of foreign trade has continued to upgrade. In 2012, China had jumped to have become Peru's largest trading partner, the largest export destination and the second largest source of import.

First, the scale of trade has shown an upward trend, and Peru has been in a surplus position. According to the statistics of the Chinese Customs, the total trade volume between China and Peru had increased from $978 million in 2002 to $12.51 billion in 2011, increasing nearly 13 times. Among them, China's export to Peru rose from $247 million to $4.653 billion, an increase of nearly 19 times; China's imports from Peru rose from $732 million to $7.857 billion, up nearly 11 times (see Table 6.26). According to the statistics of the Peruvian Customs, in 2012, the bilateral import and export of goods between Peru and China amounted to $15.49 billion, an increase of 16.2% over the previous year.[39] Among them, Peru's export to China was $7.67 billion, increasing 10.3%; Peru's import from China was $7.82 billion, increasing 22.7%.[40]

In 2009, affected by the international financial crisis, the bilateral trade volume fell to $6.55 billion, down 15.8% compared with that in 2008. However, due to the implementation of the free trade agreement and the rapid recovery of the two countries, the bilateral trade had maintained a high growth trend between 2010 and 2011. In 2010, the trade volume between the two countries rose to $9.935 billion, increasing 51.68% over the previous year.

Peru's balance of trade with China has been in a favorable state of surplus, even though China's export to Peru has increased more than its import. In 2011, Peru's surplus of trade with China was $3.204 billion, increasing 13% over the previous year. Except for a slight decline in the trade surplus between 2008 and 2009, from 2002 to 2011, during the vast majority of the years Peru's surplus of trade with China had maintained a steady growth. However, according to the statistics of the Peruvian Customs, in 2012, Peru's trade with China had changed from surplus into deficit, with a deficit of

[39] Chinese Ministry of Commerce, *Overview of Peruvian Trade of Goods and the Sino-Peruvian Bilateral Trade in 2011*, http://countryreport.mof-com.gov.cn/record/view110209.asp? news_id = 32966.
[40] *Ibid.*

Table 6.26 The Sino-Peruvian Trade Volume ($100 Million)

Year	2002	2003	2004	2005	2006	2007	2008	2009	2010	2011
Export	2.47	3.54	4.18	6.09	10.09	16.79	27.74	20.99	35.50	46.53
Growth rate (%)	39.55	43.32	18.08	45.69	65.68	66.40	65.22	−24.33	69.13	31.07
Import	7.32	7.60	15.23	22.78	29.09	43.38	44.92	44.51	63.85	78.57
Growth rate (%)	46.99	3.83	100.39	49.57	27.70	49.12	3.55	−0.91	43.45	23.05
Trade surplus	−4.85	−4.06	−11.05	−16.69	−19	−26.59	−17.18	−23.52	−28.35	−32.04
Growth rate (%)	51.09	−16.29	172.16	51.04	13.84	39.95	−35.39	36.90	20.54	13.02
Total volume of trade	9.78	11.14	19.41	28.87	39.16	60.16	72.67	65.50	99.35	125.10
Growth rate (%)	44.89	13.90	74.23	48.74	35.64	53.63	20.80	−9.87	51.68	25.92

Source: *Chinese Statistical Yearbook* (2003–2012).

$150 million.[41] In the near future, the issue of bilateral trade balance may become a concern again.

Second, Peru's exports to China are mainly mineral products, and its major imports from China are industrial products and labor-intensive products. As a traditional agricultural and mining country, Peru's main exports to China are mainly mineral products, agricultural and animal husbandry products and fishery products, and China's exports to Peru are mainly electromechanical products, mechanical equipment, chemical raw materials, high-tech products, and textile products.

The mineral products have been Peru's first major category of products exported to China, maintaining a stable and rapid growth. From 2007 to 2012, Peru's export volume of mineral products to China rose from $2.34 billion to 5.39 billion, an increase of more than two times; over the same period, the proportion of mineral products in Peru's total export to China had showed a decreasing trend, falling from 77% in 2007 to 65.8% in 2010, but from 2011 to 2012, the proportion showed a rising trend (see Table 6.27). Peru's export of food, beverages and tobacco to China has been growing, being the second large category of products exported to China; from 2007 to 2012, it rose from $540 million to $1.03 billion, growing about two times; its proportion in Peru's exports to China fell slightly, falling from 17.8% in 2007 to 13.5% in 2012.

Peru's imports of major commodities from China are mechanical and electrical products, base metals and their products, textiles and raw materials. From 2007 to 2012, Peru's imports of mechanical and electrical products, base metals and their products from China rose from to $1.63 billion to $5.08 billion, an increase of more than three times, and the proportion in imports from China fell from 66% to 60.5%. China has continued to have advantage in the export of labor-intensive products. Between 2011 and 2012, the light industrial products of textiles, raw materials and furniture and toys, and footwear

[41] Chinese Ministry of Commerce, *Overview of Peruvian Trade of Goods and the Sino-Peruvian Bilateral Trade in 2011*, http://countryreport.mof-com.gov.cn/record/view110209.asp? news_id = 32966.

Table 6.27 The Sino-Peruvian Trade Structure ($100 Million)

Year	2007	2008	2010	2011	2012
Peru's exports to China					
Mineral products	23.4	26.7	35.7	46.9	53.9
Proportion in the total export to China (%)	77.0	71.4	65.8	67.4	70.3
Food, beverage, and tobacco	5.4	8.1	9.0	11.6	10.3
Proportion in the total export to China (%)	17.8	21.6	16.6	16.7	13.5
Peru's imports from China					
Mechanical and electrical products, base metals and their products	16.3	27.1	32.4	40.9	50.8
Proportion in total imports from China (%)	66.0	66.8	63.4	64.3	60.5

Source: Statistics of Peru Customs, http://countryreport.mofcom.gov.cn/record/index110209.asp.

and umbrellas were listed the third, fifth, and eighth, respectively in Peru's imported goods (HS) from China. China's major competitors in these products are the United States, India, Brazil, and Vietnam.

Third, the bilateral free trade agreement has become the mechanism of the two countries to release the potential of economic and trade cooperation and to properly handle the frictions of the economic and trade cooperation. In April 2009, China and Peru signed a bilateral free trade agreement, which was the first package of free trade agreement between China and the Latin-American countries. The agreement covered the trade of goods, trade of services, investment, dispute settlement, trade remedies, intellectual property rights, geographical indications, cooperation, etc.[42] Under the background of the international financial crisis, the two countries of China and Peru had started to negotiate and sign a free trade agreement, which had an important significance in opening the new prospect of the trade and economic cooperation between China and Peru.

In terms of the trade of goods, China and Peru have decided to implement zero tariffs for more than 90% of the products of both sides

[42] http://www.acuerdoscomerciales.gob.pe/index.php?option=com_content&view=category&id=42&layout=blog&Itemid =59.

in different stages. All the goods of China and Peru will be classified into five kinds for the implementation of tariff concessions; China's light industry, electronics, home appliances, machinery, automobile, chemical, vegetables, fruits and other products and Peru's fishmeal, mineral products, fruits, fish, and so on will benefit from it.

In the terms of trade in services, on the basis of their commitments to the World Trade Organization (WTO), Peru will further open the sectors or departments of mining, research and development, Chinese education, Chinese medicine and martial arts to China; China will further open the sectors or departments of mining, consulting, translation, sports, and tourism to Peru. At the same time, the two countries have established a transparent standard and a simplified procedure for the temporary entry of business personnel to further facilitate the exchanges between the two countries.

In terms of investment, both China and Peru will give each other's investors and investments access to national treatment, most favored nation treatment and fair and equitable treatment, encouraging bilateral investment and providing convenience; taxes shall not be levied unless for the public interests and through the legal procedures; once collected compensation should be given to investors according to the fair market value; the investment and free remittance of income should be guaranteed; the settlement mechanism of investment disputes based on the characteristics of the arbitration of the host country has been established.

It is worth emphasizing that the Sino-Peruvian FTA has provided special provisions for the protection of the rights of intellectual property and geographical indications. China and Peru both have a long history and folk traditions, and the two sides have agreed to carry out exchanges and cooperation relating to intellectual property rights within the framework of their respective laws and regulations, taking appropriate measures to protect the genetic resources, traditional knowledge, and folk traditions.

China and Peru have promoted each other's strategic position in each other's trade pattern by signing the free trade agreement. In view of the economic complementarity between the two countries, after the implementation of the FTA, both the scale of bilateral trade and the investment have achieved a major breakthrough. Peru has greatly valued China's market potential and investment capacity, for China will undoubtedly become an important strategic partner of Peru in its diversification of the foreign economic and trade cooperation. As for China, Peru is an important emerging economy with rich resources; signing the free trade agreement is an important measure both for enhancing the bilateral relations and for deepening the economic and trade cooperation, setting an example for other Latin-American countries.

II. China's Direct Investment in Peru

China's investment in Peru began in the early 1990s. In December 1992, China's Capital Iron and Steel Corporation acquired some of the assets of the Hierro Peru Co., establishing the SHOUGANG Hierro Peru Co. Ltd. From 1993 to 1995, the China National Petroleum Corporation (CNPC) had obtained the mining rights and contract services of a number of oil blocks in Peru. At present, Peru has become one of China's major investment destinations in Latin America.

First, China's direct investment in Peru has increased rapidly, but the scale is not large. According to China's official statistics, by the end of 2011, China's investment stock in Peru was \$802 million, an increase of 22.58% over 2010 (see Table 6.28). From 2008 to 2011, China's annual FDI in Peru had increased substantially, rising from \$24.55 million to \$214 million, an increase of nearly 10 times; over the same period the direct investment stock rose from \$194 million to \$802 million, an increase of nearly 7 times.

Table 6.28 China's Direct Investment in Peru (\$10,000)

Year	2003	2004	2005	2006	2007	2008	2009	2010	2011
Investment flow	12	22	55	540	671	2,455	5,849	13,903	21,425
Growth (%)	N.A.	83.3	150	881.82	24.25	265.87	138.25	137.70	54.10
Investment stock	12,618	12,582	12,922	13,040	13,711	19,434	28,454	65,449	80,224
Growth (%)	N.A.	−0.29	2.70	0.91	5.15	4.17	4.64	130.02	22.58

Source: *Bulletin of Statistics of China's FDI in 2011*, China Statistics Press, 2012, pp. 30–40.

Second, China's investment in Peru is increasingly diversified, but still mainly in the mining industry. At present, the Chinese enterprises in Peru mainly invest in the development of mineral and oil and gas resources, processing and assembly, electronics, and engineering contracts. By the end of 2011, there are about 50 Chinese enterprises in Peru, mainly SHOUGANG Hierro Peru, CNPC, China Minmetals, China Aluminum, Huawei, the Sinohydro Corporation Limited, National Development Bank of China, Bank of China, and China Ocean Shipping Company (COSCO).

In order to promote and protect the investment of the two countries, in June 1994, the two countries signed the "Agreement on Encouragement and Mutual Protection of Investment". In September 2006, the China–Peru Entrepreneur Council was established playing a key role as the platform for the bilateral exchange and cooperation between the entrepreneurs of the two countries. With more and more Chinese enterprises entering Peru, the Chinese Enterprise Association was founded in Peru in August 2011 to strengthen the contact, communication and share of investment experiences between Chinese enterprises, so as to help Chinese enterprises to further develop the Peruvian market.

Third, China's financial institutions have actively participated in the economic and trade cooperation between China and Peru. In recent years, the China Development Bank and the China Import and Export Bank, respectively have signed a number of financing cooperation agreements with the Peru Development Finance Corporation, the International Bank of Peru and the Peru Credit Bank, which will help to enhance the level of bilateral economic and trade cooperation.

In December 2011, the China Development Bank (CDB) signed loan agreements with the Peruvian BBVA Continental Bank; CDB would provide long-term loans to the Peruvian Continental Bank for the financing of the power infrastructure project. In September 2011, CDB signed the *Peru's National Planning Consulting Cooperation Agreement* with the Peruvian National Strategic Planning Center to strengthen the economic cooperation between the two countries through the development of planning consultation and cooperation.

Table 6.29 The Sino-Peruvian Economic Cooperation ($10,000)

Year	2003	2004	2005	2006	2007	2008	2009	2010	2011
Contracted projects	1,326	9,286	6,581	5,275	8,573	7,527	18,967	11,071	21,108
Labor service cooperation	1708	2258	2169	1568	30	24	26	62	0
Total	3,034	11,544	8,750	6,843	8,603	7,551	18,993	11,133	21,108

Note: The total amount of 2007–2008 includes the income of designing and consulting.

Source: *China Statistics Yearbook* (2004–2012), http://www.stats, gov.cn/tjsj/ndsj/.

In May 2013, CDB completed the report of the Peru National Planning Consultation, of which the main content involved the planning experience of China and the fields of Peru's economic and social development plan, railway, mining, hydropower, and forestry.

Fourth, the economic and technological cooperation between the two countries has developed rapidly. From 2008 to 2011, the amount of economic cooperation completed by Chinese enterprises in Peru rose from $76 million to $210 million, an increase of nearly three times (see Table 6.29). China's economic cooperation in Peru is mainly in the form of project contracting, involving sewage treatment plants, pipelines, hydropower stations and other construction projects. From 2009 to 2011, the annual turnover of the project contracting of Chinese enterprises in Peru had maintained around $200 million. In view of the needs of Peru's infrastructure construction and financing cooperation with China, there is a great potential in China's economic and technological cooperation with Peru, such as the contracting projects.

In addition, Peru is an important country that China has aided in Latin America. From 1990 to 1999, China had provided nine batches of free material assistance to Peru, including bicycles, computers, medical equipment, etc. From 2000 to 2009, China had provided a small amount of free material assistance to Peru. From 2003 to 2010, China had provided a number of humanitarian aids to Peru. Between 2009 and 2011, China had helped the project of the expansion of Luo Ayisa Hospital in Peru. In May 2011, China and Peru signed an agreement on economic and technical cooperation, in which China would provide a free grant of 20 million RMB to the government of Peru.[43] In August 2012, China and Peru signed the agreement about China's aid to Peru between the two governments.

III. The Potential and Prospect of the Economic and Trade Cooperation between China and Peru

From the perspective of the complementarity of the Chinese and the Peruvian economy, on the basis of free trade agreements, the two countries can strengthen the cooperation in agricultural, mining, infrastructure construction and other areas, giving full play to the complementary advantages, optimizing the trade structure, and expanding the trade scale. At present, Peru's industrial policy is focused on the development of mining, energy, petrochemicals, agriculture, transportation and other industries and infrastructure. There is an important potential in these industries for China to expand investment in Peru.

In the next few years, the trade and economic relations between China and Peru will have a new breakthrough in the fields of cooperation, level and quality. Peru hopes to further expand the economic and trade cooperation with China, in particular, welcoming Chinese enterprises to invest in Peru's mining, energy, power and infrastructure. Both China and Peru need to expand opportunities for cooperation in industrial upgrading, increase mutual investments, continue to promote the facilitation of trade and investment, expand areas of cooperation making use of the long-term mechanism and diversified platforms, and properly handle the frictions in the cooperation.

First, the scale of trade will be expanded and the balance of trade and sustainability will be taken into account. Despite the differences in the statistics of the bilateral trade between China and Peru, according to the official data of Peru, in 2012, the deficit occurred in Peru's trade with China, and so the future problem of the bilateral trade imbalance cannot be ignored. In terms of Peru's scale of

[43]China's Economic and Commercial Counsellor's Office in Peru, *China and Peru Have Signed an Economic and Technological Contract*, http://www.mofcom.gov.cn/article/i/wz/201105/20110507567284.shtml.

economy and its level of competitiveness, on the one hand, China's stable growth of imports from Peru is needed to be kept; on the other hand, it is also necessary to combine the direct investment and intra-industry trade to ensure the balance of the relation between trade and investment.

In terms of China's still high future demand for mineral products and agricultural products, China will continue to be an important export market for Peru. Peru hopes to improve the trade balance through increasing the export of agricultural non-traditional products on the basis of maintaining its export of the mineral products and fishmeal. At present, Peru is an important source of China's import of grape and lemon, and its other agricultural products like avocado, dairy products, and blueberry are also likely to enter the Chinese market.

Second, the dominant position of investment and trade cooperation in the field of the mining industry will continue to be maintained. The mining cooperation is an important part in the economic and trade relations between China and Peru, and a number of large Chinese enterprises have already entered the Peruvian mining field and have accumulated many years of operating experience. Although Peru is still the world's large mining producer, but in recent years, the proportion of Peru's production of the mining industry in the global share has been declining. To achieve a steady growth in the mining production, the export expansion has become one of the focuses of the industrial policy of the government of Peru. According to the estimates of some Peruvian agencies, Peru's investment in the mining development and infrastructure was far from enough. Peru has actively attracted Chinese enterprises to invest in the mining areas, involving exploration, development and related construction of infrastructure, especially the transformation and expansion of major ports, increasing the export of mineral products and petroleum products.

Third, the two countries have important opportunities for the cooperation in the energy sector. In order to ensure the energy security, create jobs and promote growth, Peru is actively developing its energy industry. The Peruvian government has launched a number of projects to support the development of energy; its investment is mainly concentrated on power, oil and gas fields, including power generation, power grids, oil and gas pipelines, hydropower stations, etc. China's energy companies have a competitive advantage in the fields of mechanical equipment manufacturing, financing capacity and technical services. The future energy cooperation between China and Peru will go beyond the oil industry. The field of cooperation will be further broadened.

Fourth, there is a broad prospect of cooperation in the infrastructure areas of transportation, telecommunications and water conservancy. With the rapid and steady growth of Peru's economy, its backward infrastructure has become the constraints for its future economic development. From 2012 to 2021, an investment gap of Peru's infrastructure will be more than $80 billion, mainly concentrated in the infrastructure related to mining, energy and agriculture, in which the transportation field includes the network of highways, railways, ports and airports.[44] At present, the investment and research of Peru's Telecom are not enough, not matching the speed of its economic development. According to the estimation of the Peruvian Ministry of Transport and Communications, from 2013 to 2016, the investment in the field of transport and telecommunications will reach $20 billion, including the subway, highway and broadband network.[45]

IV. The Risk Factors for Investment in Peru

The investment environment of Peru is complex and the risk factors cannot be ignored. Peru's development for a period of time in the future will still rely on the development of resources (such as agriculture and mining), and the investment in the development of these industries may lead to the problems of the emergence of

[44]EL COMERCIO, *Brecha de Inversion en Infraestructura Alcanza los US$88 mil Millones*, 25 de octubre del 2012, http://elcomercio.pe/economia/1487422/noticia-brecha-inversion-infraestructura-al-canza-us88-mil-millones.

[45]http://www.fitel.gob.pe/noticia-mtc-preve-inversiones-us-20-000-millones-2016.html.

deforestation, shortage of water resources, environmental pollution, natural disasters and the tension of the relationship with the Indian residents.

First, the resource development projects face the risk of community conflicts. Between 2009 and 2012, the social contradictions around the mining development became serious and even escalated in Peru. The local residents in northern Peru and the Amazon region have always resisted the development of mining and oil and gas, frequently holding demonstrations, and violent conflicts occurred over 250 times.[46]

Second, the labor issues are still an important factor affecting the investment environment. Peru has strong trade unions, the labor welfare requirements are very high, and there are frequent strikes. Chinese enterprises in Peru often encounter problems of labor disputes. Take SHOUGANG Hierro Peru for example. Plagued by the long-term labor disputes, the production and operation of the enterprise has faced a complex social environment.

Third, the environmental standards are strict and the procedures are complicated. Environmental protection is a common problem encountered by foreign enterprises in Peru, and Chinese enterprises are no exception. Peru's environmental standards for FDI are increasingly strict, and the procedures are complex and cumbersome, involving too much content with a lot of local interests. In recent years, some of China's mining investment projects in Peru have been in a slow progress, mainly due to the impact of the environmental protection assessment. At present, the environmental protection policy has become an important factor for the multinational corporations to assess the investment environment in Peru.

Fourth, the risk of the change of tax policies cannot be ignored. The prices of the international resource products have been showing a rising trend. In Peru the voice and political pressure requiring to impose windfall tax on the mining frequently occurred and had

[46]IMF, *Peru: 2012 Article IV Consultation*, Country Report No. 13/45, February 2013, p. 10.

entered the Peruvian government's policy agenda.[47] Therefore, the Chinese enterprises investing in Peru cannot ignore the loss of benefits resulting from the change of tax policies.

Fifth, the risk of additional investment is worthy of attention. Peru's infrastructure construction related to the exploration and development of the areas of mining and energy is lagging behind; the multinational corporations upon entering Peru often encounter correlated additional investments, resulting in increased investment costs. The investment in the Peruvian mining of Chinese enterprises encountered a similar problem. For example, the relocation of the local community and the construction of related facilities involve a large amount of additional investment.

[47] IMF, *Peru: 2011 Article IV Consultation*, Country Report No. 12/26, February 2012, p. 14.

Chapter 7

Economic Reform of Venezuela and the Sino-Venezuelan Economic and Trade Relations

Zhao Lihong

Section 1 Overview of the Venezuelan Economy

I. The Natural Resources and Labor Resources

Venezuela is located in the northern part of South America, bordering the Caribbean Sea in the north, Guyana in the east, Brazil in the south and Colombia in the west. Its land area is 912,050 square kilometers (including 72 islands in the Caribbean Sea), with a coastline of 2,800 kilometers. Venezuela has a tropical plain climate. Because of the different terrains and altitudes, its regional climate differences are very large: the temperatures in the western mountains are rather low, but the temperatures in the central plains are very high. Its national average temperature is between 26°C and 28°C. The whole year is divided into the rainy season (May–November) and the dry season (December–April), with an average annual rainfall of 500–3,000 millimeters.

Venezuela has rich natural resources, such as oil, natural gas, iron ore, bauxite, gold, coal, nickel, and forests. According to the annual statistics released by the oil-exporting countries (OPEC) in 2011, with oil reserves of 296.501 billion barrels, more than Saudi Arabia, Venezuela had become the country with the most abundant oil reserve in the world.[1] The oil resources are mainly distributed in the western area of the Lake of Maracaibo, the eastern states of Anzoategui and Monagas, and the central states of Barinas and Apure. The Lake of Maracaibo is the largest lake in Latin America, covering an area of about 14,300 square kilometers, which is called the "Lake of Oil". The storage volume of the lake is about 5 billion barrels, there are 16,000 oil wells, with production of crude oil reaching more than 2 million barrels per day, and on the bottom of the lake there are 14,000 kilometers of crude oil and natural gas pipelines. The Orinoco Heavy Oil Belt is located in the south of Venezuela, including the four oilfields of Achete, Zuata, Hamaka, and Cerro Negro, with an area of 54,000 square kilometers, a reservoir thickness of 150–300 feet, and the oil density index (API) of generally 7–14 degrees. The heavy oil production has not been included in the OPEC member's oil production quotas, and the reserves of heavy oil have not yet been included in Venezuela's conventional oil reserves. Venezuela's natural gas reserves are also very rich, with about 498 million cubic meters, ranking the eighth in the world. The natural gas is mostly oil-associated gas; in the northeast of Paria Peninsula there are offshore gas fields. Its other major mineral resources are: Iron ore reserve of 4.222 billion tons, bauxite reserve of 2.4 billion tons, coal reserve of 479 million tons, nickel ore reserve of 610,000 tons, and gold reserve of 10,000 tons. Its water and forest resources are also very rich, with the forest coverage rate of 56%.

Venezuela is divided into 23 states, one capital area and one federal territory. As the political and economic center, the capital of Caracas is the largest city in the country. Other important economic centers are Maracaibo and Valencia. With a total population of 27.15 million, mainly concentrated in big cities such as Caracas, Maracaibo, Valencia, and Maracay, 68% of the population are scattered

[1] *Venezuela's Oil Reserves Rank the 1st in the World*, July 21, 2011, http://cn.latincomercio.com/investment/3268.html.

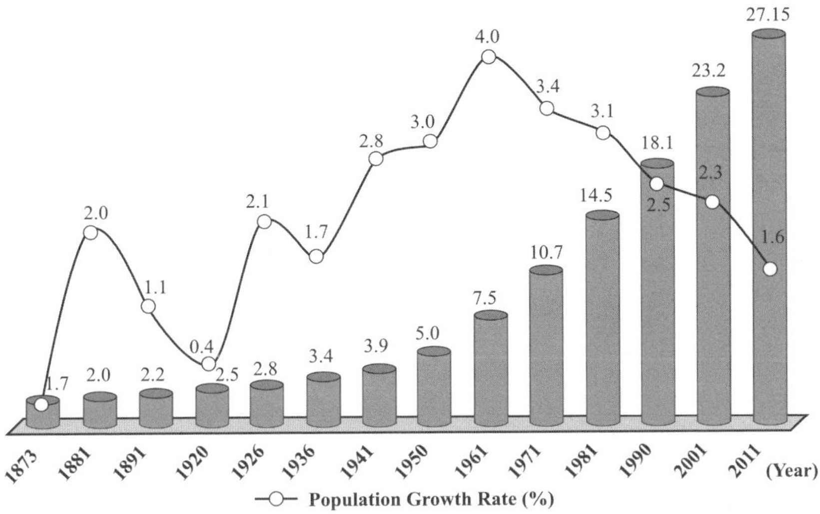

Figure 7.1 Venezuela's Total Population and Its Growth Rate (million people, %)

Source: *Instituto Nacional Estadistica, Republica Blivariana de Venezuela, Censo 2011*, Caracas, febrero 23, 2012, http://www.ine.gob.ve.

in the northern coastal areas occupying 22% of the national land area (see Figure 7.1 and Table 7.1). In 2011, Venezuela's working age population accounted for 66.6%, with the total dependency ratio of 50% (see Table 7.2 and Figure 7.2).

From the perspective of the situation of the supply and demand of the domestic labor market, its labor resources are relatively abundant, but the quality is low, lacking professional and technical personnel. Its labor wages, welfare and social security are relatively high; especially in recent years, the Chavez's government has vigorously promoted the construction of the "21st Century Socialism", continuously improving the wages and benefits — in 2010, raising the minimum wage twice, with the annual cumulative increase amplitude of 26.5%, and the monthly minimum wage increasing from 967.5 bolivars to 1,223.89 bolivars (about $470). In addition, the Venezuelan employees also enjoy social insurance, housing fund and unemployment fund.

Table 7.1 Population Distribution in the States of Venezuela in 2011

State	Population (10,000)
Zulia	370.36
Miranda	266.56
Carabobo	223.92
Distrito Capital	193.32
Lara	176.98
Aragua	162.71
Anzoategui	146.46
Bolivar	140.51
Tachira	116.36
Monagas	90.12
Falcón	90.02
Sucre	89.30
Portuguesa	87.50
Merida	82.67
Barinas	81.43
Guarico	74.62
Trujillo	68.46
Yaracuy	59.93
Nueva Esparta	49.05
Apure	45.84
Vargas	35.21
Cojedes	32.28
Delta Amacuro	16.75
Amazonas	14.44
Dependencias Federales	2.16

Source: *Instituto Nacional Estadistica, Republica Blivariana de Venezuela, Censo 2011*, Caracas, febrero 23, 2012, http://www.ine.gob.ve.

II. The Macro Economic Structure

1. The Oil Industry

Venezuela's economy is highly dependent on oil and the oil income accounts for about 30% of its gross domestic product (GDP), 50% of its fiscal revenues and 80% of its foreign exchange earnings. After the shrinking of the oil production between 2009 and 2010, the government had formulated the long-term oil production plan; in 2011 the Venezuelan export of oil (crude oil and fuel oil) increased to

Table 7.2 Changes in the Age Structure of the Population of Venezuela (%)

Year	0–14	15–65	Over 66
1990	37.3	58.7	4
2001	33.1	62	4.9
2011	27.6	66.6	5.8

Source: *Instituto Nacional Estadistica, Republica Blivariana de Venezuela, Censo 2011*, Caracas, febrero 23, 2012, http:// www.ine.gob.ve.

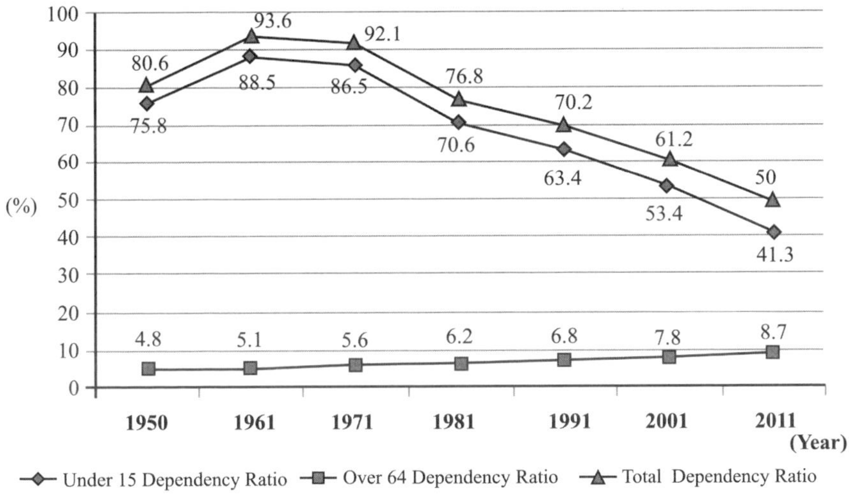

Figure 7.2 Dependency Ratio of Venezuela's Working Age Population

Source: *Instituto Nacional Estadistica, Republica Blivariana de Venezuela, Censo 2011*, Caracas, febrero 23, 2012, http://www.ine.gob.ve.

$88.1 billion. Between 2011 and 2012, the heavy oil production of the Orinoco Basin is expected to increase 15–25%, and by 2015, the oil production will increase from the current approximately 300 million barrels per day to about 400 million barrels per day. To this end, the government plans to invest $100 billion in the oil field in the next few years.[2]

[2]http://ve.mofcom.gov.cn/aarticle/jmxw/201108/20110807703685.html.

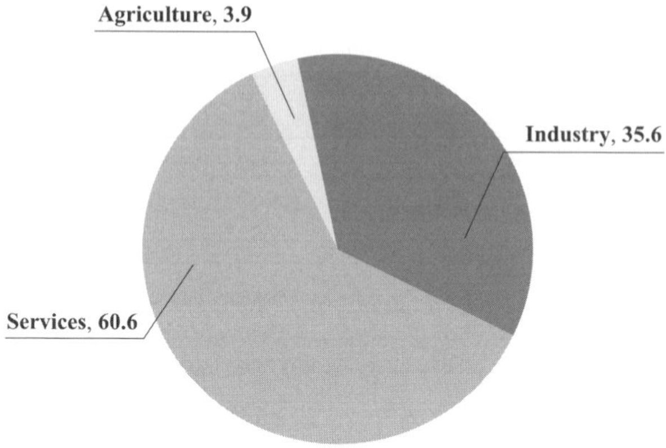

Figure 7.3 Venezuela's Industrial Structure in 2011 (%)

Source: Global Finance, *Venezuela Country Report*, http://www.gfmag.com/gdp-data-country-reports/147-veneznela-gdp-country-report.html.

After taking office, Chavez had nationalized the petroleum industry. The Venezuelan National Oil Corporation (PDVSA) is responsible for oil exploration, development, production, sales, processing and export. The company belongs to the Ministry of Energy and Oil and is the largest state-owned enterprise. According to the latest ranking of the world's major oil companies published by the US *Petroleum Intelligence Weekly*, PDVSA ranked the fourth in the world. The company's proven oil and gas reserves respectively had ranked the fifth and the sixth in the world, its oil production the sixth, its refining capacity the fourth, its sales the eighth, and its total revenue, net profit and total assets had all ranked the 12th in the world. Before the Chavez Administration, the amount of the annual investment of PDVSA was only about \$3 billion, but in recent years it has increased from \$10 billion to \$15 billion. In 2011, PDVSA's annual revenue was \$127.88 billion, an increase of 35% over the previous year, with the debt balance of \$34.8 billion; its total assets reached \$74 billion, an increase of 129% compared with 2010 (see Figure 7.3). According to the "Oil Sowing Plan" of the Venezuelan government, from 2013 to 2018, the total investment of PDVSA will reach \$236 billion, mainly from foreign investments.[3]

[3]http://ve.mofcom.gov.cn/aarticle/jmxw/201203/20120307990327.html.

In 2010, the average daily oil export of Venezuela was 2.41 million barrels, of which the export of crude oil and modified oil was 1.93 million barrels per day and the export of petroleum products was 485,000 barrels per day. North America was still the largest export market for Venezuelan oil — in 2010, its export of crude oil and modified oil to North America was 1.19 million barrels per day and oil products 95,000 barrels per day. Asia was the second largest oil export market for Venezuela — in 2010 the average daily export of crude oil was 341,000 barrels and oil products 144,000 barrels to the Asian market. In 2010, the Venezuelan export of crude oil was 206,000 barrels per day and oil products 105,000 barrels per day to the Caribbean.[4]

During the six years from 2006 to 2011, the amount of Venezuelan crude oil export to China increased by three times, from 150,000 barrels per day to 460,000 barrels per day; its export to the United States decreased from 1.5 million barrels per day in 1999 to 940,000 barrels per day in 2011. From 2013 to 2015, PDVSA will increase the export of crude oil to China from the current 460,000 barrels per day to 1 million barrels per day.[5]

2. The Agriculture and Animal Husbandry

The arable land area of Venezuela is about 30 million hectares, of which about 3 million hectares are cultivated lands, 17.13 million hectares are pastures and 3.1 million hectares are covered with forests. The agricultural employment accounts for about 13% of the total working population. The main agricultural products are rice, cocoa, coffee, sugar cane, corn, beans, potatoes, etc. Venezuela has a long history of growing coffee and cocoa, and before the rise of the oil industry, coffee and cocoa had occupied an important position in its national economy. Its coffee and cocoa have good quality and pure taste, and are well sold in the international market. The average food expenditure of Venezuelan residents accounts for about 50% of their

[4] *PDVSA 2010 Annual Report*, Caracas, Febrero 2011, http://www.petroleum-world.com/ed11032801.htm.

[5] http://ve.mofcom.gov.cn/aarticle/jmxw/201202/20120207982621.html.

wage income, but the agriculture and animal husbandry products are not self-contained — in its domestic market, 50% of the milk, 90% of the beans, 30% of the sugar, 75% of the yellow corn and 85% of the edible oil are imported from Colombia and the United States. In April 2011, the government launched the "Venezuelan Agriculture Plan" (Agro Venezuela), aiming to increase the grain production and ensure the food security at home. The specific planning includes: in 2011 to increase the production of yellow corn, white corn, and rice by 50%, 59%, and 33%, respectively, in which both the yellow corn and rice yields were to reach 1.39 million tons, and the grain yield was to increase by 70% between 2011 and 2012.[6] The government had invested 10 billion bolivars to the "Agriculture Plan", in which loans of 4.7 billion bolivars had been provided to small farmers and 150,000 farmers had been provided with tractors and raw materials for production.

3. The Construction Industry

The rental prices of land and housing are higher in Venezuela, and the real estate prices are quite different in different places. In recent years, due to the government's active promotion of the "Grand Housing Plan" (LA Gran Mision Vivienda Venezuela, GMVV), the very fast development of the construction industry has led to the tight supply and rising prices of the main building materials such as steel, cement, sand and gravel (see Tables 7.3 and 7.4).

4. The External Sectors

According to the statistics of ECLAC, in 2010, the total export of Venezuela was $116.7 billion, in which its export was $67.51 billion (including $54 billion of oil export), and its import was $49.194 billion; the annual surplus was $18.316 billion, accounting for 3.7% of GDP (see Table 7.5). In 2011, the total volume of import and export of the goods trade in Venezuela was $143.336 billion, with $9.683 billion of trade surplus. The main export commodities were petroleum

[6]http://ve.mofcom.gov.cn/aarticle/jmxw/201103/20110307472465.html.

Table 7.3 Venezuela's Land and Rent Reference Prices in 2010 (Bolivar/m^2)

Type	Sale Price	Rent Price (Month)
Land	1,550	11.5
Apartment	17,500	100
Office Building	12,000	243
Warehouse	2,520	94

Note: The reference prices are from the capital area of Caracas; there are big differences in price between different areas.
Source: www.tuinmueble.com.ve.

Table 7.4 Venezuela's Major Building Material Prices in 2010

Material	Unit	Price (Hard Bolivar)
Cement	Ton	483
Steel	Ton	4,836.39
Wood	Cubic meter	3,062
Cement Brick	15#	2.85
	10#	2.55

Note: The above prices are the ex-factory prices including taxes.
Source: http://www.infraestructura.gov.ve.

and petroleum products; the oil sector accounts for about 80% of the country's total export revenue and the main imported goods were raw materials, mechanical equipment, transportation equipment and construction materials (see Table 7.6). Venezuela's main trading partner is the United States (49% of its exports and 24% of its imports), the European Union and Brazil.

5. The Financial Sector

(1) Bank

Venezuela has a total of 59 banks of various types, including 37 commercial banks and 22 professional banks such as investment banks, mortgage banks, and savings banks. Its foreign capital accounts for about 50% of the country's banking sector. The Central Bank of

Table 7.5 Import and Export of Venezuela from 2003 to 2010 ($100 Million, %)

Year	Export	Import	Current Account Balance/GDP
2003	281.08	139.95	14.1
2004	407.82	215.18	13.8
2005	570.58	293.47	17.5
2006	671.22	395.37	14.4
2007	707.77	547.50	7.8
2008	973.00	599.98	12.0
2009	596.00	480.64	2.6
2010	675.10	491.94	3.7

Source: CEPAL, *Anuario Estadistico de America Latina y el Caribe*, 2011.

Table 7.6 The Export of Venezuela's Economic Sectors (2010–2011) ($Million, Dollar Price of 2010)

Economic Sector	2010	2011
Total	2,487	3,207
Agriculture (Vegetables)	19	21
Food, Beverage, and Tobacco Industry	40	26
Mining	557	687
Chemical Industry	437	591
Plastics and Manufacturing	46	39
Metal	1,041	1,307
Electronic Component	97	91

Source: *Instituto Nacional Estadistica, Republica Blivariana de Venezuela, Censo 2011*, Caracas, febrero 23, 2012, http://www.ine.gob.ve.

Venezuela is responsible for the formulation and implementation of the monetary policy. According to the latest report released by the Federation of Latin-American Bank (FELABAN), in 2010, the overall profit of the bank industry of 12 Latin-American countries increased by 74%, in which the Venezuelan banking sector achieved the profit of $1.5 billion, ranking the third place among the countries participating in the rankings, after Chile and Colombia. According to statistics, in the first quarter of 2010, the net profit of the five Venezuelan big banks — BBVA Provincial Bank, the Venezuelan National Bank (Banco de Venezuela), Banesco Bank, Mercantil Bank and Exterior Bank — reached 1.11 billion bolivars (about $0.43 billion), an increase of 21.8% over the previous year. The profit proportion of the five banks in the total profit of the national commercial banks increased from 62.4% to 79.6% in 2009. At present, Venezuela's Economic and Social Development Bank (BANDES) with the China National Development Bank together are implementing the financing project for the Sino-Venezuelan Joint Fund. In terms of financing conditions, the foreign enterprises and local enterprises enjoy the same treatment, but the relatively high interest rate of the banks of Venezuela, coupled with the risk of foreign exchange control and exchange, makes it difficult for foreign companies to finance in the local banks.

(2) Securities

The Caracas Stock Exchange is Venezuela's only stock exchange, managing stocks, futures, certificates of investment, derived tools and other services. By May 2010, a total of 68 enterprises or institutions had been listed in the Caracas Stock Exchange; there were a total of 63 securities broking firms.

(3) Exchange Rate

From March 2005, Venezuela had implemented a fixed exchange rate; from January 2010, a dual track system had been implemented for the exchange rate of the US dollar against bolivar, i.e., 41% of the imports enjoyed the currency exchange rate by $1:2.6 bolivars, the remaining 59% of the imported goods by $1:4.3 bolivars; on January 1, 2011, the dual exchange rate system was canceled, changing the original two official exchange rates of $1:2.6 bolivars and $1:4.3 bolivars into the single exchange rate of $1:4.3 bolivars, and the quotation of the foreign exchange rate in the security trading market by $1:5.3 bolivars remained unchanged.[7]

[7]http://www.mf.gob.ve, December 30, 2010.

6. Tourism

Venezuela has rich tourism resources. Its coastline has a total length of 3,500 kilometers, of which 1,700 kilometers are beach areas; it has 72 islands, the majority of which can be developed for tourism and leisure; its primeval forest covers an area of 430,000 square kilometers, growing a variety of plants and animals. There are the remains of the Indian culture, the world's first high Angel Falls (919 meters) and the fourth high Kukenaam Falls (610 meters). The famous tourist city of Merida has the highest and longest tramway in the world. Venezuela also has a very vast plain area of about 300,000 square kilometers. According to the data of Venezuela's Bureau of Statistics, in 2009 the number of foreign tourists coming to Venezuela for sightseeing amounted to 426,000, with 12% lower compared with the number of 486,000 in 2008. In 2009, the number of domestic tourists was 7.09 million. The tourist seasons are mainly concentrated in the carnival, Holy Week, Christmas and school holidays (July–September).

7. Infrastructure

(1) Highway

The length of Venezuela's national highways is 96,200 kilometers, of which a total of 32,300 kilometers are asphalt roads; there are totally three highways, which have 960 kilometers, 1,290 kilometers and 440 kilometers, respectively. The freight of motor vehicles accounts for 70% of the total freight volume and 90% of the passenger volume. There are 2.7 million motor vehicles altogether.

(2) Railway

The length of Venezuela's railways is 337 kilometers and the railway freight volume is 321,000 tons. The capital Caracas has three subway lines, with a total length of 42.4 kilometers and a passenger traffic volume of nearly 300 million people. According to the Venezuelan National Railway Development Plan, in 2011 the government invested a total of $22.25 billion in railway construction, with the total mileage of 1,070 kilometers to be built by the three countries of China, Cuba, and Italy. The first stage engineering of

Encrucijada — San Diego railway is to be implemented in 2012. The Encrucijada — Tuy Valley Railway and the Tinaco — Anaco Northern Plain Railway projects in the charge of China Railway Group Limited will be implemented simultaneously, in which 15% of the 468-kilometer-long Northern Plain project has been completed. The 26-kilometer-long railway section between Cagua and Mariara is to be completed in 2012; after that more stations will be added to the section of Encrucijada — Cabello Harbor so as to fully complete the railway line.[8]

(3) Airport

There are 61 commercial airports across the country, of which 7 are international airports. The largest international airport is Simon Bolivar Airport, which concentrates 90% of the country's international flights. The annual passenger volume of international civil aviation is 2.8 million passengers and the cargo volume is 27,000 tons.

(4) Port

There are 9 international ports, 34 oil ports, and iron ore ports, and 5 fishing ports. The main ports are: La Guaira, Cabello, Maracaibo and Ordaz. There are totally 60 ships with the displacement of more than 1,000 tons of various types, with a total tonnage of 630,000 tons; the total length of its inland waterway is over 1,000 kilometers.

(5) Power

Since 2009, Venezuela's frequent power shortages have had serious impacts on its domestic economic productions. The main reasons are: the long-term existence of its power source structure is unreasonable, excessively relying on hydropower, the production and supply of electricity are geographically not evenly distributed,[9] its national aging power grid equipment has led to unstable operation, its power system has poor management, its technology is relatively backward, and so on. To strengthen the unified management of the power

[8]http://ve.mofcom.gov.cn/aarticle/jmxw/201104/20110407477224.html.

[9]Venezuela's electricity distribution is very uneven: the population of the Eastern region is scarce with surplus of power exported to Brazil; but the Western region lacks electricity and needs to import it from Colombia.

industry, in July 2007, Venezuela established the national power company (*Corporacion Electrica Nacional*, Corpoelec). The six major electric power companies had been merged,[10] responsible for the production, operation and management of its national electric power industry. In October 2009, the Venezuelan government set up the State Electricity Department. The government plans to input $13.865 billion in the construction of the electric power infrastructure from 2008 to 2018 to build natural-gas thermal power stations in order to make full use of its rich oil and gas resources and to increase the existing thermal power capacity so as to change the situation of too much dependence on the hydroelectric power and the uneven distribution of power supply. In 2011, the state power company invested 21.42 billion bolivars in 13 power generation projects and a number of transmission projects, with a new installed power generation capacity of up to 1,593 megawatt. In 2012, the government planned to add the installed power generation capacity of 5,922 megawatt, of which the state power company would add 3,618 megawatts, the state oil company PDVSA would add 1,954 megawatts, and the Foundation and Mining Ministry would add 350 megawatts.[11] In February 2010, the Venezuelan government set up the National Electricity Fund, with the start-up funding of $2 billion, of which the first fund of $1 billion was assigned to the Ministry of Electric Power for the construction of 59 power generation and transmission projects and the operation and maintenance of 50 power plants. Venezuela has accelerated its import of complete sets of power equipment from Russia, Japan, China, and Germany in order to meet the needs for the construction

[10]There are six large-scale electric power companies in Venezuela's electricity industry, namely the Caroni Electric Power Company (EDELCA), the Power Management and Promotion Company (CADAFE), the Venezuelan Power Company (ENELVEN), the Eastern Coastal Power Company (ENELCO), the Barquisimeto Power Company (ENELBAR) and the ENAGEN Electric Power Company. Among them, the Caroni Power Company is Venezuela's largest power company, accounting for 62% of the total national power generation and 94% of the total amount of hydroelectric power; CADAFE is Venezuela's second largest power company, accounting for 17% of the total national power generation.

[11]http://ve.mofcom.gov.cn/aarticle/Jmxw/201104/20110407524094.html.

Table 7.7 Price List of Water, Electricity and Gas in the Area of Caracas in 2010

Type	Water Price (Bs/m^3)	Electricity Price (Bs/KVA, Bs/Kwh)		Gas Price (Bs/m^3)
Commerce and Industry	0.72	Class 1 (Low Voltage, Output Power < 100 KVA)	Fee: 10.461 (Bs/KVA) Electricity Fee: 0.066 (Bs/Kwh)	Annual Volume 5,000–50,000 Kwh: 7.84 (Bs/m^3)
		Class 2 (Low Voltage, Output Power > 100 KVA)	Fee: 8.357 (Bs/KVA) Electricity Fee: 0.049 (Bs/Kwh)	Annual Volume 50,000–100,000 Kwh: 50.87 (Bs/m^3)
		Class 3 (Medium Voltage, Output Power > 1,000 KVA)	Fee: 8.027 (Bs/KVA) Electricity Fee: 0.045 (Bs/Kwh)	Annual Volume > 100,000 Kwh: 75.84 (Bs/m^3)
		Class 4 (High Voltage, Output Power > 10,000 KVA)	Fee: 6.659 (Bs/KVA) Electricity Fee: 0.023 (Bs/Kwh)	
Apartment	0.69	Class 1	Monthly Electricity Volume < 200 Kwh: 1.608 Bs Monthly Electricity Volume > 200 Kwh: 0.16 (Bs/Kwh)	Annual Volume < 5,000 Kwh: 3.9 (Bs/m^3)
		Class 2	Monthly Electricity Volume 200–500 Kwh: 0.133 (Bs/Kwh) Monthly Electricity Volume > 500 Kwh: 0.167 (Bs/Kwh)	
		Class 3	Monthly Electricity Volume < 500 Kwh: 56.558 Bs Monthly Electricity Volume > 500 Kwh: 0.145 (Bs/Kwh)	

Source: Caracas Hydraulic Power Company, Caracas Power Company, Venezuelan National Gas Company (ENEGAS).

of new power plants and strive to add the power generation capacity of 10,000 megawatts by 2014 (see Table 7.7).

Due to the tight supply of water and electricity, the government has adjusted the balance of supply and demand in the electricity market through adjusting the prices of water and electricity. In July 2011, the price would increase by 200% for those residents whose consumption of electricity had grown 20% compared with 2009; for those industrial users with reduction of less than 10% of the electricity consumption, the price would be increased by 10% in the first month, followed by 5% up per month after the first.[12]

Section 2 Economic Reform of the Chavez's Administration

Venezuela has a typical oil economy. Its abundant petroleum resources have not become the economic engine — instead of raising the welfare level of the whole nation, they have caused distortion to the Venezuelan economy and politics, delaying the process of its industrialization, with the commodity production unable to meet its domestic demand and the stagnation of agricultural production leading to insufficient grain provision. The previous governments were only concerned about the resource taxes rather than the overall economic development, leading to the quite fragile economy with no competitiveness. In 1998, Chavez won the election, coming to power in 1999, and had been in power for 14 years. Chavez believed that Venezuela had inherited a capitalist rentier economy, the oil export income had not been reasonably allocated, and there was an urgent need of "economic revolution".[13] Therefore, since coming to power, first of all, the Chavez Administration had strengthened the state intervention in the economy. He believed that nationalization was an important condition to break the development obstacles and to

[12] "Electricity Prices in Venezuela Will Increase by 200%", June 14, 2011, http://power.in-en.com/html/power-16271627111043754.html.

[13] Agencia Venezolana de Noticias (AVN), *Chavez Considers that the Economic Model Transformation cannot be Postponed*, December 2007, http://www.avn.info.ve/go_news5.php+articulo=113471&lee=17.

realize independent development. Through the implementation of the "Bolivarian Plan" and the comprehensive nationalization policy in the strategic areas such as oil, natural gas, electricity, telecommunications and steel, the national resources and the production sector had been included in the national development process to meet the basic domestic needs. Secondly, the creation of cooperatives and land reforms had been intended to realize the economic "autonomous endogenous development" (*desarrollo endogeno soberano*) and self-sufficiency of the production of basic life necessities such as food and durable consumer goods, thus reducing the dependence on the external. In short, the "economic revolution" of the government of Chavez is the transformation of the economic mode from the free market economy and the new liberalism paradigm to the alternative mode (or quasi socialist mode) of redistribution of income and social welfare programs.

I. The Vigorous Implementation of Nationalization to Strengthen the Government's Intervention in Economy

Chavez opposed privatization, advocating that the strategic resources and strategic industries should be in the hands of the state. He believed that changing the mode of economic development needed to strengthen the country's economic intervention, so that the state could go into the field of production and the main way was nationalization. The main purpose of nationalization was to make the state to master the necessary resources, through increasing social services and public assistance to realize the redistribution of social wealth to meet the needs of the whole society so as to promote Venezuela towards the development mode of socialism. The government tried to ensure the legitimacy of nationalization through the introduction of relevant laws. The nationalization process began from the oil industry, then to strategic sectors such as telecommunications, electric power, cement, steel and banking, and even spreading to non-strategic sectors such as the food processing industry. The main measures of nationalization included: adjusting the profit sharing ratio, the re-signing of the contracts, acquisition of shares and compensation. In the specific cases of the nationalization of enterprises, the government tried to introduce the new system of "common management", i.e., the workers had the power to control the enterprise, including the election of managers, decision of production and technology and participation in the enterprise budget. Take Invepal Paper Mill for example. After it was nationalized in 2005, 51% of the shares of the enterprise were owned by the government, 49% of the shares belonged to the workers of the cooperative. Chavez believed that the "common management" encouraged greater involvement of the workers in the management of state-owned enterprises, which was an important step towards socialism in the 21st century.

1. The Nationalization of the Oil Industry

The nationalization of the oil industry is the core of the nationalization of Venezuela. Chavez believed that Venezuela must defend its oil sovereignty to use the oil revenue to improve the lives of the people, to expand investment in the production sector and to achieve the transformation of the economic mode. Since 1999, the government had gradually established the framework at the legislative level for the nationalization of the oil industry: the provisions of the Constitution in 1999 ruled that only the state had the right to explore and produce oil; the *Petroleum Law* of 2001 promulgated that all foreign investments should be in the form of setting up joint ventures with the Venezuelan oil companies to replace the forms of the operating service agreement (OSA), the risk and profit sharing agreement (RPSA) or the strategic alliance agreement, and Venezuela's PDVSA should have at least 51% of the shares; in 2006 the *Petroleum Law* was amended, ruling that on behalf of the state the Ministry of Energy and Mines was responsible for the management of Venezuela's oil exploration, development, storage, distribution and sales. By 2007, Venezuela had achieved control of all of the oil projects in the country.[14]

[14]By the end of 2006, the Venezuelan government had controlled all the oil projects except the Orinoco Oil Belt. At that time, the British Petroleum (BP),

In addition, the Chavez government also tried to increase the government revenue ratio through the oil tax reform to increase the control of the state of oil and gas resources. (1) Adjusting the income tax of oil companies. In 2001, the *Petroleum Law* adjusted the income tax rate of petroleum enterprises, ruling that the income tax rate for the enterprises engaged in the exploration and development of oil and gas and oil refining, storage and transportation and export would be lowered from 67.6% down to 50%; the income tax rate for the enterprises engaged in non-associated gas exploration and development, oil refining, storage and transportation and export would enjoy the general enterprise tax rate of 34%. In 2006, the new revision of the income tax law ruled that the income tax rate for the enterprises operating in the Orinoco Heavy Oil Belt was increased from 34% to 50%. (2) Increasing the mining royalties. In 2001 the *Petroleum Law* increased the rate of the cost from 16.6% to 30%. (3) Levying the tax on oil exploitation. From May 2006, the new mining tax was imposed on the oil and non-oil gas enterprises, with the tax rate of 33.3%. The tax was levied on a monthly basis, together with the cost and the special payment. (4) Levying additional oil windfall tax. In 2008, the *High Oil Price Special Contribution Law* stipulated that when the Venezuelan oil package monthly average export prices were between $70 and $100 per barrel, a 50% of the

Exxon-Mobil Oil Company, Chevron Oil Company and Conoco Phillips Oil Company, Total Oil Company, the Norwegian Oil Company (Statoil) cooperated with the Venezuelan oil company to develop four heavy oil upgrading projects with foreign holding. In 2007, Chavez used the warrant legislative decree to nationalize the upgrading projects of Orinoco Heavy Oil Belt, eventually winning the control of these projects. Among the six foreign oil companies, except Exxon-Mobil and Conoco Phillips, the rest of the four oil companies had renewed the partnership agreements. The two oil companies asked for international arbitration about their nationalized assets in Venezuela. By the end of 2011, according to the arbitral tribunal's ruling of the International Chamber of Commerce (ICC), PDVSA paid the companies $250 million as compensation. In addition, the government of Venezuela also faced with more than 20 disputes in the World Bank's International Center for Settlement of Investment Disputes (CIADI) caused by the nationalization of the assets of foreign companies in Venezuelan, with claims amounting to tens of billions of dollars. Therefore, the Venezuelan government withdrew from the organization in 2011.

windfall profit tax would be imposed on the oil companies for the part more than $70; when Venezuelan oil package monthly average export prices were over $100 per barrel, a 60% of the windfall profit tax would be imposed on the oil companies for the part more than $100. (5) Adding a new land surface tax and a fuel consumption tax for personal use and a general consumption tax. In 2001, the *Petroleum Law* stipulated that the non-oil and gas production mining area was levied a land surface tax, with the tax rate of 100 tax units per square kilometer every year. For the first five years, the tax rate would increase by 2% annually; five years later the annual tax rate would increase by 5%; The fuel consumption tax for personal use was applicable to the petroleum enterprises using self-produced fuel products for self-production, adopting the levy method according to amounts, with the tax base of the self-produced natural fuel volume for consumption in production and management, and the tax rate was 10% of the fuel value of per cubic meter of consumed products; the general consumption tax would be paid by the final consumer, with the tax base of the domestic market sale prices for oil products, and the tax rate of 30–50%. (6) Increasing the taxes and fees paid by joint venture enterprises. The oil joint venture enterprises operating in Venezuela also needed to pay additional taxes, including surcharges of mining royalties (3.33%), shadow tax (50% of the income of oil and gas sales minus income tax, mining royalties, municipal tax and special contributions) and the National Development Fund (1% of corporate pre-tax profit).

2. The Nationalization of the Telecommunications Industry

After the completion of the nationalization of the oil industry in 2007, the Venezuelan government began to implement the nationalization of the electricity and the telecommunications industry. The National Telephone Corporation Ltd. (CANTV) is Venezuela's largest telecommunications enterprise, with its fixed telephones, mobile communication and Internet services occupying the dominant position in Venezuela's domestic market with the US Verizon Telecommunications Company as its largest shareholder. The government believes that the company's business is mainly concentrated in Caracas and other developed regions, ignoring the demand for the development of telecommunications in other regions, and therefore has nationalized it. Through negotiations, the Verizon Telecommunications Company agreed to sell the company's shares to the Venezuelan government. From April to May 2007, the government publicly bought back the shares of the CANTV in the market, obtaining 86% of the shares of the company. After the nationalization, the company's business began to expand around the country, creating conditions especially for the economic and social development of backward areas.

3. The Nationalization of the Power Industry

The Caracas Power Company (EDC) is the largest private electricity company in Venezuela. In February 2007, on behalf of the government, PDVSA and the US AES Power Corporation (AES) signed a purchase agreement and completed the acquisition of it from April to May in the same year, with the purchase price of $0.836 billion. The proportion of government ownership was increased to 92.98%.

4. The Nationalization of the Cement Industry

Since 2008, the government began the nationalization of the enterprises of cement, iron and steel, finance and mining, so that these enterprises could be unified by the deployment of the state for production and sales to serve the national economic and social development projects. There was a large gap in Venezuela's cement market supply, resulting in high prices. In 2008, the government began the implementation of the nationalization of the Mexican Cement Company (Cemex), the Swiss Cement Company (Holcim) and the branch of France's Lafarge Cement Company, merging them into the National Cement Company (NCC), so that the government had controlled more than 90% of the cement production of the country, providing products for the country's infrastructure and residential construction.

5. The Nationalization of the Iron and Steel Industry

From 2008 to 2009, the government implemented the nationalization of the Orinoco Iron and Steel Company that had been controlled by the Argentine Techmt Group. The acquisition amounted to $1.97 billion and the government owned 80% of the shares. The nationalized Orinoco Steel Company cooperated with PDVSA to have formed the Venezuelan Steel Group. In addition, the government had also nationalized the Venprecar Company, the Comsigua Iron and Steel Company, Matesi (iron and steel raw materials company) and Tavsa (Venezuela's steel pipe company).

6. The Nationalization of the Financial Sectors

From 2008 to 2009, the government implemented the nationalization of Venezuela's third largest bank — the Bank of Venezuela, with the purchase price of $1.05 billion. In addition, the government had also restructured the Bolivar Bank, the Central Bank, the Confederado Bank and the Banfoantes Bank, establishing Venezuela's second largest state-owned commercial bank — the Bi-century Bank (Banco Bicentenario), providing preferential loans for the lower middle class people, especially providing housing loans for the vulnerable groups, helping those people who had long been excluded by the private banks to get involved in the development process.

7. The Nationalization of the Mining Industry

Since 2008, the government stopped issuing the gold mining permits to private enterprises, requiring foreign enterprises to set up joint ventures with Venezuelan enterprises, with Venezuelan enterprises as the controlling shareholders. In November 2008, Las Cristinas — Venezuela's largest gold mine controlled by the Canadian company — was nationalized.

8. The Nationalization of the Food Processing Industry

In 2009, the government nationalized a group of rice processing plants originally belonging to the US Cargill Company and Empresas Polar — a large private enterprise. Moreover, one dairy company, two coffee processing enterprises and the Cealco — the largest frozen storage and distribution enterprise — also were nationalized. In 2010, in order to deal with the price gouging behavior after the devaluation of the bolivar, the government implemented the nationalization of a number of supermarkets.

II. The Vigorous Development of Cooperatives to Promote the "Independent Endogenous Development"

Chavez hoped that Venezuela would achieve the "endogenous development" in the process of economic development, i.e., relying on their own conditions for the economic development and transforming the natural resources the to products that could be used for consumption and export to promote the social services and local production. In order to realize the "endogenous development", the government had adopted a series of measures mainly to promote the development of cooperatives and to promote the agricultural production.

1. The Vigorous Development of the Cooperatives

The Chavez government encouraged various production departments to set up cooperatives. In 2001, the *Cooperative Special Law* was issued to promote the cooperative development by means of providing loans, giving priority to purchase products produced by the cooperatives, and providing training. The Ministry of People's Economy (MINEP) provided free business training and management training for cooperatives, changing enterprises in difficulties into cooperatives. From 1998 to 2005, the number of cooperatives increased from 800 to more than 10,000, with about 1.5 million people joining the cooperatives. By 2007, the number of *cooperatives rosse* grew to 215,000, with the number of cooperative workers occupying about 18% of the population in the economic activity, and its output value accounted for 14% of the Venezuelan GDP.[15] Around 50% of the cooperatives were concentrated in the service sector and 30% of the cooperatives were concentrated in the field of production. Chavez hoped to promote the "endogenous development" through cooperatives, thus promoting a series of goals of the Bolivar Revolution, i.e., to create jobs, to achieve

[15] www.sunacoop.gob.ve.

full employment and to compete with the capitalist enterprises. As a collective ownership system, it was a way to expand the ownership of non-private ownership and to realize the transformation of the ownership of production materials. Chavez believed that the cooperatives had no exploitation, no investors lusting for profit, but workers as the owners of the enterprises paying more attention to the efficiency of enterprises; therefore, the cooperatives could better meet the needs of the people than the capitalist enterprises.

2. Actively Promoting the Agricultural Production

Venezuela has fertile land and suitable climate, suitable for the development of agriculture and the production of animal husbandry, but with the large-scale exploitation of oil resources, by 1920s, it had gone into the "oil era", with the oil economy becoming its economic entity, the agricultural production shrinking, and the economic structure growing imbalanced. Because its agricultural production could not meet its domestic demand, Venezuela soon became an agricultural-product net import country — more than 70% of the demand for food relied on imports and the domestic high food prices had resulted in a serious impact on the majority of the people, especially low-income groups. In addition, in the rural areas there was the phenomenon of widespread high concentration of land — 75% of the lands were controlled by 5% of the people, leading to the abandonment of lands. Since coming to power, President Chavez vigorously promoted the "endogenous development", promoting the diversification of its national economy. The agricultural production again had been attached importance to — the government regarded the agricultural development as the engine of the transformation of the development mode of Venezuela, through technology transfer, international cooperation and financing to promote their own food production to achieve the transformation from food-reliance to food-independence.

To promote the agricultural production, the government had adopted a series of measures: (1) Formulating a series of laws, such as the *Land Law*, the *Food Security and Food Sovereignty Law*, and the *Agricultural Credit Law*. The *Food Security and Food Sovereignty Law* stipulated that the government should establish strategic reserves of bulk agricultural products to stabilize prices and ensure food supply in case of disasters. The *Law to Ensure the People to Obtain Goods and Services* authorized the community committee to monitor the food supply and food prices and to punish food companies and retailers for illegal acts. (2) Implementing a moderate land reform. The Constitution of 1999 stipulated that a tax should be levied on the idle lands, farmers and other agricultural producers had the right to obtain lands, and the government should protect the potential of food supply; the *Land Law* of 2001 stipulated that agricultural lands should be used for food production, the land owners should faithfully declare the amount of their lands, and the government should acquire those long idled lands and then distribute them to farmers with no lands; in 2005 the "Special Land Committee" was also set up responsible for investigation of land ownership and use. If the big real estate owners' lands were not used for agricultural production, the government would acquire the lands by giving certain compensation and then allocate them to farmers' cooperatives. The State Land Bureau (INTI) was responsible for land redistribution, and the "Zamora Mission" (Misiom Zamora) was responsible for helping small and medium producers to obtain land. By 2005, one million hectares of land had been redistributed, of which 90% of the land had been used for food production; 2.2 million hectares of the state-owned land had been allocated to more than 130,000 farmer families and cooperatives. (3) Providing the support of the production capital, technology and market for the farmers and helping the development of small and medium-sized farms. The government promulgated the law requiring private banks and state-owned banks to provide farmers with low or no interest loans and set up special funds (such as the National Milk Production Fund) and the Agricultural Bank to provide loans for farmers. It reduced the debt of farmers and relieved the agricultural taxes, provided mechanical equipment and technical training for farmers, established a price stabilization mechanism to safeguard the farmers to obtain stable markets and income, and reduced the circulation chains to help farmers to directly sell their products to the state-owned enterprises and urban consumers. In 2005, the government had also implemented the "Return to Countryside Action" (*Mision Vuelta al Campo*), helping the urban poor and unemployed population return to the countryside to participate in the agricultural development.

In general, the output of major agricultural products had been greatly increased since Chavez took office. By 2008, the self-sufficiency of corn, rice, and pork had been realized (from 1998 to 2008, the production of corn, rice, and pork increased by 132%, 71%, and 77%, respectively) and the production of beef, milk, chicken, and egg had been 70%, 55%, 85%, and 80% in the domestic demand.[16]

III. Comprehensively Promoting the Social Development Project and Striving to Improve the Social Injustice

In order to change the serious unfair distribution of income and to rapidly improve the life quality of the poor people, which accounted nearly 50% of the total population, the Chavez government had implemented large-scale fiscal stimulus plans, using the oil revenues for the social development projects in the fields of medical care, education, housing, poverty alleviation, food, etc., trying to make the middle and lower classes benefited from the achievements of the economic development in order to build an inclusive and non-privileged society. Chavez believed that the main way to improve the status of social development was to redistribute the wealth of the country. Therefore, the Constitution of 1999 ruled that oil revenues should first be used in the social development projects to eliminate poverty. By the end of 2002, the Chavez Administration had successfully restructured the PDVSA to make oil revenues a major source of funding for the government to implement the social development projects. In 2005, the government set up the "National Development Fund" (FONDEN) with $6 billion. By 2008, $5.7 billion of the fund had been used for the social development projects.

[16]Anna Isaacs, Basi Weiner, Grace Bell, Courtney Frantz, Katie Bowen, "The Food Sovereignty Movement in Venezuela", http://www.venezulanalysis.com, November 26, 2009.

Table 7.8 Social Expenditure of the Venezuelan Central Government (1998–2006) (GDP, %)[a]

	1998	1999	2000	2001	2002	2003	2004	2005	2006
Total Public Expenditure	23.7	24.5	29.6	31.6	29.4	31.0	28.4	28.5	31.0
Total Social Expenditure	8.2	9.4	11.0	12.1	11.2	12.1	11.8	11.6	13.6
Education	3.4	4.1	4.5	4.8	4.8	4.6	4.8	4.1	5.1
Medical Care	1.4	1.5	1.4	1.5	1.7	1.5	1.6	1.6	1.8
Housing	1.0	0.8	1.7	1.0	0.8	1.1	0.6	1.3	1.6
Social Security	1.4	2.0	2.2	3.4	2.8	3.4	3.1	3.0	3.6
Social Development and Participation	0.8	0.9	0.8	0.9	0.8	1.1	1.2	0.9	1.0
Cultural and Social Exchange	0.2	0.1	0.2	0.2	0.1	0.3	0.3	0.3	0.3
Science and Technology	0.1	0.1	0.2	0.3	0.1	0.1	0.3	0.3	0.2
Social Expenditure/Total Public Expenditure	34.7	38.5	37.3	38.4	38.2	39.0	41.4	40.6	44.0

Note: [a]Does not include the social expenditure of PDVSA. In 2006 its social expenditures amounted to $13.3 billion, accounting for 7.3% of GDP.
Source: Sistema de Indicadores Sociales de Venezuela (SISOV) and Banco Central de Venezuela (BCV).

As can be seen from Table 7.8, from 1998 to 2006, the social expenditures of the central government increased from 8.2% of GDP to 13.6%, and the actual social spending per person increased 170% (this did not include the social spending of PDVSA; in 2006, the social spending of it reached 7.3% of GDP. If that was included, the total social spending in 2006 would reach 20.9% of GDP, and the per capita social spending would increase by 314% compared with 1998).

1. Medical Care

The most significant improvement was in the medical field. In 1998, the Venezuelan 23.4 million people had 1,628 primary care doctors; in 2008, 27 million people had 19,571 doctors. In 1998, there were 417 national emergency rooms, 74 rehabilitation centers and 1,628 basic health care centers; in 2008 there were 721 emergency rooms, 445 rehabilitation centers and 8,621 basic health care centers (including 6,500 physical examination stations in the slum areas, which are being expanded into more comprehensive primary care centers).

In 2003, the government began to implement the "Into the Community Mission" (*Mision Barrio Adentro*), providing free medical care to all the people, aiming to change the inequality in the field of medical service, getting the long-term excluded marginalized groups into the public health system. The implementation of the project was supported by the government of Cuba — a group of Cuban doctors came to Venezuela to provide medical services for the people. The "Into the Community Mission" was implemented in four steps: the first step was to establish 6,711 clinics in various parts of the poverty-group gathering areas, with nearly 8,000 doctors in them; the second stage was to establish 499 comprehensive diagnosis and treatment centers (CDI) in the country, 445 comprehensive rehabilitation centers (SRI) and 27 high-tech medical centers (CAT); the third stage was to update the existing medical instruments and equipment of the public hospitals; the fourth stage was to create a number of hospitals in the areas with poor medical conditions. In addition, the government had also implemented the "Miracle Mission" (Milagro Mision) and the "Smiling Mission" (Sonrisa Mision) to provide free ophthalmological and dental treatment for the public.

2. Education and Training

The national public schools increased from 3,620 (1999–2000) to 20,873 (2004–2005). The enrollment rates at all levels of education had increased. The gross enrollment rate of the preschool education increased by 25% from the school year of 1999–2000 to the school year of 2005–2006, the primary education by 8.3%, the secondary education by 45%, and the higher education by 44%.

In 2003, the government implemented the "Robinson Mission" (Mision Robinson) to carry out mass literacy and universal primary education, enabling about 1.48 million Venezuelans to have mastered the basic reading skills; the "Rivas Mission" (Mision Ribas) provided senior high school education for 5 million students who had dropped out of school; the "Sucre Mission" (Mision Sucre) ensured high school graduates to successfully enter the University, and the "Simoncito Mission" (Mision Simoncito) provided preschool education for the children aged 0–6. In addition, the government also implemented the "Return-to-Work Mission" (Mision Vuelvan) and the "Che Guevara

Mission" (Mision Che Guevara), providing training to those looking for jobs, or loans to help them form cooperatives.

3. Housing

From 2009 to 2010, the government launched the "New Community Program" (Barrio New) and "Big Housing Plan", investing nearly \$6 billion to promote the national housing construction to fill the gap of nearly 2 million housing units, giving priority to solving the housing problems of the poor and the middle class. By the end of 2011, under the "Big Housing Program", 26,000 housing units had been built and 25,300 housing units were under construction. In 2012, the government planned to have built 200,000 housing units and to start the new construction of 41,600 units.

4. The Food Subsidy Program

Due to the privatization of Venezuela's most food processing, storage and sales enterprises before 1998, during the strike from December 2002 to February 2003, the major food production and marketing enterprises stopped food supply, resulting in severe domestic food shortage. Some enterprises exported agricultural products that Venezuela had produced to foreign countries and after processing imported them to Venezuela to sell for profiteering, seriously damaging the interests of food producers and consumers, and a number of middlemen hoarded food and raised prices, exacerbating the shortage of food. In short, Venezuela's system of food production and sales was very fragile.

In 2003, the government began to implement the "Mercal Mission", establishing the national food supply enterprise "Mercal" (Venezuela's largest food sales enterprise and the second largest state-owned enterprise), through the form of government subsidies, in the nationwide setting up many food supermarkets, gradually establishing the Mercal state-owned discount food sales system to provide a guaranteed quality of food to the market with stabled preferential prices, blowing domestic speculation and curbing inflation to reduce Venezuela's dependence on imported food. These food supermarkets were located mainly in the poverty-population gathering areas;

part of the supermarkets were run by community residents, not only creating jobs, but also reducing the intermediate links, establishing a network of effective and safe storage, transportation and sales. In 2006, 15,726 shops were supplying main foods at subsidized prices (in 2005 and 2006 saving an average 27% and 39%, respectively than the market prices). In 2008, the government began the implementation of the "Venezuela Grain Production and Distribution" plan (PDVAL), in the charge of the Venezuelan Oil Company to strengthen the government control of food sales so as to combat domestic food hoarding behaviors by limiting food sales prices and preventing food being resold abroad. At the end of 2009, the government established the "Socialist Market Company" (Comerso), establishing state-run stores selling food and daily necessities in the market, all products coming from the "Social Production Enterprises" and the "Socialist Manufacturing Plants".

Section 3 Economic and Social Development since the Beginning of Chavez's Administration

I. The Economic and Social Development from 1999 to 2008

1. The Economic Growth Trend

From 1999 to 2008 (Chavez's 10-year administration), the Venezuelan economy grew 47.4%, an average annual growth rate of 4.3%; per capita GDP grew by 18.2%, an average annual growth rate of 1.9%. But the economic growth of the 10 years was not a process of sustained moderate growth because actually it was from the first quarter of 2003 that the Chavez's government began to control PDVSA, that is to say, in the first four years of its ruling (1999–2002), the incomes and taxes of the national oil company (accounting for about 50% of the government revenue and 80% of the total export earnings) had been controlled by the opposition. At that time, the Chavez government was simply unable to promote the economic growth; its regime had even almost been overturned. As a result, the real economic growth started only in the first quarter of 2003 after the government had controlled the country's oil companies.[17] The national strike from December 2002 to February 2003 had severely damaged the country's oil industry, causing a deep recession, but during the more than five years from the first quarter of 2003 to the first quarter of 2008, Venezuela's real GDP increased 94.7%, with an average annual growth rate of 13.5%, and per capita GDP increased by 78.8%, with an average annual growth of 11.7%. Apparently this growth rate was quite fast. Even if the recovery effect had been eliminated, the growth rate was still quite fast. We can calculate with the GDP level before the recession (i.e., from the third quarter of 2004). During the three years from the third quarter of 2004 to the second quarter of 2008, the Venezuelan GDP grew by 37.2%, with an average annual growth of 8.8%; the per capita GDP increased by 28.2%, with an average annual growth of 6.9% (see Figure 7.4 and Table 7.9). From this perspective, the economic growth in Venezuela had been successful from 1999 to 2008, and it was especially more obvious compared with the 20 years before Chavez's reign. From 1978 to 1998, Venezuela became the worst economic country in the world, with per capita GDP falling by 21.5%.

From the perspective of the structure of economic growth, due to the recovery of oil production after the strike, during the first and second quarter in 2003, the economy began to recover quickly,

[17] At the beginning of the reign of Chavez (1999) the economic was having a negative growth, with the oil price at the lowest level within 22 years. In the first quarter of 2000 the economic growth was restored, but in December 2001, the Venezuelan Chamber of Commerce (FEDECAMARAS) organized a large-scale anti-government commercial strike, followed by a military coup in April 2002 that put the government in the danger of being subverted. This was the most unstable period of political instability in Chavez's ruling, leading to massive capital flight, and hence the economy suffered heavy losses. The economy had still been in negative growth in the second quarter and the third quarter of 2002. From December 2002 to February 2003, the oil strike led by the opposition leaders again hit the economy, pushing the economy into a severe recession, during which Venezuela lost 24% of its GDP, and to the middle of 2003 the political situation tended to be stabilized (see Figure 7.4). Mark Weisbrot, Rebecca Ray and Luis Sandoval, *The Chavez Administration at 10 Years: The Economy and Social Indicators*, Center for Economic and Policy Research (CEPR), Washington, D.C., February 2009.

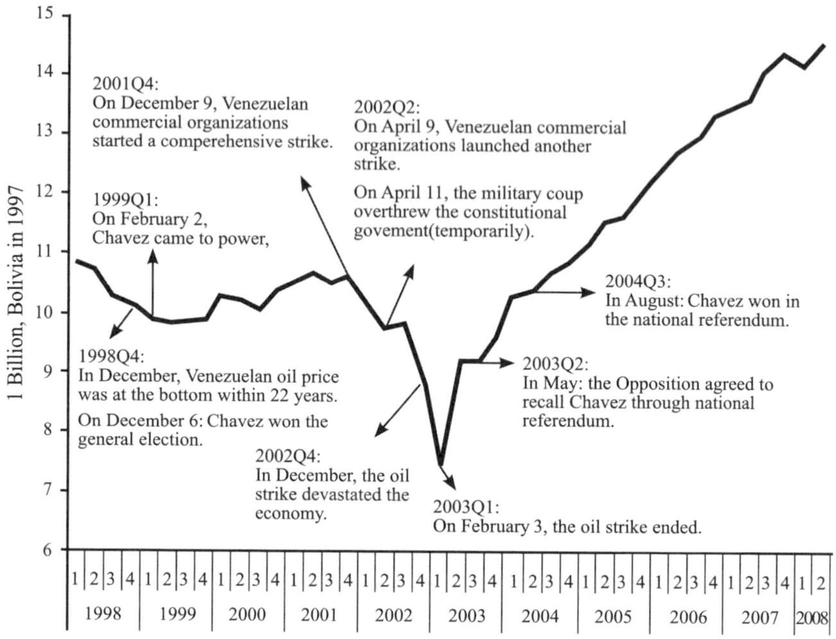

Figure 7.4 Changes of the Real GDP Growth Rate of Venezuela from 1998 to 2008

Note: The shaded part indicates the decline and recovery from 2001 to 2004.

Source: Mark Weisbrot, Rebecca Ray and Luis Sandoval, *The Chavez Administration at 10 Years: The Economy and Social Indicators*, Center for Economic and Policy Research (CEPR), Washington, D.C., February 2009.

with an increase of 18.3% in 2004, 10.3% in 2005, and 10.3% in 2006. The economy had maintained a double-digit growth till 2008. Figure 7.5 shows that the growth was mainly concentrated in the non-oil sectors of the economy; from 2005 to 2007, the oil sector had achieved a negative growth (after the ending of the strike, the production of oil was recovered; in 2004 the oil sector increased by 13.7%, but in the same year, the growth of the non-oil sectors was quicker than that of the oil sector). Table 7.10 shows the growth of various sectors of the Venezuelan economy from 1998 to 2008. In the economic expansion period (the four and a half years from the first quarter of 2003 to the third quarter of 2007), all the sectors of the economy were in growth, of which the fastest growing was the

Table 7.9 Growth Rates of GDP in Venezuela from 1998 to 2008

Time Interval	GDP		Time Span (Years)	Growth Rate (%)	
	Beginning	Ending		Total	Years
Actual GDP (1 Billion, Bolivar in 1997)					
1st Quarter of 2003–2nd Quarter of 2008	7.50	14.60	5.25	94.7	13.5
3rd Quarter of 2004–2nd Quarter of 2008	10.64	14.60	3.75	37.2	8.8
Per Capita Average GDP (Bolivar in 1997)					
1st Quarter of 2003–2nd Quarter of 2008	292.11	522.26	5.25	78.8	11.0
3rd Quarter of 2004–2nd Quarter of 2008	407(34)	522.26	3.75	28.2	6.9

Source: Mark Weisbrot, Rebecca Ray and Luis Sandoval, *The Chavez Administration at 10 Years: The Economy and Social Indicators*, Center for Economic and Policy Research (CEPR), Washington, D.C., February 2009.

financial and insurance sector (increasing 258.4%, with an average annual growth rate of 26.1%), followed by the construction industry (increasing 159.4%, with an average annual growth of 18.9%), the trade and repair services (increasing 152.8%, with an average annual growth of 18.4%), the transportation and warehousing industry (increasing 104.9%, with an average annual growth of 13.9%), the communications (increasing 151.4%, with an average annual growth of 18.3%), and the manufacturing (increasing 98.1%, with an average annual growth rate of 13.2%). In spite of this, it was not enough to realize diversification to help the economy get away from its dependence on oil. Another noteworthy phenomenon was that the private sectors had grown faster than the public sectors from 1999 to 2007; in 2007 the proportion of private sectors was considerably much higher than that before the Chavez Administration. But during the first to the third quarters of 2008, it was mainly the growth of the public sectors, and the private sectors remained almost at a standstill.

Table 7.10 Real Growth Rate of the Economic Sectors in Venezuela (1998–2008) (%)

	1998	1999	2000	2001	2002	2003	2004	2005	2006	2007[a]	2008[b]
Total real GDP	0.3	−6.0	3.7	3.4	−8.9	−7.8	18.3	10.3	10.3	8.4	5.6
Public sectors	−2.1	−5.2	3.0	−0.6	−11.1	−1.3	12.5	2.8	3.6	7.7	18.8
Private sectors	1.1	−6.9	4.2	4.9	−5.8	−8.9	17.2	12.9	11.9	7.3	0.2
Oil sectors	0.3	−3.8	2.3	−0.9	−14.2	−1.9	13.7	−1.5	−2.0	−4.2	4.1
Non-oil sectors	−0.1	−6.9	4.2	4.0	−6.0	−7.4	16.1	22.2	11.7	9.5	5.9
Mining	−7.5	−12.1	15.3	2.8	4.3	−4.4	14.2	3.0	4.5	2.0	0.4
Manufacturing	−1.4	−10.1	5.1	3.7	−13.1	−6.8	21.4	11.1	9.7	7.2	2.0
Power supply and water supply	0.5	−2.2	4.7	4.8	2.1	−0.5	8.5	11.2	5.8	2.4	3.6
Construction	1.4	−17.4	4.0	13.5	−8.4	−39.5	25.1	20.0	35.6	13.3	7.6
Trade and maintenance service	−1.5	−5.4	5.7	4.6	−13.6	−9.6	28.6	21.0	19.1	16.9	5.4
Transportation and warehousing	−5.2	−15.3	12.5	−1.3	−10.4	−8.0	24.6	14.7	10.0	13.5	3.5
Communication industry	8.2	3.6	2.1	8.1	2.5	−5.0	12.9	22.4	23.2	20.0	21.3
Finance and insurance	0.2	−15.2	−0.7	2.8	−14.5	11.9	37.9	36.4	43.9	17.0	−5.2
Real estate	0.7	−4.7	0.8	3.5	−0.7	−6.0	11.1	7.9	8.3	6.6	3.2
Community, private and non-profit services	0.3	−1.7	0.9	2.1	0.1	−0.3	9.4	8.2	16.5	10.9	9.1
Public service	−0.6	−4.8	2.8	2.5	−0.4	4.9	11.1	8.0	3.9	5.0	4.4
Other[c]	3.0	0.5	5.2	1.8	−1.0	−2.9	7.2	12.6	1.9	5.1	5.4
Government final consumption	−3.1	−7.5	4.2	6.9	−2.5	5.7	14.2	10.7	6.7	5.1	5.6

(Continued)

Table 7.10 (*Continued*)

	1998	1999	2000	2001	2002	2003	2004	2005	2006	2007[a]	2008[b]
Private final consumption	1.8	−1.7	4.7	6.0	−7.1	−4.3	15.4	15.7	17.9	18.7	8.3
Total capital formation	4.4	−10.6	6.7	13.6	−34.0	−35.5	91.3	30.5	31.6	26.6	−1.5
Export of goods and services	3.5	−11.0	5.8	−3.5	−4.0	−10.4	13.7	3.8	−4.5	−5.6	−0.4
Import of goods and services	11.3	−9.3	12.4	14.1	−25.2	−20.9	57.7	35.2	31.1	33.6	3.8

Note: [a]Means the growth rates from the first to the third quarter of 2007 and the same period of 2006; [b]means the growth rates from the first to the third quarter of 2008 and the same period of 2007; [c]means the private agricultural, food and hotel, and other public sectors.

Source: Mark Weisbrot, Rebecca Ray and Luis Sandoval, *The Chavez Administration at 10 Years: The Economy and Social Indicators*, Center for Economic and Policy Research (CEPR), Washington D.C., February 2009.

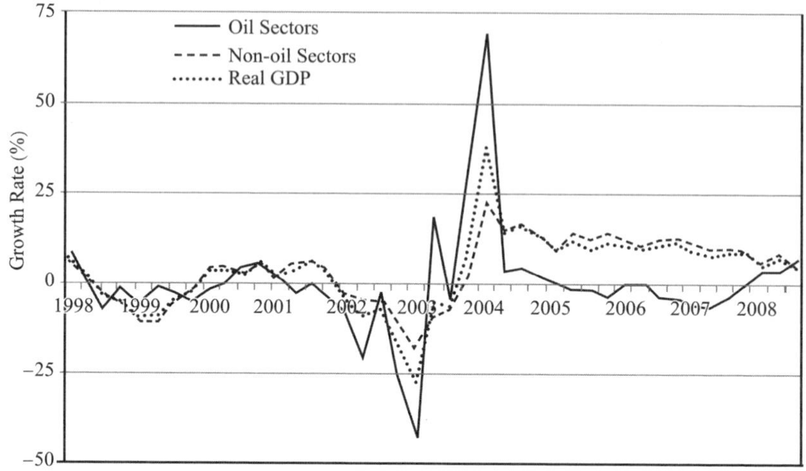

Figure 7.5 Real GDP Growth Rate and Growth Rate of the Economic Sectors
Source: BCV (Banco Central de Venezuela), "Indicadores: Informacion Estadistica", Online database, February 2009. http://200.74.197.130/c2/indicadores.asp.

2. Social Development

According to the human development index ranking of 2010 published by the United Nations Development Programme (UNDP), Venezuela's index was 0.696, ranking No. 75 in the 169 rated countries and regions. Although it ranked No. 77 in 2009, it was still a country with a "high human development index". In the past 40 years, the life expectancy of the Venezuelan people increased from 60 years to 74.2 years; the enrollment rate increased from 52% to 83%, with the average education time of 6.2 years and the per capita GDP of $11,846. At present, the Venezuelan malnourished population ratio fell from 11% in the 1990s to 3.25% (the current average ratio in the Latin-American area being 6%), the poor population fell from 49.4% in 1999 to 27.6% in 2008, and the proportion of people living in extreme poverty dropped from 21.7% to 9.9%, completing the millennium development goals ahead of schedule.

(1) Poverty and Inequality

Table 7.11 shows the change in the rate of poverty in Venezuela from 1997 to 2008 (by family and population). At the beginning of the

Table 7.11 Gini Coefficient of Venezuelan Poverty Rate and Income (1995–2008)

		Total Family Rate (%)		Total Population Rate (%)		Imparity
Year	Period	Family of Poverty	Family of Extreme Poverty	Population of Poverty	Population of Extreme Poverty	Income Gini Coefficient
1995	First Half	54.70	24.50	—	—	46.78
	Second Half	53.20	23.80	—	—	47.82
1996	First Half	70.80	39.50	—	—	48.78
	Second Half	64.30	32.70	—	—	49.22
1997	First Half	55.60	25.47	60.90	29.51	46.96
	Second Half	48.10	19.32	54.50	23.37	48.98
1998	First Half	49.00	21.01	55.40	24.66	48.65
	Second Half	43.90	17.06	50.40	20.34	47.02
1999	First Half	42.80	16.60	50.00	19.86	46.93
	Second Half	42.00	16.89	48.70	20.15	48.51
2000	First Half	41.6	16.65	48.30	19.49	47.72
	Second Half	40.40	14.89	46.30	18.02	45.07
2001	First Half	39.10	14.17	45.50	17.36	45.73
	Second Half	39.00	14.04	45.40	16.94	47.72
2002	First Half	41.50	16.58	48.10	20.13	49.44
	Second Half	48.60	21.04	55.40	25.03	47.98
2003	First Half	54.00	25.09	61.00	30.22	48.11
	Second Half	55.10	25.03	62.10	29.75	46.47
2004	First Half	53.10	23.46	60.20	28.10	45.50
	Second Half	47.00	18.60	53.90	22.50	45.40
2005	First Half	42.40	17.00	48.80	20.30	47.48
	Second Half	37.90	15.30	43.70	17.80	47.71
2006	First Half	33.90	10.60	39.70	12.90	44.22
	Second Half	30.60	9.10	36.30	11.10	43.70
2007	First Half	27.46	7.63	33.07	9.41	42.37
	Second Half	28.50	7.90	33.60	9.60	42.11
2008		26.00	7.00	31.50	9.50	40.99

Source: *Instituto Nacional de Estadistica* (INE), 2009; *Republica Bolivariana de Venezuela and Fundacion Escuela de Gerencia Social* (FEGS), 2009.

Chavez Administration in 1999, the poverty rate was 42.8%, but the poverty rate fell to 26% in 2008 and the proportion of poor families fell from 16.6% to 7%. The poverty rate was 39% at end of 2001 and it reached the highest value of 55.1% in the second half of 2003, which was mainly due to the oil strike. From 2003 to 2008, due to the rapid economic growth, the poverty rate fell from 54% in the first half of 2003 to 26% at the end of 2008, and the proportion of poor families fell by 72%.[18]

Table 7.11 also shows that the inequality of income distribution measured by the Gini Coefficient had also been greatly improved. From 1997 to 2008, Venezuela's income Gini Coefficient fell from 46.96 to 40.99. In the period of economic expansion from 2003 to 2008, the income Gini Coefficient fell from 48.11 to 40.99.

(2) Medical Treatment

After Chavez came to power, the medical treatment had been greatly improved. The infant mortality rate (per 1,000 infant mortality) fell from 21.4‰ in 1998 to 14.2‰ in 2006, dropping more than 30%; the child mortality rate (per 1,000 children mortality) fell from 26.5‰ to 17‰, also dropping more than 30% (see Figure 7.6).

From 1998 to 2008, due to the greater improvement in food security, the per capita consumption of calories in Venezuela rose from the recommended level of 91% in 1998 to 101.6% in 2007. More importantly, from 1998 to 2006, the mortality rate due to malnutrition (mortality rate per 100,000 people) fell from 4.9 to 2.3, a decrease of more than 50%. It is mainly due to two plans: the first one is

---

[18]This is the poverty rate using the cash income as measurement, without considering the health and education services that the poor have obtained. According to the conservative estimate of medical benefit value (medical expenditures of the poor in the absence of these new projects), the poverty rate should be reduced by two percentage points. The reason for the conservative estimate is that in the absence of income before, the majority of poor people did not have health care, suffering from diseases, low income and low life expectancy for a long time. Therefore, the value of these medical services is far greater than the expenditure in the absence of government projects. The obvious improvement of the poor could be measured not simply with the reduction of cash income (official poverty rate).

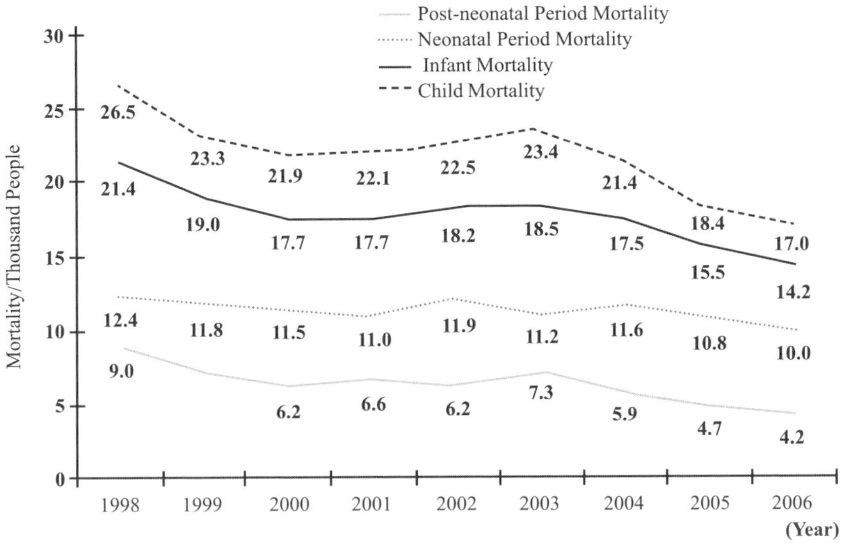

Figure 7.6 Venezuelan Infant and Child Mortality from 1998 to 2006

Note: The infant mortality refers to infants under one year old, the neonatal mortality refers to infants under one month old, the post-neonatal mortality refers to 1–11 months old infants, and the child mortality refers to the mortality of children under five years of age.

Source: *Sistema de Indicadores Sociales de Venezuela* (SISOV) 2009.

the implementation of the "School Food Program" from 1999 (Programa Alimenticio Escolar, PAE), providing free breakfast, lunch and refreshments to students; the number of benefited students rose from 250,000 in 1999 to 4 million in 2008. The second one is the state-owned "Mercal" discount food sales system established since 2003. The sales of food subsidies rose from 45,662 tons in 2003 to 1.25 million tons in 2008.

(3) Drinking Water and Sanitation

Compared with the time before the Chavez Administration, from 1998 to 2007, the improvement in drinking water and sanitation in Venezuela was also significant. As is shown in Figure 7.7, in 1998 only 80% of the Venezuelan people had access to clean drinking water, and 62% of the people had access to health services. In 2007, the two figures were 92% and 82%; compared with 1998, the number of

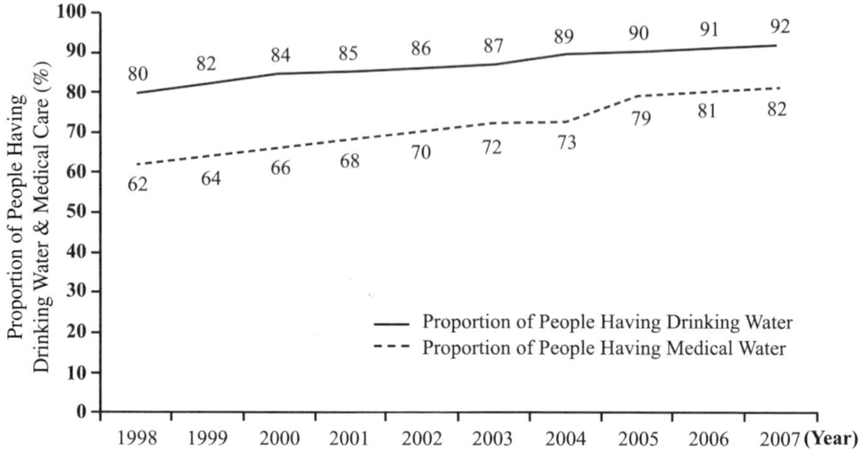

Figure 7.7 Proportion of People Having Drinking Water and Medical Care (1998–2007)

Source: *Sistema de Indicadores Societies de Venezuela* (SISOV), 2009.

people with access to clean drinking water increased over 4 million and the number of people with access to health services increased over 5 million.

(4) Education

From 1998 to 2007, as a direct result of the social investment, the improvement of education and training was also very significant. As is shown in Figure 7.8, the net enrollment rate of primary education (Grades 1–9) rose from 85% to 93.6%, nearly 50 million uneducated children going to school; the net enrollment rate of secondary education rose from 21.2% to more than 30%, with 40 million new students; the improvement of higher education was the most obvious — the enrollment increased 138% from the academic year of 1999–2000 to the academic year of 2007–2008.

In addition to the massive literacy training program, the "Rivas Mission" launched in 2003 had provided secondary education for adults; from 2003 to 2005, nearly half a million students had graduated, accounting for 3% of the adult population.

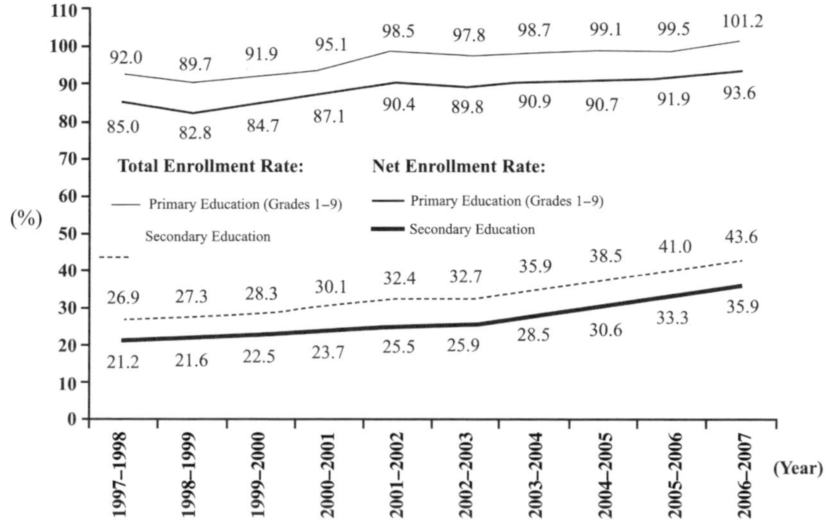

Figure 7.8 Total Enrollment Rate and Net Enrollment Rate of the Primary Education and the Secondary Education (1998–2007)

Source: *Sistema de Indicadores Sociales de Venezuela* (SISOV), 2009.

(5) Employment

From 1998 to 2008, the state of the labor market in Venezuela had continued to improve (see Table 7.12). From 1998 to 2008, 2.9 million new jobs had been created, increasing 30%; the unemployment rate fell from 11.3% to 7.8%, in which it increased to 19.2% in 2003, but after 2003 it fell by half. In 2008, 51.8% of the labor force was employed in the formal sectors, but in 1998 this proportion was only 45.4%. From 1998 to 2008, the employment in the public sectors increased by 47.2% and the employment in the private sectors increased by 30.6%. The employment growth of the public sectors and the private sectors was faster than the growth of the labor force.

(6) Social Security

From 1998 to 2008, the coverage of social security for the vulnerable groups (the elderly, elderly people living alone, orphans and the

Table 7.12 Venezuelan Labor Market Indicators (1998–2008) (%)

	1998	1999	2000	2001	2002	2003	2004	2005	2006	2007	2008
Proportion of Total Employment	88.7	84.7	85.4	86.3	84.5	80.8	83.4	86.7	89.4	90.8	92.2
By Sectors:											
Public Sectors	14.5	13.1	13.3	13.0	12.0	11.6	12.4	13.7	15.0	15.8	16.6
Private Sectors	74.3	71.6	72.1	73.2	72.5	69.1	71.0	73.0	74.5	75.0	75.6
By Nature of Sectors:											
Formal Departments	45.4	41.5	40.4	42.5	41.8	38.4	40.9	45.1	48.6	51.0	51.8
Non-formal Departments	42.8	43.2	44.9	43.8	42.7	42.3	42.4	41.3	40.9	39.9	40.4
Unemployment Rate	11.3	15.3	14.6	13.7	15.5	19.2	16.6	13.3	10.6	9.2	7.8

Source: *Instituto Nacional de Estadistica* (INE), 2009.

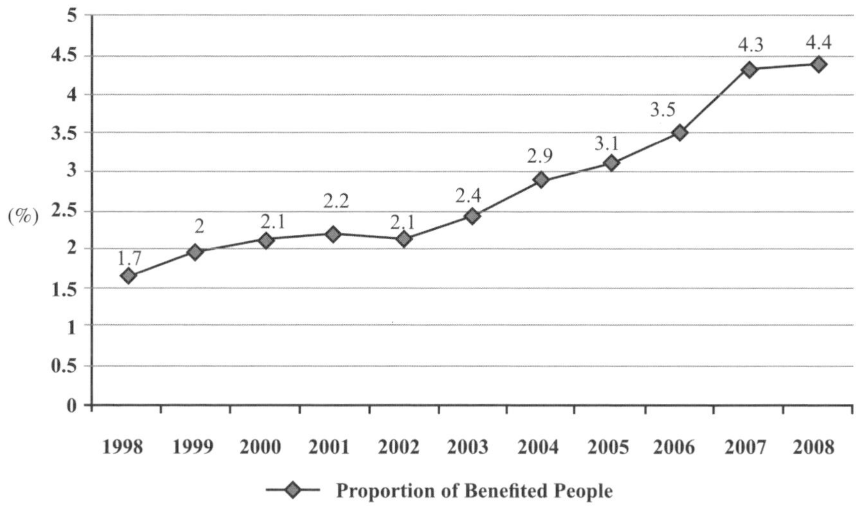

Figure 7.9 Proportion of Vulnerable Groups Benefited from the Social Security
Source: *Sistema de Indicadores Sociales de Venezuela* (SISOV), 2009.

disabled) increased from 1.7% to 4.4%, expanding more than doubled. Among them, in the early years of the Chavez Administration, the social security progressed slowly and an obvious deterioration also appeared during the strike, but since the government took over PDVSA in 2003, the social security had been improved rapidly (see Figure 7.9).

3. The Problems Existing in the Economic Development from 1998 to 2008

After Chavez took power, especially after the domestic political situation had become increasingly stable in 2003, Venezuela's economy and society had made great progress, but whether this development would continue was a problem worthy of attention because in this stage some problems were obviously existing in the process of economic development.

(1) High Inflation

Figure 7.10 shows the change in the rate of inflation in Venezuela from 1999 to 2008. From May 1998 to January 2002, the annual

Figure 7.10 Venezuelan Annual Inflation Rate (Consumer Price Index from January 1999 to July 2008)

Source: Mark Weisbrot, Rebecca Ray and Luis Sandoval, *The Chavez Administration at 10 Years: The Economy and Social Indicators*, Center for Economic and Policy Research (CEPR), Washington, D.C., February 2009.

inflation rate fell from 40% to 12%. Later, during the period of political instability (February 2002 to January 2003), the inflation rate rose rapidly to 40%. After the strike ended in February 2003, the inflation rate began to decline gradually, even in the rapid recovery period of the fourth quarter of 2003, the inflation rate was falling. But since June 2006, the inflation rate started to rise again, reaching a peak of 36% in the middle of 2008. The rising inflation rate was mainly due to the shortage of domestic supplies and the cumulative effect brought about by the four and a half years of rapid growth. According to the theory of macroeconomics about inflation, it is a critical point when the inflation rate reaches 20%; when the inflation rate is more than the critical point it will have a negative impact on the economy, and the inflation rate of Venezuela had been more than 20% at the beginning of 2008.

Severe food shortages led to a high inflation. Most grocery stores and Mercal discount food stores were unable to supply enough beef, corn oil, milk, chicken, eggs, and other foods; they could only be bought on the black markets. The food shortage was mainly due to the price control, the rapid growth of economy and consumption and the accumulation of goods. If the problem was sustained or became worse, it would become a political issue. Once the food shortage had caused serious economic and political repercussions, the government could only solve the problem of shortage through imports, leading to to a higher level of inflation rate.

(2) The Overvalued Exchange Rate

The most serious economic imbalance in Venezuela is the exchange rate. In February 2003, the government implemented the foreign exchange control; the exchange rate of bolivar against the US dollar was fixed to 1,600:1, but due to the inflation, the actual devaluation of the currency was 3,182:1. After the rapid devaluation of bolivar in 2007, the exchange rate reached 6,000:1. In 2009, the bolivar was pegged to the US dollar by the ratio of 2,150:1. The currency was significantly overestimated. If Venezuela was to seek a long-term diversified development strategy that would no longer rely solely on oil, it was necessary to adjust the exchange rate. The overvalued currency not only inhibited the development of the non-oil sectors, especially the manufacturing sector, but also led to cheaper imports and higher export prices in the international market. Therefore, the commodities of Venezuela had lost competitiveness in the international and the domestic market. This was a serious long-term development problem, reflecting the distortion and ineffectiveness of the foreign exchange management system.

(3) Lack of Investment

Table 7.13 shows the situation of the total fixed capital formation in Venezuela from 1998 to 2007. From 1998 to 2001, the total capital formation had been at a standstill. During the oil-strike period from December 2002 to February 2003, the total capital formation decreased by 57%. After the strike, the total capital formation had a rapid growth. In 2004, the total capital formation actually increased 49.7%; in 2005, it increased 38.4%; in 2006, it increased 26.6%; from

Table 7.13 Total Fixed Capital Formation of Venezuela (1998–2007) (In GDP, %)

Total Fixed Capital Formation (In GDP)	1998	1999	2000	2001	2002	2003	2004	2005	2006	2007
Total	30.7	26.5	24.2	27.5	21.2	15.2	21.8	22.6	24.7	—
Public Sector	12.2	8.0	6.1	6.5	9.3	8.3	9.1	8.1	—	—
Primary Sector	18.5	18.5	18.0	21.0	11.9	6.9	12.7	14.9	—	—
Total Fixed Capital Formation	28.6	23.7	21.0	24.1	21.9	15.5	18.3	20.2	22.5	—
Change of Investment (%)	2.1	2.8	3.2	3.5	−0.8	−0.3	3.5	2.4	2.2	—
Change of Total Fixed Capital Formation (%)	4.4	−10.6	6.7	13.6	−34.0	−35.5	91.3	30.5	31.6	22.2
Change of Total Fixed Capital Formation (%)	5.5	−15.6	2.6	13.8	−18.4	−37.0	49.7	38.4	26.6	24.6

Source: Mark Weisbrot, Rebecca Ray and Luis Sandoval, *The Chavez Administration at 10 Years: The Economy and Social Indicators*, Center for Economic and Policy Research (CEPR), Washington D.C., February 2009.

the first to the third quarter of 2007, the total capital formation increased 24.6%.

From 2002 onwards, the private capital formation had an overall downward trend, but from 2003 to 2005, the proportion of the total private capital formation in GDP increased gradually, from 6.9% and 12.7% to 14.9%, suggesting that the private investment in this period increased gradually in the economy. But after 2005, the growth rate of the public investment was much faster than the growth rate of the private investment. In 2005, the proportion of Foreign Direct Investment (FDI) in GDP was 1.8%; in 2006 the FDI was a negative, which was a major change. The economic growth could be interrupted by a downward trend of the investment rate (foreign and domestic investors thought that the invest environment was bad). According to the data of ECLAC, due to the vigorous promotion of the policy of nationalization, in 2010 Venezuela absorbed $14 billion of foreign investment, becoming the only country in the region to have absorbed negative foreign investment.

II. The Economic Recession of 2009–2010

The outbreak of the global financial and economic crisis in 2008 ended the period of five consecutive years of economic growth in the Latin-American and Caribbean region which had not happened for 40 years. During this period of growth, the economic growth rate of most Latin-American countries had increased, the poverty rate had been reduced, the macroeconomic situation had been greatly improved, and the economic vulnerability had been reduced. The Latin-American economy had lost the driving force from trade and finance because of the global economic crisis. In 2009, the trade volume of the Latin-American region decreased significantly, the remittances significantly reduced, the capital market frequently fluctuated, and the FDI remained at a standstill. According to the estimate of ECLAC, the Latin-American production fell by 1.8%. Among them, Mexico, Central American countries, and Venezuela were the most affected countries. In 2009, almost all of the large and medium-sized Latin-American countries began to restore growth; in

2010, Latin America increased about 6%. However, Venezuela was an exception — in 2009 its economy fell 3.3%; in 2010, it fell 1.6%. The level of inflation rose and there had been a serious economic recession. The main reasons are listed as follows:

1. The External Tightening

In the second quarter of 2008, the global financial crisis, marked by the collapse of the Lehman Brothers, broke out, and the bubble of the international price of commodities and other primary products was broken. The prices of the main basic products, especially oil prices, began to plummet. The oil price in June 2008 was about $130; by December the crude oil price fell to $31.55 per barrel. Within just six months, Venezuela's crude oil price fell 75%.

Although from the first quarter of 2009 the oil price began to rise, in 2009 the Venezuelan oil revenue decreased by 40%, and the current account yielded deficit the first time in six years, producing a tremendous pressure on the foreign exchange reserves (due to reduced export earnings, to the end of 2008, the Venezuelan reserves fell to its lowest level — $42.299 million). Therefore, Venezuela's economic development not only failed to break its dependence on exporting primary products, but in recent years became more and more deeply trapped in the (oil) market volatility risk.[19] In 2010, the oil export accounted for 94% of Venezuela's total export, but 10 years before, the proportion was only 68%. Nearly 50% of the revenue of the central government of Venezuela came from oil through levying the sales tax, mining tax and dividends, but 10 years before, the contribution rate of oil in the fiscal revenue was less than 37%. In addition, the factors of the significant decrease of non-oil export (the reduction of world

[19]Through the acquisition of ownership and control of the enterprise, the state became more and more involved in production activities; for the public sectors, public governance had become more complex and there were more and more financial commitments, resulting in a considerable scale of debt. The sustainability of "21st Century Socialism" seemed to depend on the increase in oil revenues. However, it was the most difficult to predict the fluctuations of the international oil market. Leonardo Vera, "Venezuela: Anatomia de una recesión profunda y prolongada", *Nueva Sociedad*, No. 228, julio-agosto de 2010.

trade and the interruption of the bilateral trade with Colombia), escape of capital, and negative net FDI had increased the external instability, leading to the external tightening.

2. The Inappropriate Policies

In response to the crisis, the package of economic policies adopted by the government had not only failed to slow the impact of external turmoil, but also magnified the impact of the crisis. In March 2009, nearly nine months after the falling of oil price, the government implemented a package of financial and revenue measures to deal with the crisis: in terms of finance, in 2009 the government cut 6.7% of its budget in the nominal spending (from 167.47 million bolivars to 156.25 million bolivars), increased the value-added tax from 3% to 12%, and increased its domestic debt from 12 million bolivars to 37 million bolivars. In terms of income, from May 1, 2009 onwards, the government decided to increase 20% of the minimum wage in two stages to make the average monthly basic salary reach 967.5 bolivars.

These measures had limited the imports. In 2009, the Venezuelan imports fell by 22%,[20] but none of the measures could slow down the impact of the potential recession brought about by the external crisis. Because 75% of the Venezuelan imports were intermediate input products and capital goods, restrictions on the imports of goods were certain to have a negative impact on the economic production. On another hand, the financial measures to maintain the balance of the public accounts would often magnify the impact of the external shocks on the domestic production. The actual expenditure of Venezuela fell 15% in 2009 compared with that in 2008, mainly in the form of the reduction of the public investment. According to the data of the Central Bank of Venezuela, in 2009 the Venezuelan total fixed capital formation fell 8.2% than in 2008. Finally, the 20% increase in the minimum wage was likely to lead to a higher inflation. In 2008, Venezuela's inflation rate had increased 26%; in 2009 Venezuela's

[20]In 2010, the total import of Venezuela increased 0.4%, but the import of capital goods still fell 5%.

inflation rate was 25.1%, ranking first in the Latin-American countries. In 2010 the inflation rate continued to rise to 27.2%, so that the actual purchasing power of the residents declined by 4% and the real purchasing power of the residents had declined for four consecutive years.

Moreover, the opacity of fiscal management had also reduced the room of the government to implement the adjustment of austerity during the recession. Since 2004, the government had created a number of mutual funds and sovereign wealth funds. Among them, the National Development Fund (Fonden) had raised a lot of money, but no regular financial statements had been submitted, not to mention the specific projects and investment records. The report of the Central Bank of Venezuela in 2008 pointed out that the fund had received a total of $46.131 million since its creation to the end of 2008, but the funding of $38.2 million was only commitments; the actual sum received was only $7.9 million, about 2% of GDP, thus reducing the room for the adjustment of austerity in the recession. In addition, most of these funds had been used in transfer payment projects and the procurement of imports for the public investment projects; therefore, the expenditure had a limited effect on pulling the domestic economy.[21]

Due to the external shocks, the nominal income of the government departments and the private sectors could not be increased. In order to avoid the impact of the decline in the purchasing power and the amplified crisis, the inflation had to be controlled; otherwise, it would cause an actual decline in the domestic demand and the consequent recession. Obviously the government had not found an economic policy to control the inflation. It had not only failed to correct the deviation of relative prices, but on the contrary had implemented a large-scale price control policy. In fact, in 2009 and the first quarter of 2010, the Venezuelan real private consumption and real wages had decreased significantly. In addition, although the foreign exchange market pressure continued to increase and the currency

[21]Leonardo Vera, "Venezuela: Anatomia de una recesión profunda y prolongada", *Nueva Sociedad*, No. 228, julio-agosto de 2010.

had been overestimated, the government departments did not adjust any official exchange rate; for nine consecutive months the exchange rate had been maintained at the level of 2.15 bolivars:$1. The policy to maintain a fixed exchange rate not only had not controlled the inflation, but also continued to have deepened the long-term trend of the overvaluation of the currency, fueling the expectation of inflation after the adjustment of the exchange rate.

In short, the external shocks had exerted an impact on Venezuela's total domestic demand or total supply and on the potential of the long-term production, but the government's policies and measures were obviously inappropriate, not only failing to mitigate the external influence, but amplifying the adverse effect, leading to a concomitant decline. For example, at the end of May 2010, the average price of crude oil in Venezuela rose to $68 per barrel ($25 per barrel higher than the average price from January to May, 2009). In theory, with the increase of the oil revenues, the government should relax its import restrictions and financial constraints and increase the public spending. But according to the statistics from the Central Bank and the Ministry of Finance of Venezuela, the imports in the first quarter of 2010 fell 38% compared with the first quarter of 2009 and the spending of the government actually fell 5%.

In January 2010, the government adjusted the exchange rate and implemented the complex exchange rate system to replace the single exchange rate system that had maintained the same in the past five years. This measure had partially corrected the deviation of the real exchange rate, but according to the past experience of the adjustment of the exchange rate, after the adjustment of the exchange rate, the depreciation tended to result in a huge loss of income and wealth, which would cause a sudden contraction of demand and production.

3. The "Crowd-Out" Effect of the Private Sectors

The implementation of the "Socialist Plan" by the Chavez's government had brought about a major change to the Venezuelan economic system and structure. The state had controlled all the production enterprises in the strategic sectors, which had produced a significant "crowd-out" effect for the private sectors. During the global financial and economic crisis, it was difficult for the private economy to make up for the effect of external instability and financial instability and to pry the economy. More importantly, the "crowd-out" of the private investment would have a serious impact on the capital accumulation and the long-term production potential.

From 2000 to 2007, about 3,000 private manufacturing companies had been reduced in the economic structure of Venezuela, including a significant portion of the manufacturing sector.[22] In the 1990s, the proportion of Venezuela's manufacturing output once reached 23% in the full value, but at present it has fallen down to nearly 11%. The latest research of the Inter American Development Bank about the Venezuelan productivity trend shows that in the process of de-industrialization, the productivity of Venezuela had showed a downward trend — the resources were turning from the higher productivity sectors to the lower productivity sectors.[23] In recent years, under the drive of the "socialist economy" (cooperatives and social production enterprises), the service economy has developed rapidly, but the problem is that the service economy has a low technological content, shorter production chain, lack of driving ability and no economic scale. Therefore, in this sense, the ownership incentive and the productive development policy have not formed a more productive economy. In addition, the policy measures of nationalization and expropriation since 2005 have led to over regulation, the foreign exchange restriction, the insufficient labor mobility, the system vulnerability and the environment lacking legal protection, seriously deteriorating the investment environment in Venezuela.[24] According

[22]L. Vera, "Cambio Estructural, Desindustrializacion y Perdidas de Productividad: Alguna Evidencia Preliminar para Venezuela" *Cuadernos del Cendes*, V. 26 No. 71, 2009.

[23]Jose Manuel Puente, Pavel Gomez, L. Vera, "The Political Economy of Productivity: The Case of Venezuela", proyecto de investigacion "The Political Economy of Productivity: Actors, Arenas and Policymaking", Banco Interamericano de Desarrollo (BID), Washington D.C., 2009.

[24]The *2010 Global Business Report* released by the World Bank shows that in the investigation of the trade and investment environment of 183 countries in the world, Venezuela ranked No. 177, becoming one of the Latin-American countries with the most unfavorable environment for investment. In the ranking of

to the report of the international balance of payments released by the Venezuelan Central Bank, the Venezuelan flight capital was $23.8 billion in 2009, and it was $19.3 billion in 2010. Since the implementation of the foreign exchange control in 2003, the accumulative total flight capital already amounted to $111.5 billion, accounting for 59% of Venezuela's GDP in 2010, equivalent to four times of its foreign exchange reserve.

III. The Economic Situation of 2011–2012

In 2011, Venezuela finally had the resumption of growth from the serious economic recession of 2009–2010, with 4% of GDP growth, mainly resulting from the growth of the non-oil sectors (4.3% of the growth of the non-oil sectors, but only 0.6% of the growth of the oil sector), and in the non-oil sectors, the growth of trade of goods and services and public services (i.e., investment in the health and educational departments) were the fastest (trade of goods and services grew 6.6%, the public service sector 5.3%, the manufacturing sector 3.5%, the construction sector 3.4%, the finance and insurance sector 11.2%, the water and electricity sector 5.5%, and the real estate service sector 3.5%).

In recent years, Venezuela's economic growth (see Table 7.14) is highly dependent on the government consumption; the large fiscal expenditure has expanded its domestic demand (but also leading to a huge budget deficit and debt). In 2011, the growth of the fixed asset investment was stalled, but the government consumption increased 4.7% and the domestic demand grew 8.9%. Its exports continued to grow, but its imports grew faster than exports, reflecting the structural imbalance of the Venezuelan economy, dragging down the economic growth.

In 2011, the current account accumulated the surplus of $27.205 billion, with $7.5 billion in the first quarter and $8 billion in the second quarter, and it maintained $7.5 billion in the third quarter

the annual global economic freedom index of 2010, Venezuela ranked No. 174 in 179 economies around the world, being the last of the Latin-American countries. http://www.doingbusiness.org/data/exploreeconomies/Venezuela.

Table 7.14 The Economic Growth of Venezuela (%)

	2009	2010	1st–3rd Quarter of 2011
GDP	−3.3	−1.5	4.2
Government Consumption	2.3	2.6	4.7
Private Consumption	−3.2	−1.9	4.2
Total Fixed Investment	−8.2	−6.3	0.4
Export of Goods and Services	−12.9	−12.9	6.7
Import of Goods and Services	−19.6	−2.9	19.7

Source: Economist Intelligence Unit, *Country Report: Venezuela*, January 2012.

(equal to 2.2% of GDP), an increase of three times over the previous year. This was mainly due to the rapid growth of exports in the third quarter of 2011, reaching $23.8 billion, an increase of 53.5% over the previous year. According to the data from the Venezuelan Central Bank, in the third quarter of 2011, the Venezuelan average oil price and exports rose by 47.8% and 5%, respectively. The non-oil exports grew by 24.6% year on year, of which the private non-oil exports increased by 31% and the public non-oil exports increased by 17.5%. The import of goods grew by 20.1% year on year. Due to the recovery of its domestic economic growth, the imports of the public and private sectors increased by 22.2% and 19.2%, respectively.

The capital account deficit of nearly $7.5 billion in the third quarter of 2011 led to the decline of $658 million in its foreign exchange reserve. Its FDI had a substantial increase in the second quarter of 2011, but in the next third quarter the net direct investment had a substantial reduction, indicating that the trend of sustained capital outflows had not been reversed. In 2011, the cumulative deficit of the capital account reached $27.619 billion.

As 2012 was the year of election in Venezuela, how the economic situation (see Table 7.15) went had a direct impact on whether President Chavez would be re-elected. Now with a look back, in 2012 the three major highlights of the Venezuelan economy played a role in Chavez's successful re-election. In other words, these highlights were precisely the pursuit of the government in the election year. First, the

Table 7.15 Account of the International Balance of Payments ($ Million)

	2010		2011			
	3rd Quarter	4th Quarter	1st Quarter	2nd Quarter	3rd Quarter	Growth Rate (%)
Current Account	1,962	3,019	7,535	8,008	7,464	280.4
Export of Goods	15,520	17,667	20,797	25,109	23,812	53.4
Import of Goods	9,939	11,196	8,883	12,444	11,934	20.1
Trade of Services	−2,300	−2,009	−2,394	−2,755	−2,714	18.0
Capital Account	−2,098	−3,071	−10,244	−6,045	−7,446	254.9
Net Direct Investment	−745	−129	−941	3,920	750	200.7
Net Securities Investment	618	2,027	2,720	532	−2,402	−488.7
Balance of International Payments Account	−221	−712	−3,743	1,340	−658	197.7

Source: Economist Intelligence Unit, *Country Report: Venezuela*, January 2012.

economic growth rate reached 5.3% and the per capita GDP growth rate was 3.7%. This growth rate not only had maintained the recovery momentum appeared in the previous year, but also was a higher level in the entire region of Latin America. Second, the inflation rate had dropped significantly, down from 29% in the previous year to 18.5%. Third, the wages of employees increased 29.7%, of which the wages of the private sectors increased by 27.2%, and the public sectors increased by 35.2%. The government raised the minimum wage twice in May and September, each time with an increase of 15%. The combination of the inflation rate falling by more than 10% and the wages increasing by nearly 30% had made the people get a strong sense of better economic situation.

However, there are some problems behind the above highlights. The fiscal policy issue was the highlight. If you look at the official statistics, in 2012 the central government's primary fiscal deficit was 1.3% of GDP, which was a very normal situation. But the problem is that the Venezuelan government's financial spending was largely at random, not subjected to budget constraints. The ECLAC had cited two prominent examples in its report of the economic situation of Venezuela in 2012. First, when Venezuela was preparing its yearly budget, the oil revenue was calculated according to the price of $50 a barrel, but the actual price was $104.7, and therefore, the government could have a lot of "extra budgetary" income to use. Second, the government had used some of the funds that were not strictly regulated for the public expenditure. The typical one was the National Development Fund (FONDEN). Its funding came from the money paid by the state oil company and the Central Bank's so-called additional reserve. This situation showed that the financial risks that Venezuela was facing were increasing.

The country's foreign exchange reserve was reduced year by year, from $43.12 billion at the end of 2008 to $25.86 billion at the end of 2012. The essence was the issue of the industrial structure and the supply of the domestic market. For example, in the first nine months of 2012, the value of the oil export increased by only 3.9% over the previous year, while the non-oil export fell by 20.4%. At the same time, the supply gap of many domestic markets was increasing, becoming an important factor to promote the rise of the consumer price. The economic growth in 2012 depended mainly on the construction industry (concentrating on the huge residential construction plan promoted by the government), business and finance, but the two major sectors of oil and manufacturing, respectively grew by only 1.4% and 1.2%. In 2012, for example, the fuel oil import grew by 88.5% year on year, mainly due to the insufficient refining capacity. The import of various daily commodities had become the basic measure for the government to reduce the inflation in 2012; therefore, the Foreign Exchange Administration and the Foreign Currency Exchange were required to reduce the foreign exchange. It could be expected that if Venezuela did not pay close attention to its industrial restructuring, its economic outlook would not be optimistic.

Another issue worthy of concern was the sharp decline of FDI. During the four years from 2009 to 2012, except for 2011, the FDI in the remaining three years was negative. According to the statistics of the Organization of Petroleum Exporting Countries, in the first three quarters of 2012, the crude oil production of Venezuela over the same period decreased by 7% than the previous year, mainly due to the decline of the investment in the oil production.

According to some international public opinions, if the Venezuelan radical nationalization policy was not changed or given up, it would be difficult to change the negative attitude of foreign investors.

Section 4 Review and Prospect of the Sino-Venezuelan Economic and Trade Cooperation

On March 5, 2013, Venezuela officially announced the death of President Chavez, who had been in power for 14 years, suffering from cancer for two years. On April 14, the first presidential election was held in Venezuela after the death of Chavez. With Chavez's political legacy and influence, Maduro, Chavez's handpicked successor, the ruling United Socialist Party presidential candidate won the election, and took the oath on April 19, officially opening the "Post-Chavez Era" of Venezuela. However, from the vote-counting result of the National Electoral Commission, Maduro defeated his main rival — opposition coalition candidate — Henrique Capriles with a marginal victory of 50.8%. This indicated that the future of Maduro's governing road would face a severe challenge. While in the short term the controversy surrounding the vote would make the political stability a pressing task, in the medium term it was still the key to the consolidation of the public opinion for the new government to boost the economy and improve people's livelihood.

I. The Economic Risk of the "Post-Chavez Era"

According to the 2012 Economic Survey of the ECLAC, the Venezuelan economy grew 5.3% in 2012. This was a high point of economic rebound after the recessions of 3.2% and 1.5% in 2009 and in 2010, respectively and the recovery growth of 4.2% in 2011, which was the same rate as in the international financial crisis in 2008 (5.3%). The high growth in the short term was mainly due to the promotion of the stimulating policies such as the high international crude oil price and the domestic large-scale housing projects. As the economy rebounded, the unemployment rate fell from 8.3% in 2011 to 8% in 2012, and the per capita disposable income increased from $8,050 in 2010 to $10,471 in 2011. All these had become the beneficial factors for the private consumption. However, the higher economic growth in the short-term could not conceal the economic risks in the medium-term.

First, the economy had the risk of stagnation. The short-term effect of stimulus gradually subsided in 2013, coupled with the global economic downturn causing crude oil prices unable to rise sharply again, the economic growth would fall down after the general election. According to the forecast of the British Economist Intelligence Unit (EIU) about Venezuela from 2013 to 2017, its economic growth momentum would be weakened, the growth rate would be less than 3.2%, and the unemployment rate and inflation rate would remain at the high level of around 9% and 25%, respectively. From the perspective of demand, the high inflation, weak employment and financial crunch would affect the household incomes and thereby affect the private consumption. Threatened by nationalization, rising capital flight, deterioration of infrastructure and the fragile financial situation, the investment in fixed assets would also decline. From the perspective of supply, the growth of industrial production would slow down and the agricultural growth would even be slower due to the government intervention and price setting. The oil sector, especially the National Oil Company (PDVSA) would face pressure from the two aspects of the operation and management and the unstable tax system.

Second, the devaluation of the currency was expected to push inflation. In January 2011, Venezuela revoked the dual track exchange rate that had been implemented nearly a year; the new single exchange rate was $1 to 4.3 bolivars. The implementation of the single currency meant that the original official exchange rate of $1 in exchange of 2.6 bolivars that was relevant to the "important imports" of the people's livelihood was adjusted to $1 for 4.3 bolivars, which was actually divided into two steps to realize the devaluation. In February 2013, the government again announced the devaluation of 32% for the bolivar-dollar exchange rate, i.e., to $1:6.3 bolivars, which was the fifth devaluation of the currency in 10 years. On the one hand, the continued overvalued official exchange rate would exacerbate the vicious circle of administrative intervention and market expectations; on the other hand, the adjusted exchange rate would push up the inflation rate. EIU expected that by the end of 2017 the official exchange rate would depreciate to $1:12 bolivars and the inflation rate would reach 23.6%.

Third, the serious fiscal deficit limited the space of the future counter-cyclical policy. Due to the large public spending, the government's fiscal deficit was severe, especially in every election year the fiscal stimulus factors led to huge increases in spending. In 2012 the budget deficit of the Venezuelan Central Government reached 3.8% of its GDP, exceeding the 3% of the international "safety warning line". The deep-seated problems such as large-scale social welfare policies and the overvalued exchange rate would keep the government budget in the state of deficit. Under this situation, the financial operating space was limited. Once subjected to external shocks, the government could not implement large-scale anti-cyclical policies to deal with the crisis as it did in 2008–2009. In addition, from 2010 to 2012 the proportion of the central government's public debt in GDP had been more than 20% for three consecutive years.

Fourth, the current account had a surplus but the foreign debt risk was gradually increasing. The trade surplus and the current account surplus were highly correlated with the international oil price. When Chavez won the election in 1998, the international oil price was at the bottom; later the oil price soared, especially from 2003 to 2008 bringing a large number of export income and trade surplus to Venezuela. However, affected by the financial crisis, in 2008 and 2009 when the oil price fell from an average of $100 a barrel to an average of $62 a barrel, the current account surplus in its share of GDP dropped from 12% to 2.6%. Therefore, how to get rid of the influence of the fluctuation of oil price was the key to the adjustment of the economic structure. In recent years, the burden of external debt increased rapidly. According to the statistics of CEIC database, by September 2012, the total external debt was $109.2 billion, in which the public sectors and the private sectors accounted for 87.6% and 12.4%, respectively; the long-term debt and short-term debt accounted for 83.1% and 16.9%, respectively. In the short-term, the current account surplus and the "Oil for Loan" program with

China could protect the government's ability to repay the external debt, but in the long term the government would have the pressure to repay its debt.

In the medium term, the economic risk of Venezuela mainly comes from the structural imbalance and policy distortion. From 1999 to 2006, Chavez replaced the new liberal reform with the "Bolivar Peace and Democratic Revolution"; since 2007, Chavez began to explore the implementation of the "21st Century Socialism". In this process, the imbalance of economic structure and economic policy mistakes were the main factors that had restricted the sustainable economic growth.

First, the economic structure with a heavy dependence on oil was vulnerable to the external shocks. From the perspective of the industrial structure, the economic structure was simple and slow to upgrade. From 1998 to 2010 the proportion of agriculture was about 5%; the development of the service industry was seriously lagging behind — in 2010 accounting for only 42% of GDP. The industry was mainly based on the petroleum industry. Since Chavez came to power in 1999, Venezuela's GDP growth rate had been positively correlated with the changes in the price of the international crude oil (or the country's oil export), reflecting Venezuela's heavy dependence on oil and the weakness of its non-oil economy. For many years, Venezuela's oil export had been accounted for about 95% of its total export, occupying nearly 30% of its total GDP, and 50% of the government's revenue had come from oil. Therefore, the economic structure with this kind of heavy dependence on oil was vulnerable to the impact of external shocks. There were two outstanding aspects: first, the oil industry strikes directly affected the economic output. For example, the large-scale oil workers' strike (from December 2, 2002 to February 3, 2003) had made the oil production and export almost paralyzed, resulting in the economic downturn of 8.9% and 7.8% in 2002 and in 2003 respectively. Second, the drop of the international crude oil price had immediately created a tight financial situation, forcing the government to maintain a large-scale social spending through borrowing, resulting in a vicious cycle of rising budget deficit and public debt.

Second, the distorted economic policy had deepened the economic imbalance. The fiscal policy emphasized on social spending. Although the government might artificially increase the local currency revenues from "oil dollars" by devaluing the currency to deal with the government's daily and social spending, the fiscal revenue growth was limited due to the stagnant oil production and the low taxes resulted from the decline of the formal sector employment and the decline of the profit of the private companies. To be able to make up the financial gap, the domestic and foreign debt were accumulated through the issuance of treasury bonds and the PDVSA company debt, resulting in a vulnerable position of the public finance. Compared with the fiscal policy, the monetary policy had been in a subordinate position. Despite the Central Bank's independence guaranteed by the Constitution, the Central Bank under the government of President Hugo Chavez had to be driven by the government policy — it was forced to keep a low interest rate from the pressure of the government, weakening its ability to control inflation. The long-term overvalued exchange rate policy had led to the decline of the competitiveness of the non-petroleum industries and the high inflation.

Third, the gradual deterioration of the investment environment had led to the insufficient investment, restraining the growth potential. Take the oil industry for example. According to the disclosure of the OPEC annual bulletin in July 2011, Venezuela's oil reserves were 296.5 billion barrels (about 40.62 billion tons), about 32 billion barrels more than the oil reserves of Saudi Arabia (264.5 billion barrels), becoming the country with the largest oil reserve in the world. However, Venezuela had suffered an embarrassment of stagnant or declining oil production with the rising oil reserve. According to EIU forecast, from 2013 to 2017 the Venezuelan oil production would remain at a level of about 2.5 million barrels per day. This was mainly due to the weakening of the technological ability of PDVSA and the deterioration of the investment environment resulting from the government's continuous tightening of the "new nationalization" policy. In the ranking of national competitiveness and business environment by the top three agencies of Lausanne International Institute for Management Development, the World Economic Forum and the World Bank, Venezuela was ranked in the back. In addition, according to the statistics of ECLAC *Economic Survey of 2012*, in Venezuela, the net FDI changed from the net inflow of $4.875 billion in 2011 to the net outflow of $759 million in 2012. This trend was particularly "alien" in the background of steadily rising attraction of foreign investment in the whole Latin-American region. Therefore, how to improve the investment environment would be an important and urgent task for the governments in the future.

In summary, the single economic structure, rigid exchange rate, severe fiscal deficit, and the deterioration of the investment environment are the four difficult problems that the government needed to overcome; if not solved properly, they would threaten the sustainability of economic growth and thereby affect the political stability.

II. Review and Prospect of the Sino-Venezuelan Economic and Trade Cooperation

1. The Sino-Venezuelan Energy Cooperation

China's diversification strategy of oil import sources has formed a perfect match with Venezuela's diversification strategy of oil export markets: on the one hand, the demand for oil is an important factor to push China to strengthen its economic and trade cooperation with Venezuela. The vigorous development of China's economy needs to expand its oil imports, and, as the world's second largest oil importer, China seeks to achieve diversification of energy supplies (to reduce its dependence on oil supplies from the Middle East). On the other hand, Venezuela hopes to realize diversification of its export markets to get rid of the passive situation of its current over-reliance on the US market for oil export. Therefore, from this economic complementarity, the cooperation of the two countries in the field of energy and the long-term development of trade are in line with the interests of both sides.

Since Chavez came to power, the two countries had signed a series of energy cooperation agreements. Especially after the signing of the "Memorandum of Understanding on a 10-Year (2001–2011) Energy Cooperation between the National Planning and

Development Committee of the People's Republic of China and the Ministry of Energy and Mineral Resources of the Bolivarian Republic of Venezuela" in May 2001, China's import volume of crude oil from Venezuela began to grow rapidly. From 2007 to 2008, the two countries had established the Sino-Venezuelan Mutual Fund (*Fondo Conjunto Chino Venezolano* (FCCV)), which had further deepened the bilateral economic cooperation. The original fund was $6 billion, of which the China National Development Bank injected the capital of $4 billion in the form of loans and the Venezuelan Social Development Bank (Bandes) injected $2 billion in the form of investment. The fund had been mainly used for the construction of Venezuela's railways, communications and shipyards; PDVSA provided the repayment guarantee through the supply of crude oil to PetroChina. Venezuela had been greatly impacted by the global economic crisis in 2008, facing the two major pressures of the decline of oil export revenues and the shortage of investment funds. In order to alleviate the impact on Venezuela, in 2009 China and Venezuela signed a "Loan for Oil" agreement of $4 billion, enabling the Sino-Venezuelan common fund to be extended to $12 billion, providing financing mainly for Venezuela's energy, mining, agriculture, housing and other development projects. In the new added $6 billion, the Venezuelan Social Development Bank injected $2 billion and the China Development Bank injected $4 billion. Venezuela directly repaid the loans from China Development Bank through increasing its trade of oil exports to China. By 2011, the fund had invested up to $32 billion in Venezuela's social development projects. In 2011, China added $4 billion to the mutual fund; the total amount of the fund reached $16 billion. This additional injection was intended to help increase the oil production in Venezuela, and also to expand the oil markets of Venezuela. Venezuela had committed to export the majority of its produced crude oil to China in the next three years, and China would pay the cash of $8 billion in advance.

At present, Venezuela has become China's fourth largest oil supplier. From 2013 to 2015, PDVSA will increase its export of crude oil to China, from the current 460 thousand barrels per day to 1 million barrels per day. During the six years from 2006 to 2011, Venezuela's crude oil exports to China had increased three times, namely from 150 thousand barrels per day to 460 thousand barrels per day, while its export to the United States fell from 1.5 million barrels per day in 1999 to 760 thousand barrels per day in 2011.[25]

The Sino-Venezuelan energy cooperation is not simply in oil supply; it also pays more attention to establishing and strengthening the cooperation in the production chain: establishing joint ventures, exploring oil in the Orinoco Oil Belt, building giant tankers, constructing joint oil refineries in their respective territories,[26] China transferring technology to Venezuela and offering personnel training, and establishing joint-venture ocean-shipping companies to transport the crude oil to Asian markets (mainly China).

The Sino-Venezuelan common fund is not a simple pool of capitals, but also a cooperative mechanism, promoting the comprehensive cooperation between the two countries in many areas centering on the energy field. For example, in the field of agriculture, China participated in the construction project of the Venezuelan national irrigation system, and Chinese petroleum enterprises cooperated with PDVSA agricultural branch to plan Venezuela's agriculture development project. In the field of communications, China's enterprises

---

[25] http://ve.mofcom.gov.cn/aarticle/jmxw/201202/20120207982621.html.

[26] Chinese petroleum enterprises have advanced refining technology that can refine and process oil for Venezuela, but need to upgrade the refinery facilities and construct specialized refineries. In December 2009, China's National Development and Reform Commission approved the construction of the large-scale refinery project in Huilai County, Guangdong Province by China National Petroleum Corporation (CNPC) and Venezuela's PDVSA. The project has the annual processing capacity of crude oil of 8 million tons with the source supply of crude oil from Venezuela; the investment of the project is close to $10 billion. In 2012, CNPC submitted to the government the project of constructing a large-scale refinery in Jieyang, Guangdong Province, with an annual processing capacity of 20 million tons. CNPC was to hold more than 60% of the shares of the refinery and the remaining shares would be held by PDVSA. The project was scheduled to start construction in 2010 and to be managed to put into operation within three years. The first phase of the project reached 20 million tons per year, with the investment of 585 million RMB; the second phase of the project would add the production capacity of 20 million tons per year and the project of millions of tons of ethylene. All of the crude oils came from Venezuela.

helped Venezuela to build optical fiber networks and produce mobile phones. In the field of manufacturing, China helped Venezuela to produce computers and oil rigs and to expand the shipyards. In the astronautic field, the two countries had completed the cooperation of the "Venezuela Satellite One" project. In the field of infrastructure, China helped Venezuela to build and update its national railway network and implement its national residential program. To sum up, the Sino-Venezuelan economic cooperation has not only enhanced the degree of China's oil security protection, but also opened up a new market for China's technology and products, and the common fund is the financial booster for the economic cooperation between the two countries.

2. The Bilateral Trade

In recent years, the bilateral trade between China and Venezuela has grown rapidly: China has become the second largest trading partner of Venezuela (Venezuela's third largest export market and third largest import source country), and Venezuela is China's fifth largest trade partner in Latin America. In 2009 the total of the Sino-Venezuelan trade was $7.2 billion, among which China's export was $2.8 billion and the import $4.4 billion; in 2010 the total bilateral trade volume reached $10.4 billion, among which China's export was $3.6 billion and import $6.7 billion, growing respectively 46%, 29%, and 42% compared with 2009 (see Table 7.16). From the

Table 7.16 The Sino-Venezuelan Bilateral Trade and Investment ($10,000)

Year	Total Import and Export	Total Export	Total Import	Venezuela's Investment to China	China's Investment to Venezuela
2007	585,681	283,286	302,395	209	—
2008	993,304	336,598	656,706	237	—
2009	719,386	281,172	438,214	2,437	27,200
2010	1,036,147	364,859	671,288	358	—

Source: China National Bureau of Statistics: *China Statistical Yearbook* in 2009, 2010, 2011, China Statistics Press.

perspective of commodity structure, the Chinese export commodities to Venezuela were mainly various kinds of industrial machinery and equipment, textile products, household appliances, computer accessories, clothing, luggage, toys, etc.; China's imports of goods from Venezuela were mainly oil (crude oil and fuel oil) and mineral products (iron ore and its products, scrap aluminum, alumina, etc.).

3. The Two-way Investment

According to the data of the Chinese Ministry of Commerce, by the end of 2009, China's investment in Venezuela was $272 million, mainly concentrated in the oil field. By the end of 2009, Venezuela had invested totally 88 projects in China, with the actual investment of $24.37 million. There were more than 30 Chinese companies in Venezuela engaged in the economic and trade cooperation, including PetroChina, the Sinopec, the National Development Bank, China Railway, Huawei, ZTE, Shanghai Bell, CAMC, CWE, CATIC, CLP, NUCTECH, Inspur Group, etc. The economic and trade cooperation projects in Venezuela were mainly concentrated in the fields of petroleum, minerals, finance, telecommunications, housing, infrastructure, agriculture, assembly industry and high-tech products.

4. Engineering Contracting

According to the data of China's Ministry of Commerce, in 2009 Chinese companies signed 58 new project contracts and the labor service cooperation contracts in Venezuela, with the contract amount of $9.645 billion, of which the amount of project contracts was $7.845 billion, and the amount of the labor cooperation contracts was $1.8 billion. The turnover completed in 2009 was $929 million, including the project contracting turnover of $929 million and the labor cooperation turnover of $80 thousand. At the end of that year there were 1,373 Chinese workers in Venezuela. The newly signed major projects included the Tinaco — Anako Railway to be built by the China Railway Group Limited, the irrigation project to be constructed by CAMC, and the social housing projects contracted by CITIC International Contract Engineering Limited. In July 2009, the China Railway Group won the general contracting contract of

Table 7.17 The Completed Turnover of the Sino-Venezuelan Economic Cooperation ($10,000)

Year	Total	Contracted Projects	Labor Service	Design Consultation
2007	67,220	67,022	135	63
2008	77,675	77,418	50	207
2009	92,855	92,847	8	—
2010	347,970	347,961	9	—

Source: China National Bureau of Statistics: *China Statistical Yearbook* in 2009, 2010, 2011, China Statistics Press.

the design and construction of the Tinaco — Anaco Railway from the Venezuelan State Railway Bureau, amounting to $7.5 billion. The turnover completed in 2010 was $3.4797 billion, of which the turnover of the contracted project was $3.47961 billion and the turnover of labor cooperation was $90 thousand (see Table 7.17). In March 2010, China Hydropower Group and PDVSA signed the total contract of EPC — an emergency power plant project, constructing an oil-gas power station with the installed capacity of 900 MW, the contract price reaching about $1.35 billion.

5. The Prospect of the Sino-Venezuelan Economic and Trade Cooperation

Maduro had made the commitment to strictly enforce the national development plan formulated by Chavez during his lifetime. Therefore, after he became the president, the domestic and foreign policies of Chavez's period could continue. However, the election result showed that the Opposition Party had almost the same power with the ruling party. It could be predicted that from the perspective of the stable political situation, in the aspects of amending the relevant laws and regulations, the reform of government agencies, and the adjustment of the economic and social policies, the Maduro Administration might make some concessions to the Opposition. Even so, the Sino-Venezuelan relationship would not be affected, continuing to develop steadily.

Since Chavez took office in February 1999, the relationship between Venezuela and China had developed rapidly. Chavez had visited China six times, becoming the Latin-American leader who had visited China the most frequently during presidency. During the reign of Chavez, the two countries had signed a total of 430 agreements and more than 200 cooperative projects. It should be acknowledged that the complementarity of the economic structure of the two countries had determined the bilateral win–win cooperation mode and potential. The Maduro Administration had provided a new opportunity to deepen the bilateral economic and trade relations.

However, the risks at the enterprise level still exist. (1) The policy risk: The continuity, coordination and transparency of the formulation of policies are not strong, which may increase the cost of investment for China's enterprises in Venezuela. (2) The foreign exchange risk: Venezuela has a strict control over its foreign exchange and practices a compulsory settlement on the dollar income. Except the import of daily necessities such as food and medicines, the foreign exchange purchasing of other imported commodities has high requirements, cumbersome procedures, and long approval time; it is different to collect export exchange earnings and operating profit remittance in Venezuela. (3) The logistics risk: The transportation of crude oil from Venezuela to China depends entirely on the ocean shipping; the Panama Canal is still a bottleneck — 300,000-ton supertankers have to bypass the Cape Horn or the Cape of Good Hope because they cannot pass through the canal; the transport cost is high because the time for one-way transportation is up to 45 days. Venezuela wants to build an oil pipeline to the Pacific port of Colombia, for it is convenient to transport oil to China. However, in recent years the pipeline cannot be built in a short period for use because the relationship between Venezuela and Colombia has been tense. (4) The labor risk: In Venezuela, the labor unions are strong, the labor quality is low, the welfare benefits are high, and the dismissals are difficult, increasing the investment costs and risks of the enterprises. (5) The administrative risk: the administrative efficiency is low and the procedure for examination and approval is complex.

Chapter 8

Study on the Economic Openness of the Latin-American Countries

Chai Yu and Li Shenggang

Section 1 Connotation and Purpose of the Study on "Openness"

The economic openness is one of the basic features of economic modernization. In different times and under different conditions, for the need of domestic politics, even those countries with higher degree of economic development will adopt the measures of trade protectionism, but the general trend of international economic openness cannot be ignored. In the 1960s and 1970s, the economies such as South Korea and Japan could take pains to protect their domestic markets, while vigorously exploring the international market with very extreme export-oriented strategies, but the current developing countries are facing a completely different international economic environment, and will never be able to get similar development opportunities. The basic mechanisms of the international economic order, such as the General Agreement on Tariffs and Trade (GATT) and the World Trade Organization (WTO), have further promoted the global trade liberalization through the gradual expansion of the scope and extent of the constraints. The result of a departure from this order or trend is to be unable to gain benefit from the markets of the opening countries.

With the development of trade liberalization and the development of international financial market, the large-scale flow of capital between the nations has become an obvious characteristic of the world economy since the 1980s, resulting in a significant impact on developed and developing countries, especially emerging market countries. Like trade openness, financial openness also has become an important content of the process of the integration of the global economy. Generally speaking, financial openness refers to the openness of a country's financial market to the whole world, with its financial business across national borders and gradually integrated into the global financial markets. In this process the country's financial activities have been expanded from inside the country to foreign countries. Financial openness is reflected mainly in two aspects: one is to allow foreign financial institutions to enter the domestic market to be engaged in financial activities; the other is the participation of domestic financial institutions in the financial activities of foreign markets. At present, the development of trade liberalization and financial globalization has greatly promoted the financial openness.[1]

On the whole, the level of economic openness of the Latin-American countries is relatively high among the developing countries. Historically, Latin America used to be a relatively open economic area, incorporated into the world system of capitalism much earlier than Asia and Africa. Therefore, the development of its regional trade and financial system pattern had been deeply impacted by Europe and the United States. From the perspective of the system model of the Central Bank, the organization of commercial banks and the development process of financial capital markets, the Latin-American countries have similarities in many aspects with the developed countries in Europe and America. However, the Latin-American countries have formed many particular system models in the process of their own development, such as the large proportion of government capital in financial industry, the important position of policy-making financial institutions in the process of financing, having

[1]Mao Minyang, Du Yulan, *Study of Chinese Financial Openness*, *Jiangsu Business*, No. 9, 2007.

a significant impact on the economic development of the country itself.[2]

Like many other developing countries, most countries in Latin America have also experienced a strategic shift from the import substitution to the export orientation. From the preliminary economic reform starting in the mid-1970s of the 20th century to the further expanded and deepened reforms in the 1990s, the Latin-American countries had firmly taken the export-oriented development strategy, implementing the reform of trade, investment and financial liberalization.[3] In terms of trade, the Latin-American countries supported the "open regionalism", implementing the unilateral reduction of tariffs and non-tariff barriers. The main content of the reform of the financial system included relaxing the control of interest rates and canceling the control of the establishment of financial institutions, and so on. The main purpose was to cancel the restrictions on capital flows and to encourage securities and Foreign Direct Investment (FDI) to enter the domestic market. During this period, the Latin-American countries had suffered their own debt crises and the global economic turmoil. Until after 2003–2004, the economy began to have a steady growth trend. Then, after years of implementation of the export-oriented strategy, to what extent has the current economic openness of the Latin-American countries reached? This is the problem that we are confused about.

For developing countries, the study of trade and financial openness is, first of all, related to the problem of economic growth. The *World Development Report* in 1987 by the World Bank had classified four kinds of trade policies of the developing countries, pointing out that developing countries had rich labor resources, needing to carry on the specialized production and export labor-intensive products so as to achieve growth. The economies such as South Korea, Singapore, and Hong Kong China have succeeded in practicing this development

---

[2]Chi Yuanji, "Review of *Latin American Finance* — A Blank-filling Book!", *World Economy*, No. 10, 1997.

[3]SU Zhenxing, *Study of the Process of the Modernization of Latin-American Countries*, Social Sciences Literature Press, 2006.

path, becoming typical cases of trade openness to promote economic growth. New classical economists, such as Ram, Kavoussi, Bhagwati, Krueger, Balasa, M. Michaely, W. Tyler, and G. Feder, have also proved from the theoretical model that through the mechanisms, such as the acceleration of the rate of capital accumulation, the improvement of the level of specialization, the scaled economy and the acceleration of technological progress, the export-oriented strategy has promoted the rapid growth of the economy of the developing countries.[4]

At the same time, the relationship between the financial deepening and the macroeconomic volatility is also a subject of academic research. The financial opening of developing countries can really have some positive effect on the economic development, such as reducing the cost of capital and promoting the optimal allocation of the resources, but the adverse effects are unavoidable, such as reducing the effectiveness of domestic policy, causing domestic financial instability and easily leading to capital outflows. Especially since the 1990s, the international financial crisis occurred frequently, most of which have occurred in the emerging market countries and regions such as Latin America and East Asia, with increasing damage and contagion, and some of them even have politically, economically and socially evolved into global comprehensive crises. Although there are causes such as the imperfect financial systems of emerging market countries leading to their poor ability to withstand the crises compared with the developed countries, the degree of their financial openness is closely related to the outbreak and the spreading of

---

[4]Sun Yanlin, *Empirical Analysis of China's Export and Economic Growth, International Trade Issues*, V. 2, 2000; Hati Ram, "Export and Economic Growth: Some Additional Evidence", *Economic Development and Culture Change,* V. 33, No. 2, 1985; Behzad Yaghmaian and Reza Ghovashi, "Export Performance and Empirical Analysis", *The American Economist,* V. 39, No. 2, 1995; M. Michaely, "Exports and Growth: An Empirical Investigation", *Journal of Development Economics,* V. 4, 1977, pp. 49–53; W. Tyler, *Growth and Export Expansion in Developing Countries, Some Empirical Evidence,* http://desafios.ipea.gov.br/pub/td/1980/td_0020.pdf, 1980; Gershon Feder, "On Exports and Economic Growth", *Journal of Development Economics,* V. 12, No. 1–2, 1983 February–April, pp. 59–73.

the crises.[5] It remains to be studied whether the relationship between the economic openness and the growth rate and the growth stability has any new features in Latin America.

Secondly, the degree of economic openness involves the core of the industrial and independent economic development of developing countries. On the basis of the study of the degree of economic openness, the problems to be solved in theory and in practice include through what kind of mechanism trade and financial openness can promote the independent development of industry and economy and what degree of trade and financial openness is appropriate for helping and not damaging the growth of the local industry and the establishment of the industrial system.

Thirdly, the trade and financial openness is closely related to the role of developing countries in the region and in the international economy. The high degree of openness of the economy and the close integration with the international economy have a high dependence on the international economic order, the high requirement of suitability for the rules of the international economy, and the high enthusiasm for promoting the perfection of the economic order, which influences the strategic arrangements of the international trade, the financial system and the regional economy. This chapter attempts to reveal the reality of the Latin-American economic openness by empirical methods in order to deepen the understanding of the characteristics and the status and the role of the Latin-American economy in the international economic pattern and the significance of the Sino-Latin American relations.

Therefore, the main purpose of this study is to do a more adequate and basic empirical research. Currently it does not discuss the norms (namely the judgment of the effect of the merits; the problem of what kind of status, strategy, policy and system is better); it only digs deeply the basic facts, clarifying the question of "what it is", providing a basis for future normative researches.

---

[5]The study of McKinnon (1973) showed the risk of increasing currency crisis for a premature opening of the capital account; Eichengreen and Bordo (1999) and Stiglitz (2000) believed that the countries with underdeveloped capital markets should adopt appropriate means to limit cross-border capital flows.

The second section of this chapter is a summary of the methods used in the analysis of trade openness and study the degree of the economic openness of the Latin-American countries from the perspective of the measurement of trade, giving the facts from the perspective of the comparison of Asian countries. The third section is the study of the degree of the financial openness of the Latin-American countries with two methods, with the comparison of the Asian emerging market countries to better reveal the current level of the financial openness of Latin America. The fourth section is a brief discussion of the empirical results, pointing out the direction of the future research.

Section 2 Study on the Trade Openness of the Latin-American Countries

I. Review of the Research on Trade Openness and the Methods Adopted

The main concern of the study of trade openness is about the entry of a country into the international market and the way, the degree and the price of the market access of the country. The trade openness refers to the level of economic internationalization of a country. The earlier literature of the study of economic openness was based on the trade dependence degree index to see if a country's trade was open to the outside world or not and on multinational comparative studies (such as Balassa, 1982); here it does not consider the effect of the differences of the countries and the domestic policies.

At present, from the domestic and foreign perspective, this study exists basically as the basic aspect of other in-depth analyses. From the perspective of research methods, there are mainly two ways: one is to regard the deviation between the real trade volume and the forecasted or analog volume as the standard. Leamer (1988) earlier wrote a classic paper, in which he did not put his focus on the tariff, but used the nine elements of the H-O Model in order to measure the trade barriers. Through the study of the ratio of the estimated net trade flow and the trade intensity of 183 kinds of commodities of 53 countries under the three-digit Standard of International Trade

Classification (SITC), he used the deviation between the estimated value and the real value of the trade intensity ratio as the trade openness index. The greater the deviation, the greater the trade distortion, and the smaller the degree of openness. On the basis of Leamer, in order to answer the question whether the trade-open countries have faster national economic growth, Wolf (1993) regarded the deviation between the real trade volume and the non-distorted level as the trade-oriented index by focusing on the opening quality of the indicators and the ultimate variables of interests. In order to investigate the same problem, Dollars (1992) studied the data of 95 developing countries from 1976 to 1985. The method of this investigation was using just the same measure formula as the real exchange rate formula to calculate the currency against the dollar, constructing the Dollars Index, also known as the index for the real exchange rate distortion. Dollars added an auxiliary index — an index of the real exchange rate change, with the annual average rate change of the real exchange rate to reflect the stability of the real exchange rate of each country — the high rate change index indicated the low degree of openness of the economy and vice versa. In order to study whether the developing countries had been more marginalized because of the globalization, Patric (1998) improved the openness index with the consideration of the national differences and on this basis set up an economic integration model to have measured the degree of the deviation and the fusion of different countries with the world economy.

The second method is treating the trade policy as the main starting point of investigation. For example, in order to study whether in the developing countries there was the economic convergence toward the economy of developed countries to test the national growth momentum of "qualified" countries and "non-qualified" countries, Sachs and Warner (1995) used one of the two sets of measures — the degree of the integration of economy in international trade, namely the economic openness. They listed five conditions to decide the trade openness: if a country had one of the five conditions, the country would belong to the non-open trade countries; on the contrary, if a country had none of the five conditions, the country would belong to the trade-open countries. These five conditions were as follows. (1) The average tariff rate was more than 40%; (2) The rate of non-tariff measures of imports was more than 40%; (3) The country had the implementation of the planned economic system; (4) There was a state monopoly in the main foreign trade enterprises; (5) The exchange rate of the black market had more than 20% than the official exchange rate. The disadvantage of this method is that the countries of the same nature cannot be distinguished, for it is difficult to accurately grasp the systemic virtual variables and there is no foundation for the standard of 20%.

Similarly, the Traditional Foundation of the United States had studied the extent of trade distortions in accordance with the tariff level and other distortion indexes.[6] The "World Development Report" of 1987 also constructed an outward index on two time points and 41 economies at the same time.[7] As to others including the average tariffs, the average coverage of quantitative restrictions, (QRs) and the actual tariff rate (CTR, namely the rate of tariff revenue and import), some scholars thought that the price premium of the black market price against the official price was a better measure of distortion. On this basis, Anderson and Neary (1994) pointed out that since the tariff was the only indicator of trade protection, "the concept of average tariff equal to the welfare" should be constructed to measure the degree of openness. They had referred to the concept of Code (1966) about the average tariff. Edwards (1992, 1998) regarded the study of the degree of trade openness as an important part in the study of the relationship between trade openness, productivity and economic growth. On the basis of Leamer, he had a comprehensive study of the trade openness index through integrating the policy measures of trade distortion.

[6]Bryan T. Johnson and Thomas P. Sheehy, *Index of Economic Freedom,* Washington, The Heritage Foundation, 1996.
[7]Also see David Greenaway and Chong Hyun Nam, "Industrialisation and Macroeconomic Performance in Developing Countries under Alternative Trade Strategies", *Kyklos,* V. 41, No. 3, 1988, pp. 419–435.

Based mainly on the research method of Patric in 1998, this chapter tries to revise and test the model according to the specific needs of this research. The main reasons for taking the method are: first, the method starts from the basic model of trade openness, continuing the widely accepted inherent logic of the model construction; second, on the basis of the basic model, the method takes into consideration the objective factors such as the size of the country and the population and the level of economic development, enabling the horizontal comparative study of countries to be carried out on the basis of a unified framework and standard; third, some methods such as the Dollars method require proxy variables, but the validity and accuracy will be affected. The rare variables with a high degree of reliability are selected to avoid the use of unreliable variables. In this chapter the modification of the model is mainly reflected in the following aspects: first, the time sequence is from 1995 to 2009, which is a new supplement and continuation of the Patric research; second, all the indexes have been adjusted with the moving average of three years in order to reduce the specific exogenous shocks in the past few years, ironing the economic fluctuation; third, from the purpose of this chapter, seven influential developing countries of Latin America have been selected with seven developing countries of Asia as the control group for the sake of both the pertinence of the objects of the study and the universality of the significance of the study.

II. Study of the Trade Openness of the Latin-American Countries — From the Perspective of the Comparison with Asian Countries

1. The Model Construction and Data Processing

We start from the basic model of trade openness. Its expression is:

$$\mathrm{TI}_i = \frac{x_i + m_i}{\mathrm{GDP}_i}. \tag{1}$$

TI_i is the basic trade openness index of the country and GDP_i is the gross national product. x_i and m_i respectively represents the country's total import and export.

There is a significant impact on the trade openness in terms of the size of the country, the population and the level of economic development. If these factors are ignored, the countries will not have comparability. For example, in 2009 Brazil had a population of 190 million people and a total economic scale of $1594.4 billion, and Costa Rica had a population of 4.58 million and a total economic scale of $29.2 billion. A simple comparison of the trade openness of the two countries not only has no sense but may be misleading. According to the current empirical research, the trade openness of small countries will be greater than that of large countries, for small countries have greater welfare effect to implement the trade policy of opening to the outside world, but large countries have the possibility of domestic trade. Therefore, in our hypothesis, large countries have less significant reaction to international trade than small countries. Similarly, it may be more likely for a country with a higher level of economic development to have a lower level of the proportion of trade with gross domestic product (GDP).[8]

A more meaningful approach should be to compare the trade openness of economies with similar country scales, similar population sizes and similar levels of economic development. If a country has a higher level than the general level of similar countries, its trade openness is higher; if lower than the general level, its degree of openness is lower. In this way, it transforms the comparison between the countries into that between the general levels of similar countries, reducing the extent of the problem of incomparability caused by the factors such as the economic scale and population to the minimum level.

In order to achieve the purpose of this study, we first construct a new trade openness model (2), which takes into account the size of the country, the number of population and the level of economic development.

$$\begin{aligned}\ln(\mathrm{TI}_{i,t}) = \beta_0 &+ \beta_1 \ln(\mathrm{GDP}_{i,t}) + \beta_2 \ln(\mathrm{GDP}_{i,t})^2 + \beta_3 \ln(\mathrm{pop}_{i,t}) \\ &+ \beta_4 \ln(\mathrm{pop}_{i,t})^2 + \beta_5 \ln(\mathrm{GDP}_{i,t}/\mathrm{pop}_{i,t}) \\ &+ \beta_6 \ln(\mathrm{GDP}_{i,t}/\mathrm{pop}_{i,t})^2 + \varepsilon_{i,t}. \end{aligned} \tag{2}$$

[8]IMF, *World Economic Outlook,* May, 1997, p. 46.

Among them, $\mathrm{TI}_{i,t}$ is the trade openness index of the country of i in the year of t, and $\mathrm{GDP}_{i,t}$ is the GDP of the country of i in the year of t, showing the economic scale; $\mathrm{pop}_{i,t}$ is the population of the country of i in the year of t, and $\mathrm{GDP}_{i,t}/\mathrm{pop}_{i,t}$ is the per capita GDP, indicating the level of economic development.

The reason for choosing the natural logarithm is to convert the heteroscedastic series of the original sequence that does not meet the homogeneity of variance into the homoscedastic sequence to solve the problem of heteroscedasticity. The reason for using the quadratic variable is to consider the possible U-type relationship. The data used here all came from the UN Development Index Database. We have made several changes about the variables: First, a three-year moving average was given to all the variables to reduce the influence of economic fluctuations on the model results. Here the five-year moving average was not used for the consideration of the not-too-long time series of 15 years; If a five-year moving average had been used, there would have been actually effective data of just 11 years, which was not enough. Second, all the data were based on the dollar price in 2000 in order to reduce the impact of the price fluctuations. At the same time, the trade data included the trade of goods and services. Third, a special treatment has been made for the GDP. Our goal is to get the GDP priced with the purchase power parity (PPP) on the basis of the US dollar price in 2000. After several transformations of the original data, we have obtained the GDP. The purpose of getting the GDP priced with PPP was to calculate all the GDPs with the same dollar price, for otherwise, each country would have lost the unified basis for the data calculation. Although there are some questions about the value of China's PPP, China is just one of the 14 countries; in order to maintain the unity of the data, this chapter still uses the GDP with the valuation of PPP. If a large deviation occurs in the result which is not in conformity with the fact, adjustment will be done separately.

In terms of Equation (2), first, there is the problem of multicollinearity; second, the regression coefficient of the population is not significant. Therefore, we change Equation (2) into Equation (3) as follows:

$$\ln(\mathrm{TI}_{i,t}) = y_0 + y_1 \ln(\mathrm{GDP}_{i,t}) + y_2(\mathrm{GDP}_{i,t}/\mathrm{pop}_{i,t}) + \varepsilon_{i,t}. \quad (3)$$

On the basis of this formula, we used the Pooled Least Squares, making multiple regressions using the statistical analysis software EVIEW6.0, e.g., the regression with the natural logarithm of the single exogenous variables and the trade openness, the regression excluding the coefficients and other detected unsatisfied variables, the test of selected regression models with the Hausman method, and so on.[9] We found that the pooled regression model was better. The direction of the regression coefficient (positive sign and negative sign) was identical with the assumption of the model result and after the statistical T-test, the probability was very small but acceptable. Regretfully the goodness of fit was not very high. At the same time, the stability of the model was tested. It could be seen that after the level value of each variable and its first and second difference were tested, the test results rejected the original hypothesis of "existence of unit root" at the significance level of 1%, namely the variables of the time series were stationary processes.

On the basis of regression, we can get the regression coefficients of each economy and every variable and then complete Equation (3). Here, we have known the relevant degree of each economy and the trade openness, or in each economy the degree and direction of these exogenous variables affecting the endogenous variables, i.e., trade openness. Even so, it is still not known what the general level of trade openness is on a given level of GDP and per capita GDP. The goal is to find the trade openness that should be achieved at a given level.

Thus, the following equation is constructed to illustrate the general level of openness at a given level of GDP and per capita GDP.

$$\hat{\mathrm{TI}}_{i,t} = \exp[\log(\mathrm{TI}_{i,t}) - \varepsilon_{i,t}]. \quad (4)$$

[9]The process of using the unit root to test stability is deleted here and in the part of the financial openness.

The actual meaning of this equation is to calculate the simulated trade openness i.e., the "standard" to be reached at a given level or general openness, making use of the real trade openness (which is Equation (1)) of each economy and the regression residuals.

Then, the revised openness index is constructed:

$$\mathrm{TI}_{i,t}^{*} = \frac{\mathrm{TI}_{i,t}}{\hat{\mathrm{TI}}_{i,t}}. \tag{5}$$

This index shows the general state the economy with the same population, GDP and per capita GDP, i.e., the deviation of the opening degree to be reached at a given level. If the value is more than 1, the country is more open than the general level. If less than 1, it is closed more than the average.

At this point, we have completed the process of the construction and calculation of the whole model.

2. The Empirical Results

The empirical results are shown in the tables and figures in the appendixes. After considering the economic scale and the level of economic development, we have obtained the calculated trade openness index, which are basically in line with the general judgment about the degree of economic openness of the Latin-American and Asian countries.

(1) From the perspective of time sequence, each economy shows the track of the change of its trade openness index. These tracks are basically consistent with the path of the economic growth.

The change of the indexes shows that, except Mexico, the change trends of the trade openness index of the other major Latin-American countries are basically the same. After Mexico joined the NAFTA in 1994, its trade openness showed a basic trend of increasing year by year. After the rapid economic growth from 1996 to 2000, Mexico experienced the economic recession from 2001 to 2003. During the high growth period, its trade openness index increased year by year, but in the recession period, the index appeared stagnant. The index declined from 2002 to 2004 and before and after 2008, which were closely related to the changes of the US economic situation. Argentina has had a low trade openness index in the Latin-American countries, which is consistent with the direct observation. Between 1997 and 2009, the index was hovering between 0.2 and 0.6. From the beginning of 1998, the Argentine economy went into a sustained downturn with the impact of the financial crises in the Southeast Asia, Russia and other places, its high domestic and foreign debt, and the serious financial deficit. Subsequently, the debt repayment crisis had a chain reaction — a large number of withdrawals of foreign capital, the stagnant production and demand, and the continued deficit of foreign trade, leading to the serious economic and social crisis from 2001 to 2002. Till 2004, the trade openness had been declining, indicating an even greater drop in foreign trade compared with the decline in GDP during and after the serious crisis. Brazil's economic vitality had remained average and in 1999 there occurred a currency crisis. Its average annual growth rate of GDP was about 2% from 1995 to 2003. In this period its trade openness index also showed a slow decline. In about 2003 its trade openness reached its lowest level. According to the ECLAC data, in 2003 its GDP growth was 0.1%. The industry, services and household consumption had all declined. But in fact that year some signs of economic recovery emerged at the same time. Its foreign trade had achieved a breakthrough of growth, becoming the world's largest exporter of soybeans and beef, with a significant trade surplus.

From 2003 to 2004, with the recovery of the global economy, the rising prices of international agricultural commodities and energy products, and the growing demand from Asia, especially from China, from 2004 the Latin-American economic and trade development began to have a rising trend. Argentina's economic growth rate in 2004 reached more than 8%, restoring its trade openness index. Corresponding to the trade openness index, since 2003, under the leadership of the Lula Administration, Brazil's economy bottomed out, entering a new period of steady growth. This trend was consistent with the change of the trade openness index of other major Latin-American countries such as Mexico, Colombia, Chile, and Peru.

China's trajectory shows the steady growth of its trade openness after the 1990s, especially after China's accession to the WTO. The other Asian countries also had basically a steady rise. The situation in India was slightly different. Its index changes reflected an increasing trend of the Indian import and export year by year from 1995 to 2000, and the growth rate of GDP was obviously greater. But after entering the 21st century, with the rapid development of IT outsourcing business, the importance of trade was further improved and the trade openness also appeared to rise.

(2) From the perspective of the cross section, the overall level of trade openness of some Latin-American countries is lower than that of Asian countries.

Compared with the Latin-American countries, the out-oriented economic features of the Asian countries are more significant.

In the 1990s, the Latin-American countries had generally entered the stage of deepening economic reform.[10] Even so, the trade openness index of the Latin-American countries since 1995 was still generally lower than that of the Asian countries. In terms of the Latin-American countries, the countries with higher trade openness (i.e., more than 1) were Mexico, Chile, and Venezuela, but none of them had reached the index level above two. The trade openness of these countries had exceeded the general level of openness of those with the same size, population and economic development. Similarly, the index of Asian countries such as China, South Korea, Indonesia, Thailand, Malaysia, and Vietnam was more than two.

It is generally believed that the Latin-American countries have a higher degree of economic openness. Historically, many of the countries were well known for exporting agricultural and mineral products in the international market. At present in some countries the proportion of the foreign currency deposits in the total bank deposits are still high (e.g., by the end of 2009 in Bolivia and Peru they were 53% and 56%, and Ecuador, El Salvador and Panama were

[10]SU Zhenxing, Latin-American Economy in the 1990s: Growth and Instability, *Latin-American Studies*, No. 1, 2000.

fully dollarized).[11] The multi-national corporation also was an important factor in the economic growth of Latin America. Although the Latin-American countries had implemented the economic development model of import substitution for a long period, in recent years, with the advance of economic reform, most countries have turned to the export-oriented development path. Even so, the Latin-American countries still have lower trade openness than Asian countries as to the average level. This also shows that the Latin-American countries still need to pay greater efforts in participating in the competition in the international market.

(3) In Latin America, it has been proved that the degree of trade openness is negatively related to the scale of GDP and the per capita GDP is positively correlated with it.

Therefore, it can be said that in relatively large and poor economies, the trade openness is more likely to be lower. This is the general trend of understanding derived from the analysis of the 14 countries, but it does not exclude the existence of special cases. In Asia, China and Indonesia have a large population, large scale, and low per capita GDP, but their degrees of trade openness have exceeded the general level. This may indicate a deviation from the general situation under open conditions, especially under the influence of a strong policy for trade promotion.

Section 3 Study on the Financial Openness of the Latin-American Countries

I. Summary and Explanation of the Research Method of Financial Openness

As one part of the study of economic openness, the finance openness is an important basis for evaluating the breadth and depth of opening to the outside world of the financial industry (or financial market) of a country or a region, which is a complex quantitative indicator. The

[11] Jose M. Cartas, Dollarization Declines in Latin America, *Finance and Development*, March 2010, IMF.

construction of financial indicators of openness is a basic part of an in-depth study of financial openness. The selection of reasonable and accurate measure indicators can better strengthen the understanding of the real situation of the financial openness of a country, and also is the premise for the subsequent empirical analysis and normative research. In terms of the researches at home and abroad at present, there are mainly two kinds of perspectives: one is the measure based on nominal openness or legal rules (*de jure*) and the other is the measure based on the facts (*de facto*).[12] In the following some representative research results in the two perspectives will be selected to be analyzed and evaluated.

1. The Study of Nominal Openness in the Research of Financial Openness

The measure of the level of nominal openness or legal rules (*de jure*) means to measure the degree of the financial openness of a country mainly through the study of the related laws, regulations and policy documents for the regulation of financial opening, which reflects the attitude and intention of the government in the field of financial opening. Currently the study of nominal openness in the theoretical circle is carried out mainly from two aspects — a country's restrictions on the cross-border capital flows and the capital market openness of the country and the measure of the corresponding nominal openness is also studied from the two perspectives of the regulation of capital account and the degree of the openness of capital market.

In order to study the government control of the capital account, Quinn and Inclan (Quinn and Inclan, 1997) constructed the CAPITAL index for the measure of the openness of capital account to measure the extent of openness of a country's capital account, through the analysis of the information of the government control of capital account every year in the AREAER, deciding the assignment of the intensity of the control of the capital account from the two aspects of

[12] Jia Qiuran, Review of Financial Openness Measurement Method and Index System, *Economic Review*, No. 3, 2011.

capital expenditure and income. Later, Quinn added a series of measure items (such as the current account openness index CURRENT), constructing a complete financial openness index and in the subsequent studies (Quinn, 2003; Quinn and Toyoda, 2008) extending the sample data to the 94 countries from 1949 to 2005. After that, Chinn and Ito (2002, 2006, 2008), following Quinn's thought, constructed a measure of the intensity of capital control index KAOPEN, using the information provided in the AREAER. This index combined four main kinds of information about the control of external account in the AREAER, including k_1: the existence of multiple exchange rates, k_2: the existence of controls on the current account, k_3: the existence of controls on the capital account, and the k_4: the existence of the requirement of turning over the export earnings. The binary dummy variable assignment method was implemented for these indicators: 1 representing completely without restrictions and 0 representing complete restrictions. At the same time, in order to better reflect the overall trend of the opening of a country's capital account, Chinn and Ito conducted a five-year moving average for K_3 in order to screed the fluctuations in special years. The method is as follows:

$$\text{SHARE}k_{3,t} = (k_{3,t} + k_{3,t-1} + k_{3,t-2} + k_{3,t-3} + k_{3,t-4})/5.$$

Then Chinn and Ito processed the index indicators (k_{1t}, k_{2t}, SHARE $k_{3,t}$, $k_{4,t}$) and obtained the index KAOPEN for the measure of the openness of capital account. The distribution of the values ranged from −1.83 to 2.50; the greater the value, the higher the openness. With respect to Quinn's method, the Chinn–Ito method is more comprehensive in terms of the measure of capital controls, with the improvement on the breadth and depth, which is an index of indicators with large samples and a long period of time,[13] becoming a method with a wide range of applicability in the area of the current study of financial openness.

In addition, the study on the nominal financial openness is carried out by examining the operation of a country's capital market. Mattoo

[13]At present, the Chinn–Ito Index has covered 182 countries from 1970 to 2010. See http://web.pdx.edu/~ito/Chinn-Ito~website.htm.

(Mattoo, 2000) measured the openness of the capital markets that the governments committed in their accession to the WTO, including the openness of banking and the insurance industry (excluding the stock market), forming a static financial openness index covering 105 WTO members. On the basis of Mattoo, Ponties (Ponties, 2002) examined the commitments made by the main APEC members after signing the "Financial Service Agreement" of the GATS and the follow-up policies, measuring the committed openness of the banks, securities and insurance markets of these countries with the Mattoo method and the actual levels of openness, but still failed to have formed the index completely reflecting the financial openness of a country. Later, Zhang Jinqing and Liu Qingfu (2007) constructed a complete, dynamic and multi-level financial openness index with a comprehensive consideration of the regulation of the financial services, but due to the high complexity and the quantity of information collection, the practicability of this method was reduced to a certain extent.

2. The Second Study Method of Financial Openness — Study on the Real Openness

The measure of real openness (*de facto*) is mainly realized through the investigation of the activities of the main participators in the market during the process of financial opening. Compared with the nominal openness, the real openness in some ways more truly reflects the depth and breadth of a country's financial opening, but due to the existence of some defects in theory and difficulties in practical operation, the measurement methods, obvious shortcomings also exist to a certain extent.

As mentioned above, the measure of the real financial opening level can be classified into the two aspects of depth and breadth: the depth of the financial openness refers to the degree of the integration of the financial market and the financial activities of a country with the global finance, which can be measured by the indicators such as the degree of the correlation of the savings rate with the investment rate, the difference between the domestic and foreign interest rate and the difference of the return rates in the stock market; the breadth of financial openness refers to the total size of the cross-border financial activities of a country which can be measured by the ratio of the total of a series of cross-border capital flows in the total size of the economy.[14] Therefore, the study of the real financial openness is mainly divided into the two types of the measure of depth and the measure of breadth.

(1) The Measure of Depth

Feldstein and Horioka (1980) used the correlation between the savings rate and the rate of investment to measure the real financial openness of a country. They believed that in a country with a completely opened financial sector, when the domestic interest rate was lower than the investment return rates of other countries and regions, the savings in the country would freely flow into those places so that the global allocation of resources had been achieved; when the domestic interest rate increased because of the shortage of savings, the foreign capital would automatically flow in to make up for the shortfall in funds, and then there would be no correlation between the domestic savings rate and the domestic investment rate of the country. On the contrary, there was a big correlation between the domestic savings rate and the domestic investment rate in a country where the financial field was completely not opened. Edwards and Khan (1985) constructed a kind of financial indicators from the differentials between the domestic interest rate and the foreign interest rates, whose core theory was the interest rate parity principle, i.e., when the financial market was fully open, the domestic interest rate and the foreign interest rates should be in line with the conditions of the interest rate parity; in this way, the real financial openness of a country could be measured through the study of the degree of the association of the level of the country's interest rate and the level of the international interest rates. Bekaert (1995) measured the financial openness of a country from the perspective of the different returns rates of the stock market, which reflected the degree of participation of a country's stock market in the integration of

[14]Jia Qiuran, Review of Financial Openness Measurement Method and Index System, *Economic Review*, No. 3, 2011.

the international finance through measuring the correlation between the country's opening stock market and the stock market returns rates of those countries (such as Europe, America, and Japan) with high openness of financial markets. But because of the focus on just the stock market of a country's financial market, it could not give a comprehensive measure of the country's overall financial opening condition.

(2) The Measure of Breadth

Based on the model about trade openness established by Patrick (1998) and Kraay (1998) constructed a flow indicator to measure the level of financial openness by using the data in the table of the international balance of payments. He measured the financial openness of a country through studying the proportion of the total of the portfolio equity in the country's annual capital account, FDI and the capital inflow and outflow of other investment projects against the country's GDP that year. This index could only reflect the short-term changes in the flow rather than the long-term trend of changes of the level of financial openness; therefore, on the basis of Kraay's research, Lane and Milesi-Ferretti (2001, 2003, 2007) proposed a new idea. They measured the financial openness of a country through studying the proportion of the total of the various financial assets such as the portfolio equity, FDI, financial derivatives, reserves, external debt, and liabilities against the country's GDP. The calculation of this method was very simple and the data sources were more convenient and credible, so it was widely applied as a measure of breadth. Currently the samples of the study have been updated to 178 countries and regions from 1970 to 2007,[15] which is a rare real financial openness index with a wide domain of data.

Generally speaking, all the above indicators of measuring the level of financial openness have various advantages and disadvantages due to the influence of the theory, method and data, none of which can be applied to all cases. Therefore, we should choose the most appropriate model for the actual situation and revise the deficiencies

[15]See http://www.philiplane.org/EWN.html.

in the research. In order to better reflect the actual situation of financial liberalization in the Latin-American countries, this chapter will use the Chinn–Ito index in the nominal openness index and the Lane and Milesi-Ferretti method in the actual openness index. The reasons for the two methods are: (1) The two methods are the indexes with rarely large samples and long time spans, which is very suitable for the transverse comparison of financial opening trends between countries. (2) Compared with other economic areas, the financial sector has the feature of strong state intervention and the will of the state is reflected more obviously in the degree of financial openness. Therefore, in the study of a country's financial openness, it is necessary to compare the country's nominal openness with the real level of openness so as to have a more accurate understanding of the country's financial openness. This is one of the important reasons why the two different index methods have been selected in this chapter. At the same time, in order to better reflect the status of the Latin-American countries in the world of finance, seven Asian developing countries and seven major Latin-American countries have been compared in this chapter so as to strengthen the pertinence and the universal significance of the research.

II. An Empirical Study of Financial Openness of the Latin-American Countries — From the Perspective of Comparison with Asia

1. The Chinn–Ito index

Since the construction of the index has been introduced in the previous literature review, here there is no need to repeat it. The Chinn–Ito indexes from 1995 to 2009 of seven Asian countries — respectively China (excluding Hong Kong, Macao, and Taiwan), India, Indonesia, Korea, Malaysia, Thailand, and Vietnam — and seven Latin-American countries — respectively, Argentina, Brazil, Chile, Colombia, Mexico, Peru, and Venezuela — have been selected in the latest research results[16] (see Appendix 2 for the generated chart).

[16] See The Chinn–Ito Index, http://web.pdx.edu/~Ito/Chinn-Ito_website.htm.

From the chart it can be seen directly that Asian countries are generally at lower levels of nominal openness and there is little change in the years between the two financial crisis (Southeast Asian Financial Crisis in 1997 and the Global Financial Crisis in 2008), which means that these countries have been insisting on the implementation of more stringent financial control policies. Compared with the Asian countries, the Latin-American countries generally have higher nominal openness, but at the same time, their annual fluctuations are greater, which have a lot to do with the several financial crises during these years and of course, also with the financial reform that the Latin-American countries have been trying to implement in recent years.

2. The Lane and Milesi-Ferretti Method

(1) Model Construction and Data Processing

To measure the level of a country's real financial openness with the Lane and Milesi-Ferretti method, the basic equation for the model is:

$$\mathrm{FI}_i = \frac{\mathrm{FA}_i + \mathrm{FL}_i}{\mathrm{GDP}_i}. \tag{1}$$

Among them, FI_i is the basic financial openness index of the country of i, GDP_i is the GDP of the country of i, and FL_i and FA_i respectively represent the external financial assets and the external financial liabilities of the country of i.

Inspired by the trade openness level model of Patrick (1998), in order to better compare the levels of financial openness between different countries, this chapter has constructed a new financial openness model after the economic scale, the population and the level of economic development have been taken into consideration, so that the method of Lane and Milesi-Ferretti has been further improved. The basic formula is as follows:

$$\begin{aligned}\ln(\mathrm{FI}_{i,t}) = \beta_0 &+ \beta_1 \ln(\mathrm{GDP}_{i,t}) + \beta_2 \ln(\mathrm{GDP}_{i,t})^2 + \beta_3 \ln(\mathrm{pop}_{i,t}) \\ &+ \beta_4 \ln(\mathrm{pop}_{i,t})^2 + \beta_5 \ln(\mathrm{GDP}_{i,t}/\mathrm{pop}_{i,t}) \\ &+ \beta_6 \ln(\mathrm{GDP}_{i,t}/\mathrm{pop}_{i,t})^2 + \varepsilon_{i,t}. \end{aligned} \tag{2}$$

Among them, $\mathrm{FI}_{i,t}$ is the financial openness index of the country of i in the year of t, and $\mathrm{GDP}_{i,t}$ is the GDP of the country of i in the year of t, representing the economic scale of the country; $\mathrm{pop}_{i,t}$ is the population of the country of i in year t; $\mathrm{GDP}_{i,t}/\mathrm{pop}_{i,t}$ is the per capita GDP of the country of i in the year of t, representing the level of economic development of the country.

In this model, the natural logarithm and square variables have been taken for all the variables (e.g., the financial openness has a negative correlation with the economic scale and the level of economic development under a small economic scale or a low level of economic development, but it has a positive correlation under a large economic scale or a high level of economic development). The data used in the model came from the IMF's Coordinated Portfolio Investment Survey (CPIS), Balance of Payments Statistics (BOPS), International Financial Statistics (IFS), UNCTAD's World Investment Report and the database of World Development Indicators (WDI). At the same time, a 3-year moving average was given to all the variables in order to reduce the impact of special-year fluctuations on the model results.

It can be seen that in model (2) there is an obvious problem of multiple linear regression, and the regression coefficient of the population is not obvious. In this case, formula (2) is changed into formula (3):

$$\begin{aligned}\ln(\mathrm{FI}_{i,t}) = y_0 + y_1 \ln(\mathrm{GDP}_{i,t}) + y_2 \ln(\mathrm{GDP}_{i,t})^2 \\ + y_3 \ln(\mathrm{GDP}_{i,t}/\mathrm{pop}_{i,t})^2 + \varepsilon_{i,t}. \qquad (3)\end{aligned}$$

Similar to the previous trade openness approach, the EVIEWS6.0 software has also been used to get the pooled regression of the above data. The results are shown in Appendix 1. At the same time, the stability of the model is tested by the unit root test. From the perspective of the panel unit root test of the level value and its first-order and second-order difference values of the variables, i.e., $\ln \mathrm{FI}$, $\ln \mathrm{GDP}$, $\ln(\mathrm{GDP})^2$ and $\ln(\mathrm{GDP}/\mathrm{pop})^2$, when the level values of all the variables are tested, the original hypothesis of "the existence of unit root" cannot be rejected, i.e., each variable is a non-stationary process. When the second-order difference value of each variable is tested, the test results reject the original hypothesis at the significant level of 5%, i.e., the time series of the second-order difference values of each variable is a stationary process.

The regression results obtained basically conform to the hypothesis of the relationship between the variables. On this basis, formula (3) is completed. In order to further determine the general financial openness under a given economic scale and the level of economic development, formula (4) is constructed:

$$\mathrm{FI}^1_{i,t} = \exp[\log(\mathrm{FI}_{i,t}) - \varepsilon_{i,t}]. \tag{4}$$

The formula is the general openness at a given level. It is obtained on the basis of the calculation of the real financial openness (formula (3)) of the economies and the regression residuals. Then, the revised financial openness index is achieved:

$$\mathrm{FI}^*_{i,t} = \frac{\mathrm{FI}_{i,t}}{\mathrm{FI}^1_{i,t}}. \tag{5}$$

This index can explain the degree of deviation of a country and the financial openness of the country that should have been achieved under a given economic scale and level of economic development. If the index is greater than 1, it indicates that the country is more open than the general level; if less than 1, it shows that the country is more closed than the general level. As a result, the financial openness of all relevant countries can be obtained (see Appendix 2).

(2) The Empirical Results

From Appendixes 2 and 5 of this chapter, it can be seen that after considering the economic scale and the level of economic development, the financial liberalization index that we have obtained is basically in line with our judgment on the real situation of the Latin-American and Asian countries.

① From the perspective of the time series, the changes of the financial openness of each economy from 1997 to 2009 basically reflected the development track of their financial sectors.

In Latin America, the Brazilian financial crisis from 1999 to 2000 and the Argentine financial crisis from 2001 to 2002 (eventually ending the Currency Board System) had influenced the entire

Latin America and the trend of financial liberalization and this time span had become the inflection point of financial openness in most countries. In fact, most of the crises in this area originated from the financial turmoils and the main reason of the turmoils came from the Latin-American dependence on the external finance, which was reflected in the net capital inflows.[17] However, at present great changes have taken place in this area. In the past ten years, the outside economic equilibrium conditions of many Latin-American countries have greatly improved, laying the foundation for the macroeconomic stability, which was an important reason why the Latin-American countries did not have serious domestic economic crises during the global financial crisis in 2008.

In Asia, after the Asian financial crisis in 1997, the financial liberalization index of some ASEAN countries originally with high economic dependence on foreign countries, such as Indonesia, Malaysia, Thailand, and Vietnam, began to go gradually downward, for these countries had relatively small national economies and not very high levels of economic development. The fact that they had early achieved higher levels of financial openness was not conducive to their defenses against external financial risks. In contrast, the financial openness of China, India, and South Korea that had relatively large sizes of economy was rising: for China (2001) and India (1995), their joining the WTO and participation in the integration of the world economy would inevitably improve their economic openness; for South Korea, after the financial crisis in 1997, the reform coming from the IMF had accelerated its embarking on the path of globalization.

② From the perspective of the cross-sectional data, the real financial openness index of most Latin-American countries is lower than that of Asian countries, which is not consistent with the result of the previous nominal financial openness index. Although most Latin-American countries started earlier in the process of economic opening, the debt pressure and higher rates of inflation resulting from

[17]Development Center of Economic Cooperation and Development Organization: *Economic Outlook of Latin America in 2010*, The Contemporary World Press, 2010, p. 20.

the import substitution model of economic development in the real economy for a long period led to the fact that their real performance in the financial markets had been worse than the export-oriented Asian emerging market countries. Generally speaking, higher levels of trade freedom will create the conditions for financial openness, e.g., the trade growth tends to bring FDI growth, providing more guarantees for bilateral debt at the same time.[18] Latin America started its financial liberalization much earlier than its liberalization of trade. The financial market without the support of the real economy is often more vulnerable in the face of crisis.

③ The degree of openness may have a U-shaped relationship with the economic scale and the level of economic development: under the condition of a small scale of economy or a low level of economic development, there is a negative correlation between the financial openness and the economic scale and the level of economic development, but a positive correlation occurs when the scale of economy and the level of economic development have reached a certain degree of measurement. However, as the assets and liabilities of the several major parts of the financial assets — securities, direct investment, debt and official reserves — have different correlations with GDP and per capita GDP, we cannot make a full affirmation of the above conclusions.

Section 4 Enlightenment and Discussion

I. Understanding of the Limitations of the Research

1. This Chapter Just Shows the Reality — An Empirical Research of the Explanation of "What the Current Situation is", Rather Than a Normative Research, With No Value Judgment

For example, it does not tell whether the high trade and financial openness is good or not. From the discussion it can be seen that

[18][US] Paul R. Krugman, [US] Moris Obstfeld: *International Economics: Theory and Policy*, the 6th Edition, translated by Hai Wen *et al.* China Renmin University Press, 2006, Chapter 22: "Developing Countries: Growth, Crisis and Reform".

Argentina had a higher trade and financial openness index in a serious economic recession period. Therefore, although general studies have shown that there is a positive relationship between the trade-and-financial openness index and economic growth or development, or have regarded the positive relation as the premise of the studies, in some special cases, the level of the positive relation itself cannot be treated as the only index for making a judgment.

2. This Chapter is a Result-research Rather than a Process-research

The so-called result-research makes use of the post-expression levels of the trade and economic activities. If the process is studied, the changes such as the economic strategy and policy, trade policy, financial policy and investment policy should be included. How to consider these changes and describe the process of these changes is still a question which is worth exploring in theory and method.

3. This Chapter is a Scale Study, not a Quality Study

What is revealed is the relationship between the overall sizes. The problem of quality is in fact closely related to the value judgment and it is not dealt with here. At the same time, this chapter is mainly a measure of the trade and financial openness without touching the problem of the depth of the participation of each country in the global economic integration, which may lead to bias of the emerged result against the real result. Therefore, a comprehensive study of the degree of economic openness depends on further study.

4. The Conclusions are not Absolute

As with other empirical analyses, the conclusions are much dependent on the hypotheses; but they are still enlightening to some extent.

II. Discussion of Problems and Enlightenment

This chapter intends to provide an in-depth analysis of the essence of trade and financial openness, namely, on the basis of considering as many known main affecting factors as possible and knowing clearly the different countries higher or lower than the general level, we can further understand the economic characteristics of these countries. In terms of theory, this chapter reveals the relationship between the trade and financial openness of the Latin-American countries and their economic scale, population and economic development from the perspective of a comparative study with Asian countries.

On the basis of this research, we can have a deep examination from multiple angles, for example, the research of the interactive mechanism of trade and financial openness. Especially for developing countries, how to deal with the order of trade and financial openness and the order of various measures during the process of financial liberalization is a major problem for the growth of the national economy.

Another important research angle is the relationship between the trade and financial openness and the position in the field of international economy. If the trade openness is relatively higher, our hypothesis is that the market access and open commitments may be more; otherwise, less. This hypothesis requires further validation. For example, we can study the relation between the trade openness of the Latin-American countries and their positions in the WTO, and compare with that of the Asian countries. If this hypothesis was proved, the change of the trade openness index might have a certain degree of direction significance to their future changes of position in WTO. At the same time, some large Latin-American countries, such as Brazil, have been very active in the discussion of the reform of the international financial system, calling for further increase of the right of developing countries to speak and vote in the international financial institutions, the promotion of the diversification of the international monetary system, and the strengthening of regional financial cooperation and assistance mechanism, but they are restricted in playing a greater role in the international governance due to their low degrees of financial openness and the strength of their currencies. China must have a cautious and in-depth observation attitude towards the possibility and its ability when making commitments concerning its global responsibility.

The relationship between the economic openness and the regional economic cooperation is also one of the problems concerned. For example, the relationship between the financial openness of Latin America and the internationalization of the RMB is the necessary thinking direction of the future development of China's foreign economic pattern. A special phenomenon in the financial system of the Latin-American countries is the existence of the US dollar. The study on the condition of the currency substitution and the potential of the internationalization of the RMB will enrich the understanding of the problems in the domain of currency circulation, providing a new perspective for the study of the internationalization of RMB.[19]

These research directions are conducive not only to knowing the trend of the economic policies of the Latin-American countries, but also to judging and analyzing the opportunities and the prospect of the economic and trade cooperation between China and Latin America.

For developing countries themselves, there is a close relationship between the economic openness and the industrial development. If the trade and the financial openness are relatively higher, the possibility of being impacted by the international market price and economic fluctuations will be bigger and the possibility of domestic economic turmoil will also be bigger. Larger-scaled markets, such as China, with a higher trade openness index but a low financial openness index, have less significant economic fluctuations (90% of China's surplus came from the United States, but the economic crisis of the United States did not result in a huge negative effect on its total economic amount and growth rate). The possible relationship here is: big power → having a sound industrial system and a big enough domestic market → having a strong ability to withstand external shocks → having a limited negative impact from the high level of trade openness. In this situation, the relationship between

[19]Chai Yu, The Study of the Internationalization of the RMB and Latin America as a Regional Object, *World Economy and Politics,* No. 4, 2013.

the development of the real economy and the economic fluctuation is much closer. The financial development is the necessary condition for the construction of the industrial system and the expansion of the domestic market. From the perspective of this sense, the most important aspect in some empirical studies has been ignored, i.e., some big powers have sound domestic industrial systems, with the ability to meet the domestic markets. This key factor may affect the degree of economic openness from several directions: First, it is the low degree of trade openness; second, the high degree of trade openness with low financial openness results in a limited negative impact during the fluctuations of the international economy; third, the extent of the impact of a high degree of the openness of trade and finance during the international economic fluctuations will change depending on the status of the domestic market.

Appendix 1 The Pooled Regression Model Results

Dependent Variable: TI
Method: Pooled Least Squares
Date: 05/31/13 Time: 21:34
Sample: 1997–2009
Included observations: 13
Cross-sections included: 14

Total pool (balanced) observations: 182

Variable	Coefficient	Std. Error	t-Statistic	Prob.
Ln GDP	−0.127184	0.017772	−7.156226	0.0000
Ln GDP/pop	0.244005	0.055096	4.428730	0.0000
R-squared	0.130461	Mean dependent var		−1.305491
Adjusted R-squared	0.125630	S. D. dependent var		0.672599
S. E. of regression	0.628932	Akaike info criterion		1.921341
Sum squared resid	71.20000	Schwarz criterion		1.956550
Log likelihood	−172.8421	Hannan–Quinn criter		1.935614
Durbin–Watson stat	0.029640			

Dependent Variable: FI Method: Pooled Least Squares
Date: 10/02/12 Time: 12:09
Sample: 1997–2009
Included observations: 13
Cross-sections included: 14

Total pool (balanced) observations: 182

Variable	Coefficient	Std. Error	t-Statistic	Prob.
Ln GDP	−7.851903	2.212928	−3.548197	0.0005
Ln GDP∧2	3.851352	1.106097	3.481930	0.0006
Ln (GDP/POP)∧2Z	0.115155	0.010643	10.81969	0.0000
R-squared	0.418716	Mean dependent var		0.058607
Adjusted R-squared	0.412222	S. D. dependent var		0.403394
S. E. of regression	0.309269	Akaike info criterion		0.507133
Sum squared resid	17.12083	Schwarz criterion		0.559947
Log likelihood	−43.14915	Hannan–Quinn criter		0.528543
Durbin–Watson stat	0.148117			

Appendix 2 The Trade and Financial Openness Index of Latin America and Asian Countries

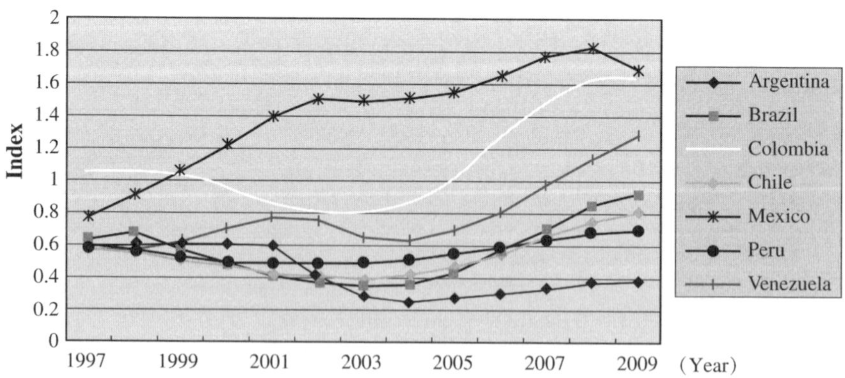

Figure A.1 The Trade Openness Index of Latin-American Countries

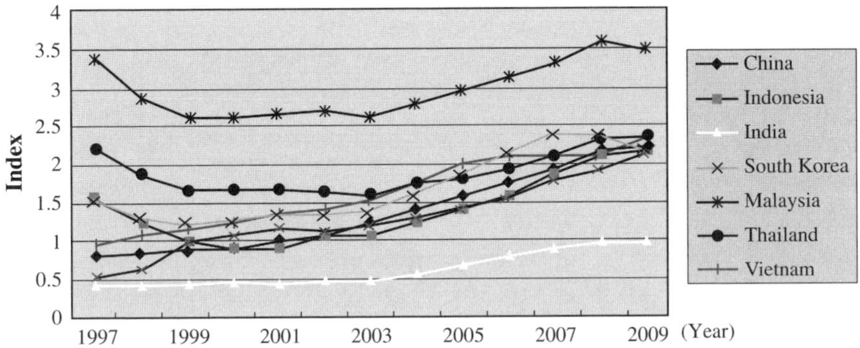

Figure A.2 The Trade Openness Index of Asian Countries

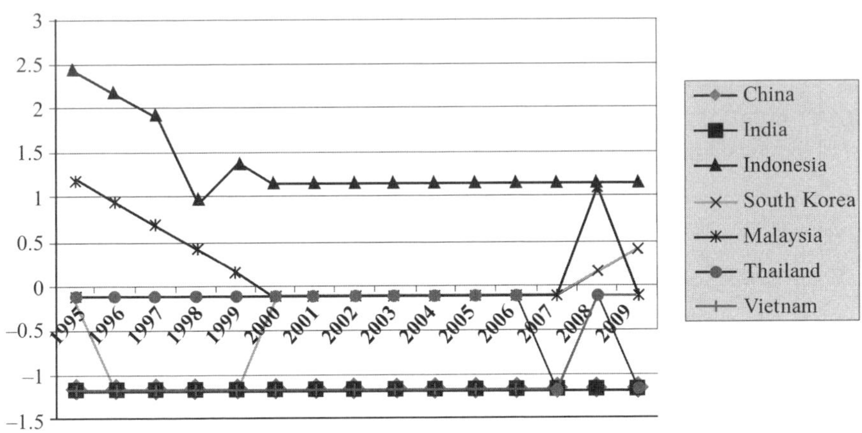

Figure A.3 Chinn–Ito Index of Asian Countries from 1995 to 2009

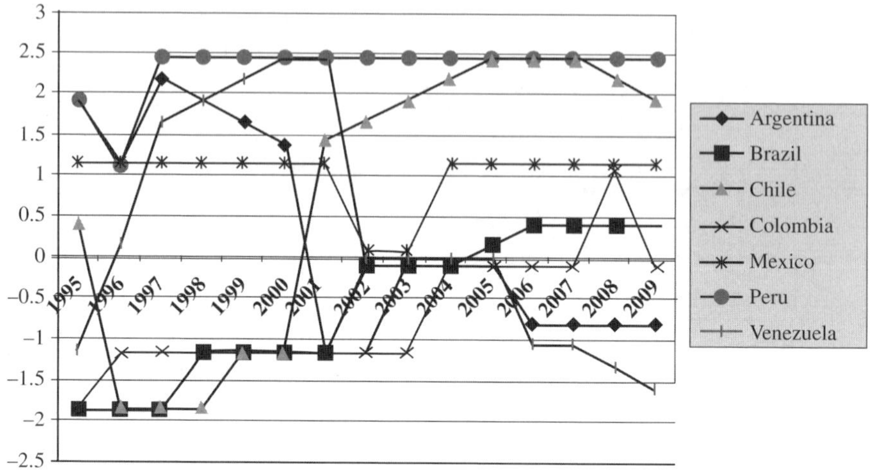

Figure A.4 Chinn–Ito Index of Latin-American Countries from 1995 to 2009

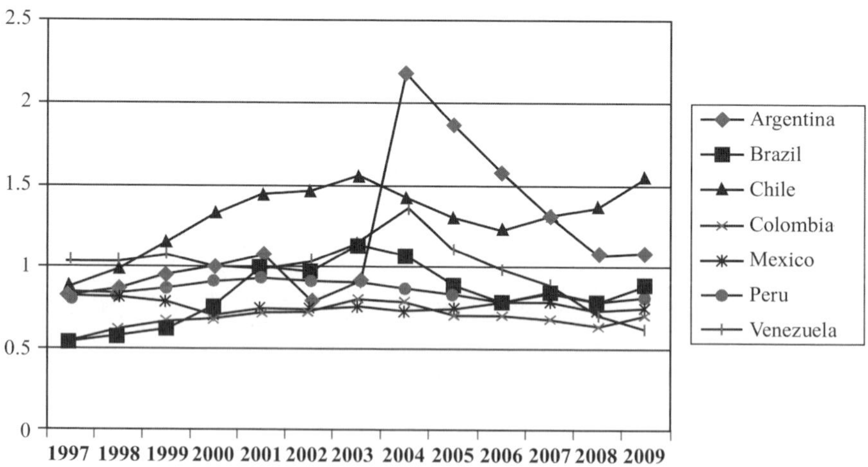

Figure A.5 The Real Financial Openness Index of Latin-American Countries from 1995 to 2009

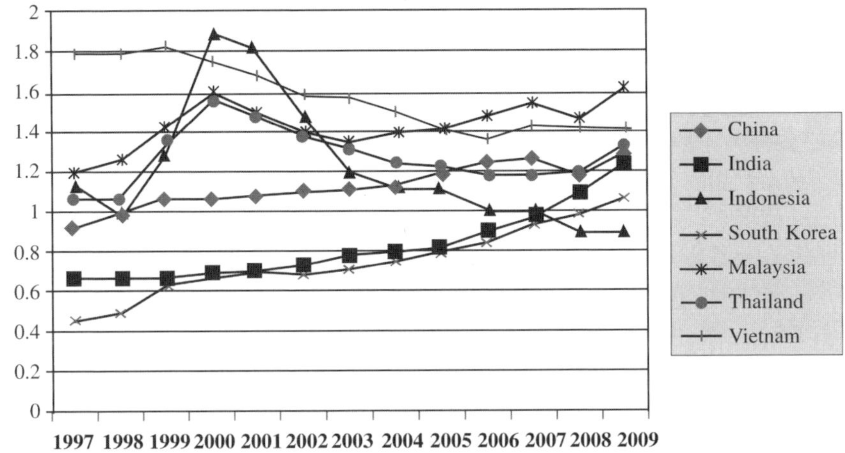

Figure A.6 The Real Financial Openness Index of Asian Countries from 1995 to 2009

Appendix 3 Trade Openness Index (2009)

Economic Body	TI: < 1	2 > TI: > 1	TI: > 2
Argentina	0.38	—	—
Brazil	0.91	—	—
Colombia	0.83	—	—
Chile	—	1.63	—
Mexico	—	1.68	—
Peru	0.70	—	—
Venezuela	—	1.27	—
Total of Latin America	4	3	—
China	—	—	2.21
India	0.99	—	—
Indonesia	—	—	2.16
South Korea	—	—	2.19
Malaysia	—	—	3.47
Thailand	—	—	2.35
Vietnam	—	—	2.36
Total of Asia	1	—	6

Appendix 4 The Chinn–Ito Index (2009)

Economic Body	Chinn–Ito Index < 0	0 < Chinn–Ito Index < 1	Chinn–Ito Index > 1
Argentina	−0.80268	—	—
Brazil	—	0.4229954	—
Chile	—	—	1.92635
Colombia	−0.10638	—	—
Mexico	—	—	1.13228
Peru	—	—	2.45573
Venezuela	−1.59095	—	—
Total of Latin America	3	1	3
China	−1.159348	—	—
India	−1.15935	—	—
Indonesia	—	—	1.13228
South Korea	—	0.422995	—
Malaysia	−0.10638	—	—
Thailand	−1.15935	—	—
Vietnam	−0.10638	—	—
Total of Asia	5	1	1

Appendix 5 Real Financial Openness Index (2009)

Economic Body	$FI^* < 1$	$1 < FI^* < 1.5$	$FI^* > 1.5$
Argentina	—	1.080554411	—
Brazil	0.887185	—	—
Chile	—	—	1.543046
Colombia	0.695481	—	—
Mexico	0.76469	—	—
Peru	0.809207	—	—
Venezuela	0.628419	—	—
Total of Latin America	5	1	1
China	—	1.274417	—
India	—	1.22725	—
Indonesia	0.90426	—	—
South Korea	—	1.057154	—
Malaysia	—	—	1.609515
Thailand	—	1.314973	—
Vietnam	—	1.409865	—
Total of Asia	1	5	1

Chapter 9

Review of the Sino-Latin American Economic and Trade Cooperation since the Beginning of the 21st Century

Zhang Yong

Since the beginning of the 21st century, the Sino-Latin American economic and trade cooperation has experienced a new phase of accelerated development. The Sino-Latin American bilateral trade volume increased from \$14.9 billion in 2001 to \$261.2 billion in 2012, an increase of 16.5 times. From 2000 to 2012, the average annual growth rate of the Sino-Latin America trade was 28.7%. By the end of 2011, China's direct investment stock in Latin America had reached \$55.17, accounting for 13% of the total stock of China's Foreign Direct Investment (FDI). The phase of accelerated development, first of all, was attributed to China's increasingly strong comprehensive national strength resulting from its sustained rapid economic growth, especially China's huge demand for energy and raw materials as the "world factory", leading to the export boom and price rising of such products in the international market, so that Latin America's exporting countries of energy and raw materials had benefited from it. At the same time, on December 11, 2001, China formally joined the World Trade Organization (WTO), creating favorable conditions for opening up a new phase in the development of the Sino-Latin American trade. Secondly, in terms of Latin America, the boom of export of energy and raw materials and rising prices had become a key factor in stimulating the economic growth at the beginning of the 21st century. In 2003, the Latin-American region had ended a period of about 20 years of economic recession and entered a new period of expansion. The export boom, a comprehensive recovery of the production, the double surplus of the public finance and the current account, and the rapid improvement of employment and income of residents had promoted the strong rebound in domestic demand. Therefore, the imports of goods of the Latin-American countries from China also had a synchronous rapid growth, constituting another important driving force to the acceleration of the development of the Sino-Latin American trade.

The purpose of this chapter is to make a comprehensive review of the Sino-Latin American economic and trade relation in the recent 10 years, including the following four parts. (1) The rise of the status of China and the Asia-Pacific countries as the Latin-American trading partners, which has brought about a historic change in the foreign trade pattern of Latin America. (2) The actual progress of the Sino-Latin American economic and trade cooperation in several major areas. (3) The experience and policy implications of the accelerated development of the Sino-Latin American economic and trade relation in the past 10 years. (4) The current main problems faced by the Sino-Latin American economic and trade cooperation.

Section 1 Historical Changes in the Foreign Trade Pattern of the Latin-American Region

Before the changes in the pattern of foreign trade of Latin America are discussed, a brief analysis of the recent economic growth in Latin America needs to be done. The statistics in Table 9.1 indicate that the economic growth of Latin America from 2003 to 2010 showed a great imbalance within the region. First, from the angle of horizontal comparison, from 2003 to 2010, the economic growth rates of the four sub-regions of Latin America were greatly different: South America — 5.0%, Central America — 4.3%, Mexico — 2.2%, and the Caribbean — 2.9%. Mexico's growth rate was only 44% of that of South America, the growth rate of the Caribbean was only 58% of

Table 9.1 GDP Growth Rates of Sub-Latin American Regions (1971–2010) (%)

	1971–1980	1981–1990	1991–1997	1998–2002	2003–2010
South America	5.6	1.0	4.1	0.3	5.0
Argentina	2.6	−1.0	6.1	−3.1	7.5
Brazil	8.8	1.7	3.0	1.7	4.0
Chile	2.8	3.1	8.2	2.5	4.0
Colombia	5.5	3.4	4.0	0.7	4.4
Central America	4.3	1.0	4.5	3.5	4.3
Mexico	6.6	1.9	2.9	3.2	2.2
Caribbean		1.6	1.9	3.0	2.9
Latin America	5.9	1.5	3.6	1.3	4.2

Note: Estimation based on the constant value of 2005. The sub-region GDP is the sum of the GDPs of the countries in the sub-region.

Source: CEPAL, sobre la base de CEPALSTAT [*base de dados en linea*], http://websie.eclac.cl/sisgen/Consultaintegrada.asp/, 2012.

South America, and the growth rate of Central America was essentially flat with the average of Latin America (4.2%). Second, from the perspective of vertical comparison, from 1998 to 2002, the average economic growth rate of Latin America was only 1.3%, known as another "lost 5 years" after the "lost 10 years" in the 1980s. Compared with the years from 1998 to 2002, the economic growth of South America had increased significantly from 2003 to 2010; the economic growth of Central America also had accelerated, but Mexico and the Caribbean which had a higher growth rate before had a dropped growth. The main reason for the difference lies in the fact that the economic growth from 2003 to 2010 was contributed to the strong demand for energy and raw materials of the Asia-Pacific countries led by China, and the South American countries had become the main beneficiaries as the exporting countries of such products. Mexico's situation was very special: it was not only one of the exporters of energy and raw materials, but also highly dependent on the US market; it rarely benefited from the strong demand in the Asia-Pacific area, but was dragged down by the US economic downturn. The Caribbean countries were not the main exporters of energy and raw materials, but highly dependent on the US market, and therefore had a worse situation than Mexico. The Central American countries also had nothing to do with the export boom of energy and raw materials, but from 2003 to 2010, the proportion of the overseas workers' remittances that they had in gross domestic product (GDP) was the highest in Latin America, with the most obvious effect on stimulating the domestic demand.

I. The Promotion of the South–South Cooperation Has Changed the Pattern of the World Trade and Economic Cooperation

The data cited above have provided a wide background for observing the changes in the pattern of Latin America's foreign trade. In fact, the international financial crisis of 2008–2009 had changed the traditional international trade system, the international monetary system and the international development system. With the center of global economic growth moving from the "Atlantic" to the "Pacific", the Latin American foreign trade and the entire foreign trade and economic cooperation pattern will continue to undergo deep adjustment, which reflects not only the rise of the status of emerging economies in the world economy, but also the closer economic ties between emerging economies and developing countries through the increase of trade and investment in the "South–South Cooperation". The ECLAC data show that in 2011 the global GDP growth was 4.4%, to which the industrialized countries (including the United States, the European Union, Japan, etc.) had contributed 1.22%, and the developing countries and regions (including Africa South to the Sahara, Latin America and the Caribbean, the developing countries in Asia, the Middle East and North Africa, and Central and Eastern Europe) had contributed 3.18%. The latter contributed 72% to global economic growth, of which the contributions of the Asian developing countries and Latin America to the global growth were 48% and 9%. This is enough to illustrate that at present Asia and Latin America have become the leading power to drive the global economic growth.

In this case, the proportion of the traditional developed countries such as the United States in the total foreign trade of Latin America was declining year by year, and the proportion of the emerging Asian countries represented by China was rising year by year, which was

Table 9.2 Proportion of Trading Partners in the Total Imports and Exports of Latin America (%)

	Asia-Pacific Region		US		EU		Latin America		Other Areas	
	2000	2010	2000	2010	2000	2010	2000	2010	2000	2010
Export	5.3	17.2	59.7	39.6	11.6	12.9	16	19.3	7.4	11
Import	10.6	27.2	50.4	29.1	14.2	13.7	15.3	22.7	9.5	7.3

Note: The Asia-Pacific region includes Australia, Brunei, Kampuchea, China, the Philippines, India, Indonesia, Japan, Laos, Malaysia, Burma, New Zealand, South Korea, Singapore, Thailand, and Vietnam.

Source: ECLAC, *Latin America and the Caribbean in the World Economy 2010–2011: The Region in the Decade of the Emerging Economies*, 2011, p. 17.

changing the traditional pattern of the long-term reliance on North America and Europe of the Latin-American foreign economic and trade cooperation. The increase in Mexico's trade with China and the Asia-Pacific region was its active adjustment in order mainly to reduce its excessive dependence on the US market. As is shown in Table 9.2, although the United States is still the largest Latin-American trading partner, its share has decreased significantly. From the perspective of exports, from 2000 to 2010, the proportion of the United States in the total Latin-American export fell from 59.7% to 39.6%; from the perspective of imports, the proportion of the United States fell from 50.4% to 29.1%, both down by about 20%. However, in the same period the proportions of imports and exports in the Asia-Pacific region and the Latin-American countries had accounted for a significant increase in the total imports and exports of Latin America.

From the perspective of a long-term trend, the proportion of the United States in the market share of the Latin-American export is expected to continue to decline; by 2020 it will be reduced to 28.4%. At that time, China's market share of the Latin-American export will be 19.3%, and the EU's will be 13.6%; over the same period, the Latin America imports from the United States, China and the EU will reach 26.1%, 16.2%, and 14%, respectively. In 2014, China will exceed the EU in the two aspects of import and export and

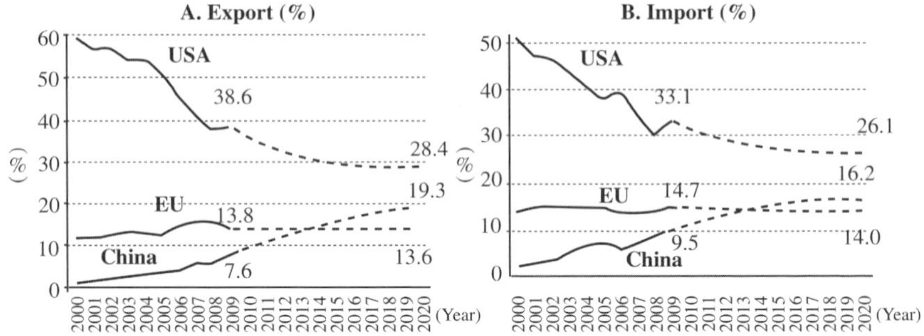

Figure 9.1 Proportion of Trading Partners in the Latin-American Foreign Trade from 2000 to 2020

Source: ECLAC, *The United States and Latin America and the Caribbean: Highlights of Economics and Trade*, March 2011, p. 5.

become the second largest trading partner of Latin America; at the same time, the gap between China and the United States — Latin America's largest trading partner — will significantly be reduced (see Figure 9.1). Moreover, in addition to China, in recent years, India, Russia, South Korea, Iran, South Africa and some of the ASEAN countries have had a rapid development in their economic and trade cooperations with Latin America both in scale and in depth.

II. Mexico Plays an Important Role in the Trade Model of Latin America with the US

The trade between Latin America and the United States is concentrated in a small number of countries. In 2010, in Latin America's exports to the United States, Mexico alone occupied 64%; the second was the Andean countries, accounting for more than 17%; the third was the Mercosur countries, accounting for 8%. In the Latin-American imports from the United States, Mexico, Mercosur countries and the Andean countries respectively accounted for 55%, 16%, and 12%. Here, it must be pointed out that both the Latin-American trade with the United States and the European Union are mainly concentrated in a few countries; such a phenomenon not solely exists in the Sino-Latin American trade because of the great differences of the sizes of the Latin-American economies.

Table 9.3 The Merchandise Trade between Latin-American Countries and the United States (2006–2010) ($ Million)

	2006	2007	2008	2009	2010
Central American Common Market (CACM)	−211	−1,788	−3,447	773	2,411
Costa Rica	−288	−638	−1,744	897	3,521
El Salvador	−301	−269	−236	−197	−226
Guatemala	−418	−1,044	−1,271	−763	−1,234
Honduras	25	−551	−808	−60	−677
Nicaragua	771	713	611	896	1,026
Andean Countries	38,143	34,949	45,836	21,282	26,234
Bolivia	147	85	122	73	171
Colombia	2,557	881	1,654	1,862	3,603
Ecuador	4,336	3,199	5,598	1,345	2,003
Peru	2,949	1,087	−328	−733	−1,657
Venezuela	28,153	29,697	38,790	18,735	22,114
Mercosur	5,538	−1,669	−6,348	−9,573	−17,533
Argentina	−801	−1,360	−1,716	−1,670	−3,607
Brazil	7,161	1,008	−2,451	−6,101	−11,439
Paraguay	−852	−1,169	−1,532	−1,296	−1,749
Uruguay	30	−149	−649	−505	−738
Caribbean Community (CARICOM)	2,256	2,193	1,171	−535	−412
Other	63,715	69,705	53,312	38,130	53,901
Chile	2,770	692	−3,905	−3,415	−3,871
Dominica	−819	−1,871	−2,624	−1,941	−2,872
Mexico	64,092	74,258	64,376	47,539	66,334
Panama	−2,328	−3,374	−4,536	−4,054	−5,690
Total	109,441	103,390	90,523	50,076	64,601

Source: ECLAC, *Latin America and the Caribbean in the World Economy 2010–2011: The Region in the Decade of the Emerging Economies*, 2011, p. 74.

The trade surplus of Latin America with the United States is mainly due to the huge surplus obtained by Mexico, followed by Venezuela. As is shown in Table 9.3, in 2010, the surpluses of the merchandise trade of Mexico and Venezuela with the United States reached $66.3 billion and $22.1 billion, respectively; the trade surplus of Mexico alone exceeded the total surplus of the Latin American region. Correspondingly, since 2007, the Mercosur countries as a whole had been in the state of growing deficits in trade with the

United States. This trend is reflected most obviously in the two largest Mercosur states of Brazil and Argentina. In 2010, the trade deficits of Brazil and Argentina with the United States reached $11.4 billion and $3.6 billion.

On the whole, in the Latin-American export to the United States, the proportion of primary products and products based on the natural resources is relatively small. This is mainly because the ratio of Mexico's exported products is very high, especially the high-tech products. If Mexico were ruled out, the region's export to the United States would be more similar to the Latin-American exports to China (mainly the export of primary products). In fact, the Latin-American countries can be divided into two categories according to the type of commodities exported to the United States: one type refers to the countries with the developed maquila industry such as Mexico, the countries of Central America and Dominica, whose proportion of the finished products (mainly low technology products such as textiles and garments) in the export is the largest; the other type refers to the countries exporting the natural resources and related processed products. For example, the exports of the Andean countries consist of almost all the primary products and natural-resources-based products, among which the main products of Venezuela, Colombia, and Ecuador exported to the United States are the crude oil. According to the data of ECLAC, from 2008 to 2010, the three Latin-American countries with the largest proportion of five kinds of goods exported to the United States annually in the total export were Venezuela (97.4%), Ecuador (89.4%), and Colombia (78.9%), while the countries with the exports of low-degree concentration of commodities are Argentina, Brazil, Dominica, Mexico, and Peru. In addition, in Latin America, Mexico was the country with the highest level of "intra-industry trade" with the United States, especially in automobile parts and the electronic machinery industry, while the other countries with a relatively high level of "intra-industry trade" were Brazil (in the automotive industry, chemical industry, etc.) and Dominica (in the electronic product, plastic, and paper industry).

III. The Mercosur Countries Have Decided the Latin-American Trade Mode with EU

Similarly, the trade between Latin America and the EU also is concentrated in a few countries — the Mercosur countries account for almost half of the trade of Latin America with EU. In 2010 the Mercosur countries, the Andean countries and Mexico were the top three countries in the Latin-American exports to EU, with the proportions of 47%, 17%, and 14%, respectively. From the perspective of import, the Mercosur countries, Mexico and the Andean countries ranked the top three in the Latin-American imports from EU, accounting for 45%, 24%, and 13%, respectively.

In addition to Mexico, the exports of other Latin-American countries or sub-regions to EU are mainly natural resources and natural-resource-based products. In Mexico and the Central American countries, the proportion of high technology products accounted for slightly over 40% in the export to EU. In the recent 10 years, there has been a very small change in the technological composition of the Latin-American exports to EU; only the countries in the Caribbean and Central America have some changes — the proportion of primary products in the former's export has increased and the proportion of high-tech products in the latter's export has increased.

The commodities of Latin-American countries exported to EU have a very high degree of concentration, mainly in the primary products such as bananas, coffee, coal, beef, copper, natural gas, iron and steel, oil, and soybeans. Mexico and Costa Rica were slightly exceptional — their first five commodities exported to EU contained more than one finished product. For example, from 2007 to 2009, the first five kinds of commodities of Mexico exported to the EU were oil (20%), passenger vehicles (18%), medical machinery (7%), telephone parts (3%), and semi-iron products (2%), accounting for a total of 50%.[1]

---

[1]ECLAC, *Latin America and the Caribbean in the World Economy 2010–2011: The Region in the Decade of the Emerging Economies*, 2011, p. 84.

IV. The Trade between Latin America and Asia Has Grown Rapidly

After the international financial crisis, the additional demands of developed countries were likely to decline, the growth rate of the world economy had slowed down compared with the time before the crisis, and the emerging economies would play a more important role in the global economic growth and partly make up the shrinking demands of the developed economies. South America had a significantly better prospect of economic recovery than Mexico and the Caribbean because of the key factor that the export markets of South American countries were more concentrated in Asia, especially China. According to the calculation of the CEIC database, by the classification of export destinations, China's share of the Latin-American exports rose from 0.7% in 1990 to 8.4% in 2010; by the source of imports, China's share of the Latin-American imports rose from 0.5% in 1990 to 13.3% in 2010. The importance of the Asian countries as Latin America's export markets was also different. As is shown in Table 9.4, in the descending order, China is the main export market for Cuba, Chile, Brazil, Peru, Argentina, and Venezuela. Japan is the main export market for Chile. As the Latin-American export markets, India, Japan, South Korea, and ASEAN are significantly less important than China. In other words, it is China that has led to the trade prosperity of Asia and the Latin-American countries.

Section 2 The Latest Development of the Sino-Latin American Economic and Trade Cooperation

I. A Leap in Trade Growth: The Main Body of Economic and Trade Cooperation

As can be seen from Figure 9.2, before 2000, the scale of the Sino-Latin America trade was very limited, but in the 21st century, the total amount of the Sino-Latin American trade had achieved a leapfrog growth, with a balance of overall imports and exports and the continuous optimization of the structure of trade. From the perspective of the total amount of trade, it soared from $14.9 billion in

Table 9.4 Trade between Latin-American Countries and Asian Countries or Sub-regional Organizations in 2010 (Proportion in the Total Exports and Imports, %)

	Export						Import					
	China	India	Japan	South Korea	ASEAN	Total	China	India	Japan	South Korea	ASEAN	Total
Argentina	9.4	2	1.2	1.1	4.8	18.4	14.4	—	2.1	1.7	3.3	22.6
Brazil	17	1.7	3.5	1.9	3.3	27.4	16.2	2.3	3.8	4.6	3.7	30.7
Chile	27.4	2.5	10.7	5.8	1.7	48	17.2	0.7	5.7	5.9	1.9	31.3
Paraguay	1	1.6	0.9	0.1	1.5	5	34.8	0.6	3.5	1.5	1.5	41.9
Uruguay	6.3	0.2	0.1	0.3	2	9	14.5	0.6	1.1	1.2	1.9	19.2
Bolivia	3.1	0.1	6.7	5.3	0	15.2	10.6	—	5.8	0.8	1.1	19.3
Colombia	5.6	0.9	1.3	0.9	1.4	10.1	14.5	1.7	2.8	2.3	2.1	23.4
Ecuador	2	0.1	2.3	0.1	1.1	5.5	9.4	0.6	3.4	4.4	2.1	19.9
Peru	16.5	0.6	5.1	2.6	1	25.8	18.3	1.7	4.6	3.5	2.5	30.6
Venezuela	9.1	5.7	0.1	0	4.4	19.3	9.8	0.5	1.6	0	0.7	12.6
Costa Rica	8.6	0.2	0.9	0.4	2.6	12.9	8.1	0.8	3.6	1.1	1.3	14.9
El Salvador	0.5	0.1	0.4	0.4	0.3	1.7	7.5	0.4	1.8	1	1	11.7
Guatemala	1	0.5	1.7	0.9	0.9	5.1	8.8	—	2	2.8	1.3	16
Honduras	3	0.2	0.9	2.3	0	6.4	5	0.5	1.3	0.8	1.3	8.9
Mexico	1.7	0.3	0.6	0.3	0.4	3.4	17.1	0.6	5	4.2	4.3	31.3
Nicaragua	2.2	1	0.8	0.3	0	4.4	9.2	1.1	2.8	3.4	1.7	18.3
Panama	0.8	0.1	0.9	0.2	0.3	2.3	32	0.6	3	2.5	14	52.1
Cuba	28.2	0	0.5	0.4	0.4	29.6	12.5	0.3	0.4	0.7	3.8	17.7
Dominica	3.1	0.9	0.2	0	0.6	4.8	11	0.6	2.1	0.9	1.6	16.2
Haiti	1.1	0.2	0.2	0.1	0.8	2.4	7	1.1	1.8	0.5	2.5	12.9

Source: ECLAC, *Latin America and the Caribbean in the World Economy 2010–2011: The Region in the Decade of the Emerging Economies*, 2011, p. 92.

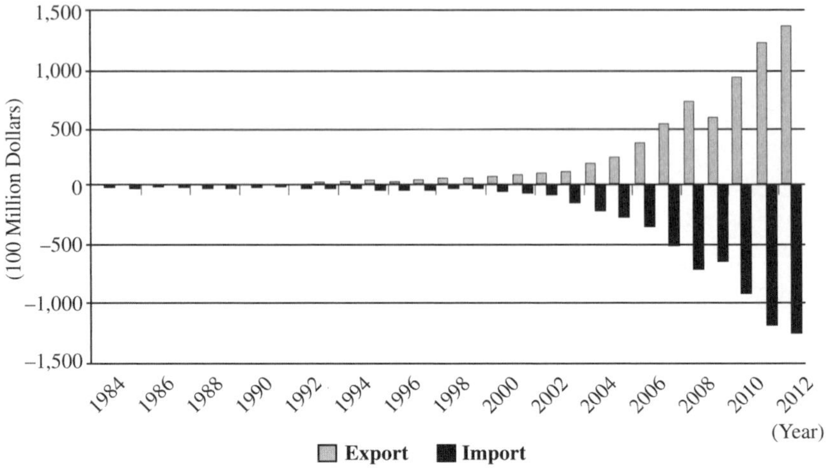

Figure 9.2 China's Exports to Latin America and Its Imports from Latin America from 1984 to 2012

Source: CEIC database.

2001 to $261.2 billion in 2012, an increase of 16.5 times. From 2000 to 2012, the average annual growth rate of the Sino-Latin American trade reached 28.7%. The overall trend shows at least: first, the international financial crisis occurred in 2008 had just suspended the growth pace (in 2009 the total trade was $121.9 billion, down 15%), without changing the growth trend of the Sino-Latin American trade. Second, the growth of trade showed a trend of accelerating growth. It took seven years from the breakthrough of $10 billion in 2000 to the breakthrough of $100 billion in 2007, and then it took only four years to break through the juncture of $200 billion in 2011. The time to enhance the platform of the Sino-Latin American economic and trade cooperation had been greatly shortened (see Figure 9.3).

1. The Proportion of Bilateral Trade Has Increased Annually in Each Other's Total Amount of Foreign Trade

From the perspective of importance, the proportion of bilateral trade in China's and Latin America's foreign trade had increased year by year, and the financial crisis objectively highlighted the status of China's foreign trade in Latin America, and even world trade. As is

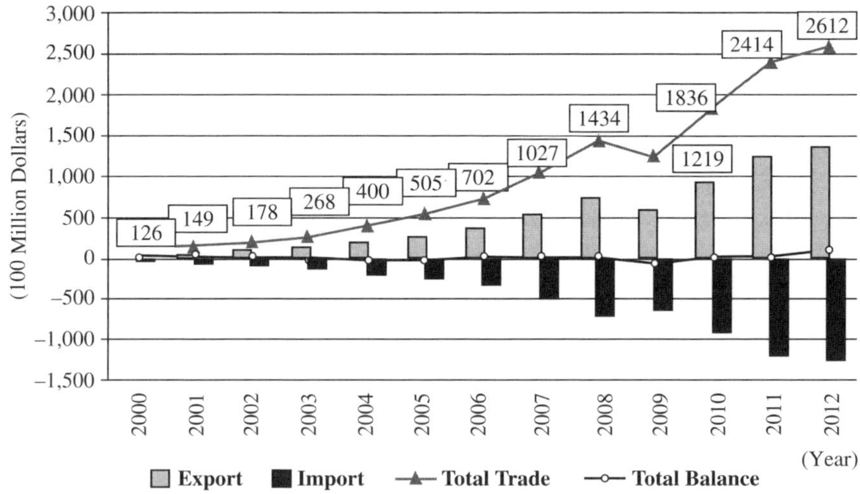

Figure 9.3 Change Trends of the Sino-Latin American Trade from 2000 to 2012

Source: CEIC database.

shown in Table 9.5, overall, the proportion of Asia and North America in China's total foreign trade volume showed a downward trend, but the proportion of Africa, Latin America, Oceania and the Pacific island countries showed a rising trend; the proportion of Europe basically did not change significantly. The proportion of the Sino-Latin American trade in China's total foreign trade rose from 2.9% in 2001 to 6.8% in 2012, while in the same period the proportion of North America in China's total foreign trade fell from 17.2% to 13.9%.[2] Specifically, in 2001–2012 the proportion of Latin America in China's exports rose from 3.1% to 6.6%, and the proportion of Latin America in China's imports rose from 2.8% to 7% (see Table 9.5).

In terms of Latin America, the proportion of the total trade of developed economies, mainly the United States, the EU and Japan, with the Latin-American countries in the total amount of the foreign trade of Latin America, was declining year by year, while the proportion of the emerging Asian economies represented by China increased

[2]The author's calculation according to the data of the China Economic Database from CEIC Data.

Table 9.5 The Proportion of Each Continent in China's Exports, Imports, and Total Trade (%)

		2000	2001	2002	2003	2004	2005	2006	2007	2008	2009	2010	2011	2012
Export	Asia	53.1	53.0	52.6	50.8	49.8	48.1	47.0	46.6	46.4	47.3	46.4	47.4	49.1
	Africa	2.0	2.3	2.1	2.3	2.3	2.5	2.8	3.1	3.6	4.0	3.8	3.8	4.2
	Europe	18.3	18.5	17.9	20.1	20.6	21.7	22.2	23.6	24.0	22.0	22.5	21.8	19.3
	Latin America	2.9	3.1	2.9	2.7	3.1	3.1	3.7	4.2	5.0	4.8	5.8	6.4	6.6
	North America	22.2	21.7	22.8	22.4	22.5	22.9	22.6	20.7	19.2	19.9	19.4	18.4	18.6
	Oceania and the Pacific Islands	1.6	1.5	1.6	1.7	1.7	1.7	1.7	1.7	1.8	2.1	2.1	2.2	2.2
Import	Asia	62.8	60.4	65.0	66.1	65.8	66.9	66.4	64.9	62.0	60.0	59.9	57.8	57.3
	Africa	2.5	2.0	1.8	2.0	2.8	3.2	3.6	3.8	4.9	4.3	4.8	5.4	6.2
	Europe	18.1	19.9	17.6	16.9	15.9	14.6	14.5	14.6	14.8	16.1	15.6	16.5	15.8
	Latin America	2.4	2.8	2.8	3.6	3.9	4.1	4.3	5.3	6.3	6.4	6.6	6.9	7.0
	North America	11.6	12.4	10.5	9.3	9.3	8.5	8.5	8.4	8.3	8.9	8.4	8.3	8.6
	Oceania and the Pacific Islands	2.6	2.6	2.3	2.1	2.4	2.7	2.7	3.0	3.6	4.2	4.7	5.1	5.1
Trade	Asia	57.7	56.5	58.5	58.2	57.6	56.8	55.7	54.6	53.3	53.1	52.7	52.3	53.0
	Africa	2.2	2.1	2.0	2.2	2.6	2.8	3.2	3.4	4.2	4.1	4.3	4.6	5.1
	Europe	18.2	19.2	17.8	18.6	18.3	18.4	18.8	19.7	20.0	19.3	19.3	19.3	17.7
	Latin America	2.7	2.9	2.9	3.2	3.5	3.5	4.0	4.7	5.6	5.5	6.2	6.6	6.8
	North America	17.2	17.2	16.9	16.0	16.0	16.2	16.2	15.3	14.4	14.9	14.2	13.6	13.9
	Oceania and the Pacific Islands	2.1	2.0	2.0	1.9	2.0	2.2	2.1	2.3	2.6	3.1	3.3	3.6	3.5

Source: CEIC Database.

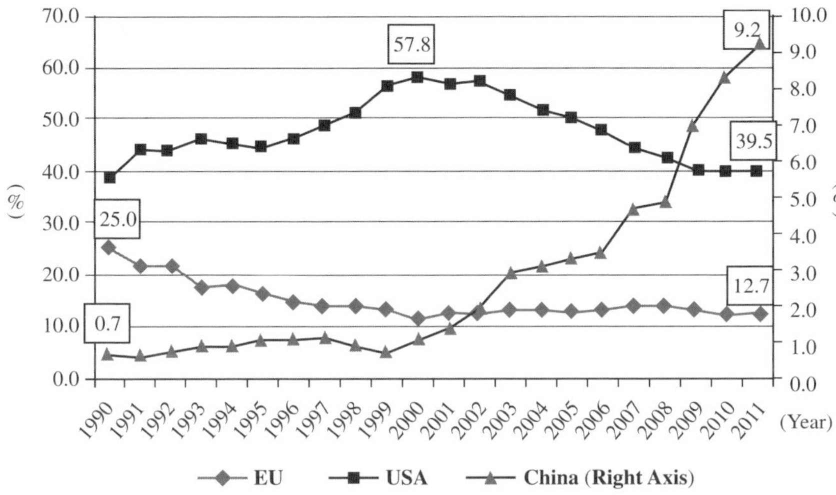

Figure 9.4 Proportions of EU, USA, and China in the Total Exports of Latin America according to Export Destinations

Source: The author's calculation according to the CEIC database.

year by year. As is shown in Figure 9.4, according to the division of export destinations, in 2000–2011 the proportion of developed economies and China in the total export of Latin America showed two opposite trends. China's proportion had risen from 0.7% in 1990 to 9.2% in 2011. If considered by the source of imports, this trend was still obvious — China's share of the total imports of Latin America rose from 0.5% in 1990 to 13.5% in 2011 (see Figure 9.5). According to the prediction of ECLAC, by 2020 the proportions of the Latin-American exports to the United States, the EU and China in its total export will have reached 28.4%, 13.6%, and 19.3%, respectively,[3] with slight variations; the importance of China to Latin America has risen further.

Given the differences between the Latin-American countries, the trade situations between China and the Latin-American countries are also different. As is shown in Figure 9.6, in general, China had maintained trade deficit with South American resource-exporting

[3]CEPAL, *La Republica Popular China y America Latina y el Caribe: Hacia una Relacion Estrategica*, mayo de, 2010.

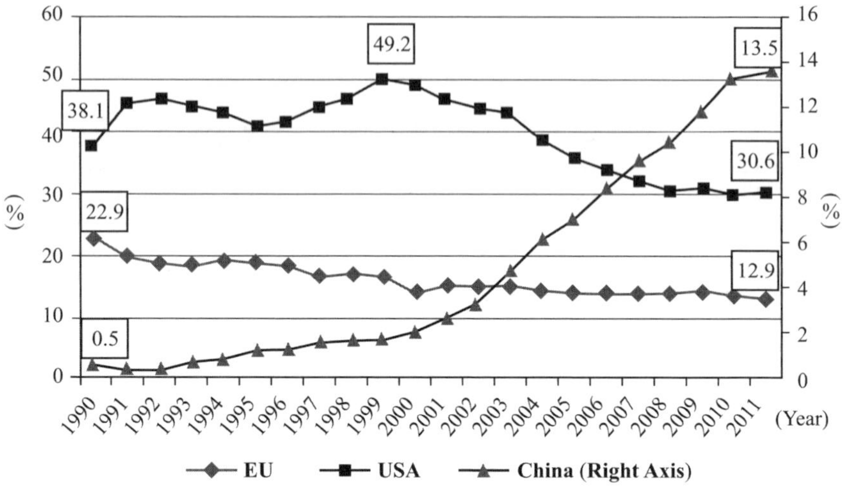

Figure 9.5 Proportions of EU, USA, and China in the Total Imports of Latin America According to Import Sources

Source: The author's calculation according to the CEIC database.

countries, while China had maintained the basic state of trade surplus with Central America and Mexico (excluding Costa Rica). In 2012, the trade deficits of China against Brazil, Chile, Venezuela, Costa Rica, and Peru were respectively \$18.6 billion, \$8 billion, \$5.1 billion, \$4.4 billion and \$3.1 billion; China's trade surplus against Mexico and Panama ranked No. 1 and No. 2 in the Latin-American region, reaching \$18.4 billion and \$15.3 billion respectively.

2. The Main Inter-industry Trade has Reflected the Complementarity of the Trade Structure

From the perspective of the trade structure, the two sides have a high complementary goods structure, mainly in the inter-industry trade. China's goods exported to Latin America are concentrated in "industrial products according to the classification of raw materials" and the "machinery and transport equipment", and its goods imported from Latin America are concentrated in the "non-food raw materials (excluding fuel)" in the primary products and "fossil fuels, lubricants and related materials". According to the report of ECLAC, except

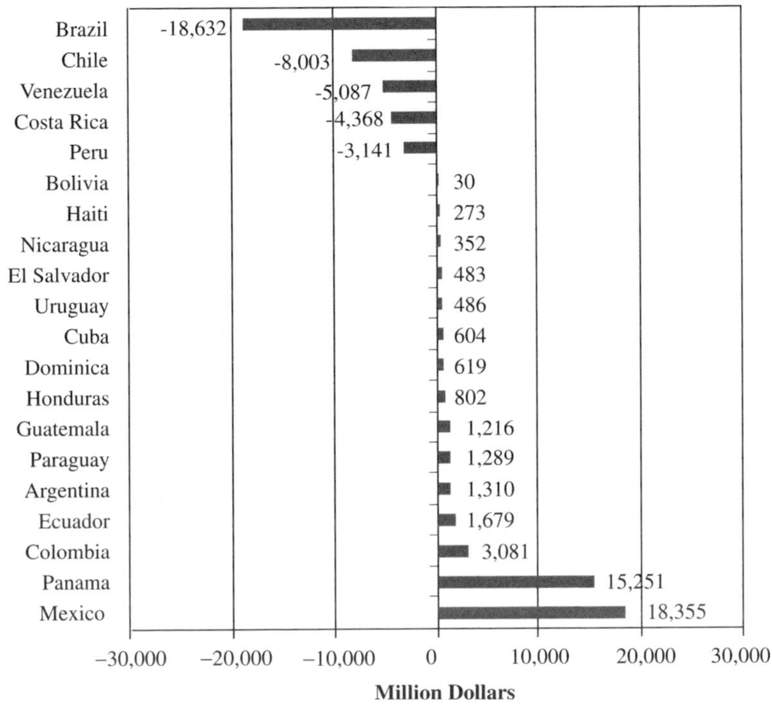

Figure 9.6 Trade Balance of China and 20 Latin-American Countries in 2012
Source: The author's calculation according to the CEIC database.

Mexico, Costa Rica, and El Salvador that have exported a large number of high-tech products to China, most Latin American countries have a very high degree of concentration on the primary products exported to China. For example, from 2007 to 2009, the proportions of the top five exported goods of Brazil, Argentina, Venezuela, Colombia, Chile, and Peru in their total exports to China reached respectively 82.2%, 92%, 98.2% and 97.6%, 92.3%, and 80.8%.[4] From this point of view, China's high economic growth demanding for the primary products is precisely one of the important factors that had

[4]ECLAC, *People's Republic of China and Latin America and the Caribbean: Ushering in a New Era in the Economic and Trade Relationship*, 2011, p. 23.

led to the earlier economic recovery of the South American countries during the international financial crisis than that of Mexico and Central America. At the same time, the Latin-American countries also recognize that China has become the platform for its Asian neighbors to indirectly export to developed countries (they are the suppliers of capital goods needed for China's manufacturing industry and the suppliers of intermediate inputs). Therefore, the Latin-American countries actively participating in the Asian supply chain and the value chain will become a powerful force in the continuous optimization of the Latin American trade structure.

Take Brazil, Mexico and Argentina, for example. In 2011, the proportions of the category of "machinery and transport equipment" were the highest in China's exports to Brazil, Mexico and Argentina, reaching 48%, 50%, and 51% respectively, while the proportions of the category of "non-edible raw materials (excluding fuel)" were the highest in China's imports from Brazil and Argentina, reaching 78% and 73% respectively. Mexico was relatively special. There was a considerable proportion of intra-industry trade between China and Mexico — the proportion of China's import of "machinery and transport equipment" from Mexico had reached 41% (see Table 9.6).

II. The Rapid Growth of Investment: A New Highlight of Economic and Trade Cooperation

1. In 2010: The Investment Exceeded $10 Billion

As shown in Table 9.7, 2010 is a year of rapid growth of the Chinese investment in Latin America. From the perspective of the volume of flow, the investment reached $10.54 billion, up 43.8%, accounting for 15.3% of China's total foreign investment that year; from the perspective of stock, the investment reached $43.88 billion, accounting for 13.8% of China's total stock of foreign investment that year. Latin America has become the second most concentrated area for China's FDI stock, after Asia.

According to the statistics of ECLAC, in 2010, China had become Latin America's third biggest country of source investment (9%) after

Table 9.6 Structure of Commodity Trade between China, Brazil, Mexico, and Argentina in 2011 (%)

	Brazil		Mexico		Argentina	
	Export	Import	Export	Import	Export	Import
Category 0: Food and Live Animals	1.74	3.98	1.88	1.44	0.46	4.67
Category 1: Beverages and Tobacco	0.01	0.84	0.01	0.07	0.00	2.17
Category 2: Non-edible Raw Materials (Except Fuels)	0.46	77.70	1.05	32.51	0.29	73.04
Category 3: Mineral Fuels, Lubricants, and Related Materials	1.19	9.32	0.33	12.55	0.09	5.11
Category 4: Animal and Vegetable Oils, Fats, and Waxes	0.00	1.18	0.00	0.00	0.00	8.31
Category 5: Chemical Products and Related Products	9.88	1.24	4.99	5.26	12.39	2.59
Category 6: Manufactured Goods by Classification of Raw Materials	19.99	3.30	20.76	3.17	15.21	3.60
Category 7: Machinery and Transportation Equipment	48.12	2.27	49.58	40.50	51.48	0.39
Category 8: Miscellaneous Manufactured Articles	18.59	0.17	21.40	4.51	20.08	0.12
Category 9: Goods and Transactions Not Classified	0.01	0.00	0.00	0.00	0.00	0.00
Total	100.00	100.00	100.00	100.00	100.00	100.00

Source: The author's estimation according to the UN Commodity Trade Statistics Database (UN Comtrade) and the standard international trade classification (SITC Rev. 4).

the United States (17%) and the Netherlands (13%).[5] From the perspective of the industry distribution, although 90% of the investment were in the field of the exploration of natural resources such as oil, gas and mining, with Huawei and ZTE entering the telecommunications industry, and BYD Auto, Chery and Jianghuai Automobile entering the automotive industry, China's diversified pattern of investment in

[5]ECLAC, *Foreign Direct Investment in Latin America and the Caribbean 2010*, 2011, p. 11.

Table 9.7 China's Direct Investment Flows in Latin America (2003–2011) ($ Million)

	Whole Area						
	Total	Proportion in the Total Flow of China's Foreign Direct Investment (%)	The Cayman Islands	The British Virgin Islands	Proportion of the Two Areas in Latin America (%)	Excluding the Cayman Islands and the British Virgin Islands	Proportion in Latin America (%)
2003	1,038.15	36.4	806.61	209.68	97.9	21.86	2.1
2004	1,762.72	32.1	1,286.13	385.52	94.8	91.07	5.2
2005	6,466.16	52.7	5,162.75	1,226.08	98.8	77.33	1.2
2006	8,468.74	48.0	7,832.72	538.11	98.8	97.91	1.2
2007	4,902.41	18.5	2,601.59	1,876.14	91.3	424.68	8.7
2008	3,677.25	6.6	1,524.01	2,104.33	98.7	48.91	1.3
2009	7,327.9	13.0	5,366.3	1,612.05	95.2	349.55	4.8
2010	10,538.27	15.3	3,496.13	6,119.76	91.2	922.38	8.8
2011	11,935.82	16.0	4,936.46	6,208.33	93.4	791.03	6.6

Note: The data of 2003–2006 are China's non-financial direct investment data in Latin America; the data of 2007–2011 are China's direct investment data for the entire industries in Latin America.

Source: The author's calculation according to the *Statistics Bulletin of China's Annual Foreign Direct Investment in 2011* by the Chinese Ministry of Commerce.

Latin America had gradually been formed; in the medium term, the manufacturing industry, infrastructure and agriculture would also be included. In short, the optimization of trade structure and the diversification of investment are the "double engines" for the overall development of the Sino-Latin American economic and trade cooperation.

According to the statistics of ECLAC, the receivers of China's direct investment (see Table 9.8) in Latin America were mainly Brazil, Argentina, and Peru, which had close trade relations with China. As is shown in Table 9.9, 2010 can be described as China's first year of high investment growth in Latin America because that year the investment soared, reaching $15.3 billion,[6] 2.1 times of the

[6]Different statistical calibers have different results from the FDI data by the Chinese Ministry of Commerce. The Latin American Economic Commission believes that China's FDI statistics in Latin America are underestimated. First, not all

Table 9.8 China's Direct Investment Stocks in Latin America (2003–2011) ($ Million)

	Whole Area						
	Total (End of Year)	Proportion in China's Total Foreign Direct Investment Stocks (%)	The Cayman Islands (End of Year)	The British Virgin Islands (End of Year)	Proportion of the Two Areas in Latin America (%)	Excluding the Cayman Islands and the British Virgin Islands (End of Year)	Proportion in Latin America (%)
2003	4,619.32	13.9	3,690.68	532.64	91.4	396	8.6
2004	8,268.37	18.5	6,659.91	1,089.38	93.7	519.08	6.3
2005	11,469.61	20.0	8,935.59	1,983.58	95.2	550.44	4.8
2006	19,694.37	26.3	14,209.19	4,750.4	96.3	734.78	3.7
2007	24,700.91	20.9	16,810.68	6,626.54	94.9	1,263.69	5.1
2008	32,240.15	17.5	20,327.45	10,477.33	95.5	1,435.37	4.5
2009	30,595.48	12.4	13,577.07	15,060.69	93.6	1,957.72	6.4
2010	43,875.64	13.8	17,256.27	23,242.76	92.3	3,376.61	7.7
2011	55,171.75	13.0	21,692.32	29,261.41	92.4	4,218.02	7.6

Source: The author's calculation according to the *Statistics Bulletin of China's Annual Foreign Direct Investment in 2011* by the Chinese Ministry of Commerce.

cumulative investment of the previous 20 years ($7.3 billion). In 2011, China's investment in Latin America would continue to grow, possibly reaching $22.7 billion.

companies have their investments registered. Second, China and the recipient countries have asymmetry information — many companies invest through holding shares of the third parties, which are usually registered as financial or service corporations. 79% of Chinese FDI is invested by the British Virgin Islands, the Cayman Islands or Hong Kong of China. In addition, there is the phenomenon of the return of investment flowing to Hong Kong back to the Mainland China, forming the "false foreign investment". Third, although the "assets for resources" in the field of natural resources have not been regarded as investment, they at least temporarily have enabled the Chinese companies to have controlled some of the resources. Moreover, China companies have invested heavily in infrastructure, and they are engaged in production and provide a variety of services in the recipient countries, but these investments are treated in statistics as exports rather than investments. Fourth, in the large mergers and acquisitions announced in 2010, many have not yet been registered in the statistics of international balance of payments in the recipient countries in early 2011.

Table 9.9 China's Direct Investment in Latin America ($ Million)

	Confirmed Investment		Planned Investment
Country	1990–2009	2010	After 2011
Argentina	143	5,550	3,530
Brazil	255	9,563	9,870
Colombia	1,677	3	N.A.
Costa Rica	13	5	700
Ecuador	1,619	41	N.A.
Guyana	1,000	N.A.	N.A.
Mexico	127	5	N.A.
Peru	2,262	84	8,640
Venezuela	240	N.A.	N.A.
Total	7,336	15,251	22,740

Source: ECLAC, *Foreign Direct Investment in Latin America and the Caribbean 2010*, 2011, p. 107.

2. The Characteristics of China's Direct Investment in Latin America

From the perspective of the three aspects of industry, business and investment, China's direct investment in Latin America has the following characteristics.

First, large investments are mainly concentrated in energy and mineral resources. From 1994 to 2010, China's total investment in Latin America in the field of oil and gas (see Table 9.10) reached \$23.6 billion, mainly concentrated in the countries rich in oil and gas resources, such as Venezuela, Brazil, Argentina, Ecuador, Colombia, and Peru. The fields of mineral deposit are mainly copper and iron ore. In recent years, the rising copper prices and the game of the iron ore pricing have urged Chinese enterprises to reserve resources in the layout of overseas metal reserves ahead of time. China's agricultural investment is mainly concentrated on Peru's fishery, Jamaica's sugar cane planting, and the soybean industry of Brazil and Argentina. Although China's investment in the agricultural sector is limited, it has an important impact on the Latin-American agricultural development, and even on its rural life. The infrastructure construction and manufacturing industry have become an important fulcrum of China's layout of investment diversification in the recent two years.

Second, the central-government-owned enterprises (central enterprises) occupy the leading position. PetroChina, the Sinopec, CNOOC and the Sinochem are the leading roles of large mergers and acquisitions. The assets of the central enterprises are larger and in a monopoly position. In general, large and monopolistic enterprises are more likely to invest in foreign companies. However, it should be noted that the state-owned enterprises have equal ability and resistance in terms of overseas acquisition; because of the nature of the "state-owned enterprises", the central enterprises have far greater resistance than that of the private enterprises.

Third, from the perspective of investment, China's investments in Latin America (see Tables 9.11–9.13) are mainly through mergers and acquisitions, with less green field investment, which is closely related to the primary phase of the implementation of the "going out" strategy of Chinese enterprises. Compared with those multinational corporations of the developed countries that have existed in Latin America for many years, the Chinese enterprises have less experience from negotiations to doing business and to risk control. Therefore, through mergers and acquisitions to take over the Latin-American assets, the Chinese enterprises can quickly get involved into the local market with reduced transaction costs. With the accumulation of practical experience and the grasp of domestic demand in Latin America, the Chinese enterprises will increase their green field investment in Latin America correspondingly. This trend may be reflected in the manufacturing sector more obviously.

Table 9.14 is a list of China's major investments in Latin America in 2011 (incomplete statistics). It can be seen that China's investment in Latin America would continue to grow and new changes had emerged, e.g., in addition to the traditional oil and gas field, the manufacturing industry (automotive, communication and machinery equipment, etc.) had become a new growth area. The investment of the manufacturing sector oriented toward meeting the demand of the Latin American domestic market and creating the platform for the export to America would be driven by "two wheels", entering

Table 9.10 China's Investment Projects in the Field of Oil and Gas in Latin America (1994–2010)

Invested Projects	Country	Year	Amount of Investment ($ Million)	By Way of	Note
			Mining Industry		
CNPC	Peru	1994	46	Franchise	In production, 6/7 of Talara Oil Field
CNPC	Venezuela	1998	>240	Franchise	In joint production with PDVSA, total investment unknown
NPC	Venezuela	1998	N.A.	Franchise	In joint production with PDVSA
CNPC	Ecuador	2003	199	Franchise	Canceled in 2010 because the change of the regulatory policy
CNPC	Peru	2004	200	Merger and acquisition	In production, 45% of Plus Petrol Norte Company
CNPC	Peru	2005	80	Franchise	In production; In the No. 111 and No. 113 Part of the Region of Madre de Dios
CNPC (55%) and the Sinopec (45%)	Ecuador	2006	1,420	Merger and acquisition	In production; Acquisition of the oil assets and pipe assets of the Canadian Oil Company (Encana)
The Sinopec	Colombia	2006	800	Merger and acquisition	In production; joint acquisition of 50% of the shares of the Colombian Omimex Company with the Indian Oil and Gas Company (ONGC)
SINOCHEM	Colombia	2009	877	Merger and acquisition	In production; acquisition of 100% of the shares of British Emerald Energy Company
The Sinopec	Brazil	2010	7,111	Merger and acquisition	Acquisition of 40% of the oil and gas resources of the Spanish Repsol Brasil in Brazil

(*Continued*)

Table 9.10 (*Continued*)

Invested Projects	Country	Year	Amount of Investment ($ Million)	By Way of	Note
SINOCHEM	Brazil	2010	3,070	Merger and acquisition	Acquisition of 40% of the shares of the Brazilian Peregrino Oil Field Held by Norway's Statoil; awaiting approval from China and Brazil
The Sinopec	Argentina	2010	2,450	Merger and acquisition	Acquisition of 100% of the shares of the US OXY Argentine Branch
CNOOC	Argentina	2010	3,100	Merger and acquisition	Acquisition of 50% of the shares of the wholly owned subsidiary — Bridas — of Argentine Energy Holdings Limited
CNOOC	Argentina	2010	3,500	Merger and acquisition	Acquisition of 60% of the shares of the Pan American Energy held by B.P by the above Bridas Joint Venture Company; plus the obtained 40% of the rights and interests of PAE, the joint venture would have 100% of the shares; not implemented
			Refining Industry		
CNPC	Costa Rica	2009	700	Greenfield investment	Announced, but not implemented
CNPC	Cuba	2010	N.A.	Greenfield investment	Announced, but not implemented
Total			23,553		

Source: ECLAC, *Foreign Direct Investment in Latin America and the Caribbean 2010*, 2011.

Table 9.11 China's Major Investment in the Mineral Field of Latin America (1992–2010) ($ Million)

Company	Sector	Year	Completed Investment	Announced Investment	Status
		Peru			
Shougang Group	Iron ore	1992	253	1,000	In operation; announced the expansion of investment
Chalco	Copper mine	2007	830	2,200	Under the environmental impact study; to begin production in 2013
Zijin Mining Group Co. Ltd. (45%), Tongling Nonferrous Metals (35%) and Xiamen Jianfa (20%) Joined	Copper mine	2007	190	1,440	Under the feasibility study; production date uncertain
China Minmetals (60%) and Jiangxi Copper (40%) Joined	Copper mine	2008	543	2,500	Under the environmental impact study; to begin production in 2014
Shandong Zibo Nan Jinzhao Group	Iron ore	2009	100	1,500	In the exploration phase
		Brazil			
Wuhan Iron and Steel	Iron ore	2010	400	5,000	Starting the iron ore mining; Announcing the construction of a steel plant, operation started, date uncertain
ECE	Iron ore	2010		1,200	Announced, to be confirmed
		Guyana			
Chongqing Bosai Mining	Bauxite	2008	1,000		In operation

Source: ECLAC, *Foreign Direct Investment in Latin America and the Caribbean 2010*, 2011, p. 107.

the fast lane. Moreover, the investments of some of the projects were the expanded re-investments based on the newly built companies in 2009–2010, showing a promising outlook of the Latin-American economy.

Table 9.12 China's Major Investments in the Latin-American Infrastructure (2009–2010)

Investors	Sector	Year of Entering	Estimated Value of Investment ($ Million)	Note
		Brazil		
State Grid Corporation of China	Transmission lines	2010	1,700	Acquisition of all or part of the 7 Brazilian transmission companies held by the Spanish Energy Company
Zhejiang Insigma	Transmission lines	2010	100	Bidding
		Ecuador		
The Sinohydro	Hydropower station	2009	2,000	The construction of the largest project for the Ecuador Government — the Coca Codo Sinclair Hydropower Station (CCS Project); China Import and Export Bank Provided the financing of $1.7b Billion to the project
		Venezuela		
The Sinohydro	Thermoelectric gas	2010	1,600	Construction of a thermoelectric gas power plant for the Venezuelan Government

Source: ECLAC, *Foreign Direct Investment in Latin America and the Caribbean 2010*, 2011.

Table 9.15 is a list of China's major agricultural investments in South American countries. The content of the projects shows the main features of China's agricultural investment in Latin America. First, China's growing investment in the agriculture of South American countries was driven by the following factors: ensuring the long-term supply of food and expanding the range of source selection; diversifying its portfolio from only buying US treasury bonds

Table 9.13 China's Major Investments in the Latin American Manufacturing (1998–2010)

Classification According to the Receiving Country	Sector	Year of Entering	Estimated Value of Investment ($ Million)	Direct Employment Created (Job)	Note
			Brazil		
ZongShen Import & Export Corp. Ltd	Motorcycle	2009	19	278	Full acquisition of the Brazilian motorcycle company Kasinski; 100,000 units
GREE	Electric appliance	1998	43	500	Sales of over 200 million Reais
China South Industries Group	Motorcycle	2007	190	181	100,000 units
SANY	Machinery	2010	200	0	Investment announced, but not implemented
			Uruguay		
Chery	Automobile	2009	100	300	Production capacity of 250 units per month
			Mexico		
Lenovo	Information and communications technology	2007	40	1,000	Indirectly creating 3,000 jobs, with an annual output of 5 million computers
Golden Dragon Precise Tube Group	Metallurgy (Brass)	2009	50	960	Annual production capacity reaching 60,000 tons

Source: ECLAC, *Foreign Direct Investment in Latin America and the Caribbean 2010*, 2011.

to investing in commodities, and easing the contradiction between the domestic supply and demand. Second, the principle of China's agricultural investment had mainly focused on the agricultural production and the infrastructure of logistics. Third, China's entering strategy had shifted from the direct purchase of land to leasing plans.

Table 9.14 China's Major Investment and Economic Cooperation Projects in Latin America in 2011 (By the End of October, 2011)

Country	Time of Signing (Or Announcing)	Sector	Project Content	Amount ($100 Million)	Note
Brazil	October	Automobile	JAC set up a factory in Camacari in the state of Bahia.	5.2	80% was funded by the Brazilian dealer SHC group; 20% was funded by JAC. Expected to be completed and put into operation in 2014, with an annual output of 100,000 units, creating 3,500 local jobs.
	October	Oil Equipment	The establishment of Brazilian Baoji Oil Machinery Company by the joint investment of Baoji Oilfield Machinery Co. Ltd. funded by PetroChina, the Brazilian PetroChina and the Brazilian energy company ASPERBRAS.		The Chinese Baoji Oilfield Machinery Company accounted for 34% of the total registered capital of the Brazilian Oil Equipment Company; the other two companies accounted for 33%.
	October	Oil Equipment	Brazilian Baoji Oil Equipment Company set up an oil exploration and mining equipment factory in Bahia, Brazil.	0.736	The new plant was expected to put into operation in the second half of 2012.
	October	Automobile	The Great Wall Motor announced its plan to establish a vehicle manufacturing plant in Brazil.		Announced, but not yet implemented.

(Continued)

Table 9.14 (*Continued*)

Country	Time of Signing (Or Announcing)	Sector	Project Content	Amount ($100 Million)	Note
	July	Automobile	Chery Automobile set up its factory in the city of Jacarei in Sao Paulo.	4	Its final annual production capacity would reach 150 thousand units; the number of direct employment would be 3,000 people; it was expected to be completed in the second half of 2013.
Argentina	August 25	Communications	Lenovo and Newsan established a notebook computer assembly plant in Tierra del Fuego.	0.14	
	August 4	Finance	ICBC acquired the Argentine branch of South African Standard Bank.	7–8	Pending the approval of the legislative bodies of the two countries.
	June 7	Automobile	The JAC Truck Co. Ltd. cooperated with the Argentine province of San Juan to construct a truck plant.	0.03	To be completed in September, 2011.
	February 16	Oil	Argentine Pan American Energy Company jointly owned by CNOOC and Argentine Bridas Energy Company acquired the Oil Refinery and Gas Station of Esso which was a branch of the US Exxon Mobil.	8–9	

Colombia	January	Agrochemicals	The Sinochem planned to buy 60% of the shares of the Israeli Makhteshim Agan industrial company so as to indirectly control Proficol Andina — the company's subsidiary in Colombia.		Proficol Andina is Colombia's main agricultural chemicals manufacturer, with annual sales of 86.5 billion pesos.
Ecuador	October 15	Infrastructure	Power Construction Corporation of China signed hydropower project of DELSI-TANISAGUA with Ecuador.	1.94	The contract contents included supplementary survey, basic design and construction design, mechanical and electrical supply and installation, civil construction, which was a complete and regular general EPC contract. The total duration was 48 months.
	August 17	Infrastructure	Xinjiang Goldwind Sci & Tech Co. Ltd. won the bid of Villonaco wind power station in Ecuador.	0.34	The construction was to be started in September; the project consisted of 11 power-generation wind turbines, a transformer substation and a 5-kilometer-long transmission line.

Source: A summary of the news from the Economic and Commercial Counselors of Chinese Embassies in the Latin-American countries and the reports of domestic and foreign media; the statistics are incomplete.

Table 9.15 2009–2011 Publically Announced China's Major Agricultural Investments in the South American Countries

Date; Type	Status; Time Span	Chinese Company	Target Company; Area	Amount	Content of Investment
June, 2011; Joint Venture	Undetermined; having signed a preliminary agreement with Cresud AS — an Argentine agricultural company.	Heilongjiang Great Northern Wilderness Agribusiness Group Corporation	Agricultural Company Cresud; Argentina	Unknown	Cooperation would be focused on soybean production. The agreement between the company, Cresud and the local partners in Rio Negro province was intended to avoid the strong domestic reaction to the ownership of farmland in Argentina (Argentina has passed legislation to restrict foreign individuals and enterprises to buy land in the rural area of Argentina — below 1,000 hectares). The Heilongjiang Great Northern Wilderness Agribusiness Group Corporation did not acquire the land directly.
June, 2011; Invest-ment/ Off-take	Undetermined; in 5–10 years	Heilongjiang Great Northern Wilderness Agribusiness Group Corporation	Rio Negro	$1.5 billion	Through the assembly of advanced irrigation facilities, the project was meant to lease and develop 30 million hectares of arable land to produce soybeans, corn and other agricultural products and sell them back to China. In addition, the project also included the construction of ancillary power generation project and the expansion of the port project.
June, 2011 Invest-ment/ Off-take	Undetermined; 5 years, Brazilian Bahia State Governor had signed an agreement of intent.	Chongqing Grain Group	Bahia, Brazil	$2 billion-$2.5 billion	The company planned to build a soybean press factory that could process 1.15 million tons of soybeans a year, a storage warehouse that could store 400,000 tons of soybeans, a fertilizer plant and a relevant logistics system. In return, the government of Bahia promised to provide tax allowances and a 100-hectare land. The project was expected to eventually employ 1,000 local workers.

May, 2011 Investment/ Off-take	Undetermined; A memorandum of understanding had been signed with Goias, Brazil.	Sanhe Huifu Grain Food & Oil Group Co. Ltd.	Goias, Brazil	$7.5 billion	Investing $7.5 billion in Brazil's soybean production, storage and transportation to ensure the supply of 6 million tons of soybeans to China every year. Chinese would also provide services such as chemical fertilizer, pesticide and seeds and other inputs to raise the yield of the state. China would also increase imports of soybeans and their byproducts.
January, 2011 Investment	Undetermined	Tieira del Fuego Energia y Quimica	Tierra de Fuego, Argentina	$1 billion	Investing $1 billion to build a chemical fertilizer plant, a thermal power station and a commercial port.
May, 2010 Purchasing Land	Undetermined; An agreement of intent had been signed.	Pallas Investment Company and the Chinese government	Bahia, Brazil	Unknown	Pallas International Group constituted by private investors signed a contract to jointly buy 20–25 million hectares of land in the state of Bahia with the Chinese government to be used in the production of renewable energy.
April, 2010 Production Agreement	Undetermined	Chongqing Grain Group	Bahia, Brazil	$0.3 billion	The company planned to buy 100,000 hectares of land for the production of soybeans. 60% of the investment would be obtained from the financing of the National Development Bank.

Source: Author's summary according to the report of the Holland Cooperative Bank (Rabobank).

In August 2010, the Brazilian government signed a decree to limit the amount of land to no more than 5,000 hectares purchased by a single foreigner or foreign company. According to the decree, all the Brazilian firms controlled by foreigners or foreign companies must declare the amount of land owned by them to the local governments each quarter; the size of the land controlled by foreigners or foreign companies should not exceed 25% of the total land area of the local city (or town). In 2011, the Brazil government introduced a new law to prohibit foreigners, foreign enterprises and foreign holdings of Brazil enterprises to purchase or acquire Brazilian enterprises with land ownerships. This was an upgraded version of the purchase-limitation order. On December 22, 2011, the Argentine Parliament passed an act to restrict foreigners to buy land. According to the act, foreign institutions and individuals in Argentina's purchase of the arable land could not be more than 15% of the country's agricultural land area, and the land purchased by the buyers of each country could not be more than 30% of the total amount of the land that foreigners were allowed to buy. In addition, the act stipulated that the land purchased by each foreign legal person or natural person in Argentina could not be over 1,000 hectares; the land with plenty of water resources could not be sold to foreigners; foreigners purchasing land in Argentina would no longer be regarded as investors. Since Brazil and Argentina had implemented the restriction on land-purchasing by foreigners, the Chinese investors had changed their mode of investment, i.e., investment in infrastructure in exchange for crop offtakes rather than direct investment in land. Fourth, it is expected that China's agricultural investment in South America (especially in Brazil) will continue to grow. As the grain stock is at the historical low point, the world will depend on the potential of the South American countries to provide more agricultural production. Compared with other countries in the world, Brazil has more resources to invest in crop production. Fifth, although China's agricultural investment is limited in size, it still has a significant impact on the domestic industry of Latin America. However, China's agricultural investment is often integrated into China's value chain, thus reducing the added value of China to stay in the Latin American countries, which is not conducive to the effect of poverty reduction in Latin America. This is the issue that China's agricultural "going out" should pay attention to.

III. Rise and Expectation: the Financial Cooperation Is Still in Its Growing Period

With the rapid growth of the Sino-Latin American trade and investment, the demand for the further development of the financial cooperation had become "ripe", and the international financial crisis objectively also had led to the acceleration of the Sino-Latin American financial cooperation. For example, as is shown in Table 9.16, on January 12, 2009, China officially became the 48th member of

Table 9.16 Content of Financial Cooperation between China and Latin America

Project	Main Content
Cooperation with the Inter American Development Bank (IDB)	1. On January 12, 2009, China officially became the 48th member of the Inter American Development Bank; 2. China Eximbank and the Inter American Development Bank jointly set up a 1-billion-dollar fund to provide financing to the 26 loan countries of the Inter American Development Bank, including China's enterprises in Latin America and the Caribbean region to carry out investment cooperation. The fund was divided into three parts: the Sino-Latin American Infrastructure Fund, the Medium-sized Enterprise Fund and the Natural Resources Fund.
Signing Currency Swap Agreement	With Argentina (¥70 billion, 2009); with Brazil (¥190 billion, 2012)
Signing the "Loan for Oil" Agreement with the Latin American Countries	Venezuela (2009, 2010, 2011); Brazil (2009); Ecuador (2009)
Establishing More Bank Branches	On November 27, 2012, ICBC (Peru) Co., Ltd. held a establishment ceremony in Lima, the capital of the Republic of Peru, becoming the first Chinese commercial bank to have successfully entered the Peru market. ICBC Peru is the first wholly owned subsidiary of ICBC formally established in the South American continent

Source: The author's summary according to the news reports.

the Inter American Development Bank; China had signed the bilateral currency swap agreement with Argentina; China had signed the "Loans for Oil" deals with Brazil, Venezuela and Ecuador; China and Venezuela jointly had established a financing fund, and the Central Bank of Chile had put RMB into its foreign exchange reserve portfolios. From these measures it is not difficult to see, first, whether it was China's participation in increasing capital to regional multilateral lending institutions, or both sides actively promoted the cooperation in the fields of currency and energy. They had reflected that the financial cooperation had become the objective demand of the rapid development of the Sino-Latin American economic and trade relation. Second, the trade financing gap resulted from the international financial crisis and the world's economic recession had provided an opportunity for the financial cooperation between China and Latin America. On the one hand, with a huge economic scale, abundant foreign exchange reserves, high financial profitability and its growing discourse power in the field of international finance, China could help the Latin-American countries actively respond to difficulties such as the trade financing atrophy, the shortage of liquidity of financial institutions and the lack of infrastructure construction funds; on the other hand, the continuous innovation of the financial cooperation model was not only conducive to the diversification of China's management of its foreign exchange reserves, but also helpful for China to overcome the "bottleneck" of resources, maintaining sustainable economic growth.

In addition to trade, investment and financial cooperation, China and Latin America had also made considerable progress in the economic cooperation in contracting projects, labor service and design consultation. According to the statistics of ECLAC, in 2007 and 2008, the average size of China's economic cooperation with Latin America reached \$2.986 billion, equivalent to 5.3% of the total size of China's economic cooperation (\$56.51 billion). Although the proportion was far lower than the corresponding index of China's economic cooperation with Asia (49.9%) and Africa (29%), with the rise of the economic status of China and the Latin-American countries,

Table 9.17 China's Foreign Economic Cooperation by Type and Region in 2007 and 2008

	Total ($ Million)	Proportion in the World (%)	Contracted Project ($ Million)	Labor Service ($ Million)	Consulting Service ($ Million)
Asia	28,192.1	49.9	24,627.8	3,248.2	320.3
Africa	16,396.8	29.0	16,062.6	230.4	103.8
Europe	3,956.3	7.0	3,442.6	494.8	18.8
Latin America	2,985.6	5.3	2,936.7	36.8	12.2
North America	862.9	1.5	786.8	68.1	8.0
Oceania	766.8	1.4	743.3	18.0	5.4
Other	28.8	0.1	27.4	1.2	0.2
China	3,314.4	5.9	0.0	3,314.4	0.0
Total	56,507.9	100.0	48,627.1	7,412.0	468.8

Source: ECLAC, *People's Republic of China and Latin America and the Caribbean: Ushering in a New Era in the Economic and Trade Relationship*, June 2011.

the opportunities for the scale of cooperation between the two sides would increase (see Table 9.17).

Section 3 Implications of the "Golden Period" of the Sino-Latin American Economic and Trade Cooperation

It can be seen from the above review that during the decade since the beginning of the 21st century, the actual progress that the Sino-Latin American economic and trade cooperation had achieved has been way beyond that in the latter half of the 20th century, and therefore, the 10 years can be said to be a "golden period" of the Sino-Latin American economic and trade cooperation. Today, China has become the second biggest economic body globally, a big trade country in the world and a new emerging country of foreign investment, marching into the world. China needs to continue to accumulate and explore the experience of participating in the global economic competition, especially the experience to carry out economic and trade cooperations in the unique environment of different regions. Looking back on the past is to better grasp the future. In terms of the Sino-Latin American economic cooperation, what are the beneficial implications that the past "golden period" has actually left us to lead the future? Therefore, this chapter will provide an in-depth exploration at this level, regarding the past achievements as a new starting point and a broader platform to push the development of the Sino-Latin American economic and trade cooperation to a higher level.

Implication 1: The new growth point is an important factor to promote the Sino-Latin American economic and trade cooperation.

During the past decade, the development of the Sino-Latin American economic and trade cooperation has been reflected mainly in two aspects: the big growth of bilateral trade and the rapid upgrading of the position of bilateral trading partners. A key factor in the development of the Sino-Latin American trade is the significant increase of the demand of China's market for energy and raw materials of Latin America. This demand had resulted in the export boom, trade price improvement and the economic growth of those Latin-American exporters of energy and raw materials, cultivating the market of the Latin-American countries, changing the additional demand of these countries into the driving force to expand their imports from China. Therefore, China's huge demand for energy and raw materials had constituted a new growth point, promoting the leap-forward development of the Sino-Latin American trade in the past 10 years.

The next 10 years, can this growth point continue to play the same role? This is a question worth serious consideration. In the foreseeable period of time, the contradiction of supply and demand of energy (especially oil), major mineral products and agricultural commodities in the international market will continue to exist, but the pricing trend of these kinds of products may have difficulty getting rid of the domination of the "raw-material-price-boom cycle". Barcena, the Executive Secretary of the Economic Commission for Latin America recently pointed out: "According to the analysis of the Economic Commission for Latin America, there are about 3–4 raw-material-price-boom cycles in the world; at present, the price-boom cycle will last at least ten years".[7] That is to say, the Latin-American countries cannot expect this resource dividend period to continue for a long period of time. This is one aspect of the problem. On the other hand, over the past decade, the phenomenon of "re-primarization" in the export commodity structure occurred in the Latin American exporters of resources. The Latin-American countries were very alert to this phenomenon, worrying about their role falling back into the "specialized production of primary products" in the international division of labor. Therefore, they had begun to make plans for the adjustment of their industrial structures, trying to revive the manufacturing industry and participating in the competition in the international market through the knowledge-and-technology intensive products with high added values. Under this background, it is obviously not enough for the bilateral Sino-Latin American trade to follow the model in the previous phase and it is necessary to have a new growth point.

The new growth point may mainly be concentrated on expanding the cooperation between the two sides in the field of industry. Generally speaking, the Latin American countries have not only a lower level in the development of the manufacturing industry than China, but also uneven development levels among themselves. As a big country of the manufacturing industry production and export, China has many advantages in its cooperation with Latin America. The main ways are to consider investing selectively in the key industries and the emerging strategic industrial departments of the Latin-American countries, expanding the strategic cooperation between the enterprises of both sides, and driving the export of the relevant technology and equipment and the transfer of the excess capacity in some industries.

It is believed that the next 10 years will be a transitional period for the model of the Sino-Latin American trade. On the one hand, China's demand for energy and raw materials of Latin America will not be reduced. For the Latin American exporters of resources, the

[7] Alicia Barcena, The Economic Development of Latin America and the Caribbean in 2012, *Latin American Studies*, No. 6, 2012, p. 4.

export of such products to China continues to be their main channel for the accumulation of funds for development. On the other hand, China is facing some kind of limited market in its commodity structure of export to Latin America and therefore has to tap the new market potential by making use of the opportunities of the adjustment of the industrial structure of the Latin-American countries. That is to say, the original growth point of the Sino-Latin American trade will continue to play a role, but a new growth point must also be cultivated in order to continue to maintain the momentum of the development of bilateral trade and achieve a rough balance of trade between the two sides.

Implication 2: China's capital advantage must be made use of appropriately.

China has a large amount of foreign exchange reserves, and the Latin-American countries in general want to get China's financial support because they are facing a shortage of funds. In the past decade, China has used its funds to promote the Sino-Latin American economic and trade cooperation in various ways with significant results. After formally joining the Inter American Development Bank in 2009, China had established a one-billion-dollar Sino-Latin American Cooperation Fund with the bank, providing financing support for 26 loan countries, so that China had formed its capital support channel at the Latin-American-region level. Since 2009, China has successively signed "Loans for Oil" agreements with Venezuela, Brazil, and Ecuador, having both met the capital needs of these countries to cope with the international financial crisis and increased the Latin-American crude oil supplies to China. The mutual fund established between China and Venezuela is also quite innovative: On the one hand, Venezuela's state oil company increased its crude oil export to China as a repayment guarantee for China's capital investment; on the other hand, the fund in Venezuela was mainly used for the development and construction of railways, telecommunications, shipbuilding, mining, agriculture, and housing. It can be said that this is a kind of extension of the "Loans for Oil" model, further expanding the scope and areas of the Sino-Venezuelan cooperation. The above example shows that as long as the amount of funds can be controlled appropriately and a more reliable repayment guarantee can be obtained, this kind of cooperation making use of the advantage of China's funds can continue to be carried out. In his speech at the UN Economic Commission for Latin America on June 26, 2012, Premier Wen Jiabao proposed that China was ready to initiate the establishment of the Sino-Latin American Cooperation Fund; China Development Bank would take the lead to set up special loans for the support of the infrastructure of the Latin-American countries; the Chinese government would set up special funds for the development of the Sino-Latin American agricultural cooperation. It was expected that these initiatives, once implemented, would have a great role in promoting the Sino-Latin American economic and trade cooperation.

Implication 3: China's investment model in Latin America in the previous phase should be correctly evaluated.

From what have been mentioned above, three features can be summarized about China's direct investment in Latin America in the previous phase. (1) Large amounts of investment had been mainly concentrated in energy and minerals; (2) The central enterprises were the main investors; (3) More investments had been put on mergers and acquisitions than on green fields. These three features precisely show that the guiding ideology and practice of China's investment in Latin America in the first phase is correct. In the past 10 years, China's investment in Latin America was still in its initial phase; to obtain energy and the supply of mineral products in Latin America was the main strategic objectives, and therefore, the main investments would naturally be concentrated in these two areas. The above second and third features were decided by the strategic goal of investment based on energy and minerals. Energy and mineral projects need large investments with high risks, of which the small and medium enterprises or private enterprises are not capable. The right to the development of resources and minerals can be obtained through the adoption of the main way of mergers and acquisitions. In the initial phase of foreign investment, it is very difficult to do mergers and acquisitions neck and neck with the green field investment.

With the passage of time, some changes have happened. For example, there is misunderstanding about China's investment in Latin America, regarding China's access to the strategic resources as the sole purpose, with doubt about the entrance of China's large state-owned enterprises and complaint about China's little investment in other sectors of the industry, and so on. From the perspective of China's domestic situation, in recent years, the pace of all kinds of Chinese enterprises "going out" for transnational business significantly accelerated, and their overseas investments will rapidly expand; in terms of the Latin-American region, as mentioned above, China must expand its industrial cooperation with the Latin-American countries in the next phase. Anyway, with the development and change of the situation, China's investment patterns in Latin America also need to be adjusted, mainly to broaden the fields of industrial investment, to increase the green field investment, and to encourage more small and medium enterprises and private enterprises to "go out". It must be emphasized that the need to correctly evaluate China's early investment model in Latin America means that the emphasis on today's adjustment is based on the changes in the subjective and objective environment, not because of any problems in the early approach. The investment in the fields of energy and mineral resources will still continue to follow the model of the early phase in the future.

Implication 4: The establishment of the bilateral free trade zone is the necessary way to promote the Sino-Latin American economic and trade cooperation.

Over the past few years, China has signed bilateral free trade agreements with Chile, Peru, and Costa Rica. These agreements cover a wide range of goods trade, services, trade and mutual investment. The mode to establish the individual bilateral free trade zones with the Latin American countries is generally based on two considerations: first, to make institutional arrangements for bilateral economic and trade cooperation through the free trade agreement is conducive to promoting the long-term and stable development of bilateral relations and cooperation; second, the conditions for China to sign such agreements with the Latin-American regional or sub-regional groups are not mature. Practice has proved that the free trade agreements that China had signed with the three countries have achieved the expected results of promoting bilateral cooperations and deepening bilateral relations. Some Latin-American scholar pointed out: "For Chile, the free trade agreement with China not only is a major step in achieving its international strategy, but also has brought a huge commercial interest. China has become the largest export market for Chile. Chile's consumers will benefit from more competitive and more diverse products from China. The higher economic growth driven by the free trade agreement will create more jobs".[8] In the same way, the economic and trade cooperation of Peru and Costa Rica with China has entered the fast lane. China has ranked the first and second place in Peru's import and export trade; China has become the largest export market of Costa Rica.

The above facts show that in the next phase, to establish bilateral free trade zones with the Latin-American countries should continue to be pushed forward actively and steadily, actively creating the conditions to establish as many as possible. According to the observation of the Chinese scholars, some of the Latin America countries with a higher level of industrial development, such as Argentina, Brazil and Mexico, are still worrying about the damage of free trade agreements to their relevant national industrial sectors with the introduction of massive China-made products in the process of the tariff reduction of commodity trade. In addition, the four countries of the Mercosur (Brazil, Argentina, Paraguay, and Uruguay) seem to have a "stick-together" tendency, having a very low positive attitude toward concluding bilateral free trade agreements with the countries outside this group. Therefore, China also needs to do some work in research to

[8]Osvaldo Rosales, Mikio Kuwayama, *China y America Latina y el Caribe, Hacia una Relacion Economica y Comercial Estrategica*, CEPAL, Santiago de Chile, marzo de 2012, p. 222.

eliminate the barriers in the process of promoting the construction of bilateral trade with the Latin-American countries.

Section 4 Main Issues Facing the Current Sino-Latin American Economic and Trade Cooperation

The Sino-Latin American economic and trade cooperation has experienced more than 10 years of accelerated development, which undoubtedly has increased China's confidence in the prospect for the future development. However, just like every coin has two sides, the accelerated development of the Sino-Latin American economic and trade cooperation has some contradictions and problems aside from the short-term data of growth and achievements. If these contradictions and problems are not promptly adjusted and solved, they will possibly become a further obstacle and resistance to the development. In the following some analyses and judgments will be given around a number of related issues.

I. The Commodity Structure of the Sino-Latin American Trade

In general, the current basic pattern of goods structure of the Sino-Latin American trade is like this: China exports manufactured goods to Latin America and Latin America exports energy, raw materials and part of the natural-resource-processed products, which is called interindustrial trade. Such a goods structure not only reflects the complementarity of the two economies, but also is decided by the respective industrial condition of the two sides. However, in recent years, the reaction of the Latin American countries to this problem has become increasingly stronger. They think that the current Sino-Latin American trade has become similar to the "North–South Trade" or the "Core-Periphery Trade", i.e., the developed countries exchange their industrial products with the primary products of developing countries so that the trend of the "reprimarization of products" has occurred in the exported-commodity structure of the Latin-American countries.

Based on this situation, the Latin-American countries have formulated the plans for the industrial restructuring, and some countries have also proposed the slogan of "reviving the industrialization", trying to further transform their modes of economic growth by expanding the export of products that are knowledge-intensive, technology-intensive and high-value-added. In terms of the economic and trade cooperation with China, the ECLAC has made it clear: "Latin American countries should take a more coordinated and consistent strategy with the groups of countries to establish a new relationship with China, i.e., both to increase the trade and investment and to form a variety of business and technology alliances in order to make use of the dynamism of Asia to promote the diversification of export and overcome the backward state of our innovation and competitiveness".[9] The above trends and recommendations of the Latin American countries deserve China's attention. In June 2012, in his speech at the Economic Commission for Latin America, Premier Wen Jiabao made a positive response: "China does not pursue the trade surplus; it not only imports the raw materials from Latin America, but also hopes to import more manufactured goods and commodities with high-added values so as to realize the balance of bilateral trade and the sustainable development".[10]

Just as the analysis in the first section of this chapter, the commodity structure of the trade between the Latin-American countries and the United States is also similar to that between the Latin-American countries and China, with the exception of Mexico, exporting mainly manufactured goods to the United States. Mexico is able to do this because its developed maquila industry has been included in the production chain of the United States in addition to the favorable conditions of being a member of the North American Free Trade Area. There are also two special examples in the Sino-Latin

[9]Alicia Barcena, Prologo al articulo de O. Rosales, M. Kuwayama, *China y America Latina y el Caribe: Hacia una Relacion Economica y Commercial Estrategica*, CEPAL, Santiago de Chile, marzo de 2012.
[10]Wen Jiabao, *Always Be Good Friends of Mutual Trust — Speech at the ECLAC of the United Nations* (June 26, 2012, San Diego), http://news.xinhuanet.com/politics/2012-06/27/c_112303984.htm.

American trade: One is Mexico and the other is Costa Rica. In 2011, China's import of the "machinery and transport equipment" from Mexico accounted for 41% of its total imports; China's import from Costa Rica was mainly electronic components. Therefore, from the perspective of Latin America, China is both a "world factory" and the export platform of Asian countries. It is likely for the Latin-American countries to expand their sales market if they can carry out the adjustment of their industrial structures, establish the strategic alliance between their industrial enterprises and Chinese enterprises, and manufacture their products according to the unified technical standards for production and make them enter the supply chain of the Asian industry.

II. The Trade Protectionism of Latin America

Trade protectionism came from the western developed countries, but the trade protectionism of the emerging economies also cannot be ignored. Recently, some Chinese scholar pointed out: "The official WTO statistics show that from 1995 to the first half of 2010, emerging economies such as India, Argentina, South Africa, Turkey and Brazil are the countries often ranking in the front of those that most frequently take the trade relief measures, usually ranking the top five in the world".[11] In the process of the development of the Sino-Latin American trade, China has had a strong sense of this situation. Mexico, Argentina and Brazil are the Latin-American countries that have launched the most anti-dumping investigations against China. Take Argentina for example. According to statistics, 1/4 of the country's anti-dumping investigation cases had been launched against the Chinese products — only in 2009 there were 19 anti-dumping investigations against China.

It is not difficult to find that in Latin America the three powers in the region are the countries that have launched the most anti-dumping investigations against China. Why? The reason is that the three countries have the highest level of industrial development in

[11] Wang Jun, "Active Trade Protectionism in Emerging Economies", *China Social Sciences News*, March 25, 2013, p. A06.

the Latin-American countries, with similar industrial structures to that of China; at the same time, because of the effect of the "de-industrialization" and the structural reform since the 1980s, they are explicitly inferior to China in terms of the level of industrial development and international competitiveness. They have the advantage of industrial development in Latin America, naturally striving to maintain and exert the advantage, but have to face the pressure of the international competitiveness of China's manufactured goods, resulting in a kind of psychological fear of China's competition. It is obvious that the trade protection measures taken by these countries tend to focus on some of China's industrial products, with the reason that the input of Chinese products has caused damage to their related industries. In fact, in addition to the purpose of protecting the domestic market, there are other purposes. For example, it was believed that China's exported products had squeezed the export markets for their products, such as the competition of Mexican and Chinese products in the US market. Therefore, the protectionism is often an indirect revenge for the China Competition. In addition, these countries often adopt protectionism to limit the import of Chinese goods under the background of the deterioration of the global environment, or the overvaluation of their currencies, or their exports being blocked and needing to compress the imports so as to maintain the balance of trade. For example, since 2009, Argentina's continuous anti-dumping investigations launched against China are directly related to the impact of the international financial crisis.

Competition is a natural phenomenon in the international trade. Proper competition should be a driving force for the development, promoting the two sides to strive to improve production efficiency and continuously carry out the technological innovation and product upgrading. To adopt trade protectionism is obviously not desirable, for it can cause damage to the rival, but it cannot automatically improve the competitiveness. On the contrary, strengthening cooperation in competition can bring about beneficial results mutually. In this sense, the above quoted suggestion by ECLAC on establishing a new relationship between China and Latin America to strengthen the industrial cooperation, forming a variety of business and technology alliance, making use of the Asian dynamism to promote the diversification of the Latin-American exports so as to improve the innovation ability and international competitiveness of the Latin-American countries, is a constructive one.

III. Labor Issues

In the investment in Latin America, labor issues are involved both in setting up enterprises and in contract labor projects. Using as many as possible the local labor to increase local employment is not only the employment trend of the transnational business enterprises but also the common aspiration of the Chinese investment enterprises and the Latin-American countries. However, in terms of the previous situation, the Chinese enterprises in the Latin American region had faced with varying degrees of the problem of labor. The so-called labor issues are mainly related to the wages of workers, welfare benefits, as well as the quality of workers and other issues. Generally speaking, most Latin-American countries have formed relatively complete systems of labor and labor laws after years of exploration, e.g., the minimum wage system, the social security payment system, the collective contract system, the working time and vacation schedule, the dismissal compensation system, and the industrial-injury accident compensation system have been expressly provided in written forms. Some countries also have set up specialized law enforcement agencies such as labor courts and labor procuratorates. Naturally, it is enough for the local foreign enterprises to strictly abide by the laws and regulations. But things are not so simple. According to some preliminary analysis, the labor problems faced by the Chinese enterprises in Latin America may have been caused mainly by the following factors.

First, the laborers do not strictly abide by the contract, often finding various reasons to ask for increasing the wages and improving the welfare. Traditionally the trade unions of the Latin-American countries have been strong, accustomed to getting involved in various kinds of labor affairs, unconditionally supporting the demands of labor wages and welfare, tending to make the general labor disputes more and more complicated.

Second, the labor law or the various provisions of the relevant labor system of the Latin American countries are too complex and cumbersome, and it is difficult for Chinese enterprises to get completely familiar with and skilled in the use of such a set of rules and regulations in the short term. Once a labor dispute case goes into the judicial process, often it can be delayed 2–3 years, and almost all the judiciary, labor consultants, lawyers and trade unions are partial to the laborers.

Third, the Latin-American countries are rich in labor resources, but the education level of the workers is generally low. Latin America's labor market has long been divided into two parts — the formal employment and the informal employment; with insufficient government investment in the vocational training, the professional quality of the labor force is not high. The Latin-American workers seem to be accustomed to the frequent change of jobs, with relatively poor stability of employment. As a result, Chinese companies tend to invest more in labor, but with lack of protection of the benefit.

To sum up, the labor problem is a realistic problem that Chinese enterprises have to face in the process of going into Latin America. On the one hand, Chinese enterprises need to experience the process of getting familiar with the local environment, and in particular, to seriously accumulate and summarize the practical experience of dealing with labor issues, and gradually become active from being passive. On the other hand, facing the big trend of China's large number of strong enterprises doing transnational business, China's legal education department seems to have the necessity to train a number of talents with a variety of legal professional knowledge familiar with all kinds of countries, including the labor law, to provide the intellectual support for Chinese enterprises going abroad. In addition, in the current phase, the Chinese enterprises can consider setting up more joint ventures with the Latin-American local enterprises to form communities of interests to deal with labor issues with the help of local entrepreneurs.

IV. The Investment Risks

The overseas investment is faced with various risks. As far as Latin America is concerned, there are two major categories of likely risks for the investment in the current phase: the political risk and the environmental risk.

Over the past decade, one of the political risks of the investment in Latin America is the implementation of the nationalization policy of some countries such as Venezuela, Bolivia, Ecuador, and Argentina. The common characteristic of the four countries is the implementation of the nationalization of oil and gas resources, and the nationalization of two countries of Venezuela and Bolivia included not only oil and gas resources, but also other industrial sectors. Among them, the measures taken by Venezuela included: increasing the fees of using mining areas of oil and gas resources; stipulating that foreign enterprises must set up joint ventures with the Venezuelan National Oil Co. (PDVSA), with foreign investment accounting for only 40% of the shares; raising 50% of the income tax of the enterprises engaged in the Orinoco Heavy Oil Belt, etc. The government of Ecuador also had taken measures such as limiting the proportion of the shares of foreign energy companies, imposing the oil windfall tax at the rate of 70%, and forcing foreign enterprises to pay 50% of their extra oil profit to the government. Therefore, the Chinese energy enterprises with investments and operations in the two countries of Venezuela and Ecuador have suffered varying degrees of economic losses.

From the perspective of the trend of the future, the author believes that the nationalization policy of the Latin-American left-wing ruling countries in the field of energy resources will continue to exist, but further radicalization of it is unlikely; the nationalization policy in other areas of the industry is very likely to have a convergence. The key problem is that the implementation of nationalization is contrary to the whole country's opening up policy, and it is likely that this local income will lead to the damage to the overall interests. Take Venezuela, for example. In recent years, the inflow of foreign capital has shown a decreasing trend, and in some years, the foreign capital inflows were negative, i.e., the foreign investment was fleeing continuously. If the foreign investment were broken off, the development of the country would be faced with difficulties. In the Summit of Latin-America and the EU held in February 2013 in Santiago, Chile, the EU gave an outspoken criticism for the nationalization policy of some Latin-American countries, complaining about the lack of legal protection for the investment in these countries. In addition, during the early reign of Chavez, due to the continued high international oil prices, the Venezuelan government could use the high oil revenues for the acquisition of foreign-funded enterprises; in the future, it will be difficult for the condition of abundant capital to recur.

Another political risk of the investment in Latin America may come from a policy shift resulting from a regime change. However, it should be seen that Latin America is currently in its historical period of political stability. Although in some Latin-American countries, the division of political forces into left and right is distinctive, alternating in power, but both sides have no difference in principle in the implementation of market economy, persisting in opening to the outside world and actively participating in the global competition. In the past decade, the phenomenon of the abnormal change of power in Latin America has been very rare; the phenomenon has rarely happened that the interests of foreign investors have been damaged due to the change of regime and the shift of policy. There is no need to be too sensitive to this issue, but prevention should not be neglected. In addition, some of the adjustments and changes of the policies in the Latin-American countries may not necessarily occur due to the change of government. For example, as mentioned above, in recent years, some Latin-American countries have made substantial adjustment of the policy for foreign investors to buy local land, strictly limiting the area of purchase, which is a major policy change for investors in agriculture.

About the environmental risk of investment in Latin America, two types of risk should be focused on. Generally speaking, any investment projects must meet the local government's environmental standards, which is the most fundamental requirement. However, the people of the Latin-American countries have very strong awareness of environmental protection and the non-governmental organizations are very active, with great social influence. Even if an investment project has been approved by the government or the state legislature, if the non-government environmental protection organization cannot accept it, the risk of this type of project in the implementation process cannot be underestimated. There is one type of investment project that may be just located in the area where the American-Indians live. Because of their unique cultural tradition, the Indians may have a negative attitude in terms of ecological environment, or do not welcome foreign investors. This means that the risks are unpredictable.

Chapter 10

Opportunities and Challenges of the Sino-Latin American Economic and Trade Cooperation

SU Zhenxing

More than 60 years ago, when the new China was founded, the diplomatic relations with Latin America was almost a blank, with no diplomatic relations established with any of the Latin-American countries. In order to break the isolation and blockade of imperialism, the Chinese government has done a long, arduous and painstaking work in Latin America to carry out various forms of exchanges and cooperations, making friends, dispelling doubts, and finally opened up vast diplomatic positions. Today looking back on this experience, the several generations of new China's leaders had shown a long-term strategic vision in the development of the Sino-Latin American relations. When the wheel of history went into the 21st century, the Latin-American relations have entered a new stage of accelerated development. Just as one Cuban scholar said, "In the first 10 years of the 21st century, China has made a great leap forward in the rise of its economy . . . its total economic output has jumped to the second place in the world, and it has become the biggest exporter in the international trade. China is still the major producer of global manufacturing and has nearly a quarter of the world's foreign exchange reserves. As a result, the great leap forward has been shown in the wide existence of China in the international fields, especially in the development of economic relations with Latin America (including trade and investment)".[1] One European scholar stressed, "China's rise and emergence as an important country in Latin America is one of the major developments in Latin America in the early 21st century... Therefore, the Latin-American countries are making decisions in order to adapt to the new international arena resulting from the rise of China".[2]

It can be said that the Latin-American countries that are seeking to accelerate their developments are eager to join in China's rapid economic development. Only 10 years ago, when China joined the World Trade Organization (WTO), the Latin-American countries had generally regarded China on the rise as a strong competitor, both worrying about China's occupation of the local markets of Latin America, and fearing China's competition in the third party market. There was even the question: Was China an "angel" or "evil" in the field of international trade? Today, the Latin-American countries have deemed the rapid development of China as an important historical opportunity. The Latin-American economic system believes, "To Latin America and the Caribbean, China means a great opportunity since it is not only an export market but also a provider of a lot of goods and services. In the financial field China is appearing as an important capital-outputting country in the world.[3] From the 'Theory of China's Competition' to the 'Theory of China's Opportunity', this mentality change of Latin-Americans is worthy of our attention".

It is believed that the development of the Sino-Latin American relations is in an important historical period of opportunity. In the

---

[1]Julio A. Diaz Vazquez (Cuba), Relaciones Economicas China-America Latina: Oportunidad o Amenaza? pp. 1–2, http://politica-china.org/imxd/noticisa/doc/1312622682.

[2]Gonzalo Sebastian Paz (Espana), "Cambio y Continuidad en las Relaciones de China con America Latina a Principios del Siglo XXI", *Revista Iberoamericana de Estudios de Asia Oriental*, No. 1, 2007, p. 2.

[3]Sistema Economico Latinoamericano y del Caribe (SELA), *Evolucion Reciente de las Relaciones Economicas entre la Republica Popular China y America Latina y el Caribe. Mecanismos Institucionales y de Cooperacion para su Fortalecimiento*, Caracas, Venezuela, octubre de 2010, p. 29.

first decade of the 21st century, the new vigor and new progress of the development of the Sino-Latin American relations is the "prelude" of this historical period of opportunity; in the next 10 years, the Sino-Latin American relations will enter a comprehensive deepening stage of development. The *China's Policy Documents for Latin America and the Caribbean* (hereinafter referred to as the DOCUMENT) published by the Chinese government in 2008 is the initiative taken to seize this historical opportunity. The DOCUMENT systematically clarified the principles and policies for China and the Latin-American countries to build a comprehensive cooperative partnership, indicating the coming of the new "climax" of the development of bilateral relations. The "climax" does not necessarily mean that the Sino-Latin American trade will maintain the high growth rate of the past 10 years, but will mainly be reflected in the further expanding and deepening of the field of cooperation between the two sides and in the greater degree of the fusion of the interests of both sides. At the same time, it must also be noted that any kind of historical opportunity is always accompanied by corresponding challenges. As far as the future of economic cooperation is concerned, not only sufficient understanding should be given to the historical opportunity, but also a clear understanding and timely response should be given to the challenges so as to take full advantage of the opportunity. The discussion of this chapter will focus on this central topic.

Section 1 The Important Period of Historical Opportunity of the Development of the Sino-Latin American Relations

In the first decade of the 21st century, the Sino-Latin American economic and trade cooperation had been accelerating (see Chapter 9 of this book). For the emergence of the new situation in the bilateral cooperation between China and Latin America, the reasons should be explored from the perspective of the two sides in cooperation. In terms of China, its comprehensive national strength has increased significantly over the past 30 years since its reform and opening up, injecting new impetus to the development of the Sino-Latin American economic and trade cooperation, which is the most fundamental reason. However, this statement does not explain why in the first 20 years of the reform and opening up the momentum of the acceleration of the development of the Sino-Latin American economic and trade cooperation did not appear. It is believed that the emergence of the period of the historical opportunity of the development of the Sino-Latin American relations is closely related to the transformation of China's opening up strategy. China's opening up to the outside world has been in the process of expanding and deepening, which contains the gradual adjustment and transformation of the strategy of opening to the outside world. The adjustment and transformation would have different effects on different types of countries and regions. Here are a few examples: (1) The early target of China's strategy of opening to the outside world was to attract external funding and technology. Therefore, the western countries, China's Hong Kong and Taiwan, and some Asian countries naturally became the key partners. China has become a pivotal role in the field of international trade after becoming a "world factory" and joining the WTO; in particular, it has become a country with a huge demand for energy and industrial raw materials. This huge demand is the most important driving factor in the Sino-Latin American economic and trade cooperation in the recent 10 years. (2) In the process of rapid development, China has gradually accumulated huge foreign exchange reserves. Therefore, China has changed its role from a debtor to a creditor in the world, with a strong ability of foreign investment. China's opening up to the outside world has changed from the way of simple "welcoming in" into the approach of "welcoming in" and "going out" simultaneously, encouraging Chinese enterprises to invest overseas to carry out cross-border operations. In the eyes of the Latin-American countries, China not only is no longer "competing" with them for foreign investment, but also has become a new foreign investor in the emerging countries. Over the past few years, China's direct investment in Latin-America, as well as financial cooperation with the Latin-American countries, has been rapidly expanding. (3) With the rising labor costs and land prices, China is stepping up its structural adjustment and the transformation of modes to upgrade its industrial level, from a single export-oriented mode to the mode of focusing on domestic demand and opening up the markets both at home and abroad. Therefore, the competition of the labor-intensive products between China and the Latin-American countries has showed a decreasing trend in the third markets, and the diversification of Chinese market capacity and import demand is rapidly expanding, forming a huge attraction in Latin America.

The report of the Eighteenth National Congress of the Communist Party of China pointed out, "With an overview of domestic and international trend, China's development is still in an important period of strategic opportunities, which can accomplish a great deal".[4] The size of the opportunity of the economic and trade cooperation between countries depends on the degree of mutual satisfaction with each other's demands for interests. Judging from this perspective, there is a sufficient reason to support the idea that the Sino-Latin American bilateral economic and trade cooperation is still in a period of opportunity hitherto unknown in history.

I. The Bilateral Cooperation in the Fields of Energy and Resources Will Continue to Expand and Deepen

Being a resource-rich region, Latin America "has 1/3 of the land area and 1/3 of the freshwater resources in the world, 31% of the production of bio-fuels and 13% of the oil production in the world; in addition, it has 44% of the world's copper, 65% of the world's lithium, 49% of the world's silver, 32% of the world's molybdenum, 23% of the world's zinc and nickel, 48% of the world's soybeans, 31% of the world's meat products, 23% of the world's milk and 16% of the world's corn".[5] As a "world factory" with a large population,

[4]Hu Jintao, *Advance Firmly along the Road of Socialism with Chinese Characteristics and Strive to Build a Well-off Society in an All-round Way — Report at the 18th National Congress of the Communist Party of China* (November 8, 2012), *Collection of the Documents of the 18th National Conference of the Chinese Communist Party*, People's Publishing House, 2012, p. 15.

China's development will confront the problem of the shortage of energy and resources in the long term. Therefore, the Latin-American region is no doubt one of China's long-term cooperative partners for the supply of energy and resources. This cooperation is of strategic importance to China and also essential for Latin America. Currently, with a substantial increase in the amount of resource exports and a sustained high price of resource products, the Latin-American countries are in a period of "resource dividend". "The economic growth from 2003 to 2008 and the subsequent rapid recovery from the international financial crisis of Latin America and the Caribbean, to a large extent, are due to its increasingly close connection with the Asia Pacific region, especially with China ... China's huge demand for food, energy, metals and mineral products has enabled the Latin-American countries that output such products to have benefited from a substantial improvement in the trade prices and the rapid growth of exports".[6] The Latin-American economists have called the double effect of the export boom and a substantial improvement in trade price "China Effect" (*efecto China*). According to the ECLAC statistics, from 2001 to 2010, the Latin-American and Caribbean exports of goods valued at an average annual growth of 10.8%, of which the price effect was 5.5% and the export volume effect was 5.3%. Despite the rich resources, in its development history of 200 years, Latin America has had few opportunities to promote the rapid development of the country by the "resource dividend". The first time was from the 1870s to the eve of World War I, when the flourishing industrialization and modernization of the European countries had formed a huge demand for Latin America's resources. The prosperity of the export of primary products of Latin America, which had lasted nearly half of the century, was a strong impetus to the early industrial development and urban expansion. After entering the 21st century, Latin America

[5] Alicia Barcena, The Economic Development of Latin America and the Caribbean in 2012, *Latin American Studies*, No. 6, 2012, p. 6.

[6] Osvaldo Rosales, Mikio Kuwayama, *China y America Latina y el Caribe, Hacia una Relacion Economica y Commercial Estrategica*, CEPAL, Santiago de Chile, marzo de 2012, p. 84.

ushered in the second historical opportunity. China's huge demand for resources as a representative of Asia's rapid economic growth has become one of the important factors of pulling the economic growth of Latin America in the last 10 years. The Latin-American countries might worry about the phenomena of the "reprimarization" in the export commodity structure and the "Dutch Disease" resulted from the export boom of primary products, but eventually they would not abandon the "resource dividend" because all these worrying phenomena could be avoided or defused by taking corresponding measures.

II. The Domestic Markets of Both Sides are Showing the Trend of Rapid Expansion

China is accelerating the transformation of its economic development mode, especially in the stimulating effect of increasing domestic demand in the economy, but as an economic power, China can never ignore the importance of the international market in its development. Latin America has a population of 600 million people with a higher level of economic development. At market exchange rates, in 2010 the group domestic product (GDP) of the total area reached $4,897.4 billion, with per capita GDP of $8,404.[7] Especially since 2003, the Latin-American economy has got rid of the state of an over-20-year low growth, with a sped-up economy (average annual growth rate of 4.2%), an expanded employment, the increased income of residents, the improved financial situation, a reduced debt, a flourishing domestic demand, and a booming export and an expanding import. Take the years from 2005 to 2009 for example. The growth rate of China's import and export trade with Latin America was far higher than other areas (see Table 10.1). For both sides, the original small trade volume and the relatively low starting point was one of the reasons, but mainly it was because of the very strong demands of both sides. The Latin-American economy was expected to remain a growth rate of around 4% in the next few years; therefore, Latin America also had a great potential for China's

[7]ECLAC, *Statistical Yearbook for Latin America and the Caribbean 2011*, pp. 81–82.

Table 10.1 Annual Growth Rate of China and Its Major Regional Partners (2005–2009) ($ Million, %)

	2005	2006	2007	2008	2009	Grow Rate
			Export			
Latin America and the Caribbean	23,259	35,396	51,060	71,045	56,449	24.8
Asia-Pacific	140,443	165,871	202,705	246,407	203,988	9.8
The United States	163,180	203,801	233,169	252,844	221,295	7.9
Other areas	289,458	373,789	487,563	567,033	483,473	13.7
EU	145,613	189,978	245,563	293,360	236,442	12.9
			Import			
Latin America and the Caribbean	26,664	34,072	51,004	71,417	64,132	24.5
Asia-Pacific	259,677	309,645	365,432	414,786	375,533	9.7
The United States	48,741	59,314	69,548	81,586	77,755	12.4
Other areas	250,898	297,789	359,164	432,129	360,367	9.5
EU	73,972	90,641	110,967	132,646	127,769	14.6

Source: ECLAC, according to UN statistic database of commodity trade (comtrade).

commodity export market. For Latin America, it was undoubtedly a great news that China had announced to build a moderately prosperous society by 2020, achieving the goal to double the GDP and the per capita income of urban and rural residents of that of 2010. In the next 10 years, China's economy will maintain the growth rate of 7.5–8%, although somewhat slower than the previous stage, but still a leader in the world. All these clearly show that China's domestic consumption will be greatly improved and its consumer demand will be more diversified. When the markets of Europe and the United States continue to be in a recession, the magnetic effect of the Chinese market for Latin America is further highlighted. Barcena, the Executive Secretary of ECLAC, recently pointed out, "In international trade, from 2017, the 'North–North' trade will gradually be replaced by 'South–South' trade... the 'South–South' economic interaction will exceed the 'North–North' trade in 2017. From 2013 to 2017, the emerging economies are expected to contribute 2/3 of the world economic growth. In fact, we will see great changes in the world geopolitics: the economic center will shift from the Atlantic to the Pacific, from the 'North' to the 'South"'.[8]

III. The Bilateral Investment and Financial Cooperation are in the Ascendant

Compared with China's trade status in Latin America,[9] China's investment in Latin America can only be said to be in the initial stage. According to China's official statistics, by 2011, China's direct investment stock in Latin America was $55.17 billion, accounting for 13% of China's total stock of foreign investment, but out of the $55.17 billion, $51 billion of the investment was in the two "tax havens" of the Cayman Islands and the British Virgin Islands, and therefore, the actual investment in Latin America was only about $4 billion.[10] Compared with the investment of any western big country in Latin America, China's amount of investment was negligible. China is the country with the world's largest foreign exchange reserves and it has become a popular concern how China will use these reserves. It may be a good choice to pay close attention to the foreign investment so as to form overseas assets.

Latin America has not only a wide range of industrial areas suitable for China's investment choice, but also a high demand for foreign investment in the region. From 2007 to 2011, the Latin-American average annual absorption of Foreign Direct Investment (FDI) had exceeded $120 billion (about 10% of the total global FDI), basically still in the stage of emphasizing the amount of foreign capital. The Latin-American demand of FDI is mainly based on the following three reasons. One is because Latin America's investment rate is low, i.e., the so-called "internal shortfall of savings", which needs

[8]Alicia Barcena, The Economic Development of Latin America and the Caribbean in 2012, Studies on Latin America, No. 6, 2012, p. 4.

[9]At present, China is Latin America's third largest trade partner after the US and EU (27 countries); in terms of individual countries, China has become Latin America's second largest trade partner.

[10]Chinese Ministry of Commerce, National Bureau of Statistics, State Administration of Foreign Exchange, *Statistics Bulletin of China's Foreign Direct Investment in 2012*, China Statistics Press, 2012.

external savings to be added to. In the fifties and sixties of the 20th century, the fixed capital formation rate of the Latin-American countries occupied an average of 20.3% of GDP; from 1970 to 1982, it rose to 24.3%; from 1983 to 2003, it fell to 18%; in the recent five years (from 2006 to 2011) it rose to 20.7%,[11] and compared with the current about 40% of the investment rate of Asian developing countries, this is rather small. The second is due to the huge demand for funds for infrastructure construction. In the 80s and 90s of the 20th century, due to the decrease of the investment rate and the advance of the market reform, the public investment in Latin America was greatly compressed. The proportion of the public investment in GDP dropped from 6.7% in 1980 and 1981 to 3.9% from 1999 to 2003; since 2004 it gradually rose to 4.8%.[12] During the 1980s and 1990s, due to the sharp decline in the proportion of the public investment and the too strong social spending rigidity, all of the governments generally had significantly reduced the investment in infrastructure, resulting in the situation of the infrastructure construction seriously lagging behind, which had already become one of the main bottlenecks restricting the economic and social development. The current investment in the construction of infrastructure in Latin America accounted for only 0.8–0.9% of GDP. The relevant forecasts show that the Latin-American infrastructure investment has to reach at least 5% of GDP each year in the next 15 years in order to meet the basic needs. China has obvious advantages in the financing, design and construction of large infrastructure projects. The third reason is that the construction of the emerging strategic industries basically had to rely on foreign investment. The Latin-American region experienced a process of "de-industrialization" in the 1980s and 1990s. The most prominent consequence of the process is that the construction of the emerging strategic industries of the Latin-American countries generally did not catch up. Many countries had put forward their planning of related industrial policies, but currently with constraints

[11]CEPAL, *Cambio Estructural para la Igualdad: Una Vision Integrada del Desarrollo*, San Salvador, 27–31 de agosto, 2012, p. 125.
[12]*Ibid.*, p. 129.

of the domestic investment capacity, the development of emerging strategic industries mainly depends on foreign investment.

Over the past 10 years, the financial cooperation between China and Latin America has increased significantly, with continual innovations in the cooperation modes. China has already become an official member of the Caribbean Development Bank and the Inter American Development Bank, China has signed a 70-billion-yuan currency swap agreement with Argentina, China has signed the "Money-for-Oil" agreement of a total of $19 billion with Brazil, Venezuela and Ecuador, and China has established the "Bilateral Joint Investment Fund" of a total of $12 billion with Venezuela. In June 2012, during his visit to South America, Premier Wen Jiabao again made a commitment: China had initiated to set up the Sino-Latin American Cooperation Fund, in which China's financial institutions would provide the initial contribution of $5 billion and China Development Bank would lead to establish a special loan of $10 billion for the cooperation in the infrastructure construction between China and Latin America. "China is considering the signing of a local currency swap agreement with more Latin-American countries to carry out the local currency trade settlement and set up mutual bank branches".[13]

Another factor that cannot be ignored is that the multinational corporations in Latin America have grown fast in the last 10 years. According to the study of Spanish scholars, at present, the foreign investment of the first batch of 65 Latin-American multinational corporations (multilatinas) has accounted for 38% of the total investment. The field of management involves the processing of agricultural products, aviation, alternative energy, construction, business, cosmetics, mining, telecommunications, metallurgy, etc. In 2011, the sales of these companies reached $710.2 billion, an increase of 6% over the previous year. The characteristics of the current activities of these large companies are "Reconquista" (referring to the purchasing back of some of the local enterprises pre-acquired

[13]Wen Jiabao, *Always Be Good Friends of Mutual Trust — Speech at the ECLAC of the United Nations* (June 26, 2012, San Diego), http://news.xinhuanet.com/politics/2012/06-27/c_112303984.htm.

by foreign capitals) in the Latin-American region, the acquisition of assets in Europe and the United States, and entering into Asia and Africa.[14] This shows that the capacity of the foreign investment of the Latin-American countries is also growing.

IV. The Bilateral Industrial Cooperation Has a Great Potential

From the perspective of industrial cooperation, there are several important factors worth our attention. First, the current Sino-Latin American trade is characteristic of the trade among the industrial sectors, i.e., China mainly outputs manufactured goods, while Latin America mainly outputs raw materials and primary products. The Latin-American countries worry about the trade pattern, wondering whether this trade pattern can be sustained and if the situation has been sustained for a long time, it will be difficult for the Latin-American countries to upgrade their industrial structures, and even may make their economies go back to the time of the "specialized production of primary products". Second, China has become the export platform of its Asian neighbors; in other words, Asia has formed a relatively complete industrial chain with China as the center. The Latin-American countries have a strong desire to enter into the Asian production or supply chain by strengthening the industrial cooperation with China in order to drive the production and export of their own manufacturing industries, thus leading to the transformation of the Sino-Latin American trade from the trade between industries to the trade within the industrial sectors. Third, currently China and the Latin-American countries alike are going through the adjustment and optimization of industrial structure to enhance the level of economic development. At present, China's manufacturing industry as a whole has been obviously more advanced than that of Latin America, and the enterprises of the manufacturing industry of China are in the climax period of "going out" to carry out transnational operations.

[14]Mercedes Temboury (Espana), El Viaje de Vuelta: La Expansion de las Empresas Latinoameri canas, http://www.realinstitutoelcano.org/wps/portal/rielcano/contenido?WCM_GLOBAL_...2012-12-10.

Therefore, similar enterprises in Latin America can benefit from several aspects such as capital, technology and market through the strategic alliance with Chinese enterprises.

One of the Latin-American scholars pointed out, "The leading role of China in the world economy shows that the Latin-American and the Caribbean countries should establish a strategic alliance with this trading partner and strive to make the bilateral relations a pillar of improving the quality of their international participation. Considering the huge risks still hidden in the world economy and the changing of the economic geography of the world, increasingly moving to concentrate in the Asia-Pacific area, especially to focus on China, Latin America and the Caribbean area should redouble their efforts to ascertain the complementarity between them and make use of it. It is imperative to strive to promote the diversification of export through the establishment of the enterprise alliance of the two sides".[15] The author also believes that it is undoubtedly a key option in the current deepening of the economic and trade cooperation for the two sides to strengthen cooperation between the industrial sectors and the alliance of manufacturing enterprises. When announcing the establishment of the Sino-Latin American Cooperation Fund, Premier Wen Jiabao also stressed that "Latin-American countries are welcome to participate in the construction of the fund to jointly invest in the projects of bilateral cooperations, such as manufacturing, high technology and sustainable development".[16]

V. Both Sides Have a Long Way to Go in the International Multilateral Diplomatic Cooperation

At present, emerging market countries and developing countries as a whole have improved their economic strength, leading to significant changes in the comparison of the economic strength of the north

---

[15]Osvaldo Rosales, Mikio Kuwayama, *China y America Latina y el Caribe: Haii una Relacion Economica y Commercial Estrategica*, CEPAL, Santiago de Chile, Marzo de 2012, p. 121.

[16]Wen Jiabao, *Always Be Good Friends of Mutual Trust — Speech at the ECLAC of the United Nations* (June 26, 2012, San Diego), http://news.xinhuanet.com/politics/2012/06-27/c_112303984.htm.

and the south. But at the same time, there are also a lot of challenges, such as the global climate warming, the environmental degradation, frequent disasters, the food crisis, the slow economic recovery of the world, the rise of trade protectionism, the western countries passing the crisis, the slow progress of the reform of the international monetary and financial system, and how to give full play to the leading role of the United Nations in the maintenance of world peace and security. In short, in terms of how to strengthen the construction of global governance to construct an environment more conducive to the survival and development of human beings, there are more and more common interests between China and the Latin-American countries. The Latin-American countries and China are both in the period of the rapid increase of their international status; China, Argentina, Brazil, and Mexico are members of the Group 20; China and Brazil are among the Brazil, Russia, India, and China (BRIC) countries. Therefore, both sides should not only accelerate their own development and deepen the bilateral cooperation, but also strengthen the communication and coordination of positions in the international multilateral diplomatic arena, striving to safeguard the common interests of the emerging markets and developing countries.

The above is a rough summary of the history of the Sino-Latin American cooperation from five aspects. Any historical opportunity is composed of many factors, and therefore it is called a "rare opportunity". But at the same time it also should be noted that the opportunity of the Sino-Latin American economic and trade cooperation over the past 10 years had come mainly from the development of China; in the next 10 years, whether this opportunity will continue depends on whether China can continue its development. If China's development continues, the "magnetic effect" composed of China's huge market, China's rapid growth of foreign funds and technological cooperative ability will be able to be more fully played out, so that all kinds of positive factors in Latin America can be further mobilized to carry out the cooperation with China.

Section 2 From the "China Competition" Theory to the "China Opportunity" Theory

At the end of the 1970s and the beginning of the 1980s, both the Chinese economy and the Latin-American economy were at an important historical juncture. The great historical process of the reform and opening up in 1978 is the starting point of China's farewell to the long-term planned economic system to establish a socialist market economy. The outbreak of the Latin-American debt crisis in 1982 had become a direct cause of the Latin-American countries to promote structural reforms, marking the transformation of the development model of the Latin-American countries from the inward development to the outward development of the import substitution industrialization. In the entire 1980s, due to the serious problem of the debt crisis and the very small scale of the Sino-Latin American economic and trade cooperation, in the view of most Latin-Americans, China's reform and opening to the outside world was the story occurring in a distant country in the East, and seemed to have little to do with them; therefore, they did not have much interest. After entering the 1990s, the Latin-American public opinion began to give increasing attention to China's sustained rapid economic growth and increasing international influence. At that time, the mainstream tendency of the public opinion was that the rising China was a new competitor that should be treated with caution and even with fear. This mentality became even stronger when China officially joined the WTO in 2001. This psychological attitude could be generalized as the "China Competition" theory. At that time, the main issues that were worried about involved the following three aspects.

First, it was the worry about the damage that the Chinese export of cheap manufactured goods to the relevant industrial sectors of the Latin-American countries, leading to the reduction of the employment opportunities of their own labor force. It was just like what Eduardo Lola, the chief economist of Inter American Development Bank, said, "Since China joined the WTO in 2001, people have been worrying about the competition of the Chinese products which might cause devastating effects on the Latin-American garment industry, electronic industry and other industrial products produced by thousands of companies in the region".[17] A Spanish scholar also pointed out that even if China was welcome in South American countries as a big buyer of primary products, "there also exists the resistance (to China) of the industrial sectors and the workers' movement".[18]

Second, it was the fear that China had become a strong competitor in the third party market against Latin America, especially in the US market, and even there was the so-called idea that "China will replace Latin America in the next few decades". This sentiment was particularly strong in Mexico and Central American countries whose exports were highly dependent on the US market. Some scholar wrote, "Mexico is the first to resist the expansion of China in Latin America. One of the reasons is that its maquila industry has suffered a major loss of jobs. For this reason, Mexico is the last country to accept China's entry into WTO. In Central America, the acceptance (of China) is much more controversial than in South America. It is believed that the driving force of the countries of Central America and the Dominican Republic to have signed the free trade agreement with the United States lies in the fact that they regard it as a means of defense against China's competitiveness in the US market, especially in the field of textile industry".[19]

Third, China was thought to have absorbed too much FDI, thus reducing the number of foreign capital inflows to Latin America. In the early 1990s, this view was quite popular in Latin America; until the early 21st century it was still popular because the foreign-capital inflow of Latin America had been volatile. "Mexico's FDI inflows fell

[17]Eduardo Lora (the Inter American Development Bank): *Should Latin America be Afraid of China?* Originally from *Economic Quarterly (Trimestre Economico)* V. 72, No. 3, July–September; later collected into *The Visible Hand of China in Latin America* edited by Javier Santiso *et al.*, translated by Wang Peng, Zhao Chongyang, World Knowledge Press, 2009, p. 8.
[18]Gonzalo Sebastian Paz (Espana), "Cambio y Continuidad en las Relaciones de China con America Latina a Principios del Siglo XX1", *Revista Iberoamericana de Estudios de Asia Oriental*, No. 1, 2007, p. 6.
[19]*Ibid.*

from $26.6 billion in 2001 to $11 billion in 2003; a total of 960 companies had left Mexico, and thus the estimation of job losses would reach more than 300,000 (single garment industry reducing 250,400 jobs). This trend had partially been reversed in 2004, with FDI increased to $14.4 billion, and the export processing zone created about more than 70,000 jobs. However, when the FDI again dropped to $11.3 billion in 2005, this concern again had intensified".[20]

From around 2004 to 2005, the direction of the Latin-American public opinion about China was gradually changed: more emphasis was put on China as the Latin-American economic and trade partner and more emphasis was put on the rise of China as an opportunity for the development of Latin America. Therefore, the author called this new public opinion the theory of "China Opportunity". The reasons for this change of the public opinion may be varied, but among them three factors should be emphasized. First, since 2003, the Latin-American region had got rid of the sluggish state of more than 20 years of recession, with the momentum of a strong expansion. One of the main factors driving this round of the Latin-American economic expansion was the tremendous demand for raw materials and primary products of the emerging Asian economies with China as the representative. The related Latin-American countries have gained tremendous profits from the rapid growth of exports and the sharply rising prices of these products. Second, in November 2004, President Hu Jintao visited Latin America and made a speech in the Brazilian Congress, putting forward three objectives for the development of the Sino-Latin American relations: politically becoming trustworthy all-weather friends with mutual support, economically becoming mutually beneficial and win–win cooperative partners at a new starting point with complementary advantages, and culturally becoming a model of dialogue among different civilizations through enhancing

---

[20]Eduardo Lora (the Inter American Development Bank): *Should Latin America be Afraid of China?* Originally from *Economic Quarterly (Trimestre Economico)* V. 72, No. 3, July–September; later collected into *The Visible Hand of China in Latin America* edited by Javier Santiso *et al.*, translated by Wang Peng, Zhao Chongyang, World Knowledge Press, 2009, p. 8.

cultural exchanges. At the same time, President Hu Jintao also proposed an inspiring goal that the Sino-Latin American trade would break through $100 billion in 2010.[21] This goal had been achieved three years in advance. President Hu Jintao's visit caused a stir in the Latin-American public opinion, being called an "offensive" of China against Latin America. Third, it was under the background of this new "upsurge" in the development of the Sino-Latin American relations that scholars in Latin America, Europe and the United States started a debate whether China had constituted an opportunity or a threat in the field of economy and trade for Latin America, with a number of quite fruitful research reports published.[22] These studies generally believed that the growth of the Chinese economic strength had brought far more opportunities to Latin America than challenges and from a professional point of view criticized some obviously biased prevailing views about the problems in the Sino-Latin American economic and trade cooperation.

Let's take a look at some of the basic ideas raised by these reports. (1) "The impact of China on the trade of Latin America is positive in the short and medium term.... The Latin-American trade will benefit from China's strong demand and accelerated growth". (2) The complementarity is more than competitiveness in the trade structure of the two sides. "Most of the trade structures of the Latin-American countries are usually more complementary than competitive with China's trade structure. Because of the difference in the export structure, the possibility of damaging the trade transfer effect is reduced".[23] (3) In the local market of Latin-America, China's

[21]Hu Jintao, Create a New Situation of Friendship between China and Latin America — Speech at Brazilian Congress (November 12, 2004, Brasilia), *People's Daily*, November 24, 2004, p. 1 and p. 3.

[22]This batch of research reports include five reports from *The Visible Hand of China in Latin America* edited by Javier Santiso *et al.*, *China's Influence: Opportunities and Challenges Facing Latin America and the Caribbean* published by three scholars including R. Devlin from the Rockefeller David Center for Latin-American studies, Harvard University, *Latin America Encountering China and India: Prospects and Challenges in Terms of Trade and Investment*, written by O. Rosales, Mikio Kuwayama from UN ECLAC, etc.

products have not formed any fierce competition with the local manufacturing industry. China "is becoming more and more competitive in a series of products of low technology and high technology. Latin America is still far from this process".[24] In other words, the growth of the manufacturing industry of the Latin-American countries depends on their further adjustment of the industrial structure and enhancement of the international competitiveness of their products. In terms of employment, take Brazil, for example, "the obtained employment research results indicate that the trade with China and India had produced only a small negative impact on employment in the industrial sector".[25] (4) The competition between China and Latin America in the US market is not so serious as some news media had propagandized. Mexico's competition index of products against China's products in the US market is 50%, Brazil's is less than 30%, and Colombia's, Argentina's, Peru's, Uruguay's, Chile's and Venezuela's are no more than 20%.[26] If the Chinese competitive advantage is in labor cost and the relatively low cost of intermediate inputs, Mexico and Central American countries enjoy the advantages of short distance from the US and bilateral preferential trade arrangements with the US. The researches of Devlin and other scholars show that in the production of clothing the labor cost in Nicaragua was 34% higher than that in China, and in Mexico it was 96% higher than in China; the average annual nominal wage of the manufacturing industry in Mexico was five times (1998) as much as in China, in Brazil it was

[23]Santa Haya Rari, John Vis, "China and Latin America: Trade Competition (1990–2002)", from *The Visible Hand of China in Latin America*, translated by Wang Peng and Zhao Chongyang, world knowledge Press, 2009, p. 101.

[24][Spain] Javier Santiso *et al.*, "An Angel or a Devil? China's Impact on the Trade of the Emerging Markets in Latin America", from *The Visible Hand of China in Latin America*, translated by Wang Peng, Zhao Chongyang, World Knowledge Press, 2009, p. 101.

[25]Gonzalo Sebastian Paz (Espana), "Cambio y Contunuidad en las Relaciones de China con America Latina a Princpios del Siglo XXI", *Revista Iberoamericana de Estndios de Asia Oriental*, No. 1, 2007, p. 61.

[26]Javier Santiso (Espana), "La Emergencia de China y su Impacto en America Latina", *Politica Exterior*, V. 19, No. 107, p. 102. http://dialnet.unirioja.es/servlet/articulo?Codigo=1237354.

three times (2002) as in China; in 2003, it took 24 days to ship a standard container of goods from China to the United States, with the transportation cost of $4,300; in contrast, it took only four days from Mexico, with the transportation cost of only $1,750.[27] According to the estimates of Lopez Cordoba and other scholars, "Free trade in the western hemisphere will enable the Latin-American export to the US to have increased by about 3%, while the Central American export to the US will rise more significantly (21%)". They believe, "The lagged productivity growth is the main reason for the poor performance of the Latin-American export".[28]

In terms of foreign investment, there is no "zero-sum game" between China and Latin America. First, the reason for the up-and-down state of Latin America's inflow of FDI comes not from outside, but from Latin America itself. For example, in the first half of the 1990s, the influx of FDI into Latin America (see Figure 10.2) was identical with the wave of the large-scale privatization in Latin America. When the climax of privatization passed in 1997, the FDI inflow naturally began to show a decreasing trend. Another example, from 1998 to 2002, the Latin-American economy as a whole had been in a state of recession, known as the "lost 5 years", during which the inflow of foreign capital was naturally reduced. With the Latin-American region entering the new period of economic expansion in 2003, the inflow of FDI also had a strong rebound. In 2004, for example, China's absorption of FDI reached over $60 billion, an increase of 8% over the previous year, and the absorption of foreign capital of the four countries of Brazil ($18 billion), Mexico ($16 billion), Chile ($5 billion), and Argentina ($4 billion) together reached more than $43 billion, an increase of 50% over the previous year.

[27]Robert Devlin, Antoni Estevadeordal, Andrez Rodrlguez-Clare (Estados Unidos), *El Impacto de China: Oportnnidades y Retos para America Latina y el Caribe*, Editores BID y David Rokefeller Center for Latin-American Studies, Harvard University, Washington, D.C., 2007, pp. 205, 207, 226.

[28]Ernesto Lopez, Cordova, Alejandro Mikko, Daniel Ken Molina, "Fighting with the Dragon: Export of Latin America and China to the US Market", from *The Visible Hand of China in Latin America* edited by Javier *et al.*, translated by Wang Peng, Zhao Chongyang, World Knowledge Press, 2009, p. 124.

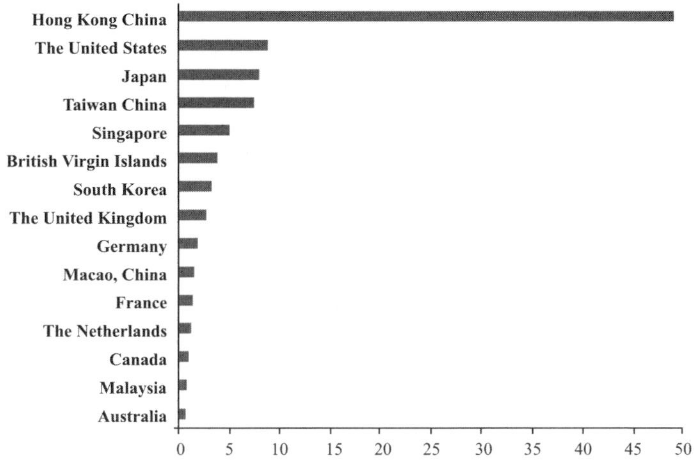

Figure 10.1 The Cumulative FDI into China by 2000 (%)

Note: From China National Bureau of Statistics (2003).

Source: Robert Devlin, Antoni Estevadeordal, Andres Rodriguez-Clare, *El Impacto de China: Oportunidades y Retos para America Latina y el Caribe*, Banco Interamericano de Desarrollo, David Rockefeller Center for Latin-American Studies, Harvard University, julio de 2007, p. 176.

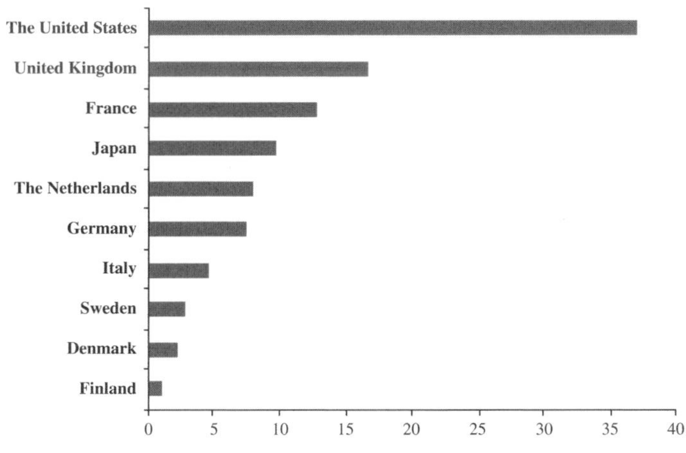

Figure 10.2 The Cumulative FDI into Latin America (1997–2001) (%)

Source: Robert Devlin, Antoni Estevadeordal, Andres Rodriguez-Clare, *El Impacto de China: Oportunidades y Retos para America Latina y el Caribe*, Editores BID y David Rockefeller Center for Latin-American Studies, Harvard University, julio de 2007, p. 176.

Secondly, foreign scholars have made comprehensive researches on whether China is in the form of direct competition with Latin America in attracting FDI. They mainly analyzed the main sources of FDI of the two sides and the coincidence index of industrial sectors (*indice de coincidencia sectorial*) that received the FDI. Santiso pointed out that China's four major sources of FDI in turn were China Hongkong, Japan, China, Taiwan, and Singapore, of which only Japan was also one of the main sources of Latin America's five FDI sources.[29] Devlin and other scholars had obtained essentially the same results through the analysis of the FDI stocks of the main foreign investors in China and Latin America respectively (see Figures 10.1 and 10.2).[30] In a special research report, Alicia Garcia-Herrero and Daniel Santabárbera pointed out, "The results of the study show that during the long period from 1984 to 2001, there was no evidence that the FDIs had shifted from Latin America to China... The large inflow of foreign capital to China might have a negative impact on Mexico and Columbia, but similar impact would not be on other Latin-American countries".[31] The negative effect on Mexico and Colombia mentioned here was based on the coincidence index of the industrial sectors absorbing FDI. China's absorption of FDI (see Figure 10.1) mainly was concentrated in the manufacturing sector, and 56% of Mexico's FDI and 21% of Colombia's FDI were invested in the manufacturing sector. Although the two authors had put forward the above views, they also made it clear that the use of this method to analyze the competition in the field of foreign investment of the two sides was just an attempt.

[29]Javier Santiso (Espana), "La Emergencia de China y su Impacto en America Latina", *Politica Exterior*, V. 19, No. 107, p. 104. http://dialnet.unirioja.es/servlet/articulo?codigo=1237354.

[30]Robert Devlin, Antoni Estevadeordal, Andres Rodrlguez-Clare (Estados Unidos), *El Impacto de China! Oportnnidades y Retos para America Latina y el Caribe*, Editores BID y David Rockefeller Center for Latin-American Studies, Harvard University, Washington, D.C., 2007, p. 176.

[31]Alicia Garcia-Herrero, Daniel Santabárbera, Does China Have an Impact on Foreign Direct Investment to Latin America? from *The Visible Hand of China in Latin America* edited by Javier Santiso, translated by Wang Peng, Zhao Chongyang, World Knowledge Press, 2009, pp. 153–154.

In 2007, Osvaldo Rosales, Director of the Department of the International Trade and Integration of ECLAC, and Mikio Kuwayama, the agency's Asia expert, jointly published an article titled "Latin America Encountering China and India: Prospects and Challenges of Commerce and Investment", which made a systematic assessment of China's position in the international economy and China's impact on the trade and investment in Latin America. The authors believed that this article had a symbolic significance in the process during which the Latin-American public opinion about China had changed from the early relatively negative to positive. The article emphasized that (1) China is the main engine of growth for the next several years in the global economy. In 2005, according to the parity of purchasing power, China's contribution to the global GDP growth was more than 27%, exceeding the sum of the contributions of the United States, the European Union and Japan. (2) The role of China in maintaining the balance of the world economy is growing. The output of a flood of cheap Chinese goods has enabled the developed countries to maintain a high demand while obtaining low inflation, China's huge foreign exchange reserves have helped the United States to ease its current account deficit, and any moves in China's huge international reserves are sufficient to cause vibrations in the international financial market. (3) China has played the leading role in the world trade. In 2006, China's export grew by 27%, with the export value reaching $969 billion, which was 1.5 times of the equivalent value of the export of Latin America and the Caribbean. China has become the platform for its Asian neighbors to export to the markets in Europe and America and has become one of the world's 10 top import and export countries of service trade. (4) China is a major buyer of primary products and manufactured goods from Latin America and the Caribbean. China ranks the third in the world as a consumer of the 14 kinds of products out of the 15 kinds of important primary products exported by Latin America, excluding the natural gas. From 1999 to 2005, the world auto market sales increased 7 million, of which 46% of the increase appeared in the Chinese market. China's consumer demand for electronic products and mobile phones had exceeded that of the US market. (5) China is becoming an important foreign investment country. By the end of 2004, China's non-financial overseas investment stock had reached \$33.2 billion. In the same year, China's foreign investment was \$5.5 billion, of which 32% was invested in Latin America. Therefore, it is suggested that the Latin-American countries should deepen relations with China, such as signing trade agreements or establishing other forms of trade and investment alliance, increasing bilateral economic complementarity so as to enter the Chinese market to a greater extent and join the Asian production and export chain.[32]

The first section of this chapter described the role that the Sino-Latin American economic and trade cooperation had played in promoting the economic growth of Latin America and in coping with the international financial crisis in the past 10 years. This positive role has been generally recognized by the Latin-American countries and the international public opinion and become the most valid proof for the theory of "China Opportunity". It was mentioned previously that the huge demand of China had stimulated the substantial growth of the export of primary products and the prices to continue to rise in Latin America, forming the so-called "Chinese Effect" (efecto China). This is a convincing example. According to the statistics of the Latin-American scholars, "From 2001 to 2010, Latin America and the Caribbean had achieved an average annual growth rate of 10.8% of the values of exports of goods. Among them, the factor of the rising of export price accounted for 5.5%, and the factor of export growth accounted for 5.3%. If Mexico was not included, the average annual growth rate of the region's export value would be 13.5%, of which the factor of price increase and export growth accounted for 7.9% and, 5.6% respectively".[33] Mexico's exports of commodities are mainly industrial manufactured goods. To exclude

---

[32]Osvaldo Rosales, Mikio Kuwayama, America Latina al Encuentro de China e Idia: Perspectivas y Desafios en Comercio e Inversion, *Revista de la CEPAL*, No. 93, Diciembre de 2007.

[33]Osvaldo Rosales, Mikio Kuwayama, *China y America Latina y el Caribe: Hacia una Relacion Economica y Comercial Estrategica*, CEPAL, Santiago de Chile, Marzo de 2012, p. 74.

Mexico, the proportion of price increase would have a substantial rising, indicating that it was the raw materials and primary products that had mainly contributed to the rising of the prices. Therefore, most of the substantial growth in export revenues of the Latin-American countries outputting resources in the past 10 years came from the rising prices.

The British scholar Rhys Jenkins believes that the rising of prices of raw materials and primary products is an "indirect effect" of China's demand growth. A study that he had conducted showed that on the basis of the total export value of \$260.579 billion of the 15 kinds of primary products outputted from Latin America in 2007, it was estimated that the income brought about by the so-called "China Effect" (i.e., price factor) was about \$56.295 billion.[34] It is no exaggeration to say that the increase of the annual income of tens of billions of dollars due to the increase of the price of primary products in the Latin-American region is the key factor for most of the governments in the region to maintain surplus in the current account for consecutive years.

The "China Opportunity" theory becoming the mainstream of the Latin-American public opinion about China is a kind of important and far-reaching change, which had weakened the negative impact of the "China Threat" theory and the Chinese "New Colonialism" by some western media, and enhanced the foundation of the public opinion about the Latin-American governments actively promoting cooperation with China. Thus, facing the new situation that China has become a global power of economy and trade, with rapid expanding foreign economic cooperation and trade, China needs to strengthen the investigation on related foreign public opinions and increase the external propaganda so as to create a favorable public-opinion environment for China to enter the world.

[34]Rhys Jenkins, "El Efecto China" en los Precios de los Productos Basicos y en el Valor de las Exportaciones de America Latina", *Revista de la CEPAL*, No. 103, abril de 2011, p. 88. The 15 listed basic products are: crude oil, iron ore, copper, aluminum, zinc, soybeans, soybean oil, fish meal, coffee, sugar, bananas, beef, poultry, timber, and pulp.

Section 3 The Main Focus of the Current Public Opinion on the Sino-Latin American Economic and Trade Relations

The last section is a review of the reaction of the public opinion of Latin America and western countries about the rise of China and the Sino-Latin American economic and trade cooperation in the last 20 years. Obviously this reaction was not static, but would change with the development of the objective environment and the cooperation between the two sides. This change is not necessarily symbolized by a big shift in the public opinion, but more by the change of the "focus" of the public opinion, or change in the interests of the public opinion. In terms of the current situation, the "China Opportunity" theory as the mainstream of the Latin-American public opinion will not change in the short term, but the focus of the public concern is changing. The current focus of the public opinion is the new "Center–Periphery Theory".

The "Center–Periphery Theory" appeared in the 1950s of the 20th century, as one of the basic concepts of the Latin-American School of Structure represented by Raul Prebisch, and later was adopted by the School of Attachment Theory. The Latin-American School of Structure believed that the world economic system was a whole composed of the center (centro, i.e., developed countries) and periphery (periferia, i.e., less developed countries). The trade between the center and the periphery was the exchange of the industrial products and the primary products. Prebisch said, "For the periphery, when its technical and economic disadvantages have not been overcome, apart from the primary products, what else can it export? ... For the center, there are obvious benefits to export these products with a huge comparative advantage to the periphery, and import those that do not have this advantage or have a very low advantage from the periphery".[35] Therefore, in the eyes of the Latin-American School of Structure, the pattern of international division

[35]Raul Prebisch, *The Peripheral Capitalism: Crisis and Reform*, translated by SU Zhenxing and Yuan Xingchang, The Commercial Press, 1990, p. 175.

of labor between the center and periphery would lead to the result that the process of the industrialization of countries at the periphery would be delayed to be in the status of a long-term "specialization of the production of primary products".

Currently in the commodity structure of the Sino-Latin American trade, the major Chinese outputs are manufactured goods, while Latin America mainly exports raw materials and primary products. Therefore, ECLAC believes that "Latin America and China's trade in essence has the property of the trade between industrial sectors (interindustrial). In this mode, the main exports of China are manufactured goods and the Latin-American and the Caribbean outputs are mainly primary products. It will hinder not only the enterprise alliance of the two sides, but also the Latin-American countries more effectively into the Asia-Pacific production chain".[36]

It seems that in the recent period the response of the Latin-American public opinion on the trade structure between the industrial sectors is even much stronger. Alicia Barcena, Executive Secretary of the ECLAC, said, "The increase in trade and investment with China does not mean that Latin America has a qualitative improvement in global trade. The expansion of the sectors related to the natural resources is not enough to promote the formation of the new technical capabilities in Latin America, and the productivity gap between Latin America and the advanced countries continues to expand. In this sense, the business relationship between Latin America and China provides both opportunities and challenges. In terms of challenges, in particular, we should avoid re-shaping and strengthening a Center–Periphery Model of trade in the growing trade with China, i.e., China becomes the new center, and the Latin-American countries become the new periphery".[37] This is undoubtedly the most representative point of view of the new "Center–Periphery

[36]CEPAL, *La República Popular China y America Latina y el Caribe: Hacia una Relacion Estrategica*, Santiago de Chile, mayo de 2010, p. 5.

[37]Alicia Barcena, *Prologo de China y America Latina y el Caribe: Hacia una Relacion Economica y Commercial Estrategica*, CEPAL, Santiago de Chile, marzo de 2012, p. 12.

Theory", but Ms. Barcena as a UN official has paid great attention to artistic expression, putting forward the problem from the perspective of avoiding the Center–Periphery Trade Model between Latin America and China. In contrast, the Argentine scholar J. Sevares was much more straightforward. He said, "The relationship between Latin America and China is repeating some paradigms in the relations between Latin America and its old suzerain. This relationship is pushing the Latin-American economies to reprimarization of products, so that the future of the region is being met with a number of yellow lights".[38]

This section intends to focus on the several issues that the Latin-American public opinion is concerned about in the Sino-Latin American economic and trade cooperation. These issues are actually the current conflicts of interests of the two sides in the bilateral economic and trade cooperation, and thus they deserve attention and need to be solved through joint efforts of both sides.

I. The Huge Demand of China Has Led to the "Reprimarization" of the Latin-American Export Commodities

What is the "reprimarization" (reprimarizacion) of the Latin-American export commodities? In short, it refers to the phenomenon that after a long process of industrialization of the Latin-American countries, the proportion of primary products in exports originally had dropped significantly, but in recent years has increased sharply again. The Latin-American countries usually classify export goods into five types: the high technology products, the medium technology products, the low technology products, the natural-resource-processed products and the raw materials, of which the natural-resource-processed products (such as the preliminarily refined copper, iron and other minerals, as well as food, beverages, tobacco, etc.) and the raw materials belong to the category

[38]Julio Sevares, "El Ascenso de China: Oportunidades y Retos para America Latina", *Nueva Sociedad*, No. 235, septiembre-octubre de 2011, Buenos Aires, Argentina, p. 35.

of primary products. For example, in the early 1980s, in the structure of the Latin-American export commodities, the raw materials accounted for 51.5%, dropping to 27.6% between 2001 and 2002, and rising again to 38.8% between 2008 and 2009. During the same period, the change of the curve of the proportion of the natural resource-processed products was basically the same as that of the raw materials. This shows that the Latin-American export commodity structure was being "re-primarized". The reason for this phenomenon is that, since entering the 21st century, the demand for primary products and raw materials in the international market has continued to rise. As can be seen from Figure 10.3, Japan, China, South Korea, and ASEAN countries are the main targets of the output of the Latin-American raw materials. Among them, Japan's proportion of imports of raw materials from Latin America is the highest, but because the scale of trade between Japan and Latin

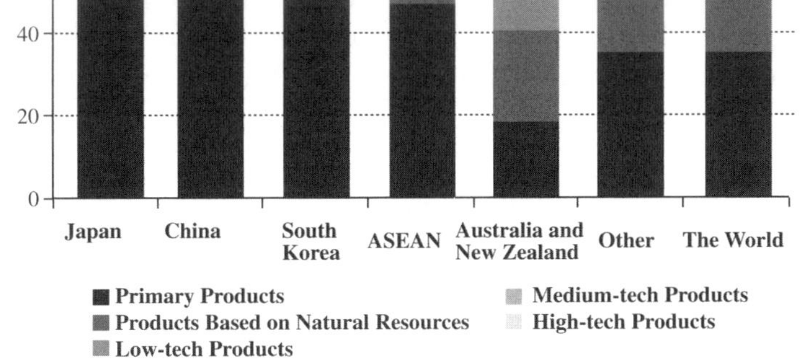

Figure 10.3 Exports of Latin America and the Caribbean to Asia by Technology Concentration (2005–2008) (%)

Note: ASEAN consists of only five countries: Indonesia, Malaysia, Philippines, Singapore, and Thailand.

Source: Osvaldo Rosales, Mikio Kuwayama, *China y America Latina y el Caribe: Hacia una Relacion Econdmica y Comercial Estrateica*, CEPAL, p. 99.

America is smaller than that of the Sino-Latin American trade, in terms of individual country, China is the largest buyer of the Latin-American raw materials and primary products. Therefore, there is the so-called China being the "decisive factor" for the reprimarization of the Latin-American export commodity structure.[39]

As mentioned earlier, in the past 10 years, the Latin-American countries outputting raw materials and primary products have acquired large benefits from the strong demand for such products and the increases of price and effectively stimulated the growth of the entire national economies. Then why were these countries worried about this kind of phenomenon and even such a concern has become a focus of current public opinion? In early 2005, the Spanish scholar Javier Santiso pointed out, "The China Effect will result in further deepening of the special traditional pattern of the products with less additional value, of low-level processing, and subject to the global cyclical fluctuations of Latin America". "Once the Chinese economy slows down, Latin America will be directly hurt".[40] These words basically summed up the two main factors of the above concern: first, it is the worry about the economy to go backward; the second is the worry about the sustainability of the trade with China.

The reason is very simple: the more profitable the resource-based industries become, the more the industry sectors in the country are able to get the opportunity to develop and become hot industries to attract domestic and foreign investment. However, the prosperity of the resource-based industries also has brought two obvious negative effects. First, the exploration and exploitation of oil, coal, and metal ore belong to capital-intensive industries with a very high proportion of foreign investment. These sectors are hotspots attracting the foreign investment, becoming the departments with the most foreign profits and the most repatriation of profits. At the same time, there

[39]Osvaldo Rosales, Mikio Kuwayama, *China y America Latina y el Caribe: Hacia una Relacion Economica y Commercial Estrategica*, CEPAL, Santiago de Chile, Marzo de 2012, p. 96.

[40]Javier Santiso, La Emergencia de China y su Impacto en America Latina, *Politica Exterior*, V. 19, No. 107, 2005, pp. 100–101. http://dialnet.unirioja.es/servlet/artlculo?Codico=1237354.

is little space for these sectors to create jobs, but the effect of the destruction of the environment is very prominent. Second, it is the "Dutch Disease" syndrome. With the substantial growth in export earnings, the increase of foreign investment, and especially a large number of short-term speculative capital inflows caused by the US "quantitative easing" policy, the appreciation of currency and the rising inflationary pressure appeared in the Latin-American exporters of primary products generally continued. The above two kinds of negative effects have an adverse impact on the development of the manufacturing and output of products, which runs counter to the wish of the "reindustrialization" of some Latin-American countries. A Colombian scholar pointed out that, in recent 20 years, Columbia has focused on the development of oil and coal industries, which had brought about the so-called "mining boom", but at the same time resulted in three consequences: first, the national economy has been enabled to be further focused on the three primary products of oil, coal, and coffee; second, Colombia has become the recipient of foreign investment, but the foreign investment is concentrated in minerals and petroleum, resulting in the damage to the development of the manufacturing industry; third, the mining boom will not help to solve the unemployment problem of the country, forcing a large number of labor force to go overseas to earn a living.[41] Obviously, the author's worry is that the "reprimarization" of the structure of export commodities will lead to the "reprimarization" of the entire national economy, i.e., gradually returning to the position of the production of raw materials.

The doubt of the Latin-American public opinion on the sustainability of the Sino-Latin American trade is mainly based on the characteristics of the three "high concentrations" in the trade pattern of the Sino-Latin American trade. Firstly, the current Sino-Latin American trade is over concentrated in a few Latin-American countries. According to the data of ECLAC, calculated according

[41] Ricardo Bonilla Gonzale (Colombia), "Apertura y Reprimarizacion de la Economia Colombiana: Un Par also de Corto Plazo", *Nueva Sociedad*, No. 231, enero-febrero de 2011, Buenos Aires, Argentina, p. 58.

to the average value of four years from 2005 to 2008, 86% of the total value of exports to China from Latin America had been concentrated in five countries, of which Brazil accounted for 33%, Chile 25%, Argentina 12%, Mexico 9%, and Peru 7%; 80% of the total import from China had been concentrated in four countries in Latin America, of which Mexico accounted for 48%, Brazil 20%, Argentina 6%, and Chile 6%.[42] Because the economic scales of Latin America are different, it is difficult to avoid the phenomenon that their trades with China are relatively concentrated in a small number of major countries, but this concentration is indeed somewhat high. Secondly, the Latin-American exports to China are highly concentrated in the primary products. According to the ECLAC calculation of the average export values of three years (2007–2009), of the 20 kinds of main products exported to China from Latin America (export value $53.982 billion, 85.7% of the total $62.974 billion), 19 kinds were raw materials or primary products, and only the integrated circuit belonged to manufactured goods (from Costa Rica, with an annual export value of $2.805 billion).[43] Thirdly, the exports of the Latin-American countries are concentrated in a few commodities. The statistical data of ECLAC show that in all of the Latin America's exports to China, the proportions of the export values of five kinds of main products had reached 80–100% in the total export value, with the exception of only three countries — Mexico (37%), Venezuela (64%) and Panama (78%).[44] On the basis of the characteristic of a high degree of concentration, large fluctuations of the demand, supply or price of one or several main products could cause a great impact on the bilateral trade. Obviously, the Latin-American countries are more concerned about how to change the situation of a single export of raw materials and primary products to China and gradually increase the output of the industrial manufactured goods to China.

[42]Osvaldo Rosales, Mikio Kuwayama, *China y America Latina y el Caribe: Hacia una Relacion Economica y Commercial Estrategica*, CEPAL, Santiago de Chile, Marzo de 2012, p. 91.
[43]*Ibid.*, pp. 101–102, Cuadro II. 8.
[44]*Ibid.*, pp. 104–105, Cuadro II. 9.

II. The "Exclusion Effect" of the China-Made Products on the Latin-American Products in the Latin-American Market

In the field of trade, the worry of the Latin-American public opinion about the "China Competition" still exists, but the focus has changed. For example, with the increase of labor costs in China and the decrease of the proportion of labor-intensive products in China's export commodities, in recent years the degree of the concern of the Latin-American public opinion about the competition between China and Latin America in the United States, Europe and other third-party markets has decreased. The current problem is that some of the countries in Latin America that have better industrial base consider that China's exports of manufactured goods to Latin America are producing a exclusion effect on their manufactured goods. In April 2012, several scholars in Brazil co-published an article entitled "The Performance of the Exports of China and Brazil to Latin America, 1994–2009", giving a more systematic exposition of the above points of view.

The article believes that export is the key to the implementation of the internationalization strategy of China and also the key to guaranteeing the stability of the process of modernization of China. In the post-crisis period, as the United States and Europe are facing great difficulties, the emerging markets, including the Latin-American countries, have become the targets of intense competition. The Latin-American markets, especially the South American markets, are the key markets for Brazil's manufactured goods, while China's exports are being pushed to the markets that were previously occupied by Brazil. "By the measurement of some indexes of international trade and competitiveness it can be confirmed that China's exports, especially the exports of manufactured goods, are trying to exclude Brazilian exports of manufactured goods in the Latin-American market, which may pose a threat for Brazil".[45] The

[45]Marcos Tadeu Caputi Lelis, Andre Moreira Cunha, Manuela Gomes de Lima, "Desempeno de las Exportaciones de China y el Brasil hacia America Latina, 1994–2009", *Revista de la CEPAL*, No. 106, Abril de 2012, p. 57.

author's research shows that the expansion of China's export market mainly lies in the substantial adjustment of its export commodity structure, its rapid upgrading of products and the obvious improvement of its technical content. From 1994 to 2002, the proportion of China's export in the total value of the imports of the Latin-American countries (excluding Brazil) had been lower than that of Brazil, but since 2003, China's proportion began to exceed Brazil's, and in 2008, the proportions of China and Brazil respectively were 11% and 9%.[46] In terms of the country market, for example, compared with 2004, in 2009, in the industrial products that Argentina had imported, the ratio of Brazilian products decreased while 16 kinds of Chinese products were found in the rising-ratio list; over the same period, in Venezuela's imports of industrial products, the ratio of Brazilian products decreased while 13 kinds of Chinese products were found in the rising ratio list.[47]

Latin-American countries have different levels of industrial development. Brazil, Mexico and Argentina are considered to be the Latin-American manufacturing countries with the highest levels of development and relatively complete industrial systems. In recent years, these countries have issued industrial development plans, having ambitions to revive the industrialization of their countries. Looking back on the Latin-American anti-dumping cases against China in the past 10 years, it is not difficult to find that the three countries ranked the forefront. The reason is that the manufacturing industry occupies an important position in the national economy. With many products, once the input of Chinese products was considered negative to the domestic industry, or the import needed to be restricted because of the poor economic situation, often they would take anti-dumping measures. The Brazilian scholars' article cited above shows that the conflicts of interest between Brazil and China in the trade of manufactured goods are extending from Brazil's domestic market to the Latin-American market. This new trend is worth attention. For the countries with a low level of the development of the

[46] *Ibid.*, p. 67, Cuadro 3.

[47] *Ibid.*, pp. 69–70, Cuadro 6 y Cuadro 7.

manufacturing industry, the current focus is to selectively develop some emerging industries, and the original industries such as textiles, clothing, footwear and toys will continue to be fully protected because these industries have much to do with solving the supply of the domestic market and providing jobs.

III. China's Direct Investment in Latin America Being "to Obtain Natural Resources as the Main Purpose"

The reactions of the Latin-American public opinion on China's investment in Latin America also experienced some changes before and after. For example, the claims about China's competition for foreign investment internationally with Latin America currently have disappeared. In recent years, the pace of China's investment in Latin America has accelerated, but the Latin-American public opinion is not contented, emphasizing that the Latin-American and Caribbean countries have very high expectations, but China's investment has been tardy. The Latin-American public opinion also has criticized the phenomenon of the large number of China's capital into the Caribbean "tax havens". Some scholars pointed out that by 2009, the stock of China's direct investment in Latin America was about \$31 billion, of which more than 90% had been invested in the British Virgin Islands and the Cayman Islands. These capitals flowed back to China in the form of Latin America's investment to China, but only about 7% of the capital had truly been invested in the Latin-American countries.[48]

However, the current focus of the public opinion on the issue of investment is that the main purpose of China's investment is to obtain natural resources in Latin America. The Argentine scholar J. Sevares said, "The Chinese direct investment in Latin America has been in the departments of primary products and enterprises

---

[48]Osvaldo Rosales, Mikio Kuwayama, *China y America Latina y el Caribe: Hacia una Relacion Economica y Commercial Estrategica*, CEPAL, Santiago Chile, marzo de 2012, pp. 112–113.

and infrastructure related to the export of natural resources, promoting the production specialization of local primary products. This is the same as the investment of economic powers in Latin America in the 19th century. The challenge confronting Latin America is becoming more serious because of China's import substitution and export policies, which are squeezing the opportunities of the products of high degree of processing in Latin America into the market".[49] The scholar also quoted the US. "Wall Street Daily", "China's growth is making the development models of many economies transform from the manufacturing sector to the production of raw materials".[50]

The two previously quoted ECLAC scholars are of the view that China's direct investment in Latin America is pursuing three objectives: to acquire natural resources, to expand export markets (including the markets in Latin America and the US market), and to improve production efficiency. They also has taken Argentina as an example to stress that China's investment in the natural resources in Latin America have the characteristic of covering all the value chains while making the "acquisition of natural resources" as the primary goal. According to their opinion, China is seeking to secure a stable supply of grain, meat and their by-products from Argentina. China has signed a deal with Argentina on beef imports and plans to directly invest in the agricultural production of Argentina. In addition, China and the Belgrano Freight Company have jointly built a railway to transport goods such as grain products to the port.[51]

Some European and American scholars also have directly linked China's participation in the infrastructure construction of the Latin-American countries with China's acquisition of the supply of natural resources. The American scholar Devlin believes that there are two

---

[49] Julio Sevares, "El Ascenso de China: Oportunidades y Retos para America Latina", *Nueva Sociedad*, No. 235, Septembre-Octubre de 2011, Buenos Aires, Argentina, pp. 35–36.

[50] David Wessel, Paulo Prada, "El Ascenso de China Trastoca al Resto de las Economias del Mundo", *The Wall Street Journal.* Reprinted by the Argentine *National Daily*, March 11, 2011.

[51] Osvaldo Rosales, Mikio Kuwayama, *China y America Latna y el Caribe: Hacia una Relacion Economica y Commercial Estrategica*, CEPAL, Santiago de Chile, marzo de 2012, pp. 115–116.

characteristics in the current Chinese investment in Latin America: one is that the main purpose of investment is to establish a platform for export in order to ensure the supply of natural resources; the other is that the investors are mainly big companies in China.[52] The Spanish scholar Santiso stresses that China "not only seeks supply of raw materials to support its rapid growth, but also wants to ensure a normal and reliable supply, and therefore needs the support of ports, railways, gas pipelines, oil pipelines and other infrastructure. In the supply of raw materials, Latin America also has become a region to attract investment in infrastructure".[53] The Spanish scholar Paz also said, "Compared with trade, the (Chinese) investment is still small... In fact, as in Africa and elsewhere, the (Chinese) investment seems to have a clear pattern: to ensure the supply of raw materials needed for China's economy. Investment in the infrastructure sector is also focused on the protection of the supply of primary products".[54]

IV. Central America and Mexico — the Weak Link in the Economic and Trade Relations between China and Latin America

From the perspective of the development of the Sino-Latin American economic and trade relations in the past 10 years, as a sub-region, Central America has become a weak link in the bilateral cooperation between China and Latin America. First, because this stage of the Latin-American economic growth was driven by China's huge demand for raw materials and primary products in Latin America, while the Central American countries were also the importers of such

[52]Robert Devlin, Antoni Estevadeordal, Andres Rodrlguez-Clare, *El Impacto de China: Oportunidades y Retos para America Latina y el Caribe*, Editores BID y David Rockefeller Centre for Latin American Studies, Harvard University, Washington, D.C., 2007, p. 182.

[53]Javier Santiso, "La Emergencia de China y su Impacto en America Latina", *Politica Exterior*, V. 19, No. 107, Espana, p. 105. http://dialnet.unirioja.es/servlet/artlculo?Codigo=1237354.

[54]Gonzalo Sebastian Paz, "Cambio y Continuidad en las Relaciones de China con America Latina a Principios del Siglo XXI", *Revista Iberoamericana de Estudios de Asia Oriental*, No. 1, 2007, p. 7.

products. "China's growing need has promoted the growth of South American countries and the improvement of trade price. The most benefited is the countries outputting oil and minerals. The effect of the increasing prices of the export products is greater than the effect of the growth of export, especially in South American countries. In contrast, in Mexico and Central America (excluding Costa Rica) only exports increased... Those that have strengthened the trade links with China through the basic products have become the countries with the most benefit from the trade price. On the contrary, the Central American countries have suffered a deterioration of terms of trade"[55] (see Figure 10.4). Second, as importers of energy and food,

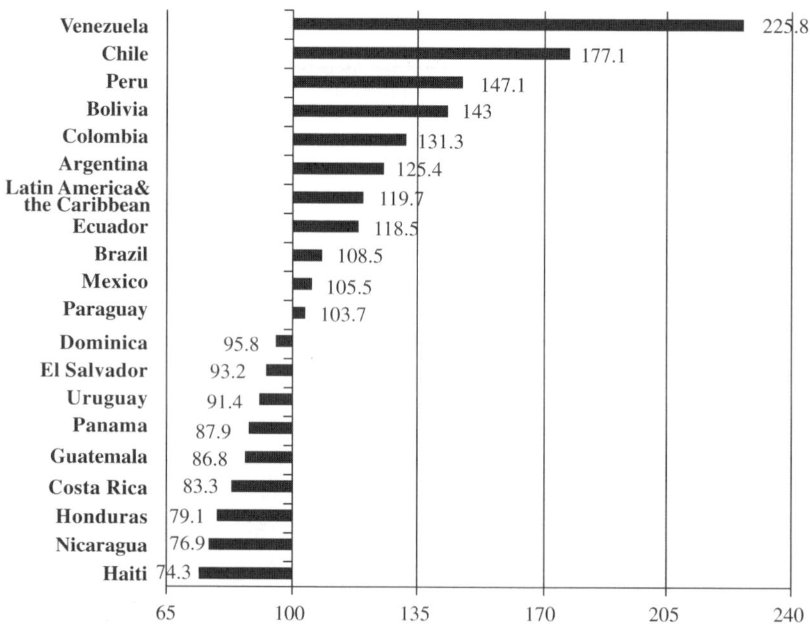

Figure 10.4 Changes of the Trade Price of Commodities of the Latin-American and Caribbean Countries (2007–2008) (index of 2000:100)

Source: Osvaldo Rosales, Mikio Kuwayama, *China y America Latina y el Caribe: Hacia una Relacion Econdmica y Comercial Estrategica*, CEPAL, p. 75.

[55] Osvaldo Rosales, Mikio Kuwayama, *China y America Latina y el Caribe: Hacia una Relacion Economica y Commercial Estrategica*, CEPAL, Santiago de Chile, marzo de 2012, pp. 74–75.

the Central American countries have to bear the imported inflation pressure because of the increased international prices for these products. Third, except Costa Rica, the other five countries in Central America have been in a deficit position in their trade with China. Fourth, the statistics of China's Ministry of Commerce show that so far China only has had a small amount of direct investment in Panama, with no investment in the remaining five Central American countries. Fifth, in the US market, although the competition between China and the Central American countries has been weakened, the two sides are still rivals.

At present, the outstanding problem in the Sino-Mexican economic and trade relations may be the phenomenon of trade imbalance. As it has been quoted in the above article by Rosales from the ECLAC, Mexico is China's largest export market in Latin America — from 2005 to 2008, Mexico had accounted for an average of 48% of the Latin-American imports from China. This is the result obtained from the statistical data of ECLAC. According to China's statistics, in recent years, Mexico's imports from China consistently ranked the second place, after Brazil, with the annual trade deficit of more than $10 billion (in 2011, for example, with exports of $9.38 billion to China and imports of $23.98 billion from China), becoming the Latin-American country with the largest deficit in trade with China. Some scholars have stressed that Mexico's method of statistics of its foreign trade was different from that of China, with the problem of a possible statistical exaggeration of the imports from China. However, the author believes that it is very difficult to require the implementation of the same trade statistics from the Mexican side. If the trade between the two sides can achieve a general equilibrium, the impact of the difference in statistical methods can be relatively limited. In addition, for the government of Mexico, there is also the problem of a re-balance between its diplomatic relations with the US and the Asia-Pacific area. Since joining the North American Free Trade Zone, Mexico has become more and more dependent on the US market for its exports, reaching more than 80%. In recent years, the US economy has suffered a serious blow from the financial crisis, which also hit Mexico. From 2003 to 2010, Mexico's economy grew at only an average annual rate of 2.2%, being the lowest in Latin America. The government of the Mexican Revolutionary Institutional Party (PRI), which has come into power recently, is facing a favorable opportunity to improve relations with China.

Four problems have been summed up in the above. Obviously, the first three problems, i.e., the so-called "reprimarization" in the Latin-American export commodity structure resulted from China's demand, the "exclusion effect" of China's manufactured goods to the Latin-American manufactured goods in the Latin-American market, and China's investment in Latin America "for the acquisition of natural resources as the main purpose", are directly related to the new "Center–Periphery Theory" by the Latin-American scholars. However, what is needed to be emphasized is that these problems have been summarized from the response of the Latin-American public opinion and they have reflected the interest demands of the Latin-American countries in their economic and trade cooperation with China, but whether these problems are practical and those interest demands are reasonable also need to be further argued and analyzed. This will be dealt with in the last chapter of this book.

Section 4 Competition between Great Powers and the Sino-Latin American Economic and Trade Cooperation

In the current progress in the economic and trade cooperation with Latin America, in addition to the challenges listed in the last section, China also has to face the challenges resulted from the competition between big powers. Some foreign scholars believe that the rising China, together with other Asian countries, constitutes the third pivot (*un tercer punto de apoyo*) of the Latin-American diplomacy. In the 20th century, the United States and Europe were the two major economic pivots of Latin America, and the two "pivots" were both in the Atlantic. "With the rise of China, an unprecedented third pivot has come out, and a new tropism (*tropismo*) has been confirmed, i.e., more and more eyes from the American Continent are focusing on the Pacific side... For Latin America, China's re-rising is a very important geo-economic change. This Asian tropism means that the Latin-American region is now more dependent on the floating RMB and the demand from Beijing or Shanghai. This is good news because there has been a greater geographical diversification of the demand for Latin America".[56]

Back in the 1970s, the Latin-American countries had proposed the policy of diversification of external relations, with the key orientation for Asia, especially for Asia's economic stars — Japan and the "four little dragons", but the real progress was relatively limited. In recent 10 years, the Latin-American diplomacy of "Asia-Pacific-orientation" (including Asia and Oceania) has made remarkable progress, while China is the top priority of its Asia-Pacific diplomacy. The Latin-American leaders frequently visited China, establishing many kinds of cooperation mechanisms for cooperation with China, including the bilateral free trade area, trade, investment, finance, technology, and so on. The Sino-Latin American entrepreneurs have held five summits, and the 11 Pacific coast countries in Latin America have founded the "Latin-American Pacific Arc Ministerial Forum"; the four countries of Colombia, Chile, Mexico, and Peru have formed a "Union Pacific" (Costa Rica and Panama as observers). The aims of them are to work together to promote relations with China and Asia. During the 10 years, the trade between Latin America and Asia has been greatly expanded, which is the best witness to the above efforts. In 2000, the Latin-American exports to Asia accounted for only 5% of its total export, but in 2010 they accounted for 6%, in which the proportion of China rose from 1.1% to 8.3%; over the same period the Latin-American imports from Asia rose from 10.9% to 26.9% in the total imports, in which the proportion of China rose from 1.8% to 3% (see Table 10.2).

Some scholars believe that the Latin-American countries have two basic reasons for promoting the diplomatic relations with China: one is the enlightenment of history, and the other is the need of reality. From the historical point of view, since the 19th century, the

[56]Javier Santiso, "La Emergencia de China y su Impacto en America Latina", *Politica Exterior*, V. 19, No. 107, 2005, p. 98.

Table 10.2 Latin America and the Caribbean: Changes of Export Destinations and Import Sources in 2000, 2006–2010 (%)

	2000	2006	2007	2008	2009	2010
			Export			
Destination						
Latin America and the Caribbean	19.0	17.2	18.2	19.6	18.9	18.9
Asia	5.0	9.7	11.5	12.2	15.2	16.6
China	1.1	3.4	4.7	4.9	7.1	8.3
Asia and other countries	3.9	6.4	6.8	7.2	8.1	8.3
US	61.0	50.0	46.2	43.3	41.5	41.0
EU	11.8	14.2	15.0	15.2	13.9	13.1
Other areas in the world	3.2	8.9	9.2	9.8	10.5	10.5
			Import			
Source						
Latin America and the Caribbean	15.1	20.5	20.5	21.2	20.7	19.7
Asia	10.9	22.0	23.1	13.3	24.7	26.9
China	1.8	8.4	9.6	10.5	11.8	13.3
Asia and other countries	9.1	13.6	13.4	12.9	12.9	13.6
US	55.0	34.9	32.7	31.2	31.5	30.8
EU	12.1	14.3	14.6	14.7	15.1	14.3
Other areas in the world	6.9	8.2	9.1	9.6	8.0	8.3

Note: Data in the table cover Argentina, Bolivia, Brazil, Chile, Colombia, Costa Rica, Ecuador, El Salvador, Guatemala, Honduras, Mexico, Nicaragua, Paraguay, Peru, the Dominican Republic, Uruguay, Venezuela and the Caribbean. The information from the "espejo statistics" (estadisticas espejo). The data of Venezuela came from the IMF Trade Statistics Department.

Quoted from Osvaldo Rosales, Mikio Kuwayama, *China y America Latina y el Caribe: Hacia una Relacion Economica y Commercial Estrategica*, CEPAL, Santiago de Chile, Marzo de 2012, p. 71.

Source: ECLAC (based on official data), EUROSTAT, USITC, DOTS of FMI.

influence of the United States on Latin America has been ubiquitous. Because of the US intervention in the Latin-American sovereign matters regarding Latin America as its own backyard and the unsuccessful development mode recommended by the United States, Latin America has the desire to get rid of the control of the United States to break the "Center–Periphery Circle". From the perspective of reality, China's demand for primary products has not only greatly expanded the Latin-American export market, but also enhanced the international price of such products. China pursues the principle of peaceful coexistence, not to interfere in other countries' sovereignty and internal affairs, which makes China not to take western practices in the economic exchanges with other countries and not to revenge because of the problems of human rights or democracy.[57]

Some scholars have emphasized the role of China's diplomatic strategy. "From peaceful rise to peaceful development, from multi-polarization to multilateralism, the "harmonious world" proposed by President Hu Jintao means to seek consensus through dialogue. This thinking and policy are based on the following judgment: the main impact factor of China is economy rather than defense. However, this policy is gaining more and more influence, for people are seeing that the interests of China are covering more and more extensive areas beyond its territory".[58]

However, in recent years, there has been a phenomenon worthy of our attention. Whether it is a new development of the Chinese relationship with Latin America or with Africa, the response of western countries has been much stronger than that of Latin America or Africa itself. This phenomenon is expected to continue to exist in the future. This phenomenon must be understood in the broad context of the adjustment of international relations. Since the beginning of the 21st century, most emerging economies have experienced accelerated economic growth in the world. Western developed economies have generally suffered heavy losses in the international financial crisis. The US economic recovery is faltering and the Euro zone has been in deep debt crisis, but some of the major emerging economies are still maintaining the momentum of strong growth. The growth and decline of the economic powers of the East and West will inevitably lead to the corresponding adjustment of the international relations.

[57]Juan Carlos Trivino Salasar (Argentina), *Relaciones Comerciales entre China y America Latina: Un Matrimonio de Conveniencia*, Centro Argentino de Estudios Internacionales, www.cael.com.ar.

[58]Xulio Rios (Espana), *El Impacto de China en el Futuro de Asia y del Mundo*, http://www.polltica-china.org, 9 de enero de 2009, p. 5.

Take the Latin-American region for example. With the rapid development of the Sino-Latin American economic cooperation in the last 10 years, China has replaced Japan to have become Latin America's largest trading partner in Asia. According to the prediction of ECLAC in May 2010, the United States, the statuses of the three Latin-American major trade partners of the united States, the European Union (27 countries) and China will undergo great changes in the next 10 years. In 2009, the exports of Latin America (16 countries) to the United States, the European Union and China accounted for 38.6%, 13.8% and 7.6%, respectively of their total export, but in 2020 they will become respectively 28.4%, 13.6%, and 19.3%; over the same period, the imports of Latin America (16 countries) from the United States, the European Union and China respectively will change from 33.1%, 14.7%, 9.5% to 26.1%, 14%, and 16.2% of the total imports. In 2014 and 2015, China will become Latin America's second largest trade partner with the increase in import and export over the EU, and at the same time, the gap between China and Latin America's largest trading partner — the United States — will greatly be narrowed (see Figures 10.5 and 10.6). In addition to China, in recent years, the scale and depth of economic and trade cooperation of India, Russia, South Korea, Iran, South Africa and some of the ASEAN countries with Latin America is also developing rapidly. In the face of this situation, in order to safeguard their vested interests in Latin America, western countries have used some of the political means, such as the "China Threat" theory, the "Neo-Colonialism" theory and the "Plundering of Resources" theory, to supplant and strike the new competitors.

The United States has always regarded Latin America as its own "backyard", having a strong resistance towards emerging powers such as China into Latin America. As some scholars have pointed out, after President Hu Jintao's visit to Latin America in November 2004, the American news media, Congress, the military and the government are on high alert to China's influence in Latin America. The news media "often portray the existence of China in Latin America as a threat to the US interests in the region. On the Internet, the blogs of many conservatives attack the new role of China in Latin America

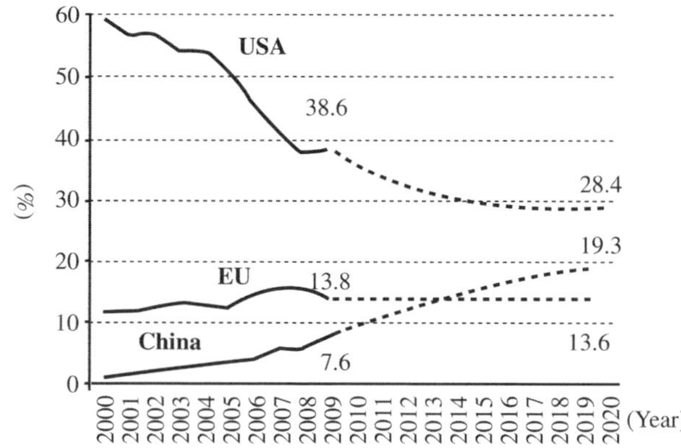

Figure 10.5 Proportion of the Major Export Destinations of Latin America and the Caribbean Region (16 Countries) in the Total Export (2000–2020)

Note: The data came from CEPAL, the UN Comtrade and the global national statistics. The 16 countries are: Argentina, Bolivia, Brazil, Chile, Colombia, Costa Rica, Ecuador, El Salvador, Guatemala, Honduras, Mexico, Panama, Paraguay, Peru, Uruguay, and Venezuela. The estimates and projections are based on the growth rates of GDP in Latin America and the Caribbean, Asia-Pacific, China, the United States, the European Union and other countries of the world from 2000 to 2009. The forecast of trade growth rate was based on the long-term economic growth rate.

Source: CEPAL, *La República Popular China y America Latina y el Caribe: Hacia una Relacion Estrategica*, mayo de 2010, p. 13.

and the lack of action of the Republican government".[59] Many congressional committees work closely with the news media, frequently holding hearings about the "security threat" to the United States that China has posed in Latin America, in which politicians, academics, the press, senior military generals have made testimonies. The issues involved in these hearings include: the military personnel exchanges between China and the Latin-American countries, China's export of weapon equipment to Latin America, the military purposes of the joint development of satellites by China and the Latin-American countries, the possibility that China may monitor and steal

[59]Gonzalo Sebastian Paz (Espana), "Cambio y Continuidad en las Relaciones de China con America Latina a Principios del Siglo XXI", *Revista Iberoamericana de Estudios de Asia Oriental*, No. 1, 2007, p. 8.

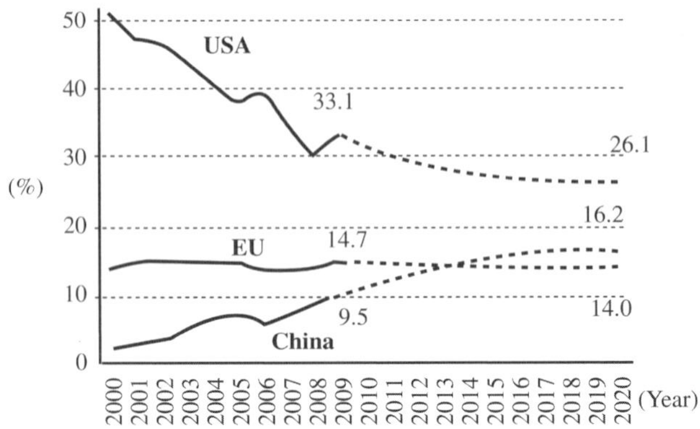

Figure 10.6 Proportion of the Major Import Sources of Latin America and the Caribbean Region (16 Countries) in the Total Imports (2000–2020)

Note: The data came from CEPAL, the UN Comtrade and global national statistics. The 16 countries are: Argentina, Bolivia, Brazil, Chile, Colombia, Costa Rica, Ecuador, El Salvador, Guatemala, Honduras, Mexico, Panama, Paraguay, Peru, Uruguay and Venezuela. The estimates and projections are based on the growth rates of GDP in Latin America and the Caribbean, Asia Pacific, China, the United States, the European Union and other countries of the world from 2000 to 2009. The forecast of trade growth rate was based on the long-term economic growth rate.

Source: CEPAL, *La Republica Popular China y America Latina y el Caribe: Hacia una Relacion Estrategica*, mayo de 2010, p. 13.

information by means of the former Soviet base in Cuba, the threat that China poses to the American oil safety and the navigation of the Panama Canal, the possibility that China may establish special relationships with the Latin-American left-wing governments, and so on. For a time, the theory of China's "threat" in Latin America has become a hot topic.

Just under this background, in April 2006, when he was Secretary of the US State Department responsible for Western Hemisphere Affairs, Thomas Shannon, assistant Secretary of State, came to visit China to have a dialogue with officials from the Chinese Foreign Ministry on the policies of both sides for Latin America. Since then, the officials of the two governments have conducted five dialogues under this mechanism, which has played a positive role in reducing misunderstandings of the two sides and cooling the American "threat theory" about China in Latin America. Although the United States now has admitted that the Sino-Latin American economic and trade cooperation can promote the prosperity and stability of Latin America, which is in line with the interests of the United States, it is expected that the US suspicion about and interference in the development of the Sino-Latin America relations will continue in the future. First, with the expansion of Chinese economic interests in Latin America, the commercial competition between China and the US in Latin America is likely to get intensified. Second, the United States may require China to take more "responsibilities" in Latin America and even encourage the Latin-American countries to raise the prices in cooperation with China. Third, the high alert psychology of the United States against China in terms of its so-called "security interests" in the Western Hemisphere will not be relaxed at any time.

The European countries have different attitudes from the US towards China's entry into Latin America. The European countries see emerging powers entering Latin America as new commercial competitors; however, the Europeans always have disgust for the US attempt of hegemony in Latin America. Therefore, it is not a bad thing for the Europeans that there are more roles in the competition in the Latin-American region. For the last 10 years, there have been positive and negative public reactions in Europe towards the rapid warming relations between China and Latin America. For example, the in-depth analyses in the several articles cited in this chapter of the economic and trade cooperation between China and Latin America have mostly come from the hands of European scholars. The basic conclusions drawn from them are positive. At the same time, there are some political forces in Europe that have negative views about the development of both the Sino-Latin American relations and the Sino-African relations. The argument of the so-called China's "threat" in Latin America also exists in Europe. Although the current economic recovery in the European Union has been seriously troubled by the sovereign debt crises of some member states, but the relationship between Europe and Latin America has never been ignored because of it. Marked by the EU-Latin America Summit held in May 2010,

EU increased its aid efforts in Central America, restarting the free trade negotiations with Mercosur, establishing three funds: the Latin-American Investment Fund, the Caribbean Infrastructure Investment Fund, and the EU-Latin America and the Caribbean Fund to promote bilateral investment and cooperation in the fields of energy, environment and infrastructure. The German government introduced a new policy for Latin America on August 4, 2010, emphasizing its identity with the Latin-American values and cultures, intending to strengthen technology transfer to and cultural exchanges with Latin America.[60] The cooperation of military and weapon supply between France and Brazil has taken a major step; Spain has deepened cooperation with Latin America with its unique history, cultural origin and "Iberian American Summit" as the carrier, and so on.

The relative decline of Japan's status as a Latin-American economic and trade cooperation partner has caused the alert of the Japanese government. On August 25, 2010, the "Department of Emerging Nations" was established under the Ministry of Foreign Affairs of Japan, intending to increase its diplomatic efforts with emerging market countries, including the Latin-American countries. According to the Latin-American public opinion, Japan has launched new strategies to deepen its economic ties with Latin America, taking the form of an alliance between the public sectors and the private sectors to seek cooperation opportunities to make use of the natural resources, energy, infrastructure, and food security. The main ways are to combine signing economic agreements with the Latin-American countries and providing official development assistance. The former aims at deepening the trade liberalization, while the latter emphasizes the strengthening of the development of infrastructure and human resources, joining the regional and global value chain to restore the production sector and to promote foreign trade and attract investment by the aided Latin-American countries.[61]

---

[60] Newsletter Punto Europa, *Nueva Estrategia Alemana para America Latina*, No. 6, 17/08/2010.

[61] See CEPAL, *Panorama de la Insercion Internacional de America Latina y el Caribe 2009–2010*, Capltulo V, Santiago de Chile, septiembre de 2010.

To sum up, the following judgment can be made: in the near future, between the developed countries, including emerging powers, the competition around Latin America's resources and markets will be showing a growing trend. Therefore, in the process of China's entering into the Latin-American market, whether it is the design of government policy, or the enterprise business strategy and management behavior, must fully take into account the environment of the fierce competition between big powers, trying to take the initiative.

Chapter 11

Continuing to Deepen the Cooperation and Realizing Common Development

SU Zhenxing

The previous chapter has discussed the opportunities and challenges that the Sino-Latin American economic and trade cooperation is facing, with special emphasis on the fact that the current period is in an important historical opportunity. The theme of this chapter is to explore how to seize the opportunity to further expand and deepen the economic and trade cooperation between China and Latin America. This chapter includes the following four parts: (1) On the basis of the analysis of the Chinese pursuit of interests in the Sino-Latin American economic and trade cooperation, it will focus on the basic guidelines for the win–win cooperation that China has to abide by when carrying out its foreign trade and economic cooperation. (2) It will give an analysis of the path of industrial structure adjustment that the Latin-American countries have selected in the next 10 years. (3) It will investigate the potential converging interests in the economic and trade cooperation between China and different types of the Latin-American countries in the next 10 years. (4) It will offer policy recommendations for deepening the bilateral economic and trade cooperation between China and Latin America.

Section 1 Following the Principle of Win–Win Cooperation

I. Scientific Assessment of the Status of the Latin-American Region in China's Foreign Trade and Economic Cooperation

During the 60 years since the founding of the new China, the economic and trade cooperation between China and Latin America has long been in a marginal position for both sides. For a long time since China started its reform and opening up, this situation also had changed little. For example, by 2001, the Sino-Latin American annual bilateral trade volume was just about $15 billion. Geographically the far distance between them is undoubtedly one of the most important reasons, but more importantly it is the fact that both economies lacked complementarity, or in other words, there was very little converging interest, both in their pursuit of the export market or seeking for funding and technical sources. But this situation could be changed. As has been talked about in the previous chapter, at the beginning of the 21st century the Sino-Latin-American economic and trade cooperation entered a period of rapid development, resulting from the changes of their respective development stages and the external demands. Compared with the rapid development of the Sino-Latin-American economic and trade cooperation in recent 10 years, the Chinese local governments and business communities probably still have not paid enough attention to the promotion of the status of the economic and trade cooperation with Latin America, and their traditional concept of focusing on the markets of Europe, the United States and Asia is not easy to change. This is clearly unfavorable for us to make full use of the historical opportunity of the Sino-Latin American bilateral economic and trade cooperation.

At present, what aspects of the Latin-American region can meet China's pursuit of interests? The author believes that this mainly involves the following four aspects: (1) Latin America is an important supplier of energy and resources. China's development is faced with the constraint of resources and environmental protection; the way to overcome the resource constraint is both to look for new sources and to reduce expenses simultaneously, and the acquisition of foreign supply of resources is one of the main selections of the "new sources". Latin America is a region with rich resources, with both large reserves and complete varieties. The resources available there involve oil and natural gas, ferrous and non-ferrous metal ore, and agricultural, animal husbandry and fishery products. Latin America has been and will continue to be one of the important strategic supports of China's access to the external supply of resources. (2) Latin America is one of the priorities in China's efforts to "stabilize and expand the international market". From 2001 to 2011, the average annual growth rate of the value of the Sino-Latin American trade reached about 30%, increasing from less than \$15 billion to \$241.5 billion. This rapid development is due to both China's huge demand for the Latin-American raw materials and primary products and the substantial increase in the purchasing power of Latin America to buy Chinese goods (mainly industrial manufactured goods). In 2012, Premier Wen Jiabao proposed that both countries should try to achieve the bilateral trade volume of over \$400 billion in the next five years. (3) Latin America is an important place for China to expand foreign investment. The Report of the 18th National Congress of the CPC stressed "to accelerate the pace of internationalization of enterprises and to enhance the ability of enterprises in international operations so as to foster a number of world-class multinational corporations".[1] The region of Latin America has many favorable conditions for Chinese enterprises to achieve this strategic objective. (4) To further deepen the economic and trade cooperation is conducive to strengthening and expanding China's diplomatic positions in Latin America. 12 countries in Latin America still have not established diplomatic relations with China, making it the area in the world where there are the most countries with which China has not established

[1] Hu Jintao, *Advance Firmly along the Road of Socialism with Chinese Characteristics, and Strive to Build a Well-off Society in an All-round Way — Report at the 18th National Congress of the Communist Party of China, Collection of the Documents of the 18th National Conference of the Chinese Communist Party*, People's Publishing House, p. 22, 2012.

diplomatic relations. To deepen the economic and trade cooperation and strengthen the relation of interests between countries is an effective way to improve the political relations between countries.

In addition, a series of important changes of the situation in Latin America recently also need to be paid close attention to. For example, since 2003 Latin America has got rid of the longest period of economic downturn in the history of its development, entering into a new stage of economic growth; the influence of the "Washington Consensus" in Latin America has gradually declined, the economic policy of each country has turned to be prudent and pragmatic, the differences in economic policy between the ruling and opposition parties have been significantly reduced, and the stability of economic policy has been strengthened; with the economic situation improved and the active social policies taken by the governments, the poverty rate in the region has continued to decline, leading to enhanced social stability; the consensus of various political forces on maintaining the representative democracy has been strengthened, with respect for the rules of the game under the system and for the election results, realizing the transfer of the political power through regular elections; all the countries have strengthened regional cooperations to achieve the goal of common development; the establishment of the "Community of the Latin-American and Caribbean States" is recognized as one great achievement, which is expected to become the regional representative office for coordinating their foreign positions and safeguarding the common interests of the region; the diversification of diplomacy centering on Asia is actively being promoted; after the establishment of the "Arc of Pacific Latin America" by 11 countries along the Pacific coast in Latin America, Mexico, Colombia, Chile and Peru had formed the "Pacific Alliance" (Costa Rica and Panama as observer countries); the traditional diplomatic pattern of Latin America's excessive inclination to the Atlantic (North America and Europe) is changing rapidly, and so on. All of these changes are reflected in the fact that the political situation in Latin America has entered a relatively stable period of development and the international status of Latin America is in a new rising period.

II. The Basic Principle of Win–Win Cooperation

It must be admitted that the relationship between countries is always a kind of benefit relation, and the economic and trade cooperation between countries is even more so. Such a cooperation in which both parties can benefit and achieve the win–win purpose can have a lasting vitality. The "win–win cooperation" is not only the basic principle by which the Chinese government abides by when carrying out foreign trade and economic cooperations, but also a basic experience of the great achievement in the Sino-Latin American economic and trade cooperation.

First, the win–win cooperation is in accordance with the requirements of the present era. The Report of the 18th National Congress of the CPC pointed out, "The human race has only one earth, and all the countries live in one world. History shows us that the jungle law is not the way of the coexistence of the human race, and it is unable to bring about a better world to exhaust all the resources to build up military powers. It is the common aspiration of the people of all countries to pursue peace instead of war, to pursue development instead of poverty, to pursue cooperation instead of confrontation, and to promote the building of a harmonious world of lasting peace and common prosperity".[2] It is an irresistible trend of the times to pursue peace, development, and cooperation. This win–win cooperation is precisely in line with the trend of the times and the common aspirations of mankind. Any action against this trend of the times, such as the continued implementation of the policy of the jungle law and the building of military powers, will naturally be opposed and resisted by the people of all countries, and it is doomed to failure. An important feature of the current international economic situation is the continuation of the global financial crisis that broke out in 2008. The severity of the crisis is not less than that of the

[2]Hu Jintao, *Advance Firmly along the Road of Socialism with Chinese Characteristics, and Strive to Build a Well-off Society in an All-round Way — Report at the 18th National Congress of the Communist Party of China, Collection of the Documents of the 18th National Conference of the Chinese Communist Party*, People's Publishing House, 2012, p. 43.

crisis in the 1930s. The Western powers fell into an unprecedented predicament; the world economy recovered slowly; the protectionism of investment and trade came about again, and some countries had implemented the quantitative easing monetary policy without control, causing many problems to the emerging markets and developing countries, leading to more serious imbalances of the global development. The Chinese scholar Zheng Bijian pointed out, "What should be done to deal with these contradictions, difficulties and conflicts? From the perspective of international trends, in the final analysis, there are three ways: the first one is to continue the Cold War mentality, the second is to launch a local war, and the third is to seek common development, mutual benefit, and build 'converging interests' and 'community of interests'".[3] Thus, the advocacy of the win–win cooperation in today's international communication is conducive to awakening the people of all the countries to resist the acts of beggar-thy-neighbor and transferring crises so as to promote the international economic recovery as soon as possible.

Second, the win–win cooperation is an important part of China's peaceful diplomacy. The peaceful diplomacy is decided by the goal pursued by China's development and the path selected by China's development. The goal pursued by China's development is to let the Chinese people live a happy life and to build China into a prosperous, democratic, civilized and harmonious modern socialist country. The road of peaceful development is the inevitable choice of socialism characteristic of China. China's development first relies on its own effort to find a development path suitable to China's national conditions through unremitting explorations, and on Chinese people's diligence and wisdom to turn the grand blueprint gradually into reality. However, with China's sustained and rapid economic development and gradually increased comprehensive national strength, the constantly-made so-called "China-Threat Theory" in the world doubts whether China's "peaceful development" is true and reliable, and even there is speculation that China will take the old road of

[3]Zheng Bijian, *The 18th National Congress of the CPC Has Opened a New Chapter in China*, *Shanghai Social Sciences Newspaper*, November 22, 2012, p. 1.

aggression and expansion like some of the emerging powers in the history of the world. In this regard, the Report of the Eighteenth National Congress of the CPC again declared, "Peaceful development is the inevitable choice of socialism with Chinese characteristics. We shall adhere to the principles of open development, cooperative development and win–win development and strive for a peaceful international environment to develop ourselves and with our own development to safeguard and promote world peace, to expand the convergence of interests of all parties, and to promote the construction of a harmonious world of lasting peace and common prosperity".[4] Under this guiding ideology, China has offered to establish a new type of major-power relation with the United States; China has advocated to solve various international disputes through negotiations; China has committed to the implementation of continuous expansion of the policy of opening to the outside world. Considering the different situations of the developed countries, the neighboring countries, and the developing countries, China constantly looks for the confluence of interests of both sides and a new model of mutual cooperation, striving to bring new vigor and vitality into the development of bilateral relations and promoting the interests of both sides to achieve a greater degree of convergence.

Third, the win–win cooperation is the inevitable choice of the national economic development of the era of globalization. In today's world, the process of economic globalization is continuing to develop, and the degree of the overlapping and convergence of interests between countries is becoming increasingly deepened. The whole world has increasingly become a community of destiny. From the perspective of national development, there is no way out for seclusion; it is imperative to open to the outside world. Select the "cooperation" and both sides will benefit; select the "conflict" and each will suffer. Under the complicated situation of the world economy and global problems, no country is immune from it. From the perspective of overcoming the common challenges facing humanity, many of the major problems facing the world today cannot be solved simply by

[4] *Report at the 18th National Congress of the Communist Party of China*, p. 14.

means of relying on a few powers and some traditional measures; the only way out is to cooperate with each other and to pull together in times of trouble. Therefore, the promotion of cooperation and the win–win concept mean to promote the awareness of the human community of destiny — to give attention to the legitimate concerns of other countries in the pursuit of one's national interests and to promote the common development of all the other countries in the pursuit of one's own development so as to establish a more equitable and balanced new global partnership for development.

Considering the relationship between China and the Latin-American countries, the Chinese government has attached great importance to the arrival of the historical period of opportunity of the development of the Sino-Latin American relations with the very clear policy of the cooperation and the win–win principle. On November 5, 2008, the Chinese government first published *China's Policy Documents for Latin America and the Caribbean*, clarifying that "the Chinese government treats the Sino-Latin American relation from a strategic perspective, focusing on the establishment and development of a comprehensive cooperation partnership of equality and mutual development with the Latin-American and Caribbean countries", emphasizing that "the Sino-Latin American relations are facing a new development opportunity", advocating that both sides should "have mutual respect and mutual trust" and "expand consensus" in the field of politics, "have mutual benefit and deepen cooperation" in the field of economy and trade, and "have mutual learning and common progress and close exchanges" in the field of humanities.[5]

Less than half a month after the publication of the documents, President Hu Jintao went to Costa Rica, Cuba and Peru for state visits, and delivered an important speech at the Peruvian Congress entitled *Work Together to Build the Sino-Latin American Comprehensive Cooperative Partnership in the New Era*. President Hu made a brilliant exposition on how to enable both sides to seize the opportunity to achieve the win–win cooperation, "Development is a fundamental

[5]China's Policy Documents for Latin America and the Caribbean, http://www.gov.cn/jrzg/2008-11/05/content_1140303.htm.

way to improve people's well-being and to promote the social progress. Development is the most urgent task for China and Latin America, and the development of China and Latin America is in a critical period. Both China and Latin America are also each other's development opportunities". "China is the largest developing country in the world and Latin America is the world's most important region of development. Both sides should be united more closely together to carry out the cooperation at higher ranks, in wider areas and at higher levels. This is the trend of the times and the need of their own development". "China is willing to strive to build a comprehensive cooperative partnership of equality, mutual benefit and common development with the Latin-American and Caribbean countries".[6]

In June 2012, during his visit to Brazil, Uruguay, Argentina and Chile, Premier Wen Jiabao made a speech at the Economic Commission for Latin America, once again stressing the win–win policy of the cooperation with the Latin-American countries. Premier Wen pointed out, "Under the perplexing international situation, the common interests of China and the Latin-American countries are expanding, the mutual demands are increasing, and the desire for enterprises to strengthen cooperation and for people to promote exchanges is increasingly growing. Deepening cooperation, complementing each other, and seeking a win–win development conform to the fundamental interests of the people of both sides, and are conducive to the world's balanced development, prosperity and stability. China is willing to work with the utmost sincerity to push forward the partnership of all-round cooperation between China and Latin America to enhance the bilateral pragmatic cooperation to a new level".[7] Premier Wen proposed to deepen the strategic cooperation between China and Latin America on the basis of mutual political trust, to expand the common interests of China and Latin America

[6]Hu Jintao, Together Build a New Era of Comprehensive Cooperative Partnership — Speech at the Peruvian Congress (November 20, 2008, Lima), *The People's Daily*, p. 3, November 22, 2008.

[7]Wen Jiabao, *Always Be Good Friends of Mutual Trust — Speech at the ECLAC of the United Nations* (June 26, 2012, San Diego), http://news.xinhuanet.com/politics/2012/06-27/c_112303984.htm.

with the focus on the economic and trade cooperation, to maintain the food security of China and Latin America with the agricultural cooperation as the starting point, and to enhance the friendship of the people of China and Latin America through cultural exchanges. In the four cooperative initiatives, there are a series of major measures to promote the bilateral cooperation between China and Latin America. For example, the establishment of a cooperation forum; the increase of imports of high value-added products and manufactured goods from Latin America, trying to achieve the bilateral trade volume of over $400 billion over the next five years; the strengthening of investment and financial cooperation, establishing the cooperation fund with China's investment of $5 billion in the first phase, and China's special loan of $10 billion to promote the cooperation in the infrastructure construction and industrial cooperation; the expansion of currency swap and trade settlement currency with the Latin-American countries; the establishment of the Sino-Latin American Forum of Ministers of Agriculture; the establishment of food emergency reserve mechanism of the scale of 500,000 tons for China and Latin America; the establishment of a special fund for the development and cooperation in agriculture of China and Latin America with China's injection of $50 million into the fund; the establishment of cultural centers in Latin America, with the offer of 5,000 scholarships for the Latin-American students to study in China over the next five years; the establishment of the Sino-Latin American Technology Cooperation Forum to strengthen cooperation in aerospace, new energy, resources and environment, and marine and polar research; the establishment of the tourism promotion mechanism for China and Latin America, etc.

From May to June in 2013, during his visits to Trinidad and Tobago, Costa Rica, and Mexico, President Xi Jinping made a speech in the Mexico Senate. On the relationship between China and Latin America, he stressed, "At present, the Sino-Latin American relations are in an important period of opportunity of rapid development. We should keep pace with the times and consolidate the traditional friendship, strengthening all-round exchanges, enhancing the level of cooperation, pushing the comprehensive partnership of cooperation of equality and mutual benefit of China and Latin America to achieve a new and greater development". Therefore, President Xi further elucidated the basic principles of deepening the Sino-Latin American cooperation in the fields of politics, economy, culture, and the desire for "the early completion of the Sino-Latin American Cooperation Forum". He once again stressed, "The development process of the relationship between China and Latin America has and will continue to prove that the development of bilateral relations is the development of open, inclusive, cooperative, and win–win development".[8]

To sum up, it can be seen clearly that the Chinese government has viewed and planed the development of the Sino-Latin American relations from a strategic height and a long-term perspective, implementing the policy of full cooperation between the two sides and the focus on the economic trade, adhering to the implementation of the policy of mutual benefit and win–win cooperation and offered a series of cooperation initiatives of making full use of the current favorable opportunities. It is reasonable to expect: first, the Latin-American countries can seize the opportunity to give a positive response to China's initiatives by taking drastic actions; second, the local governments in China and the vast majority of Chinese entrepreneurs will increase understanding of and attach importance to the Latin-American region, actively participating in the process of the promotion of the Sino-Latin American cooperation and the exploration of the Latin-American markets.

Section 2 The Path Choice for the Adjustment of the Industrial Structure of the Latin-American Countries

I. Background of the Adjustment of Industrial Structure

In the next 10 years, the Latin-American countries will enter a stage of continuous adjustment of the industrial structure. It is very

[8]Xi Jinping, Promote Common Development and Create a Better Future — Speech at the Mexican Senate (June 5, 2013, Mexico City), http://news.sohu.com/20130606/n378193678.shtml.

important to know this point because this is an important perspective to observe the basic trend of the Latin-American economies in the next 10 years and then determine the basic needs of these countries in the fields of international trade, investment, finance and technological cooperation. Why will the adjustment of industrial structure become a basic task for the economies of the Latin-American countries?

During the last 25 years at the end of the 20th century, the Latin-American countries had carried out a large-scale economic reform in order to get rid of the crisis of the structural development caused by the long-term inward development model of import substitution. This reform had realized the change of the mode from the inward development to the outward development, but under the guidance of the "Washington Consensus", the reform had put too much emphasis on the market level, such as trade liberalization, financial liberalization, and privatization of state-owned enterprises, while ignoring the adjustment of the industrial structure. For example, in the export-oriented development mode, the Latin-American countries only chose the so-called "specialization" according to the static comparative advantages of resources and labor. As a result, the two modes of "production specialization" had been formed, i.e., the South American countries followed the mode of processing natural resources — the industrial production of primary products, and Mexico, Central America and some Caribbean countries formed the "maquila" (customer) industrial mode. In the 1980s and 1990s, the Latin-American countries also experienced the process of "de-industrialization", resulting in the failure of the development of strategic emerging industries and the significant improvement of the labor productivity of original industrial sectors (see Table 11.1). The investment in research and development has fallen way far behind — from 2002 to 2006, the proportion of the investment in research and development in the Latin-American countries accounted for only 0.57% of their gross domestic product (GDP).

After entering the 21st century, especially from 2003 to 2008, either due to the benefit from the boom of resources of exports and the rising prices of trade, or due to the pulling of maquila industry by the American economy, the above two specialized production

Table 11.1 Labor Productivity of Latin America (Selected Countries) (Compared with US, %)

Sector	1990	1998	2003	2008
Agriculture, hunting, forestry, and fishery	14.2	13.3	10.7	7.0
Mining and quarrying	40.9	59.2	51.5	70.2
Manufacturing	25.0	20.7	16.1	14.6
Electricity, gas and water supply	23.4	34.4	31.0	34.8
Construction	21.0	22.2	23.7	33.5
Business, catering and hotels	27.4	17.1	13.2	14.4
Transportation	19.2	18.2	13.8	11.2
Financial institution	18.1	17.9	19.7	22.0
Community, social and personal services	18.5	18.1	18.2	18.8
Total	18.4	17.0	15.4	16.2

Source: CEPAL, *America Latina y el Caribe, Series Histdricas de Estadisticas Economicas 1950–2008*, Cuadernos estadisticos, No. 37 (LC/G.2415-P), Santiago de Chile, 2009. Public acion de las Naciones Unidas, No de venta: S. 09. 11. G. 72; OIT: Laborsta, 2009.

modes have made significant achievements in the actual operations. However, with the passage of time, the implied risk of these two kinds of specialized production modes has emerged. First, as for the resource output countries in South America, on the one hand, the "resource bonus" period has resulted in the emergence of a substantial increase in the proportion of resource products in export, and the focus of the domestic and foreign investment on the departments of resource development; on the other hand, the continued appreciation of the currency has made the export of manufacturing industry at a disadvantageous position. Therefore, strong concerns about the national economy "going back to primary products" have appeared in these countries. Second, the two specialized production modes have one thing in common: the specific export goods are highly dependent on specific markets, such as the reliance of the maquila industry on the US market and the reliance of resource exports to the Chinese market. Therefore, the main export of commodities in Latin America is greatly affected by the changes of external demands. For example, after the outbreak of the financial crisis in 2008, the maquila industry of Mexico and Central America had been dragged by the US economy; in 2012, due to the economic slowdown of EU and China, the export volume of Latin America fell by 18% over the previous year. From the perspective of the trade settlement in Latin America, the industrial sectors have had successive years of foreign trade deficit, having to be compensated by the trade surpluses of the agriculture and the mining sector (see Table 11.2). This indicates that the current mode of economic growth of the Latin-American countries does not have a long-term sustainability.

Table 11.2 reflects a long-term structural problem facing the Latin-American countries. As is shown in the statistics of 1980, the implementation of import substitution industrialization before 1982 led to the increasing trade deficit in the industrial sector, which could not be made up by the trade surplus of the agricultural and mining sectors. The "de-industrialization" after the outbreak of the debt crisis in 1982 resulted in a significant reduction of the trade deficit in the industrial sector, and the overall trade surplus increased, becoming an important source of funds to repay the foreign debt at the time. By 1998 the situation had reversed again — the trade deficit of the industrial sector reached more than $60 billion. Since 2003, with the arrival of the export boom of agricultural and mineral products, the foreign trade had improved, but after 20 years of reform, the industrial sector had remained to be the main sector spending foreign exchange rather than earning foreign exchange.

Recently, Alicia Barcena, the ECLAC Executive Secretary, emphasized the necessity of the adjustment of industrial structure from the perspective of the long-term trend of the development of the international economy. She focused on the following three problems. First, it is the technological revolution. The technological revolution had brought about changes for different industries, products and production processes, and redefined the pattern of international competition. The rise of the Asia-Pacific region came, to a certain extent, from seizing this opportunity to make good use of the achievements of science and technology, but Latin America did not catch up in this regard. Second, it is the environmental issue. She believed that it was not enough only by the recycling and reuse technology; the establishment of a new paradigm of the production and consumption

Table 11.2 Latin America: Trade Settlement (Unit: $1,000)

Sector	1970	1980	1990	1998	2003	2008
Agriculture	1,302,191	3,229,446	8,053,713	12,045,198	14,048,738	28,384,653
Mining	2,594,776	15,345,835	18,048,226	17,696,919	40,372,224	150,455,987
Industry	−3,585,818	−22,486,471	−6,810,511	−60,463,927	−30,168,729	−148,563,691
			Knowledge-intensive			
Industrial sector	−4,974,309	−24,229,565	−20,033,217	−43,815,418	−19,375,174	−102,246,840
			Natural-resource-intensive			
Industrial sector	1,958,858	2,759,600	12,702,086	−7,918,827	−676,687	−10,028,422
			Labor-intensive			
Industrial sector	−570,367	−1,016,507	520,620	−8,729,681	−10,116,868	−36,288,428
Total	311,149	−3,911,191	19,291,428	−30,721,810	24,252,233	30,276,949

Source: CEPAL, *Sobre la base de informacion del Banco de Datos del Comercio Exterior de America Latina y el Caribe* (BADECEL).

pattern was the key to the problem. Third, it was the changes of the international economic pattern. The developed economies continued to fall into crises and the rise of the importance of Asian economies required the Latin-American countries to re-examine the international economic situation and the way to participate in international cooperation. The Latin-American countries should not just play a role in the export of raw materials. To change the industrial structure was the key to solve these problems.[9]

II. The Planning and Design of the Adjustment of the Industrial Structure

Since entering the 21st century, with the withdrawal of the new liberalism in the Latin-American region, the Latin-American economists and some Latin-American governments began to attach importance to the adjustment of industrial structure, and even put forward the problem of "reindustrialization" (reindustrializacion). In this background, the ECLAC tried to exert its influence on providing theoretical and policy support for the future economic and social development in the Latin-American region, and put forward two important reports. The first report was entitled *The Era of Equality: The Gap to Be Filled, the Road to Be Opened Up* (*LA Hora de la Igualdad: Brechas por Cerrar, Caminos por Abrir*), which had comprehensively discussed the development path to social equality through the adjustment of industrial structure. The report was submitted to the 33rd Member Congress of ECLAC for discussion, which was held in Brasilia from May to June in 2010, and was given great attention to by the Latin-American governments. "The suggestions of ECLAC have been widely adopted, and created a continuation of the chain effect".[10] The second report was entitled *Structural Adjustment with the Goal of Equality: An Integrated Vision of Development* (*Cambio Estructural para la Igualdad: Una Vision Integrada*

[9] Alicia Barcena, The Economic Development of Latin America and the Caribbean in 2012, Latin American Studies, V. 6, 2012, pp. 5–6.

[10] Alicia Barcena, Prologo de *Cambio Estructural para la Igualdad: UnaVision Integrada del Dessarrollo*, CEPAL, San Salvador, 27–31 de agosto de 2012, p. 13.

del Desarrollo). On the basis of the previous report, this report had a more in-depth and systematic exposition of the strategic objectives, theoretical basis and supporting policies of the adjustment of industrial structure, forming a relatively complete planning and design of the adjustment of industrial structure. The report was submitted to the 34th Member Congress of ECLAC for discussion, which was held in Salvatore in August 2012, and caused widespread positive response. In the following the main viewpoints of the report will be introduced emphatically.

The ECLAC stressed that the report had presented a comprehensive concept of development, namely, the development of a variety of factors organically synthesized together, such as the control of the economic cycle, the strategic adjustment of industrial structure, macroeconomic policy, the integrated use of the industrial policy and the social policy, the vigor of enterprises to promote the labor productivity constantly closer to the high level, the diffusion of high-quality employment to all the economically self-sustaining population, and so on. The report highlighted three main points: (1) Equality is the value and strategic approach of the pursuit of development; (2) The adjustment of industrial structure is the key to achieve the strategy; (3) The right choice of the public policy is the tool to ensure the smooth adjustment of industrial structure.

According to the report, Latin America is a highly unequal society. Equality requires the spreading of enhancing the ability, job opportunities and access to social services to the whole society. Equality is the essential condition of the civil society, i.e., to ensure that the citizens enjoy civil, political, social, and environmental rights. This requires that in the democratic order each social stratum should fully participate in the governmental and political affairs and express their views, and this requires that the government ensure all the rights that the citizens enjoy, and this requires that the government ensure the redistribution of the fruits of development through the social contract and financial contract to make sure that all aspects of social inclusion are put into practice.

The author of the report emphasized that the equality put forward as the strategic objective of development had fitted into the "historic turning point" of the situation in Latin America. This historic turning point was expressed as follows: (1) The systematic accumulation of the unmet demands of the citizens finally had led to the reorganization of the political landscape of Latin America in the first 10 years of the 21st century. This obviously refers to the rise of a group of left-wing governments in Latin America. (2) Many countries and governments were more likely to increase the social investment and use the redistribution mechanism in the specific expression of the systematic increase of social spending and the implementation of the active counter-cyclical policy after the global financial crisis occurred in 2008 to reduce the social cost. (3) The policy emphasizing on the universal rights was being gradually strengthened, reflected in such fields as health care, retirement pensions and old-age pensions.

On the adjustment of industrial structure, the report pointed out that the industrial structure of the Latin-American countries had a high heterogeneity (*heterogeneidad*), specifically reflected in the very low proportion of high productivity sectors and the great proportion of low productivity sectors (see Table 11.3). The small- and medium-sized enterprises (SMEs) and micro-enterprises were huge in number, but generally weaker in strength; large-scale enterprises were rare in number, but very high in monopoly (see Table 11.4). If the continuous adjustment of industrial structure was not implemented, the effective participation in the international competition would be impossible, and on this basis continuous investment could only aggravate the labor market segmentation, aggravating the employment quality, labor productivity and differences in wage incomes. It is because of the labor market segmentation that led to the existence of the scale of the informal employment in Latin America, the difficult improvement of the coverage of social security and labor, and the inequality in the field of social security and the continuing expansion of the gap.

The adjustment of industrial structure means to regard the qualitative change of the production structure as the center of the drive of growth. In today's world, it has its special requirements to do so; the open economy today needs to have its specialized characteristics due to its participation in the global market. In order to achieve a better global participation, in order to have a benign internal

Table 11.3 Latin America (Selected Countries): Employment Structure[1] (1990–2008) (%)

	1990	1998	2003	2008
High-productivity sectors[2]	7.9	7.0	7.3	8.1
Medium-productivity sector[3]	23.1	20.7	19.7	20.0
Low-productivity sector[4]	69.0	72.3	73.0	71.9
Total	100.0	100.0	100.0	100.0

Note: [1]The estimation was obtained with the use of the economic self-reliance population of the sectors by the International Labor Organization, and adjusted by the unemployment rates of the sectors. [2]High-productivity sectors refer to mining, energy and finance. [3]Medium-productivity sectors refer to industry and transportation. [4]Low-productivity sectors refer to agriculture, construction, business, and community and personal services.

Source: CEPAL, *America Latina y el Caribe, Series Historicas de Estadisticas Economicas 1950-*, Cuadernos Estadisticos, No. 37 (LC/G.2415-P), Santiago de Chile, 2009, Publicacion de las Naciones Unidas, No. de venta: S. 09. 11. G. 72 y OIT, Laborsta, 2009.

Table 11.4 Latin America (Selected Countries): Contributions of the Employment of Different Types of Enterprises, GDP and Export (%)

	Micro-Enterprises	Small Enterprises	Medium Enterprises	Large Enterprises
Employment	30.4	16.7	14.2	38.7
GDP	7.3	9.8	11.4	71.5
Export	0.2	1.8	6.4	91.6

Note: This table reflects the proportions of employment, GDP and export of various types of enterprises in the formal sectors. The table was made with the simple averages of the official data of Argentina, Brazil, Chile, and Mexico. The standards of enterprise classification were based on the standards used by the relevant agencies of various countries (see Ferraro and Stone Park, 2009).

Source: ECLAC.

vitality in productivity and employment, the proportion of the knowledge-intensive industry needs to be increased more and more in the whole production process. This requires promoting capacity building, increasing knowledge and promoting the learning process by coordinating the production with investment in the whole economy and society. Therefore, the structural adjustment will only be benign if the two interrelated dimensions are combined. On the one hand, the proportion of knowledge-intensive industries is increasing higher and higher in the participation of production and trade; on the other hand, the industries of rapid growth in the production sector along the internal and external demand are moving towards diversification. When these needs can be met by the internal supply, exports and imports will be growing in a balanced manner rather than forming a high pressure in the balance of payments. That is to say, the structural adjustment requires combining two efficiencies. One is the so-called "Schumpeterian Efficiency", i.e., the production sectors with the highest productivity and highest growth rate and with the ability to disseminate more knowledge and more skills to the economy and the whole society are becoming more and more dominant, leading the innovation process, driving the growth of productivity in these sectors themselves and spreading the productivity growth to other departments. The other one is the so-called "Keynes Efficiency" (also known as "Growth Efficiency"), referring to a specialized production mode, in which the production departments benefit from the high growth of the internal and external demand and produce a positive effect on the production and employment. The structural adjustment is to make those departments full of vitality, stronger not only from a technical point of view but also from the perspective of demand. The productivity growth without the demand growth may lead to underemployment or unemployment. The two kinds of efficiency can usually be realized at the same time because the knowledge-most-intensive sectors in the long term are often the departments with more vitality of demand and more vitality of international specialization.

The adjustment of industrial structure makes the productivity difference narrowed, a general increase in the diversification of industrial sectors and productivity, and the workers benefited in equality because wage differentials are narrowed; the social protection will be expanded as the decent employment scope is expanded; the state finance gets improved because of the rich living force of growth and the effect of national redistribution will be strengthened. With the improvement of infrastructure, the availability of all kinds of social service will increase. When an economy achieves a high degree of integration around a more diversified and specialized production system, it means that the society has progressed and the contract of reaching a more equal share of the fruits of development in all walks of the social life is more feasible politically.

In terms of the policy options related to the adjustment of industrial structure, the report highlighted the industrial, macroeconomic and social policies. This also means that the country should play a leading role. According to the report, the industrial policy pointed to two complementary directions: one was to give a greater production capacity and competitiveness to those existing production sectors with the potential of specialization and the potential of the absorption of the technological progress; the other was to achieve the diversification of the industrial structure through establishing emerging industrial sectors with a high productivity and a greater environmental sustainability. In addition, the productivity of the small, medium-sized and micro-enterprises should be vigorously improved and such enterprises should become the center of the dissemination of knowledge and the absorption of technology. If just high-tech enterprises were increased or just the tip part of the production system was adjusted, there would be no benign adjustment of the industrial structure. The adjustment of industrial structure should be coordinated in the whole economy, including both forward and backward extension, and the focus on supporting the transformation of those departments from the secondary productivity to the high productivity. In the downward driven and bottom-up upgrade process, the employment structure would change, and the labor force would gradually be transferred from the sectors with a low productivity to the sectors with a medium-and-high productivity.

The main mission of the macroeconomic policy is to maintain the economic stability, support the adjustment of industrial structure, and implement a progressive redistribution of income. The basic goal is to maintain a high economic growth rate. Only by maintaining a high economic growth rate can the necessary jobs be created for the increasing labor force and can the production capacity be fully utilized, encouraging the investment and deepening the process of the adjustment of industrial structure.

The report pointed out that the positive social policy is indispensable at any time. In terms of the process of the adjustment of industrial structure, there are at least two kinds of cases in need of positive social policies to escort. On the one hand, the positive effect of redistribution resulted from the adjustment of industrial structure often requires a long time; therefore, in the short-term it is necessary to improve the income distribution and reduce the social vulnerability through social policies. Second, in the process of adjusting the industrial structure, the so-called "short-circuit period", i.e., some industries may just have to face a structural reorganization, resulting in the phenomenon of unemployment, which requires active social policies to protect those who may be temporarily affected.

The above is the basic content of the report of the ECLAC. From the perspective of the reaction of the public opinions, it is generally believed that the Latin-American countries feel it urgent to transform the mode of economic growth. It is correct and timely for the report to propose to adjust the industrial structure as the central link to promote the economic and social development in the next 10 years. The Latin-American governments also have a basic consensus on the necessity of the adjustment of industrial structure. It can be said that in the next 10 years the Latin-American countries will enter the stage with the center of the change of the mode of economic growth. This process contains a huge demand for funds, technology, equipment and training of the human resources, which also determines that Latin-American countries must follow the road of expanding opening up and carrying out the extensive international cooperation. Among them, the status and role of the economic and trade cooperation with China will be further increased, and the interests of the Latin-American countries will correspondingly be changed, for instance, the importance of industrial cooperation, emphasizing the greenfield investment, the establishment of joint ventures, technology transfer, and the access to the export market of manufactured goods. If the change cannot be seen in time, the increase of the interests of both sides may be affected. At the same time it should be seen that, as a policy advisory body, the reports by ECLAC offered just a roadmap for the adjustment of the Latin-American regional industrial structure, which is not the same as to the adjustment plan of the industrial structure of each government. Therefore, it has become more and more important to strengthen the research on the adjustment plan of the industrial structure and the industrial policies of the Latin-American countries, particularly major Latin-American countries such as Brazil.

Section 3 Actively Exploring the Bilateral Converging Interests

Premier Wen Jiabao pointed out, "The relation of interests is the essence and the core of the Sino-Latin American relations".[11] The author believes that this is a real and honest expression about the essence of the relationship between countries. This honesty originated from the fact that China's pursuit is legitimate national interests in the development of its relations with other countries, and from the principle of equality, mutual benefit and win–win cooperation, trying to meet the other's legitimate interests and concerns. In today's world, not all countries can take this kind of honest attitude, for example, those countries that seek hegemonic interests in the world often try to interfere in others' internal affairs in the guise of protecting human rights, or form cliques in the world, sow discord, show off force, and curb the development of emerging countries. In our view, since the relationship between countries is a kind of relation of legitimate interests, the "converging interests" of both sides should continue to be explored in the development process, through deepening cooperation to build different levels of "common interests" between countries.

China and the Latin-American countries have the foundation of many years of cooperation in economy and trade. At present, the

---

[11] Wen Jiabao, *Always Be Good Friends of Mutual Trust — Speech at the ECLAC of the United Nations* (June 26, 2012, San Diego), http://news.xinhuanet.com/politics/2012/06-27/c_112303984.htm.

problem is how to further expand and deepen the cooperation. This requires both sides to actively explore the new convergence of interests, and especially to give a calm and objective analysis for some seemingly conflicts of interest issues in the exchanges between the two sides to avoid putting the original converging interests into conflicts of interest. The exploration of the converging interests of both sides contains several layers of meaning. First, the convergence of interests is the foundation or premise of the economic and trade cooperation. Second, the convergence of interests is dynamic, not immutable and frozen. Third, from the perspective of the cooperation between Latin America and China, the converging interests are hierarchical, with converging interests of the whole region's cooperation with China, and those with the sub-regions and each country. Fourth, the emphasis on active exploration means to hope that the two sides in cooperation, especially the think tanks of both sides, should continue to put forward new converging interests for both decision-makers to discuss. If the two sides can reach a consensus it may become the basis for cooperation.

I. How to Look at the Latin-American Output of Energy and Raw Materials to China

Many Latin-American scholars pointed out that in the recent 10 years due to China's demand for energy and raw materials of Latin America, the phenomenon of "Reprimarization of Products" (reprimarizacion) occurred in the export commodity structure of the Latin-American countries. According to the research of these scholars, the reasons for the phenomenon are: (1) Due to the strong international demand for energy and raw materials, the export growth rate is higher than other commodities; (2) The production sectors of energy and raw materials have obtained development opportunities because of the high profits, attracting a large number of domestic and foreign investment, which is not conducive to the other sectors, especially the development of the manufacturing sector; (3) The boom of the export of energy and raw materials has brought trade surplus and large amounts of foreign investment, plus a large number of "hot money" flowing in due to the "Quantitative Easing" monetary policy of western countries, resulting in the increasing appreciation of the currencies of the resource-exporting Latin-American countries, harming the export of manufactured goods. People do not question the authenticity of the "Dutch Disease" phenomenon, but the problem is: should China shoulder the responsibility for this phenomenon?

The mainstream view of economists in Latin America is that China's huge demand for energy and raw materials has led to a substantial increase in the amount of the export of these products and the rapid growth of the export price; this "China Effect" has become a major factor boosting the economic prosperity of Latin America since 2003. It can be said that it is the rapid development of China and other Asian countries that has ushered in a "Resource Bonus" period for the Latin-American countries. This historical opportunity does not often occur. The "Reprimarization of Products" in the structure of export commodities is an "indirect" effect resulted from the export boom of energy and raw materials, which is the problem for the resource-output countries to solve by adopting corresponding policies. It should be noted that, as a developed economy, Australia is also a major resource-export country. According to the reports of the Chinese media, Australia currently is also discussing how to break the "Resource Curse", proposing the main way of the adjustment of its domestic industrial structure.[12] The intention of the roadmap for the design of the adjustment of industrial structure for the Latin-American countries by ECLAC in Section 2 of this chapter is to show the essential way of adjusting the industrial structure to avoid the phenomenon of the "Dutch Disease", and therefore, it is worthy of affirmation. In addition, it is understandable that the Latin-American countries do not want to be in the status of exporters of raw materials in their trade with China, but the increase in the export of high value-added products also relies on their own adjustment of the industrial structure to achieve.

[12]Zheng Ou, Zhang Mengying, Australia Seeking the Means to Break the "Resource Curse", *Chinese Social Sciences*, November 2, 2012, p. A-03.

The adjustment of industrial structure needs not only long-term efforts to produce results, but also a lot of financial support in the process. It should be seen as a favorable opportunity for the Latin-American countries to make use of the accumulated funds in the price boom of raw materials to support the adjustment of industrial structure. Wilson Pastor Morris, Ecuador's Minister of Non-renewable Resources, in his interview with the "China Today" in Beijing said that it was Ecuador's strategy to have a responsible development of the oil and minerals, with its profits to be spent in the development of other high added-value industries. On this path, China is Ecuador's "priority partner" (*aliado privilegiado*).[13] It is estimated that, in the next 10 years, with the slowdown in economic growth and the adoption of a series of policies and measures to overcome the constraints of energy and resources, the growth of China's demand for raw materials and energy will also slow down, but there is no doubt that the demand is still an important convergence of interests in China's cooperation with the Latin-American region.

II. How to Deal with the Problem of the Bilateral Competition of Industrial Products

To some degree China competes with Latin America in the industrial manufactured goods, both in the third markets (such as the market of the United States) and in the local markets of Latin America. This competition is caused by the fact that both sides are generally at a similar stage of development and have close levels of industrial development. It needs to be acknowledged that it is not a bad thing that there is a certain degree of competition between the two sides. Justified international competition is a driving force for development, promoting the competitors to attach importance to technological innovation, to save cost, to improve efficiency, and to accelerate the upgrading of products.

The competition of the two sides in the US market mainly involves the Latin-American countries with more developed maquila

[13]Rafael Valdez Mera, "Eguador Buscaun Cambio Profundo y China es su Aliado", *China Hoy*, mayo de 2013, p. 33.

industries. The international academic circles have done a large number of researches on this issue, stating that the two sides have their respective advantages: China mainly has a relatively low labor cost, but the Latin-American countries not only enjoy the preferential trade system with the United States, but also have a geographical advantage. For example, according to the research of Robert Devlin, in 2003, it took 24 days to transport a standard container of goods from China to the United States, with the transportation cost of $4,300, but from Mexico to the United States it just took four days, with the transportation cost of only $1,750.[14] In recent years, with the rise in labor costs, land prices and prices of raw materials, China's competitive advantage has tended to have weakened, with the enterprises in coastal areas that had been engaged in export processing transferred in succession to the Central and Western regions or its Asian neighbors. Therefore, today it has not too much sense to emphasize the competition of both sides in this area. Under this new situation, the two sides can consider how to encourage the export processing enterprises in China to be transferred to Mexico, Central America and the Caribbean region, or have cooperation in the establishment of export processing zones or industrial parks to make use of the accumulated experience of China in the recent 30 years.

At present, the problem with a relatively high degree of concern may be how to transform the Sino-Latin American trade from the "inter-industrial" trade to the "intra-industrial" trade. The bilateral trade structure reflects the current industrial structures of both sides to a great extent; the transformation of the product structure fundamentally depends on the adjustment of industrial structure. Therefore, if the Latin-American countries can really put the adjustment of industrial structure as a major strategy into practice, it will not only have a far-reaching significance for improving their own economic strength and international competitiveness, but also greatly help the

[14]Robert Devlin, Antoni Estevadeordal, Andres Rodriguez-Clare, *El Impacto de China: Oportunidades y Retos para America Latina y el Caribe*, Editores BID y David Rockefeller Center for Latin American Studies, Harvard University, Washington, D.C., 2007, pp. 205, 207, 226.

transformation of the trade pattern of China and Latin America. China naturally will explore new converging interests of both sides in terms of the new situation.

China's current development has entered the stage centering on accelerating the transformation of the mode of economic development, resulting in a series of important changes. To accelerate the transformation and upgrading of industrial structure is one of them. In the industrial field it is to promote the healthy development of strategic emerging industries and the advanced manufacturing industry and to accelerate the transformation and upgrading of traditional industries with the support of modern science and technology. This means that China is seeking to increase the proportion of high-tech products in its output of industrial products and to gradually reduce the low technology products, thereby reducing competition between China and Latin America in terms of the latter two kinds of products. China's mode of economic growth has turned mainly to domestic demand, focusing on improving people's livelihood, which means that China's market demand will be further expanded. In the next five years, the amount of China's imports will reach $1,000 trillion. Just as Premier Wen Jiabao pointed out in 2012, "China does not pursue the trade surplus, not only importing the Latin-American raw materials, but also hope to import more manufactured goods and high value-added products so as to achieve the bilateral trade balance and sustainable development".[15] The expanding and diversified needs of China can provide important market support for the upgrading of the adjustment of industrial structure of the Latin-American countries.

Another noteworthy change is that China is changing from mainly relying on the absorption of foreign capital to both the absorption of foreign capital and the investment in foreign countries. In the next 10 years, China is expected to become an important foreign investor and there will be more and more Chinese enterprises

[15]Wen Jiabao, *Always Be Good Friends of Mutual Trust — Speech at the ECLAC of the United Nations* (June 26, 2012, San Diego), http://news.xinhuanet.com/politics/2012/06-27/c_112303984.htm.

going abroad to do international business, which indicates the coming of the trend of "change of export to investment". The website of "The Atlantic" recently published an article stating that China is changing from a trade center into an investment center. It may be a new "bright spot" in the next stage of the Sino-Latin American economic and trade cooperation to combine the Chinese capital advantage with the upgrading of the adjustment of the industrial structure of the Latin-American countries. The expansion of investment cooperation is the material basis for both sides to further develop industrial cooperation, scientific and technological cooperation and enterprise cooperation. Over the past 10 years, the Sino-Latin American bilateral economic and trade cooperation was driven mainly by China's great demand for energy and raw materials. In the next 10 years, if the driving force continues to be relied on solely, it not only cannot meet the actual needs of the new situation for the bilateral development cooperation, but also will be difficult to reach the goal of broadening and deepening cooperation. Therefore, expanding investment cooperation will inject a new and important driving force for the next phase of the bilateral economic and trade cooperation.

III. China's Investment Interest beyond the Limit of the Field of Resources

In recent years, China's direct investment in Latin America grew rapidly, but had caused some reactions of the public opinion. There is a perception that China's investment "has focused on acquiring resources of Latin America". In fact, so far, China's direct investment in Latin America is still in the initial stage, with relatively few enterprises, relatively small amount of investments, and relatively narrow fields of investment. There is a relatively high proportion of investment in the fields of energy and resources. It is believed that if China's capital can widely participate in the upgrading process of many industries of the Latin-American countries the situation will soon change.

During the past 10 years, China has obtained oil, metals and non-metallic minerals, soybeans and other products from Latin America mainly through the trade channel and the way of "funds for oil" with some countries, with a small proportion of the development of energy and resources by the Chinese direct investment. During the process of China's purchase of the Latin-American energy and resources with high prices, the Western multinational corporations have become important beneficiaries. Some Latin-American scholars pointed out that, from 2003 to 2008, in those South American countries that produce and export oil, metal and mineral products, since the right to develop these resources mainly lies in the hands of western multinationals, the profits from the subsidiaries of multinational companies were remitted to the parent companies with substantial growth, resulting from the sharp rise in the international prices of these products. For example, from 1990 to 1999, in Chile and Peru the profit remittance of foreign companies reached an average of 1.3% in GDP, and from 2003 to 2008, this proportion rose to 7.6%; over the same period, the proportion of Ecuador, Bolivia and Colombia rose from 0.8% to 2.5%; in other Latin-American countries it rose from 0.6% to 1.2%.[16] Thus, to a large extent Western multinational companies have controlled the development rights of natural resources of the Latin-American countries, and obtained a lot of benefits from the rapid growth in demand for resources of the big emerging economies such as China. At the same time, they had created the public opinion of China's "exploitation of resources" in Latin America.

Two related issues are involved here. First, to the Latin-American countries, China, India, and other emerging powers entering the fields of the development of energy and resources can break the monopoly of the multinational corporations from the west, which is beneficial and harmless. Second, the Latin-American countries are eagerly looking forward to strengthening cooperation with China in the manufacturing sector, establishing strategic alliances by the manufacturing enterprises of both sides to promote the industry chain of the Latin-American manufacturing industry to enter Asia.

[16]Osvaldo Kacef, Rafael Lopez-Monti, "America Latina, del Auge a la Crisis: Desafios de Politica Macroeconómica", *Revista de la CEPAL*, No. 100, abril de 2010, p. 45.

In fact, Chinese enterprises have been taking a positive attitude toward the investment in the Latin-American manufacturing industry and the Chinese government has also made a positive response. Premier Wen Jiabao made the initiative that "China has proposed to set up a cooperation fund and Chinese financial institutions will offer $5 billion as the first investment. The Latin-American countries are welcome to participate in the construction of the fund to jointly invest in the bilateral cooperative projects in the fields of manufacturing, high-tech and sustainable development".[17] Under the background of the great adjustment of industrial structure in the Latin-American countries, the industrial cooperation is undoubtedly an important convergence of interests for the two sides. In the joint efforts to implement the initiative by Premier Wen Jiabao, at the same time, the Latin-American countries also need to make their industrial development plans and industrial policies as soon as possible.

IV. Continuing to Promote Cooperation in the Field of Infrastructure Construction

Latin-American countries are currently facing the development bottleneck caused by the seriously lagged infrastructure construction. According to the analysis of the ECLAC, the main reason for this situation is that since the 1980s there has been a serious shortage of the public investment in the field of infrastructure construction in the Latin-American countries. In 1980, the Latin-American public infrastructure investment accounted for about 3.4% in GDP, with continuous declines in the two decades after 1980; from 2003 to 2008, the level of the public investment in infrastructure construction rebounded slightly, but with only 9% in GDP.[18] It is estimated that, in the next 10 years or more, the public investment

[17]Wen Jiabao, *Always Be Good Friends of Mutual Trust — Speech at the ECLAC of the United Nations* (June 26, 2012, San Diego), http://news.xinhuanet.com/politics/2012/06-27/c_112303984.htm.

[18]CEPAL, *Cambio Estractural para la Igualdad: Una Vision Integradad el Desarrllo*, San Salvador, agosto de 2012, pp. 130–131.

in infrastructure construction in the Latin-American region needs to reach 5% in GDP, indicating that the gap in funding is the key problem.

For the Latin-American countries, the current infrastructure construction can generate multiple positive effects. From the short-term perspective, it is conducive to overcoming the "bottleneck" constraint facing the development, stimulating economic growth and increasing employment; from a long-term perspective, it is conducive to sustainable economic growth and improving the efficiency of the production departments. In August 2012, the Brazilian government launched an ambitious plan of a total investment of 133 billion reais ($65 billion) to construct 7,500 kilometer highways and 10,000 kilometer railways. In fact, the plan of the investment funds is not fully implemented, clearly providing the opportunity for the domestic private capital and the foreign capital to participate in the public investment. The case of Brazil shows that it is feasible to solve the problem of the funding shortage in infrastructure construction by the government's planning and development of relevant policies to attract the domestic private capital and the foreign capital to participate in.

The related Chinese enterprises have accumulated rich experience in the design and construction of large-scale modern infrastructure projects and also have relatively strong advantages in project financing. Therefore, the Sino-Latin American cooperation in the field of infrastructure is one of the important converging interests. Therefore, Premier Wen Jiabao has said, "China's National Development Bank will take the lead to offer a special loan of $10 billion to promote the Sino-Latin America cooperation in infrastructure construction, including railways, highways, ports, power plants, power grids and telecommunications facilities that are closely related to the production and people's livelihood".[19] If this initiative can be implemented as soon as possible, it may lay a good start for the next phase of cooperation in infrastructure construction.

[19]Wen Jiabao, *Always Be Good Friends of Mutual Trust — Speech at the ECLAC of the United Nations* (June 26, 2012, San Diego), http://news.xinhuanet.com/politics/2012/06-27/c_112303984.htm.

In terms of the cooperation in infrastructure construction, the governments of the Latin-American countries may need to exclude the interference of some misleading publicity. In Europe, the United States and Latin America it is argued that China's purpose in participating in the infrastructure construction of the Latin-American countries is to solve the problem of transportation of resources that China needs. Where is the evidence for this argument? It is hard to find the answer. The constructions, such as highways, railways, pipelines, ports and docks, belong to the so-called large-scale engineering projects. The constructions of these types of projects are decisions to be made by the governments or the legislatures of the host countries, which cannot be replaced by others. According to international practice, this kind of large engineering constructions needs to go through the bidding procedures to determine. In this case, is China likely to build a specialized infrastructure service system for its own sake in the Latin-American countries? If China's companies were involved in the construction of a project, such as the construction of a railway or highway, after the completion of the railway or highway, would the transportation involve only materials that China needed, but not any other supplies? China has participated in the construction of Brazil's natural gas pipelines, but China had not bought gas from Brazil. How should this be explained? Therefore, such irresponsible public opinion like this not only causes harm to China, but also is negative for the Latin-American countries to attract investment.

V. The Increasingly Prominent Importance of the Sino-Latin American Financial Cooperation

The rapid expansion of the scale of the Sino-Latin American bilateral economic and trade cooperation requires the active financial cooperation between the two sides. In recent years, with the increase of China's ability to carry out international financial cooperations, and its official joining in the Caribbean Development Bank, the Inter-American Development Bank and other major financial institutions, the Sino-Latin American financial cooperation is playing a role of an important booster in the bilateral economic and trade cooperation.

Both sides have a lot of innovations in the ways of financial cooperation, for example, the bilateral currency swap, implementation of the deal of "Loans for Oil", the establishment of a joint investment fund, China's providing of financing for the construction of some projects of the Latin-American countries, and so on. In the next 10 years, the two sides will greatly expand the scale of economic and trade cooperation in bilateral trade. For example, the bilateral trade is expected to reach $400 billion by 2017. If both sides further extend the direct currency for trade settlement, the bilateral monetary cooperation scale required only by this one will be much larger than the previous period. In the series of initiatives that Premier Wen Jiabao had put forward in 2012, there are a number of initiatives involving establishing cooperation funds, special loans, special funds, etc., which require the financial sector to directly participate in. More and more enterprises of the two sides will go to each other country to be engaged in business directly. Anyway, the greater development of economic and trade cooperation objectively requires the financial departments of the two sides to have a greater degree of participation, requires the financial cooperation to be further deepened, and requires more branches of financial institutions to be set up mutually to achieve more convenient financial services. In a certain sense, the active participation of financial institutions will play a leading role in promoting the bilateral cooperation. There is good reason to believe that the Sino-Latin American financial cooperation will become one of the important converging interests of both sides in the next stage.

VI. Making Good Use of the Cooperation Potential of Both Sides in the Field of Agriculture

No matter for China or the Latin-American countries, the development of agriculture is directly related to the security of food supply and food safety of the residents of the country and it is a major issue related to a long period of national stability. In the recent 30 years, with the rapid development of China's industrialization and urbanization, China's not enough rich land resources have decreased and the influence brought about by the global climate change and the deterioration of the environment on the agricultural production also cannot be ignored. It is a long-term necessity for China to adhere to the guidelines to actively carry out international cooperation in agriculture while insisting on solving the food problem of the 1.3 billion people through its domestic production.

From the perspective of agricultural resources, the Latin-American countries can be divided into two types: South American countries and Mexico are rich in agricultural resources, while Central America and the Caribbean countries have relatively limited agricultural resources. The two types of countries both have the traditional advantages of the output of certain agricultural products and most countries have varying degrees of some problems in solving domestic food supply. The climate change and environmental degradation are the challenges that all the Latin-American countries also have to face. Therefore, in the discussion of the Sino-Latin American agricultural cooperation, the first consideration is how to achieve the complementary advantages of both sides, with emphasis on the technical level, such as the establishment of the center of the research and development of agricultural science and technology, the demonstration district of agricultural processing, the development zones of agricultural investment, and the exchange of agricultural experts and technical personnel. The purpose is to achieve common commitment to the effective use of agricultural resources, to improve the agricultural production technology, to deal with the climate change, to protect the ecological environment, to realize high and stable agricultural yields, and to let the agricultural sector play a greater role in improving the lives of the people and promoting the economic development.

In terms of the Sino-Latin American trade in agricultural products, at present a trend worthy of concern is that, along with the increase of the level of income and the quality of life of the residents, the demand for agricultural products in the Chinese market is becoming increasingly diversified, which should be the focus of the Latin-American countries in the future to develop the market of agricultural products in China. Therefore, relevant enterprises in the Latin-American countries need to strengthen the researches on the changes of the Chinese market demand for agricultural products, developing more marketable products and striving to occupy more market shares in China.

The converging interests of the Sino-Latin American bilateral economic and trade cooperation have been analyzed from the above six aspects. This analysis has given only some examples, meaning that the converging interests of two sides are not limited in these several aspects. The converging interests are dynamic, which will increase with the expansion of the bilateral cooperation, or be adjusted with the deepening of cooperation between the two sides. The converging interests also vary from one country to another. The converging interests of a region may not necessarily be the converging interests of a specific country because of the different pursuits of interests of each country. The important problem is that it is necessary to constantly seek bilateral converging interests from the regional and national level, to gradually achieve the integration and expansion of the interests of both sides through the process of cooperation and ultimately to form the relatively stable community of interests.

Section 4 Policy Recommendations for Deepening the Sino-Latin American Bilateral Economic and Trade Cooperation

From the perspective of the history of the development of the economic and trade cooperation between China and the Latin-American countries, in the 50 years from the founding of the new China to the early 21st century, the cooperation between the two sides was basically confined to trade with each other, and the growth rate was also very slow, with their respective foreign trade always in a marginal position. In the recent 10 years, the Sino-Latin American economic and trade cooperation has experienced a rapid development stage, with the rapid growth of bilateral trade and the rapid expansion of areas of cooperation in investment, finance, and infrastructure construction. Within a few years, China has become Latin America's third largest trading partner and an important source of investment. This situation has occurred due to the confluence of many favorable factors at a particular point in time. Our study shows that the development of the Sino-Latin American economic and trade relation in the next 10 years will be not only the simple extension of the development of the past 10 years, but also an important "period of deepening bilateral cooperation", which will show many new characteristics. For example, while energy and resources continue to be the key areas of cooperation, the industrial cooperation of the two sides with the manufacturing industry as the center will significantly be strengthened; with the increase of the investment in the industrial sector of the two sides, the cooperation at the enterprise level is expected to become an important mode of cooperation; the commodity structure of bilateral trade in goods will be further optimized in order to gradually change the current pattern of inter-industry trade; the proportion of bilateral trade in services will have increased significantly; the bilateral cooperation in the field of infrastructure construction will have been greatly expanded; the financial cooperation, agricultural cooperation, and scientific and technological cooperation will rise to become key areas in bilateral cooperation. The arrival of the "deepening period" of the economic and trade cooperation is not only in accordance with the stage of development of Latin America centering on the transformation of the mode of economic growth after entering the period of the comprehensive adjustment of industrial structure on the basis of its basically completed reform of the economic system, but also coincides with China's becoming a big trade country and a new emerging country of foreign investment in the world. The process of deepening bilateral economic and trade cooperation will lead to a qualitative leap in bilateral relations, which can lay a material foundation for a long-term healthy and stable development of bilateral relations.

The selection of policies must be based on the changes of the situation and the environment. On the basis of this principle, the following policy recommendations have been put forward.

I. Adhering to the Basic Principle of "Comprehensive Cooperation with the Focus on Economic Trade"

In the discussion of policy choices to deepen the Sino-Latin American economic and trade cooperation in the next 10 years, first of all, the *Policy Documents of China for Latin America and the Caribbean* (hereinafter referred to as the "DOCUMENT") must be reiterated, which was published by the Chinese government in November 2008, for the basic policies presented in this document have a long-term significance on the development of the Sino-Latin American relations. The DOCUMENT states, "The Chinese government regards its relations with Latin-America from the strategic height and is committed to working with the Latin-American and the Caribbean countries to establish and develop a comprehensive cooperative partnership of equality, mutual benefit and common development".[20] The "comprehensive cooperation with trade as the basis" is the basic principle of this document. The DOCUMENT has elucidated the overall policy goals of China for Latin America, emphasizing the all-round cooperation with Latin America and the Caribbean countries from dozens of fields, such as politics, economy, culture, society, peace and security, judiciary, and the relations between regional organizations. This fully embodies the three important foundations for the development of the relations between the two sides: to enhance political mutual trust through the close political exchanges to consolidate the political foundation of bilateral relations, to set up the foundation of interests with a wide range of bilateral relations through wide-ranging and multi-level cooperations, and to establish the public opinion foundation of a deep bilateral relationship through expanding the exchange of humanities and social exchange. The DOCUMENT has positioned the Sino-Latin American relationship as a "comprehensive partnership", with particular emphasis on the nature of the relationship of "equality, mutual benefit and common development". President Hu Jintao believes that common development is the theme of the

[20] *China's Policy Documents for Latin America and the Caribbean*, November 5, 2008, http://www.gov.cn/jrzg/2008-11/05/content_1140303.htm.

Sino-Latin American relations and the basic principles of equality and mutual benefit should be adhered to in the Sino-Latin American relations. He stressed that, "Development is the most urgent task for China and Latin America, for China and Latin America are both in a critical period and both sides are also the development opportunities for each other. China is willing to expand pragmatic cooperations in various fields with the Latin-American countries to promote development with cooperation, and to promote common development with each other's development".[21] This means that the economic and trade cooperation has been given a specially important position in the Sino-Latin American relations. Premier Wen Jiabao more clearly pointed out, "Common interests should be expanded with focus on economic and trade cooperation". Therefore, the "comprehensive cooperation with focus on economic trade" is the long-term guideline for the development of the Sino-Latin American relations.

II. The Implementation of "Dual-wheel Drive" between the Regional Cooperation Platform and the Inter-country Bilateral Mechanism

So far, the Sino-Latin American bilateral economic and trade cooperation is mainly through bilateral cooperation between countries. With the establishment of the national community of the Latin-American and the Caribbean, the conditions for establishing the platform of the regional economic and trade cooperation between China and Latin America are becoming mature. For some time, the voice of the Latin-American countries requiring a coordinated strategy in their cooperation with China has been high. "The political dialogue that Latin America and the Caribbean have with the Asia-Pacific region, particularly with China, must be institutionalized. The importance of the relationship of trade and investment between the two regions should be paid attention to, and a coordinated strategy should be adopted between the countries and

[21] Hu Jintao, Together Build a New Era of Comprehensive Cooperative Partnership — Speech at the Peruvian Congress (November 20, 2008, Lima), *The People's Daily*, November 22, 2008, p. 3.

groups of countries to work closely in trade and investment with the Asia-Pacific region".[22] The community of Latin America and the Caribbean countries was established as the senior coordinating mechanism for the integration of the Latin-American region with the main targets to strengthen the internal communication and coordination of the area and to strengthen the dialogue with other countries, groups of countries and regional organizations to promote the cooperations within the region and between the region and other countries or regions.[23] From China's point of view, the establishment of a platform for cooperation with Latin America, which is a representative regional organization, is conducive to having dialogues and communication from the district level to understand the desires and demands for cooperation of the countries (including countries with no diplomatic relations), and to the overall planning and the layout of regional cooperations. China has the experience of setting up the platform of regional cooperation with Africa, which can provide some reference. However, the vitality of the regional cooperation platform between China and Latin America will depend on whether the platform is consistent with the characteristics of the Latin-American region and whether it can meet the actual needs of the development of the Sino-Latin American relations.

Why the "dual-wheel drive" was emphasized is because, in our opinion, when China carries out economic and trade cooperation with a region covering dozens of countries, the regional cooperation platform must have its unique role, but after all, it cannot replace the mechanism of bilateral cooperation between countries. Therefore, it is very important how to locate the function of the regional cooperation platform, which may require a trial and improvement process. The aim is to form a "dual-wheel drive" with the regional cooperation platform and the bilateral cooperation mechanism between the

[22]Alicia Barcena, Prologo del Articulo de Osvaldo Rosales, Mikio Kuwayama, *China y America Latina y el Caribe: Hacia una Relacion Economica y Commercial Estrategica,* CEPAL, Santiago de Chile, marzo de 2012, p. 12.

[23]Francisco Rojas Aravena, "La Celac y la Integracion Latinoamericana y Caribena: Principales Claves y Desaftos", *Nueva Sociedad*, No. 240, julio-agosto de 2012, Buenos Aires, Argentina, p. 21.

countries, promoting each other and complementing each other. In addition, it must also be seen that although there are many countries in Latin America, the differences in the scale of economies between countries and in the market sizes are very prominent, and the economic and trade cooperation between China and Latin America will in the long run be in the form of the cooperation between a number of the major countries in Latin America. Similarly, whether the idea to build the regional cooperation platform between China and Latin America can be in smooth progress will also depend on what attitude the major Latin-American countries hold towards it.

III. Implementing the "Initiatives" Proposed by the Chinese Premier

During his visits to four countries in South America in June 2012, Premier Wen Jiabao made a speech in the UN ECLAC, putting forward four suggestions, including a number of specific recommendations, such as the building of the Sino-Latin American Cooperation Forum, the establishment of the Sino-Latin American Cooperation Fund, the special loans for the Sino-Latin American cooperation in infrastructure construction, and the special fund for the development of the Sino-Latin American agricultural cooperation. The author believes that, at present, China should implement the initiatives by Premier Wen Jiabao as the priority to promote the Latin-American relations. First, from the perspective of our research on the problems that the Sino-Latin American economic and trade cooperation is facing, the above initiatives by Premier Wen Jiabao had fully responded to the concerns of interests of the Latin-American countries in their cooperation with China, reflecting the spirit of win–win cooperation with the Latin-American countries that the Chinese government hoped to realize. Second, these initiatives meant that China's economic and trade cooperation with Latin America had changed in the layout. In the next 10 years, the cooperation in the fields of energy and resources is still one of the priorities of the Sino-Latin American cooperation, but at the same time, as important areas, the industrial cooperation, agricultural cooperation, cooperation in infrastructure construction and financial cooperation have been in the agenda of bilateral cooperation. The relevant government sectors and enterprises should understand and follow these changes through the implementation of these initiatives. Third, the implementation of these initiatives is likely to be a good start, exerting a profound impact on deepening the Sino-Latin American bilateral economic and trade cooperation for the next 10 years.

IV. Increasing the Industrial Investment in the Latin-American Countries

At present, the main concern of the Latin-American countries, especially South American countries, is how to change the present status of trade between the sectors in the Sino-Latin American trade. It is hoped that the adjustment of domestic industrial structure can be promoted through outputting more manufactured goods and high value-added products to the Chinese market. Therefore, this concern of South American countries does not mean that they are reluctant to export energy and resource products to China; on the contrary, they hope to make use of the current period of resource bonus to increase domestic investment, improve infrastructure, accumulate human capital, update technology and equipment, and speed up the adjustment and upgrading of industrial structure so as to improve the international competitiveness of their economies. Just as Barcena, Executive Secretary of ECLAC said, "We should make use of the present historical opportunity to increase investment in the fields of infrastructure, innovation and human resources with a view to convert the benefits of natural resources to various forms of human capital and international competitiveness. Therefore, it is a pressing matter of the moment to promote innovation and the endogenous development of technical ability to reach a higher level".[24] Obviously, the fields of energy and resources will continue to be the focus of the Sino-Latin American bilateral economic and trade cooperation.

[24]Alicia Barcena, Prologo del Articulo de Osvaldo Rosales, Mikio Kuwayama, *China y America Latina y el Caribe: Hacia una Relacion Economica y Comercial Estrategica*, CEPAL, Santiago de Chile, marzo de 2012, pp. 12–13.

Faced with this situation, it may be a better choice for China to increase the industrial investment in Latin America. China has advantages in funds and increasing investment in foreign industries can better play the advantages, adapting to the needs of the adjustment of industrial structure of the Latin-American countries. The specific areas of investment must be selected according to the needs of the domestic market or the matching of industry chains. Therefore, the increase of industrial investment may not only help to drive the export of some technical equipment to further expand the foundation of bilateral trade, but also be conducive to promoting a number of small and medium enterprises to go into the Latin-American market.

V. Continuing to Promote the Construction of the Bilateral FTA Zones

Signing bilateral free trade agreements and building free trade zones are the important carriers to promote the relations between China and the Latin-American countries to a higher level. Over the past 10 years, the signing and smooth implementation of three free trade agreements — the Sino-Chilean FTA, the Sino-Peruvian FTA, and the Sino-Costa Rican FTA — has played the role of models in the whole Sino-Latin American relations. However, in 21 Latin-American countries that have established diplomatic relations with China, these three countries are still a minority. Bilateral free trade zones not only have opened up more space for mutual trade and investment and achieved a higher degree of integration for the interests of both sides, but also have been conducive to the prevention of some power interference on regional cooperation. In the next 10 years, the construction of bilateral free trade zones between China and the Latin-American countries need to continue to be promoted. The author believes that in the signing of bilateral free trade agreements, on the whole, China's attitude is positive, but differences of attitude exist among the Latin-American countries due to their different demands for their own interests. This requires us to study all the countries one by one, finding out the specific problems and trying to solve them with joint efforts. In short, we should continue to actively promote rather than wait for the objective conditions to become ripe.

VI. Strengthening the Sino-Latin American and the Caribbean Sub-regional Cooperation

As a sub-region of Latin America, Central America and the Caribbean area have many characteristics of their own, for example, there are many small countries and island countries with small economic scales and relatively limited market potentials; with the shortage of energy, mineral resources and agricultural resources, many of the countries belong to the countries importing energy and food; most countries rely on the maquila industry or tourism as a key industry. Due to their geographical closeness to the United States and the institutional arrangements of the "Caribbean Basin Initiative" with the United States and the bilateral free trade agreement, their foreign trade has a very high degree of dependence on the market of the United States. As for China, this area is the most concentrated area where China has not established diplomatic relations. Therefore, it is significantly important not only to strengthen China's economic and trade cooperation with Central America and the Caribbean area, but also to promote the bilateral economic and trade cooperation based on the characteristics of the region different from South America.

As mentioned earlier, if China and Latin America has established a regional cooperation platform, the contact and communication channels between China and Central America and the Caribbean countries are expected to be improved. From the perspective of the key points of bilateral cooperation, it is believed that the choices of the fields of cooperation are very extensive. First, there are many countries in the region engaged in export processing production; China has accumulated a lot of experience in this area in the recent decades, so both sides can explore the possibility of cooperation in the construction of export processing zones. Second, the regional agricultural foundation is generally weak, and natural disasters are very frequent; therefore, it is of strategic significance for these countries to solve the food problem, and the prospect for the two sides to carry out the agricultural science and technology cooperation is broad. Third, the insufficient infrastructure is also the prominent problem in the current development of Central America and the Caribbean countries, and there are demands in project financing, project design and construction. Fourth, in terms of the Caribbean countries, it is undoubtedly an important option to carry out cooperation in the tourism industry, including attracting Chinese tourists and the construction and operation of the tourism infrastructure.

The above policy suggestions are mainly thoughts based on some problems that need to be focused on by the current economic and trade cooperation between China and Latin America. It is believed that from the government level policies should mainly be formulated focusing on the key issues. As for the specific ways or mechanisms in the economic and trade cooperation, there are various available ones and the continuous exploration and innovation of them can be done by various sectors and enterprises in the process of practice.

Bibliography

Agosin, M. R., "Trade and Growth in Chile", *CEPAL Review 68*, August 1999.

Alicia Barcena, *Prologo de China y America Latina y el Caribe: Hacia una Relacion Economica y Commercial Estrategica*, CEPAL, Santiago de Chile, marzo de 2012, p. 12.

Alicia Barcena, Prologo al articulo de O. Rosales, M. Kuwayama, *China y America Latina y el Caribe: Hacia una Relacion Economica y Commercial Estrategica*, CEPAL, Santiago de Chile, marzo de 2012, pp. 12–13.

Alicia Barcena, Prologo de *Cambio Estructural para la Igualdad: UnaVision Integrada del Dessarrollo*, CEPAL, San Salvador, 27–31 de agosto de 2012, p. 13.

Anderson, J. E. and P. Neary, "Measuring the Restriction of Trade Policy", *The World Bank Economic Review* 8(1): 151–169, 1994.

Aravena, Francisco Rojas, "La Celac y la Integracion Latinoamericana y Caribena, Principales Claves y Desafios", *Nueva Sociedad*, No. 240, Julio-agosto de 2012, Buenos Aires, Argentina.

Banco Central de Reserva del Peru, *Reporte de Estabilidad Finaciera*, Noviembre 2009.

Banco Central de Reserva del Peru, *Reporte de Estabilidad Finaciera,* Noviembre 2010.

Barcena, Alicia, "The Economic Development of Latin America and the Caribbean in 2012", *Latin American Studies*, No. 6, 2012.

Bardález, Paul Castillo, Daniel Barco Rondán, "Crisis Financieras y Manejo de Reservas en el Peru", *Revista Estudios Económicos*, Banco Central de Reserva del Peru, No. 17, Junio 2009.

Bekaert, G., "Market Integration and Investment Barriers in Emerging Equity Markets", *The World Bank Economic Review*, 9(1): 75, 1995.

Bouzas, Roberto, "Perspectivas de La Politica Comercial Argentina: Es Posible Sobrevivir a las Buenas Noticias?", Revista *Brasileira de Comercio Exterior*, septiembre-octubre de 2008.

BP, *BP Statistical Review of World Energy*, June 2011.

Cartas, J. M., "Dollarization Declines in Latin America", *Finance and Development* March 2010, IMF.

Castillo, Paul and Fernando Perez Forero, "Los Mecanismos de Transimsion de la Politica Monetaria en Peru", *Revista Estudios Econdmicos, Banco Central de Reserva del Peru*, No. 21, Junio 2011.

CEPAL, *America Latina y el Caribe: Series Historicas de Estadisticas Economicas 1950–2008*, 2009.

CEPAL, *Anuario Estadistico de America Latina y el Caribe*, 2010.

CEPAL, *Anuario Estadistico de America Latina y el Caribe*, 2011.

CEPAL, *Balance Preliminar de las Economias de America Latina y el Caribe 2004*, Santiago de Chile, 2004.

CEPAL, *Balance Preliminar de las Economias de America Latina y el Caribe 2005*, Santiago de Chile, 2005, p. 51.

CEPAL, *Balance Preliminar de las Economias de America Latina y el Caribe 2010*, Santiago de Chile, 2010.

CEPAL, *Balance Preliminar de la Economia de America Latina y el Caribe 2008*, 2008, pp. 14, 68.

CEPAL, *Balance Preliminar de las Economias de America Latina y el Caribe 2012*, Santiago de Chile, 2012.

CEPAL, *Cambio Estructural para la Igualdad: Una Vision Integradad del Desarrollo*, San Salvador, 27–31 de agosto, 2012.

CEPAL, *Estudio Economico de America Latina y el Caribe 1998–1999*, p. 140.

CEPAL, *Estudio Economico de America Latina y el Caribe 1999–2011.*

CEPAL, *Estudio Economico de America Latina y el Caribe 2002–2003*, p. 144.

CEPAL, *Estudio Economico de America Latina y el Caribe 2008–2009: Peru.*

CEPAL, *Estudio Economico de America Latina y el Caribe 2010: Peru.*

CEPAL, *Informe Macroeconomico, julio 2012.*

CEPAL, *La Inversion Extranjera Directa en America Latina y el Caribe 2010*, 2011.

CEPAL, *La República Popular China y America Latina y el Caribe: Hacia una Relacion Estrategica*, Santiago de Chile, mayo de 2010.

CEPAL, *Panorama de la Insercion Internacional de America Latina y el Caribe 2008–2009*, 2009.

CEPAL, *Panorama Social de America Latina 2009*, Santiago de Chile, 2009.

CEPAL, *Panorama Social de America Latina 2012*, Santiago de Chile, 2012.

CEPAL, *Perfiles de Infraestrutura y Transporte en American Latina: Caso Peril*, Unidad de Servicios de Infraestrucutura de CEPAL, 2012.

CEPAL, *The Reactions of the Governments of the Americas to the International Crisis: An Overview of Policy Measures upto 31 August 2009,* September 2009.

CEPAL, sobre la base de CEPAISTAT [base de datos en linea]. http://websie.eclac.el/sisgen/ConsultaIntegradad.asp/, 2012.

CEPAL, sobre la base de J.M. Davis R. Ossowski y A. Fedelino, *Fiscal Policy Formulation and Implementation in Oil-Producing Countries*, Washington, D.C., Fondo Monetario Internacional, 2008.

Chaffee, Wilber Albert, *Desenvolvimento: Politics & Economy in Brazil*, Lynne-Rienner Publishers, Inc. 1998.

Chavez, Daniel, "Hacer o No Hacer, Los Gobiernos Progresistas de Argentina, Brasil y Uruguay Frente a las Privatizaciones", *Nueva Sociedad*, No. 207, enero-febrero d 2007.

Chi Yuanji, "Review of *Latin American Finance* — A Blank-filling Book", *World Economy*, No. 10, 1997.

China National Bureau of Statistics, *China Statistical Yearbook*, 2010, 2009, 2011, China Statistics Press.

China's Policy Documents for Latin America and the Caribbean, http://www.gov.cn/jrzg/2008-11/05/content_1140303.htm.

Chinese Ministry of Commerce, China National Bureau of Statistics, State Administration of Foreign Exchange, *Bulletin of the Statistics China's Foreign Direct Investment in 2012*, China Statistics Press, 2012.

Chinn, M. D. and H. Ito, "Capital Account Liberalization, Institutions and Financial Development: Cross Country Evidence", *NBER Working Paper 8967*, 2002.

Chinn, M. D. and H. Ito, "What Matters for Financial Development? Capital Controls, Institutions, and Interactions", *Journal of Development Economics*, 81(1): 163–192, 2006.

Chinn, M. D. and H. Ito, "A New Measure of Financial Openness", *Journal of Comparative Policy Analysis: Research and Practice*, 10(3): 309–322, 2008.

DATA CEIC Database, "Chinese Economic Sub-database and Latin American Economic Sub-database".

David Wessel, Paulo Prada, "El Ascenso de China Trastoca al Resto de las Economias del Mundo", *The Wall Street Journal*. Reprinted by the Argentine *National Daily*, March 11, 2011.

Development Center of Economic Cooperation and Development Organization, *The Economic Outlook of Latin America in 2010*, Contemporary World Press, 2010.

Development Center of Economic Cooperation and Development Organization, *The Outlook of Latin America in 2011*, translated by Zhao Lihong and Zhao Chongyang, Contemporary World Press, 2011.

Development Center of Economic Cooperation and Development Organization, *The Economic Outlook of Latin America in 2012*, translated by Wang Wenxian, Zhao Lihong *et al.*, Contemporary World Press, 2012.

Development Research Center of the Organization Economic Cooperation and Development, *The Outlook of Latin American Economy of 2011*, Chinese version, translated by Zhao Lihong & Zhao Chongyang, Contemporary World Press, 2011, p. 28.

Devlin, Robert, Antoni Estevadeordal and Andres Rodriguez-Clare (Estados Unidos), *El Impacto de China: Oportunidades y Retos para America Latina y el Caribe*, Editores BID y David Rokefeller Center for Latin American Studies, Harvard University, Washington, D.C., 2007.

Dollars, D., "Outward-oriented Developing Economies Really Do Grow More Rapidly: Evidence From 95 LDCs 1976–1985", *Economic Development and Cultural Change*, 523–544, 1992.

Dumas Damas, Roberto, "The History and Prospect of the Brazilian Economy", *Economic Studies of Big Powers*, V. 2, 2010.

ECLAC, *The Reactions of the Governments of the Americas to the International Crisis: An Overview of Policy Measures up to 31 December*, January 2010.

ECLAC, *2010–2011 Economic Survey of Latin America and the Caribbean*, 2011.

ECLAC, *2010–2011 Latin America and the Caribbean in the World Economy: The Region in the Decade of the Emerging Economies*, 2011.

ECLAC, *Foreign Direct Investment in Latin America and the Caribbean, 2010*, 2011.

ECLAC, *Peoples Republic of China and Latin America and the Caribbean: Ushering in a New Era in the Economic and Trade Relationship*, June 2011.

ECLAC, *Statistical Yearbook for Latin America and the Caribbean 2011*, 2011, pp. 81–82.

Economist Intelligence Unit, *Country Report*: *Venezuela*, January 2012.

Edwards, S., "Openness, Productivity, and Growth: What Do We Really Know?", *Economic Journal*, 108(147): 383–398, 1998.

Edwards, S., "Trade Orientation, Distortions, and Growth in Developing Countries", *Journal of Development Economics*, 39: 31–57, 1992.

Edwards, S. and M. S. Khan, "Interest Rate Determination in Developing Countries: A Conceptual Framework", *International Monetary Fund Staff Papers*, 32(3): 377–403, 1985.

Eichengreen, B. and M. Bordo, "Is Our Current International Economic Environment Unusually Crisis Prone?", in David Gruen and Luke Gower (eds.), *Capital Flows and the International Financial System*, 1999.

EIU, *Country Report — Brazil*, May, 2012.

FAO, *Evaluacion de los Recursos Forestales Mundiales 2010*, Roma, Italia, 2010, p. 234.

Feder, Gershon, "On Exports and Economic Growth", *Journal of Development Economics*, 12(1–2), February–April, 59–73, 1983.

Feldstein, M. and C. Horioka, "Domestic Saving and International Capital Flows", *The Economic Journal*, 90(358): 314–329, 1980.

Ffrench-Davis, R., "El Impacto de las Exportaciones sobre el Crecimiento en Chile", *Revista de la CEPAL*, No. 76, abril de 2002.

Garcia-Herrero, Alicia and Daniel Santabárbera, "Does China Have an Impact on Foreign Direct Investment to Latin America?" from *The Visible Hand of China in Latin America*, edited by Javier Santiso, translated by Wang Peng, Zhao Chongyang, World Knowledge Press, 2009.

Gonzalez, Raul, "Tres Decadas de un New Orden Economico: Chile, 1973–2003", *Revista Europea de Estudios Latinoamericanos y del Caribe*, CEDLA, Amsterdam, Paises Bajos, No. 77, octubre de 2004.

Gonzalez, Ricardo Bonilla (Colombia), "Apertura y Reprimarizacion de la Economia Colombiana: Un Paraiso de Corto Plazo", *Nueva Sociedad*, No. 231, enero-febrero de 2011, Buenos Aires, Argentina.

Granda, Alejandro, Cesar Liendo, and Carlos Rojas, *El Indicador de Balance Estructural*, Ministerio de Economia y Finanzas del Peru, Junio de 2012.

Greenaway, David and Chong Hyun Nam, "Industrialization and Macroeconomic Performance in Developing Countries under Alternative Trade Strategies", *Kyklos*, 41(3): 419–435, August 1988.

Grottola, Leonardo, *Neo-desarrollismo y rol del Estado (Argentina 2003–2010)*, julio de 2010.

Grugel, Jean and Maria Pia Riggirozzi, "The Return of the State in Argentina", *International Affairs 83*, enero de 2007.

Harrison, A., "Openness and Growth: A Time-series, Cross-country Analysis for Developing Countries", *Journal of Development Economics*, 48: 419–447, 1996.

Haugh, David, Roselyne Jaminand Bruno Rocha, *Maximizing Mexico's Gains From Integration in the World Economy*, OECD, December 2008.

Haya Rari, Santa and John Vis, "China and Latin America: Trade Competition (1990–2002)", *The Visible Hand of China in Latin America*, edited by Javier Santiso, translated by Wang Peng and Zhao Chongyang, World Knowledge Press, 2009.

Herrera, German and Andres Tavosnanska, "La Industria Argentina a Comienzos del Siglo XXI", *Revista CEPAL 104*, agosto de 2011.

Hu Jintao, Create a New Friendship between China and Latin America — Speech at the Brazilian Congress (November 12, 2004, Brasilia), *People's Daily*, 3rd Edition, November 24, 2004.

Hu Jintao, Together Build a New Era of Comprehensive Cooperative Partnership in the New Era — Speech at the Peruvian Congress (November 20, 2008, Lima), *People's Daily*, November 22, 2008.

Hu Jintao, *Advance Firmly along the Road of Socialism with Chinese Characteristics and Strive to Build a Well-off Society in an All-round Way — Report at the 18th National Congress of the Communist Party of China* (November 8, 2012), *Collection of the Documents of the 18th National Conference of the Chinese Communist Party*, People's Publishing House, 2012.

Hu Lifa, "Re-estimation of China's Trade Openness", *World Economic Studies*, No. 5, 2004.

Huang Hongzhu, "The Gradual Integration of Latin America's Finance with the World", *Latin American Studies*, No. 1, 1994.

Huang Ling, "Is Capital Control an Effective Means to Prevent the Financial Crisis?", Working Paper of the School of Economics, Peking University, September 10, 2010.

Illescas, Javier, Felipe Jaramillo, *Export Growth and Diversification: The Case of Peru*, World Bank, Policy Research Working Paper 5868, November 2011.

IMF, *World Economic Outlook*, 1997.

IMF, *Peru: 2006 Article IV Consultation*, Country Report No. 07/54, February 2007.

IMF, *Peru: 2009 Article IV Consultation*, Country Report No. 09/40, February 2009.

IMF, *Peru: Staff Report for the 2010 Article IV Consultation*, Country Report No. 09/40, February 2010.

IMF, *Peru: 2011 Article I Consultation*, Country Report No. 12/26, February 2012.

IMF, *Peru: 2012 Article IV Consultation*, Country Report No. 13/45, February 2013.

Instituto Nacional Estadistica, Republica Blivariana de Venezuela, *Censo 2011*, Caracas, febrero 23, 2012, http://www.ine.gob.ve.

Jenkins, Rhys (Inglaterra), "El 'Efecto China' En los Precos de los Productos Basicos y en el Valor de las Exportaciones de America Latina", *Revista de la CEPAL*, No. 103, abril de 2011.

Jia Qiuran, "Review of the Financial Openness Measurement Method and the Index System", *Economic Review*, No. 3, 2011.

Jiang Shixue (ed.), *Reflections on the Argentine Crisis*, Social Sciences Literature Press, 2004.

Jiang Shixue, *Prediction of the Prospect of Latin American Development*, China Social Sciences Press, 2011.

Johnson, Bryan T. and Thomas P. Sheehy, *1996 Index of Economic Freedom*, Washington, The Heritage Foundation, 1996.

Juan Carlos Trivino Salasar (Argentina), *Relaciones Comerciales entre China y America Latina: Un Matrimonio de Conveniencia*, Centro Argentino de Estudios Internacionales, www.cael.com.ar.

Justino, Patricia and Arnab Acharya, *Inequality in Latin America: Processes and Inputs*, PRUS Working Paper No. 22, April 2003, Poverty Research Unit at Sussex, University of Sussex.

Kacef, Osvaldo and Rafael Lopez-Monti, "America Latina, del Auge a la Crisis: Desafios de Politica Macroeconomica", *Revista de la CEPAL*, No. 100, abril de 2010.

Katz, Jorge, "Cambios Estructurales y Productividad en la Industria Latinoamericana, 1970–1996", *Revista de la CEPAL*, No. 71, agosto de 2000, p. 66.

Kehoe, Timothy J. and Kim J. Ruhl, *Why Have Economic Reforms in Mexico Not Generated Growth?*, Federal Reserve Bank of Minneapolis, November 2010.

Kevin, Gallager and Roberto Porzecanski, *The Dragon in the Room: China and the Future of Latin American Industrialization*, Stanford, 2010.

Kosacoff, Bernardo (ed.), *Crisis, Recuperacion y News Dilemas, la Economia Argentina 2002–2007*, CEPAL, noviembre de 2007.

Kosacoff, Bernardo and Mercado, Ruben (eds.), *La Argentina ante la Nueva Internacionalizacion de la Produccion: Crisis y Oportunidades*, CEPAL, PNUD, Buenos Aires, 2009.

Kraay, A., *In Search of the Macroeconomic Effects of Capital Account Liberalization*, Unpublished World Bank Working Paper, 1998.

Krugman, Paul R. and Moris Obstfeld, *International Economics: Theory and Policy*, the 6th Edition, translated by Hai Wen *et al.* China Renmin University Press, 2006.

Lane, P. R. and G. M. Milesi-Ferretti, *International Financial Integration*, IMF Staff Papers, 50(3): 82–113, 2003.

Lane, P. R. and G. M. Milesi-Ferretti, "The External Wealth of Nations, Measures of Foreign Assets and Liabilities for Industrial and Developing Countries", *Journal of International Economics*, 55(2): 263–294, 2001.

Lane, P. R. and G. M. Milesi-Ferretti, "The External Wealth of Nations Mark II: Revised and Extended Estimates of Foreign Assets and Liabilities, 1970–2004, *Journal of International Economics*, 73(2): 223–250, 2007.

Leamer, Edward, E., "Measures of Openness", in Robert E. Baldwin, (ed.) *Trade Policy Issues and Empirical Analysis*, (pp. 145–204), The National Bureau of Economic Research, University of Chicago Press, 1988.

Lelis, Marcos Tadeu Caputi, Andre Moreira Cunha and Manuela Gomes de Lima, "Desempeno de las Exportaciones de China y el Brasil hacia America Latina, 1994–2009, *Revista de la CEPAL*, No. 106, abril de 2012.

Lodha, Mary, *Brazil: Development Path of Neo-liberalism and New Economic Dependence*, abridged translation by Zhou Tong, Foreign Theoretical Trends, No. 3, 2003.

Lopez, Andres and Daniela Ramos, "A la Sombra del Gigante Chino: Hay Lugar para la Argentina en el New Mundo?", *Boletin Informativo Techint 326*, mayo-agosto de 2008.

Lopez-Cordova, Ernesto, Alejandro Mikko, and Daniel Ken Molina, "Fighting with the Dragon: Export of Latin America and China to the U.S. Market", from *The Visible Hand of China in Latin America*, edited by Javier Santiso, translated by Wang Peng, Zhao Chongyang, World Knowledge Press, 2009.

Lora, Eduardo (Inter American Development Bank): "Should Latin America Be Afraid of China?", from *The Visible Hand of China in Latin America*, edited by Javier Santiso, translated by Wang Peng, Zhao Chongyang, World Knowledge Press, 2009.

Low, Patrick, Marcelo Olarreaga, and Javier Suarez, "Does Globalization Cause a Higher Concentration of International Trade and Investment Flows", *World Trade Organization Staff Working Paper ERAD-98-08*, 1998.

Lv Yinchun, *Economic Development and Social Justice*, World Knowledge Publishing House, 2003.

Mao Minyang and Du Yulan, "The Study of Chinese Financial Openness", *Jiangsu Business*, No. 9, 2007.

Mattoo, A., "Financial Services and the WTO: Liberalization Commitments of the Developing and Transition Economies", *World Economy*, 23(3): 351–386, 2000.

McKinnon, R., *Money and Capital in Economic Development*, Brookings, Chapters 2, 1973.

Mercedes Garcia Escribano, *Factores que Impulsan la Desdolarizacion en el Peru*, Banco Central de Reserva del Peril, No. 21, Junio 2011, pp. 23–40.

Michaely, M., "Exports and Growth: An Empirical Investigation, *Journal of Development Economics*, 4: 49–53, 1977.

Ministerio de Economia y Finanzas, Evaluacion Global de la Gestion Prespuestaria 2008.

Ministerio de Economia y Finanzas, Evaluacion Global de la Gestion Prespuestaria 2009.

Ministerio de Economia y Finanzas, Evaluacion Global de la Gestion Prespuestaria 2010.

Nacht, Pablo Alejandro, "China y Argentina: 'Oportunidades y Desafios', o Cristalizacion de una Asociacion Dependiente", *Relaciones Internacionales* No. 20, GERI-UAM, junio de 2012.

Narodowski, Patricio and Demian Panigo, *El New Model o de Desarrollo Nacional y su Impacto en la Provincia de Buenos Aires*, Cuadernos de Economia de Ministerio de Economia de la Provincia de Buenos Aires No. 75, julio de 2010.

Novick, Marta, Carlos Tomada, Mario Damill, Roberto Frenkel, and Roxana Maurizio, *Tresla Crisis: El New Rumbo de la Politica Economica y Laboral en Argentina y su Impacto*, Instituto Internacional de Estudios Laborales de OIT, 2007.

OECD Perspectives: Mexico Key Policies for Sustainable Development, May 2010.

Osvaldo Kacef, Rafael Lopez-Monti, "America Latina, del Auge a la Crisis: Desafios de Politica Macroeconomica", *Revista de la CEPAL*, No. 100, 2010, p. 43, 44.

Ouyang Nao, Zhang Yabin, and Yi Xianzhong, "The 'Shared' Growth of China's Foreign Trade with the BRIC Countries", *Chinese Social Science*, No. 10, 2012.

Oviedo, Eduardo Daniel, *Modernizaciones, Intereses y Relaciones Estrategicas entre Argentina y China,* ponencia presentada al Seminario Internacional: "Como Enriquecer la Asociacion Estrategica entre China y Argentian ante las Nuevas Situaciones Internacionales", Instituto de Relaciones Internaciona les Contemporaneas (CICIR) Beijing, China, octubre de 2011.

Paz, Gonzalo Sebastian (Espana), "Cambio y Continuidad en las Relaciones de China con America Latina a Principios del Siglo XXI", *Revista Iberoamericana de Estudios de Asia Oriental*, No. 1, 2007.

PDVSA 2010 Annual Report, Caracas, febrero 2011, http://www.petroleumworld.com/ed11032801.htm.

Pensar, Fundacion, *Un Modelo Agotado, La Economia Argentina bajo Cristina Fernandez de Kirchner, 2008–2011*, Abril de 2011.

Peres, Wilson and Annalisa Primi, *Theory and Practice of Industrial Policy: Evidence from the Latin American Experience*, CEPAL, February 2009.

Pontines, V., "The Role of the General Agreement on Trade in Services (GATS) — Financial Services Agreement (FSA) in the Financial Liberalization Efforts of APEC Economies", Philippine APEC Study Center Network (PASCN) Discussion Paper, 2002.

Prebisch, Raul, *The Peripheral Capitalism: Crisis and Reform*, translated by SU Zhenxing and Yuan Xingchang, The Commercial Press, 1990.

Quinn, D. P., "Capital Account Liberalization and Financial Globalization, 1890–1999: A Synoptic View", *International Journal of Finance & Economics*, 8(3): 189–204, 2003.

Quinn, D. P. and A. M. Toyoda, "Does Capital Account Liberalization Lead to Growth?", *Review of Financial Studies*, 21(3): 1403, 2008.

Quinn, D. P. and C. Inclan, "The Origins of Financial Openness: A Study of Current and Capital Account Liberalization", *American Journal of Political Science*, 41(3): 771–813, 1997.

Qv Lingyun and Wen Hui, "Analysis of the Relationship between China's Foreign Trade and Economic Growth", *Contemporary Economy*, No. 7, 2009.

Rafael Valdez Mera, "Eguador Buscaun Cambio Profundo y China es su Aliado", *China Hoy*, mayo de 2013, p. 33.

Ram, Rati, "Export and Economic Growth: Some Additional Evidence", *Economic Development and Culture Change*, 33(2), 1985.

Ran Zongrong, "The Anti-dumping Motivations of Developing Countries Against China and China's Countermeasures", *International Trade Issues*, No. 4, 2005.

"Reference News", March 16, 2013, p. 6.

Regional Development and Regional Inequality, "An Overview of the Brazilian Economy", http://www.econ.fea.usp.br/nereus/eae0503_1_/hadch199.pdf.

Reid, Michael, "Brazil's Unfinished Search for Stability", *The Washington Quarterly*, Autumn 1998.

Rosales, Osvaldo and Mikio Kuwayama, America Latina al Encuentro de China e Idia: Perspectivas y Desafios en Comercio e Inversion, *Revista de la CEPAL*, No. 93, Diciembre de 2007.

Rosales, Osvaldo and Mikio Kuwayama, *China y America Latina y el Caribe: Hacia una Relacion Econdmica y Comercial Estrategica*, CEPAL, Santiago de Chile, marzo de 2012.

Sachs and Warner, *Economic Convergence and Economic Policies*, CASE, Harvard University, 1995.

Santiso, Javier, "La Emergencia de China y Su Impacto en America Latina", *Politica Exterior*, V. 19, No. 107, p. 108, 2005.

Santiso, Javier, "Preface" of *The Economic Outlook of Latin America in 2009*, translated by Yue Yunxia *et al.*, World Knowledge Press, 2009.

Santiso, Javier, *The Pragmatic Nature of Latin American Economic Policies* (Chinese version), Contemporary World Press, 2009.

Santiso, Javier *et al.*, "An Angel or a Devil? China's Impact on the Trade of the Emerging Markets in Latin America", from *The Visible Hand of China in Latin America*, edited by Javier Santiso, translated by Wang Peng, Zhao Chongyang, World Knowledge Press, 2009.

Sevares, Julio, "ElA Ascenso de China: Oportunidades y Retos para America Latina", *Nueva Sociedad*, No. 235, septiembre-octubre de Buenos Aires, Argentina.

Shen An, *Review of and Reflections on the Crisis of Argentina*, World Knowledge Press, 2009.

Sistema Economico Latinoamericano y del Caribe (SELA), *Evolucion Reciente de las Relaciones Economicas entre la Republica Popular China y America Latina y el Caribe. Mecanismos Institucionales y de para su Fortalecimiento*, Caracas, Venezuela, octubre de 2010.

Stiglitz, Joseph E., "Capital Market Liberalization, Economic Growth, and Instability", *World Development*, 28(6): 1075–1086, June 2000.

SU Zhenxing (ed.), *Study of the Process of the Modernization of Latin American Countries*, Social Sciences Literature Press, 2006.

SU Zhenxing, *Anthology of Su Zhenxing*, Shanghai Dictionary Press, 2005.

SU Zhenxing, *Economic Development of Latin America*, Economic Management Publishing House, 2000.

SU Zhenxing, "Chile's Economic Policy and Development Model", *Latin American Studies*, No. 5, 2005.

SU Zhenxing, "Latin American Economy in the 1990s: Growth and Instability", *Latin American Studies*, No. 1, 2000.

SU Zhenxing, Zhang Yong, "Twists and Turns of the Transformation of Latin American Economic Growth Mode and Its Process of Modernization", *Latin American Studies*, No. 5, 2011.

Sun Yanlin, "Empirical Analysis of China's Export and Economic Growth", *International Trade Issues*, V. 2, 2000.

Tyler, W., "Growth and Export Expansion in Developing Countries, Some Empirical Evidence", 1980, http://desafios.ipea.gov.br/pub/td/1980/td_0020.pdf.

Ursell Abdenour, Adriana, "The Brazilian Economy Has Walked Out the Shadow of the "Lost Decade", *Chinese Social Sciences*, December 5, 2012.

Vazquez, Julio A. Diaz (Cuba), *Relaciones Economicas China-America Latina: Oportunidad o Amenaza?*, http://politica_china.org/imxd/noticias/doc/1312622682.

Vera, Leonardo, "Cambio Estructural, Desindustrializacion y Perdidas de Productividad: Alguna Evidencia Preliminar para Venezuela" *Cuadernos del Cendes*, V. 26 No. 71, 2009.

Vera, Leonardo, "Venezuela: Anatomia de una recesión profunda y prolongada", *Nueva Sociedad*, No. 228, julio-agosto de 2010.

Vergara M., Sebastian, "The Dynamic of Employment in Chilean Industry", *CEPAL Review 86*, August 2005.

Vidal, Gregorio, *Privatizationes en America Latina: Flujos Internationales de Capital, Regiolizacion y Desarticulacion Productiva, Consecuencias Financieras de la Globalizacion*, Universidad Nacional Autonoma de Mexico, Instituto de Investigaciones Economicas, Mexico, 2005, pp. 73–99.

Waldkirch, Andreas, *The Effects of Foreign Direct Investment in Mexico since NAFTA*, Colby College, March 2008.

Wang Jun, "Active Trade Protectionism in Emerging Economies", *China Social Sciences News*, March 25, 2013, p. A06.

Weisbrot, Mark, Rebecca Ray, and Luis Sandoval, *The Chavez Administration at 10 Years: The Economy and Social Indicators*, Center for Economic and Policy Research (CEPR), Washington, D.C., February 2009.

Weiss, Eli and David Rosenblatt, *Regional Economic Growth in Mexico Recent Evolution and the Role of Governance*, the World Bank Latin America and Caribbean Region, July 2010, WPS5369.

Wen Jiabao, *Always Be Good Friends of Mutual Trust — Speech at the ECLAC of the United Nations* (June 26, 2012, San Diego), http://news.xinhuanet.com/politics/2012/06-27/c_112303984.htm.

Winkelried, Deigo and Jose Enrique Gutierrez, "Dinamica Inflacionaria Reional y el Esquema de Metas de Inflacion de el Peru", *Revista Estudios Economicos*, Banco Central de Reserva del Peru, No. 24, diciembre 2012.

World Bank, *Doing Business 2011 in Latin America: Making a Difference for Entrepreneurs*, 2011.

World Bank, *Public Expenditure Review for Peru: Spending for Results,* Report No. 62586, June 6, 2012.

World Bank, *Doing Business 2013: Peru*, 10th edition, 2013, pp. 5–9.

Wylde, Christopher, "Continuidad o Cambio? Politica Economica Argentina Posterior a la Crisis y el Gobierno de Nestor Kirchner, 2003–2007," *Revista de Ciencias Sociales*, Num. 43, FLACSO-Sede Academica de Ecuador, Quito, mayo 2012.

Xi Jinping, *Promote Common Development and Create a Better Future — Speech at the Mexican Senate* (June 5, 2013, Mexico City), http://news.xinhuanet.com/world/2013-06/06/c_116058743.htm.

Xiang Jun, "Why People in Brazil Protest", *United Morning Post of Singapore*, June 29, 2013, p. 21.

Xie Wenze and Liu Huayi, "Analysis of the Growth Trend of Latin American Economy from 2005 to 2010", *Latin American Studies*, No. 5, 2005.

Xu Wenyuan, Chen Shunying, and Liu De, *The Argentine Economy*, People's Publishing House, 1983.

Yaghmaian, Behzad and Reza Ghovashi, "Export Performance and Empirical Analysis, *The American Economist*, 39(2), 1995.

Yalan, Cesar Carrera, "El Canal del Credito Bancario en el Peru: Evidencia y Mecanismo de Transmision", *Revista Estudios Economicos*, Banco Central de Reserva del Peru, No. 22, diciembre 2011.

Yamada, Gustavo, Juan F. Castro, and Jose L. Bacigalupo, "Desigualdad Monetaria en un Contexto de Rapido Crecimieto Economico: El Caso Recient del Peru", *Revista Estudios Economicos*, Banco Central de Reserva del Peru. No. 24, deciembre 2012.

Ying Jian and Zhang Guolin, "Study of the Economic Openness and Its Measurement Method", *Study of Financial Issues*, V. 10, 2002.

Yu Yang's compiled translation, *Regulations on Administrative Procedures for the Implementation of Anti-dumping Measures in Brazil*, http://www.cacs.gov.cn/cacs/newcommon/details.aspx?articleId=38558.

Zhang Jinqing and Liu Qingfu, "Measurement of China's Financial Openness and International Comparative Study", *International Financial Research*, No. 12, 2007.

Zhang Jinqing, Liu Qingfu, and Zhao Wei, "Review and Comparison of the Measure of Financial Openness", *Study of Industrial Economy*, No. 3, 2007.

Zhang Jinqing, Zhao Wei, and Liu Qingfu, "Analysis of the Intrinsic Relationship between the 'Opening of Capital Account' and 'Financial Opening'", *Journal of Fudan University* (Social Sciences Edition), No. 5, 2008.

Zhao Wei *et al.*, "A Review of the Measurement of the Degree of Openness", *International Trade Issues*, No. 6, 2005.

Zheng Bijian, "The Eighteenth National Congress of the CPC Has Opened a New Chapter of China", *Shanghai Social Sciences Newspaper*, November 22, 2012, p. 1.

Zheng Ou, Zhang Mengying, Australia Seeking the Means to Break the "Resource Curse", *Chinese Social Sciences*, November 2, 2012, p. A-03.

Zhou Zhiwei, "Brazil: The 'Domino' Worry of the Cabinet Corruption Case", Wu Baiyi (ed.): *Report on the Development of Latin America and the Caribbean (2011–2012)*, Social Sciences Literature Publishing House, 2012.

Index

C

N

T